BEETHOVEN

THE MUSIC

AND THE LIFE

Lewis Lockwood

W. W. Norton & Company

New York   London

For information about permission to reproduce selections from this book, write to
Permissions, W. W. Norton & Company, Inc., 500 Fifth Avenue, New York, NY 10110

Manufacturing by The Maple-Vail Book Manufacturing Group
Book design by Blue Shoe Studio
Production manager: Andrew Marasia

Library of Congress Cataloging-in-Publication Data

Lockwood, Lewis.
Beethoven : the music and the life / by Lewis Lockwood.
p. cm.
Includes bibliographical references (p.) and indexes.
ISBN 0-393-05081-5
1. Beethoven, Ludwig van, 1770–1827—Criticism and interpretation. I. Title.

ML410.B4 L597 2002
780'.92—dc21

[B]   2002075397

ISBN 0-393-32638-1 pbk.

W. W. Norton & Company, Inc., 500 Fifth Avenue, New York, N.Y. 10110
www.wwnorton.com

W. W. Norton & Company Ltd., Castle House, 75/76 Wells Street, London W1T 3QT

1 2 3 4 5 6 7 8 9 0

To Ava

CONTENTS

The symbol *W denotes a music example in score, located on
W. W. Norton's Web site at www.wwnorton.com/trade/lockwood.
The first such reference appears on page 55.

Note to the paperback edition: In this edition I have corrected a number of typographical and other errors, some of which were pointed out to me by readers. Among them are Jaime Urrea, Franz Schulze, G. W. Spence, and, especially, Robert Levin, to all of whom I am grateful.

ILLUSTRATIONS

PREFACE

᚛ᚑᚋᚐ᚜

This book attempts to portray Beethoven as man and artist, with a primary focus on his music but with ample attention to his life, career, and milieu. My aim is to present his life mainly through his development as a composer, rather than to devote each chapter to a biographical narrative combined with a partial overview of his artistic growth. The complex question of how to interweave the two dimensions—the musical and the biographical—and to what extent they can be interwoven is itself an issue that is discussed in the book and that hovers over it throughout.

Although separate chapters are devoted to biography and to critical discussion of the music, my hope is that readers who care more about Beethoven's life will also read those that deal with works and genres; and that readers interested mainly in the music will cross the bridge to the biography. As for readers most interested in the historical, political, and cultural framework in which Beethoven came of age—the turbulent Europe of the French Revolution, the Reign of Terror, the years of war before and during the reign of Napoleon, and the vast turning of the wheel that brought on the Industrial Revolution and the age of Romanticism—this book is meant to give such readers access to Beethoven's works both as reflections of outer influences and as imaginative products of a richly endowed musical mind.

I have found models for this approach in two biographies: Abraham Pais's *"Subtle is the Lord:" The Science and the Life of Albert Einstein* (1982), and Nicholas Boyle's *Goethe: The Poet and the Age* (1992–2000). In Pais's biography chapters with titles in italics provide "an almost entirely nonscientific biography of Einstein," while the nonitalicized chapters (most of them) are the equivalent of a scientific biography. In Boyle's book on Goethe, biographical matters and criticism of the poetry and drama alternate with one another, sometimes as separate sections within chapters. I have not used italics or any other way of differentiating chapter titles, but have written on Beethoven's works with the lay reader in mind at what I hope will be a highly accessible descriptive level.

Although some chapters reflect my interest in the study of Beethoven's creative process, much of the musical discussion in the book consists of short critical accounts of a large number of works, including his most important ones in every genre. These commentaries are inevitably brief, as they must be in a book of moderate length, but I have tried to bring out salient and important aspects of the works and to frame my comments within the context of Beethoven's changing styles and changing ways of shaping larger musical compositions over the course of his lifetime. The earlier chapters reflect on the special problem that Beethoven faced as a young and gifted artist who found that his contemporaries hoped that he would become a "second Mozart," a role that was not only prescribed for him by his teachers and knowledgeable patrons but that he willingly took on in his early years. The difficulty for the young Beethoven of being a truly rebellious original and of accepting his destiny as the main successor to Mozart—as lofty a model as has ever existed in music—is a crucial aspect of his early development, and it plays out through his entire career in different ways. The later chapters, in a partial parallel, show us Beethoven in his last years, with great achievements behind him, now surmounting the crisis of finding still another new artistic path on which to continue, reaching back through several generations and finding new models in the music of Handel and, especially, Bach.

Within every specialist lurks a generalist yearning to get out—a sensation I have never felt more keenly than while writing this book. Accordingly, this broad survey can be read as a précis of many specialized monographs, many already written and some still unwritten. Throughout the book, in text and footnotes, I have tried to take account of the current specialized scholarly literature on Beethoven. To make the discussion of Beethoven's works as accessible as possible, music examples within the book have been kept to the barest minimum, but a large number of examples in score will be found on a special Web site for this book maintained by the publisher at www.wwnorton.com/trade/lockwood.

Each reference to an example on the Web site is marked by *W and a number in the text.

Growing up in New York City in the 1940s, I first heard Beethoven's orchestral works, and much other music, played by the New York Philharmonic at Young People's Concerts at Carnegie Hall. As a young cellist I played his cello sonatas, trios, string quartets, and symphonies, first in the incomparably stimulating atmosphere of the High School of Music and Art, and later at Queens College of the City of New York. The Queens College faculty then included, among others, Edward Lowinsky, Karol Rathaus, Leo Kraft, Sol Berkowitz, John Castellini, and other eminent teachers in history, philosophy, and literature. Many years later, after having taught Beethoven at undergraduate and graduate levels at Princeton University and at Harvard University, I still play Beethoven's chamber music, and thinking and writing about him has become a main professional activity. I found out in my teenage years that there was a substantial critical literature on Beethoven, starting with the essays of Donald Francis Tovey, which I discovered on the shelves of the Bainbridge Avenue Public Library in the Bronx. And I can remember wondering, while playing the A major Cello Sonata, Opus 69, why certain parallel passages in the exposition and recapitulation of the first movement didn't exactly agree in their intervals, although every other parallel pair was identical. Many years later, when I was studying Beethoven's compositional methods through his sketches and autographs, the answer came into my hands unexpectedly when I was given the opportunity to study Beethoven's autograph manuscript of the first movement of this very cello sonata. The manuscript was then owned by the late Felix Salzer, an eminent theorist and former student of Heinrich Schenker, who invited me to study it at his home in New York and to decipher its many complex revisions and alterations. This experience taught me firsthand what it means to follow the complexities of Beethoven's notation as direct evidence of his restless, exploratory musical thinking.

At graduate school in Princeton in the 1950s, among seminars in music history that I took with Oliver Strunk, Arthur Mendel, and Nino Pirrotta, a graduate course on Beethoven biography was offered by Elliot Forbes, then a member of the Princeton faculty. At that time Forbes was well along in his work on a new edition, published in 1964, of the great nineteenth-century *Life of Beethoven* by Alexander Wheelock Thayer that I was fortunate enough to read in manuscript before it appeared in print. My indebtedness to Elliot Forbes, later my colleague at Harvard, is many-sided. In 1977 I renewed my early friendship with Maynard Solomon, whose brilliant Beethoven biography, published that same year, broke new ground in its blending of close scholarly discussion of Beethoven's life with new insights drawn from Solomon's psychoanalytic background.

A question any reader will ask is how this book fits into the current spectrum of works on Beethoven, including those of Solomon, William Kinderman, David Wyn Jones, Barry Cooper, and others. The best analogy I can give is that of several painters making portraits of the same subject. Despite certain obvious resemblances, the differences will outweigh the similarities. For no matter how faithfully painters work to present their subjects, they also present themselves. Each has an individual point of view, a vision of the subject that determines what the essential proportions, colors, and textures will be, what features will be thrust into the foreground and what will remain in the shadows or be omitted altogether. Since this book springs primarily from my experience of the music, it inevitably reflects my own viewpoint and interests. It also illustrates my preference for making a portrait of the composer in which the music looms larger than the life, the composer dominates the man, but in which both have a place.

What is the nature of the relationship between the life and works of a great artist? This mysterious question comes up for discussion in the earlier part of the book and can never be plumbed deeply enough. To what extent the events of the artist's life can, or cannot, be connected meaningfully to the works differs in various periods of Beethoven's life and with the character and meaning of individual compositions. Beethoven's greater works often give the impression that they directly reflect the deepest aesthetic, philosophical, and at times political currents of his age, but also that in their powerful artistic individuality they transcend all outer causes. Some of his lesser works, on the other hand, were clearly written to make money, to capitalize on current tastes in the musical marketplace, or in some cases to respond directly to political events. A blatant example of the latter is *Wellington's Victory*, a potboiler that Beethoven wrote as a patriotic gesture to celebrate Wellington's military defeat of the French in 1813.

Such direct outer influences, of all kinds, are more nearly traceable in earlier and later periods than in the middle period, and partly for this reason I have adopted a different strategy for that phase. For what I am calling the "Second Maturity," roughly from 1802 to 1812, which embraces many of the most famous works, my approach is by genre: that is, first the symphonies, then the concertos, then the stage music, the vocal music, the keyboard chamber music, and finally the string quartets. I have chosen this plan because it makes more sense to me to deal with the major genres in this period one at a time. In the earlier and later periods, on the other hand, a much more nearly chronological approach fits the music better than it does in the Second Maturity because Beethoven tended to compose in his principal genres in a more consistent way when he was young and when he was an old master.

I cannot close this introduction without acknowledging the help and advice of various colleagues and others from whom I have benefited during the writing of this book. First, my warmest thanks go to Maynard Solomon, Charles Rosen, Mark Kroll, and Robert Marshall. All four colleagues read the book in manuscript and all gave me sound and frank advice on matters large and small. In a larger sense I am grateful to a broad range of colleagues, some of whom I have known professionally for many years, some of whom were once graduate students of mine at Princeton and at Harvard, and forty-eight of whom, twelve at a time, were members of four summer seminars for college teachers that I gave on Beethoven in the 1980s and '90s, sponsored by the National Endowment for the Humanities.

I am especially indebted to Michael Ochs, formerly the Richard F. French Music Librarian at Harvard and later Music Editor at W. W. Norton, who invited me to undertake this book and whose thoughtful, painstaking editing and criticism have been exemplary. For any and all errors and shortcomings I alone am responsible.

Finally, my thanks and love to my wife, Ava Bry Penman, whose knowledge of music and of the art of healing have been profoundly meaningful to me over the past ten years.

Brookline, Massachusetts

BEETHOVEN

THE MUSIC
AND THE LIFE

YOUTH, MATURITY, OLD AGE: THREE LETTERS

❦

1787: The Death of Beethoven's Mother

In mid-September 1787, the sixteen-year-old Ludwig van Beethoven wrote a letter of apology to Dr. Joseph Wilhelm Freiherr von Schaden in Augsburg. He had stayed at von Schaden's home in late April, more than four months earlier, on his journey back to Bonn from Vienna. The young pianist-composer had gone to Vienna in the hope of making contact with Mozart, but his stay had been brief and he had rushed back to Bonn as fast as he could when he received urgent letters from his father telling him that his mother was seriously ill. Now, after his mother's death on July 17, he wrote to von Schaden in mid-September:

> I can easily imagine what you must think of me, and I cannot deny
> that you have good grounds to think of me unfavorably. But before
> apologizing I will first explain the reasons that led me to hope that my
> apologies will be accepted. I must tell you that from the time I left
> Augsburg, my joy and with it my health began to decline. For the
> nearer I came to my native town, the more frequent were the letters
> from my father telling me to travel faster than usual because my mother
> was not in very good health. So I hurried as much as I could, the more
> so as I myself began to feel ill. My longing to see my sick mother once
> more overcame all obstacles and helped me surmount the greatest diffi-
> culties. I found my mother still alive but in a dreadful state of health.
> She had consumption, and finally she died about seven weeks ago after
> a great deal of pain and suffering. She was such a kind, loving mother

to me, and my best friend. Oh, who was happier than I when I could still utter the sweet name, mother, and it was heard—and to whom can I say it now? To the silent images of her in my imagination? As long as I have been here I have had very few happy hours. For the whole time I have been plagued by asthma, and I am afraid that it may develop into consumption. To this is added melancholy, which for me is almost as great an evil as my illness itself. Put yourself in my place, and then I shall hope to receive your forgiveness for my long silence. You showed me extreme kindness and friendship in lending me three carolins in Augsburg. But I must ask you to bear with me for a little longer. My trip cost me a great deal of money and I have no hope for any compensation here. Fate is not favorable to me here in Bonn. You must forgive me for taking up so much of your time with my chatter, but it has all been very necessary for the purpose of my apology. I beg you not to refuse from now on your dear friendship. There is nothing I wish so much as to deserve it, even to a small degree.

*With the greatest respect I remain your obedient servant and friend
L. v. Beethoven Court Organist to the Elector of Cologne*[1]

This letter, ostensibly about an unpaid debt, is an expression of pain and loss.[2] His mother's death in mid-July, along with his father's chronic alcoholism and hopeless abdication of family responsibility, had left Beethoven a virtual orphan at sixteen. These two psychic injuries, one of them continual, the other sudden and unexpected, inflicted suffering that reverberated throughout his lifetime. In an immediate sense they left him, the oldest son, as surrogate parent responsible for the welfare of three younger siblings—his two brothers Caspar Anton Carl, then thirteen, and Nikolaus Johann, then eleven, along with a baby sister one and a half years old, Maria Margaretha, who died two months later, of unknown causes. The household from then on had no guiding and protecting mother at the center of family life and no little sister.

Beethoven's family had suffered earlier losses of children. His mother, Maria Magdalena Keverich Leym, had lost a baby in infancy in 1764, a year before the death of her first husband, Johann Leym. After marrying Johann

Beethoven's letter of September 15, 1787, to Joseph Wilhelm von Schaden explaining his unpaid debt and mourning his mother's death a few months earlier; the earliest personal correspondence from Beethoven that is preserved. (Beethoven-Haus, Bonn)

van Beethoven in January 1767, she bore in seventeen years a total of seven children, of whom Ludwig van Beethoven was the second. The first, a son named Ludwig Maria, was born in April 1769 and died in less than a week. After Ludwig's birth in December 1770 she gave birth to two more sons who grew to manhood, Caspar Anton Carl (born 1774) and Nikolaus Johann (born 1776), but the last three children all died young. These were

Anna Maria Franziska (born in February 1779, died after four days); Franz Georg (born in January 1781, died in August 1783); and Maria Margaretha (born May 1786, died November 26, 1787). The result was that, by the time of the child Maria Margaretha's death, the family had lived through the painful death of four children in addition to the loss of Maria Magdalena as wife and mother.

So from this early age, Beethoven lived in a womanless house, as he would all his life, despite his yearning to find love in a relationship with a woman. This predicament was all the more bitter because his mother had been, as he put it, not only his nurturing parent but his best friend. The family crisis and his new struggle to take on responsibility for his brothers was a harbinger of Beethoven's later relations with his family members—his brothers, their wives, and, much later, his nephew Karl. His entanglements with all of them in his later years would grow to take the form of obsessive interference.

But now in the immediate aftermath, embarrassed by not having written to von Schaden before this, he gives news of his mother's death but also stresses, repeatedly, his own ill health and the morbid depression he associates with it. Going well beyond what we might expect in a letter of apology to a benefactor, he speaks intensely of sickness, anxiety, and depression. Fear of mortal illness and early death, emotional abandonment in the wake of losing his mother and the love she had provided, shame over his unpaid debt—all these are etched into the text of this highly personal letter. His persistent references to his poor health can be linked to a litany of similar complaints about illness that come up again and again in his letters throughout his life, and we must remember that in 1787 he had as yet no sign of the deafness that would begin to descend on him ten or eleven years later. We see, then, that his sense of personal health and wholeness, his feeling of the rightness of fit between himself and the outer world, were compromised by an onset of physical and emotional infirmity at the time of his mother's death, long before his deafness, which emerged between about 1797 and 1802. These feelings would later be intensified as he covered his morbidity with the irascible outward manner of a proud, uncompromising artist forced to come to grips with a barely comprehending world.

Significantly, he hardly mentions his father, Johann van Beethoven, in the letter, nor does he refer to his father's loss and bereavement. Everyone familiar with musical life at Bonn knew that Johann, a tenor and violinist in the Bonn Hofkapelle, was a ne'er-do-well and alcoholic whose ambitions for his son ineffectively covered his own failures as father, as provider, and as professional musician.

Just as telling is young Beethoven's remark, "Fate is not favorable to me here at Bonn." Although as a pianist and a composer he was the most gifted prodigy that the seasoned musicians of the Bonn court chapel had ever seen, already advertised as a "second Mozart" who seemed to enjoy the benevolent approval of the Elector, Beethoven knew that to embark on the great career for which he was preparing he would have to leave provincial Bonn for Vienna or another European capital. By the time of this letter he had just really begun to produce some promising works, especially his three piano quartets of 1785. Very likely he had brought these quartets and perhaps some other juvenile works with him to Vienna to show to Mozart, and he may have had an opportunity while there to play for Mozart and to show off his skills as keyboard improviser. With good reason, Beethoven regarded Mozart as his early musical god, and his central ambition was to launch his career as Mozart's pupil. Still, it took until November 1792 before he could leave Bonn for Vienna. By that time the opportunity was lost, as Mozart's death, just ten months earlier, left Beethoven's further training "in the hands of Haydn," as his friend Count Waldstein put it in a farewell message to him on his departure.

Looking once more at the crisis months of 1787, it is striking to find this sixteen-year-old describing his emotional burdens and physical afflictions so openly, and with such an interplay of allusions to body and mind. Certainly his mourning for his mother, just when her steady care of him and his siblings would have eased his path to independence, deflected his energies for the next few years into family matters, forcing a conflict between his musical career and the practical demands of family life and creating emotional conflicts that remained unresolved in later years. In managing his family in Bonn he had some degree of support from friends, and he remained indebted to the family von Breuning for the help he received from them. As a pianist he made continued progress, but he may have lost some momentum in his development as a composer—we would know more clearly if the chronology of a number of his early works were reliably established. Yet by 1790 he had expanded his early efforts beyond piano music and songs, writing a powerful and original work for chorus and orchestra, his *Cantata on the Death of the Emperor Joseph II.* He had come to the attention of Haydn, who was then, even with Mozart still alive, the foremost figure in European music; and within two years he was ready for his permanent move to Vienna.

1812: Letter to a Child

By 1812 Beethoven, at age forty-one, had fulfilled his early ambitions. He had taken on the burden of history to the fullest possible degree, had succeeded Haydn and Mozart as the most acclaimed composer of instrumental music in Europe, and in twenty years had transformed the musical language of his time. He already had behind him all his symphonies except the Ninth; all the concertos he was ever to write; the piano sonatas up through Opus 81a (*Lebewohl*); the keyboard chamber music through the "Archduke" Trio; the string quartets up through the F-minor Quartet Opus 95; his major opera *Leonore* (which later became *Fidelio*) in its first versions of 1805–6; several works of sacred music; and a substantial number of songs. This year, 1812, was emerging as another hard passage, perhaps the most troubled after the crisis that in 1802 had spawned Beethoven's Heiligenstadt Testament, his early and private revelation of the psychological trauma caused by his oncoming deafness and his determination to overcome and persevere. On July 6–7, 1812, while at the spa at Teplitz in Bohemia, he wrote an agonizing letter to an unnamed woman who has been christened by history the "Immortal Beloved." For now, however, let us turn to another letter that Beethoven wrote very shortly afterward, on July 17, 1812, to "Miss Emilie M. at H." (possibly Hamburg). The young Emilie M., apparently a child about eight to ten years old who played the piano, had embroidered a pocketbook and had sent it to Beethoven as a gift with an admiring note.[3] Although he did not know her, Beethoven sent this reply:

My dear, kind Emilie, my dear friend!

My reply to your letter to me is late in arriving. A great amount of business and persistent illness may serve to excuse me. The fact that I am here for the recovery of my health proves the truth of my excuse. Do not rob Handel, Haydn, and Mozart of their laurel wreaths. They are entitled to theirs, but I am not yet entitled to one.

Your pocketbook will be treasured among other tokens of a regard that many people have shown me but that I am still far from deserving.

Persevere, do not only practice your art, but endeavor also to fathom its inner meaning; it deserves this effort. For only art and science can raise men to the level of gods. If, my dear Emilie, you should ever desire to have anything, do not hesitate to write to me. The true artist has no pride. He sees unfortunately that art has no limits. He has a vague awareness of how far he is from reaching his goal; and while others may perhaps admire him, he laments that he has not yet reached the point to which his better genius only lights the way for him like a distant sun. I should probably prefer to visit you and your family than to visit many rich people who betray themselves with the poverty of their inner selves. If I should ever come to H. I will call on you and your family. I know of no other advantages than those which entitle one to be numbered among one's better fellow creatures. Where I find them, there is my home.

If you want to write to me, dear Emilie, just address it directly to Teplitz, where I will be for another four weeks. Or send it to Vienna. It really doesn't matter. Look upon me as your friend and the friend of your family.

Ludwig van Beethoven

No letter from Beethoven to anyone is more generous, more poignant, or more self-effacing. His tone is that of a benevolent teacher but it is also intensely personal. Again, he apologizes for his lateness in replying and writes of his ill health, now to a child, as if beckoning for sympathy in view of the persistent precariousness of his physical well-being. To Emilie's apparent flattering comparison of Beethoven to Handel, Haydn, and Mozart he offers a gentle correction and modestly proposes that the widespread admiration he receives on all sides is still undeserved. This touch of humility resonates with a much earlier statement, in a letter of 1797 to the singer Christine Gerhardi, in which he had said that "it is a peculiar feeling to see and hear oneself praised and at the same time to realize one's own inferiority as much as I do. I always treat such occasions as admonishments to strive toward the inaccessible goal that art and nature have set us." It also links to a passage in the "Immortal Beloved" letter, in which Beethoven had written movingly of being "pursued by the goodness of mankind here and there," of being undeserving, of feeling the "humility of man toward man."[4] The letter to Emilie—and we must remember that he is writing to a child he does not know—speaks of his seeming uncertainty about his true place in the light of history, his awareness of potential for growth, and a sense of mystery about his qualities as a man and as an artist. It hints of his striving to look deeply into himself and to deflect everything in his life that might obstruct his artistic progress. Writing in the wake of his passionate letter to the "Immortal Beloved," he seems aware of the price he had already paid and would continue to pay for renouncing female companionship and love as he pulled his emotional energies back toward his work and career. The artistic sermon he preaches to Emilie in so kindly a manner carries conviction as he tells her not only to practice the piano but to devote herself to fathoming the inner meaning of her art, "for only art and science can raise men to the level of gods." We think of Prometheus, of Kant and the Enlightenment philosophers, of Schiller's *Letters on the Aesthetic Education of Man*, and of Beethoven as a bearer of belief in the potential of human development and the exploration of the widest range of human capacities.

Eight years later, in 1820, Beethoven copied down a quotation from Kant that rings with significance for his entire life and work—"the moral law within us and the starry skies above us." This pithy phrase sums up the image by which later generations saw Beethoven, the solitary artist, accepting his fate and confronting the eternal, both in his personal outlook and in his music. That there is more to it emerges from the Kantian idealism that dominated German thought at the time.[5] Kant's view of human knowledge presupposes a decisive distinction between objective reality, that is, the world of *phenomena* as we experience it, and an unknowable world of *noumena*—of things as they exist "in themselves" that underlie the fleeting world of appearances. As moral agents we are governed by what is eternal, we are "morally free active subject[s] independent of the causal order of nature."[6] This Kantian epigram, portraying a connection between the firmament and human morality, epitomizes Beethoven's whole sense of his artistic enterprise, whereby the artist—earth-bound, frail, and vulnerable but possessed of moral purpose—strives through art toward the transcendental world of the higher order of things, characterized in imagination as the realm of God but materially visible to all humanity as the starry heavens. This image as a collective desire vividly appears in Schiller's *Ode to Joy*:

Ihr stürzt nieder, Millionen?	Do you prostrate yourselves, you millions,
Ahnest du den Schöpfer, Welt?	Do you sense the Creator, World?
Such ihn überm Sternenzelt,	Seek him beyond the canopy of stars,
Über Sternen muss er wohnen.	Beyond the stars he must surely dwell.

That Beethoven in 1812 had reached the end of a long and profoundly important phase of his career and was poised on the threshold of a new path is clear to us and must have been clear to him as well, because he tells Emilie that "art has no limits; he [the artist] has a vague awareness of how far he is from reaching his goal." Beethoven's feeling for the contradiction between artistic and ordinary values emerges in his comparison of her and her family, clearly bourgeois people, to the wealthy classes "who betray themselves with the poverty of their inner selves." Writing from Teplitz, a spa frequented by royalty and the aristocracy, he found himself surrounded by rich aristocrats whose daily social behavior revealed their aimless lives. It was the time and place at which Goethe is said to have bowed as a royal carriage went by, while Beethoven belligerently strode away and turned his back.[7] We are also reminded of what Beethoven supposedly wrote in 1806 to Prince Karl Lichnowsky, one of his most reliable patrons and supporters:

"Prince, you are what you are through the accident of birth; what I am, I am through myself. There have been and will be thousands of princes; there is only one Beethoven."[8]

1826: The Old Child

On December 7, 1826, four months before his death, beset with illness and a sense of foreboding, Beethoven wrote to his old friend, the medical doctor Franz Gerhard Wegeler, at Coblenz on the Rhine, a boyhood companion from Bonn whom Beethoven had not seen in thirty years.[9] The letter speaks eloquently of Beethoven's reawakened feelings for Wegeler as he recalls their childhood friendship. "I remember all the love you have always shown me, for instance, how you had my room painted white and thus gave me such a pleasant surprise."[10]

> *If we drifted apart, that was due to the nature of our lives. Each of us had to pursue his intended purpose and seek to attain it. Yet the eternally unshakable foundations of what is good always held us strongly together. . . . My beloved friend! . . . I need hardly tell you that I have been overcome by the remembrance of things past and that many tears have been shed while the letter was being written.*

This message reveals the sick and aging composer's nostalgic vision of his early years at Bonn and his memories of old friends—not only Wegeler, no doubt, but also others close to Wegeler. They would have included Helene von Breuning, later Wegeler's mother-in-law, who had welcomed the young Beethoven into her house and her circle and had helped guide him through his difficult late teenage years. It would also have included Helene's daughter, Eleonore von Breuning, just his own age, to whom Beethoven dedicated a set of early variations and whom he called "my dearest friend" in a letter of 1793.[11]

Now in 1826, finishing his last complete string quartet, Opus 135, Beethoven was feeling the weight of the journey of a lifetime and a premonition that this illness might be his last. "I still hope to create a few large-scale works and then like an old child [*ein altes Kind*] to finish my days on earth among kind people." Beethoven was seeking comfort in memories of his childhood. He suppressed or avoided mentioning the many painful aspects of his early years, above all his mother's death, his rage at his alcoholic father, and his having had to become the head of his family while still in his teens. Less than three months earlier, he had gone through the trauma of his nephew Karl's abortive attempt at suicide. This crisis ended his years of striving to turn Karl, the central attachment of his later years, into a virtual son; thus he failed once more to find stability and warmth in a family relationship.[12]

But no hint of this problem appears in Beethoven's letter to his old friend Wegeler. Instead, his remembrance of things past suggests a spiritual homecoming in these last months, a lingering retrospective vision that might connect his youth and old age and enable him to look back at the wrenching emotional crises and dislocations he had suffered throughout his life. As he pondered his enduring infirmities, from parental abandonment, early illnesses, and melancholia to deafness to old-age sickness and isolation, he also knew that through it all he had persevered, had created a body of artistic work of monumental significance, and was recognized as an artist for the ages.

The dramatist Franz Grillparzer's funeral oration of 1827 is shot through with references to the divided character of Beethoven's visible persona, his social alienation contrasted with the wide human reach of his music and all the clear implications in the music of his love for humanity. Grillparzer was only thirty-six when he wrote this oration, and had really known Beethoven only in his later years, so it is not surprising that he stressed the painful aspects of Beethoven's existence, stated in the flowing rhetoric of the age:

> *The thorns of life had wounded him deeply, and as the castaway clings to the shore, so did he seek refuge in thine arms, O thou glorious sister and peer of the Good and the True, thou balm of wounded hearts, heaven-born Art!*[13]

Grillparzer mentions Beethoven's afflictions, seeming misanthropy, and loneliness precisely in order to contrast them with his role as "heir and amplifier" of the fame of Handel, Bach, Haydn, and Mozart, and his status as an artist to rank with the "immortals." The funeral oration establishes the basic narrative of later Beethoven literature, which has always stressed his deafness, his lingering physical ailments, and his pervasive psychological distress. Yet to balance the inevitable biographical emphasis on his limitations, it is at least as important that through perseverance he maintained the strength to thrust them aside, and endured them in order to follow the light of what he described to little Emilie as his "better genius."

Thinking back over his works, as he had done more than once while contemplating the idea of a complete edition, he could also have been aware of parallel connections between youth and old age in his artistic development, despite the distance he had traveled and the massive enlargement of his musical language over the years. Such connections between early and late works are hardly considered even by those who know the works deeply and intimately, owing to the profound changes in compositional procedure that gave rise to the famous "three periods." This tripartite division of his works became an early watchword in Beethoven biography and later served as a basic paradigm for understanding his development.[14] It tends to mask the connections between works from different periods, but they exist nonetheless.

An astute critic once compared Beethoven's artistic growth to a great column resembling a tree, composed of a "basal columnar mass surmounted by another, broader, higher cubical one, itself topped by still another mass of even greater width and depth and height. The three homogeneous but distinct forms are the three sections into which the prodigious work falls."[15]

Although we can trace far-reaching changes in Beethoven's music, we can also catch glimpses of the column through the thick foliage of his artistic development. His sense of purpose was clear from very early on. In each period, even his earliest, Beethoven was a resolutely original and forward-looking artist, not simply an early and gifted imitator of Mozart and Haydn who later found a ruggedly independent way to his own greatness. No matter how much his later compositions differed from his early ones, he always found ways to reach back to his own previous stages and to the works of his predecessors—above all, in his late phase, to Bach and Handel—in order to chart his way into the next stage represented by new and demanding compositional projects. This gathering up of earlier tendencies in order to move forward is apparent in many aspects of his creative process and we find it documented in his sketchbooks, in which initial ideas for compositions often look like regressions to historically earlier phases of musical style that are then elaborated, sharpened, modernized, and given strong individual profiles. When he can find the right ways to make use of them, these first versions of musical ideas are sculpted into forms clear enough to be expanded musically and strong enough to bear the weight and pressure of well-developed compositions. In reviewing his early training, first maturity, and influences from contemporary musical life, we have to strike a balance between his awareness of strong outer influences, above all those of Mozart and Haydn, and that inner, self-critical drive toward originality that characterizes his youthful development and every later phase of his life.

Life and Works

Another critical question remains. With Beethoven as with every great artist, drawing immediate connections between "life" and "works" is difficult. The difficulty may be even greater for composers than for writers or painters, especially for a composer such as Beethoven, whose music was preponderantly instrumental, because the "subject matter" of many of his instrumental works is virtually synonymous with their formal structures and emotional content. Of course, we can study the formal dynamics of his compositions and analyze their generic and stylistic features, but framing exact meanings for individual instrumental works, however much we are driven by intellectual necessity to do so, remains a distant and elusive task. As Schopenhauer puts it, music among all the arts—and he particularly meant instrumental music—directly articulates the noumenal, the inner essence of things, rather than the phenomenal.[16] In a striking passage, Schopenhauer, whose feeling for musical experience surpassed that of almost any other philosopher of the nineteenth century, argues that music's capacity to render experience is far greater than what Leibniz had imagined, namely, that music "is an occult exercise in the counting of numbers in which the mind does not know it is counting."[17] Schopenhauer dissents: If music "were nothing more, the satisfaction it affords would inevitably resemble what we feel when a sum in arithmetic comes out right, and could not be that profound pleasure with which we see the deepest recesses of our nature find expression. . . . We must attribute to music a far more serious and profound significance that refers to the innermost being of the world and of our own self." And shortly afterward, "The composer reveals the innermost nature of the world, and expresses the profoundest wisdom in a language that his reasoning faculty does not understand." And now Schopenhauer comes to the crux for the artistic biographer: "Therefore in the composer, more than in any other artist, the man is entirely separate and distinct from the artist."[18] Still later, in a chapter "On the Metaphysics of Music," he claims that music, "the most powerful of all the arts, . . . attains its ends entirely from its own resources." And he chooses as the summa of instrumental music "a symphony of Beethoven," from which "all the human passions and emotions speak: . . . joy, grief, love, hatred, terror, hope, and so on in innumerable shades, yet all, as it were, only in the abstract and without any particularization; it is their mere form without the material."[19]

A fair number of Beethoven's works—more than most of us realize—have texts or programmatic associations indicating particular aesthetic qualities, and there is evidence that Beethoven aimed not only to render such qualities in a general sense, but to bring out specific traits of character in individual works. Especially in his later works, he developed a musical language in instrumental music that at times paralleled the eloquence of human rhetoric and even, in some cases, approximated it—for example, the speechlike instrumental recitatives in the Ninth Symphony finale. Moreover, certain features of his life, such as his persistent illnesses and his depression, are apparently mirrored to some degree in early works such as *La Malinconia* ("Melancholy"), the title for the finale of his String Quartet Opus 18 No. 6, and even more explicitly in a late work, the "Holy Song of Thanksgiving to the Divinity by a Convalescent, in the Lydian

Mode," the famous slow movement of the Quartet Opus 132. But although generations of commentators have sought to find literary analogues and to portray in language what often seems beyond description in the gestural power and psychological subtlety of his music, for many of his most important instrumental works such meaning eludes translation into words. Furthermore, when it comes to attaching individual works to the biographical background, we are often unable to say, apart from occasional connections, what congeries of circumstances in his outer life may have generated a particular composition at a particular time.

What then, broadly speaking, is the relationship of life to works? The question has aroused endless responses, but the more authoritative ones have been largely negative. One extreme view, voiced by the writer and critic Donald Francis Tovey, took this form: "to study the lives of great artists is often a positive hindrance to the understanding of their works, for it is usually the study of what they have not mastered, and thus it undermines their authority in the things which they have mastered."[20] Another writer, Carl Dahlhaus, opens his interpretive Beethoven book with a chapter on "Life and Work" that could hardly be more skeptical about the relevance of "a biographical narrative that runs along beside the interpretation of the work without making any important intervention in it."[21]

The reasons for pessimism are clear enough. What we call the "life" of an artist, in all its ramifications, is more or less what is left over from the artist's immersion in the working projects, present and future, that fill his or her consciousness and force daily life into patterns of concentration and sacrifice beyond the routines of other people. That most people have an intuitive awareness of this pressure is precisely why biographies of artists are of interest; they form a bridge by which we can sense the ways in which artists are like everyone else and those in which they stand aloof and apart, driven by necessities that we would like to understand. Accordingly, the relevant "life" for biographical purposes is made up in only small part of the events and encounters that form the artist's calendar. Much of the remainder concerns the parts of the life that are squarely aimed at producing and disseminating the artist's works. For these parts we would do better to speak of "career" than "life." At the same time we sense that an element of inner character always underlies the artistic enterprise and gives it staying power as the individual artist faces the vicissitudes of life and career. With Beethoven we feel a granitic inner strength that sustained him through all his physical and psychic troubles.

Our awareness of separation between outer life and inner life is reinforced by testimony from artists who feel a profound sense of psychological division, as if they were two persons, not one. We get the sense of this from many reports. The poet and writer Marge Piercy puts it this way:

> [O]nce I am working on a poem, it becomes molten ore. It becomes "not me." And the being who works with it is not the normal, daily me. It has no sex, no shame, no ambition, no net. It eats silence like bread. I can't stay in that white-hot place long, but when I am in it, there is nothing else. All the dearness and detritus of ordinary living falls away, even when that is the stuff of the poem. It is as remote as if I were an archaeologist working with the kitchen midden of a 4,000-year-old city.[22]

For Beethoven, creative necessity dominated everything else. It utterly determined his outer life, constantly interfered with it, and rendered it perpetually erratic, as it does for most artists on his level. When he wrote his music manuscripts in fair copy his attention to details and nuances of notation is astonishing in its precision and care, a virtual mirror of the structural and gestural properties of the music itself. But when he wrote letters, his writing was a scrawl that hardly anyone could read.[23] His artistic involvement was so intense that it tended to reduce the rest of his life to a struggle for equilibrium in which the pressure of the work could cause the life almost to wither away, "like some organ they no longer require," as Rilke said of Tolstoy and Rodin.[24]

Because the feeling of separation can be intensified in times of crisis, biographers are often surprised to find that during periods of despair and near breakdown, artists can use their gifts to create works that seem to bear no trace of their current afflictions—a famous example is Beethoven's completion of the Second Symphony at the time of the Heiligenstadt Testament. Here we come to a boundary problem that defies us to find connecting pathways between biographical facts and artistic work and, if we find them, to interpret them. We accept as an act of faith that there must be connecting threads, but they are labyrinthine, buried below the surface and rarely visible except as hints given in runic remarks, letters, diaries, or the rare testimony of contemporaries. This predicament holds especially for Beethoven, who was not given to overt descriptions of his purposes and certainly not of his works. The unleashing of his creative imagination through improvisation at the keyboard and through sketching was so instinctive that we should hardly be surprised that he would not, or could not, furnish any verbal accounts of what he was doing. Nevertheless, the logic of his artistic aims is partly revealed from what we find in the thousands of pages of sketches he left behind, and to a lesser degree in remarks on art in his letters and *Tagebuch*, his diary.

Yet despite all these problems, the theory of an absolute separation is self-defeating and will not hold. Works do not materialize out of nothing. They are created, and always by individuals carrying out specific imaginative purposes; they are not made by abstract processes or algorithms. Accordingly, we can acknowledge that deeply rooted elements in the creative individual's personality, angle of vision, speech habits, interactions with people, and ways of dealing with the world find resonance in many of the artist's works. Such elements combine to shape what one writer calls the artist's "creative character," the inner being that leaves an indelible personal imprint on works that in some way seems unmistakable, even if we cannot define it in detail.[25] This idea comes close to what Flaubert meant when he wrote, "The author in his works should be like God in the universe: always present, but nowhere visible."[26]

The sketchbooks Beethoven used throughout his life furnish rich evidence of his creative character, by virtue of their content and their very preservation. They also provide us with the equivalent of an artistic diary in many volumes that lasted from his early years to the end of his life in 1827 and cover a multitude of his works, great and small. After having used single leaves and sheets for sketching in his earlier years, Beethoven began to use sketchbooks regularly in 1798, at the time he began work on his first string quartets. From then on he organized his creative routine in such a way that on any given day he could lay his hands on his current "desk" sketchbook, a bound or hand-sewn book of oblong music paper in which he planned and worked out the larger shape and more detailed content of

a given composition, whatever its size or importance. He also used loose
leaves apart from these sketchbooks, and after 1814 he carried pocket-sized
booklets of music paper to use out of doors, as the spirit moved him. As
one contemporary quoted him, referring to Joan of Arc, "without my banner I dare not come."[27] But the mass of sketchbooks of both kinds continued to grow. That he kept his sketchbooks so carefully over so many years,
more carefully than he kept his finished autograph scores, suggests that he
was, in effect, creating a record of his own development. He protected the
precious sketchbook hoard from loss or damage despite the chaos of his
daily life and the need to haul them from place to place when he moved his
lodgings in Vienna, as he frequently did.[28] Instead of destroying his preliminary ideas for his works or allowing them to become dispersed and
lost, as almost every one of his major predecessors from Bach to Mozart
had done, Beethoven kept the bulk of his precompositional material intact,
in principle making it possible for him to look back at any time over the
details of his own development as reflected not only in the finished works
but in their formative background.[29] As one scholar put it, "many of the
homely, cluttered leaves that had accompanied him on the long journey
from Bonn to Vienna in 1792 were still within his reach when he died."[30]
The chaos of his daily life is reported by a long line of visitors and
observers. Thus Baron de Trémont, who visited Beethoven in 1809, wrote
later:

> Picture to yourself the dirtiest, most disorderly place imaginable—
> blotches of moisture covered the ceiling; an oldish grand piano, on
> which the dust vied for a place with various pieces of engraved and
> manuscript music; under the piano (I do not exaggerate) an unemptied
> chamber pot; beside it, a small walnut table accustomed to the frequent
> overturning of the secretary placed upon it; a quantity of pens
> encrusted with ink, compared with which the proverbial tavern-pens
> would shine; then more music.[31]

The dazzling contrast between quotidian disorder and artistic order,
between utter carelessness in matters of daily life and fanatic zeal in preserving the record of his personal artistic history and seeing to the last

detail in his work, captures a basic paradox. What Beethoven would have regarded as the essence of his life lay in the works themselves; they testify, not to his life as it was forced on him by the necessities of survival, but to the abiding imaginative visions by which he sought to rise above contingency. He was self-consciously aware, as he wrote to Prince Galitzin in 1825, that "unfortunately we are dragged down from the other-worldly element in art only too rudely into the earthly and human sides of life."[32] We can hope that the deciphering and publication of the sketchbooks in all their detail—a massive project that, one hundred fifty years after the first attempts, still has a long way to go—may enable future readers and listeners to come to a better understanding of Beethoven's artistic character than we have had till now. If his "creative character" is found in the finished compositions, after all, it is also found to some degree in the process that gave them life, in the ceaseless labor to generate and improve his works that is embodied in the vast mass of sketches, drafts, and revised autographs. In this book my primary concern is with the artistic side of the equation, that is, with Beethoven's artistic development, while at the same time I try to give a balanced overview of Beethoven the man.

PART ONE

※━◆━◆━❦█❦━◆━◆━※

THE EARLY YEARS
1770–1792

CHAPTER 1

BEGINNINGS

Bonn as a Musical Center

Bonn, Beethoven's birthplace, was and is in essence a small town in Germany. In modern times the capital of the West German Republic from the end of World War II in 1945 until 2000, Bonn remains today what it has always been, a small, prosperous commercial station on the west bank of the Rhine south of Cologne. It is not a major center to rival Cologne, Frankfurt, or Munich, nor is it even as developed as Mannheim, once its cultural rival. An air of comfortable provinciality has always pervaded its civic life, all the more now since the capital of reunited Germany has moved to Berlin, and Beethoven as historic native son remains Bonn's principal cultural attraction.

Yet for centuries the city had political importance out of proportion to its size because it was the long-established seat of the archbishops of Cologne.[1] The prince holding this position was, by designation, a vassal of the Austrian branch of the Holy Roman empire, still ruled by the Habsburg dynasty with its principal capital in Vienna. The archbishop, as an imperial Elector, was one of the seven original ecclesiastical princes of the ancient empire—more a loose collection of states than a geographic entity—that sprawled across central Europe and claimed the allegiance of millions. Its long history notwithstanding, the role of the empire in power politics had been virtually nullified for more than a century before Beethoven's birth in 1770 by the rising dominance of Britain, France, and above all Prussia under the Hohenzollern, especially Frederick the Great. In 1770 the empire was still ruled by the aging empress Maria Theresa, but after the death of her husband Francis I in 1765, her son Joseph II became her coadjutor. Taking power in 1780, Joseph in time gained a reputation as an enlightened reformer, pursuing his anticlerical policies in a regime that shrewdly combined state despotism with paternal reforms aimed at improving education and the common welfare.

No such ambitions were nourished in the Rhineland by the Elector of Cologne during Beethoven's earliest years. The Elector from 1761 to 1784 was Maximilian Friedrich, a member of the Swabian house of Königseck-Rothenfels that for several generations had held the deanship of the cathedral of Cologne. Max Friedrich, as an English visitor put it in 1780, was an "easy, good-tempered, indolent, friendly, man . . . very merry and affable . . . easy and agreeable, having lived all his life in ladies' company, which he is said to have liked better than his breviary."[2] As governing Elector, Max Friedrich left affairs of state to his strong-minded minister, Kaspar Anton von Belderbusch, who managed the court with a tight fist for expenditures. Belderbusch must also have been unusually adept in political maneuvering, since he was said not only to have shared a mistress with the Elector but to have fathered the woman's children.[3]

Bonners in this period took pride in their town's status as a provincial capital, and visitors were impressed by its imposing Electoral palace, its favorable location on the Rhine with the hills of the *Siebengebirge* across the river, and its pleasant surrounding countryside. Although its churches were venerable Catholic institutions, cultural life centered mainly on the Electoral court, whose tradition of music making went back to the seventeenth century. Its singers and instrumentalists were regularly and routinely engaged in producing music for the church, theater, and, in the sense of the period, concerts attended by the local aristocracy and burghers. A few of the wealthier families cultivated music at home, and some of these, above all the von Breunings, played important roles in Beethoven's early development.

Bonn's emerging status as a musical stronghold should be seen in the light of regional competition. Its main musical rival was the court of Mannheim in the Palatinate, in many ways more important than Bonn for most of the eighteenth century. At Mannheim music had sprung to life as early as the 1720s under the Palatine Elector Carl Philip. It gained further

Beethoven's birthplace in Bonn, now a museum and the seat of the Beethoven-Haus. (Beethoven-Haus, Bonn)

momentum in the 1740s when his successor, Carl Theodor, engaged the Bohemian violinist and composer Johann Stamitz, who set about raising the quality of its orchestra to European heights. When the British music critic and historian Charles Burney visited Mannheim in 1772 he called the Mannheim orchestra "an army of generals." He could have said the same about its opera company, under the direction of Ignaz Holzbauer (whom Mozart once praised), which flourished from the 1750s to the 1770s while Bonn's still lagged behind.

Growing up in Bonn, the young Beethoven could feel that local musical life had long been a family affair, since the court musicians were led by his grandfather, also named Ludwig van Beethoven. Grandfather Ludwig was not known as a composer but was reported by contemporaries to be an excellent singer and keyboard player, and as paterfamilias of the musical forces he cut a formidable figure. Wegeler described him, in a passage that could equally fit his grandson, as "a short, muscular man, with extremely animated eyes . . . greatly respected as an artist," and this impression is reinforced by his portrait painted from life.[4] He suffered the pain of having to place his wife, Maria Josepha Poll, in a sheltered cloister, apparently because she was an alcoholic. Further, Old Ludwig had to cope with the same proclivity toward alcoholism on the part of his only son, Johann van Beethoven, who had some competence as a music teacher but stumbled through a troubled career as a court singer and violinist, a weak and forlorn link between father and son. Fortunately, Johann in turn married a woman of quality who until her death held the family together with affection and imagination. His long-suffering wife was Maria Magdalena Keverich Leym, daughter of a court cook. She bore seven children, of whom three survived to adulthood and among whom Ludwig was the second. For years the grandson kept the portrait of his grandfather and namesake on his walls, though he scarcely ever spoke of his father.[5] Although Johann inherited an estate of some size from his father in 1773, by 1784 he had squandered most of it and was described in a court memoir as having a "deteriorated voice" and as being "very poor."[6]

Bonn under Max Friedrich had a modest operatic life that was to grow larger in the later decades of the century. One local opera company was led by Andrea Lucchesi, a capable Venetian composer who brought Italian singers to Bonn in 1771 and performed several of his own operas; in fact, Beethoven's father and grandfather had both sung in at least one of them. When Grandfather Ludwig died in December 1773, the Elector preferred Lucchesi to Johann van Beethoven as his successor, paying him twice the salary that had been paid to Ludwig. Thereafter Lucchesi's career rose and fell with the tides of local rivalries. His main rival was Christian Gottlob Neefe, a very different kind of musician, who became the young Beethoven's principal teacher. Still, Lucchesi managed to stay at Bonn until his death in 1801, surviving the French occupation that began in 1794. In Lucchesi and in Cajetan Mattioli, the court concertmaster, Bonn had two solid Venetian musicians and thus a strong link to Italian performing traditions that balanced the rise of German opera at Bonn and the increasing emphasis at the court on instrumental music.[7]

In 1781–82, when Beethoven was turning eleven, as many as sixteen operas were rehearsed, if not all produced, at court, by composers as diverse as Florian Gassmann, André-Ernest-Modeste Grétry, Georg Benda,

Holzbauer, and Neefe. And in the following year, no doubt because of the coadjutor Max Franz's admiration for Mozart, the season included that composer's brilliant new Singspiel, *Die Entführung aus dem Serail* ("The Abduction from the Seraglio"). Singspiel—vernacular opera with spoken dialogue, homely plots, and simple songs in German that had popular appeal—was on the rise, and with *Entführung* Mozart effectively lifted the whole genre onto a higher plane. Since its premiere had just taken place in Vienna in July 1782 (where it had been a raging success and received sixteen performances), its production in Bonn so soon thereafter shows Max Franz's ambition to make the Rhineland town a little Vienna, a distant provincial reflection of the cultural life of the capital. The robust energy and subtlety of *Entführung,* far beyond the reach of the other Singspiel composers, must have made a powerful impression on the young Beethoven, for whom playing and hearing Mozart's operas and other works when they were new remained of lasting importance.[8]

The musical reputation of the Bonn court rested mainly on its orchestra, whose rise in quality after 1778 coincided, probably not by accident, with a decline at Mannheim.[9] In 1783 the orchestra was big for a small court, with more than twenty-seven regular players, including eleven violinists, three violists, two cellists, two contrabass players, two flutists, four horn players, and three bassoonists, plus trumpeters and percussion players.

But more important than their numbers was the quality and professional experience of its leading players. The principal violinist was Franz Anton Ries, who except for a short stay in Vienna, remained a faithful Rhinelander and citizen of Bonn. Born in 1755, a year before Mozart, he outlasted not only Beethoven but also his own son Ferdinand Ries, who was close to Beethoven as piano pupil, copyist, agent, and biographer. A Bonn memoir of 1784 said of the elder Ries that he was the "best violinist, especially for solo playing, plays extremely well, and is still young."[10] More telling is a 1791 account by Carl Ludwig Junker: "He is an outstanding score reader, sightreads splendidly, conducts from the violin chair," is as good a musician as Christian Cannabich, his celebrated rival at Mannheim, and "gives spirit and liveliness by means of his strong, decisive bowing." Junker also reported that the setup of the orchestra at Bonn for a Paisiello opera was "like no other I have seen, but very effective," with Ries standing in the middle and with the string sections on one side and the winds on the other. In 1790 Ries was joined by Andreas Romberg, another excellent violinist, who remained for three years until the impending dissolution of the court drove him on to Hamburg and a successful career as violinist and composer.[11]

For years the leading cellist was Joseph Reicha, a Bohemian like the Stamitzes, who joined the orchestra in 1784 and became court opera director in 1790. Joseph was known as a virtuoso and something of a composer; his cello concertos display his facility in high registers and difficult passage work.[12] He was the uncle of Anton Reicha, who, exactly Beethoven's age, came to Bonn as a boy of fourteen, played violin and flute, studied with Neefe alongside Beethoven, and later had an influential career as composer and theorist in France. Andreas Romberg was joined by his cousin Bernhard Romberg, later the most famous cellist of his time in a field crowded with competitors. After a few years in Bonn Bernhard Romberg toured as a soloist from England to Russia, and was a prolific composer of mediocre works.[13] Present too was the horn player Nikolaus Simrock, who founded his music-publishing firm in Bonn in 1793 and stayed in contact with Beethoven for years thereafter. Simrock was the first publisher of several important Beethoven works, including the "Kreutzer" Sonata, Opus 47; the Piano Sonata Opus 81a, *Lebewohl*; and the cello sonatas of Opus 102.[14]

For a smaller musical center the array of talent was remarkable, and playing viola in the orchestra with such performers gave Beethoven a first-class introduction to the major orchestral literature of the time, including symphonies by Haydn, Mozart, and many other composers. He also took part in operatic performance as seen and heard from the orchestra pit. He may have had violin and viola lessons from Franz Ries. By adding the violist's experience of playing inner-voice string parts within the orchestral ensemble and probably also in quartets he undoubtedly gained a stronger feeling for orchestral sonorities and idiomatic playing than he could have had in his more limited role of keyboard virtuoso. Certainly after the years in Bonn there is no evidence that he ever played a stringed instrument in an orchestra again, and only on special occasions in later life did virtuosi of the caliber of these Bonn players turn up in any numbers to perform his orchestral works. After leaving Bonn and establishing himself as a free-lance composer, he had occasional limited access to orchestras assembled and paid for by a few wealthy patrons, such as the Lobkowitzes, but never had a regular court orchestra at his disposal for any length of time. For each of his own later public concerts of orchestral works he had to put the orchestra together himself. It often included a fair number of amateurs playing alongside a few top professionals such as the violinist Ignaz Schuppanzigh and the cellist Joseph Linke.

Bach from the Hands of Neefe

Christian Gottlob Neefe counts as Beethoven's only important teacher at Bonn.[15] A musician of solid attainments, Neefe came to Bonn in 1779 as the head of an operatic troupe, settled down, and in 1781 moved into the role of court organist. Though not a gifted composer, he was a devoted teacher and a stern critic of current musical trends that fell below the standards of craftsmanship he brought from his background at Leipzig—where, before Neefe's time, Johann Sebastian Bach had been the dominant figure. Such standards implied an emphasis on principles of strict composition, up to and including fugue, as codified by Johann Philipp Kirnberger in his *Kunst des reinen Satzes* ("Art of Strict Composition") and by Friedrich Wilhelm Marpurg, especially in his *Abhandlung von der Fuge* ("Treatise on Fugue"). Neefe had a typical north German musician's opinion of his Italian rival Lucchesi at Bonn: "He is a light, agreeable, and lively composer, whose counterpoint is cleaner than that of most of his countrymen."[16] Having studied composition with Johann Adam Hiller, who had worked in Leipzig in the post-Bach years, Neefe primarily composed and produced operas, especially *Singspiele*, in the 1770s. His strength as a teacher rather than a composer may have been an advantage for Beethoven, who could profit from Neefe's rigorous standards and apparent generosity. We have no reason to doubt Beethoven's sincerity laced with self-confidence when in October 1792, on the eve of his departure from Bonn for Vienna, he wrote to Neefe, "I thank you for the advice you have

C. G. NEEFE.

Christian Gottlob Neefe, Beethoven's first important teacher, to whom Beethoven wrote, about 1793: "If I ever become a great man, you too will have a share in my success." (Beethoven-Haus, Bonn)

very often given me about making progress in my divine art. If I ever become a great man, you too will have a share in my success."[17] Something of the same resolute, self-confident attitude speaks from a silhouette of Beethoven at about age sixteen, made by a local artist named Joseph Neesen.

Not only did Neefe's encouragement partly compensate for Johann van Beethoven's failings, but his serious engagement with current literature and intellectual affairs played a part in the young Beethoven's intellectual growth. At Leipzig Neefe had made contact with the poets Christian Gellert and Johann Christoph Gottsched, and he took an interest in aesthetics. It was probably through Neefe that the young Beethoven first encountered the German literary movement, the *Sturm und Drang* ("storm and stress"), which took its name from a play written in 1776 by Maximilian Klinger.

LUDWIG VAN BEETHOVEN

in seinem 16ten Jahre.

Beethoven at about age sixteen, in court dress and with pigtail, in a silhouette attributed to Joseph Neesen. (Beethoven-Haus, Bonn)

Sturm und Drang aimed at a new kind of poetry and drama that stressed natural feeling and exuberant originality in opposition to neoclassical formal language. Neefe was a member of the Illuminati, a radical group of Freemasons who promoted the progressive ideas then sweeping Germany in response to the political crises that were coming to a head in France.[18] And Neefe also belonged to the local *Lesegesellschaft* ("reading society") that was formed in 1787 after the Illuminati were suppressed in Bonn, as they were elsewhere in Germany.

Beyond his role as a mentor and teacher of modern styles, Neefe earned his place in history by introducing the young Beethoven to the music of Johann Sebastian Bach. His burnishing of Bach's image emerges in a very important notice that Neefe published about the young prodigy Beethoven as early as March 1783, when the boy was only twelve:

> *Louis van Beethoven* [sic], *son of the tenor singer mentioned, a boy of eleven years, and of most promising talent. He plays the clavier very skillfully and with power, reads at sight very well, and—to put it as simply as possible—he plays chiefly* The Well-Tempered Clavier *of Sebastian Bach, which Herr Neefe put into his hands. Whoever knows this collection of preludes and fugues in all the keys—which might almost be called the* non plus ultra *of our art—will know what this means. So far as his duties permitted, Herr Neefe has also given him instruction in thorough-bass. He is now training him in composition and for his encouragement has had nine variations for the pianoforte, written by him on a march—by Ernst Christoph Dressler—engraved at Mannheim. This youthful genius is deserving of help to enable him to travel. He would certainly become a second Wolfgang Amadeus Mozart if he progresses as he has begun.*[19]

This is no mere plea for support of a talented beginner. It is a profession of faith in J. S. Bach as a supreme musical model—and this at a time when the greater part of Bach's output was still little known and hard to find, except for copies that circulated among groups of enthusiasts who included Bach's sons, a handful of surviving Bach pupils, and a few theorists wedded to Bach's achievements, as well as some lay admirers. It is indicative of Neefe's knowledge of Bach and devotion to his music that in 1800 Simrock commissioned him to furnish a corrected text of *The Well-Tempered Clavier* for local publication.

In the Germany of 1783 the name Bach for most people referred either to his best-known son, Carl Philipp Emanuel, then rounding out his career at Hamburg—or to his youngest son, Johann Christian, who had just died in England in 1782. Musicians knew of old Sebastian's reputation as a legendary patriarch of music, but in the age of *galant* homophony, his music, though of transcendent quality to Bach enthusiasts, seemed arcane and difficult to average musicians. In Bach's lifetime only two cantatas and a handful of his keyboard works had been published, because music prints were expensive to produce in the earlier part of the century. For thirty years after his death in 1750 there were only twelve Bach editions, mainly his late and contrapuntally "learned" works—*The Art of Fugue* in 1750, the *Musical Offering* and the third part of the *Clavierübung* in 1761.[20]

It was only from about 1800 on that more publications of Bach's music began to appear, their production picking up momentum throughout Beethoven's lifetime. What little of Bach was known in these early years was regarded by most musicians as formidably difficult to perform and to understand. That Beethoven could learn to know and play *The Well-Tempered Clavier* so early gave him direct exposure to Bach's unparalleled command of musical logic and depth of expression, even if he could hardly integrate it into this embryonic stage of his own compositional development, which was inevitably aimed at mastering much easier contemporary styles and techniques. Bachian counterpoint remained a latent influence for many years before it reemerged in Beethoven's later life, when he was ready to accept the very different artistic responsibility of coming fully to grips with the intricate mysteries of Bach's art.

Kant, Schiller, and the Enlightenment

Some of Beethoven's mentors and patrons were caught up in the Enlightenment—which in Germany remained a loose constellation of progressive social and intellectual ideals, clearly not a political movement. The young composer could also shape his aspirations along progressive lines in other ways. One strand of the German Enlightenment was anchored in the work of Immanuel Kant, whose reformulation of idealistic philosophy was in full swing by the 1780s. Beethoven may not have read contemporary philosophy widely and painstakingly, but we have to reckon seriously with his contention, made years later, that although he did not consider himself "learned," from childhood on he had always striven to be acquainted with what the best and wisest intellectuals of his age had thought and written.[21] Kant's treatises were lively subjects of discussion at the university in Bonn in the later 1780s, the leading local Kantian being a philosopher named Elias van den Schuren.[22] And the interest in Kantian idealism coincided with the radical political teachings of the local pedagogue Eulogius Schneider, as well as the fiery new spirit of social revolution and personal liberation that Friedrich Schiller was promoting in his dramas.

A new world of German literary experience, in poetry, fiction, and drama, had arisen in the works of Goethe, followed swiftly and dynamically by Schiller. Goethe's plays and early novels, classics of *Sturm und Drang*, broke through established narrative conventions to place sensuous and personal emotional experience at the center—above all in his 1774 novel *Werther*, in which young Werther, "lost in fantastic dreams" and hopelessly in love with his Charlotte, ends by taking his own life. Along with a new focus on the emotional fate of the individual, Goethe's dramas express hatred of tyranny and the virtues of freedom, responding to the political transformations in Europe and America in these decades that for Beethoven's generation were raising the "revolutionary fever" that he later mentioned in a latter.[23] Goethe's *Egmont*, *Tasso*, and *Iphigenia* all entwined the theme of personal sacrifice with that of political liberty. So did the even stronger plays of Schiller, beginning with *The Robbers*, a drama of heroic rebellion against societal norms. The protagonist in this work, Karl Moor, inspired by Plutarchan heroes, becomes the leader of a band of robbers to fight the injustices he has suffered from the evils of society. That Moor ultimately fails to convert his dreams to reality does not lessen the strength of Schiller's portrayal or its image of a single man's striving to change the world as he found it. The first production of *The Robbers* at the German National Theater in Mannheim in January 1782 caused an uproar:

> *The theater was like a madhouse—rolling eyes, clenched fists, hoarse cries in the auditorium. Strangers fell sobbing into each other's arms, women on the point of fainting staggered towards the exit. There was a universal commotion as in chaos, out of which a new creation bursts forth.*[24]

A public response of such intensity manifests Schiller's revolutionary impact, and his plays could easily fire ambitions in younger artists, including musicians, to find their own ways to evoke similar audience reactions. The passion, the architecture, and the rhetorical strength of Schiller's five-act dramas made them the most potent theater works of their time. As such they could very well have been important aesthetic models for the young Beethoven as he imagined ways of expanding the scale and intensifying the emotional content of his larger and more powerful works, above all his symphonies, after settling into his first years in Vienna.

Schiller's later plays, including *Love and Intrigue* and *Don Carlos*, all appeared during Beethoven's teenage years, and every one embodied libertarian themes and a plot in which a male hero follows his destiny, however tragically, in the name of freedom. It was no accident that Beethoven thought of setting Schiller's *Ode to Joy*—an appeal to human brotherhood in an imagined ideal state—as early as the 1790s, and that he held on to the plan throughout his life until he finally realized it decades later in the Ninth Symphony. The long gestation of the Ninth Symphony marks the underlying persistence of his basic liberal ideals.

Besides these general trends of the 1780s, which were felt in every German city and region, local developments at Bonn opened access to new ways of thinking. In 1785, his first year as Elector, Max Franz raised the Bonn academy to the status of a university, and four years later Beethoven and Anton Reicha both matriculated on the same day, May 14, as students in the faculty of philosophy.[25] The faculty included Eulogius Schneider as professor of classical Greek and belles lettres.[26] Schneider was a charismatic ex-Franciscan who became passionately involved in current politics and in 1790 published poetry shot through with praise for the revolution in France, including the recent fall of the Bastille.[27] We get a glimpse of Schneider's rhetoric from a remark of his to the duke of Württemberg: "Enlightenment has reduced the power of the ruler to certain limits, and has taught the rulers that they wear their crowns only for the common welfare."[28] A peripatetic dissident, Schneider went on to Mainz, where he ran into trouble with the leading Catholics, and eventually to Strasbourg, where he espoused Jacobin views and, as public prosecutor, saw to executions. Later a victim of these tumultuous times, he himself went to the guillotine during the years of the Terror. At Bonn Schneider had taken the lead in 1790 in organizing a local memorial service for the death of Emperor Joseph II, whose socially progressive views were well known. It was for this ceremony that Beethoven wrote his cantata on the death of Joseph.

The German princes were shaken to their roots by the revolution that swept over France in 1789. Some of them were sincere in professing noble ideals and promoting religious and intellectual freedom—but when it came to political action by revolutionary sympathizers they drew the line. In Germany and Austria it was anything but prudent to preach or foment opposition. Not that Beethoven, despite his liberal beliefs, was seriously committed to revolution or anything approaching it, certainly not to the degree represented by Eulogius Schneider. On the verge of his career as a musician, inevitably dependent on the public success of his work and on the good will and largesse of the nobility, Beethoven authentically believed in freedom as a political and artistic credo but he also recognized, early and late in his life, that "the world is a king and must be flattered."[29] Notwithstanding his basic faith in liberal ideals, Beethoven in later life uttered many contradictory political remarks that somehow seemed to support the ideals of freedom and human rights and, at the same time, accept the role of the aristocracy in the furthering of his career.[30] Still, to the end of his life Beethoven maintained his faith in the doctrines of individual human rights and of collective enlightened representative government. Writing the Ninth Symphony in the 1820s, a time when such ideals were under heavy attack from the restored monarchies after the Congress of Vienna, he found in Schiller's *Ode* and its declaration that "all men shall be brothers" a Utopian message that he had been ready to deliver all his life but that now seemed more urgent and relevant than ever before.

Max Franz and the Mozart Legacy

Neefe's notice of 1783 called the young Beethoven potentially a "second Mozart." By this Neefe surely meant not only or even principally Mozart as composer but Mozart as the European *wunderkind* of the

The Elector Max Franz, Beethoven's principal patron at Bonn. (Beethoven-Haus, Bonn)

1760s, the celebrated child prodigy who had sat on the laps of patrons across Europe under the watchful tutelage of his father Leopold. Of course it dawned on patrons at Bonn that a similar prodigy was in their midst, and it occurred to Johann that he might become a second Leopold, and might reap from his son's talent a comparable degree of fame and what he hoped would be fortune. But neither Johann nor anyone else at Bonn could match Leopold Mozart's entrepreneurial skills, nor could the young Beethoven, despite his gifts, live up to the golden image of the child Mozart. That his father and others spared no effort in trying is evident from efforts to conceal the boy's real age and thereby to make him seem younger than he was; thus the rumor floated for some years that Beethoven was born in 1772, two years later than the actual year.

The levers of court patronage lay with the Elector. In 1784 the new incumbent was the twenty-eight-year-old Archduke Maximilian Franz, youngest son of Maria Theresa, who had been Max Friedrich's coadjutor for several years. With his accession a new wave of support for music could clearly be felt, and Neefe in 1789 praised his patronage to the skies.[31] As a younger brother of Joseph II, Max Franz seemed to represent a force for the new Enlightenment trends in conservative, Catholic-dominated Bonn. And most important for the young Beethoven was his enthusiasm for Mozart.

Max Franz, who had some musical ability himself, had known Mozart since he made a state visit to Salzburg in the 1770s, saw *Il Re Pastore*, the *festa teatrale* that Mozart had composed for the occasion, and heard the young man play the piano. He met Mozart again in 1781 when the composer made the decisive move of his career and came to live permanently in the capital. As Mozart wrote in his letters (which include disdainful remarks about Max Franz's stupidity and corpulence), the archduke tried to promote his interests whenever he could; if Mozart had had more such supporters in the aristocracy his later career might have been very different. Thus he wrote to Leopold on January 23, 1782: "he [the archduke Max Franz] thinks the world of me. . . . [H]e shoves me forward on every occasion, and I might almost say with certainty that if at this moment he were Elector of Cologne, I should be his Kapellmeister."[32] Indeed, after just one year in office, Max Franz actually tried to induce Mozart to accept the position. His failure to get Mozart may have spurred his support for Beethoven as a local prodigy, and it was probably Max Franz who paid for the sixteen-year-old Beethoven's trip to Vienna in the spring of 1787 for the purpose of making direct contact with Mozart.

Beethoven's access to the world of contemporary music, in its rich profusion of techniques and genres governed by the prevailing musical language that history has called the "classical style," came primarily through exposure to local performance of a wide range of music, from chamber and orchestral music to sacred music and opera. That the Bonn orchestra rehearsed and played every day, providing a wealth of exposure to contemporary styles, is not just a reasonable assumption but is confirmed by witnesses, including Anton Reicha, perhaps the young Beethoven's worthiest peer. Brimming with expectations of a musical career, Reicha was exposed to exactly the same musical environment but eventually showed that his talents lay more in theory and pedagogy than in composition, despite his many finished works. Reicha later said of his years in Bonn that

playing and hearing good music every day, instrumental and vocal, I
became completely devoted to music. . . . [U]p to then I had been a
simple performer and quite an ordinary musician; now the passion for
composition came over me and became a veritable fever.[33]

Performing forces at Bonn depended for their music mainly on the excellent court library, which contained a large cross-section of music by contemporary composers from all over continental Europe—from France to Bohemia, from northern Germany to Italy. The collection offered extensive holdings in opera, sacred music, and instrumental music, according to a 1784 inventory.[34] The operatic scores were predominantly Italian, seventy-nine in all compared to only thirteen in French. This preponderance reflected the leading role of Italian opera across Europe, despite the growing interest in Vienna and a few other German centers in promoting Singspiel as a competing art form, a trend strongly supported by Joseph II. Sacred music in the library ranged from Antonio Caldara to Johann Albrechtsberger, and included masses by Joseph Haydn and his contemporaries.

The symphonies and *symphonies concertantes* consisted of seventy-five works that embraced every current type of orchestral composition. The main composers, French, Italian, Bohemian, German, and Austrian, were among the best of the many musicians then writing orchestral music for audiences across Europe, as concert life grew and prospered. The symphony was gaining ground, not simply as an opening and closing piece for concerts that featured concertos, arias, and other solo turns; it was becoming the primary large form of the period for public performance. And above all other composers of symphonies stood Joseph Haydn, whose consistent development of the symphony as a formal genre, beginning in the 1760s, was a wonder of fertility, imagination, and command of form and content.

In the listing, no other composers approach Haydn in numbers or in quality. Every composer represented by a symphony in this library was alive in 1784 when the inventory was made, and many were only in their thirties or forties. If the absence of Mozart is in any way surprising, it may simply reflect that up to 1784 his orchestral works were not so readily copied in a Rhineland court such as Bonn, though other works of his, certainly operas and chamber music, were well known. But since Mozart's fortunes soared in Bonn when Max Franz arrived as elector in that year, we can be sure that from then on Beethoven's exposure to Mozart's music was strong and meaningful.

The library also contained chamber music, especially for the keyboard, at which Beethoven first tried his hand as a teenage composer. Here too contemporaries were well represented, and in this sector Beethoven's budding works show the impact of Mozart beyond all others. Outside the court library, Beethoven almost certainly had access to some important private collections of music in Bonn. One such collection belonged to Johann Gottfried von Mastiaux, a local official and passionate musical amateur highly praised by the fastidious Neefe.[35] Neefe reported in 1783 that Mastiaux was in correspondence with Haydn and possessed in his personal library some eighty Haydn symphonies along with thirty Haydn quartets and forty trios, plus fifty piano concertos by various composers. He also owned a collection of fine Italian violins and violas. Between the court library and the Mastiaux collection, the young Beethoven could hardly avoid coming to know many of the Haydn symphonies and quartets composed before 1792, whether or not he was yet able to assimilate Haydn's characteristic features into his own style. Beethoven's natural bent at this time was toward keyboard music, much more Mozart's terrain, and he took his time before attempting quartets and symphonies that would inevitably put him in competition with Haydn.

Family, Friends, and Patrons

If the death of Beethoven's mother in July of 1787 inevitably threw him and his younger siblings into shock and turmoil, his father's further lapse into alcoholism and depression intensified the family's problems. In the close atmosphere of a small city like Bonn, Johann van Beethoven's behavior was notorious and pitiable, and on more than one occasion young Ludwig had to struggle with the local police to prevent them from locking up his father for disorderly conduct.[36] In 1789 Beethoven had to petition the Elector to direct half of his father's annual salary to him so he could support himself and his brothers, with the further condition, if Johann did not agree, that in case of nonpayment Johann would be exiled to a village somewhere in the Elector's lands. As it turned out these drastic steps were not needed because, as Beethoven later explained in a 1793 letter to the Elector, "my father earnestly beseeched me not to do this." Out of shame Johann offered instead to pay half his salary to his son in quarterly installments, and in fact "this was always punctually done."[37] The domestic situation from mid-1787 to Beethoven's departure in November 1792 must have been barely endurable: an incapacitated father, two younger brothers in need of nurturing, schooling, and guidance; and the young Beethoven forced into the role of an adult provider just when he was ready to pursue his own dreams of a musical career. After some musical training, Carl took a job in Vienna as clerk in the imperial financial service while continuing to help his brother in his dealings with publishers. Johann, the younger of the two, also gravitated to Vienna and became a pharmacist, eventually moving to Linz in 1808 to open his own shop.

As for father Johann, he died on December 18, 1792, just one month after Ludwig's departure for Vienna. It is striking that Ludwig made no effort to return to Bonn for his father's funeral or to be with his younger brothers at this second stage of parental bereavement; nor, apparently, did he mourn his father's death. A diary of his expenses from the period November 1792 to January 1794 records his payments for "boots, shoes, piano, desk," and the like, as well as the costs of lessons with Haydn, but yields nothing at all about his father's funeral. An entry probably made in 1794 as a New Year's resolution shows his continued awareness of his precarious physical health combined with determination to persevere. He wrote, "Courage. Despite all weaknesses of body, my spirit shall rule. You have lived twenty-five years. This year must determine the complete man—nothing must remain undone."[38] The entry anticipates the stoic, resolute, and self-conscious comments that he entered into his diary of 1812 to 1818, a time when he faced far more troubling physical and emotional ailments.[39]

To keep up his income from Bonn he wrote to the Elector some four months after his father's death to ask for the renewal of the half salary that he had received after his father's retirement, and in May this amount was added to his current stipend from Bonn. All these arrangements were apparently facilitated by Franz Anton Ries, acting on Beethoven's behalf in Bonn.[40] In the immediate domestic crisis of 1787, friends stepped in to help, especially the Ries family (as Beethoven later acknowledged) and the benevolent von Breunings. The family head was Helene von Breuning, widowed since 1777, along with her daughter Eleonore and sons Stephan, Christoph, and Lorenz. Stephan in particular formed a close friendship with Beethoven, not an easy task then or later. Probably preferring the von Breunings' home to his motherless and virtually fatherless household, Beethoven spent a good deal of time with them, as mother Helene was one of the few who could influence this "stubborn and unsociable boy," as Franz Wegeler later described him.[41] Wegeler, five years older, was also a frequent guest in the von Breuning household; he and his brother Lorenz both renewed contact with Beethoven in Vienna in 1794–96, before returning to Bonn, where Franz eventually married Eleonore von Breuning in 1802.[42]

Wegeler was a true friend. It was to him that Beethoven first revealed his fears over early signs of deafness, in letters written from Vienna in 1800. Although the two did not see one another for many years, Beethoven from his sickbed wrote Wegeler the deeply moving letter of December 7, 1826, quoted earlier, recalling their childhood friendship. Wegeler's book, whose title translates as *Biographical Notes about Ludwig van Beethoven*—written with Ferdinand Ries and published in 1838—was the first important biographical work on Beethoven.[43]

Among his patrons at Bonn in addition to Max Franz was Count Ferdinand Ernst Gabriel von Waldstein, who came to the city in 1788 as a companion of the Elector and was ceremoniously inducted into the Teutonic Order, a social and political organization of German noblemen that gathered periodically. Beethoven wrote a "Knight's Ballet" (WoO 1)[44] for a meeting in 1791 of the Order at Bonn, and let it appear that the author of the music was Waldstein.

This ambitious young Bohemian aristocrat, who also admired Mozart, could help Beethoven gain access to the Austrian and Bohemian nobility, through whom career chances might open up. Waldstein could well have

Count Ferdinand Ernst von Waldstein, in a silhouette from the farewell album that he and others prepared for Beethoven when the composer left Bonn for Vienna in November 1792. (Oesterreichische Nationalbibliothek, Vienna)

heard about Beethoven through acquaintances who knew about music in Bonn, and he may have been in Vienna in the spring of 1787 when the young Beethoven arrived there.[45] The later dedication to Waldstein of the Piano Sonata Opus 53 probably reflects Beethoven's gratitude for Waldstein's early support rather than any obligation incurred at the time he composed the work in 1804. In fact their relationship by then was fading, as Waldstein left Vienna for many years (he later went bankrupt and died in poverty).[46] But in furthering Beethoven's ambitions in the later Bonn years and helping him establish himself in Vienna, probably no one was more important.

To Vienna in Search of Mozart

Although Wegeler later wrote that Beethoven's trip was paid for by Waldstein, the costs were probably met by the Elector or by a consortium of local supporters. With letters of recommendation in his pocket, Beethoven came to the great city, like many a young artist before him, anxious to show off his talents, to meet Mozart, and to make the contacts that would ensure his advancement. If he accomplished any of these things he did so in a mere two weeks. Still, the visit was productive; Gerhard von Breuning, son of Stephan, later wrote that Beethoven did meet "the great art-loving aristocratic families of the Vienna of that time" and compared the composer's visit to that of the young Wegeler, who came to Vienna in September of the same year and successfully made contacts to pursue medical studies. Wegeler's letter of recommendation from the Elector opened the doors of the "most famous physicians and professors of the era of Joseph II," according to von Breuning.[47] The same may have been true for Beethoven.

In 1787 Viennese musical life was flourishing, with ample performances of opera, ballet, and theater that were supported and attended by the nobility, the diplomatic corps, and the rising bourgeoisie. Public concerts were infrequent, but music-making in salons was on a scale beyond anything Beethoven could have imagined in Bonn or encountered in any other continental city except Paris, Berlin, and Prague. Musicians from all over Europe swarmed to Vienna and competed for employment, seeking audiences and auditions with aristocratic patrons or their representatives that might lead to permanent positions, though these were hard to come by.

Mozart, in April 1787, was at the first height of his operatic glory, having launched *The Marriage of Figaro* in Vienna the previous April and having just returned from Prague (January–February 1787), where *Figaro*'s sensational success had spurred a commission for *Don Giovanni*.[48] At the time of the young Beethoven's arrival, Mozart was composing his string quintets in C Major, K. 515, and G Minor, K. 516. Beethoven may have met him, but the famous remark that Mozart is said to have made about Beethoven—"Keep your eyes on him—some day he will give the world something to talk about"—is uncorroborated. In any case, Beethoven almost certainly heard Mozart play: according to Beethoven's own piano pupil Carl Czerny, writing many years later, Beethoven told him that Mozart's playing was "fine but choppy, [with] no *legato*."[49] Mozart's death in December 1791 precludes Beethoven's having heard Mozart play at any other time.

As to Beethoven's receiving any instruction in theory or composition from Mozart, it is utterly doubtful, and we cannot rely on Ries's report to this effect in his later *Biographical Notes*. Mozart's teaching methods, well attested to in these years by the notebooks of his British pupil Thomas Attwood, would have included exercises in strict composition and counterpoint, and approaches to composition by easy stages.[50] Beethoven presumably brought some of his Bonn compositions to show Mozart, such as his piano quartets of 1785, which reveal unmistakable signs of his close study of Mozartean models, above all several violin sonatas. Yet, however brief, the visit must have been memorable. Even if he managed only to hear Mozart play, the opportunity to walk the streets of Vienna, see the palaces and townhouses of the aristocracy, and take in the ambience of the capital, inevitably confirmed the provincial narrowness of Bonn and whetted his readiness to leave. No wonder that little more than five years later Waldstein wrote that returning to Vienna was for Beethoven "a wish that has long been frustrated."

The Last Years in Bonn

Despite all the difficulties of these last Bonn years, the conditions he faced were not so bad as he had feared.[51] If life as court organist and uniformed orchestral violist was menial and routine, at least it was steady, and in these years the Elector was ambitiously expanding his support. In 1788 he founded a National Theater in Bonn to produce German plays and operas, compete with Mannheim, and imitate the theater established by his older brother in Vienna. Knowing that good opera productions required his best musicians, the Elector put Joseph Reicha in charge of the theater orchestra. Between 1789 and 1792 the troupe produced operas by Grétry, Antonio Salieri, Domenico Cimarosa, and Mozart, including *Figaro* and

Don Giovanni.[52] To these were added the regular performances of symphonies and concertos by the orchestra, with its ambitious players such as the Rombergs in prominent roles.

A major local event took place at Christmas of 1790 with the arrival in Bonn of Joseph Haydn, then on his way to England accompanied by his impresario, Johann Peter Salomon. Since Salomon was himself a Bonner and in earlier years had played the violin in this same Electoral orchestra, for him to bring Haydn to Bonn was a doubly prestigious homecoming. The Elector saw to it that the great man would be properly received. Haydn was then fifty-eight, at the height of his powers, just released from decades of service to the Esterházys and ready to reap the admiration of Europe. He was on the way to his finest decade of productivity and the writing of his ripest quartets, symphonies, keyboard sonatas, and piano trios, along with his late masses and his two oratorios. The Elector's hospitality included an unexpected banquet to which "the most capable musicians had been invited,"[53] perhaps including Beethoven. Wegeler reports that during this visit in 1790—though it may have been on Haydn's return through Bonn in July 1792—Beethoven showed Haydn a cantata, either the funeral cantata for Joseph II, WoO 87, or its companion, his cantata for the elevation of Joseph's successor, Leopold II, WoO 88.[54]

Regardless of which one and when Haydn may have seen it, Haydn was impressed enough to give Beethoven strong encouragement. Informal arrangements were made in July 1792 for Beethoven to come to Vienna to be Haydn's pupil, which he did four months later. Indicative of Beethoven's originality is a recollection by Simrock that when the orchestra tried out the cantata they found it too difficult to perform, "because all the figures were completely unusual."[55] Junker, a reliable witness, published a glowing report on the Bonn Hofkapelle in 1791 after hearing the orchestra perform a new work by Paul Anton Winneberger of Wallerstein, as well as symphonies by Mozart and Pleyel and a double concerto played by the two Rombergs:

> *Such perfection in the pianos, fortes, rinforzandos—such a swelling and gradual increase of tone and then such an almost imperceptible dying away . . . all this was formerly to be heard only at Mannheim. . . . The*

members of the chapel . . . form truly a fine sight, when one adds the
splendid uniform in which the Elector has clothed them—red, and
richly trimmed with gold.[56]

Junker then makes special mention of the young Beethoven, one of the
greatest of pianists—"the dear, good Bethofen . . . [who showed in his
improvising] an almost inexhaustible wealth of ideas, the altogether characteristic style of expression in his playing, and the great execution which
he displays. I know therefore, no one thing that he lacks, that conduces to
the greatness of an artist."[57]

Beyond the Rhineland and its principalities and cities, France since
1789 had cracked apart in the bloodiest revolution of the century. Even the
somewhat insulated members of an Electoral court felt the reverberations
of this cataclysm, let alone one as close to the French border as Bonn; and
by 1792 the postrevolutionary armies of France were on the march, occu-
pying and attacking Rhineland cities.[58] Like some other German princes
Max Franz tried to stay as neutral as possible, hoping he might be able to
negotiate a reprieve from disaster and somehow remain in power.[59] But in
October 1792 Mainz fell, the west bank of the Rhine was overrun by French
troops, and the Elector hastily moved to Münster, where he remained from
December 1792 to April 1793. Accordingly, when Beethoven left Bonn in
November, the court in which he had grown up was in the process of dissolution. Throughout 1793 and 1794 French and German armies were in
battle all across the Rhineland, and in October 1794 the Elector himself left
Bonn for the last time, ending the regime. By then his talented young musical prodigy, the pride of the Bonn establishment, had been gone for almost
two years. Beethoven never again wore the uniform of a liveried servant.
Fired up by his temperamental resistance to servitude, he maintained his
bearing as an independent artist, bound by necessity to keep on good terms
with the aristocracy but fiercely proud of his self-determined status in society. It is hard to find other musicians of the time who displayed such feelings so openly or attempted to act on them.

Waldstein's Prophecy

No early Beethoven document is more telling or more frequently quoted than the entry in his personal album written by the young Count Waldstein in November 1792, as Beethoven prepared to leave:

> *Dear Beethoven! You are going to Vienna in fulfillment of a wish that has long been frustrated. Mozart's genius is still in mourning and weeps for the death of its pupil. It found a refuge with the inexhaustible Haydn but no occupation; through him it wishes to form a union with another. With the help of unceasing diligence you will receive* the spirit of Mozart from the hands of Haydn.[60]

This album entry stands out for its language and imagery. Unlike most of the others, which are homely but sincere bits of poetry sprinkled with quotations from Klopstock and Schiller, Waldstein's rhetoric is serious and thoughtful, framing this journey not only as the departure of a friend and artist but as an event in the music history of his time. Its central point is the passing of Mozart, whose death was like another parental loss for Beethoven, the death of his spiritual and artistic father—leaving him with only the pathetic figure of his biological father Johann, who in turn died a month later.

However neglected Mozart may have been by Viennese patrons in his last years—as his simple and unceremonious burial is sometimes thought to show—his death at thirty-five was felt in Viennese and, gradually, in European musical circles, as an incalculable loss. His widow Constanze began immediately to mount subscription concerts that would help pay off her many debts, and over the next few years she raised substantial sums from benefactors across Austria and Germany at concerts in various stops on the musical highroads from Vienna to Prague, Leipzig, and Berlin.[61] Haydn, then in London in the midst of his first great success there, eloquently mourned Mozart's loss—"posterity will not see another such talent for a hundred years" he wrote to Marianne von Genzinger. The better journalists lamented the loss of a "master above all masters," as one of them put it as early as twelve days after Mozart's death, and during the next few years a wave of admiration for Mozart began, coupled with many performances of his works. This surge of interest soon led publishers to issue a number of his compositions, thus gathering attention and stimulating commemorations of many kinds, including the first biographies.[62]

Waldstein's entry, which breathes this spirit of reverence for Mozart the newly departed hero, is unfairly slanted against Haydn, who, although "inexhaustible," is recognized not for his own true greatness but only as a medium for transmitting the spirit of Mozart. Waldstein tells the young Beethoven, on the threshold of a great career, that he will have to work hard to earn his inheritance, but also says that his reward will not be recognition as Haydn's pupil but rather his emergence as Mozart's heir. In this canonic pronouncement the Mozart legacy is not just a generalized mark of potential status but is a sign that Waldstein and other like-minded patrons expect Beethoven to rise to Mozart's level and to take on musical leadership in the future. For such patrons the death of Mozart had thrown the future of serious music into crisis. They could not envisage Haydn as providing such leadership, if only because of his age—he was sixty in November 1792. So, as if he were being habilitated for a spiritual succession, Beethoven's future assumption of the mantle might guarantee the salvation of music as a higher art. In circles of musical connoisseurship in the early 1790s, perhaps influenced by the radical political and philosophical transformations of the preceding ten years and more, there was a sense that the tradition of high art required a new leader, a new figure of unquestioned originality and universality who could become the protagonist of a new musical age. The situation reminds us of many similar moments in the music history of a period and culture, as in Italy after Verdi, in Germany after Wagner and Brahms, and in late-twentieth-century America, when directly following the death of Aaron Copland in 1990, the venerated music critic Arthur Berger wrote of

> that sense of being left adrift, a realization that one of the last links with the lofty tradition of a recent past had been severed. Also, a sense of losing a leader. . . . [W]e not only mourn him but also become more aware that an invaluable segment of the recent past, of a most vital period of musical creativity, is rapidly slipping away.[63]

Waldstein's remarks seem especially prejudiced in view of the central fact that Beethoven was on his way to Vienna to apprentice himself to Haydn. The original plan was that Beethoven would study with Haydn, perfect his craft, and eventually return to Bonn, where Max Franz dreamed of fame, with Beethoven as the Electorate's star. As it turned out, the political avalanche that buried the Bonn court cut Beethoven off from any possible return, even supposing that he intended one. Despite appeals from Beethoven and some help from Haydn in dealing with the Elector, his remittances dwindled and by March 1794 stopped entirely.[64] But by that time Beethoven was well installed at Vienna.

CHAPTER 2

MUSIC OF THE BONN YEARS

>‑‑‑‑‑‑‑‑‑‑

Early Keyboard Music

B eethoven's earliest music grew naturally from his keyboard flu-
ency and skill as an improviser, talents that amazed his contemporaries. His first efforts, solo keyboard variations and
sonatas, began with the "Dressler" Variations of 1782, published that year
bearing the falsified age of ten. To these he added a few juvenile attempts to
set German poetry, guided by Neefe, who was something of a lieder composer.[1] In all Beethoven wrote some twenty songs between the ages of
eleven and twenty-one, almost all of them artless and diminutive, of which
Schilderung eines Mädchens ("Description of a Girl") and *An einen Säugling*
("To an Infant") are the earliest.[2] The second of these shows a slight touch
of originality in its brief major-minor mixture, but both reflect the pretty,
homely sentimentality of the contemporary German lied. Marginally more
ambitious were his *Trinklied* ("Drinking Song") and *Elegie auf den Tod
eines Pudels* ("Elegy on the Death of a Poodle") written about 1787.

In the "Dressler" Variations of 1782, WoO 63, Beethoven takes a simple, laborious C-minor march theme through nine variations that display
diminished note values in the right and sometimes left hand, all of them
slavishly following the basic contour and harmonic pattern of the theme in
conventional ways. Inevitably primitive by his later standards, the
"Dressler" Variations are impressive enough for an eleven-year-old, though
they hardly suggest the genial power he would develop in this genre within
the next eight years, for example in the far more polished "Righini" Variations of 1790. What is surprising, however, is that more than twenty years

Title page of the "Dressler" Variations for piano, WoO 63, printed at Mannheim in 1782, the first publication of music by Beethoven, then eleven years old. (University Library, Geneva, Collection A. Mooser)

later, in 1803, when he was in the flush of maturity and starting full-scale work on the *Eroica* Symphony, Beethoven agreed to a new edition of the "Dressler" Variations, with only some light improvements made by him or someone else.[3] This initiative is an early indication of his lifelong inability to pass up publication of older and sometimes trifling works in order to pocket a publisher's fee. It also suggests the possibility that in 1803, as he moved into a new phase of his mature creative mastery, he marked it by quietly agreeing to the reappearance of this little piece that had begun his juvenile career as a composer. The reprint removes the name of Dressler but repeats the fiction of 1782 that the work had been written by Beethoven at the age of ten!

After the "Dressler" Variations Beethoven's first comparable efforts to write keyboard sonatas are the three "Electoral" Sonatas WoO 47, composed in 1782–83, published in a handsomely decorated edition dedicated to Max Friedrich and with a proud indication in the title that they are the product of "Ludwig van Beethoven, eleven years old."[4] Again Neefe's hand is evident in these little works that reflect the late sonata style of C. P. E. Bach intermingled with elements derived from the lighter keyboard sonata literature of the 1760s and '70s that had been poured out by a horde of composers, including the young Mozart. Short, undeveloped, and crowded with stereotyped figures, still these three little works show that the barely adolescent Beethoven could spin coherent phrases and short paragraphs as capably as many an adult professional. The first movements are in perfectly competent small-scale sonata form, in which the first theme of the exposition reappears at the beginning of the diminutive development section and leads to an abbreviated recapitulation. The slow movements are in simple forms of statement, contrast, and reprise, with slight variations on this formula; and the finales are in the regular rondo forms current at the time. Here and there moments of surprising interest appear, either in the turn of a phrase or in brief motivic elaboration. And as for Beethoven's ability to shape a principal melody, the opening of the 6/8 Rondo Vivace of the Sonata No. 2 in E-flat Major compares favorably with many a contemporary 6/8 rondo theme, even Mozart's finale for his fourth Horn Concerto (*W 1), written four years later in June 1786 when Mozart was at the height of his career.

"This passage has been stolen from Mozart"

By far the most ambitious products of these years are the three Quartets for Piano and Strings WoO 36, which were not published until after Beethoven's death and which so surprised even knowledgeable observers, including Ferdinand Ries, that they doubted Beethoven had written them at all, let alone at age fourteen.[5] Fortunately a surviving autograph manuscript attests to their authenticity. That the movement plans differ in all three works suggests a modest conceptual scheme behind the entire group, surely a progressive tendency for a fourteen-year-old.[6] Their three-movement layout follows common practice in late-eighteenth-century keyboard sonatas and keyboard chamber music.

Despite the limitations of these works, remarkable features crop up everywhere, above all in melodic inventiveness and in the larger layout of individual movements. The juvenile composer shows a surprising ability to generate effective thematic ideas, and a precocious sense of proportion. This combination, which buds forth here for the first time, later became one of his greatest strengths in far more mature and developed contexts. As a major step forward from the little piano sonatas of 1783, these ensemble works show signs of maturity in the making.[7] Indeed, had he written them as straight piano sonatas their weaknesses would have been far less apparent, since their failings are largely in the string writing and in his inability to integrate piano and strings effectively and idiomatically. But their strengths outweigh their defects. They stand up not despite their direct indebtedness to Mozart—above all certain Mozart violin sonatas—but precisely because of it. Though far below Mozart in level of imagination and control, they possess the voice of a beginner of genius who is steeping himself in Mozart's ways and is trying to imitate them.[8] Thus the C Major Piano Quartet is clearly modeled on Mozart's C Major Violin Sonata, K. 296, the E-Flat Major Piano Quartet on his G Major Violin Sonata, K. 379. These connections appear not only in their larger movement plans but in their choices of key, movement types, and tempos—and to some extent in thematic material and harmonic planning as well.

These piano quartets are the first and clearest examples of the teenage Beethoven's dependence on Mozart. They mark the beginning of a relationship to Mozart that remained a steady anchor for Beethoven over the next ten years as he moved into his first artistic maturity. Just as Mozart himself had once told his father that he was "soaked in music," so Beethoven was soaked in Mozart. His invention of new ideas sometimes began with his asking himself if what he was writing was his own, or something

Wolfgang Amadeus Mozart, in an unfinished portrait by his brother-in-law, Joseph Lange. (Mozart-Haus, Salzburg)

he might have heard or seen in a work by Mozart, or partly both. Of course, his central influence in the 1780s was not solely Mozart, in view of Haydn's importance and the availability of Haydn's works in Bonn, but it was primarily Mozart at this time. It is no accident that on a sketch leaf from about October 1790 Beethoven wrote down a brief C-minor passage in 6/8 meter, in two-staff piano score, and then wrote down these words, between the staves, about the little phrase: "This entire passage has been stolen from the Mozart Symphony in C, where the Andante in six-eight from the . . ." (he breaks off here). Then Beethoven writes the passage again just below and a little differently, on the same sketch page, and signs it "Beethoven himself."[9] The passage he thought he was quoting cannot be traced to any Mozart symphony that we know. (It slightly resembles the slow movement of the "Linz" Symphony, but only slightly.) But it shows that Beethoven, in the act

A musical passage written by Beethoven on a sketch leaf around 1790 and inscribed, "This entire passage has been stolen from the Mozart Symphony in C, where the Andante in 6/8 from the . . ." (breaks off); below he has rewritten the passage and inscribed it "Beethoven's own version." (British Library, London, Ms. Add. 29801, fol. 88r)

Transcription of the passage (Source: The "Kafka" Sketchbook, *ed. Joseph Kerman [London, 1967], 2:228):*

diese ganze Stelle ist gestohlen aus der Mozartschen Sinfonie in c wo des Andante in 6 8 tel aus den [. . .]

of composing, discovered, or thought he discovered, that he had unwittingly plagiarized Mozart, then rushed swiftly to make amends and declare his independence, then wrote himself an ironic note about it. Nothing could be more revealing of his anxiety about Mozart, his musical god and artistic father, whose music he knew and heard in his mind so well and clearly that he must have felt he had to work his way through the Mozartian landscape to find his own voice.

Anton Reicha confirms what we would have suspected in any case, that Beethoven played Mozart piano concertos with the Bonn orchestra. He also reports that he and Beethoven, then inseparable comrades, after hearing an aria from Mozart's *Idomeneo* (Electra's passionate D-minor aria) talked of nothing else day and night for weeks thereafter.[10] We must remember that in 1790, Mozart was still alive, had recently completed *Così fan tutte*, had not yet written *The Magic Flute*, and so far as he or anyone knew, had years of productivity ahead of him. And at this time of writing down the little C-minor passage he feared was Mozart's, Beethoven was chafing to leave Bonn and study with the master in Vienna.

Nor is this "fear of theft" an isolated case. About thirteen years later, in 1803–4, while starting his work on the *Eroica* Symphony, Beethoven found himself inadvertently quoting the main theme of the finale of Mozart's B-flat Major Piano Concerto, K. 595, though not in its original key and meter but in the key and meter of the first movement of the *Eroica*![11]

His long-term relationship to Mozart passed through several phases. It began with a phase of "imitation" that characterized this early formative period. Then came a phase of "appropriation," during Beethoven's rapidly increasing maturation in the first Vienna decade, 1792–1802, when he was truly asserting his individuality to a high degree but nevertheless had Mozartian works and modes of procedure locked into memory. A prime example from the first Vienna phase, though it has been somewhat misunderstood, is his String Quartet in A Major, Opus 18 No. 5, which is often characterized by its relationship to Mozart's A Major Quartet K. 464.[12] Later, in his middle period, other examples show Beethoven's occasional recourse to Mozartian models. Touches of Mozart account for what have been called regressions to classical procedures in certain works, such as the C Major Quartet Opus 59 No. 3. This quartet is indebted to Mozart in its first-movement layout and some turns of phrase, deriving above all from the "Dissonant" Quartet in C Major, K. 465. Yet it is unmistakably Beethovenian in every lineament.[13] We will see that an essential aspect of Beethoven's development is his ability to turn back to aesthetic models, and even musical ideas, that are characteristic of Haydn and Mozart, then elaborate and transform them. In doing so he follows no single track but shows constant evidence of spreading in many directions, from all of which he reaches back explicitly to one or the other of these two central figures. In later years he reaches back even further, to Handel and Bach. Yet even then he did not abandon his lifelong connection to Haydn and Mozart but extended his powers of assimilation in new ways and in deeper contexts.

In fields in which Beethoven felt ambitious but not as well grounded—above all opera—he also sought to compete directly with the few contemporaries, such as Cherubini, from whom he could learn. His paths to maturity encompass a much broader range of influences than most biographers have been inclined to admit. The first signs of this wide approach to models is already manifest in these little piano quartets. These works were good enough that ten years later Beethoven helped himself to ideas from them for his first works published with opus number—his Opus 1 piano trios, and, even more, his Opus 2 piano sonatas. The connections are these:

1. A nine-measure passage from the E-flat Major Piano Quartet is lifted bodily and used in the C Minor Piano Trio, Opus 1 No. 3, in a comparable cadential situation.[14]

2. Thematic material from the first movement of the C Major Piano Quartet is used in literal form in the first movement of the big Piano Sonata in C Major, Opus 2 No. 3, with a shift in the sequence of musical ideas from the earlier exposition. The main point is that in the earlier piece, composed at age fourteen, Beethoven was able to come up with a "pathetic" theme as well formed as this one in G minor that was worth salvaging for the much more developed piano sonata composed in 1794–95.[15]

3. The entire second movement of the C Major Piano Quartet, an F-major Adagio con espressione, is the immediate source for the more compact and intense Adagio of the Piano Sonata Opus 2 No.

1 in F Minor. In 1785, Beethoven worked out good thematic material in simple schematic terms. Ten years later, in 1794, now a bold young master, he took the same material and fashioned from it a poetic, expressive slow movement, replete with the dramatic tension that had been completely lacking in the earlier work.

To take one movement of these piano quartets as a signal of early originality, we need look no further than the Allegro movement of the Quartet in E-flat Major, WoO 36 No. 1. First, the movement is in the extreme key of E-flat minor, rare in this period and, with its six flats, especially difficult for string players.[16] The thematic material with which it opens is strangely uneven in its phrase structure and striking in its shift of accents (*W 2). The six-measure phrase—terse, intense, asymmetrical—is the earliest example we have of an opening thematic gambit that Beethoven may have

Autograph of the Piano Quartet in D major, WoO 36 No. 2, dating from 1785, showing the end of the second movement and the beginning of the finale. (Staatsbibliothek, Berlin)

picked up from Mozart. It can also be seen as an example of what came to be called a "Mannheim rocket": a theme that rises through the tones of the minor triad, that is, 1–3–5–1–3. Mozart used the formula decisively to begin his C Minor Wind Octet, K. 406, of 1782, his late C Minor Piano Sonata, and also the finale of the G Minor Symphony, a movement that Beethoven knew well and even wrote down when he employed the same rising pattern for the Scherzo of the Fifth Symphony. Beethoven tried out this same early E-flat minor theme, idiosyncratic as it is, to open a "Sinfonia" in C minor that he sketched around 1787–88, an astonishing draft that presages his "C-minor mood" and also links to Mozart.[17] The spirit of Mozart found refuge in these works.

Composing and Sketching

The very idea of a second Bonn period owes essentially to Beethoven's quest for a meeting with Mozart in Vienna in April 1787, and those compositions that we can date with confidence show him seeking new challenges in wider spheres. His primary works were, again, keyboard variations, keyboard chamber music (especially the first piano trios), some other chamber music for strings or for winds, and the two cantatas. Of the keyboard trios one is for winds and piano; the other (WoO 38), for the usual strings and piano, is a three-movement work that might have found its way into his Opus 1 trios but is not so fully realized as the three that did.

In instrumental genres the only progressive work is a massive set of twenty-four variations on the arietta "Venni amore" by Vincenzo Righini, a journeyman composer from Bologna who forged a career in Germany, visited Bonn in 1788, and contributed a Mass for Leopold II's coronation in 1790. Thus by composing these variations the young Beethoven, in a typical challenge to the current establishment, was competing with Righini both directly and indirectly for public recognition. Beethoven thought enough of this work, which exceeds his earlier sets in size and heft, to revise it in 1802. The variations demand substantial virtuosity from the performer, develop the simple theme well beyond its seemingly modest possibilities, and show real flair. Possibilities latent in the theme are exploited here with imagination and freedom that go far beyond the "Dressler" Variations; the shifts in tempo, mode, and character are handled with impressive skill. The ending of the twenty-fourth variation even brings a "farewell" effect that anticipates the much later *Lebewohl* Sonata. Although some of the more striking effects may have been added to the work in a revision between 1791 and 1802, we are sure that the first edition, now lost, also had twenty-four variations, so the odds are good that it was not much less elaborate than the 1802 version. Beethoven played these variations in 1791 for the celebrated pianist Abbé Sterkel while in Mergentheim with the Bonn court musicians, and he not only rose to the technical challenge offered by Sterkel but toyed with Sterkel by deliberately imitating his delicate keyboard manner. As Wegeler put it, "that is how easy it was for him to imitate someone else's style of playing."[18]

Beethoven started writing a curiously adventurous "Romance cantabile" for solo flute, bassoon, and pianoforte, with orchestra (Hess 13) in 1786 or '87 but abandoned it after a promising start.[19] Choosing the elegiac key of E minor and setting up a type of *concertante* work for two wind instruments plus piano with orchestra—a combination he never used again—Beethoven got only far enough to show that the work could have been an important one if he had completed it. That he did not suggests an inability at this stage to finish a fully formed concerto or concerto-like work, let alone one for three solo instruments, and adequately develop the quasi-Mozartian ideas with which he started it. Several years earlier, in 1784, he had tried his wings with a juvenile piano concerto in E-flat (WoO 4), and a few years later he would get down the full orchestral and solo expositions of the first movement of a violin concerto in C major. But this early violin concerto, like the Romance, remained unfinished.[20]

More important in the broader sense is the large array of loose sketch leaves that Beethoven began to fill with music in the second half of the 1780s and that he continued to pile up until he started to make use of bound sketchbooks in the late 1790s. These loose single and double leaves, which survive as a substantial collection of 124 sheets, later found their way into the hands of a Viennese collector and musician named Johann Nepomuk Kafka, who sold them to the British Museum in 1875.[21] They are made up of a few autographs, a few copies of works by others (Handel and

Mozart), and a large mass of closely packed sketches, patches of musical ideas, little pieces, unfinished torsos like that of the Romance, exercises, some verbal memoranda, and jottings of all kinds. They provide a window into Beethoven's early workshop and the ferment of musical material with which he was beginning to forge his professional identity, reflecting his aspirations as composer, pianist, and improviser. The portfolio contains links to some other bundles of leaves from the same period, but taken by itself it shows that Beethoven planned and worked out his ideas for movements and entire works from the very beginning of his career, and that he kept this inchoate mass of early music papers as long as he lived, along with his sketchbooks. As a result we have some preliminary compositional material for a number of early works, both those he wrote in Bonn and a number of the more important works—those with opus numbers—from the earlier Vienna years.

One striking feature of the "Kafka" papers is the mass of keyboard "exercises" or jottings that he wrote down on his sheets of loose music paper wherever he could sandwich them in among other musical ideas for actual compositions. These exercises, which cover about ninety pages in a modern edition of the whole material, range from two or three to about twenty measures. They are always written for keyboard two hands, and almost none of them can be traced directly to any of his sonatas, keyboard chamber works, or other finished compositions, although they often resemble some of the figuration patterns that he needed for his piano works.[22] They form an arsenal of ideas for keyboard writing that he could use for either composition or for improvisation—the two were not fully divided, then or ever in Beethoven's creative life—and he probably wrote them out to fix them in memory and create a written mass of material that he could examine, study, and use as a stimulus to framing means of continuity and contrast in keyboard works.

Cantatas for Two Emperors

The two cantatas stand as the capstones of the Bonn years. Not only do they show the young Beethoven reaching for powerful rhetoric in works for solo voices, chorus, and orchestra, but they implicitly bid for recognition in royal and aristocratic patronage circles, as the ambitious young composer from Bonn presents his credentials in weighty and serious works. The Joseph cantata anticipates important elements in *Leonore* of 1805, the first version of *Fidelio*. Especially telling are the tragic choral outbursts that open the cantata with the words "Tod! Tod!" ("Death! Death!") in sustained harmonies, alternating with orchestral sonorities dominated by the woodwinds, foreshadowing Florestan's dungeon scene. The streaming melody of the soprano aria "Da stiegen die Menschen ans Licht" ("Thus mankind rose to the light") returns in *Leonore* as the noble closing melody with which Leonore celebrates her and Florestan's liberation by the benevolent Don Fernando (*W 3). By means of this quotation Beethoven could privately connect Joseph II with the operatic father figure who, like Sarastro in *The Magic Flute*, brings freedom and love together at the end of the opera. He could also resurrect a beautifully sculpted melody that perfectly fitted both cantata and opera.

The Leopold cantata, though less majestic, possesses the expressive chorus "Stürzet nieder, Millionen" ("Prostrate yourselves, O millions"), which textually associates with Schiller's Ode and the Ninth Symphony by means of its passage asking the question "Stürzet nieder, Millionen?" ("O ye millions, do you fall prostrate?"). More important is that the Leopold cantata forms a positive, optimistic counterpart to the tragedy of the Joseph cantata, anticipating in this early period Beethoven's later way of contrasting two opposed expressive domains in consecutive works in the same genre. Because he never published or performed these works during his lifetime, they remained essentially unknown until 1884, when the critic Eduard Hanslick wrote about them enthusiastically. One result was an astonished letter of praise from Brahms, who said of the Joseph cantata, "It is Beethoven through and through." Brahms, encountering this work, was profoundly impressed by its "noble pathos . . . its feeling and imagination, the intensity, perhaps violent in its expression, also the voice-leading and declamation, and, in the two outer sections, all the features that we may observe in and associate with his later works."[23]

PART TWO

THE FIRST MATURITY

1792–1802

CHAPTER 3

THE FIRST YEARS IN VIENNA

>◦×◦×{||◘◖◗||}×◦×◦

The Political Atmosphere

E arly on the morning of November 2, 1792, Beethoven left Bonn by coach on his way to Vienna. He divided the trip into stages, crossing the Rhine at Ehrenbreitstein, arriving at Frankfurt the next morning, then enduring about a week on the long route through Nuremberg, Regensburg, Passau, and Linz along the Danube to Vienna.[1] Dangers hung over travelers in these times of incessant war and military movements, with the armies of revolutionary France battling Austrian troops massed in the Rhineland and with worsening political conditions throwing Europe into upheaval.[2] Beethoven reports in his diary that he tipped the driver "one small thaler . . . because the fellow drove us at the risk of a whipping right through the Hessian army, going like the devil." Though Beethoven had good personal reasons to leave the Rhineland and move to Vienna, his journey was also a move to safety at a time when a French invasion and annexation of the Rhineland seemed imminent.

The political situation was momentous. In September 1792 the new French constitutional convention had abolished the monarchy and declared France a republic. To ensure that the world understood that a new epoch was dawning, the French prepared for the introduction of a new calendar that would declare September 22, 1792, the first day of Year 1. King Louis XVI was now held hostage while the revolutionary deputies decided what to do with him. In December they indicted him; in January 1793 the deputies voted for execution. On January 21 he was beheaded with the newly invented guillotine. Europe would not be the same again.

Once in Vienna Beethoven was there to stay. He would never return to Bonn and probably never intended to. The imperial city must have seemed even more imposing than it had during his brief visit in 1787. Vienna boasted twenty times the population of Bonn and brimmed with opportunities for a young musician looking to make a mark in the salons of the central European aristocracy that formed the core of Viennese society. Even if the nobility was in collective shock over the events in France, its members were insulated by distance and instinctive denial from the French revolutionary tidal wave, which had buried the *ancien régime* and put an end to hereditary privilege in the oldest and most centralized of the European monarchies. The upheaval shook the neighboring regimes to their foundations. It signaled to the German and Austrian princes that their comfortable world was now under a death sentence. Between hope and fear they wondered how to protect their financial and political power from the wreckage they saw in France, anxious to see what the new European balance of power would bring. As it turned out, the Terror that erupted in 1793 and the aggressive military policies of the new French government justified the nobles' worst fears and launched a period of invasion and instability in western Europe that would last through the reign of Napoleon.

German artists and intellectuals, aware that the uprisings in France were epoch-making and might spread to Germany and the Austrian empire unless repressed, spoke out loudly and clearly on both sides of the question. As early as 1788–89, when Louis XVI summoned the Estates General in a well-meant but futile attempt to carry out reforms and stave off violence, the poet Klopstock wrote an ode declaring the king's gesture "the most important event of this century."[3] To idealistic German writers of even moderately liberal viewpoints, as to their counterparts elsewhere in Europe, the revolution in its earlier stages seemed to signal a new phase of history—"Bliss was it in that dawn to be alive," said Wordsworth—in which political freedom, equality, and brotherhood seemed at last to be on the verge of triumph. "Sie und nicht Wir" ("They and Not We"), the title of another Klopstock poem, expressed the envy felt by German artists and intellectuals that the French *citoyens* had broken the barriers of class and wealth that formed the basic social edifice. Only later, as the grand revolutionary ideals crumbled in the wake of the Terror, did their hopes and illusions begin to fade. And as the German-speaking aristocracy, led by the

Austrian monarchy, worked to prevent revolutionary propaganda and stirrings from emerging in their midst, an atmosphere of political repression
settled on Vienna in the 1790s and created the basis for a virtual police
state, thick with spies, informers, and fears of conspiracies.

In fact the repression had already begun in the last years of Joseph II's
reign, when the spread of revolutionary beliefs, clearly subversive in the
eyes of the monarchy, led to the strengthening of police powers and the
suppression of seditious movements. As far back as 1786, before the French
Revolution had broken out, the Austrian police received instructions

> *to unobtrusively investigate what the general public is saying about the*
> *Emperor and his government, how public opinion is developing in this*
> *respect, whether among the upper or lower classes there are any mal-*
> *contents or perhaps even agitators . . . all of which is to be consistently*
> *reported to headquarters.*[4]

In 1789 the regime severely curtailed freedom of the press and watched
carefully for any signs of treason and sedition. These policies continued
under Leopold II and Francis II, despite the efforts of Joseph von Sonnenfels, councilor of the Court Chancery, to prevent the secret police from
amassing ever greater power. The outbreak of war between Austria and
France in 1792 made the atmosphere in Vienna still worse.[5] During Beethoven's first Viennese years the political atmosphere became even more
constricted. Austrians who sympathized with the ideals of the French Revolution and who gathered for discussions at coffeehouses and in private
homes came under increasing suspicion. In the summer of 1794 a group of
revolutionary sympathizers were arrested, tried, and convicted. In January
1795 two were hanged; several others were given long prison sentences.[6]

Beethoven was well aware of these growing threats to civil freedom. In
May of 1793 he entered some verses from Schiller's *Don Carlos* into the personal album of a lady in Vienna, a certain Theodora Johanna Vocke, and
followed them with a set of "precepts":

> *I am not wicked—hot blood is my fault—my crime is that I am young.*
> *I am not wicked, truly not wicked. Even if wildly surging emotions*
> *assail my heart, my heart is good—*

> *Precepts: To do good whenever one can; to love freedom above all else; never to deny the truth, even before the throne.*[7]

In a 1794 letter back to Bonn, Beethoven cavalierly dismissed the Viennese public's interest in the burning political issues of the day, but he quietly registered concern over the Austrian police and their repressive measures:

> *Here various important people have been locked up; it is said that a revolution was about to break out. But I believe that so long as an Austrian can get his brown ale and his little sausages, he is not likely to revolt. People say that the gates leading to the suburbs are to be closed at ten p.m. The soldiers have loaded their muskets with ball. You dare not raise your voice here or the police will take you into custody.*[8]

Although German cultural and political thinkers were at odds over how to interpret the transformation in France, no one could deny its significance. The beheading of Louis XVI and Marie Antoinette sent a tremor through Europe and the Americas. Goethe later remarked in his diaries that the atrocities of Robespierre had shocked the world.[9] Schiller not only denounced the "depraved generation" of revolutionaries for the bloody acts of the Terror but undertook a deeper philosophical inquiry as to how the failures of the revolution should be understood; ultimately he found their causes not merely in the violence of French politics but, more broadly, in the failure of the Enlightenment. It seems beyond doubt that Schiller's *Letters on the Aesthetic Education of Man* informed Beethoven's view of the potential power of art (and music) to enlighten individuals and society in a new way and to bring them to higher levels of understanding and behavior. If Schiller as innovative playwright had been a potential model for him in the 1780s, Schiller the philosopher-artist of the 1790s became an even more potent influence on Beethoven's moral and political outlook.[10]

Vienna as a Musical Center

For a young musician in pursuit of a successful career, outspoken liberal beliefs had to be tempered by prudence and necessity. Beethoven believed in the enlightened political principles for which the revolution had been fought, but he was surely as shocked as most Germans were when the Terror sent sixteen thousand French people to their deaths in nine months, and he was aware, of course, that the beheaded Marie Antoinette had been the sister of his own Elector, Max Franz. For Beethoven, lacking a salaried position, aristocratic patronage remained the primary system of support. Even in hard and dangerous times, it was easier to find such support in Vienna, where his known patrons were, than to look elsewhere. And although Vienna did not then rival Berlin, Paris, and London in the scope of its concert life—it had no public concert hall or friends of music organization that could sponsor regular concert series—it was still a hive of music and music making.[11]

The core of the patronage network was the imperial court. Its *Hofkapelle*, or court orchestra, traced its origins back to the Renaissance and had flourished as a major musical institution for almost three centuries. In the earlier eighteenth century the court had become the mecca of Italian opera, its official poet, Pietro Metastasio, furnishing dozens of *opera seria* librettos that were set to music by every important opera composer from the 1730s to the 1790s, including Hasse and Mozart. In the 1750s the court had taken over the operation of the Burgtheater and the Kärntnertortheater, two of the most important in the city. With an eye to popular appeal and national pride, the imperial cultural managers under Joseph II had turned to *Singspiel*, thus giving rise to a new Viennese tradition that Mozart enriched with *Die Entführung* in 1782 and *The Magic Flute* in 1791, the high points of the burgeoning wave of German opera.

Alongside opera, instrumental music had also expanded, mainly in the music rooms of the nobility. Their salons reflected their passion for music as higher recreation and entertainment, furnished a way of competing for cultural prestige, and gave some of them opportunities to show off their personal musical attainments (some of which were quite genuine) by having their own companies of hired musicians and at times joining them on keyboard or stringed instruments.

By the 1790s private patronage in Vienna had fallen into decline, but growing numbers of public concerts in music rooms and pleasure gardens were thriving. A correspondent around 1800 noted that concerts were being put on in the halls in the Augarten or in the Mehlgrube, "At the sign of the flour shop," where Viennese bakers bought their flour. Mozart in 1785 took the financial risk of putting on six subscription concerts in the Mehlgrube, paid for by an estimated two hundred fifty to three hundred subscribers for each concert, hiring an orchestra, and performing his own concertos—an unusual step at the time.[12] Such concerts were either arranged by an individual performer who hoped to reap the profits or were mounted to benefit a worthy cause. More rarely they were part of a series set up by an association of supporters of music or an individual entrepreneur.[13] All of these opportunities for public performance were still flourishing when Beethoven came to Vienna, and they were beginning to supplant private concerts in importance. And although fewer nobles kept musicians on regular payrolls, they found ways to hire musicians for special occasions.[14] Professionals played side by side with competent amateur players of stringed and wind instruments. Such mingled ensembles and choruses, combining dilettantes and professionals, remained a feature of Viennese concert life throughout Beethoven's lifetime.

Confronting the Viennese Aristocracy

Discerning Viennese patrons saw the young Beethoven as a brilliant talent, a "new Mozart" in the several meanings they attached to that title. Among these patrons were many to whom the composer dedicated important works and from whom he received financial support in varying degrees. Of thirty-odd noble patrons listed in one sociological study of music patronage around Beethoven, at least twenty received dedications from him, and he was certainly in touch with at least a dozen more.[15] Among the most active were the strongly conservative Baron von Swieten; Count Ferdinand Waldstein, Beethoven's supporter at Bonn; the Count and

Countess von Browne; Prince Karl Lichnowsky; the prince's younger brother Count Moritz Lichnowsky, and Karl's wife, Princess Christiane; and Prince Franz Joseph Maximilian von Lobkowitz, whose imposing palace contained a salon grand enough for orchestral performances. Beethoven's spreading personal network included female patrons, piano pupils, and friends, among them two sisters of the Brunsvik clan, Therese and Josephine Brunsvik. Josephine married Count Joseph Deym in 1799 and, after his death in 1804, was on intimate terms with Beethoven for several years, as we know from his love letters to her written between 1804 and 1807.[16]

Beethoven's attitude toward most of his patrons in these years fluctuated openly between burning ambition to succeed in their eyes and fierce, surly independence. These impulses were perpetually in conflict, not only in his early years but throughout his life. As a free-lance composer and per-

The palace of Prince Franz Joseph Maximilian von Lobkowitz, one of Beethoven's wealthy Viennese patrons, in a painting by Bernardo Bellotto. Here the prince's private orchestra held rehearsals of the Eroica *Symphony before its first public performance in 1805. (Kunsthistorisches Museum, Vienna)*

former without a fixed position, he needed his patrons' support to advance his career and gain recognition. But he demanded respect in no uncertain terms, and his impetuous, sometimes violent, temper spilled over again and again. His more far-seeing admirers were willing to forgive his brusque and insolent style as the price of his talents, and some of them probably even took perverse pleasure in it as a mark of artistic temperament. Prince Karl Lichnowsky, the most generous among them, gave Beethoven an annual pension of six hundred florins in 1801 and continued to pay it until 1806. Lichnowsky, a friend of Waldstein's, had been close to Mozart and had tried to help Mozart through the difficult financial struggles of his last years (1789–91). He had arranged Mozart's tour to Prague, Dresden, Leipzig, and Berlin in 1789. Exactly seven years later he arranged the same tour for Beethoven, introducing him to the same local patrons and some of the same performers who had known Mozart. In these ways Lichnowsky furthered the artistic project by which the young Beethoven sought to fulfill his role as Mozart's successor.[17]

Like Waldstein, Karl Lichnowsky was older than Beethoven—Mozart's exact contemporary. Lichnowsky was a well-trained musician who played chamber music by day and pursued women by night. A female member of his social world later called him "a cynical degenerate and a shameless coward" who fathered many illegitimate children. His death in 1814 was attributed to venereal disease. His wife, Princess Christiane, also one of Beethoven's devoted admirers, endured a marriage so painful that, according to rumor, she once disguised herself as a prostitute in order to surprise her husband in a brothel.[18] Nor were these extravagant lifestyles abnormal among Vienna's upper classes. A friend of Beethoven's described Count Browne, to whom Beethoven dedicated four works, as "one of the strangest men, full of excellent talents and beautiful qualities of heart and spirit...[but] full of weakness and depravity."[19]

It seems curious and strange that Beethoven's most attentive patrons at this time included several characterized by Solomon as "hardly free of personality difficulties and even bizarre tendencies."[20] In the light of history we can imagine how keenly the Austrian nobility felt the pressure of the times, knowing that they were living on borrowed time and that the current state of foreign revolution, war, and even benign political change in their own country signaled dangers to their sheltered status that could not be warded off. Isolated from participating in the major political and social events of their times, they looked for ways to put meaning into their private lives. For some of them this effort meant whiling away their time in hunting, balls, receptions, gossip, amorous affairs, and other diversions —the traditional patterns of life typical of their social class. For some it meant music, their anodyne. In 1813 the acerbic Madame de Staël described the Viennese aristocracy in a nutshell:

> *All the best people go* en masse *from one salon to another, three or four times a week. Time is wasted on getting dressed for these parties, it's wasted on travelling to them, on the staircases waiting for one's carriage, on spending three hours at table; and in these innumerable gatherings one hears nothing beyond conventional phrases. This daily exhibition of individuals to one another is a clever invention by mediocrity to annul spiritual faculties.[21]*

Of the Austrian nobility as a whole Beethoven could well have said to their faces, as Beaumarchais's Figaro had said privately about the Count Almaviva, "Because you are a nobleman you think you are a great man! What did you do to deserve it? You took the trouble to be born!"[22] Yet the patrons around Beethoven—as around music generally—were a relatively enlightened subset of the larger aristocratic population, if only because many of them cultivated music with enthusiasm, varying degrees of skill, and in some cases genuine concern for aesthetic quality. Looking outward from the hollow shells of their lives to their own dreams, the music lovers among them could see in the young Beethoven an artistic commitment they could never emulate. Here was a musician totally bound to the values and necessities of his art who would stand as far apart as he could from their carefully organized lives of social pleasantry while he shamelessly used their wealth and status as springboards to his own career. Inevitably he harbored ill-concealed anger at them, at himself, and at his need to accept their largesse while struggling to free himself from the servitude that had been the lot of musicians from time immemorial. It is even possible that his occasional adoption of a "nobility pretense"—in which he lapsed into a fantasy or allowed it to be thought from time to time that he might actually be of noble birth—stemmed in part from resentment, from the feeling that he, as an artist, really deserved but would never obtain the material advantages that his patrons took for granted.[23]

A memoir later written by Frau von Bernhard, who had come to Vienna as a young girl to complete her piano studies, tells the story, both in her disdainful description of Beethoven and in the elements that she chooses to stress:

desc. of B.

> When he came to us, he used to stick his head in the door and make
> sure there was no one there whom he disliked. He was small and
> plain-looking with an ugly, red, pock-marked face. His hair was quite
> dark and hung shaggily around his face. . . . [H]is clothes were very
> commonplace, not greatly different from the fashion of those days. . . .
> [H]e spoke in a strong dialect and in a rather common way. . . . [H]e
> was without manners in both gesture and demeanor. He was very
> haughty. I myself saw the mother of Princess Lichnowsky, Countess
> Thun [a patron of Haydn and Mozart, the mother-in-law of Lich-
> nowsky], go down on her knees to him as he lolled on the sofa, begging
> him to play something. But Beethoven did not. . . .

And she continues:

> I still remember clearly Haydn and Salieri sitting on a sofa. . . . both
> carefully dressed in the old-fashioned way with wig, shoes, and silk
> stockings, while Beethoven would come dressed in the informal fashion
> of the other side of the Rhine, almost badly dressed.[24]

Contrasting models—comfortable dependency and uncomfortable independence—had been provided by his two great spiritual mentors, Haydn and Mozart. Haydn had spent more than thirty years in service to the Esterházy family, emerging only when nearly sixty as an older master but never a rebel against the system. Haydn seems to have accepted that his development as an artist had been not only facilitated but conditioned by the enduring support of Prince Nikolaus. As he later put it to a biographer, Georg August Griesinger:

> *My prince was content with all my works, I received approval, I could,*
> *as head of an orchestra, make experiments, observe what enhanced an*
> *effect and what weakened it, thus improving, adding to, cutting away,*
> *and running risks. I was set apart from the world, there was nobody*
> *around me to confuse and annoy me in my course, and so I had to*
> *become original.*[25]

Griesinger, one of two reliable contemporaries who left memoirs of Haydn, claims that for years Haydn had resisted invitations to go to England, where his success seemed assured, saying that "so long as his Prince was alive, he could not leave him."[26] Other anecdotes, reported by him and by Albert Christoph Dies, another contemporary, give us a firm sense of Haydn's personal allegiance to his patrons and, equally, their loyalty and generosity to him. Each understood what he had to gain from this long and happy association, and Haydn was by nature balanced and thoughtful. Dies reports that Haydn's house in Eisenstadt burned down twice and that Prince Esterházy hurried to Haydn, "comforted him, had the house rebuilt, and provided the necessary furnishings. Haydn, deeply moved by the Prince's generosity, could repay him only with love, attachment, and with the offspring of his muse."[27]

After his early years of confinement in oppressive Salzburg, Mozart, partly leavened by his international fame as a former child prodigy and his several long tours abroad in the 1770s, had spent his last eleven years in Vienna (1781–91) as a free-lance teacher, pianist, and composer. In the absence of a court or church appointment his professional situation was precarious and uneven. Even so, the formerly prevailing portrait of Mozart as perpetually poor is a distortion; his income in his Vienna years fluctuated considerably, leaving him sometimes in financial embarrassment and sometimes well off. Yet though he was greatly admired by patrons in Prague, Bonn, and elsewhere, he never received from the imperial court or any other important patron in Vienna the appointment he clearly deserved.

Haydn in a generous letter bemoaned the fact that Mozart had not yet been given a major post commensurate with his "incomparable talents."[28]

Beethoven at first accepted the hospitality of the Lichnowskys. Prince Karl, his wife, and his brother treated him as a pampered and honored guest. His first apartment was located in a building owned by the prince, who lived on an upper floor, and Beethoven later chose his own lodgings so as to be near them. Yet though Prince Karl gave him a set of rare Italian stringed instruments (now preserved at Bonn) and also an annuity of six hundred florins, Beethoven resented their expectations. He refused to appear each day at four o'clock at Lichnowsky's house for dinner and said to Wegeler, "Am I supposed to come home every day at half-past three, change my clothes, shave, and all that? I'll have none of it!"[29] His anger broke out again in 1802 when he received a gift from Countess Susanna Guicciardi, the mother of his pupil Giulietta Guicciardi. Taking her present as the equivalent of a payment, he vehemently rebuked her and read her a stern lesson in Beethovenian pride and morality, saying in a letter that her gesture had "immediately put the little I had done for dear J. [Julia] on a par with your present, and it seemed to me that you wanted to humble my pride by wanting to show me that you wished more to put me in your debt than to have the appearance of being in mine."[30] Characteristically, however, he stopped short of severing the relationship and managed to find a way to keep the gift after all by saying that he had only decided to accept it after reading the words accompanying it ten times. He warned her that if she ever repeated this sort of thing, she would "never again see me in your house." And, tellingly, he assured her that, although he has been very open and free in his behavior in her house, where he wished no payment for his time, "I adopt the same frankness everywhere, even where I work only for payment."

Haydn

It was important for Beethoven to get to know the best string and wind players then established in Vienna, performers who frequented the salons of the same patrons as he did. Lichnowsky's passion for chamber music brought in the rising young violinist Ignaz Schuppanzigh, leader of

Franz Joseph Haydn, who agreed to take the young Beethoven as his pupil, portrayed by the English painter Thomas Hardy in 1791 during Haydn's first stay in London. (Royal College of Music, London)

a newly formed string quartet that included the violist Franz Weiss and the cellist Nikolaus Kraft.[31] Thus by the mid-1790s, having begun fully to establish himself but having not yet written a single string quartet, Beethoven was able to hear Haydn's and Mozart's quartets in the hands of excellent players. Beethoven's reputation as a pianist and improviser also put him into immediate competition with the other keyboard virtuosos of the day. As soon as he arrived in Vienna, he was beset by invitations to play for the nobility, most of which he snubbed and avoided as much as he could. Beethoven displayed anger over such situations; Wegeler reports that during the mid-1790s, when asked to play,

> [H]e would fly into a rage. He often came to me then, gloomy and out of sorts, complaining that they had made him play even though his fin-

gers ached and the blood under his nails burned. . . . I would try to divert and calm him. . . . I could never cure him of his obstinacy, which was often the source of bitter quarrels with his closest friends and patrons.[32]

The same stubborn personal resistance seems to have troubled his relationship to Haydn, though here it was mingled with reverence for authentic genius. Always generous and courteous, Haydn did what he could to further Beethoven's development. In the past he had taught competent pupils such as Ignaz Pleyel and Sigismund Neukomm, but no one with either Beethoven's talent or his explosive temperament. What complicated their relationship most of all was the new expansion of Haydn's already long and enormously successful career, marked above all by his visits to England in 1791–92 and again in 1794–95; his reception in England as a great artist; the major commissions he received for new works to perform at his English concerts, primarily the London symphonies; and the spirit of freedom that followed his release from long years as a princely Kapellmeister. No one could reasonably have expected Haydn in the 1790s to devote himself wholeheartedly to correcting counterpoint exercises, no matter how talented the pupil, and Haydn hardly had the time or inclination to do so. By early in 1793 Beethoven was getting nowhere in his counterpoint studies with Haydn. According to a later remark by Johann Schenk, he had been at it "for more than six months [*sic*] and was still at work on the first exercise."[33] Sometime in 1793 Beethoven began studying with Schenk, a decent journeyman composer, who put Johann Joseph Fux's classic *Gradus ad Parnassum* into his hands and worked hard at correcting Beethoven's counterpoint exercises for a few months, "by which time he finished double counterpoint." According to Schenk's later testimony, it was he who insisted that this arrangement be kept secret from Haydn, with whom Beethoven apparently continued to have lessons. In January 1794, when Haydn returned to London without taking Beethoven along (as rumor had it he would), Beethoven turned to the celebrated theorist and teacher Johann Georg Albrechtsberger for further counterpoint lessons, with or without Haydn's knowledge. Beethoven had three sessions a week with Albrechtsberger and also with Schuppanzigh, perhaps for violin lessons.

Johann Georg Albrechtsberger, a celebrated theorist of the late eighteenth century, who became Beethoven's counterpoint teacher in 1794. (Bibliothek der Gesellschaft der Musikfreunde, Vienna)

Albrechtsberger's conscientiousness and care in details of pedagogy were exemplary. In one place Beethoven wrote an unprepared chord and asked in a marginal note, "Is it allowed?"[34] The entire experience of studying the most demanding and rigorous of compositional disciplines—tonal counterpoint—was salutary, as it provided a form of discipline Beethoven could not derive from keyboard playing, improvisation, and free composition, all of which he was mastering with ease by 1793–94. As Nottebohm put it in a valuable summation, this period of study

> enriched him with new forms and means of expression and . . . effected
> a change in his mode of writing. The voices acquired greater melodic
> flow and independence. A certain opacity took the place of the former
> transparency in the musical fabric. Out of a homophonic polyphony of

two or more voices, there grew a polyphony that was real. The earlier
type of accompaniment gave way to an obbligato style of writing that
rested to a greater extent on counterpoint. Beethoven has accepted the
principle of polyphony; his part-writing has become purer, and it is
noteworthy that the compositions written immediately after the lessons
are among the purest that Beethoven ever composed. True, the Mozart
model still shines through the fabric, but we seek it less in the art of fig-
uration than in the form and in other things that are only indirectly
associated with the obbligato style. Similarly we can speak of other
influences—that of Joseph Haydn, for example. . . .[35]

A fugue for keyboard in C major in the early "Kafka" collection may well come from the Albrechtsberger study period. Some early fragmentary fugues for string quartet, along with the many examples of fugal passages in finished works, also show us the importance of Beethoven's work on counterpoint.[36]

As to Beethoven's feelings about Haydn, we have to distinguish artistic from personal judgments. On musical grounds there is no doubt that Beethoven revered Haydn as a master on the highest level. That he learned greatly from him we see from much of Beethoven's music as well as from later testimony such as the letter to "Emilie M." Although the child Beethoven had been brought up to emulate Mozart, he knew and valued Haydn's symphonies and chamber works; he copied some of them; he learned from Haydn ways of sharpening the wit and enhancing the vigor of musical ideas, phrases, and paragraphs; and he directly imitated some of Haydn's formal and expressive innovations. On the personal side their relationship seems not to have been easy, and Haydn was probably reacting to Beethoven's truculence when he referred to the fractious young man as a "Grand mogul."[37] Certainly Haydn had grounds for annoyance. After arriving from Bonn, Beethoven took financial support from Haydn when in need and enlisted his help in dealing with the Elector, but misled him about when certain of his own works had been written—whether in Bonn, or since Beethoven's arrival in Vienna.

There was an unbridgeable generation gap between them, and strong differences in social, intellectual, and political outlook as well as in personality. Yet Haydn continued to accept Beethoven as a protégé after returning from his second visit to England. He had Beethoven play at one of his concerts, and he continued to show him favor despite Beethoven's touchiness. Haydn criticized the C Minor Trio Opus 1 No. 3, explaining to Ries that he had done so because "he had not believed that this Trio would be so quickly and easily understood and so favorably received by the general public."[38] That Beethoven interpreted Haydn's reaction as jealousy fits all too well with his extreme sensitivity to criticism, certainly from Haydn. Ruffled feelings on both sides stemmed from innate artistic differences. Beethoven's sweeping originality and high emotional tension in some of his works was so strong that it would have been hard for Haydn to accept them entirely.[39] Yet Beethoven must have felt a need for Haydn's blessing, not just because of his fame and seniority but because of what Beethoven knew instinctively was Haydn's experience, resourcefulness, and originality. Striking in this respect is Seyfried's remark that Beethoven displayed "a kind of apprehension, because he realized that he had struck out on a path for himself of which Haydn did not approve."

Within less than four years after arriving in Vienna Beethoven was acknowledged as its young musical hero. We see this judgment plainly in a 1796 publication by Johann Ferdinand von Schönfeld that surveys the current Viennese musical world and devotes a chapter to brief critical accounts of active composers. They range from veterans such as Albrechtsberger and Johann Baptist Vanhal, both born in the 1730s, to a full array of composers in their forties and fifties, such as Joseph Weigl, Ignaz Umlauf, Leopold Kozeluch, Antonio Salieri, and Anton Wranitsky, and a younger set that includes Franz Xaver Süssmayr and Joseph Wölffl, a pupil of Leopold Mozart. Wölffl was a brilliant pianist, slightly younger than Beethoven and clearly his rival, though in 1793 he showed his admiration for Beethoven by dedicating a set of piano sonatas to him. In 1799 a piano contest was staged between Beethoven and Wölffl at the home of Baron Wetzlar, with the principals seated for a time at two pianos improvising alternately on themes they gave each other.[40] As Seyfried put it, "even then Beethoven did not deny his tendency toward the mysterious and gloomy," while Wölffl, "trained in the school of Mozart, was always equable."[41]

Mozart is missing in Schönfeld's hierarchy because it deals only with living composers. The longest article and highest praise are reserved for Haydn, portrayed as the greatest living master by virtue of his undiminished productivity. Probably reflecting the views of patrons seeking to manipulate opinion in favor of Beethoven (but not at the risk of offending Haydn), Schönfeld gives the young "musical genius" the top rank below Haydn, singling him out beyond anyone else of his generation. Of the forty-odd composers described in the volume, about half appear in retrospect to be of any real importance, and of these about eight now merit serious study (a result that should give us pause when we read critics' evaluations of composers in our own time). But among the creative few Beethoven is clearly Haydn's heir apparent:

> Beethoven, a musical genius, has chosen Vienna as his residence for the past two years. He is widely admired for the unusual velocity of his playing, and is astounding in the way he masters the most formidable difficulties with the greatest of ease. He seems already to have entered into the inner sanctuary of music, distinguishing himself for his precision, feeling and taste; consequently his fame has risen considerably. A living proof of his true love of art lies in the fact that he has put himself in the hands of our immortal Haydn in order to be initiated into the holy secrets of the art of music. The latter great master, during his absence, has turned him over to our great Albrechtsberger. What cannot be expected when such a great genius places himself under the guidance of such excellent masters! There have already been several beautiful sonatas by him, among which his latest are regarded as particularly outstanding.[42]

Playing for an Elector and a King

Early in 1796 Beethoven journeyed to Prague and then to Berlin, with stops at Dresden and Leipzig, on a concert tour that was supposed to last six weeks and turned into six months. He made these plans in collaboration with Lichnowsky, who accompanied him to Prague but not farther, just as this same patron had accompanied Mozart on the identical itinerary.[43] When Beethoven arrived in Prague he knew that the beautiful and historic Bohemian capital had welcomed Mozart, had been enamored of *Figaro*, and had witnessed the premieres of *Don Giovanni* in 1787 and of *La Clemenza di Tito* in 1791. Staying at an inn in Prague named *Das goldene Einhorn* (The Golden Unicorn), he slept in the same hostelry in which Lichnowsky and Mozart had stayed in 1789, conceivably in the same bed as Mozart. He wrote back to his brother Johann from Prague:

> First of all I am well, very well. My art is winning me friends and renown, and what more do I want? And this time I shall make a good deal of money.[44]

While in Prague he composed a major concert aria on a Metastasio text, *Ah, perfido*, Opus 65, for soprano and orchestra. Although dedicated to Countess Josephine de Clary, a Prague singer and patron, it was likely intended for Josefa Dussek, who gave its first performance in Leipzig that year. Mozart admired Dussek and wrote a superb concert aria for her, "Bella mia fiamma," which became a model for Beethoven.[45] In Prague Beethoven also wrote a few minor works, including the Wind Sextet Opus 71 and the easy Piano Sonata Opus 49 No. 2, and played at least one concert, on March 11, 1796. From Prague he moved on in April to Dresden and then to Leipzig, both cities with rich traditions and the latter especially important for the career of Johann Sebastian Bach.[46] In Dresden, where he stayed for a week and won general acclaim, he played for the Elector of Saxony, on one occasion for an hour and a half.[47] Of the Leipzig stay we know little, but surely he visited the Thomaskirche, Bach's main scene of activity and already a shrine to his memory.

In May Beethoven arrived in Berlin, the Prussian capital and by far the most sophisticated of German cities. He stayed there a surprisingly long time, until July, making contact with musicians and new patrons. The court was an attractive center for music, thanks to the personal talent and interest of the recently crowned king of Prussia, Friedrich Wilhelm II. This nephew and successor to Frederick the Great, though not much of a political figure, was a devoted amateur musician. He had studied cello with Carlo Graziani in his earlier years. On ascending to the throne he associated himself with excellent players, including other famous cellists. One was Luigi Boccherini, who contributed more than fifty works for the court from his base in Spain; another was Jean Pierre Duport, who moved from France to Berlin and became first the prince's cello teacher, and later his royal superintendent of chamber music. An even greater virtuoso was Jean Pierre's brother, Jean Louis Duport, who left France in 1790 and joined his brother in Berlin. Beethoven encountered the two Duports in the late spring of 1796, and for Jean Louis he wrote the two cello sonatas of Opus 5, among his most original early accompanied sonatas, and performed them with him at court.[48]

In Berlin, where Carl Philipp Emanuel Bach had been the leading figure from mid-century until his death in 1788, court music was only part of the scene. There was a lively opera theater, much private chamber music, and sacred music, often sung in patrons' homes.[49] In June Beethoven was invited to play before the Berlin Singakademie, a major choral society, and he "fantasized" for them on a fugue theme so successfully that he was called back a week later for a second appearance.[50] When copies of his Piano Sonata in A major, Opus 2 No. 2, reached him after it had been published in Vienna a few months earlier, he sent an inscribed copy to the director of the Singakademie, Carl Friedrich Christian Fasch.[51]

This journey gave Beethoven exposure in four important musical centers, one of them a seat of royalty, all of them having patrons who might be of use to him if he ever decided to leave Vienna. Later that year he went to Pressburg (now Bratislava) and Pest (now part of Budapest) to play concerts. Two years later, in October 1798, he returned to Prague to perform his first piano concertos. He had consolidated his position in Vienna; now he was aiming to spread his reputation as the most brilliant of the current composer-pianists.

Entering the Publishing World

Beethoven's first Vienna years culminated in July 1795 with his first publication—his Opus 1—the three piano trios in E-flat, G, and C minor, dedicated (appropriately enough) to Lichnowsky. The road to the music market was now open, and with these first works in print his reputation leaped forward. Just as he was the first composer through whom so many patrons became well known by virtue of their association with him, he was also the first major composer whose music was regularly printed during his lifetime by a host of publishers, sometimes in rival editions. They could read the market, and they rushed to profit from his works.

His dealings with publishers occupied a good deal of his attention over many years. They became more and more complex as his career developed, and eventually resulted in some of the most bizarre business arrangements that any artist ever had with those who disseminated his works. Fiercely proud and dependent for his living on the sale of his music, he worked very hard all his life on managing, or trying to manage, his publications.[52] In the 1790s his rising image brought printers swarming around him. He wrote to Eleonore von Breuning as early as November 1793, sending her the dedication of his variations on Mozart's "Se vuol ballare," WoO 40, and telling her that "people in Vienna have been pestering me to publish this little work."[53] By seven or eight years later, a steady stream of his new works were coming out from local printing shops.

His main outlet in the first years was the prestigious house of Artaria, established in Vienna in 1766. Artaria had published more than three hundred editions of works by Haydn and as many as eighty-three first editions of Mozart. That Beethoven opened his career with them was a clear sign of status; that the relationship was a good one is indicated by the fact that of his works with opus number—throughout his life the ones he considered important—the first eight were brought out by Artaria between 1795 and 1797. Even later, when he was publishing on a Europe-wide scale, Artaria issued a number of minor works but also the very important first edition of Opus 106, the *Hammerklavier*, in 1819. In the later 1790s Beethoven moved on to rival Viennese publishing entrepreneurs such as Johann Traeg, Giovanni Cappi, Johann Eder, Franz Hoffmeister, and Tranquillo Mollo. These smooth paths of publication, closed to many a contemporary such as Schubert, went hand in hand with his productivity. As he wrote to Wegeler in June 1801,

My compositions bring me in a good deal; and I may say that I am offered more commissions than it is possible for me to carry out. More-

The Kohlmarkt *(Coal Market)*, an important street in Vienna. Visible in the right foreground is the music shop of Domenico Artaria, the publisher who brought out a number of Beethoven's earliest piano sonatas and chamber music (Opp. 1 through 8). (Historisches Museum, Vienna)

> over, for every composition I can count on six or seven publishers, and
> even more, if I want them. People no longer come to an arrangement
> with me, I state my price and they pay.[54]

As a result of all these dealings, he thought about composition and publication from early on as a single large-scale enterprise. Very few finished works remained in his pile of manuscripts for good, even if they were not of high quality. Often succumbing to a need to make money and an impulse to present himself publicly in as many guises as possible, he deliberately and indiscriminately published a long list of these minor works without any opus numbers (abbreviated in German WoO).[55] He tried to manage the sequence of opus numbers but in dealing with so many publishers there were a few lapses, from which it came about that four opus numbers of the total of 135 issued in his lifetime are spurious. Thus, Opus 41 and Opus 42 are hack arrangements by others of two of his earlier trios for piano and another instrument, Opus 63 and Opus 64 are unauthorized arrangements of string chamber works. And although Beethoven tried to reserve the opus numbers for important works, now and then he slipped new but unimportant compositions into the sequence—for example, the little song, "Merkenstein," Opus 100, published by Steiner in Vienna. Even in later years he still gave in to the temptation to release early second-rate works. The Wind Octet, Opus 103, which had actually been written in Bonn and had been revised as the String Quintet Opus 4, was supposed to be issued in 1819 by Artaria though it did not actually appear until 1830, when Breitkopf & Härtel designated it Opus 103. The Quintet Opus 104 (Artaria, 1819) is an arrangement of the early Piano Trio in C Minor, Opus 1 No. 3, originally made by a certain Herr Kaufmann and "raised from the most abject misery to some degree of respectability" by Beethoven himself, as he noted ironically on the score.[56]

We must remember that in this era of little or no control over authors' rights, before copyright laws existed, all that a composer could derive from any publication was a one-time payment. Publishers could only hope for a rapid sale directly after publication but had no way of protecting themselves or the author from pirated editions by other entrepreneurs who paid nothing to the composer and undercut the original price if they could. As Gottfried Christoph Härtel lamented to Beethoven in 1802, "in Germany, with [the publication of] every interesting work, the pirate reprinters often now follow suit, so that the legitimate printers, who cannot set such low prices on them, often cannot sell a tenth as many copies as the pirate can."[57] Accordingly the risks run by publishers were substantial, and their reluctance to issue long, complex, and difficult works was understandable. Beethoven would try to induce them to take on less salable larger compositions by promising them easier works, and his correspondence is peppered with offers to publishers of works that he declared ready although they were still unfinished. He would frequently offer bundles of works as a unit for a fixed sum in return, in order to get the larger works, especially sacred works, off his hands. This explains why his oratorio of 1803, *Christus am Ölberge* ("Christ on the Mount of Olives") was not published until 1811, after years of effort to get it accepted by Breitkopf & Härtel, then his main publishers.

The standard method of printing music was by hand engraving, that is, incising of the music on copper plates by specialists whose work required them to rule the staves on the plates, punch in the note heads, engrave every detail of the notation, and, if there was a text, insert it using letter punches. The publishers kept the plates and struck off as many copies as they thought they could sell. Thus each "issue" was a batch made up at a certain time by the publisher, and the sizes of the issues differed in keeping with the potential sale of the work. The two Piano Trios Opus 70, for example, had a first issue of one hundred copies, while the first printing of the Piano Sonata Opus 81a (*Lebewohl*) was five times that figure; however, that edition was printed by the recently invented method of lithography.[58] For the most part, errors could remain in printed versions for a long time after Beethoven or others had detected them. Many of his letters to publishers included lists of errata that he found while proofreading (and his proofreading itself was far from exact and painstaking) but they made very few corrections, fearing loss of sales to pirated editions that would soon appear. In 1809, correcting early copies of his Cello Sonata in A Major, Opus 69, he sent Breitkopf & Härtel a list of misprints, told them that he would publish the misprints "in the newspaper" in Vienna, and try to see to it that

> all who have bought the work already may obtain it. This again confirms what I have experienced before, that works published from my own manuscripts are the most correctly engraved ones. Presumably there are many misprints in the copy which you have, but in looking over the music the author actually overlooks the errors.[59]

The problems were never really resolved in his lifetime. In a letter of 1811, apropos of a solo piano arrangement of the *Egmont* Overture, he excoriated Breitkopf & Härtel: "Mistakes—mistakes—you yourself are a unique mistake! I will have to send my copyist, or go there myself, if I want to ensure that my works don't come out as just a mass of mistakes."[60] Aside from these tribulations, his earlier works had come out rapidly through the efforts of local publishers in Vienna, and in view of the poor quality of some of these editions (especially Artaria's, whose engraving standards were not of the highest) we can imagine Beethoven's frustration.

CHAPTER 4

Music of the
First Vienna Years

❧

Revising Earlier Works

In the later eighteenth century a young composer's path to maturity depended on natural ability; an intuitive grasp of contemporary genres, forms, and styles; and a solid foundation in traditional musical disciplines—above all the still disparate sectors of harmony and counterpoint. By the time Beethoven arrived in Vienna he had all these credentials in abundance except mastery of counterpoint, and he set out to remedy this deficiency through assiduous work. Carrying out contrapuntal studies first with Haydn, then with Schenk, and finally with Albrechtsberger, he made decisive progress during his first two years in Vienna. He completed endless counterpoint exercises, made new efforts to integrate a contrapuntal dimension into his work, and studied such classics of music theory as C. P. E. Bach's *Essay on the True Manner of Playing Keyboard Instruments*, Kirnberger's *Kunst des reinen Satzes* ("Art of Strict Composition"), and treatises by Daniel Gottlob Türk and Albrechtsberger.[1] All of this work followed up on his earlier exposure to theoretical writings afforded him by Neefe, along with his previous introduction to Bach's fugal mastery in *The Well-Tempered Clavier*.

A handful of Beethoven's works associated with his first years in Vienna had been started in Bonn or even completed there in early versions. When Haydn wrote to the Elector in November 1793 to help the young Beethoven obtain further financial support, he sent along a number of pieces that he thought Beethoven had composed during the previous months in Vienna—including a quintet, an "eight-voice Parthie" (a wind octet, presumably Opus 103), an oboe concerto, a set of variations, and a fugue. The Elector indignantly replied a month later to say that except for the fugue, all of these works had actually been composed and performed in Bonn before Beethoven's departure. Since there is no reason to doubt Max Franz's memory, given his respectable prowess as a musical amateur, Beethoven had evidently built up a portfolio in Bonn of new works to take with him to Vienna when the time finally came. Those that survive, such as the wind octet, show his improvements in compositional technique since the earlier 1780s.

Anecdotal evidence plus sketches and revisions allow us to estimate the pace of Beethoven's development prior to his first Vienna publication, the three piano trios of Opus 1, which came out in the summer of 1795. In Bonn he had begun a B-flat-major piano concerto that became the Second Piano Concerto, though most of his work on it predated the first. This concerto in B-flat had been drafted between 1787 and 1789, for his own performance with the Bonn Hofkapelle.

The first versions of several other works may well date back to 1793, his first full year in Vienna, among them the Piano Trio, Opus 1 No. 1, which might have been the earliest of this group.[2] At this time Beethoven was probably also at work on the first of the three piano sonatas of Opus 2—the powerful Piano Sonata Opus 2 No. 1, with its turbulent contrasts, striking patterns of tension and release, and clear reflections of the new and massive styles of keyboard writing then being developed by Dussek, Clementi, and Haydn.

That the three piano sonatas of Opus 2 marked a decisive step forward makes it all the more notable that for two of them, as we saw earlier, he lifted material directly from his piano quartets of 1785. His deployment of this material shows that the deeper roots of his first maturity go back about a decade before the early Vienna years. If we look closely at what he accomplished in Bonn, then some of the earlier Vienna works, including the F Minor Piano Sonata, no longer look like somewhat radical precursors of later styles but, rather, like highly charged and integrated culminations of earlier efforts to write cyclic sonatas and chamber works. His youthful works of 1785, now seen in retrospect, show remarkable originality for a fourteen-year-old. Beethoven's early compositional style shows him "multiplying the resources of Mozart into those of Haydn,"[3] as Tovey once suggested. The point is valid, and its stress on Mozart as the underlying model helps to correct the impression that in 1794–95 Beethoven was working primarily under the spell of Haydn's string quartets and his first six London symphonies (Nos. 93 through 98), even though these compositions also influenced him significantly.

Especially revealing of Beethoven's musical growth from the final apprentice years to his first true maturity in Vienna is his revision of the Wind Octet, Opus 103, as a string quintet (Opus 4).[4] The quintet was offered in response to a commission in 1795 for a string quartet from Count Apponyi, a well-known Haydn patron, together with the String Trio, Opus 3, as if Beethoven were studiously avoiding the quartet target, missing it by one voice on either side. In the quintet each movement is longer and harmonically more enlarged than in the wind octet; yet the quintet is also tightened and made more cogent in its flow of ideas and in the contrapuntal animation of the subordinate parts. A telling change is Beethoven's addition of a second Trio section to contrast with the original Menuetto, a short twenty-four-measure addendum marked *dolce* and *piano*. Just as Mozart had conspicuously omitted one voice—the clarinet—in a Trio section of his Clarinet Quintet, Beethoven omits the second viola, making this his first completed movement for string quartet. But more important is the smoothness and authority with which the quiet half-step motion of the opening phrase is twice repeated, each time an octave lower, with added sonority in each statement. The whole revision—which is no mere arrangement but a true recomposition—exemplifies Beethoven's command even more than does his use of Bonn material in the piano sonatas of Opus 2.

Another work that underwent revision in the first Vienna years was the Opus 3 string trio, still essentially a *divertimento* but a clever sample of his craftsmanship. An English commentator, William Gardiner, knew an early incarnation of the work that may have been brought to England in 1792, and a surviving variant finale in Beethoven's handwriting probably belongs to a version that was circulating prior to the trio's publication early in 1796.[5] A draft score of the finale also contains a number of variants showing Beethoven's improvement of the idiomatic features of the string writ-

A leaf containing the autograph of a "second Trio" for the Scherzo of Beethoven's String Trio in G Major, Opus 9 No. 3. Below the fourth staff, Beethoven wrote "the second Trio must be written out and inserted [into the work]." (Beethoven-Haus, Bonn, Bodmer Collection)

ing in this work, along with changes in compositional details (such as the omission of single measures or short phrases) that show him tightening the material and shedding redundancies. These changes are consistent with his methods of revision in all periods of his career.

Chamber Music and Piano Sonatas

With his Opp. 1 and 2—three piano trios and three piano sonatas—Beethoven came out boldly with works that combined strong originality with shrewd career-building implications. By opening his record of publications with keyboard works he was advertising his compositional skills and capitalizing on his reputation as a performer. Through landmark contributions by both Haydn and Mozart, plus a host of contemporaries, the piano sonata and piano trio were gaining ground, though they still lagged behind the string quartet in aesthetic stature. Mozart's piano sonatas and a handful of trios from the 1780s included some works of high distinction, but few of them matched his violin sonatas, string quartets, quintets, concertos, and the last half-dozen symphonies, all of which in turn were greatly enriched by their subtle connections to Mozart's operas. Haydn was at his peak in the 1790s, producing not only his London symphonies, his quartets from Opp. 71 to 77, and other works, but also a series of highly imaginative keyboard-centered piano trios and his last piano sonatas, many of them among his most brilliant late compositions. The rising popularity of piano music in the same decade brought on a wave of solo sonatas and other keyboard works by composer-pianists working in central Europe, France, and above all England. There the manufacture of the newly strengthened pianoforte, with its larger range and finer timbral gradations, stimulated ambitious competitors such as Clementi and Dussek to proudly explore the instrument's new capacities.

Beethoven certainly knew Mozart's and Haydn's earlier piano sonatas, but he also learned from Dussek and Clementi, as we can see from passages in his works that mirror their expanded ways of writing for the piano.[6] His own growing command of pianistic figurations and sonorities is visible on every page of Opus 1 and Opus 2, setting the stage for the larger frameworks and wider expressive range of his later keyboard chamber music, not to mention his concertos. The works that followed up to 1798 show him gradually advancing from the safer ground of keyboard music to the less familiar symphony and string quartet.

Opus 2 Piano Sonatas

Although they were dedicated to Haydn and so might have been expected to conform to familiar expectations, Beethoven's Opus 2 piano sonatas came across to the public of 1796 as original in content and unorthodox in plan. Following the familiar pattern of placing two works in major with one in minor, Beethoven broke tradition by putting the minor-mode sonata first and by establishing the four-movement sonata as a norm. Opus 2 No. 1 in F minor is an intense, tightly woven masterpiece.

The rising arpeggiated contour of its famous opening, which cannot but remind listeners of the finale of Mozart's G Minor Symphony, actually traces back to the first theme of Beethoven's 1785 E-flat Major Piano Quartet, written three years before Mozart's symphony. In the piano sonata, the theme, which has been altered to duple time, moves with decisive logic from its opening arpeggio through its turn figure and moves harmonically from its opening tonic to its first pause on the dominant, thus setting the stage for dramatic consequences. That a little turn figure in the second measure should prove usable as a developmental motif is a highly progressive sign that foreshadows later works built up from small motivic cells; it is a feature not found much at all in Mozart and only occasionally in Haydn.[7]

Even more revealing of Beethoven's individuality is the slow movement, which transforms thematic material written in 1785 from a plain, square-cut sectional design into a pre-Romantic Adagio, with more elaborate figuration patterns later in the movement, stronger dissonances, and an expressive intensity that transcends anything he had been capable of writing ten years earlier. The third movement, labeled Menuetto, is actually a scherzo with strong dynamic contrasts between its first part (*piano*) and immediate juxtaposition of *pianissimo* and *fortissimo* in the second part—the latter a typical example of Beethoven's decisive and emphatic way with dynamics in his early works. The finale brings similar contrasts in its opening measures, with strongly chopped chords in hammering rhythms over running triplets; this combination pervades much of the movement, gives way for a time in the lyrical middle section, but returns to give its stamp to the *fortissimo* close, where the triplets and chord patterns have now switched hands.

The next two sonatas contrast both with the first and with each other. No. 2, in A major, moves through a wide span of affects in its four movements and exits with grace and charm in a beguiling finale marked "Rondo, Grazioso." It immediately reassured amateur pianists that the *Sturm und Drang* of the F Minor Sonata, Opus 2 No. 1, was not Beethoven's only voice but that he could also write with charm and verve. The third, a big, bravura sonata in C major, uses 1785 material in its first movement but deftly rearranges the thematic ideas into a better and more cogent design, all of which is shaped to give free rein to dazzling virtuosic passages that anticipate the first piano concerto and some of the later sonatas, including the

"Waldstein."[8] The opening, with its highly profiled motivic figure—abrupt, energetic, and cut off by a rest (as in the opening of the Quartet Opus 18 No. 1)—is soon extended into a movement on a very large and imposing scale that is then matched by the rest of the work. Its massive technical demands, its vivacity and brilliance, round out this first sonata "opus" by delivering the message that a major pianist and composer had arrived in the crowded world of keyboard-sonata composition.

Opus 1 Piano Trios

The dedication of the Opus 1 Trios went to Prince Karl Lichnowsky rather than to Haydn, who may have admired them but was wary of the fierce idiosyncrasies of the third, in C minor. Here as in the three piano sonatas we find two works in major, quite different but both emotionally

The title page of Beethoven's three Piano Trios, Opus 1, his first publication to carry an opus number. Beethoven reserved opus numbers for his more important works, leaving the others unpublished or publishing them without opus number. (Beethoven-Haus, Bonn)

tempered, and one in minor that breathes fire. Opus 1 No. 3 is the first published example of Beethoven's intense C minor, a key to which he returned over a lifetime in a long series of works that share certain thematic contours and aesthetic affinities.[9] Opus 1 No. 1, in a conservative vein, reflects Mozart's E-flat-major piano quartet of 1785. It is the first of many Beethoven compositions in E-flat major to open with a figure that moves up the scale steps 1–3–5 (here extended through two octaves). This feature is so ubiquitous in his E-flat-major works in all genres that he might, consciously or unconsciously, have had in mind the overture in E-flat to *The Magic Flute* and its solemn, opening three-fold chords, which move up through the same 1–3–5 triad. The remainder expands in other ways: the slow movement is an ample and well-developed lyrical rondo; the C-minor Scherzo is a brilliant tour de force whose quiet opening becomes boisterous, laden with rhythmic ambiguity and unexpected turns of phrase; and the finale is Haydnesque in its wit and surprise, kin to many a Haydn quartet finale.

The second piano trio, in G major, also starts in a conservative vein but in its glorious slow movement breaks out into the world of the Romantic. This Largo con espressione is unexcelled by the slow movement of any piano trio written up to this time, and for sheer lyrical beauty it outdoes those of his early piano sonatas. Here for the first time in Beethoven's keyboard chamber music the strings achieve complete parity with the piano, sharing the leading role so fully that we can no longer speak of the work as a keyboard composition with an important violin part and a subordinated cello part (as in Haydn's late trios). Instead, the strings emerge as leading voices in significant portions of the movement, one of the most poignant of his earlier slow movements.

The C Minor Trio caps the set as a tumultuous, four-movement work that brings a space for relaxation only in its Andante cantabile, a set of variations. Turbulence dominates the other movements from start to finish. The first begins with a quiet two-measure motivic themelet that opens out into an asymmetrical larger phrase and then a long exposition that works its way through rushing sixteenth-note passages, contrasting thematic elements, and a whirlwind of emotions. The finale is even more decisive and emphatic in the rhythmic shape of its opening motifs, moving from its passionate *fortissimo* outburst to another C-minor murmuring first theme. The C-minor theme eventually closes into a fine secondary theme, a melodic arch rising to an apex and then descending from it, a sample of that "absolute melody" that is one of the most striking features of Beethoven's first maturity (*W 4).[10]

Opus 5 Cello Sonatas

Up to the turning points represented by the "Pathétique" Sonata, Opus 13, and the two sonatas of Opus 14, the works with opus number in the years 1792–98 show a pattern of deliberate diversity. Beethoven's main line includes the serious keyboard chamber works and the string trios of Opus 9. Despite his ability to endow even lesser works with memorable ideas and high technical finish, already in this early phase we can distinguish pieces that aim at career building and audience approval from those in which the young composer is listening to his inner conscience. We will consider the latter group first.

The two Cello Sonatas Opus 5 were evidently written in Berlin during Beethoven's visit there in the early summer of 1796, though they were probably touched up in Vienna before being published in February 1797. These works break new ground. Although Mozart had established the rich classical tradition of the accompanied violin sonata in the 1780s, no comparable sonatas for the cello had ever been written. This is true in the face of plentiful contributions to the attractive wallpaper literature by cellist-composers such as Luigi Boccherini, who was a great player and a favorite of Friedrich Wilhelm II as well as a fertile producer of pleasant but stereotypical sonatas, concertos, quintets, and other works. But there was no genuine precedent for Beethoven's attack on the problem of composing a full-scale cello sonata by bringing the entire range of his piano writing into a working reciprocal relationship with the cello in its varied registers and expressive voices.

The Opus 5 pair emerged as the first true cello sonatas worthy to rank with Mozart's violin sonatas, the first steps in Beethoven's long-term project of liberating the cello from its subordinate and supporting functions and giving it a leading role.[11] That this effort coincided with his getting to know Jean Louis Duport is not an accident. Although the two Duports were both virtuosi, Jean Louis was the more famous player and had grand didactic ambitions as well. Some years later he was the first to codify a new approach to the technique of the instrument.[12] His achievements for the cello rank historically with those of Viotti for the violin in opening up and normalizing a new spectrum of technical achievements. Duport brought to the cello the violinist's range of brilliant new technical effects: arpeggios and figuration patterns, difficult bowings, double stops, complete facility in higher registers; in short, his playing marked the cello's emergence as a major new sonorous resource. Apparently Beethoven sent him an inscribed copy of Opus 5, for in a letter Duport thanked Beethoven for the dedication and expressed the wish to play them with him. It is Duport's personality as a performer that Beethoven captured to animate both works.[13]

The two cello sonatas differ significantly, although they share the same formal plan, one that Beethoven probably borrowed from Mozart's Violin Sonata in C Major, K. 303. The idea is to begin auspiciously with a slow introduction of some length that arrives at the dominant and then breaks into a full-scale Allegro first movement, followed by a bright Rondo finale to close the form. Each sonata has its own way of joining piano and cello in varied textures that can generate a larger work. Thus in the F Major Sonata, No. 1, Beethoven utilized the idea of thematic reciprocity that he found in the later Mozart violin sonatas, in which every important theme is stated twice; here each is given once with the piano as leading voice, once with the cello, or vice versa. The Allegro sets the pattern, for the good, square-cut theme (virtually plagiarized by Weber in a bassoon concerto of 1811) appears first in the piano in middle register, then in the cello, leading to further elaborations and consequences. This thematic reciprocity culminates at or near the end of the movement, when the two instruments will climactically present the main theme together in octaves. This principle, which never fails to make an effect, underpins many a later Beethoven sonata as well, not only for cello. The sonorous potential of the cello's C string is evident from beginning to end, and the 6/8 Rondo finale offers episodes that contrast effectively with its main theme.

The G Minor Sonata, No. 2, is one of Beethoven's most extended works of these years, more intellectually ambitious than its companion. Here the slow introduction is long and complex, with lights and shadows, lyrical subthemes, and near the end, surprising silences—pauses on unresolved chords—that prepare us for the start of the G-minor Allegro with considerable drama. In the Allegro first movement the main principle of organization is the exact opposite of thematic reciprocity. Now each instrument has its own material. The piano plays rolling triplets almost throughout the movement, one of the longest sonata movements Beethoven ever wrote, while the cello plays no triplets whatever but sustains long lines against the incessant rhythmic figures in the piano. This scheme maximizes the cello's ability to spin long legato phrases, rising and falling in crescendo-decrescendo patterns, and helps extend the movement to full length by developing principal and secondary thematic groups and even inserting a new theme in the middle of the development section. Then the courtly finale enters from another sphere: it is a charming G-major Rondo redolent of the social world of the contredanse though much more developed, and foreshadowing the finale of the Fourth Piano Concerto (also in G major!) in its lightness of manner, humor, and even its opening on the subdominant.

Opus 12 Violin Sonatas

The three violin sonatas of Opus 12 written in 1798 also stem, as we should expect, from Beethoven's direct engagement with Mozart's late violin sonatas. They were dedicated to Salieri, with whom Beethoven was studying vocal composition and Italian text-setting methods, clearly with operatic ambitions in mind. Apart from the dedication of Opus 2 to Haydn, the sonatas represent the only case in which Beethoven dedicated a work with opus number to a teacher; there are no dedications to Neefe, Albrechtsberger, or Schenk. In view of Salieri's position as the Imperial *Hofkapellmeister* and his political role in Viennese musical life, the dedication had obvious career implications, though nothing came of it. Salieri, like Albrechtsberger, found Beethoven self-willed and difficult, and he was probably bewildered by the new features of these works.[14]

The first sonata, in D major, anticipates in its first movement the figuration patterns of the String Quartet Opus 18 No. 3, a work in the same key

Antonio Salieri, opera composer and Imperial Court Kapellmeister, with whom Beethoven studied the setting of Italian texts to music. (Bibliothek der Gesellschaft der Musikfreunde, Vienna)

and written around the same time, though it lacks the quartet's emotional range. Like its companions in this group, the sonata holds to the three-movement template in the familiar layout of Allegro first movement, full-length slow movement, and rondo finale, unlike the four-movement trios and piano sonatas of 1795. The second and third works improve the landscape. No. 2, in A major, combines a brilliant first movement with a bleak but expressive A-minor Andante, closing with a full-bodied Allegro piacevole. The first movement shows Beethoven's early facility in forming a theme from arpeggiated repetitions of a simple two-note figure in the piano right hand (in this case moving downward through an octave and a half) while the violin steadily pulsates on chord tones in the middle register (*W 5). Thus one instrument holds the harmonic rudder steady while the other traverses a defined harmonic space against it. In the finely spun course of the first movement new figures and patterns emerge as contrasts to the opening; and at a wonderful place in the coda the two-note figure emerges in exchanges between the piano right hand and the violin plus the piano left hand to form the movement's climax (*W 6).

The third of the set, in E-flat major, is more elaborate and ambitious in its first movement and contains one of Beethoven's best early slow movements, a C-major Adagio con molt'espressione (typically he gives a much more detailed tempo marking than we find in Haydn or Mozart) that is a relative of the Largo of Opus 7 and of the Adagio of the String Trio Opus 9 No. 3, both also in C major. The work closes with an energetic Rondo in E-flat major, reminiscent in some details of the finale of Opus 3. Both derive in character from Haydn, above all some of Haydn's quartet finales. Beethoven at this stage was probably studying Haydn's late quartets assiduously as he prepared to embark on quartet composition. These movements show that although he could imitate Haydn's surface features to perfection, he could not yet capture Haydn's subtle wisdom and high humor.

Keeping in mind what we now see as the hybrid character of the Opus 12 sonatas—caught between Beethoven's early exuberance and the higher quality of his models in Mozart's violin sonatas and Haydn's quartets—we can understand a contemporary reviewer of 1799. He writes pointedly that he had not known Beethoven's early piano music but complains that these violin sonatas are "heavily laden with unusual difficulties" and that they made him feel like a man who had wandered through an alluring forest and at last emerged tired and worn out."[15] Reviewers tended to be conservative at the time. Beethoven was a brash newcomer, and the emphatic rhetorical style of these works, with their elaborate figuration patterns and well-defined motivic ideas passing between keyboard and violin, was more than salon-music enthusiasts could accept.

Piano Sonata Opus 7

Opus 7 is a single piano sonata in E-flat major, published as "Grande Sonate" by Artaria in October 1797 with a dedication to Countess Babette von Keglevics. This society lady, who became Princess Odescalchi on her marriage in 1801 to an Italian nobleman, was one of Beethoven's admiring piano pupils who played unusually well. She received the dedications of the First Piano Concerto in 1801 and the F-major Variations, Opus 34 two years later. This important sonata strides beyond the advances Beethoven had already made in Opus 2. A critic in 1806 praised it as being "full of great effects" and compared it favorably to Mozart's C Minor Fantasy and Sonata, "to which in a certain sense it forms an appendage."[16] He may have been thinking of the slow movement, a C-major Adagio of deep feeling and nobility, but other high points in the work could have stimulated the comparison. In the ample first Allegro the flow of ideas in the exposition is so smooth that we realize only with some effort how different they are melodically, motivically, and rhythmically. Beethoven is now learning to emulate Mozart's miraculous way of making diversities cohere in a sonata exposition. The coda at the end of the movement brings a return to the opening combination of pulsating left-hand tonic repetitions with rising tonic chords above. And now the eighth notes intensify into sixteenths, the dynamic gradually rises from *pianissimo* to *fortissimo,* and the final crash tells us that this is no Mozart but is the forceful and assertive young Beethoven (*W 7).

Piano Sonatas Opus 10 Nos. 1–3

With the three piano sonatas of Opus 10, Beethoven moved on to new discoveries. These strongly contrasting sonatas in C minor, F major, and D major were published in September 1798 and were dedicated to another female patron, Countess Anna Margarete von Browne, wife of Count Browne-Camus. From the taut agitation of the C minor sonata to the forthright and energetic Sonata in F major, Beethoven displays his full range of imagination and control of the content as he works out two different types of three-movement sonatas. The C minor compares favorably in its first movement, Allegro molto, with the C Minor Piano Trio, Opus 1 No. 3, but shows greater tightness and lyricism. The slow movement is conventional in its placid lyricism, but the little sonata-form finale, marked Prestissimo, bristles with nervous action as it manipulates an opening figure that has the characteristic properties of an early Beethoven motif expanding into a theme (*W 8). Its way of repeating the neighbor-note figure C–B–C while varying the closing notes of the figure in successively higher pitches reflects the thematic model A–A^1–A^2, which became a staple for many a theme in the works of the major Romantic composers after Beethoven.

The tiny middle section of this finale suggests a link between this opening figure and its much more powerful C-minor consequent, namely the opening of the Fifth Symphony; and the coda conclusively integrates both first and second subjects of the movement (*W 9a,b).

There is a lot to say about the capacity of the Sonata Opus 10 No. 2 in F major to make much from little, a very strong Beethovenian feature. Thus the first two notes of the opening figure suffice to generate much of the later thematic content while always relating back to this germ idea. A mere glance at the first measure and later thematic beginnings suffice to show this principle at work. And this early ability to build from molecular figures is equally evident when the whole development section turns out to be based on a simple three-note descending figure that ends the exposition.[17] In the Scherzo shades of darkness prevail, while in the beautiful *pianissimo* Trio we hear unmistakable echoes of the poignant E-major Trio of Mozart's E Minor Violin Sonata K. 304.

Opus 10 No. 3 in D major, in four movements, is the grandest and most powerful of the group. Its slow movement, in D minor and marked Largo e mesto, breathes an air of desolation whose only parallel from the time is the great slow movement of the Opus 18 No. 1 Quartet, a movement we know Beethoven associated with the tomb scene in *Romeo and Juliet*. That he has death and mourning in mind here is evident from the unusual word *mesto* ("mournful") in the tempo marking; the only other time he uses this word is for the F-minor darkness of the Adagio of Opus 59 No. 1, marked Adagio molto e mesto. In earlier piano sonatas he had written "Largo" slow movements but none in the minor mode nor any that reach the emotional depths of this one.[18] The movement reminds us of Beethoven improvising at the keyboard, able to move his listeners to tears, and it is not surprising that the work still loomed large in discussions around Beethoven in the last years, as we hear from Schindler and read in the Conversation Books.[19] It is always a question whether or not we can believe Schindler (whose prevarications and falsifications in the Conversation Books have become a cause célèbre) but it is at least possible that Beethoven actually replied when asked why he had not indicated the poetic idea on the first pages of this or other sonatas. Schindler reports that

> the period when he [Beethoven] had composed this sonata was a more poetic one than the present [the 1820s] and so such annotations were unnecessary. Everyone at that time could sense in this Largo a description of the spiritual condition of a melancholy person, with all the various nuances of light and shadow in its depiction of depression and its stages of feeling, without having titles written in to tell him.[20]

The connection of this Largo to the expressive world of the Opus 18 No. 1 Adagio and to the finale of Opus 18 No. 6, which Beethoven titled *La Malinconia*, speaks for itself.

Other Chamber Works

Of the lesser works, designed for popularity and little more, the most developed are the Clarinet Trio Opus 11 and the Quintet for Piano and Winds Opus 16. On its publication in 1798 Beethoven dedicated the clarinet trio to a Countess Thun, presumably the oldest one of several by that title, who a few years earlier had gone on her knees to implore him to play.[21] For her pains she now received a light and flashy reward that moved from a glittering first movement and slow movement to the circus style of its finale, made up of variations on the hit tune "Pria ch'io l'impegno" from a recent comic opera by Joseph Weigl. In once more forcing an inevitable comparison with Mozart, whose E-flat Major Clarinet Trio, with viola, had been another quiet masterpiece, Beethoven did well to make his piece attractive to audiences and performers, especially cellists, but he was fully aware that instead of attempting a really serious work that could stand up to Mozart's, he was trolling the surface for easy dividends.

Somewhat the same must be said about his E-flat-major Quintet for Piano and Winds of 1796–97, of which a quartet version for piano and strings was published with the first edition in 1801. Like all his keyboard chamber music, the quintet descended directly from Mozart: his quintet of

1784 for the same combination, K. 452, "the best [work] I've written in my entire life."[22] Curiously, the autograph of Mozart's quintet was owned around 1800 by Beethoven's jovial friend Zmeskall, which might have had more than a little to do with Beethoven's interest in this combination.[23] By prefacing his 3/4 Allegro first movement with a long 4/4 slow introduction Beethoven provides an outward resemblance to the G-minor Cello Sonata Opus 5 No. 2, but neither of those movements generates the drama and passion of the cello sonata. The quality improves in the beautiful opening theme of its slow movement, and the finale is a conventional 6/8 Rondo on a main theme reminiscent of Mozart but—and by now we see it is inevitable at this stage—lacking Mozart's perfect blend of imagination and restraint.[24]

After his String Trio Opus 3 Beethoven returned to this secondary genre with the Serenade Opus 8, published in October 1797 with no dedication. Like Opus 3 it is a lightweight divertimento that features some attractive ideas and at times, as in the Scherzo, wit and cleverness. But with the three String Trios of Opus 9 we come to a higher level. These were published in July 1798 and were dedicated to Count Browne-Camus. Generous to Beethoven, he also received the dedications of the important Piano Sonata Opus 22; the Cello Variations on the "Bei Männern" duet theme from *The Magic Flute*; the three Marches Opus 45 for piano four hands; and the six Gellert Lieder Opus 48.

These three trios are the best of Beethoven's string chamber music before the Opus 18 quartets; Beethoven himself declared them "la meilleure de [mes] oeuvres." Especially No. 3, in C minor, stands up as the most fully realized early work in this key, a full step beyond its C minor companions, the Piano Trio Opus 1 No. 3, the Piano Sonata Opus 10 No. 1, or even the Quartet Opus 18 No. 4.[25] In this work there appeared for the first time in Beethoven's output the opening figure in minor using the scale tones 1–7–6–5, which was to play a significant role in both middle-period and late works, above all the last quartets (*W 10). The first movement grips our attention from beginning to end. Its material is charged with vital energy and varies remarkably in character within the small space of its sonata-form exposition. From the opening phrase to the end, it conveys a sense of controlled urgency, of material that cunningly elaborates its opening ten-measure phrase or dramatically contrasts with it, of ideas expanded within a tightly bounded C-minor tonal orbit. Especially striking is Beethoven's covering the start of the recapitulation as the movement comes back to the tonic with its opening descending fourth, as the violin is rising to a crescendo in flowing sixteenth-note groups that reach the tonic five measures later than the other instruments. This way of phasing in a recapitulation, as Beethoven does in the enigmatic and intense first movement of Opus 59 No. 2 at the corresponding place, anticipates a middle-period approach. The Adagio of the string trio anticipates many a middle-period slow movement, with its opening chorale-like simplicity giving way to exceptionally elaborate embellished phrases in all instruments. The Scherzo resumes the character of the first movement, and the finale anticipates in minor mode the theme of the finale of Opus 18 No. 1 but with a darker character, holding this color fast to the end where the codetta closes the whole work in a hushed C-major *pianissimo*.

Throughout this trio Beethoven interweaves the three voices of the ensemble in ways that match the best of the Opus 18 quartets, works on which Beethoven lavished fierce concentration and revision. Achieving balance and fullness in the string ensemble without a fourth voice—the second violin—is especially challenging, but in this work it is carried out with high imagination and without any registral strain on the violin, viola, or cello. Knowing that he had achieved a tightly knit work he could be proud of in this secondary genre—in which, once again, Mozart alone had wrought a masterpiece, in his E-flat-major Divertimento for String Trio, K. 563—Beethoven felt free for the rest of his career to drop the string trio and move on to the higher ground of the string quartet.

CHAPTER 5

YEARS OF CRISIS

⭑⭒⭑⭓⭑⭓⭑⭒⭑

Deafness

"Crisis" and "triumph over adversity" are the watchwords most often used to describe Beethoven's life and development in the years between 1798 and 1802. The new adversity emerged gradually, apparently as early as 1797, when Beethoven began to have intimations of deafness and then the growing fearful realization that his loss of hearing for both music and speech was not a passing experience but was becoming a chronic condition. Yet in these five years his compositional output expanded and gained momentum as he worked to strengthen his position as the leading younger composer of instrumental music. He nourished and deepened his capacity to discover new approaches to the genres he had already mastered, and he widened his reach to challenge tradition in the two categories he had not yet mastered—the symphony and the string quartet. His ability to nurture his creative psyche and protect it from the physical and psychological anguish of his growing deafness is one of the more remarkable features of his life. Approximate parallels seem to exist with at least some other artists who suffered in earlier life from severe physical and psychological illnesses and who overcame them to go on to strong productive years of development. A comparison can be made with Francisco Goya, twenty-four years older than Beethoven. In 1792–93, at the age of forty-six, Goya became permanently deaf after a life-threatening illness. He suffered later bouts of illness and depression but maintained his artistic staying power and fertility. For Beethoven, as for Goya, the relentless pursuit of his art had healing func-

tions: concentrating intensely on the most difficult artistic tasks strengthened the artist's ability to maintain his career at full speed.[1] We will never
find a simple explanation for the psychic sources of his strength and resolve
in overcoming his illnesses, above all his deafness, but no study of his life
and work can avoid the issue.

Although at least one early biographer attributes the onset of his deafness to a severe illness that he apparently contracted in the summer of
1796, there is no corroborating evidence that this ailment was the immediate cause.[2] The first symptoms of hearing loss probably appeared in 1798,
for Beethoven wrote to his old friend Wegeler on June 29, 1801, that "for
the last three years my hearing has become weaker and weaker." That he
speaks of buzzing and humming in his ears suggests the onset of tinnitus.[3]
This letter contains other revealing remarks. He complains to Wegeler
about his Viennese physicians, one of whom had tried to "tone up my con-
stitution with strengthening medicines and my hearing with almond oil,
but much good did it do me!" And he complains of another "medical ass
who advised me to take cold baths." Reporting his symptoms of hearing
loss and intestinal disorders (which several doctors thought were connected in some way), telling all this to Wegeler, who was after all a physician, Beethoven appeals for sympathy:

> I must confess that I lead a miserable life. For almost two years now I
> have ceased to attend any social functions, just because I find it impos-
> sible to say to people, I am deaf. If I had any other profession I might be
> able to cope with my infirmity, but in my profession it is a terrible
> handicap. And if my enemies, of whom I have a fair number, were to
> hear about it, what would they say?

In the theater, he writes, he has to sit close to hear what an actor is saying,
and "when I am at a concert I cannot hear the high notes of instruments or
voices." His ears "continue to hum and buzz day and night." Understanding
speech was easier, but if anyone spoke softly he could not make out the
words. At the end, enclosing a picture of himself, he apologizes to Wegeler
for his earlier silence and says that "writing was never my strong point."
"Even my best friends have had no letters from me for years." Deafness and
isolation were beginning to blend as characteristic features of his life.[4]

Yet at the beginning of this letter to Wegeler Beethoven takes pride in his productivity. He tells Wegeler that if they could meet again now (almost nine years after his departure from Bonn) "you will certainly see that I have become a first-rate fellow, not only as an artist but also as a man you will find me better and more fully developed." And near the end of the letter, he offers to send Wegeler "all my works, which, I must admit, now amount to quite a fair number, a number that is daily increasing." It looks as though he was striving to balance strength and weakness, to connect his recollection of himself as he had been during his childhood years in Bonn with his new and powerful self-image as a young artist in the full flush of his artistic maturity.

Meanwhile, the agonizing prospect of finding that he was progressively losing touch with the world around him was spurring him on to concentrate more fiercely and produce more abundantly than ever. Aware that he had long had a tendency to distance himself from his surroundings and to sink into a reverie of absolute concentration on his work, he asks Wegeler to tell Helene von Breuning that "I still have now and then a *raptus* [a sensation of being transported into a dreamlike state]." He tells Wegeler that he dreams of giving the proceeds of his music "to the poor"; that Lichnowsky has furnished him the promised annuity; and that he is earning sizable sums from his compositions, for each one of which he can find six or seven publishers who will pay what he asks. He continues:

> *I live entirely in my music; and hardly have I completed one composition than I have already begun another. At my present rate of composing, I often produce three or four works at a time.*

That this claim is no exaggeration is clear from the seven major sketchbooks that Beethoven used during much of this time, from mid-1798 to 1802, in which he worked out all but one of the Opus 18 quartets, the piano sonatas Opus 26 to Opus 31, the violin sonatas of Opp. 23, 24, and 30, the *Prometheus* ballet, the Second Symphony, and the two sets of piano variations, Opus 34 and Opus 35. And that this wave of creative energy coincided with deepening anxiety over his deafness is one of the essential facts of his early maturity. Whether deafness and fear of further illness were causal factors, his steady absorption in his creative work shows the reserves of will he could summon up in overcoming the threat to his ability to hear music, to further his performing career, and to maintain normal relations with everyone around him.

Three days after the letter to Wegeler he wrote an equally poignant letter to another close friend, the violinist Karl Amenda, then in Courland in Latvia, blending revelations about his deafness with a bitter mixture of remarks about his "true friends," such as Amenda, and his "Viennese" friends, among them the "egotistical" Zmeskall and Schuppanzigh, "whom I regard merely as instruments on which to play when I feel inclined."[5] Thus the Hamlet in him suddenly emerged—a young, proud, distrustful, pensive prince, laden with doubt and anxiety, struggling with a perpetual choice between death, perhaps self-destruction, and staying alive to face difficult courses of action. Like Job he says he has often cursed his Creator "for exposing his creatures to the smallest of hazards, so that often the most beautiful blossom is thereby crushed and destroyed." He tells Amenda of his increasing deafness and the misery of his current life, "seeing that I am cut off from everything that is dear and precious to me." He says he is grateful to Lichnowsky for his financial support, and again takes pride in his rising fame and productivity—"everything I compose now can be sold immediately five times over and be well paid for too."

But he returns to his fears that his deafness, isolation, and illness will cripple his work:

> *[I]n my present condition I must draw away from everything and my best years will rapidly pass away without my being able to achieve all that my talent and my strength have commanded me to do—sad resignation, in which I am forced to take refuge. Needless to say, I am resolved to overcome all of this, but how can that be done?*[6]

Yet he also says that "when I am playing and composing my affliction hampers me the least; it affects me most when I am in company." He even claims that "my piano playing . . . has considerably improved" and, in his emotional vulnerability, he voices the fantasy that, if his deafness should turn out to be incurable, then Amenda might perhaps become his traveling companion on concert tours. Doing so would "perhaps enable you to make your fortune as well; and then you will stay with me forever."

Two more documents attest to Beethoven's crisis and its revelations: a second letter to Wegeler of November 16, 1801, and the Heiligenstadt Testament, written nearly a year later, dated October 1802.[7] Although he had experienced some improvement by the end of 1801, he was still complaining to Wegeler about both abdominal pains and deafness—"what an empty, sad life I have had for the past two years." There was a gleam of hope, though an uncertain one; his infatuation with "a dear charming girl who loves me and whom I love." This was Giulietta Guicciardi, then seventeen, one of his piano pupils, to whom he dedicated the "Moonlight" Sonata.[8] But nothing came of it; there was no possibility of a lasting relationship, and in 1803 Giulietta married and left for Italy.

The most memorable part of this second Wegeler letter is Beethoven's longing to be rid of his affliction, his feeling of being pursued by sickness while still comparatively young—"was I not always a sickly fellow?"—and the struggle between growing artistic strength and weakening hearing and illnesses. Yet the feeling comes through that the artist in him will win out. He writes, "my physical strength has been increasing more and more, and therefore my mental powers also." There follows a statement from the heart: "Every day brings me closer to the goal that I feel but cannot describe. And it is only in that condition that your Beethoven can live." And finally, a sentence for the ages: "I will seize Fate by the throat; it will certainly not bend and crush me completely—Oh, it would be so lovely to live a thousand lives."

The Heiligenstadt Testament

The best-known document on his deafness is the Heiligenstadt Testament, one of the most moving statements by an artist ever made.[9] It is a private narrative of his suffering and of his determination to overcome suicidal impulses and fulfill his artistic destiny. If Hamlet's question, "to be or not to be," was in his thoughts, as we see from the Amenda letter, the confessional Testament becomes his central soliloquy in this personal drama, a means of rebuilding his shattered confidence and facing the bleak life of a lonely, socially alienated artist. It has had many interpreters, from Schindler to our time, and will have many more. No serious study of Beethoven can pass it over without comment.

The so-called Heiligenstadt Testament, a private letter and will written by Beethoven to his brothers and to humanity at large on October 6, 1802, at Heiligenstadt near Vienna. In the document he confesses his deafness and resolves to overcome it for the sake of his art. (Staats- und Universitätsbibliothek, Hamburg)

Johann van Beethoven, youngest brother of the composer, who became an apothecary at Linz and later a landowner at Gneixendorf in Austria. (Historisches Museum, Vienna)

Beethoven wrote the document in the fall of 1802 after a secluded stay of six months in the town of Heiligenstadt, then a quiet, wooded village near Vienna. He kept it hidden among his private papers all his life, probably never mentioned it to anyone, and certainly did not rewrite it in later years, since it is addressed to both his brothers, Carl, who died in 1815, and Johann, who lived on until 1848. After Beethoven's death in March 1827 it was discovered in his effects by Anton Schindler and Stephan von Breuning and was transmitted by them to Friedrich Rochlitz, who published it for the first time that October.[10] Addressed to "my brothers Carl and [name left blank] Beethoven" and bearing the dates October 6 and 10, 1802, it is a confessional statement in the form of a testament, a letter to his brothers should they survive him.

Since it is, by Beethovenian standards, a carefully written statement that shows some signs of corrections and was probably copied from earlier drafts, the omission of brother Johann's name at three places in the document has occasioned much speculation. The simplest and plainest explanation is that it reflects nothing more than Beethoven's uncertainty, in writing this "quasi-legal" document, as to whether he should call his brother by one or both of his given names; Johann's formal name was "Nikolaus Johann." Beethoven calls his other brother "Carl" even though his full name was "Caspar Carl," and both brothers shortened their double names to the single "Johann" and "Carl" after moving to Vienna.[11] A more compelling interpretation is offered by Solomon, who observes that all his life Beethoven tended to avoid using his brother Johann's name in letters and documents in which it would have been perfectly normal to insert it. He further suggests that this practice reflects Beethoven's deeply contradictory feelings about Johann, his lifetime inability to overcome his obsessive attachment to both brothers, and his incessant meddling in their lives in later years. Finally, he notes that the unnamed brother carried the patronymic "Johann," the same name as their dead but unlamented father, whom Beethoven remembered with rage when he remembered him at all.[12]

Yet from the beginning this private testament is also, and primarily, addressed to the world at large; its first words are "O you people" ("O ihr Menschen"), and most of its text is meant for the public even though the document remained among Beethoven's most private papers. It is a written act of testimony to both his surviving family members and to posterity, a declaration concerning what he now believes will be a lifetime affliction that handicaps him in two ways. For him as a musician it brings the heavy burden of deafness; for him as a man in the world it brings the stigma of his seeming to be "malevolent, stubborn, misanthropic," isolated, and misunderstood.

Beethoven seeks first to justify his antisocial behavior, explaining his withdrawal from social contacts. "Though born with an active, fiery temperament, and receptive to the diversions of society, I was soon compelled to withdraw, to live life alone." His loss of hearing has cut him off from easy intercourse with others—"yet it was impossible for me to say to people, 'speak louder, shout, for I am deaf.'" The affliction was the more painful because it affected "a sense I once possessed in the highest perfection, a per-

fection such as few in my profession have or have ever possessed." His con-
flicted feelings spill out in the remark that his current doctor had ordered
him to "spare my hearing as much as possible" and thus the physician
"almost encouraged my present natural inclination, though indeed when
carried away now and then by my instinctive desire for human society, I
have let myself be tempted to seek it."

But the torment of deafness is unbearable: "[W]hat a humiliation for
me when someone standing next to me heard a flute in the distance and *I
heard nothing* or someone heard a shepherd singing and again I heard
nothing."[13] And now the central point:

> *Such experiences brought me close to despair; a little more of that and I
> would have been at the point of ending my life. The only thing that
> held me back was my art. Oh, it seemed to me impossible to leave the
> world until I had produced all the works that I felt the urge to compose.*

He vows to "endure this wretched existence, a truly wretched existence, seeing that I have such a sensitive body that any quite sudden change can
plunge me from the best feelings to the worst." And later:

> *Perhaps I shall get better; perhaps not. I am ready. Forced to become a
> philosopher in my twenty-eighth year—though it was not easy, and for
> the artist much more difficult than for anyone else. Almighty God, who
> looks down into my inmost soul, you know that it is filled with love for
> humanity and a desire to do good.[14]*

From there to the end Beethoven turns again to his brothers Carl and
Johann—still unnamed—requesting them as his survivors to ask his physician to write a description of his malady and "attach this written document
. . . so that as far as possible at least the world may become reconciled to me
after my death." He declares them the heirs to his "small fortune," enjoin-
ing them to "divide it fairly" and adding a special note of thanks to Carl for
"the attachment you have shown me in recent years"—perhaps here deliberately omitting Johann once more. He asks them to thank his friends,
especially Prince Lichnowsky and Professor Schmidt, his physician, and

hopes that one of them will preserve the set of stringed instruments given him by Lichnowsky. He wishes them a better life than his, reminding them that "virtue alone can make a man happy. Money cannot do this. . . . It was virtue that sustained me in my misery." In the last paragraph Beethoven reaffirms his sense of tragedy coupled with resolve.

> *Well, that is all. Joyfully I go to meet death. If it comes before I can develop all my artistic capabilities, then in spite of my hard fate it will still come too soon and I shall probably wish it later. Even so, I should be content, for will it not release me from a state of endless suffering? Come then, Death, whenever you will and I will meet you with courage.*

And in a postscript of October 10, after mourning his abandonment of the hope he had brought to Heiligenstadt, that he might be cured "to a degree, at least," he completes the testament:

> *As the leaves of autumn fall and are withered—that hope has faded for me. I leave here almost in the same condition in which I came; even that buoyant courage that often inspired me in the beautiful days of summer has vanished. O Providence! Grant me but one day of pure joy! It is so long that the inner echo of real joy has been gone from me—Oh when—oh when, Almighty God—shall I hear and feel it again in the temple of Nature and humanity?—Never?—No—Oh, that would be too hard.*

The depth of feeling is unmistakable. Despite the occasionally high literary tone there is no reason to believe that the rhetorical style betokens any lessening of sincerity; rather, it may be Beethoven's way of framing a formal document that he intends to be a lasting statement, therefore conveying a quasi-legal character as well as a personal one.[15] The references to suicide can be associated with Goethe's *Werther*, in which the sorrows of the youthful hero over the loss of his beloved had been portrayed so powerfully that, as the book became popular, it spawned a wave of actual suicides by young men. The reference to the Temple of Nature evokes Tamino before the priests, and thus suggests the Masonic rituals of undergoing the tests of fire and water to enter the brotherhood. So does the stress on the word "virtue" (*Tugend*). Both reflect Beethoven's belief in steadfastness and endurance as the highest personal qualities, a belief that surfaces later in the sufferings of Florestan in *Leonore/Fidelio* and in his *Tagebuch* (private diary) of 1812–18.

The *Tagebuch* opens with a quiet declaration of "submission, deepest submission to your fate," and similar affirmations of stoicism run through it.[16] In Act I of *The Magic Flute* Tamino had sought Pamina before the three temples of Reason, Wisdom, and Nature, but was rebuffed by the Masonic brotherhood because he was not yet purified. Only after reuniting with her in Act II did he undergo the trials that brought him to the higher plane of manhood. Tamino was a prince, like Hamlet, and *The Magic Flute* reverberated in Beethoven's consciousness, musically in both direct and indirect ways, and philosophically as a tract on human brotherhood. Whether Beethoven had himself joined a Masonic lodge we do not know; several of his friends from Bonn had certainly been inducted. But the last part of the Testament is shot through with the resolution to endure ordeals, face down adversity, and accept death with courage, essential elements of the Masonic ideal of what it meant to be a man.[17]

What threads connect the Testament to Beethoven's work? In the broad sense, many; in the narrow, none that we can trace with certainty. The deafness crisis to which the Testament was a primary response is certainly the major shaping event of Beethoven's early maturity, and it could not help having a broad, far-reaching effect on his work. But particulars are harder to find. Certainly in key works of this period the topics of mourning and death emerge in several highly expressive slow movements. Depression is one half of the explicit subject of the Adagio finale of the Quartet Opus 18 No. 6, *La Malinconia* ("Melancholy"; the other half is exuberant joy). If Schindler can be believed, emotional darkness is the subject of the D-minor Largo e mesto of the Piano Sonata Opus 10 No. 3. Death, loss of love, suicide, and abandonment seem to pervade the Adagio of Opus 18 No. 1, whose sketches allude to *Romeo and Juliet*. And death and heroism are directly evoked in the "Funeral March for the Death of a Hero," the slow movement of the Piano Sonata, Opus 26 (1800), and in the solemn *Marcia funebre* of the *Eroica* (1803–4). As for the lesson in perseverance he wrote in the Testament, it certainly bears on some of the later works, in which dark struggle and conflict in an earlier movement (typically the first) passes through other stages of aesthetic and emotional turmoil and gradually emerges in the light of affirmation and triumph in the last movement. The Fifth and Ninth Symphonies are the most celebrated examples, but in various ways the same sequential narrative emerges in other works, at times explicitly, as in *Fidelio*.

To sum up, the deafness crisis had a lasting and debilitating effect on Beethoven's ability to deal with the world around him, most of all on his social life and performing career, and it undoubtedly had a powerful effect on the character and content of his work. Yet there is no clear evidence that it seriously interfered with his ongoing productivity as composer or that it counts as the central reason for the major stylistic changes that come about in 1802–4. Those changes might have had to happen as part of his artistic growth, whether or not he had lost his hearing. Paradoxically, Beethoven in deafness may have found a way to protect his inner creative world from the intrusions of the social world around him. Deafness may have helped provide him with a socially acceptable reason for the violent surliness with which he held the greater world of people, business, and money in contempt. It also gave him a way of justifying to himself his lifelong rage and alienation—characteristics that may have stemmed primarily from the emotional deprivation he had experienced in his teenage years, when the death of his mother and the survival of his hopeless father left him unexpectedly in charge of a family before he could work out his own personal destiny. Perhaps deafness offered him a way of transferring this pain from outer social irascibility into a private world of solitude in which he could literally shut out the irritable features of the world around him while, at the same time, perpetually and mournfully yearning to be loved and admired.

He may never have been able to find a single "pure day of joy." But in later years, even as his hearing deteriorated, his continuing pursuit of new artistic goals and his ability to maintain his artistic integrity—even if he abandoned it at times in minor popularizing works—must have reinforced his feeling of self-realization and personal wholeness. As a man he found himself imprisoned by deafness. As an artist, he broke free, continuing on a trajectory marked by significant acts of renewal and stages of stylistic transformation, while his deafness remained a heavy burden, a gradually worsening handicap for him to overcome as best he could. The letter to "Emilie M." of 1812, written at a time of deep depression, mentions sickness but not deafness, and only rarely does he specifically speak of his deafness in the many later letters in which he mourns his ill health.[18] If, over the years, he ever took out the Heiligenstadt Testament from its secret drawer and read it over, he must have understood that it expressed both his despair and his deeply rooted resolution to endure, the two in precarious balance like everything else in his life.

CHAPTER 6

MUSIC FOR AND WITH PIANO

❦

The "New Way" and the Early Sketchbooks

From Carl Czerny, writing in 1852, comes this anecdote:

> Around the year 1803 Beethoven said to his friend Krumpholz: "I am
> not satisfied with what I have composed up to now. From now on I
> intend to embark on a new path." Soon thereafter the three sonatas of
> Opus 29 [i.e., 31] were published.[1]

Because the Opus 31 sonatas came out in 1802, not 1803, Beethoven's
remark can be dated to that year. Czerny's testimony, though written much
later, has the ring of truth, not only because these piano sonatas are indeed
pathbreaking but also because the violinist Wenzel Krumpholz was a solid
musician, a long-time friend of Beethoven's, apparently the sort of person
to whom he might have spoken in this way. Krumpholz was also the young
Czerny's mentor; it was he who introduced the ten-year-old Czerny to
Beethoven, and it seems likely that Czerny would have had the anecdote
directly from Krumpholz.[2] The story of the "new path" has had an
extended run, as anecdotes go, but it stands up because it refers to a change
in Beethoven's approach to form, certainly apparent in these years, and to
ways of shaping musical content that generate formal innovations.

That the "new path" coincides with the deafness crisis and the Heiligenstadt Testament has also attracted commentary. Received opinion,
based primarily on the "crisis and triumph" narrative of Beethoven's life
and works, centers the major artistic turning point on the *Eroica* Sym-

phony. Written in 1803–4, this massive landmark launches the "heroic style" and the new symphonic ideals that are generally accepted as essential to the basic Beethovenian paradigm. Yet despite the undeniable importance of the *Eroica*, a longer view of Beethoven's career shows that its revolutionary features are subtly foreshadowed by path-breaking works written in the preceding five years. That period, from 1798 to 1802, closes the large phase of his development that I call Beethoven's "first maturity."

Supporting this view are a set of important piano sonatas, along with his First Symphony and earliest string quartets. Although the First Symphony is timorous by the standards of Beethoven's more original works of the 1790s, the six quartets of Opus 18 are landmarks on which Beethoven concentrated his fiercest and most self-critical labor in sketch preparation, composition, and revision. They are also the works that occasioned a basic change in his compositional procedure—the first steady and regular use of sketchbooks.

As we saw earlier, Beethoven had already amassed and kept in a portfolio a large quantity of loose sketch leaves and bundles of leaves dating back to 1786.[3] His jottings on these early leaves look pretty much like ones we find in the later sketchbooks, except that the early leaves tend to be filled to the brim with notations, with very few spaces left empty. The musical ideas in the later Bonn and first Vienna years range from short themes and phrases to extended passages and whole movements, from impulsive musical thoughts of the moment to extensive layouts of whole sections. But despite resemblances in the musical ideas, a sea change in his habits took place when he began to use whole, bound, or gathered sketchbooks to organize his working procedures, a method that he then maintained assiduously all his life. It is not too much to say that from 1798 on his regular recourse to the sketchbooks and his care in preserving them constituted an important biographical turning point, a way of bringing discipline into his working methods that contrasted dramatically with the disorder and turbulence of the rest of his daily life. Because this change in working methods coincided with the onset of his deafness and the end of his first maturity, the newly established control and overview that the sketchbooks gave on his compositional work conferred a sense of order and stability that might have compensated for some of the frustration and stigma brought on by his deafness. While the man suffered, the artist in him found ways to recoup his losses.

Both the zealous care he took in his work and the disorder in his life increased as he grew older. His sketch work became more and more comprehensive as his music became more recondite and his everyday life became more reclusive, eccentric, and chaotic. In a letter of 1815, answering a request for his score of a song on the poem "Merkenstein," he explained that he had actually written two melodies for it, both of which had been "buried under a pile of other papers . . . [but] since nothing in my house is, as a rule, ever lost, I will let you have the other setting too, as soon as I find it."[4]

Once he began to use sketchbooks the miscellaneous jottings of the earlier years, which he had tended to scribble on any open staves of a given page, became less frequent. The use of a single main sketchbook at a given time enabled Beethoven to concentrate his efforts on the large-scale and small-scale planning of whole movements and entire works in a much more systematic way, and it enabled him to manage his output more effectively. At the same time he was increasing his ability to plan and realize larger compositions, so that changes in the working materials and his growing capacity to write more complex music went hand in hand. In view of his busy role as composer, pianist, prominent city musician, and sometime teacher of piano pupils such as Czerny, Ries, and some younger members of the Viennese aristocracy, the new way of working accelerated his productivity. It props up his claim that he could find himself composing "three or four works at a time."

The sketchbook format allowed him to work systematically on the quartets, and at the same time use portions of the sketchbook for other compositions that came up or had to be finished during the same period. He could return to composing with greater ease after the inevitable daily diversions and interruptions by returning to a single large-format book that served as his primary working space for current compositions, instead of having to rummage through piles of separate leaves and bundles of leaves to find his sketches for projects at hand.

The first two sketchbooks, now known as "Grasnick 1" and "Grasnick 2" (from the name of a later owner), contain much of the surviving sketch material for the Opus 18 Quartets. Because all final autograph manuscripts of Opus 18 are lost, these sketchbooks show us most of what we know at present about the origins and genesis of these works.[5] They also contain much other material, for example, jottings for the Piano Sonata Opus 14 No. 1 and for the first two piano concertos, variations, songs, the Septet Opus 20, and lesser works.

A close look at these two sketchbooks shows us how Beethoven worked at this time. First, he bought a batch of ninety-six oblong leaves of ruled sixteen-staff music paper, which came either as two forty-eight-page sketchbooks or as a large single bundle that he himself then divided in half. From 1798 to 1808 he seems to have used preassembled sketchbooks of this kind; later he stitched such books together himself or used more irregular ones.[6] Although in its present form Grasnick 1 has only thirty-nine leaves, scholars have been able to piece together its original first gathering from separate leaves or fragments now located in Bonn, Paris, Stockholm, and Washington. These can now be "restored" to the original, like a missing thumb from an ancient marble hand, thanks to studies of the paper types, watermarks, and content of the sketchbook and sketch leaves.[7] Grasnick 1 contains material for a few important compositions, with lesser projects or marginal jottings interleaved before and after the works that were his main focus.[8]

After working out some refinements in the Piano Sonata in E Major, Opus 14 No. 1, on the first pages of the sketchbook, he turned to his main new project, the D-major String Quartet that was the first of the Opus 18 series to be composed but later became No. 3. As the central project in the first portion of the book, it was almost certainly begun in the summer or fall of 1798 and continued in the later months of that year. Grasnick 1 remained his primary sketchbook until about February 1799, a period of about six or seven months, allowing us to estimate the larger rhythm of his work on Opus 18 No. 3 in its earlier phases. Interleaved with the quartet sketches are jottings for a cadenza to his First Piano Concerto, a couple of songs ("Der Kuss," Opus 128, and "Opferlied," WoO 126), as well as the G-major Rondo, Opus 51 No. 2, and several isolated entries for the Septet, Opus 20. More extensive are some further sketches for all movements of the B-flat Piano Concerto and a few more entries for songs and minor works, including the Piano Variations WoO 73 on Salieri's "La stessa la stes-sissima" from the opera *Falstaff*. Beethoven probably worked on it in that part of the book (fols. 30–36) shortly after the opera was premiered on January 3, 1799. The only item of importance that follows the variation set is made up of initial sketches for the F-major string quartet that was to become Opus 18 No. 1, sketches for which he then brought over directly into Grasnick 2, where he carried out the bulk of his work on it.

The great mass of his sketchbooks forms a significant context for understanding his works, as they contain the cumulative artistic diary of his progress.[9] This context is especially important for Beethoven, in whose opinion instrumental music by most of his immediate peers and contemporaries, however competent, was largely below his artistic standards. His letters are bereft of any complimentary references to works by such solid composers as Ignace Joseph Pleyel, Jan Ladislav Dussek, Muzio Clementi, and Daniel Steibelt. We have few anecdotal comments by contemporaries to suggest that he regarded them as anything more than capable adversaries. In 1817 he recommended to Steiner that he publish "the enclosed quintets, since they are written by a man who understands composition," probably Georges Onslow; but such remarks are exceptionally rare, and the phrasing of the letter suggests that a positive opinion of this kind from Beethoven was unusual.[10] He competed readily with such contemporaries, largely with the knowledge that he could outdo them in every genre except opera. But for him the more significant context by far lay in the work of his major predecessors, Mozart and Haydn, much of whose music was still being absorbed into the current mainstream by performers and the public. Haydn, it is true, was still alive in 1798, in the last ripe years of his career, but with the completion of his final masses and his two great oratorios, *The Creation* in 1798 and *The Seasons* in 1801, his output was ending. He wrote his last completed quartets, the two of Opus 77, in 1799, and when he tried to add a third in 1802 he had to leave it unfinished (two movements of this B-flat-major Quartet appeared in 1803 as his Opus 103). Though Haydn lived on until 1809 his creative career was over by the time Beethoven was working on the *Eroica* Symphony.

Beethoven appears to have gained knowledge of at least some orchestral music by composers working in France in the wake of the Revolution, but none of them, in their instrumental music, did more than confirm a new aesthetic of the powerful, characterized by the use of massive instrumental and choral forces performing music for the general public that glorified military heroism and aroused national pride. In contrast, French opera in the hands of Cherubini and Méhul was cutting a deeper path, one that Beethoven could admire but not yet emulate. Beethoven's professed admiration for Cherubini stemmed from uncertainty about his own prowess as a dramatic composer, but it was probably sincere, and as late as 1824 he praised an opera by Méhul and lamented the composer's recent death.[11] In instrumental music he probably sized up his rival pianist-composers such as Dussek and Clementi as professionals. In string writing he certainly did appreciate the French school led by Kreutzer, Rode, Baillot, and Duport, but he could easily surpass all of them in quality of musical thought. At a later phase of his life, his only possible rival would have been Schubert. But Schubert, born in 1797, was younger by a full generation, with a completely different temperament and aesthetic bent. Schubert's marvelous creative pathways were rooted primarily in the lyrical, from which he worked assiduously to move out into the larger instrumental forms of the period, not without feeling perpetually in the shadow of Beethoven's preeminence. By the time of Schubert's high maturity—the 1820s—Beethoven was living in his own inner world and Schubert was gaining ground as a favorite in Viennese musical circles.[12] Although Beethoven's artistic development was important to Schubert as he grew in earlier years toward artistic independence, there is no evidence that Beethoven knew Schubert's works, apart from some songs that he may have seen in his last years, if we can believe Schindler, the only source for this anecdote. If Schindler was for once telling the truth, he showed Beethoven a collection of Schubert's songs early in 1827, during the master's final illness. The songs astonished Beethoven, eliciting the celebrated remark—if it is genuine—"Truly he has the divine spark!" A few weeks later Schubert was a torchbearer at Beethoven's funeral.[13]

A Laboratory of Invention: More Piano Sonatas

Between 1798 and 1802 Beethoven wrote eleven piano sonatas. They fall into two groups, Opp. 13–28 and Opus 31 Nos. 1–3. The first contains the deservedly famous "Grande Sonate Pathétique" in C minor, Opus 13, probably written in close proximity to its sturdy C-minor companion, the String Quartet Opus 18 No. 4. Forming a pendant to the "Pathétique" are the paired Sonatas in E major and G major, Opus 14 Nos. 1 and 2. Then came five more sonatas that marked still further stages and varieties of maturity. The first four, written between 1799 and 1801 but published in March 1802, became Opp. 22, 26, and Opus 27 Nos. 1 and 2 (the two Sonatas "Quasi una fantasia"). Opus 28, in D major, was labeled "Grande sonate" in its first edition of August 1802 but soon called "Sonate pastorale" in a subsequent London edition. Within two more years, as he continued to move along the "new path," still another new turn emerged in the three sonatas of Opus 31, in G major, D minor (the "Tempest" Sonata), and E-Flat major, composed in 1801–2. These emerged in the context of several other ambitious projects, including two works of unusually high intensity—the "Kreutzer" Sonata and the Second Symphony—and the massive "Prometheus" Variations Opus 35.

"Pathétique" Sonata

The eleven piano sonatas from Opus 13 to Opus 31 No. 3 showed that Beethoven's command of the genre rose to levels of originality, aesthetic power, and rightness of proportions that no rival pianist-composer could approach. Though public recitals of piano sonatas were hardly yet known, private performances of the "Pathétique" immediately guaranteed it a wider audience than any of his earlier sonatas, for reasons deep in the marrow of the work. The unleashed power of its first movement amazed contemporaries, even those who were becoming aware of Beethoven's C-minor mood. The strong rhetoric of the Grave introduction dramatically prepared the way for the intense Allegro first movement, which whipped up a storm of excitement not previously heard in his—or anyone else's—piano sonatas. Yet the Allegro also harbors strange and subtle moments, such as the rumbling *pianissimo* passages in the development section.[14] Lyrical composure and melodic subtlety are regained in the beautiful Adagio cantabile in A-flat, and the C-minor rondo finale restores the work to the pathos that is its dominating affect.

The term *pathétique* had intertwining meanings, deriving from *pathos* as a term in rhetoric. Many writings of the late eighteenth century applied rhetorical terms to music, an approach to music theory that had in fact been cultivated for centuries but flowered fully once again in this age of expanding aesthetic theory and listeners' widening aesthetic expectations.[15] This sonata uses musical equivalents of some of the motivic gestures of the rhetorical "pathetic," a tradition that also helps to account for such features as the return of the opening Grave in the middle and end of the first movement. In Beethoven, thematic returns of this kind within a movement always have the purpose of dramatic recall, comparable to situations in which a major character introduced early in a drama makes a striking reappearance in a later act; the return of the Commendatore as the speaking statue in *Don Giovanni* is the most famous contemporary example. We see such reappearances in selected Beethoven movements in all periods, including the programmatic and rhetorically "melancholy" finale of the Quartet Opus 18 No. 6; the first movement of the Trio Opus 70 No. 2; and, in the far-off world of Beethoven's late style, the first movement of the E-flat-major Quartet Opus 127.

Sonatas Opus 14

In the two sonatas of Opus 14, other, less extreme modes of expression prevail. The first, in E major, may have begun life as a string quartet and then became a piano sonata. In 1802 Beethoven himself arranged the sonata as a quartet, transposing it to F major to take advantage of the viola's and cello's open C strings while adjusting sonorities and dynamics to fit the medium and make the work idiomatic for quartet. He proudly declared, in a letter to Breitkopf & Härtel, that only the composer of a work could properly make a true arrangement of this kind. The letter adds to all the other testimony about his real feelings for his two great predecessors:

*I firmly maintain that only Mozart himself could translate his works
from the keyboard to other instruments, and Haydn could do this
too—and without wishing to compare myself to these two great men, I
claim the same about my keyboard sonatas.*[16]

The two Opus 14 sonatas are paired opposites: the E major is a sturdy,
well-made, three-movement work with a poignant Allegretto in E minor
sandwiched between its two Allegro movements. The second, in G major,
often a lighter key for Beethoven, is a foray into the smaller-sonata world;
it is almost a sonatina, with a charming first movement in the manner of
the 2/4 finale of the Cello Sonata Opus 5 No. 2, followed by a slow, simple
C-major variation movement and a curt finale marked Scherzo that is
actually a rondo.

Sonata Opus 22

These works were followed by a very important group of five piano
sonatas, Opus 22 to Opus 28, written at the same time that Beethoven was
composing and revising the Opus 18 quartets. That they form counterparts
to Opus 18 has not been generally recognized because the publishing traditions of string quartets led to their being grouped in threes and sixes, like
most of Haydn's sets and Mozart's of 1785. Their composite opus number
makes it difficult to see the Opus 18 quartets as highly individual works,
though indeed they are. Conversely, it is just as hard to see these piano
sonatas as forming a consistent group.[17]

Their movement plans and formal strategies vary as widely as their
expressive qualities. Opus 22 is in B-flat major, a key that Beethoven
favored for subtlety. It follows the four-movement plan, which includes a
Minuetto and a Rondo finale, that he had set up in Opus 2. This progressive plan is shared in this group only with Opus 28, while the others deviate. Thus Opus 26, in A-flat major, has no movement in sonata form: it
begins with an Andante variations movement, continues with a Scherzo in
A-flat major, a funeral march in A-flat minor, and an Allegro finale that is
essentially a rondo. The next pair, the two sonatas of Opus 27, are both
marked "Quasi una fantasia" but differ in new ways. The first has a complex
movement plan in which the opening Andante in E-flat major, gives way to

an Allegro in C major and brings the E-flat Andante back at the close. It also incorporates a C-minor scherzo, an Adagio in E-flat, and an Allegro vivace finale with a brief return of the Adagio slow movement before the end. To this work Beethoven added as a companion Opus 27 No. 2, the "Moonlight" Sonata, with its tremendous range of contrasts, from its deeply moving Adagio in C-sharp minor to the idyllic scherzo in D-flat (the enharmonic equivalent of C-sharp) and the passionate, stormy finale in C-sharp minor.

About Opus 22 Beethoven told his publisher "this sonata is a terrific piece" (diese Sonate hat sich gewaschen), and when he talks this way we have to pay attention. In craftsmanship and smoothness of finish, Opus 22 is on a pinnacle. For works of this time it has an unrivaled intricacy of thematic invention and sequential linking of ideas, both within movements and across the whole work. Its elegance of detail maximizes the grace and beauty of lines and figuration patterns. There is a kinship here to the Quartet Opus 18 No. 6 aside from their sharing the key of B-flat. Both begin with an arpeggiated first theme with a turn figure on the fourth beat that has developmental possibilities. And indeed the sketchbook Beethoven was using then reveals some crossing of preliminary ideas for this sonata and Opus 18 No. 6. Thus the theme that finally became that of the sonata finale started life as a possible finale theme for the quartet. It was also sketched once in A major, and therefore was briefly a candidate for a finale to another work in A major or minor, perhaps the Sonata for Violin and Piano in A minor, Opus 23.[18] At deeper levels the sonata employs the descending-third pattern that Beethoven had picked up from Haydn and Mozart—in this case, I believe, from Mozart's A Major Quartet, K. 464, which Beethoven openly admired and used in a different way as a template for Opus 18 No. 5.

Piano Sonata Opus 26

An early reviewer saw the Opus 26 Piano Sonata as "doubtless one of [Beethoven's] most fully realized masterpieces in the genre . . . grand, noble and sublime."[19] Its opening with variations has evoked comparison with Mozart's A Major Piano Sonata, K. 331, but the resemblance is only skin deep. The first movement foreshadows Schubert's way with intimate themes of this kind, as in his A-flat-major Impromptu. Pianists took to it at once. One was a young pianist named Anne Caroline Oury, née de Belleville, who as a child of eleven in 1819 played it for Beethoven, "who sat by the hour, with his long trumpet to his ears, listening to her inimitable touch of his divine adagios."[20]

But the touchstone of this work is its slow movement, titled "Marcia funebre per la morte d'un Eroe," ("Funeral March for the Death of a Hero"), written in the exceptionally rare key of A-flat minor. We have no reason to think that Beethoven intended reference to any specific hero. His aim is to import into the piano sonata an overtly programmatic movement, a *Charakterstück*, or "characteristic piece," as Beethoven called it in his sketched movement plan for the sonata. After jotting down an idea for the first movement, he writes, "poi Menuetto o qualche altro pezzo character-istica come p.E. una Marcia in as moll" ("then a minuet or another charac-teristic piece such as a march in A-flat minor").[21]

Czerny and Ries both thought that this funeral march could have been derived from Ferdinando Paer's opera *Achille* of 1801. The connection has some plausibility, since Beethoven obviously knew Paer's *Leonore* and probably looked at other Paer operas. Paer's C-minor march—mourning the fallen hero Patroclus, who is brought to the tent of Achilles—makes extensive use of dotted rhythms that bear an obvious relationship to Beet-hoven's march (*W11).[22] But there are reasons why Beethoven's march is unforgettable whereas Paer's is exhumed only for the sake of comparing the two. Beethoven's greater depth in every dimension is evident from begin-ning to end. This movement introduces the elegiac mode into Beethoven's keyboard sonatas, thereby enlarging the genre in a new way and foreshad-owing the *Eroica* slow movement as well as later movements that imply funeral corteges. The next great examples are the C-minor slow movement of Schubert's E-flat Trio and the funeral march in Chopin's Sonata No. 2 in B-flat Minor.

Piano Sonatas Opus 27 Nos. 1 and 2

That both of these works were titled "Sonata quasi una fantasia" puts them in a special category, mitigating the notoriety of the "Moonlight" and the obscurity of its companion. "Quasi una fantasia" means, though not in a simple and direct sense, "in the manner of an improvisation." It also means that these hybrid works share one important feature of fantasias by Mozart, Haydn, and others, namely, that a fantasia has an unpredictable number of sections that use different kinds of figuration patterns. It also means that all sections are played without pause or final stop, each going directly on to the next. Beethoven makes the most of this feature here and in some other middle-period works. One result of employing it is to blur the impression that each movement is an autonomous whole with a full cadence at the end, and so it also blurs the notion that individual movements are the main units of organization. This effect is especially true in Opus 27 No. 1, with its cyclic return of earlier material later in the work. There is no return of thematic material in the "Moonlight," but the first movement passes on directly to the second and the second to the third. Furthermore, the hypnotic first movement, a world classic from the day of its publication, possesses the quality of an immense, slow improvisation. It then progresses from the dreamlike C-sharp-minor Adagio sostenuto to the graceful D-flat Allegretto[23] and on to the tragic and powerful Presto finale. Though the sonata has no movement in "Allegro" tempo, its sonata-form Presto agitato finale completes the formal architecture of the cycle with enormous energy. The work begins almost *in medias res*, as if the pianist had been quietly improvising before it starts.[24] Over the first movement Beethoven writes, "si deve suonare questo pezzo delicatissimamente" ("this piece should be played in the most delicate manner"), a heading similar to the one he placed over *La Malinconia* in Opus 18 No. 6: "questo pezzo si deve trattare colla più gran delicatezza" ("this piece should be performed with the greatest possible delicacy"). We have no basis for assuming a defined programmatic intention behind the C-sharp-minor sonata, despite almost two centuries of interpretation by various hands. But no one can doubt that the work presents a succession of intense emotional atmospheres unlike any other early Beethoven sonata.[25]

Piano Sonata Opus 28

The pastoral connection of Opus 28 springs from figures and effects whose roots lie far back in the Baroque; the celebrated pastoral interludes in Bach's *Christmas Oratorio* and Handel's *Messiah* are only the most

famous of many examples. Pastoral movements and compositions regularly exhibit such features as drone bass effects (sustained bass notes on the
first and fifth scale steps) and motivic repetitions lasting over whole
phrases, and arpeggiated thematic ideas, all of which Beethoven used a few
years later in his *Pastoral* Symphony. The choice of the pastoral archetype
shows still another attempt at forging a "new path," to give a piano sonata
a special expressive aura as well as subtle connections of material between
movements. These are not direct quotations, as in Opus 27 No. 1; rather,
they are motivic allusions and contour associations of the kind that
abound in the higher class of Beethoven's works in every period. The
pianistic effects show the composer expanding the limits of the keyboard
sonorities of the time. This sonata associates through its movement plan
with other works in D major that have a D-minor slow movement, such as
the String Trio Opus 9 No. 2, the Piano Sonata Opus 10 No. 3, and later, the
"Ghost" Trio, Opus 70 No. 1. And its connects in structural ways to the Second Symphony.[26]

These works confirm that for Beethoven the three- or four-movement
piano sonata was ripe for experimentation and for new ways to unfold
ideas. Except for variation sets and fantasias, the piano sonata remained the
genre most closely tied to improvisation. With these five sonatas Beethoven
moved from rhetorical passion and abruptness to a more personal voice
and to the direct exploitation of programmatic and "characteristic" pictorial devices. He used these devices as springboards for new compositional
thinking about the sonata as a musical category, seeking and consolidating
a wider expressive range. He also showed in these five works a wide gamut
of aesthetic models within the same genre: one gentle and smooth in B-flat
major (Opus 22); one radical in formal plan and with a tragic funeral
march (Opus 26); two more that were "quasi una fantasia," of contrasting
character (Opus 27 Nos. 1 and 2); and one "pastoral" (Opus 28). An analogy with the six mature symphonies of the second period, from the *Eroica*
to the Eighth, is not far-fetched. As in his later life, the piano sonata served
as a laboratory for innovations that he could deploy in other, more public
genres.

Piano Sonatas Opus 31 Nos. 1–3

With these works we come to the border of Beethoven's first maturity. Intimations of change are everywhere, with these sonatas advancing even further into unmapped, early Romantic territory. Composed in the spring and summer of 1802, these sonatas had a peculiar publication history. Beethoven accepted a commission from a Swiss publisher, Hans Georg Nägeli of Zurich, who issued them in April 1803 in an edition so careless and arrogant that it contained four extra measures inserted by Nägeli himself at the end of the first movement of the first sonata. When Ries played Nägeli's version for Beethoven, "[he] jumped up in a rage, ran over and all but pushed me away from the piano, shouting, 'Where the devil does it say that?'" And then he had the sonatas correctly published by his old friend Simrock in Bonn and by Cappi in Vienna.

The openings of all three speak a new language, each presenting a new and original mode of entry into a large sonata-form movement. In the first sonata, disruption rules. The whole point of the opening is to throw the rhythmic relationship of right and left hands into conflict when the left hand punches a downbeat in immediate apposition to the tied-over sixteenth-note upbeat of the upper line, which in turn then continues with the descending figures of the opening motif (*W 12a). The second motif that follows again displays the same disruptive right- and left-hand upbeat/downbeat combination, which becomes a basic issue in the whole movement, worked out with abrupt humor in the development section and in the preparation for the recapitulation. Just as striking is Beethoven's unusual choice of key scheme for the exposition, in which the tonic, G major, moves not to its dominant for the second group but to B major (the key based on the third step of the scale), which then finds its way to the expected D major. This progression is a harmonic pathway that appears here for the first time in his sonatas and resurfaces, more dramatically, in the "Waldstein" first movement. And in the recapitulation, the B major key, a third above the tonic, is replaced by the key a third *below* the tonic— E major, which then finds its proper goal, the tonic. The syntax of the opening rhythmic displacement of right and left hands, played out to the hilt in the coda, is matched by an extraordinary sequence of short phrases, all using its basic figures. These phrases are first heard *pianissimo* for many measures, then erupt in *fortissimo* near the end, and as a final gesture, after a full measure's rest, the work ends softly in *piano* with two abrupt tonic chords in wide and close positions, the second on the off-beat of its 2/4 measure. It should not surprise us that Nägeli failed to understand this ending, but by trying to fix it, he joined the ranks of historic blunderers. Luckily he left the second and third movements alone, though he might have been tempted to tamper with the end of the finale, where again quiet *pianissimo* chords close the work in the tonic in a way that elaborates on the ending of the first movement.

In the second sonata, the "Tempest," a parallel contrast of two thematic ideas in two tempos opens the action, but far more dramatically and evocatively than it does in the first sonata (*W 12b). Here, after a quasi-improvisational, harmonically unstable arpeggio on the dominant, *pianissimo,* that ends with a long-held note, or pedal, the Allegro theme arrives with its hurtling two-note figures, leading to a second pause on the dominant. Then the same Largo-Allegro contrast resumes, now with the arpeggio chord on C major and the Allegro contrasting theme in F major. From this point on the "tempest" breaks out, returning to D minor and exploring all the ramifications of the opening statement and counterstatement with unprecedented concentration. For some listeners the movement evokes a Hegelian concept of "becoming," the emergence of a totality through complex elaborations of statement and counterstatement leading to an eventual synthesis.[27] At the beginning of the development the rising Largo chords return in an upward sequence, now three times instead of two, and moving from D major to arrive at a new place—F-sharp major—from which the development can take off. Most poignant of all in this movement is the two-fold recitative at the recapitulation of the opening Largo chords: here the piano becomes a high alto singing voice improvising in the guise of a keyboard player. The first recitative remains in the tonic D minor but the second, after the return of the "tempest" theme, moves into distant harmonic regions. These moments bring a poetic quality to the piano sonata beyond all past imaginings, by Beethoven or anyone else. They presage the instrumental recitatives of such late works as the Ninth Symphony and the A Minor Quartet, Opus 132.

The same evocative character governs the two movements that follow. The B-flat Adagio, opening like the first movement with a rising arpeggio chord is by turns given to lyrical expression and beautiful atmospheric effects in various piano registers, at times employing distant registral attacks in close proximity to each other—even at the end, where the final low B♭ is struck alone after an apparent close in high register on the same note a full four octaves higher. Typical for the innovative feeling of this work is the absence of a formal close with chords in both hands. The Allegretto finale builds a dramatic sonata-form continuity through hurtling repetitions of running sixteenth notes in both hands, as if it were a celestial exercise piece. It truly inherits the tradition of concentrated D-Minor movements that Beethoven could have traced back to Mozart's D Minor Piano Concerto and other celebrated Mozartian antecedents that he knew very well, apart from the fact that its opening motif happens to coincide with an important theme from Mozart's G Minor Quintet. But this D-minor movement completes and grounds the whole sonata with a demonic fury that is entirely his own.

Finally, the third beginning, that of Opus 31 No. 3, opens another door into a new landscape. It begins not only on an "off-tonic" harmonic progression but on an unstable chord built on the second note of the scale, with a brief motif in the top voice; it poses a question once, twice, and then goes on to a slowly rising chromatic motion, pausing on a I 6/4 chord that prepares the cadential return to the tonic (*W 12c). The whole of this introductory statement is an experiment in shades and degrees of harmonic color that suggests resolution to a possible tonic but postpones it for seven measures, by which time the tonic arrival becomes the starting point for further harmonic and thematic adventures. Suspending our attention and postponing resolution have come into the foreground and do not relinquish center stage until the end of the movement.

The later movements of Opus 31 No. 3 are equally original. Its Scherzo is a brilliant early experiment with a 2/4 movement of this type, a rare exception Beethoven would not try again for a long time to come. The Scherzo is matched by a graceful Minuet third movement, and the whole is capped by a manic Presto con fuoco finale in 6/8.

In these three works of Opus 31, the piano sonata enters the world of early Romanticism, and it does so by different portals that lead to divergent destinations. The sense of the eighteenth-century tradition of the sonata as a formal entity is loosened and displaced by the poetic and evocative qualities that Beethoven now wanted to bring to instrumental music. Undeniably, these sonatas look forward to the great middle-period piano works, the sonatas and concertos, more than they hark back to their antecedents. Already distanced from his earlier sonatas by a considerable margin, they show us the long road Beethoven was traveling toward a new and richly developed idea of what the piano sonata could now become.

From Convention to Originality: Piano Variations

To make money and keep his hand in as a major figure in the current music life of amateurs as well as professionals, Beethoven also churned out several more sets of piano variations during these years, based on themes ranging from Salieri's *Falstaff* (WoO 73) to Singspiel tunes by Peter Winter and Franz Xaver Süssmayr. But then, dissatisfied with repeating himself, he found a way to raise the conventional bravura variations type to a higher level in the two innovative sets to which he assigned opus numbers: Opus 34 and Opus 35. Beethoven told Breitkopf & Härtel that both were composed "in an entirely new manner, each in a different way." The idea was to do for variations what he had done in his four-movement piano sonatas and keyboard chamber music: reshape expectations and make the public sit up and take notice.

The Opus 34 Piano Variations

The major innovation of this set is that, unlike traditional sets, in which a prevailing tonic key was maintained (at most deviating to its parallel minor), each variation is in a different key. Successive keys are separated by descending thirds, a pattern sometimes associated with development sections of sonata-form first movements. The whole moves from the basic

F major down through successive major keys, arriving at C minor, which then easily converts to C major as dominant of the home tonic:

$$F \longrightarrow D \longrightarrow B^\flat \longrightarrow G \longrightarrow E^\flat \longrightarrow C \text{ minor} \longrightarrow C \quad F$$

| *Theme* | *Var. 1* | *Var. 2* | *Var. 3* | *Var. 4* | *Var. 5* | *Var. 6 & Coda* |

The "Prometheus" Variations

More important by far is the big set of variations that received the opus number 35. This great work, the culmination of Beethoven's early variations sets, is often miscalled the "Eroica" Variations, because its introduction and thematic material directly foreshadow the finale of the *Eroica* Symphony. But Beethoven also used the same material in two other works: (1) the finale of the Twelve Contradances (WoO 14) that he wrote for ballroom use in Vienna during the winter of 1800–1801; and (2) the finale for the *Prometheus* ballet, Opus 43. Beethoven specifically asked Breitkopf & Härtel to put a reference to *Prometheus* on the title page of the variations, but they did not comply; making the relationship explicit in that way would have forestalled any criticism that might come up if critics noticed the connection themselves.

In any case, Opus 35 is a milestone in the history of variation. Its introduction dramatically unfolds several elements in order, as if Beethoven, at the keyboard instead of writing in a sketchbook, was sequentially building the thematic material before the very ears of the listener. First we hear only the bass of the theme; then come multiple counterpoints to it in successively higher registers; then the theme, the upper-line melody, sails in at last in a high register, completing the basic material on which fifteen very elaborate and virtuosic variations can be based. The climax of the work is a closing fugue on the theme's bass line, crowned at last with a great peroration that reintroduces the theme in high register and then carries it to a ringing climax as it falls to the bass register amid resounding figuration patterns. The whole anticipates the *Eroica* finale in broad outline, but there, of course, it is recomposed as a grand symphonic finale. The "Prometheus"

Variations are the grandest of all Beethoven's early variations sets, a work that matches and overshadows such earlier efforts as the "Righini" Variations. It points the way to the orchestra-like keyboard writing of his middle period and his later piano writing, including that of the later piano concertos.

New Violin Sonatas

In the by-now familiar domain of keyboard chamber music Beethoven continued to make strides, above all in the violin sonata, composing two works in 1800 (Opus 23, in A minor, and Opus 24, the "Spring" Sonata, in F major). At the end of this phase, in 1802, he returned to the violin sonata with the important set of three published as Opus 30, in A major, C minor, and G Major. And as early as 1802 he capped the climax with the first version of the most brilliant of all his earlier accompanied sonatas, the "Kreutzer" Sonata in A minor, revised and eventually published as Opus 47 in 1805. These six violin sonatas form the largest body of accompanied sonatas that he ever wrote in so short a time. Differing sharply from each other in stylistic character and means of organization, they all share the same basic problem of achieving a balance of sonorities between the violin, as a middle- and high-register instrument, and the keyboard, with its fullness of range. They show us Beethoven modernizing an inherited genre in the light of the same new powers of integration that we feel in the five piano sonatas of the Opus 20s and in the quartets of Opus 18.

Opp. 23 and 24 are a contrasting pair, like individuals with cold and warm personalities. Opus 23, in the rare key of A minor, is bleak, odd, and distant, a neglected child in the family of Beethoven violin sonatas, despite its original and experimental moments. The "Spring" Sonata, Opus 24, is clearly meant to be a work of great beauty; it is one of the most ingratiating and beguiling works Beethoven ever wrote. Beloved by performers and the public ever since it appeared, this sonata exemplifies Beethoven's use of thematic reciprocity, meaning that the musical material is balanced between the two instruments and this equilibrium is perpetually maintained. The keyboard of 1800 for which this sonata was written still had the resonance of the late-eighteenth-century *fortepiano*, although the instrument was gradually growing in volume as piano makers met the demand for greater sonorous resources. Still, the balance of function between violin and keyboard is exquisitely achieved in this work, from the very opening to the very end. Avoiding or minimizing the abrupt percussive effects found in many of Beethoven's earlier works, it may be an answer to the critics who refused to believe that he could lure them with the smooth and beautiful as effectively as he could frighten them with the bizarre and unexpected.

In the Opus 30 sonatas the same principles are evident, now with more developed substance, wider formal and harmonic range in the first movements, and stronger rhetorical contrasts. The opening of Opus 30 No. 2 brings a sculpted rhythmic figure (long-held note plus four sixteenths plus abrupt quarter note), foretelling the new and larger scheme of Beethovenian sonata form that can unfold from the possibilities latent in such a single figure. It is less quirky than the similar effect at the opening of Piano Sonata Opus 31 No. 1, but shows Beethoven moving in the same direction. He was now experimenting consciously with the idea of building works in which large movement forms evolved not from symmetrical phrase patterns or long-breathed melodies but from abrupt, terse figures stated early and then composed out to far-distant consequences through the wide range of a sonata-form movement. Beethoven thought back to this way of opening an accompanied sonata as late as 1815 in beginning his D Major Cello Sonata, Opus 102 No. 2, whose first motif is a virtual inversion of this one, with a four-sixteenth figure preceding the held note instead of following it.

With Opus 47 we reach the summit of his earlier violin sonata style, now raised to a brilliant pitch of virtuosity in the most difficult violin writing of the period. The work, which is even labeled "scritta in uno stilo molto concertante, quasi come d'un concerto" ("written in a highly concerto-like style, almost in the manner of a concerto"), was originally written for the violinist George Augustus Polgreen Bridgetower, who played it with Beethoven in 1803.[28] Later the dedication was offered to Rodolphe Kreutzer, the famous French violinist who taught at the Paris Conservatoire, and whom Beethoven met in Vienna in 1798. In an act of modernization Beethoven lifted the finale he had originally intended for the A

Major Sonata Op. 30 No. 1 and moved it to the "Kreutzer" Sonata, replacing it with a more placid variation finale. The whirlwind finale as rewritten for the "Kreutzer" is a tour de force, as is the entire work, which blends elements of concerto and sonata in a new and brilliant synthesis. No amateur violinist could master this work, then or since. It amazed audiences down through the nineteenth century, gaining fame as the most dazzling of all violin sonatas. Berlioz called it "one of the most sublime of all violin sonatas," and for Tolstoy in his story titled "The Kreutzer Sonata" it was the supreme example of the power of music (a dangerous power, in his view) to arouse erotic feelings.[29] With the "Kreutzer" Beethoven reached the last stage of his first major phase of composing accompanied sonatas for any instrument. As he had in the Opus 31 piano sonatas, he had driven the genre to unheard-of expressive limits, reshaped it along new dialectical lines, and moved it entirely beyond the Mozartian models that still lurked behind his earlier sonatas. When he returned to the accompanied sonata some years later, he did so not in groups of works but with single compositions of exceptionally high distinction and restraint: the A Major Cello Sonata Opus 69 of 1808–9 and the G Major Violin Sonata Opus 96, a richly developed work in a wholly different spirit from the "Kreutzer," written in 1812. But by then accompanied sonatas were no longer his main focus.

The Earlier Piano Concertos

During the same span of years, Beethoven at last completed the first two piano concertos and composed the third. The first to be finished was actually the B-flat Piano Concerto, Opus 19, labeled No. 2 when published in 1801, although it had reached its final form in 1798 after much revision. The much stronger C Major Piano Concerto, finished in 1800, was published as Opus 15 and thus became No. 1. Although ideas for the Third Piano Concerto, in C Minor, actually appeared as early as 1796, it remained an embryo until 1802, when he set to work on it in earnest, no doubt in preparation for performing it in public. He apparently completed it in the course of 1802 and early 1803, and played it for the first time at a concert that April along with his Second Symphony and *Chri-*

stus am Ölberge, plus a repeat of the First Symphony, first heard three years earlier.[30]

In these works Beethoven took center stage as virtuoso and as the leading composer of piano concertos. Despite his deafness he played them all in public except the Fifth, which was given its premiere by Friedrich Schneider in 1811. Though not as a concerto soloist, Beethoven aspired to play the piano in public or semipublic settings as late as January 1815, when he appeared at the Congress of Vienna as a song accompanist. But in the early years he guarded his concertos as his own property and did not publish them until he had performed them himself at least once and in some instances several times. Conceived in the compositional and performing tradition of the Mozart piano concertos, they combine high artistry of design with demands for keyboard virtuosity.

The status of the first three concertos differed considerably from one to the other, as Beethoven moved from the safe and conservative orbit of No. 2—"not one of my best," he confessed to the publisher Hoffmeister—to the firmly grounded brilliance of No. 1 and on to the more experimental and emotionally more colorful No. 3, with its eccentricities of form and key scheme. In Concerto No. 1 the traditional three-movement form brings an expressive but not path-breaking slow movement in the key of the flat sixth, A-flat major (not a highly unusual choice for a slow movement at this time, though certainly a progressive touch). In the Third the two C-minor movements frame a slow movement in the surprising key of E major, providing a calculated shock for concert audiences at the beginning and end of this movement, above all when the finale opens with a theme that wrenches the hushed chords of E major back into C minor by reinterpreting the high closing G♯ of the Largo (which ends *fortissimo*) as an A♭ in the wide-spanned Allegro theme that sparks off the finale (*W 13).

Concerto No. 1 is shot through with dramatic oppositions of ideas, themes, and sonorities of piano and orchestra in short-range and long-range dialogue that bear witness to the new Beethovenian style now finding its way for the first time into the concerto. Properly speaking, this work matches the Second Symphony, completed at about the same time, in dramatizing all the basic elements—ideas and sonorities—as if they were actors in a serious play. In the concerto format, of course, the soloist and the orchestra are naturally pitted in such roles, as they had been since Mozart's masterpieces, ranging from early gems such as K. 271 in E-flat to the glories of his late concertos and ending with the balanced wisdom of K. 595 in B-flat, a work that Beethoven certainly knew well.[31]

CHAPTER 7

MUSIC FOR ORCHESTRA AND THE FIRST QUARTETS

❧❦❧❦⊰⊰∘⊱⊱❦❧❦❧

The First Symphony and the Prometheus *Ballet*

In 1795 Beethoven sketched some ideas for the first movement of a C-major symphony, then let the project lie fallow. He picked it up again in 1799, revised and completed it, and had it performed as his First Symphony at a concert in April 1800, along with a Mozart symphony, an aria from Haydn's *Creation*, and other new compositions of his own, including his Septet. The 1795 torso is of interest only as it foreshadows some material in the finished First Symphony. Realizing that the main C-major theme in the sketched first movement would not work in his more developed conception, Beethoven transferred it to the symphony's finale, where in altered form it became the sprightly first theme. By presenting the initial tonic C major chord as a dominant seventh, Beethoven maintains and dramatizes the idea of opening with a short slow introduction, clearly in the manner of Haydn's London symphonies. This way of beginning was celebrated as a coup, although it is in fact a harmonic condensation of a familiar opening gambit inherited from Mozart and Haydn.[1]

In all, the First Symphony contains attractive features within an essentially simple larger design. Its first movement displays some progressive touches, such as the elegant use of antiphonal solo wind instruments in the second thematic group of the exposition and the darkly colored *pianissimo* modulatory episode that follows. And the climax of the first movement is built on the same harmonic sequence we heard at the opening of the slow introduction, which returns to form the culmination of the coda.[2] The slow movement is perfunctory when compared with those of the piano sonatas and piano trios of these years, let alone those of the Opus 18 quartets.

But the third movement stands out. This "Menuetto" is really the first Beethoven symphonic scherzo. Marked Allegro molto e vivace, it is a long, brilliant, ambitious movement with a far-reaching modulatory scheme in its second section and a fullness of realization that eludes the other movements. No other composer of the time could have written even a phrase of the Menuetto, which leaps out of the symphony as its most memorable movement. The finale, all lightness and wit, is a clever 2/4 sonata-rondo that pairs well with the finale of the First Piano Concerto even if it lacks the sharp contrasts by which the concerto's solo and tutti exchanges enliven the action.

Alongside the more adventurous works of these years, the First Symphony fails to impress. As he prepared to give the public a first taste of his prowess as a symphonic composer, Beethoven played it safe rather than provoke his audience. He avoids the quirks and eccentricities (such as the abrupt contrasts of dynamics, accents, tempos, and musical ideas) that had come to be the order of the day in his sonatas and chamber music but that annoyed his critics. So the First remains a trial run, not a work that comes up to the standard of the "sublime" that Johann Georg Sulzer and other aestheticians had set for the symphony nor, in practical terms, the artistic standard set by Haydn and Mozart in their later symphonies. The same ambition to please is written all over his Septet, Opus 20, a divertimento companion to the First Symphony intended for salon performance. In his later symphonies Beethoven took the entire genre into his hands, remolded it, and flung it beyond all earlier boundaries, putting unheard-of demands on performers and listeners and transforming the parameters of the symphony. In later years the First remained a distant memory of an earlier, attractive and domesticated Beethoven that survived only in his lighter compositions intended for amateurs. As late as 1821 a critic could refer to the First with unwitting irony as "one of his earlier, more comprehensible instrumental works." If the critic had sympathetically followed Beethoven through the immense development of the later years, he would have had to agree that, except for the third movement, it lacked anything truly new. Berlioz minced no words in a review included in his *A Travers Chants*:

[I]n this symphony the poetic idea is completely absent, even though it is so grand and rich in the greater part of the works that followed. Certainly it is music admirably framed: clear, vivacious, although only slightly accentuated; cold, and sometimes even mean, as in the final rondo, a true example of musical childishness. In a word, Beethoven is not here.[3]

The path from the First to the Second Symphony is not direct but runs through *Prometheus*, the ballet that Beethoven wrote in the winter of 1800–1801 for the Italian ballet master Salvatore Viganò, who premiered it on March 21, 1801, in the Hofburgtheater. Though the music is attractive enough, the work is more important for its dramatic qualities. It shows Beethoven's acquiescence in the current view that ballet music was primarily intended for entertainment and must be easier and lighter than music for the concert hall. Only later, in writing incidental music for *Coriolanus* and *Egmont*, would he turn to the more serious modes of expression demanded by music for spoken drama, which meant vastly more to him than ballet. Still, *Prometheus* is of interest precisely for its special effects and limitations: it shows Beethoven exploiting instruments and coloristic orchestral effects that would never appear in his symphonies or serious dramatic overtures. Among them are No. 5 (from Act II), in which the muse Euterpe plays the flute, presumably with a simulated musical performance by the demigods Arion and Orpheus, famous musicians of antiquity. Here Beethoven opens with an Adagio introduction for solo harp with rolled chords, probably strummed by Orpheus; then strings provide a pizzicato accompaniment to concertante wind passages (Euterpe's solo). At last the whole gathers to a climax. Here a solo cello cadenza takes over the ensemble and leads the orchestra through a handsomely melodic Andante quasi Allegretto that in another context could have been the slow movement of a popular and beautiful cello concerto in Beethoven's most ingratiating first-period style.

Elsewhere the score abounds with scenic effects, from the opening storm ("La Tempesta"), in which Prometheus runs through the forest, to an Allegretto "Pastorale" (No. 10) that dimly foreshadows the finale of the Sixth Symphony. But the *pièce de résistance* is the Finale, in which the E-flat ballroom contredanse in 2/4 receives extended orchestral treatment; it even uses another of his contredanses, in G major, as its middle section. But the dance sticks tight to its simple binary form, receiving no development—for in ballet there could be none.

What Viganò's *Prometheus* meant to contemporaries is worth considering, so far as we can piece it together from scant evidence. The full title is *The Creatures of Prometheus*, and it is labeled "a mythological allegorical ballet." The protagonist is the Titan Prometheus, portrayed here not as suffering victim but in his benign role as the molder of human civilization. Prometheus literally shapes humankind by bringing to life two clay statues, a man and a woman. From an 1838 synopsis of Viganò's plot we learn that "the two statues come to life . . . [then] Prometheus beholds them with joy . . . but cannot awaken any feeling in them that shows the use of reason."[4] Prometheus despairs of his mute creatures and plans to enlighten them by exposing them to the "higher arts and sciences." In the second act, set on Parnassus, the stage is filled with a parade of mythological figures: Apollo, the nine Muses, the Graces, Bacchus, Pan, then Orpheus, Amphion, and Arion. At the end, Melpomene, the muse of tragedy, appears and abruptly shows the inevitability of death by killing Prometheus before their eyes. But the necessary happy ending of neoclassical drama occurs just as suddenly, if hardly more credibly, when Thalia, the muse of comedy, "holds her mask over the faces of the two mourning creatures . . . while Pan, leading his fauns, calls the dead Prometheus back to life, and so the tale ends with festive dancing."[5]

Prometheus was called in the original playbill a "heroic, allegorical ballet." The term "heroic," as applied here, has been associated with Beethoven's use of the ballet finale material in the *Eroica* finale, and thus the identity of the ballet's theme with the symphony's finale might seem to extend the allegory to both. But the Prometheus of the ballet is not the rebellious Titan who brought fire to humanity and then suffered Zeus's punishment by being bound to a rock while his liver was gnawed by a vulture. He is not the monumental Prometheus of Aeschylus, nor that of Goethe or Shelley, who stands up to the gods. This Prometheus is presented rather as an Enlightenment philosopher and teacher who brings reason and knowledge to the unlettered and ignorant "creatures"—Rousseau's noble savages on the ballet stage—men and women in a pre-civilized, preliterate state.

Behind Viganò's work lay a more current subtext. By 1800 Napoleon Bonaparte was the talk of Europe. As a military hero he had risen to fame with his lightning victories at Toulon and in Italy, where, at twenty-five, he had become commander of the French armies. Italian patriots glorified Bonaparte as the champion of their long struggle against Austrian despotism, and in 1797 the poet Vincenzo Monti hailed him as the liberator of Italy in an epic poem called, significantly, *Prometeo*. It is possible that Beethoven's decision to use the *Prometheus* finale in the fourth movement of his Third Symphony, which was not only dedicated originally to Bonaparte but was even intended to carry his name, reflected his awareness of a connection between Prometheus as mankind's mythic liberator and Napoleon as a modern hero.[6] This possibility is not undermined by the indirect path from *Prometheus* to the *Eroica* through the Opus 35 Piano Variations, which in turn laid the basis for his first concrete ideas for the symphony.

The French Dimension and Military Music

Stirred like all his contemporaries by the upheavals in France, Beethoven was receptive to the vigor and power of French Revolutionary and post-Revolutionary music, above all in two domains. One was French opera. He admired the operas of Cherubini, which with others from France were becoming increasingly popular in Vienna between 1802 and '04, so much so that Beethoven could tell Rochlitz in January 1804 that "Schikaneder's empire has really been eclipsed by the light of the brilliant and attractive French operas."[7] He knew Cherubini's *Médée* (1797) and *Les deux journèes* (1800), serious and effective works that brought a new and powerful voice to French opera.

The other domain was the new school of virtuoso French string playing. Beethoven's acquaintance with the new generation of violinists had begun in Bonn but continued in Vienna, where he met Franz Clement and even studied violin with Schuppanzigh. But he soon became fully aware of the new traditions that had been established in France by Viotti and his followers, especially Pierre Baillot, Pierre Rode, and Rodolphe Kreutzer, with whom he played a violin sonata at a private concert at Lobkowitz's in April 1798.[8] When Baillot came to Vienna in 1805 he met Beethoven at a tavern and later expressed surprise when he found the celebrated composer to be quite friendly, "although his portraits always show him to be so unattractive and almost fierce."[9] Similarly, Beethoven's exposure to Jean Louis Duport in Berlin in 1796 had stimulated his awareness that the new French virtuosity now extended to the cello.

The music of postrevolutionary France aroused and inspired the whole European world. Traditional French music, certainly French opera, had been available in Bonn in the 1780s, and continued to be heard in Vienna in the 1790s as musicians rapidly adjusted to the cultural and political currents of these years. Responding to the new national fervor and mindful of the volatile swings of domestic politics, French composers quickly developed popular idioms that caught the spirit of the times—whether in works that directly reflected the new ideology of political liberation plus French military exuberance, or in grandiose works designed to symbolize the national pride and mass solidarity on which the leaders of the new regime depended for support. Thus propaganda songs, choral hymns dedicated to liberty, equality, and fraternity, and, most important, stirring military marches and marching songs were the order of the day. A government decree directed that *La Marseillaise* and other songs were to be sung before every performance in theaters all over France, thereby sparking the singing of a popular song or anthem before sports events and, in some countries, theatrical performances, that has lasted down to our time. Stage works and festivals commemorating Revolutionary milestones, such as the taking of the Bastille on July 14 or the founding of the Republic on September 22, served as pretexts for large-scale public assemblies marked by patriotic pageants, of which there were seven or eight every year in France between 1790 and 1800.[10]

By far the most famous single piece, the one that the world could never forget, was *La Marseillaise*, written on the night of April 25, 1792, by the soldier, poet, and composer Claude-Joseph Rouget de Lisle, and first called *Chant de guerre pour l'armée du Rhin*. Rouget de Lisle was a young lieutenant in the French army and also a violinist and singer, assigned to duty at Strasbourg, when he wrote both the words and music of this amazing piece. When it was immediately adopted by a battalion from Marseilles, it became wildly popular under the name *The Marseillaise's Hymn*. It swept the field in all of France just five months later, when François-Joseph Gossec orchestrated it and inserted it into a lyric scene called *Offrande a la Liberté* that was put on at the Paris Opéra. No music or text more completely captures the military spirit of its time, or any time; it is a "tune to set the pulse racing and the blood coursing."[11] Embodying in one stroke the surge of national and military pride then felt across France, and sung by French soldiers marching to battle in their first major campaigns against the enemy states of Europe, *La Marseillaise* remained a perfect symbol. It has stood ever since as the epitome of a militaristic national anthem, as we see from countless arrangements; quotations of the melody in songs or concert works by Schumann, Wagner, Liszt, Tchaikovsky, and others; and its emotional pull when sung by French citizens in film scenes reflecting French national pride, as in *Grand Illusion* and *Casablanca*.

In Beethoven's time everyone knew it and writers as far removed from France as were Klopstock and Goethe admired it. After a battle in which it was sung, August von Kotzebue, a German dramatist, praised Rouget de Lisle by asking, "Brute, barbarian, how many of my brothers have you not killed?"[12] Although the *Marseillaise* faded in France during the Napoleonic and Restoration eras, it came back in the 1830s, by which time it had been translated and taken up abroad, had even been given German words, and had become a German popular favorite.

Beethoven knew a great deal about popular songs, especially national ones, and wrote variations sets on several, including "Rule Britannia" and "God Save the King." He also composed military marches throughout these years. When it came to the battle scene in his *Wellingtons Sieg* ("Wellington's Victory") of 1813, he had the British march to "Rule Britannia" and celebrate at the end with, appropriately, "God Save the King." The French army in this work marched not to the strains of *La Marseillaise* but to the old-fashioned though equally durable "Malbrouck s'en va-t'-en guerre" ("Marlborough Goes Off to War").[13] In the heady atmosphere of the Austrian victory celebrations of 1813 *La Marseillaise* would have been subversive and probably illegal, and the older tune fitted the losing side.

Composing marches for military band, or with words as marching songs, or for civilian bands to play in order to arouse patriotic fervor, was then a widespread popular pastime. As armies all over Western Europe marched into battle year after year, French soldiers sang the *Marseillaise* and other tunes by François-Joseph Gossec, André Gretry, Jean-François Le Sueur, Etienne Méhul, and Luigi Cherubini. British battalions marched to music by Thomas Busby, John Callcott, William Crotch, James Hook, at times even Handel and Haydn. Both Handel and Haydn, if anyone asked, could be considered adopted Britons in the wake of their personal successes in England, but it was ironic that the Britons could sing Haydn, considering that he had composed the great "Kaiser-Hymne" ("Emperor Hymn") in 1797 at the request of Austrian ministers who were anxious to revive the flagging national will to continue the country's war against France. Austrian infantrymen in the Napoleonic years could counter with marches by Süssmayr, Paer, Hummel, and Beethoven.[14]

Included in Beethoven's large catalogue of minor works are four quick-step marches for military band, plus a polonaise and two ecossaises, all written between 1809 and 1816. As a genre, the rapid march plays a telling role in some of the works on a higher level: witness the pithy, brilliant military march for Pizarro's soldiers in *Fidelio*; the march in the wonderful cadenza for the piano version of the Violin Concerto; and the up-tempo, stylized marches sprinkled among his instrumental works, even late works such as the Piano Sonata Opus 101, the Ninth Symphony finale, and the A minor Quartet, Opus 132. Military elements, especially march-like rhythms, found their way into concertos of the period, to some extent in Mozart and certainly in Beethoven, right down to the "Emperor" Concerto.[15] It almost seems as if the dramatic confrontation of solo instrument with orchestra in the classical concerto may have spurred a sense of contentious striving and of force of oppositions that suggested an affinity with the rhythms of military music.

In this bloody era cursed with incessant war and with chauvinism rampant on all sides, national anthems sprang into being, literally for the first time in history. The earliest anywhere had been "God Save the King," first heard in 1745 after a British military defeat. For a long time this sturdy English melody grew so popular that other countries, faute de mieux, made use of it with appropriate words as their own version of a national anthem—the list included Denmark, Sweden, Switzerland, Russia, and even the United States. In Germany it was sung as a patriotic anthem in various German states from the 1790s through 1871, the year of German unification, and it was still being used as late as the First World War with the words "Heil Dir im Siegenkranz" ("Hail to Thee in the Wreath of Victory").[16] Only in 1922 was it superseded in Weimar Germany by the proleptic adaptation of Haydn's hymn for the kaiser as "Deutschland, Deutschland, über alles," which, with words purged of seeming German claims to international domination, is still in use today. But "God Save the King" was still preeminently British in Beethoven's time, as he knew when he used it to celebrate Wellington's victory over the French at Vittoria. Precisely at this time musicians were creating new anthems for their own countries, and all through the nationalistic nineteenth century new European anthems sprang up on demand; in some cases—"The Star-Spangled Banner," for example—these anthems were not formally and officially adopted until the twentieth.[17]

The spirit of national urgency in the *Marseillaise* colored much French music of the time, and the widespread adoption of march rhythms, overtly in some "heroic" works and more subtly in others, arose from the growing awareness of music as a public art that could powerfully express contemporary political and spiritual energies. This feeling was sparked by French revolutionary fervor in 1789 and continued to blaze as France embarked on its European campaigns that seemed never to end. Even during peacetime the new France, first under the Directories and then under Napoleon, continued to spawn new modes of musical expression, most grandly in choral compositions designed for public performance but also in opera, orchestral works, and piano music. During Beethoven's most impressionable years, from the late 1780s to about 1800, French works for public political celebrations were often performed outdoors with extravagant numbers of performers that could rise into the hundreds, sometimes the thousands. Such music had to be "simple, direct, striking, memorable, and—most of all—flexible. . . . [I]t breathes the spirit of a new age . . . frankly directed to large audiences, to simple, communal sentiments."[18]

Whatever the absolute musical quality of the works stemming from

France, they showed composers seeking higher and more arcane forms of expression in the hope that they too could address audiences beyond the chamber music rooms of patrons, and even beyond the theaters and concert halls in which crowds of several hundred could hear symphonies. It became clear that a composer seeking to represent the spirit of this new age and be a major voice in that representation had to produce music that reached large audiences, and do so in bold strokes that would ring out far beyond the immediate confines of music-making spaces. The music, of course, would need to have enough force and cogency to address not just immediate listeners but the world beyond. And of all composers active around 1800, Beethoven was the one most capable of expressing this élan, with its new aesthetic of power and complexity. The latent connection to French music and to national and military music in his style—later called the "heroic" style—was subtly apparent to knowledgeable musicians and commentators of the time. At the same time, works such as the *Eroica* and Fifth Symphony, which manifest this style in its strongest form, carried the heroic aesthetic to heights of which no French or other contemporary could dream.

The Second Symphony

Beethoven began work on the Second Symphony as early as 1800 and continued sketching it through 1801 and into 1802, although it was probably not ready when his brother Carl offered it to Breitkopf & Härtel at the end of March. Beethoven came back to it later that year in time to get it ready for its premiere in April 1803. Then it took another year for its publication, in March 1804. These dates are important because it appears that Beethoven often took the publication of his previous symphony as a springboard for intensive work on the next one. Thus he was certainly working on the Second when the First Symphony was published in December 1801, that is, published in parts, not score, following the custom of this time. Similarly, when the Second appeared, he was deep in the toils of composing the Third. The publication dates also carry weight because Beethoven often revised his works after their first performances, especially orchestral works, which took time to publish, and he often kept on revising as long as he possibly could, that is, until the work was actually in print. Thus the final touching-up of the Second Symphony, which was extensive, must have taken place while he was in the midst of working on the Third.

From the sketches we can see that the idea of a slow introduction was integral from the start, though originally in duple not triple meter. The early ideas for the introduction include a slow-tempo version of the march theme that he later transferred to the Allegro exposition as the main sec-ond-group theme. Accordingly, the spirit of the military march was firmly established from very early on, and however expanded the first movement became, it never lost this spirit. The first Allegro theme was originally a simple triadic figure (1–3–1–5–1–3–1) but there is more to it than first appears: its interval sequence is nearly identical to the one that Beethoven later used for the opening of the first theme of the *Eroica*. In the sketches for the Second this theme is rhythmically too static to serve his purposes. In these sketches it evolves into what became the final version, which main-tains the linearized tonic triad as its basic frame but cuts the material neatly into well-defined segments that can function both together and apart. The final version has a rhythmic form typical of the early middle period, with a long-held first note and four brisk sixteenths at the end of the measure.

(a) Sketch for Symphony No. 2, first movement, main theme, from sketchbook Lands-berg 7, p. 38 (Source: Ein Notierungsbuch von Beethoven, *ed. Karl Lothar Mikulicz [Leipzig, 1927]):*

(b) Symphony No. 2, first movement, main theme:

The first movement leaps far beyond anything in the First Symphony, even the earlier work's excellent Menuetto, in dynamic action and dramatization of ideas. The slow introduction is the widest ranging in harmonic span that Beethoven had written up to this time, and it glows with touches of orchestral color he had never tried before. By marking it Adagio molto (the same as for the short introduction to the First Symphony) he brings a strong tempo contrast between introduction and the main section, marked Allegro con brio.[19] The main Allegro exposition then surprises us by presenting the first theme not as a complete melody in an upper register but as a partial theme in the lower strings, a theme that then invites development of its strongly profiled motivic units and energetically pursues a wealth of contrasts.

The slow movement, one of the most sensuous of all Beethoven's Larghettos (a tempo that Mozart had reserved for his most beautiful slow movements), sank deeply into the musical consciousness of contemporaries and subsequent generations, becoming, as Tovey said, the touchstone of what is beautiful and childlike in music. For Beethoven the tempo Larghetto is new in his instrumental music (if we exclude the little "Electoral" Sonatas of 1783), and he used it elsewhere for delicate works and movements such as the song "Adelaide," the slow movement of the Violin Concerto, and the introduction to the finale of the Quartet Opus 95. The opening theme, in its pure sonorities of strings all in middle and high register, and its repetition with clarinets, bassoons, and horns, all *piano*, anticipates the Romantic orchestral effects of Schubert and Mendelssohn. For Berlioz this movement was "a delineation of innocent happiness hardly clouded by a few melancholy accents."[20] A vast step beyond its counterpart in the First, this slow movement is a large-scale sonata form that finds room within its lyrical expansions and contrasting thematic elements for a full development section, plus a retransition to the home tonic and the main theme that is as beautiful and nostalgic as anything Beethoven ever wrote.

That Beethoven labored to achieve this quality we could easily infer, but Ries tells us so explicitly. He says that this slow movement was "so beautiful, so purely and happily conceived, and the voice-leading so natural, that one can hardly imagine anything in it was ever changed"—but Ries also says that in the autograph score the second violin and viola parts at the beginning were so heavily covered with corrections that he could hardly make out the original notes.[21] To which Beethoven replied, when Ries queried him, "it's better that way."

The manic finale of the Second outdoes the first movement in energy and originality. It opens with a wild and powerful figure on the dominant that stops with an abrupt accented two-note motif on the downbeat, then touches off a rapid continuation that ends again with the same two-note whiplash figure (*W 14). Essential to the conception is that the finale should open in high tension and then extend and hold the hot current in motion right to the end, culminating in a final peroration that amazed contemporaries and evoked such criticisms as "colossal" (in a negative sense), "tumultuous," and "untamed."[22] The symphony crosses new boundaries, moving into a range of dramatic expression in which the strongest possible contrasts occur in unexpected immediacy—movement to movement, section to section, idea to idea. Breaks in texture, breaks in continuity, powerful motoric rhythms that suddenly stop—these erupt before the listener's ear with a violence that had never been heard in symphonic writing up to this time. No wonder the critics found it bizarre—it was too much for traditional ears accustomed to gentler, more gradual contrasts. This symphony signaled that from now on in Beethoven's orchestral works power and lyricism in extreme forms were to be unleashed as never before, that the stark dramatization of musical ideas was to be fundamental to the discourse, and that contemporaries, ready or not, would have to reshape their expectations to keep up with him.

Opus 18: "I have now learned how to write string quartets"

Since its emergence as a genre, essentially created singlehandedly by Haydn in the 1760s and later brought to its first maturity by him and by Mozart, the string quartet had grown in stature to be the highest and most demanding of musical categories, a "noble genre," as Seyfried called it.[23] That it stood apart was not just a matter of idle preference or snobbish taste. The new schools of violin playing that had risen to virtuoso heights in the last forty years of the century, led by Leclair and Viotti, were followed ambitiously by cellists and even a few violists. All of this was reflected in expanded writing for strings in all genres but nowhere more strikingly than in the string quartet. This new type of ensemble, divorced from the vestigial Baroque keyboard continuo, made up exclusively of homogeneously blended string instruments that had the widest range and quality of tone, warmth, expressivity, and flexibility, aroused a strong response from performers and patrons that composers soon rushed to fulfill. The quartet became a test of compositional ability for young composers, a way of showing their skill in writing idiomatically for four equally important parts with no fillers or patchwork to hide deficiencies in imagination or dull material. And by the time Beethoven came around to quartet writing in the later 1790s, Mozart's mature quartets were all very recent classics, prominent on

Sketches for the slow movement of the String Quartet Opus 18 No. 1, containing references in French to scenes from Shakespeare's Romeo *and* Juliet. *(Staatsbibliothek, Berlin)*

A set of Italian stringed instruments given to Beethoven by Prince Karl Lichnowsky around 1800. (Beethoven-Haus, Bonn, on permanent loan from the State Institute of Musical Research, Preussischer Kulturbesitz)

the horizon. Haydn, the law-giving master of the genre from its inception, was still turning out new quartets on the same high level to which he had accustomed the musical world since the early 1770s, when his Opus 20 had set a very difficult standard for all his contemporaries and successors to meet.[24]

Beethoven was probably wary of the high expectations that musicians held for him in this genre above all, and no doubt also saw Haydn's masterly Opp. 71 and 74 Quartets directly before him. Those works had been commissioned by Apponyi in 1793 and published in London in 1795 and 1796, just when Beethoven was publishing his first trios and piano sonatas. Writing a string quartet, he would have felt even more keenly, as John Keats put it, the high cliff of tradition towering above him. To heighten the inevitable competition with Haydn, the commission for Beethoven's first six quartets actually came in the fall of 1798 from Prince Lobkowitz, who also asked Haydn at the same time for another new set of six. But Haydn, now aging, was able to produce only two, the pair of Opus 77, followed by the unfinished Opus 103 a few years later.

Beethoven began work on his own quartets in 1798. After massive preparatory work and extensive revisions, they were ready for publication in two sets of three in June and October 1801. Aside from No. 4 in C minor, the order of composition, to judge from the sketchbooks, was: No. 3 in D major, No. 1 in F major, No. 2 in G major, No. 5 in A major, and No. 6 in B-flat. The C Minor, No. 4, remains the orphan of this group, and because we have no sketches for it in the surviving sketchbooks, some believe that it might go back to Bonn antecedents and might have been written much earlier than the others.[25] But there is no positive basis for this assumption, and all the anecdotal remarks denigrating the quartet come from later and not trustworthy observers. The only story that rings true comes from Ries, who reports that he asked Beethoven about a contrapuntal passage in No. 4 that he thought violated traditional procedures, to which Beethoven replied, "I allow them."[26]

The odds are good that the C Minor Quartet was written at about the same time as the others of Opus 18, but for some reason simply not worked out within the sketchbooks he was then using. He may have worked on it in a hypothetical lost sketchbook of 1799–1800, or on separate sketch leaves that are now lost.[27] It has, after all, substantial affinities with other C-minor works of this time; the first and last movements, especially, evoke the comparable movements in the "Pathétique," written just before work on the quartets began. The clever and intricate Andante scherzoso bears some resemblance to the slow movement of the First Symphony, though the quartet Andante is of finer workmanship.

The most imposing quartet of Opus 18 is No. 1, one of Beethoven's longest four-movement cycles before the *Eroica*. The material in the first movement is characterized by a short, memorable motif, recognizable from its rhythmic form alone. Except where the second group in the dominant provides relief through smoothly flowing eighth notes, the motif serves as the leading factor throughout. But this primary motif, though always well defined, appears in many guises. Sometimes its pitches are entirely different; sometimes it acts as accompaniment to other thematic figures; sometimes it lacks its first note but, like a puzzle in a Gestalt formation, is still recognizable.

String Quartet Opus 18 No. 1, first movement, beginning, violin I only:

The first Allegro is thus an early instance of an amply developed movement that is permeated by a single motif, anticipating the Fifth Symphony, by far the most famous Beethovenian example (*W 15a). The main motif can either be heard as if it were a picaresque figure in a narrative, which enters into varied situations and encounters, yet maintains its own form; or else as if it were a recurrent emblematic figure that runs like a red thread through an entire complex tapestry. The sketches show that it began life in 4/4 time and was then transformed into its characteristic triple meter (*W 15b).

A window onto the genesis of this quartet is provided not only by its extensive sketches but also by the chance survival of a complete early version of the entire work.[28] Beethoven gave this version to his old friend Karl Amenda, who preserved it among his papers after receiving a letter from Beethoven telling him not to circulate it because he had now revised the entire composition, "having now learned how to write quartets."[29] The two versions are instructive, both for their contrasts and as an example of Beethoven's not only sketching but working through to complete drafts of works in early versions, few of which survive. In the second version we see Beethoven, especially in the first and last movements, tightening the content, improving the voice leading, and making the string writing more idiomatic—in all, he gave the work the mature profile and idiomaticity that he now saw was essential to a higher level of quartet writing. That sketching and revising the Opus 18 quartets cost Beethoven intense effort does not in principle distinguish them from many of his other works, but it confirms the exceptionally high standards he associated with this genre.

Striking in Opus 18 No. 1 are the fugal passages in the first and last movements. Fugue is more characteristic of the quartet than of the piano sonata. It remained a mark of the more developed, intellectual character of quartet composition, in which composers were expected to show off their contrapuntal accomplishments both in creating interesting inner and lower parts and in the learned disciplines of fugue and fugato, even when used as episodes within sonata-form or sonata-rondo structures.[30] The same prominent use of fugal textures appears in other works that Beethoven regarded as truly serious, lofty accomplishments, such as the Third, Fifth, Seventh, and Ninth symphonies. In each of these major orchestral works, all of epic character, fugue or fugato occurs in at least one movement, sometimes more, typically as a way of extending the developmental range by treating one or more themes contrapuntally. And although we find no fugal episodes in the even-numbered symphonies and in most of the piano sonatas before the late period, this lack in no way lessens the quality of those works but simply signals that their aesthetic models make no room for fugal development and proceed in other ways; the Fourth Symphony is a prime example.

Celebrated for expressivity is the slow movement of Opus 18 No. 1, known also for its associations with the tomb scene from Shakespeare's *Romeo and Juliet*. These connections arise from remarks that appear in French at particular places in the sketches near the end of the movement: for example, "il prend le tombeau" ("he comes to the tomb") followed by "désespoir" ("despair") —the word is hard to decipher; "il se tue" ("he kills himself"); and "les derniers soupirs" ("the last sighs") (*W 16). The final remark is attached to a closing segment for the movement and uses a traditional "sigh" motif. Beethoven often wrote in Italian or French in his sketchbooks when he was thinking out passages and, at times, larger plans for movements or works.[31] The association with Shakespeare's *Romeo and Juliet* is also supported by other evidence: Amenda recalled telling Beethoven that this movement induced thoughts about the separation of two lovers, to which Beethoven is said to have replied, "[For this movement] I was thinking of the burial vault scene in *Romeo and Juliet*."[32]

The large-scale sonata form of this Adagio gives it a weight and gravity beyond all but a few of Beethoven's earlier slow movements. If Beethoven was thinking of *Romeo and Juliet*, then the main theme, in D minor, and the principal second theme, in F major, may represent the two conflicting principles of Romeo's despair and Juliet's beauty. If the burial vault scene from the play was a generating idea for the movement, as it may have been, the important point is that Beethoven, not wanting to be literal, destroyed all traces of any such program in the finished work. What evidence he left exists only by chance in the sketches, which he never expected the world to know. Essential in the movement is the expressive conflict of these two basic musical ideas. Oppositions between paired and contrasted themes, gestures, motifs, and segments always with clear-cut rhythmic profiles —become a vital means by which Beethoven generates drama, action, and larger shape in his sonata-form movements, increasingly so as he moves from early to middle-period works.

The other quartets of Opus 18 offer varied perspectives on Beethoven's hard-won virtuosity as a quartet composer. Thanks to Amenda, we know about his revision of No. 1, which has in fact been published and recorded. He also revised No. 2 and possibly No. 3.[33] Quartet No. 2 is built along different lines from No. 1. It is light and graceful, and has an elaborated slow movement that alternates Adagio and Allegro segments, perhaps following a Haydn model, and anticipating the tempo alternations in *La Malinconia*, the finale of No. 6. No. 2 is the epitome of the charming, not the forceful, as different from No. 1 as it can be. In Beethoven's first sketchbook, in which he worked out Opus 18 No. 3, the first of the set to be composed, he entered the annotation "le seconde quatuor dans une style bien legère excepté le dernier" ("the second quartet in a light style, except its finale").[34]

No. 3, striking out in other directions, prizes legato linear motion in its first movement beyond all else. In the opening phrase, after a solo upward seventh leap, the first violin moves down in graduated phases, alternating smooth eighth-note figuration with long points of arrival, falling a ninth from high G to lower F♯. The undulating motion of the material in the third measure and its many ramifications recall Mozart more than Haydn; sure enough, in the course of the movement, we find possibly unconscious reminiscences from the finale of Mozart's A Major Quartet, K. 464, which we know Beethoven copied. The pace and flow of this movement is also akin to that of the "Spring" Sonata, Opus 24, in which a similar ebb and flow of melodic lines is the primary feature of the first movement.

No. 5 is often taken as the main inheritor of Mozart's K. 464, because it shares with Mozart's quartet its key, its movement plan (with the Menuetto second), its position in the cycle of six quartets, and certain other features. Actually, though, it is quite independent of the Mozart work if we look below the surface, as it omits all the characteristic structural underpinning of the Mozart quartet, namely its use of descending-third chains in both first and last movements.[35]

The cycle closes with the Quartet No. 6, a small-scale, compact, intimate work of high craftsmanship. With its opening in a Haydnesque texture, the first movement unfurls a main theme that contains a "folded arpeggio," that is, a theme in which the notes of the tonic chord are presented in this order: 1–5–3–1–5–3–1. But instead of moving downward, as this sequence of figures implies, the notes zigzag upward, alternating small-scale up-and-down motions to form a theme (*W 17). Beethoven employs this means of thematic formation in later works as well. The whole first movement of No. 6 makes witty use of the turn figure on the fourth beat, as we could expect. It also finds room for rolling, questioning phrases, as in the preparation for the recapitulation, where a dying away leads to a measure of silence and then a *pianissimo* pause on the dominant.

The Adagio ranks with the most expressive of the early slow movements, yet harbors surprises, as when a sudden *fortissimo* erupts in the reprise, disclosing powerful feelings that had been hidden below the lyrical surface. The Scherzo is a tour de force of syncopation, like no other early Beethoven movement, an explosion of rhythmic eccentricity after the more nearly straightforward rhythmic patterns of the first two movements. But the crux of the whole work is its finale, labeled *La Malinconia*. The movement comprises four sections: (1) Adagio; (2) Allegretto quasi Allegro; (3) a return of (2), preceded by brief returns of Sections 1, 2, and 1; and (4) Prestissimo (preceded by a brief Poco adagio). In Section 3 Beethoven plays out returns of previously heard contrasting material, each return shorter than the one before. The sense is that of indecision as to what will happen to these opposed emotional states—the melancholic and the sanguine—and how their opposition can be resolved. The question is then settled and the movement stabilized by the Allegretto, which now returns in Section 4 and finds its way back to the tonic. The movement ends in a manic close taken at the fastest tempo marking found in Beethoven's works.

What does the title *La Malinconia* mean? A partial clue is found in the special performance direction, which recalls the "Moonlight" sonata: "Questo pezzo si deve trattare colla più gran delicatezza" ("This piece is to be played with the greatest possible delicacy"), which means that Beethoven wants the strongest shades of light and darkness in the phrasing and dynamics. The words *La Malinconia* have traditionally been taken to refer only to the Adagio, as a representation of melancholia, reflecting Beethoven's personal depression as his deafness increased.[36] The long Adagio gropes through darkness, beginning with the bare outlines of periodic structure in its rhythm and phrase organization which is then undercut by sudden contrasts of high and low chords, *pianissimo* and *fortissimo* (*W 18). The Adagio then gradually loses its original rhythmic profile as it wanders through distant harmonic regions. Finally it clings to the figure of a strong quarter note preceded by a sixteenth-note-triplet turning-motion upbeat in its last measures, again alternating *forte* and *piano*. In its last phrase the slow crescendo from *pianissimo* to *fortissimo* is held together by the cello while the other strings rise through a succession of chromatic harmonies, searching for a harmonic foothold but not finding it until they reach the final dominant.

But another way of looking at *La Malinconia*, which might have roots in both the deafness crisis and in the idea of representing two temperaments, two states of the soul in melancholia and sanguinity, is to see it as a bold extension of the programmatic into the string quartet, a genre it had not penetrated before. Beethoven's use of this title, with all its implications, is a departure from Haydn and Mozart, and it goes beyond his reticence regarding the *Romeo and Juliet* allusion in the first quartet. Haydn and Mozart never used representational titles in their quartets even when they might conceivably have been appropriate. Certainly in some of Haydn's and Mozart's quartets, strongly profiled and virtually nameable emotional states stand right at the border of consciousness—of the performer, of the listener, and probably of the composer. We need only think of Haydn's profound slow movement of Opus 76 No. 5 or the introduction to Mozart's "Dissonant" Quartet, K. 465, the strangest harmonic experiment in all of Mozart's chamber music. That Beethoven could have had the "Dissonant" Quartet in mind, directly or as distant recollection, as a potential background to *La Malinconia* may seem at first far fetched. But in fact the affinities between this slow introduction and the modulatory scheme of the finale of K. 465 are real, though generally unrecognized.[37] At all events, this movement rises like a great peak out of the postclassical landscape of the Opus 18. It foreshadows the wider emotional world that Beethoven would explore several years later in the Opus 59 trilogy, by which time composing string quartets had taken on for him a greatly enlarged range of meanings.

CHAPTER 8

THE FIRST MATURITY: AN OVERVIEW

❧❧❧⊰⊱❧❧❧

In 1776, Charles Burney defined music as "an innocent luxury, unnecessary, indeed, to our existence, but a great improvement and gratification to the sense of hearing."[1] He also called music "the art of pleasing," listing as its valued qualities "the ingenuity of the composition, the neatness of the execution, the sweetness of the melody, and the richness of the harmony, as well as the charms of refined tones, lengthened and polished into passion."[2] The vocabulary is telling, the viewpoint is conservative. Music's aim is to "please"; its inner qualities can be evoked by terms such as "sweetness of melody," "richness of harmony," "charm of refined tones" and the like. Burney's viewpoint is that of a listener seeking solace and pleasure, not mystery, in the musical experience.

That such a view held the center of aesthetics, a new branch of philosophy that was rapidly growing in the later eighteenth century, is clear from formal philosophical writings. Edmund Burke, in his treatise of 1757 on the "sublime" and the "beautiful," had opened up a much wider spectrum of aesthetic categories, in which the "great and sublime in nature" is contrasted with the "smooth and polished" character of the "beautiful." But it took several decades before these precepts were translated into musical aesthetics by J. G. Sulzer and by Christian Friedrich Michaelis, a Beethoven contemporary, who argued that the composer could express the sublime "through the use of the marvellous . . . [by means of] unconventional, surprising, powerfully startling, or striking harmonic progressions or rhythmic patterns."[3] When Haydn's biographer Georg August Griesinger summed up Haydn's aesthetic views, he wrote that "Haydn's theoretical *raisonnements* were very simple: A piece of music ought to have a fluent melody; coherent ideas; no superfluous ornaments; nothing overdone; no deafening accompaniments, and so forth."[4] Although Haydn's general outlook was undoubtedly conditioned by the view that the aim of music was expressive in the widest sense, there is nevertheless a quality of restraint in Griesinger's summary, written in 1809. One wonders if the "deafening accompaniments" that should be shunned could obliquely refer to the louder orchestral music of, say, Beethoven's *Leonore* Overture No. 3 or the Fifth Symphony.[5] A similar emphasis on expression and restraint is found in Mozart's scattered references to music and the emotions it arouses in listeners. Witness Mozart's famous description of Osmin in a letter he wrote to his father on September 26, 1781, about *Die Entführung aus dem Serail*:

> *[P]assions, violent or not, must never be expressed to the point of disgust, and music must never offend the ear, even in most horrendous situations, but must always be pleasing . . . in other words, always remain music."*[6]

And in a letter of 1782 Mozart justifies the qualities he tried to combine in his Piano Concertos K. 413–415 and what he hopes their public reception will be:

> *These concertos are a happy medium between what's too difficult and too easy. They are brilliant, pleasing to the ear, natural, without becoming vacuous. There are passages here and there that only connoisseurs can fully appreciate—yet the common listener will find them satisfying as well, although without knowing why.*[7]

Music must not only give pleasure, therefore, but is at its best when it is "natural," a basic notion that goes far back in Western thought to the idea of art as the "imitation of nature."[8] Mozart stresses both of these factors. Clearly enough his music, in all its fertility, formal perfection, and wide range of expression, conveys the sense that its emotional life is contained within well-defined boundaries. Raising this notion of emotional moderation, balance, and restraint to the level of an aesthetic category, we can argue that it is a primary factor in Mozart's aesthetic philosophy.[9]

Contrary to much popular belief, Mozart—despite his incredible fertility, imagination, and ability to shape works in his head before writing them down—spent countless hours planning and polishing his works, at times beginning large and important compositions and leaving them incomplete until the right opportunity came along for him to finish them.[10] All this effort was expended in the service of his role as a universal master whose range included all current genres and modes of expression and who was able to provide music that could please the public while its higher properties could be heard and enjoyed by trained listeners. That he succeeded so completely remains a miracle we can hardly understand, and we have to imagine what anxiety of influence such a model must have presented to a young musician raised to be Mozart's heir and successor.

As Beethoven grew to early adulthood, music began to be seen not as a marvelous craft but as an inborn, basic means of human expression. Signs of change were in the air, reflecting attendant transformations in taste, style, and ideology, all of which were coming under pressure from the political and social revolutions that were altering the European world. Stirrings are felt in Sulzer's comprehensive 1771–74 treatise on a general theory of the fine arts in which we see a decisive turn toward the view that music's aim is the powerful arousal of the emotions.[11] The practitioners of *Sturm und Drang* insisted on strength of expression as a primary factor in art and literature, and a widespread impetus to enlarge the frameworks of artistic forms and to capture the flux of powerful human emotions was in the air.

Johann Gottfried Herder, the historian and philosopher who took on himself the task of writing cultural history as what would later be called anthropology, saw music as a primary human capacity, an art that reached into the human spirit in all ages and countries:

The music of a nation . . . and favorite tunes, display the internal character of the people, that is to say, the proper tone of their sensations, much more truly and profoundly, than the most copious description of external contingencies.[12]

And elsewhere Herder wrote:

> *Music rouses a series of intimate feelings, true but not clear, not even*
> *perceptual, only most obscure. You, young man, were in its dark audito-*
> *rium; it lamented, sighed, stormed, exulted; you felt all that, you*
> *vibrated with every string. But about what did it—and you with*
> *it—lament, sigh, storm? Not a shadow of anything perceptible. Every-*
> *thing stirred only in the darkest abyss of your soul, like a living wind*
> *that agitates the depths of the ocean.*[13]

The definition of music's purpose has shifted. Now there is no talk of "pleasing" but rather of arousing deep and intimate personal feelings, of listeners swept up in the storms and calms of musical emotion, not just hearing but feeling music as a bodily experience in which their soul's are transported. If sexual experience had been the subject, in an age when sex was rarely discussed explicitly by novelists or philosophers, the language would probably not have been very different. The same stress on music as stimulating the passions of the soul comes from Wilhelm Wackenroder, the brilliant young novelist and essayist who died in 1798 at the age of twenty-five. In his novel of 1797 on the musician Joseph Berglinger, clearly a portrayal of Wackenroder himself, all the new tendencies are tightly concentrated. First he portrays the young Joseph, who longs to "live in a realm of grand imaginings and exalted dreams" but is forced to live in prosaic reality, listening to church music:

> *Expectantly, he would await the first sound of the instruments—and*
> *when it came bursting forth, mighty and sustained, shattering the dull*
> *silence like a storm from Heaven, and when the sounds swept over his*
> *head in all their grandeur—then it was that his soul spread great*
> *wings, as if he were rising up from a desolate heath, as if the curtain of*
> *dark cloud were dissolving before his mortal gaze, and he were soaring*
> *up to the radiant Heavens. . . . [T]he present receded, and his very*
> *being was purged of all that earthly ballast which is the very dust upon*
> *the polished mirror that is the soul.*

Joseph is equally overwhelmed at a concert, the music of which envelops his soul:

> *Many passages were so vivid and engaging that the notes seemed to speak to him. At other times the notes would evoke a mysterious blend of joy and sorrow in his heart, so that he could have either laughed or cried. This is a feeling that we experience so often on our path through life and that no art can express more skillfully than music. . . . That is the marvelous gift of music, which affects us the more powerfully and stirs all our vital forces the more deeply, the vaguer and more mysterious its language is.*[14]

We are now on the high road of Romanticism, with its insistence on the power of immediate emotional experience and response, its openness to aesthetic states that are parallel to, even informed by, physical and sexual passion, the feeling not just of the listener's auditory experience of pleasure but of a oneness with the music as a mysterious art that can evoke such altered states. Wackenroder directly anticipated E. T. A. Hoffmann, whose commentaries on Beethoven's Fifth Symphony, *Coriolanus*, and other instrumental works shaped for generations a view of Beethoven as a seer who had the power to unlock deeply rooted emotional secrets and states of inwardness, to move his listeners to the depths of their souls.

The larger progression of thought that leads from the aesthetic of gratification to that of involvement took place precisely during the years of Beethoven's early maturity. It was an intellectual change that he understood and in which he felt himself to be a protagonist. That it finds partial resonance in his own earlier development seems to me self-evident, even though the works that his contemporaries saw as its strongest expressions—the Third and Fifth Symphonies—were still to come. But the piano sonatas and other chamber music of the later 1790s breathe an atmosphere akin to that of the Romantics, especially in stormy and passionate works such as the Piano Sonata Opus 2 No. 1, the slow movement of the Piano Trio Opus 1 No. 2, and all of the C-minor works—the Piano Trio Opus 1 No. 3, the String Trio Opus 9, and the "Pathétique" Sonata. A little further on, the same spirit inhabits the Piano Sonata Opus 10 No. 3 and the String Quartet Opus 18 No. 1, especially their tragic slow movements, not to mention the hypnotic Adagio of the "Moonlight" Sonata. And by 1802, the year of the Heiligenstadt Testament, mystery and emotional transport are evident in the Piano Sonatas Opus 31 No. 2 (The "Tempest") and the E-flat major Sonata Opus 31 No. 3, as well as the Piano Variations Opp. 34 and 35. The Second Symphony is the most ambitious product of the same intensified atmosphere.

If Beethoven's career had ended in 1801, ten years after Mozart's death, he would still be regarded as the most important composer of his time. Except for opera, he had composed in every major genre, from choral music (the two Bonn cantatas) to songs to chamber music with and without piano, string quartets, and symphonies. His role as Mozart's successor was no longer a prophecy but a truth, though he never lost his awareness of how far he still had to travel or his wonder at Mozart's mastery. Eleven years later, in 1812, he was writing that "Haydn and Mozart [have] their laurel wreaths [and] are entitled to theirs, but I am not yet entitled to one."[15] Whatever his personal problems with the aging Haydn in matters of career, temperament, and ambition, Beethoven saw Haydn as a true mentor, the creator of the modern language of tonal composition in the later-eighteenth-century sense. By the 1790s Beethoven had learned enough from both Mozart and Haydn to see that his own path to the future lay no longer in assimilating but in augmenting their methods and achievements with his own innovations, despite occasional bluntness and rough edges. Still, it would take time for him to become fully comfortable with his own accomplishments, the more so since his instrumental music continued to inhabit the same genres as that of Haydn and Mozart.

For Beethoven as pianist and composer, Mozart's late piano concertos formed Olympian models that he sought at first to emulate in his own concertos, inevitably falling short of Mozart's balance, finish, and fertility, but in the process discovering his own strengths. The Second Piano Concerto comes off as a hybrid, partly his own, partly still a Mozartian imitation. The First is a substantial step forward in strength and vigor, and the Third breaks new ground in regions where Mozart had never traveled—in its dramatization of musical ideas, its juxtapositions of intensity with lyricism, its decisive contrasts that differ from those of Mozart's C Minor Concerto, its obviously strong model. We can readily believe that Beethoven said to J. B. Cramer a few years later, when hearing the Mozart C Minor Concerto, "Ah, Cramer, we will never be able to do anything like that." Beethoven's Mozartian problem was once summed up by Brahms, apropos of these very works, in a conversation reported to have taken place in 1896:

> Yes, the C Minor [Mozart] Concerto: a marvelous work of art and filled with inspired ideas! I also find that, for example, Beethoven's C Minor Concerto is much smaller and weaker than Mozart's. You know how much I revere Beethoven! I perfectly understand that Beethoven's new personality and the new viewpoint that his works disclosed to the public, seemed to them greater and more significant. But already fifty years later [c. 1850] one had to alter that opinion. One had to distinguish the excitement of what was new from its inner value. I admit that the Beethoven concerto is more modern, but it is not as significant! I also see that Beethoven's First Symphony seemed so colossal to its first audiences. It has indeed a new viewpoint! But the last three Mozart symphonies are much more significant. Now and then people realize that this is so.[16]

Brahms's interlocutor, Richard Heuberger, continued by suggesting that the best Mozart quartets are more important than Beethoven's chamber music up to Opus 24, the "Spring" Sonata. Brahms agreed, and continued:

> Yes, the Razumovsky quartets, the later symphonies, that is another world. One can feel it already in the Second Symphony.[17]

Yet nevertheless, if Beethoven could possibly have imagined what his great successor might later say about the Third Piano Concerto, he might also have added (perhaps under his breath), "But even if my concerto as a formal and expressive whole doesn't stand on the same plateau with Mozart's C Minor Concerto, still, in some ways, and in my way, I have gone beyond him."

Beethoven's first maturity saw a marked separation between career aims and inner growth, because his burning ambition to achieve public recognition led him to publish a fair number of minor works written merely to please his audience. We can identify at least three strains in Beethoven's larger works. The first consists of those written for worldly success, in which he aimed to inaugurate an independent career but not to shock patrons or listeners too radically. This group comprises the first two piano concertos, the Septet, and the First Symphony. Then there is an intermediate class of works that show signs of higher imagination, though they were still designed to ingratiate. This group includes the songs, the many sets of variations, the easier sonatas and keyboard pieces, and some of the chamber music. A good example is the Quintet for Piano and Winds Opus 16, artfully but weakly modeled on its great Mozartian forebear, the Piano Quintet K. 452.

To the third category we can assign Beethoven's really original compositions, those produced entirely from within. Some of these break new ground, such as the Cello Sonatas Opus 5, or are radical contributions to sectors in which Mozart had excelled, such as the piano trios of Opus 1 and the violin sonatas of Opus 12. In this main line are the works that show the younger Beethoven in his first maturity, of which by far the most important are the early piano sonatas and the first string quartets. The sonatas show Beethoven at the keyboard as the master of all he can survey. Their counterparts are the Opus 18 quartets, in which he steps forward in another way as the successor of Haydn and Mozart.

If we look beyond genres to formal principles we see that the promise of the early piano quartets was fulfilled in the decade between 1790 and 1800. Extending a number of three-movement genres to four movements—the piano sonatas and early trios—Beethoven explored myriad uses of the sonata principle in the first movements of three- and four-movement cycles. At times beginning with terse, seemingly unpromising short ideas punctuated by rests and pauses, he is able to develop such short themes in larger sections and paragraphs that build his movements additively, section by section, without resorting to the simpler repetitions and sequences that mark the work of so many of his contemporaries. Enlarging inherited frames and planning his works as wholes, he balances longer and highly developed first movements with varied later movements, especially enlivening his finales with new formal schemes. Many early slow movements, either sectional forms or variations, display a sureness of touch in melodic writing and elaboration that rivals that of his predecessors, while his ability to move listeners to introspection through memorable melody is manifest in such compositions as the singing slow movements of the Piano Trio Opus 1 No. 2 and the "Pathétique" Sonata. The scherzi or fast minuets are imaginative, ingenious, and anything but perfunctory. The range of character he achieves in finales, as he either replicates the basic Allegro tempo of a first movement or moves on to still faster tempos, brings many an early work to a convincing close, rounding out the whole with the fulfillment of all expectations built up along the way.

The sketch process enabled Beethoven to plan the shape of entire sections rapidly, then fill out the substance after he had conceived the outline. It also enabled him to work out alternative strategies of development, whether of single motives, thematic units, larger sections, or even entire expositions and development sections. We can see this technique in many a bundle of sketch pages for works as early as the late 1780s, and we see it intensified as the pile of finished major works rose higher during the 1790s. That Beethoven accepted the basic formal conventions and movement types of his predecessors in no way implies a conservative view, since he was bursting with ways to fill these formal husks with surprising and original content.

The picture is partially revealed if we take a measured look at the reviews of his early works in contemporary musical journals, including the *Allgemeine Musikalische Zeitung*, a conservative journal founded by the ambitious Friedrich Rochlitz in 1798 and published by no less a firm than Breitkopf & Härtel. To some reviewers the young Beethoven, appearing with his first published works in 1795, seemed a brilliant new star, but within a few more years they thought he had veered far off course. Thus the Opus 1 piano trios of 1795 were praised in 1806 as being "strong, powerful and moving," but the same review holds that his "later piano works"—meaning works such as the "Waldstein" and "Appassionata" sonatas, have become "incomprehensible, abrupt, and dark . . . much of it is enormously difficult without there being some exceptional beauty to compensate for it."[18] Similar complaints were lodged over the Second Symphony, as when a Leipzig critic in 1805 reported that "we, like others in

Vienna and Berlin, find the whole too long and some things over-written. . . . [T]he frequent use of all wind instruments hinders the effect of many fine places and we regard the finale . . . as all too bizarre, wild, and ugly."[19]

To others Beethoven was a dangerous radical from the start. A full-bodied trifle such as the Clarinet Trio Opus 11 was reluctantly praised by a conservative reviewer in 1799, who found it "more flowing than many other works by this composer."[20] And some of the more difficult works evoked cries of horror, like those expressed in print about the Opus 12 violin sonatas. Beethoven was very angry with his reviewers, and in 1801 he wrote to Breitkopf & Härtel to complain, asking them to

advise your critics to be more circumspect and intelligent, particularly with regard to the productions of young authors. For many a one may become dispirited who otherwise might have risen to higher things. For myself, far be it from me to think that I have attained such a degree of perfection as to be beyond criticism. The outcry of your critics against me was humiliating. Yet when I began to compare myself to other composers, I could hardly bring myself to pay any attention to it. Still I remained quite quiet, and said to myself, "they do not know anything about music." And I had all the more reason for being quiet when I saw how certain people were being praised to the skies who here [in Vienna] have very little standing.[21]

PART THREE

THE SECOND MATURITY

1802–1812

CHAPTER 9

BEETHOVEN IN THE NEW AGE

❧•⊷⊶≺∣∋⊷⊶•❧

Napoleon and Self-Made Greatness

The new age promised by the French Revolution was soon darkened, first by the Terror and then by the rise of Napoleon, who pledged republicanism and delivered despotism. France expanded its ambitions with successive attempts to dominate the Continent by force, while the loosely allied opposing powers—mainly Britain, Prussia, and Austria—struggled desperately to stop Napoleon's armies. The Austrian regime faced the dual problem of mounting a war effort to resist France's political and military ambitions, and of stemming subversive Jacobin sympathies within its own population.

By 1800, Napoleon had risen from obscurity to glory in just a few years, astounding Europe with his ferocious energy and military brilliance and arousing fear and admiration on all sides. He gained power in successive stages. After the ruling Directory had run its course from 1795 to 1799, he became First Consul in 1799 on the 18th Brumaire (November 9) by ruthless means. Over the next five years he seized increasing personal control of government. In 1804 he crowned himself emperor, creating a new regime that reframed and modernized French political and cultural life while he launched further military campaigns across Europe. After years of victories, his glory peaked around 1810, by which time the "Greater French Empire" included all of Spain, most of Italy, much of western and central Germany, the Swiss cantons, and a large part of modern Poland. His main enemies were now Britain and Russia, plus a few Mediterranean territories. But in large measure Europe lay in Napoleon's hands until 1812, when his

Napoleon as emperor, in an 1812 oil portrait by Jacques-Louis David. (National Gallery, Washington, D.C., Kress Collection)

ill-fated invasion of Russia started his downward spiral, ending in his abdication and exile in 1814, when the French Senate recalled Louis XVIII. Ten months later came his famous escape from Elba, the "Hundred Days," and Waterloo in June 1815.[1]

Throughout these years a lasting Napoleonic myth was in the making, firing the imaginations of contemporaries and of later apostles of individualism and self-reliance such as Thomas Carlyle and Ralph Waldo Emerson. The image of Napoleon, associated at first with military and political genius, stood essentially for self-made greatness. This image lived on and even grew in stature after 1814, when his fading career became an epic tragedy that ended with the downfall of the hero and the return to political stagnation. What remained was the universally admired image of the little Corsican who had come up from nothing to make himself emperor of Europe. His career implied that liberty, equality, and fraternity were unquestioned abstract virtues, but that real power could flow into the hands of one man if that man was intelligent and ruthless enough and if he made the most of every possible opportunity. As one modern historian put it:

> The great known world-shakers of the past had begun as kings like Alexander or patricians like Julius Caesar, but Napoleon was the "little corporal" who rose to rule a continent by sheer personal talent. . . . Every young intellectual who devoured books, as the young Bonaparte had done, wrote bad poems and novels, and adored Rousseau could henceforth see the sky as his limit, laurels surrounding his monogram. Every businessman henceforth had a name for his ambition; to be . . . a "Napoleon of finance" or industry. All common men were thrilled by the sight, then unique, of a common man who became greater than those born to wear crowns.[2]

In this time of accelerating political and cultural change, no one could remain aloof. To younger artists, poets, and writers everywhere, Napoleon evoked hope and fear, hero-worship and dislike, but above all a triumphant example of individual achievement. It was true that his march to power and the implacable character of that march—especially his overthrow of the government in November 1799 and the deliberate murder of the Duc d'Enghien for being a supposed member of a Bourbon plot against Napoleon—disillusioned the liberals among his admirers. Among artists it confirmed an innate distrust of politicians and their feeling of dissociation from the brutal realities of politics. Dreaming of their imagined ability to influence their times, they consoled themselves with their self-concept as "unacknowledged legislators of the world," a phrase from Shelley that resonates with Beethoven's feeling about himself. Witness his remark to his friend Krumpholz about Napoleon, "It's a shame that I do not understand the art of war as well as I do the art of music. I would conquer him."[3] Beethoven's lifelong attitude to Napoleon oscillated between admiration and dislike, between approval and revulsion, but it always carried a feeling of strong personal identification with a contemporary whose colossal ambition, will to power, and sense of destiny, however differently revealed, seemed to mirror his own.

For those living in the states opposed to France, censorship made open expression of sympathy difficult. Police spies and agents were everywhere in imperial Vienna. The publisher Hoffmeister asked Beethoven in April 1802 to write a sonata with a program embodying ideas or events drawn from the French Revolution. The composer answered in the sharp manner of a disenchanted liberal:

> *Has the devil got hold of you all, gentlemen?—that you suggest that I should compose such a sonata?—Well, perhaps at the time of the revolutionary fever—such a thing might have been possible, but now, when everything is trying to slip back into the old rut, now that Bonaparte has concluded his Concordat with the Pope—to write a sonata of this kind? Ho, ho—there you must leave me out—you won't get anything from me.*[4]

Yet in the fall of 1803, as Beethoven worked on his Third Symphony, he planned to take the unprecedented step of associating it publicly with Napoleon, as we know from an October 22 letter from Ferdinand Ries to Beethoven's old friend Simrock in Bonn and from the symphony's original title page.[5] Ries declares that Beethoven was "very much inclined to dedicate it to Bonaparte," or, if Prince Lobkowitz were to pay him a higher fee and keep it for six months as his own, then Beethoven would give him the dedication but would name the work after Bonaparte.

Although there is good reason to connect this proposed dedication and title with Beethoven's hopes of an appointment in Paris, reflecting his characteristic way of blending personal idealism with practical calculation, it was nevertheless an unusual gesture on his part to recognize Napoleon as a military hero and now as First Consul, effectively the ruling figure of France. The French, after all, had defeated the Austrians in Italy two years earlier in a victory that had led to the Treaty of Lunéville. This agreement humbled the Austrian regime and forced the Emperor Francis II to cede vast imperial tracts to French control, especially in Italy. Austrian war weariness and financial weakness had already been visible in the 1790s, when the war of the "first coalition" nearly brought the imperial treasury to bankruptcy and led to Austria's cessation of hostilities in 1796. Then in March 1799 war broke out again, lasting three more years. From 1802 to

1805, however, another period of comparative peace reigned, during which Austria once more struggled to regain its financial stability and find ways to meet the threat from France. In these years, Austrian foreign policy may even have leaned more toward neutrality and acceptance of Napoleon's conquests up to this time than toward further resistance.[6]

It is noteworthy that Beethoven never thought to name any work, let alone this symphony, after the emperor of Austria, nicknamed "Francis the Good."[7] The glow of the Napoleonic image was all the more apparent when seen against the mediocrity of his opposite numbers who headed the regimes he was aiming to overthrow. Although Francis was liked by his subjects for his simple manner and lack of grandiose ambitions, nothing about him stirred the contemporary mind with anything like the astonishment and admiration felt for Napoleon all across Europe.[8]

Even though Beethoven withdrew the dedication to Napoleon in the following year, the main point at this stage is that in the autumn of 1803 he

Title page of a manuscript copy of the Eroica *Symphony showing Beethoven's autograph annotations and his erasure of the original dedication to Napoleon Bonaparte. (Bibliothek der Gesellschaft, der Musikfreunde, Vienna)*

still considered it appropriate to attach Bonaparte's name to a new and monumental symphony that, according to Ries, he considered "the greatest work he has yet written."[9] Even apart from Beethoven's disillusionment with Napoleon after he had made himself emperor in 1804 and abandoned all pretense of republicanism, any remotely lingering idea of naming or dedicating a work to the great political and military nemesis had evaporated by the time the symphony was published—in October 1806, when Austria was once again at war with Napoleon.

In any case, the original idea of naming so important a work after a living political leader reflects Napoleon's personal stature and Beethoven's enormous respect. It meant that the work would in some way embody the spirit Beethoven saw or hoped to see in the man. Almost every published work by Beethoven carried a dedication, always intended to gain favor from the recipient, sometimes to obtain money and on rare occasions as an expression of genuine affection, as with the sonata Opus 81a for his gentle and gifted royal pupil Archduke Rudolph and his dedication of the *Diabelli* Variations to Antonie Brentano. But at no other time did Beethoven contemplate naming a major instrumental composition for a living patron, no matter what dividends he might have hoped to reap from it. Thus, the "Waldstein" Sonata was dedicated to Count Waldstein but not named for him. *Wellingtons Sieg* (Wellington's victory), a seeming exception, is really in a separate category, since it is hardly a musical composition in the higher sense; rather, it is a sound-effects example of descriptive program music celebrating a specific military event, not a symbolic "representation" of the higher qualities of a hero.[10] Two earlier examples, the funeral cantata for the Emperor Joseph II and its companion cantata for Leopold II, were not symphonic works but texted tributes that marked the death of one emperor and the crowning of his successor. French postrevolutionary composers of the time wrote similar compositions to commemorate public figures, civilian or military, who had passed away. Such works include Gossec's *Marche lugubre* for the funeral of Mirabeau and Cherubini's *Hymne et marche funèbre* for the death of General Hoche. But although both have been associated with the *Eroica* Funeral March, neither was an abstract symphony named for a living hero.[11]

If the idea of a "Bonaparte" symphony had lasted, it would have been a more radical departure for the genre than the eventual title *Sinfonia Eroica* turned out to be. Napoleon in these years seemed to be a worldly counterpart of what Beethoven imagined his own role in the world of music could become, thus his ambivalence in later years. Although he tore up his dedication of the symphony in 1804, five years later a French official, Baron de Trémont, visited Beethoven and wrote:

> [T]hrough all his resentment I could see that he admired [Napoleon's] rise from such obscure beginnings. . . . [H]e said, "if I go to Paris, will I have to salute your Emperor?" I assured him that he would not, unless commanded for an audience. This question made me think that, despite his opinion, he would have been flattered by any sign of distinction from Napoleon.[12]

Much later, on learning of Napoleon's death at St. Helena in 1821, Beethoven was heard to say, "I have already composed the music for that catastrophe." Three years after that, Czerny reports accompanying Beethoven to a coffeehouse in Baden. Reacting to a newspaper announcement of Sir Walter Scott's *Life of Napoleon*, Beethoven is quoted as saying, "Napoleon; earlier I couldn't have tolerated him. Now I think completely differently."[13]

Beethoven and His Milieu

In 1803 Beethoven was thirty-two years old. Despite his troubling deafness he was a confident artist, the new and apparently unrivaled master of instrumental composition, stepping forward on the Viennese and European musical stages as the new century began. His self-assurance was now so great that he could already envision a complete edition of his works.[14] Such an edition would give him leverage with publishers, provide a steady income, and enable him to establish control over the definitive texts of his works, a nagging problem in view of the publishers' perpetual mistakes. The project came to nothing, as did similar attempts in later years. But the point of strongest interest is that in 1803, before completion of his Third Symphony, his Opus 59 Quartets, or the "Waldstein" and

Beethoven in 1802 in a miniature on ivory by Christian Horneman. (Beethoven-Haus, Bonn, Collection H. C. Bodmer)

"Appassionata" sonatas, publishers were vying for his works, knowing that profits were in it for them. In little more than ten years since coming to Vienna he had fully established himself in instrumental music despite mixed reviews from conservative critics; and he was making plans to break into opera. On March 30 he put on a concert in the Theater an der Wien that included his First and Second Symphonies, the Third Piano Concerto, and the hastily composed oratorio *Christus am Ölberge*.[15] The critics had varied reactions, as usual, but one of them admired the oratorio and offered the prescient remark that "it confirms my long-held opinion that Beethoven in time can effect a revolution in music like Mozart's. He is hastening toward this goal with great strides."[16]

To envisage Beethoven the man, we can begin with his physical appearance, which to later generations became the stuff of legend, as the standard image in the public mind prominently featured his stocky, muscular frame, resolute facial expression, and aura of power. This depiction fits the heroic idea of Beethoven that was cultivated in the later nineteenth century, of which Max Klinger's Beethoven monument of 1902 is the quintessential expression.[17] The first mature portrait of Beethoven, painted by Willibrord Joseph Mähler in 1804–5 is an exercise in myth creation.[18] It is the first of two portraits by Mähler, who did the second a decade later (three versions of the second portrait survive).[19] The earlier picture, which stems from classical formulas for portraying musicians of rank, shows a strong, sturdy young man, sitting erect on a chair, his gaze intensely fixed on the viewer, holding a species of lyre in his left hand while (as Mähler put it in a later description) his right hand appears to beat time. The hands, with long tapering fingers, are very prominent, reflecting the subject's pianistic virtuosity. The lyre connects with the temple of Apollo in the background (Mähler's description) and a mysterious landscape with a blasted tree—thus combining neoclassical and early Romantic background symbols in a portrait in which the primary figure dominates the pictorial space.[20] That Beethoven prized the portrait is clear from a letter he wrote to Mähler in 1804; having lent the painting to the artist, he asked for its return: "I have promised it to a stranger, a lady who saw the portrait at my place, so that she may have it in her room for a few weeks while she is in Vienna—and who can resist such charming advances? It is clearly understood, of course, that if all kinds of favors are going to be bestowed on me for this, your share will not be forgotten—Wholly your Bthvn."[21]

That the portrait could charm a female admirer only underscores how much it idealized his actual appearance, which was not nearly so captivating. His Bonn acquaintances Gottfried and Cäcilia Fischer, whose family had owned the house in which Beethoven grew up, described Beethoven later as being "short and thickset, broad across the shoulders, short neck, large head, rounded nose, dark-brown complexion; he always leaned forward a little in walking. In his boyhood they used to call him 'der Spagnol' in our house."[22] From other descriptions we know that he was short, that is, about Napoleon's height, and that his face bore marks, perhaps from smallpox. However, a medical description of a life mask made in 1812 reported that his face also showed other lesions and indentations.[23]

These physical features—a man short, stocky, powerfully built, a "genial savage" in Alessandra Comini's words—reappear in some later likeness, for example in an engraving by Blasius Höfel made around 1814. By this time Beethoven was forty-three, and Höfel's portrait shows us the composer in his maturity; his face is fuller and he appears, handsomely dressed, in an attitude of intense and severe concentration, his eyes sharply focused. From then on other portraits, like a slowly unfolding film sequence, depict a progressively aging man, ill and debilitated, hair whitening, facial expression less resolute and more resigned. We see this figure in many of the later portraits, above all Mähler's of 1815 and Waldmüller's of 1823, in which Beethoven has aged almost beyond recognition.

Beethoven's deafness, his most lasting physical ailment, was the one with the strongest psychological consequences. Other deaf artists, such as Goya, were not impeded by it in their professional lives in anything like the same degree as a composer-pianist like Beethoven.[24] His other ailments also pursued him throughout his life, some having started in Bonn in his troubled teenage years. Because he speaks of them repeatedly in his correspondence, as he probably did in his conversations with friends, we know that they not only loomed large in his daily life but were prominent in the eyes of contemporaries, forming an image that was transmitted first by his students and others close to him and later by his biographers and other commentators. His hearing difficulties, from their inception in the late

Beethoven, holding a lyre and depicted against a Romantic landscape, in an 1804 portrait by Willibrord Joseph Mähler. (Vienna, Historisches Museum)

1790s, continued as a chronic condition, sometimes worsening and sometimes stabilized; but his hearing was not wholly destroyed. His situation was probably something like that described by the twentieth-century poet David Wright, who became deaf in boyhood and wrote, forty years later:

> I do not live in a world of complete silence. There is no such thing as
> absolute deafness. Coming from one whose aural nerve is extinct, this
> statement may be taken as authoritative. . . . [T]he list of things audible
> or at least interfering with the silence . . . [includes] . . . gunfire, deto-
> nation of high-explosive [sic], . . . carts clattering over cobblestones. . . .[25]

Beethoven suffered from earaches and ringing in the ears, a form of tinnitus. Loud noises were painful to him. His fear and depression over losing social contact through deafness, a leitmotif in his letters to Wegeler and Amenda and in the Heiligenstadt Testament, probably never abated, but at times he may have felt that his increasing isolation from some of the frivolity and hypocrisy of the social world could have its benefits. On a sketch leaf of 1806, when he was busy composing the second version of *Leonore* and the Quartet Opus 59 No. 3, Beethoven wrote:

> Even as you tumble into the whirlpool of society here, even so it is pos-
> sible for you to write operas despite all social obstacles—Let your deaf-
> ness no longer be a secret—even in art.[26]

Between about 1803 and 1812 he could still play marvelously, and his ability to improvise continued for many years thereafter. In 1808 he was still able to play the first performance of the Fourth Piano Concerto. It is true that the premiere of the Fifth, in 1811, was given by Friedrich Schneider, but by then the work had already been published by Breitkopf & Härtel, and since the performance took place in the publisher's city, Leipzig, far away from Vienna, Beethoven could not have played it there in any case. His ability to perform in public certainly declined by about 1811–12, but his last known public appearance as a pianist was as late as 1815, when he played for the assembled heads of state at the Congress of Vienna, accompanying a singer in his early song "Adelaide." Yet despite his limitations he conducted rehearsals of the *Eroica* and of *Leonore*, and he could still hear and judge details of piano performance by others.

It was only after 1812 that his perception of speech deteriorated to the point that people had to shout; beginning around 1816 he had to use an ear trumpet. In 1818, at the age of forty-seven, he began to use conversation books. These were tablets or bundles of note paper, sometimes single folded sheets, on which visitors would write down questions and remarks of all kinds, with Beethoven answering aloud, unless he wanted not to be heard, as he sometimes did, in which case he wrote an answer himself. He continued to play the piano, at least for himself, all his life, and on a sketch leaf of 1811 he wrote a memo to himself to procure a "small piano for composing."[27]

Other nagging physical complaints persisted, some probably psychosomatic. He complained of abdominal distress during the Bonn years and told Wegeler in 1801 that in Vienna it had become worse.[28] He suffered from intermittent illness and recurrent bouts of bronchitis. But the real deterioration of his health took place after 1815, the year of his brother Carl's death from consumption at the age of forty-one. From then on Beethoven's health plummeted, resulting in a series of infections, probably a form of colitis, that lasted until his death in 1827. Assessing the known evidence of Beethoven's health, Edward Larkin concluded that "the whole story is consistent with connective tissue disease and immunopathy."[29] Larkin doubts the theories of chronic alcoholism, despite the evidence of cirrhosis; tales of syphilis, along with other theories, have been widely advanced but never confirmed. What is certain is that Beethoven's health in his mature years was marked by recurrent physical ailments, some of them quite debilitating, by emotional stress, hypochondria, and an aggressiveness that, at times, spiraled out of control.[30]

Regarding his illnesses and deafness, the central point to keep in mind is that despite all his troubles during these years, Beethoven maintained a rigorous schedule of work, virtually without significant lapses; he produced a consistent body of works of unparalleled quality in a variety of genres (along with many less important works); and he continued to advance artistically, far beyond even his most original earlier work. Thayer writes eloquently that

> there is something in truth nobly heroic in the manner in which Beethoven at length rose superior to his great affliction. The magnificent series of works produced in the ten years from 1798 to 1808 are no greater monuments to his genius than to the godlike resolution with which he wrought out the inspirations of that genius under circumstances most fitted to weaken its efforts and restrain its energies.[31]

Nor was there yet in evidence the stone deafness, the pathetic isolation, the eccentricity, and the serious loss of emotional equilibrium that came in the later years as he moved inward to a silent world of musical thought.

Despite his tendency to isolation and his afflictions, Beethoven's circle of friends expanded between 1802 and 1812. It included literary figures such as Heinrich Joseph von Collin, the Viennese playwright, for whose tragedy *Coriolan* Beethoven wrote his overture and whom Beethoven addressed in letters as his "brother in Apollo."[32] Another trusted friend, and there were not many, was Ignaz von Gleichenstein (1778–1828), who worked in the same government office as Beethoven's old friend from Bonn, Stephan von Breuning, and to whom he dedicated the Cello Sonata Opus 69.[33] A different kind of personal chemistry, typical of Beethoven's bearish and aggressive style with his acquaintances, bound him to Nikolaus Zmeskall von Domanovecs, a Hungarian cellist, chamber music enthusiast, and sometime quartet composer, who had received the dedication of Haydn's Opus 20 Quartets in an Artaria edition of 1800 and to whom in 1816 Beethoven dedicated his Opus 95 (like Haydn's Opus 20 No. 5 also in F minor), naming him as "among my oldest friends in Vienna."[34] Zmeskall, who had a family title of baron, made himself available for help with petty tasks; his jovial manner could alleviate Beethoven's blacker moods. All this is clear from the booming jocularity of Beethoven's many notes and letters to him over the years, calling him "Count of Music" and "Baron Dirt-Driver," and blaming him for his "Zmeskallian-Domanoveczian gabble."[35]

On a far less intimate level, for the most part, were his male aristocratic patrons, a few of whom generously gave him financial support; other patrons, whom he treated with the deference and disdain with which a self-absorbed and ambitious artist treats amateurs; and the many others to whom he simply offered dedications. His financial support came from the princes Kinsky and Lobkowitz, and from the young Archduke Rudolph. Among them they bestowed an annuity of four thousand florins on him in 1809, when there was danger that he might accept a position from Jerome Bonaparte, the younger brother of Napoleon who had been installed in Kassel as "King of Westphalia." Even though in the long run only the arch-duke kept his financial promise, the gesture by these three indicated where Beethoven stood in the eyes of Vienna's music patrons, above all in such troubled times.

Then there were patrons whom he flattered with dedications, expect-ing that they would respond with gifts of money or something else of value. For the most part Beethoven decided on a dedication when a work was accepted for publication, whereupon he would tell his publishers to whom each work should be inscribed on the decorative title page. Big and impor-tant works, such as symphonies, went to wealthy and powerful patrons, such as Prince Lobkowitz, who received the dedications of the *Eroica*, the Triple Concerto, the Quartet Opus 74, and the song cycle *An die ferne Geliebte*; Lobkowitz also shared with Count Razumovsky the dedications of the Fifth and Sixth Symphonies. It was of course Razumovsky whose name became attached to the Opus 59 Quartets in 1806, but the following year, Beethoven thought for a while of transferring them to Prince Lichnowsky, his former generous patron, who also happened to be Razumovsky's brother-in-law. But the plan fell through, and the quartets remained the "Razumovskys."[36]

Beethoven was often ready to negotiate: he "gave" the Fourth Sym-phony to Count Oppersdorf, a wealthy country nobleman, for a fee of five hundred ducats on the usual understanding that after six months Beetho-ven was free to publish it. He had originally promised the count the Fifth Symphony and received a fee for it but changed his mind and offered it to Breitkopf, apologizing to the count in a letter.[37] Sometimes the publishers would act on their own regarding a dedication, as when Breitkopf & Här-tel went ahead and dedicated Beethoven's Choral Fantasy, Opus 80, to King Maximilian Joseph of Bavaria, whereupon Beethoven complained about being bypassed. "If you intended by this action to pave the way for an honorable present to me, then I thank you for it; but if not, then such a dedication does not suit me at all. . . . [O]ne is not supposed to dedicate anything to kings without their permission."[38] He dedicated many works, important and unimportant, to members of aristocratic families, keeping up contacts and perhaps receiving gifts accordingly. Some works he dedicated sincerely to fellow artists, such as the poet Friedrich Matthison and the playwright Heinrich Joseph von Collin, or to personal friends, without any thought of money. Some works were published without any dedications at all, including the Piano Sonata Opus 54 and, surprisingly, the Eighth Symphony.

Since Beethoven's financial well-being and the growth of his reputation depended essentially on his success in selling his music, he spent great energy on negotiating with publishers. He demanded the highest initial payment he could for each work and kept publishers' interest alive with accessible works while trying to sell them his larger and less salable ones. In short, he maintained a full-scale business correspondence, aided by a few close friends and by his brothers. The two major local firms for him in the middle years were the Bureau d'Arts et d'Industrie in Vienna, which published many of his works with opus numbers in the fifties, and Breitkopf & Härtel in Leipzig, which published many of his major works bearing opus numbers from the sixties through the eighties, including the Fifth and Sixth Symphonies, the Cello Sonata Opus 69, the two Trios Opus 70, the Choral Fantasy, and the two large choral works, the oratorio *Christus am Ölberge* and the Mass in C.

Relations with Women

Beethoven's relations with women have become the stuff of endless speculation, some of it poignant and some of it prurient. Articles, books, and films have explored what is known and believed about his love affairs, focusing above all on a quest to identify the "Immortal Beloved," to whom Beethoven wrote the most famous, most notorious of all his letters.

Much of the literature on this subject reflects the assumption that a lonely male genius of Beethoven's artistic stature had a lifelong yearning to establish a permanent loving relationship with a woman who could in some way redeem him from his misery. That he did have such yearnings is hardly in doubt; that he also remained incapable of establishing any such relationship, and that he never did so, is undeniable.

To make a long and complex story short, we begin with the hardly surprising fact that in his youth in Bonn, Beethoven pursued love affairs with local girls. Franz Wegeler, no doubt being discreet about an old friend, wrote, "Beethoven was never out of love," and Ries allows that "he was very frequently in love but usually only for a short time."[39] Once in Vienna, Beethoven continued as before but his affairs were usually with women of higher social standing than his own, perhaps as a way of fulfilling his upward-striving ambitions but keeping marriage out of the question. The essential character of Beethoven's relations over his lifetime with women seems to have combined perpetual quest for love and perpetual avoidance of any long-term commitment that might change his life and rob him of the time and energy he needed for his work. Women could be part of his life but not part of his career. This ambivalence was no doubt exacerbated by his deafness, which made him increasingly irascible and difficult. His rising fame and achievements should have made him an attractive catch, but some women, at least, saw him as a less than ideal lover and most of them must have seen that he would be a difficult husband. Thus Magdalena Willman, a singer from Bonn, to whom he proposed in 1795, before the onset of his deafness, turned him down (as her niece later told Thayer) "because he was so ugly and half crazy."[40]

We know of further involvements. A mutual infatuation with his young piano student Giulietta Guicciardi began in 1801, when she was sixteen, and faded in 1803, a year after he had dedicated the "Moonlight" Sonata to her. In 1804 he went through a period of intense attachment to the recently widowed Countess Josephine Deym, née Brunsvik, whose older sister, Therese Brunsvik, was also an occasional piano student of Beethoven's. That Beethoven fell in and out of love with his female piano students should surprise no one, but Josephine did not reciprocate his feelings and, as she made clear in a letter, would not agree to sleep with him. In an affectionate and poignant letter, she wrote to assure him of her love for him, and continued:

> Do not tear my heart apart—do not try to persuade me further. I love you inexpressibly, as one gentle soul does another. Are you not capable of this covenant? I am not receptive to other [forms of] love for the present.[41]

And soon afterward she wrote again:

> Even before I knew you, your music made me enthusiastic for you—the goodness of your character, your affection increased it. This preference that you granted me, the pleasure of your acquaintance, would have been the finest jewel of my life if you could have loved me less sensually. That I cannot satisfy this sensual love makes you angry with me, [but] I would have had to violate holy bonds if I gave heed to your longings.[42]

When Josephine left Vienna for Budapest in 1806, their relationship dwindled, and in 1807, when she returned to Vienna, they broke off contact after a few more letters.[43]

Still other disappointments included his futile courtship of Therese Malfatti in 1810, who turned down his proposal. As he said of himself in a bitter note to Gleichenstein in 1810, "For you, poor Beethoven, no happiness can come from outside; you must create it in yourself. Only in the ideal world can you find friends."[44]

Seeking love and companionship but fearful of commitment, unable to form a lasting relationship with any one woman but moving impulsively into liaisons that failed to prosper or lead to marriage—this was the pattern of pursuit and separation that characterized Beethoven's romantic life during this most productive period of his life. His perpetual need to concentrate on his work in isolation and privacy, coupled with his fear of loneliness and lack of physical and psychic fulfillment, came to a crisis in 1812. At Teplitz he poured out his heart in a passionate love letter to the unnamed "Immortal Beloved," as he called her in the letter, which like the

Heiligenstadt Testament, was discovered in his private papers after his death. Efforts to identify the woman have brought on an avalanche of speculative commentary, predictably the largest on any subject in the Beethoven literature. By 1964, the year of Elliot Forbes's revision of Thayer's biography, the list was headed by four candidates: Giulietta Guicciardi, Amalie Sebald, Therese von Brunsvik, and Josephine von Brunsvik-Deym-Stackelberg. Since then more articles and books have rained down on this subject, but by far the most plausible and convincing case has been made by Solomon, whose proposed candidate, Antonie Brentano, has the strongest claim in the light of the available evidence.[45]

Antonie Brentano, née Birkenstock, who was ten years younger than Beethoven, belonged to a prominent Viennese family; her father had been court secretary to Emperor Joseph II. She married the Frankfurt merchant Franz Brentano in 1798 at the age of eighteen, moved with him to Frankfurt, and then returned to Vienna in 1809, remaining there until 1812. It was during these three years in Vienna that her intimate friendship with Beethoven and her enormous admiration for him would have grown, culminating in a love relationship they could not fulfill. As a sample of her esteem, consider this excerpt from a letter she wrote to Bishop Johann Michael Sailer in 1819, trying to enlist his help in finding a mentor for Beethoven's nephew Karl:

> *This great, excellent person, whose name I enclose herewith, who is greater as a human being than as an artist, has made it the greatest concern of his life to provide the best possible conditions [for his nephew] but with his soft heart, his glowing soul, his faulty hearing, with his deeply fulfilling profession as an artist . . . not even a tolerable patchwork has resulted.*[46]

"Greater as a human being than as an artist"—no one else in the panorama of Beethoven's friends and acquaintances ever characterized him that way. Quite the contrary, those who knew him well tended to justify his misanthropy and reclusiveness as consequences of his deafness and physical suffering. They also shared in the widespread belief, which certainly still persists, that an artistic genius is virtually expected to be narcissistic and anti-social, as demonstrated in Grillparzer's funeral oration:

> *Because he withdrew from the world they called him a man-hater, and because he held himself aloof from sentimentality, unfeeling. . . . He fled the world because, in the whole range of his loving nature, he found no weapon to oppose it. . . . He dwelt alone because he found no second Self.*[47]

If nothing else, Antonie Brentano's letter to Sailer conveys the sense that the writer was a woman who had the highest degree of affection and sympathy for Beethoven and could characterize him with unusual insight. Furthermore, Antonie was not only personally close to Beethoven but was also, as Solomon discovered, the recipient of the autograph manuscript of his song "An die Geliebte" ("To the Beloved") WoO 140. Among the recipients proposed for the "Immortal Beloved" letter, she is the prime candidate.[48]

Surely the most important biographical consequence of this letter is that it signals Beethoven's renunciation of any further attempt to marry or form a lasting love relationship. Nor was it accidental that the summer of 1812 coincided with a critical turning point in his creative career—the completion of the Eighth Symphony and the end of what we have come to see as his second maturity. By this time he had arrived at a crossroad in his artistic career. Even if he had stopped writing music after that, we would still have to reckon his achievements as the basic foundation for musical developments of the later nineteenth century. It is not surprising that Beethoven was showing signs of exhaustion. Quite possibly the personal crisis embodied in the "Immortal Beloved" letter was connected to his awareness of having arrived at this artistic turning point. The letter seems to say that he has reached an emotional impasse, with no clear indication of what his road might be. In music he would have the strength and resilience to make new discoveries, but only after a decline in productivity and an eventual change of direction. But in his relationship to women, there could now be only renunciation and stoic acceptance. Solomon notes that at the end of the main text of the letter Beethoven actually exhorts the woman to "cheer up—remain my true, my only treasure, my all as I am yours. The gods must send us the rest, what for us must and shall be."[49] Again he was relearning the Plutarchan lesson of resignation that had enabled him to come through the deafness crisis of 1801–2. That acceptance of his personal destiny, that equation of the heroic with endurance, had pointed the way to some of his most compelling musical achievements of the previous ten years.

CHAPTER 10

NEW SYMPHONIC IDEALS

>⊶⊷⊷⊱⟪⊰⊷⊷⊶⊷

The Heroic and the Beautiful

In the five years from 1798 to 1802 Beethoven transformed his style; in the next four he transformed music. Like Bach in Cöthen from 1717 to 1723, Haydn at Esterházy in the early 1770s, and Mozart in his first five years in Vienna, Beethoven now came fully of age, working imaginatively along new pathways while drawing organically on his earlier achievements. The consequences are writ large over all his major works between 1803 and 1806, and, in other ways, in those that followed up to about 1812. This long "second period" has been accepted as a unit—and as a unity—since Wilhelm von Lenz coined the idea of "Beethoven and his three styles" in 1852. It is the central phase of Beethoven's career, the time of origin of many of his most famous compositions. Among these are major orchestral works for the broadest possible public, above all the Third through the Eighth Symphonies and the three principal concertos—the Fourth and Fifth Piano Concertos and the Violin Concerto. This phase also witnessed his main theater music, including his opera, *Leonore*, the *Coriolanus* Overture, and the incidental music for Goethe's *Egmont*. In 1807 he wrote the Mass in C, his first true sacred work; and he published several important song collections on poems by Gellert, Goethe, and others. The principal second-period piano sonatas are the "Waldstein," Opus 53, the "Appassionata," Opus 57, and *Lebewohl*, Opus 81a, written for Archduke Rudolph. From his first phase as a quartet composer in Opus 18 he now moved on to the formidable "Razumovsky" Quartets, followed a few years later by the "Harp" Quartet in E-flat Major, Opus 74, and the F-minor

Quartet, Opus 95. He also produced important keyboard chamber music: the pair of Opus 70 Trios, the Opus 69 Cello Sonata, the Violin Sonata in G major, Opus 96, and the "Archduke" Piano Trio, Opus 97.

For many listeners this series forms the central experience of Beethoven. Launching one major artistic achievement after another, something like contemporary Napoleonic victories, he took command of the musical world and aroused an immense response. Once these works were in place, it was clear that he had found a range of voices that enlarged musical expression, pointed to the future, and reframed understanding of what had come before, both in his own earlier work and in that of his predecessors. With these compositions Haydn and Mozart became "classics." With these works, Beethoven's boldness and innovation in the 1790s almost began to look like a genial apprenticeship, although the best works of the first period stand up very well and are not displaced by anything that came later. Still, there is no doubt that what Beethoven achieved in the second period overwhelmed the musical world and established a new standard of emotional and intellectual completeness that has never been lost.

Mid-nineteenth-century listeners, for whom the works of the second period became an essential canon, found that they could not identify the same qualities in the more arcane and difficult works of his third period, above all the late piano sonatas and quartets, which even in the early twentieth century struck many as the products of a deaf genius buried in an inaccessible world. Although in later times we have come to entirely different assessments of the two outer periods, seeing in the first the seeds of much that came later and in the third glimpses of earlier ways of thought, the second-period Beethoven still holds the center of what could be called the ordinary experience of concert music. As Donald Francis Tovey put it in the early twentieth century:

> The distinguishing features of Beethoven's second style [using von
> Lenz's term] are the result of a condition of art in which enormous new
> possibilities have become so well known that there is no need for stating
> them abruptly, paradoxically, or emphatically, but also no need for
> working them out to remote conclusions. Hence these works have
> become for most people the best-known and best loved type of classical

*music. In their perfect fusion of untranslatable dramatic emotion with
every beauty of musical design and tone they have never been equaled.*[1]

The point is well taken. A number of works after Opus 30—the Piano
Sonatas Opus 31, the Opus 34 and Opus 35 piano variation sets, the Second Symphony, and above all the Third Piano Concerto—are studded
with moments and passages that split them off sharply from their late-
eighteenth-century antecedents, including Beethoven's own early works,
almost defining them as wayward and quixotic children of normal and tidy
parents. They abound in sudden and abrupt shifts of tone, key, and character of the musical material—witness the juxtaposition of keys in the Third
Concerto, with its E-major slow movement flanked by C minor in the first
and last, and, as noted earlier, with a deliberate play on the pitch equivalent
G♯ = A♭ as the slow movement ends and the finale begins. Similarly intense
contrasts appear in the Second Symphony, where the most boisterous of
first and last movements are able to contain a slow movement of unsurpassed smoothness and beauty. In the later, mainstream compositions of
the second period, however, these traits have largely disappeared, having
been assimilated into more balanced, mature, richly developed artworks.

The Third Symphony (Eroica)

As early as the summer of 1802, while finishing his sketches for the
E-flat Piano Variations, Opus 35—the "Prometheus" Variations, as
he called them—Beethoven jotted down some ideas for a possible third
symphony in E-flat.[2] That these first ideas for a cyclic work in the same key
directly follow his final sketches for Opus 35, in the same sketchbook, gives
the strong impression that the new plan is an immediate outgrowth of the
Variations. The sketches show a plan for the first three movements of a
cyclic work, but no finale. They begin with a patch of an idea for a slow
introduction; then an Allegro first movement, worked out to the end of the
exposition; then an Adagio sketch in C major marked "seconda" (second
movement); then ideas for a "Menuetto serioso" in the tonic with a Trio in
G minor. We can reasonably assume that Beethoven had no need to write

in an idea for the finale because the material of the "Prometheus" Variations was intended from the beginning to be used for the finale of the new work, and that is in fact what later happened.

Accordingly, we can regard the finale as the springboard for the plan of the symphony, the fixed point against which Beethoven elaborated the other movements.[4] It has long been obvious that the *Eroica* finale is in fact closely derived from the Opus 35 Variations.[3] It is also well understood that the last movement abandons the more rigid form of the classical variation set (which is still present though expanded in Opus 35) and becomes a blended form for which we have no name. The *Eroica* finale consists of a large introduction (labeled as such in Opus 35) that builds up the basic thematic material of the movement in stages. First, as in the piano variations, Beethoven establishes the bass of the theme—he literally calls it "Basso del Tema"—creating an expectation that must be fulfilled; then he handsomely fulfills it by adding the upper-line melody itself. The whole process is something like a mirror of Beethoven's compositional process in small, laid out for the world to see, in its gradual assemblage of an intelligible bass and melody in a simple song form. It could well have derived from an improvisation in which he first presented a bass, elaborated it as a bass with other voices, and then combined it with a main theme. The introduction also anticipates those other instances in which a great theme arrives as the culmination of a gradual process of preparation—two later examples are the slow movement of the Seventh Symphony and the long and complex preparation for the arrival of the "Ode to Joy" in the finale of the Ninth.

In the *Eroica* finale, this thematic preparation is followed by a set of variations on the theme and bass that include two fugato sections and a G-minor Alla marcia, then at length a large-scale Poco andante in the tonic E-flat major that serves as a special kind of formal and harmonic return. The Andante leads to remarkable excursions into remote harmonic regions, evoking memories of the most distant wanderings of the first movement and the coda of the massive slow movement. The later sketches show that Beethoven embarked on the final stages of working out the symphony's finale only after he had laid out his plans for the earlier movements in some detail, but always with Opus 35 in the background of the whole project.

In the winter of 1803–4 Beethoven plunged into full-time work on the symphony. It now grew to a length that dwarfed any previous symphony by him or anyone else. The first movement alone is almost the length of an entire early Haydn symphony, nearly seven hundred measures in Allegro con brio 3/4 (not counting the repeat of the exposition), during which it spans vast arches of musical space and traverses a wide range of keys. The first edition actually carried the composer's warning that, since "this symphony having been written to be longer than is usual, it should be performed closer to the beginning than near the end of a concert, because, if it is heard too late, after an overture, an aria, and a concerto, it may lose for audiences something of its own proper effect."[5] It is not only the first movement that is unusually long. Each movement is developed on a grand scale and each has its own contrasts and byways, producing the impression that four monumental pillars create the whole. The work expanded the time space of the symphony as never before, demanding an unprecedented degree of patience and concentration from concert audiences.

But what marks the *Eroica* as pathbreaking is not only its epic length. At least equally important is the unity of musical ideas that marks the first movement. Here Beethoven intensifies the relationships among the themes and motives of the first movement by placing at the beginning a small vocabulary of melodic intervals that present the main ideas of the movement (*W 19). He then draws on the same vocabulary to construct all the other themes, motives, and even transitions in the movement, including a new theme that appears in the development section. What results is a chain of subtly related ideas, giving this long work a unity that could not have been achieved by traditional means. In a larger sense, he has also greatly increased the developmental potential of the symphonic sonata form.

The exposition divides into six well-defined segments, five of them closing with an emphatic cadential passage that lands firmly on the tonic (*W 20). The exception, the third segment, is launched by a transition figure that lands on an unstable chord.[6] In the recapitulation, the same transition figure and segment reappear as a normal part of the return in the tonic of all the material that had been presented in the exposition in the dominant key. The *coup de théâtre* is reserved for much later.[7] The coda, as culmination, encompasses five segments of its own, building up from restatements of the first theme with new counterpoint through the return of the "new theme" from the development section, still more returns of other figures from the exposition, and finally, a peroration on the opening triadic theme that begins in the solo horn, traverses the first violins and the lower strings, and finally appears in full grandeur in the winds and trumpets as the music moves to what is expected to be the great cadence that ends the movement.[8] But one more stroke remains to be accomplished: in sudden *piano*, the third segment returns, in contrary motion, virtually the same as in the exposition and recapitulation, but now instead of leading to a diminished seventh, as always before, it lands squarely on a full-range dominant seventh, an arrival that serves as a long-range "resolution" of the moments of instability heard much earlier (*W 21). That this resolution comes so late, near the very end of the movement, shows the magnitude of the time span over which this connection is extended. Beethoven uses this connection to hold the fate of this passage at maximum tension, like a coiled spring, before releasing it at the last possible moment.

Another significant factor in the first movement, besides its motivic density, is its harmonic range, above all in the development section, by far the longest of any symphony written up to this time. This section also has room for another formal anomaly—the introduction of the new theme, which appears first in E minor and then in E-flat minor en route to the long dominant preparation that precedes the recapitulation. And just before that moment of formal return, we encounter a long preparation as the retransition prolongs the extended dominant harmony, gradually building up anticipation of the long-awaited tonic. While the strings are still playing a dominant seventh chord, the second horn enters with the first theme in the tonic. The resulting dissonance has us believe that the horn came in two bars too soon. That is exactly what Ries thought, and at the first rehearsal he burst out with the remark, "The damned horn player! Can't he count?"[9] Whereupon, as Ries recalls, Beethoven very nearly slapped him in the face. In fact, the horn entrance is not wrong but right, as it rubs a dissonant touch of the tonic into the prevailing dominant, seemingly breaking the tension but actually prolonging it, as if the hornist must break out of the dominant because the suspense is too great. Beethoven's sketches show that he worked out this passage in many different ways, but they also show that the idea of a tonic harmony inserted into the prevailing dominant was part of his conception from early on. Many other details are intelligible as part of a broad scheme in which elements in conflict arouse expectations of resolution that are then dramatized or postponed. This essential aspect of Beethovenian second-period formal design reaches its first great height in the *Eroica* first movement.

The slow movement shifts the perspective from heroic epic to tragedy and to the portrayal of heroism. The 1802 sketch models the slow movement as an Adagio in C major, but by the time of the "Eroica Sketchbook" of 1803–4 a lengthy Funeral March had taken its place. This change of plan clearly coincided with Beethoven's enlarging the "heroic" concept of the whole work, and in the sketchbook, the funeral music has become integral to the whole. The final result is a "Marcia funebre" of the highest seriousness, in C minor. No textbook formal scheme fits this expansive movement, yet its large-scale statement, counterstatement, and return, fit the current patterns of Beethoven's larger slow movements well enough.

1. First section, C minor, mm. 1–68 (Funeral March)
2. Second section, C major, mm. 69–104 ("Maggiore")
3. Partial return of first theme, C minor, with new fugal extensions and elaborations, mm. 105–172
4. Shortened recapitulation of first section, C minor, theme in oboe and clarinet, over ostinato in strings, mm. 173–209
5. Coda, beginning in A-flat, closing into C minor; at the end, the fragmentation of the first theme

Though various sequential and metaphorical narratives for the whole symphony have been proposed, none truly satisfy. The most grotesque is Paul Bekker's idea that since Beethoven in effect mourned the dead hero in the slow movement and then brought him back into action in the third, performers might reverse the order of the two inner movements![10] Berlioz said about the whole work, "I know few examples in music of a style in which grief has been so consistently able to retain such pure form and such nobility of expression."[11] That representing grief in this way was Beethoven's aim emerges clearly enough from a predecessor to the slow movement, his A-flat minor "Marcia funebre per la morte d'un eroe" ("Funeral March for the Death of a Hero"), in the Piano Sonata Opus 26, written in 1800. As we saw earlier, it has often been claimed that the *Eroica* slow movement may have been drawn from Paer's funeral march, also in C minor, from his opera *Achille*, which had been performed in Vienna in 1801.[12] The parallel is visible but too limited to be of value, as Paer's march is so much simpler than Beethoven's visionary movement, even when we allow for the difference between journeyman and master and between an operatic march and this grand symphonic Adagio.

At all events, if Beethoven had a "picture" in his mind as a guiding concept when writing this movement, it was that of a slow processional march for a fallen hero being taken to his grave—that much is clear from the triplet drumbeats simulated in the basses at the beginning and end. The disintegration of the theme at the end signifies not the literal death of the hero, as it does a few years later at the end of *Coriolanus*, but that mourning and grief have reached a stage at which the theme itself can no longer be uttered in full but is reduced to broken whispers.

Of all Beethoven's works, the Third Symphony, by virtue of its final title, its character, and its magnitude, has been the mainspring behind the notion of a "heroic style" and the labeling of the years from 1803 to 1812 as a "heroic period."[13] As a result, the whole period is named for one of its conspicuous parts, at the expense of a higher valuation of works that do not fit the mold and are clearly not heroic, yet are essential products of the same period. Accordingly, to regard the heroic as a primary but not wholly dominating aesthetic term for Beethoven's work from this time frees us to see the heroic as only one among various models that Beethoven was pursuing in instrumental music and even in opera.[14]

Inevitably, "hero" and "heroic" have undergone drastic changes in meaning over the centuries. In our pessimistic, self-consciously postmodern and certainly nonheroic age, we can hardly imagine what it meant to nineteenth-century artists and writers to portray the "hero" as the self-reliant male warrior, the brave man whose virtue consists in overcoming all obstacles and, if need be, dying for the cause to which he has pledged his being. Occasionally, a creative artist breaks with tradition and casts a woman in the role of hero. *Leonore*, on a subject Beethoven accepted because of its moral seriousness, realism, and lack of the usual operatic artificiality, actually has two heroes. One is the courageous title character, who risks her life by disguising herself in order to save Florestan, her imprisoned husband. The other is Florestan himself, the victim of political oppression, who exhibits the heroism of endurance and bears up stoically under the ordeal of torture and starvation, kept alive by his hope for salvation. It is fitting to his time that most of Beethoven's personified "heroes" (and all of them in second-period works) are men, and specifically, men who endure suffering: Jesus in *Christus am Ölberge*, Florestan, Coriolanus, Egmont. The unnamed figure whose death is mourned in Beethoven's funeral marches and glorified in the Eroica is "a great man," one who has conceivably battled for noble ideals; the symphony, as its published title tells us, "celebrates the memory" of such a hero. The image of the masculine hero as the embodiment of virtue pervaded the social culture of Beethoven's time, and a serious attempt to see the work in anything like its true historical context must accept the relevance of that image. Since this symphony is at the root of Beethoven's "heroic" style and, even more, of "Beethoven hero," we need to grapple with the term as Beethoven would have understood it.

First, there is no evidence that the term *Eroica* was known or used for this symphony before its publication in October 1806.[15] Second, Beethoven used the term *Eroica* in 1806 in this way: "Sinfonia eroica . . . composta per festeggiare il sovvenire di un grand Uomo . . ." ("Heroic Symphony . . . composed to celebrate the memory of a great man"). In brief terms, the known facts about the symphony's title and dedication are as follows:

- October 22, 1803. Ries writes to Simrock in Bonn, "He will sell the symphony to you for 100 ducats. In his own testimony it is the greatest work he has yet written. Beethoven played it for me recently, and I believe heaven and earth will tremble at its performance. He is very anxious to dedicate it to Bonaparte; if not, if Lobkowitz wants it for half a year and will give 400 ducats for it, he will [dedicate it to Lobkowitz and] entitle it 'Bonaparte.' "[16]
- May 18, 1804. First public announcement by the hand-picked French Senate that the government of the French Republic is to be

entrusted to Napoleon as hereditary emperor, free to establish an imperial court.[17]

- August 26, 1804. Beethoven offers the symphony to Breitkopf & Härtel, writing that "the title of the symphony is actually Bonaparte."[18]

- December 2, 1804. In Nôtre-Dame de Paris, Napoleon takes the imperial crown from the hands of Pope Pius VII and sets it firmly on his own head, after which he swears an oath to uphold liberty and equality. A close observer in France wrote later, "In those days the history of the Revolution was as remote for us as the history of the Greeks and Romans."[19]

- Sometime after December 2, 1804. Beethoven crosses out the words "titled Bonaparte" in his own copy of the score. However, he leaves intact the message "written on [the subject of] Bonaparte" in pencil at the bottom of the title page.[20]

The trail between August 1804 and October 1806 runs cold; despite many hypotheses, some of them political, some more nearly psychological, we have neither letters nor documents to show us how Beethoven reached the final wording. All we have is the final title "Sinfonia eroica" in the published parts of 1806. The dedicatee is Prince Lobkowitz; no individual's name is included in the title, certainly not Bonaparte's, and the subtitle says that the symphony is "composed to celebrate the memory of a great man." So the final title leaves all identities open. Perhaps deliberately, it is open to more than one interpretation. On the one hand, in the political context of the time it could be taken to refer to Napoleon as he had been before he crowned himself emperor. But the wording also raises the title to a more abstract level, at which the subject is not any specific individual but the idea of "the memory of a great man." We are invited to see the work as elegiac, as symbolizing what it means to commemorate a hero. So the final title indicates the breadth, grandeur, and expressive nobility of the whole symphony, while the subtitle's reference to celebrating "the memory of a great man" alludes directly to the funeral march. The implication is that, rather than presenting scenes from the life of a hero, the work offers an elaborated set of perspectives on the idea of the heroic, including the hero's death.[21]

This explanation fits well with the classicizing viewpoint embodied in so much of the art and symbolism that were created around Napoleon as the dominating figure of the age. The embrace of the classical both glorified the upstart Corsican and gave him a mythic stature borrowed from Caesar and Augustus. Napoleon was thus aping and continuing the quest for legitimacy pursued for centuries by the Holy Roman emperors, who could imagine themselves to be the heirs of the Roman empire. In fact, when Napoleon proclaimed himself emperor in 1804, his action directly threatened the Austrian emperor's claim to the same title, and for this reason Francis II immediately demanded recognition of his own legal status as emperor of Austria, to counter Napoleon's move.[22] Liberal hopes for a more democratic age, in the spirit of the American and French revolutions, were dealt a double blow.

The emergence of this new French potentate, with his universal claims to power and authority, fostered an imperial style in art, architecture, sculpture, and the domestic arts, including furniture and clothing, as artists and intellectuals fell under the Napoleonic spell. The principal image maker was Napoleon's "First Painter," Jacques-Louis David, who began as a revolutionary and a friend of Robespierre's. He later joined Napoleon's entourage and gave the world vivid images of the emperor as ruler, along with scenes from antiquity that were understood as analogues to contemporary life.[23] The neoclassic strain in David had originated before the Revolutionary period, but in the heyday of the Revolution the imitation of the ancients in manners and dress flowed directly into the work of the major French painters. David had turned in this classicizing direction even before such allegorical works as *The Grief of Andromache, The Oath of the Horatii, The Death of Socrates,* and *Brutus,* all dating from the 1780s. Later, while in Napoleon's service, he painted *The Rape of the Sabines* and *Leonidas at Thermopylae.* The sculptor Antonio Canova brought many of the same themes to his figural works, emulating the classics in his *Amor and Psyche* and feeding at the trough of Napoleonic patronage in his erotic representation of Pauline Bonaparte as Venus on her bed. Canova even had the idea of a sculptured Washington, dressed in a toga, giving a speech to Congress.[24]

This broad wave of enthusiasm for classical models informs the ideological background of Beethoven's concept of the heroic. It is as significant as his deafness in providing Beethoven with the impetus for certain works, despite the true sense in which he could feel his career threatened by his affliction, and resolve to overcome it—as in fact he could and did. In the "heroic" he finds an aesthetic model that resonates perfectly with one of the dominant cultural strains of the time, thus enabling him to be both a highly individual artist and at the same time a representative one, in tune with the aesthetic sensibilities that were sweeping Europe. Thus the *Eroica* Symphony can be seen not only as a personal testament to his own capacity to overcome but as a work devoted to the "heroic" as a partly classical idea, in which the protagonists are the Greek or Roman heroes. These are exactly the figures who had been described by Plutarch in his *Parallel Lives*, the book Beethoven said taught him resignation.

The "hero" of the *Eroica* is not a single figure but a composite of heroes of different types and different situations. In the first movement the heroic is felt in musical images that evoke grandeur, conflict, and nobility of spirit; in the slow movement a fallen hero is mourned and brought to final rest; in the Scherzo and above all the Trio, we hear horn calls to battle, along with "a strange voice" at the end, a return to the chromatic mystery of the symphony's opening ideas.[25] And the finale evokes a "Promethean" hero who (in the ballet, its direct antecedent) brought wisdom and the arts and sciences to the world. To rigorous music theorists such as Heinrich Schenker, Beethoven is the hero. Later contextual discussions of the work have run the gamut, from the *Eroica* as Beethoven's personal statement of his own response to deafness to the work as a depiction of the life and death of a single individual.

When Ries said that Beethoven admired Napoleon as First Consul, we should remember that he added, "[Beethoven] held him in the highest regard *and compared him to the greatest Roman consuls* (my italics)."[26] Beethoven's love of classical literature included Homer, whom he placed alongside Goethe and Schiller as his favorites and lamented that he could read Homer only in German.[27] Homer reappears in other letters written by Beethoven and in his Conversation Books; he copied passages from the *Odyssey* and from the *Iliad* in his diary. As to Plutarch, his references are always cast in terms of admiration for what he has learned from the *Paral-*

lel Lives, and when he turned to this monumental collection of biographies it was undoubtedly to dwell on the attitudes to life he found in distinguished figures of antiquity. When J. R. Schultz wrote in 1824 about his visit to Beethoven, he said, "He is a great admirer of the ancients. Homer, particularly his *Odyssey*, and Plutarch he prefers to all the rest; and, of the native poets, he studies Schiller and Goethe, in preference to any other."[28]

The Fourth Symphony

Though many writers and listeners regard the Fourth Symphony as a regression, they could hardly be more mistaken. Once the Eroica had enlarged the landscape of the symphony, Beethoven's next four-movement symphony was inevitably compared with it, and connoisseurs looked long and hard to see whether the composer had tried to match it or had shifted his ground. His decision to return to a smaller scale, to reduce length and density but also to invest a smaller framework with subtlety, action, and lyricism, showed that, paradoxically, he was aiming to broaden his new symphonic framework still further by showing that the epic, heroic model was only one of a number of potential aesthetic alternatives. The Fourth showed that less could be as much, perhaps more.

The first difference is one of scale. All four movements are shorter than their counterparts in the *Eroica*. As in the Second Symphony the first movement opens with a harmonically adventurous, but now deliberate and slow-moving Adagio introduction that mingles B-flat major and B-flat minor, then packs a far-flung modulatory scheme—entailing the transformation of the flat-sixth $G\flat$ into $F\sharp$, its pitch equivalent, with varied consequences—into its second half before slipping back to the home dominant and clearing the way for the Allegro main section.[29] The intervallic relationship of $B\flat$ to $G\flat$ plays a role throughout the entire work, emerging in different ways in each movement. The first movement exposition spins out a set of vigorous contrasting themes, a sequence in which one rhythmically profiled theme after another sweeps across the landscape. After remarkable elaborations of its motivic material in the development, one of the movement's most striking passages comes at the long preparation for the recapitulation. Instead of a lengthy stay on the dominant, the harmony settles down to the tonic, B-flat major, well before the actual start of the recapitulation. The tonic harmony is anchored by having the tympani hold the tonic pitch, B♭, in a long steady roll while the strings slowly build up a crescendo based on the upbeat figures that have been prominent from the beginning. The whole gradually grows in volume to its climax, tonic harmony giving way to louder tonic, and all at once the moment of recapitulation has arrived as part of a vast sweep of events, all of which took place over the single tonic harmony.

In this work the basic condition is that of direct gestural action at various speeds, much more than of the pensive, logical, developmental side of symphonic thought, as in the *Eroica*. A key to this aspect of the Fourth, when compared with the Third, is the work's complete avoidance of fugal writing, for which it literally has no time as it moves forward to new, rhythmically well-defined ideas in each movement rather than making room for a contrapuntal exegesis built on just one of them. As it turns out, the same absence of fugal writing characterizes each of the even-numbered symphonies (4, 6, and 8) as opposed to the odd-numbered (3, 5, 7, and, ultimately, 9). The aesthetic dualism of the even- and odd-numbered symphonies starts here.

A second difference is in the instrumentation. In the Fourth, Beethoven reverts to the orchestra of late Mozart or Haydn: one flute, the other winds in the usual pairs, two horns (instead of three as in the *Eroica*), trumpets, tympani, and strings. The wind writing brings new orchestral colors as early as a bassoon solo in the Adagio introduction, a canon between clarinet and bassoon in the first movement, gorgeous wind writing in the slow movement foreshadowing Schumann and Brahms, and virtuosic passage work for the bassoon again in the finale. The emergence of the tympani as a dramatic factor in the first movement has already been noted, but the tympani play an equally important role in the slow movement and Scherzo.

The Fourth stands out for its grace, energy, and lightness, for its feeling of godlike play among delicately poised forces. Schumann, whose affinity for it seems so natural in the light of his own instrumental style, called it "the Greek-like slender one" among the Beethoven symphonies.[30] Rhythmic, melodic, and harmonic features of high subtlety inhabit every movement. Occasionally we sense what Theodor W. Adorno called a virtual suspension of time in certain passages—"as they swing back and forth, the passages become the pendulum of time itself."[31] Different speeds and energies of motion dominate the first movement, the Scherzo, and the finale; contemplative beauty governs the Adagio. The slow movement, a sensuous slow rondo, inaugurates the Romantic type of expressive major-mode orchestral Adagio, replete with contrasts between sharply defined rhythmic figures and sweeping, beautiful melodic lines. Its progeny include the triple-meter slow movements of Schumann's "Spring" Symphony and of Brahms's First.

The Scherzo breaks a new formal path that Beethoven later followed in a number of middle-period works. It is made up of five parts instead of three, with a second return of the Scherzo and Trio following the normal Scherzo-Trio-Scherzo da capo form. Syncopation in the Scherzo theme immediately recalls the Scherzo of Opus 18 No. 6, another B-flat major work, and the gentle contrast of wind-dominated Trio to string-dominated Scherzo evokes late Haydn, whose own last symphonies in this key, Nos. 98 and 102, could not have been far from Beethoven's mind. But the work remains wholly Beethovenian, never more so than in the surprising gestures that conclude the slow movement and the Scherzo: both end not with quiet cadences but with powerful fortissimo strokes.

The finale, a perpetuum mobile in running sixteenth notes almost from start to finish, brings back humor and wit to Beethoven's symphonic finales, surpassing the First Symphony's 2/4 finale in this and other respects. That the opening four-note figure can be a subject for development comes as no surprise in itself, but the lights and shadows in which it is later seen are an unsurpassed source of wonder. A pair of sketches for the finale, entered as early as 1804 in leaves that originally belonged to the main sketchbook for *Leonore*, show what are probably the earliest ideas sketched for the symphony.[32] That Beethoven may have been thinking about it while working on *Leonore* is suggestive, in view of the dominating importance in the symphony of pace and tempo and in light of the focus on contrasting speeds in the Allegros and on lyricism in the Adagio, as if it picked up hints from Beethoven's heightened awareness of stage time during his work on the opera.[33] Because a sketchbook from about this time is lost, we are not well informed about the genesis of the Fourth, but Beethoven probably held off full concentration on the symphony until he had finished his labor on the opera from autumn 1805 to the middle of 1806. By early September of that year he was offering the symphony to Breitkopf along with the Opus 59 Quartets and the Fourth Piano Concerto.

The Fifth and Sixth ("Pastoral") Symphonies

By 1807–8, when Beethoven returned to work on new symphonic projects, the Fourth was being engraved and the *Eroica* had appeared in print quite recently, in October 1806. During this long period of sustained creative energy Beethoven continued his practice of starting work on a new symphony within one to two years after completing the last one, aware that by the time the previous work was actually published and

Beethoven's autograph score of the Fifth Symphony, showing the opening page. (Staatsbibliothek, Berlin)

gradually getting to be known and performed across Europe, he would have a new one under way.

Since the *Eroica* he had turned out new works in various categories. The most time-consuming had been *Leonore*, in its two versions of 1805 and 1806 and its two versions of the C-major overture later known as Nos. 2 and 3. But he had also completed three piano sonatas, the Fourth Piano Concerto, and the Opus 59 Quartets, as well as the *Coriolanus* Overture, a work that bridges the *Eroica* and the Fifth symphonies. In 1807 and 1808 he determined not to plan one symphony at a time but to embark on two. Despite their strongly profiled individuality the Fifth and Sixth were paired in various ways from the start, and their similarities, which now command more attention than their manifest differences, "relate to aspects of the narrative design, as well as to style and character," in the words of one writer. "Like the 'Waldstein' and 'Appassionata' sonatas, the Fifth and Sixth symphonies represent disparate musical worlds that . . . complement one another."[34] To which I would add that these two worlds, despite their affinities, belong to systems that move at different speeds. Their relationships to musical time are entirely different.

As to chronology and genesis, it looks as if Beethoven began the main work on the Fifth before he embarked on the Sixth. He sketched an embryonic plan for it in the later pages of the *Eroica* sketchbook as early as 1804, so the gestation period for the Fifth in broad terms took as long as four years. This idea made its way into the Beethoven literature after Nottebohm published extracts from the sketchbook and has since become part of popular lore.[35]

But the bulk of his work on the Fifth took place in 1807 and early 1808, followed by his composition of the Sixth in the spring and summer of 1808. Both symphonies (with their numbering reversed) were premiered at a benefit concert that Beethoven presented on December 22, 1808, at the Theater an der Wien, the only time Beethoven premiered two symphonies together, directly exposing their contrasts.

Their similarities include the use of cumulative instrumentation. The Fifth adds three trombones, piccolo, and contrabassoon in the Finale, widening the span of volume and pitch in the winds. In the Sixth, the first two movements use only the orchestral winds, strings, and horns but no trumpets or tympani; the Scherzo adds two trumpets, and the fourth movement (the Storm) adds a piccolo, two trombones, and tympani, keeping the trombones (though not the piccolo and tympani) for the quiet finale. In both works the final movements (two in the Fifth, three in the Sixth) are contiguous, moving without pause from one to the next. Both first movements employ 2/4 meter (the only two symphonies till now to do so), and both open with a short phrase that leads to a fermata on the dominant. The tempo of the slow movement in the Fifth is Andante con moto in 3/8 meter, that of the Sixth ("Scene by the brook") is Andante molto moto in 12/8. Incidentally, after the expressive Adagio of the Fourth Symphony, no later symphony until the Ninth has a slow movement that is really slow—they are all Andante or faster. As Beethoven increased the proportions and complexity of the symphonic slow movement, he apparently wished to ensure that its greater length would in some degree be compensated by its more active, faster tempo.

Yet despite these similarities, their differences mattered much more to Beethoven's contemporaries, as they still do to us. A basic generating idea behind the Fifth is that it should dramatize Beethoven's by-now famous "C-minor mood" in a new way. It is as if Beethoven shut down an invisible roof on his material in this first movement, subjecting it to an unprecedented state of compression, using the celebrated "motto" of the first two measures to bind the continuity of the whole, then deploying this motif in different guises for later movements. The dominating motto and the rhythmic and harmonic compression create the force behind the first movement, which unleashes a tragic power in the symphonic domain that audiences had not known before. Just as audiences in 1787 had been shaken by Schiller's *Die Räuber*, they were now shaken in somewhat the same way by Beethoven's Fifth.

The Fifth Symphony

In an 1810 review of the Fifth Symphony, the novelist and critic E. T. A. Hoffmann voiced the opinion, then current, that Beethoven's instrumental music was built on that of his two great predecessors, Haydn and Mozart, who "were the first to show us the art in its full glory."[36] In the true Romantic spirit of Hoffmann's writings, he now accepted Haydn as a "cheerful" classic, whose music is "full of love and . . . happiness . . . [but] there is no suffering, no pain." Mozart "leads us into the inner depths of the realm of the spirits. Fear envelops us but does not torment us; it is more a premonition of the infinite." And now comes Beethoven, whose instrumental music "opens the realm of the colossal and the immeasurable for us. Radiant beams shoot through the deep night of this region, and we become aware of gigantic shadows which, rocking back and forth, close in on us and destroy all within us except the pain of endless longing. . . . Beethoven's music evokes terror, fright, horror, and pain, and awakens that endless longing that is the essence of romanticism."[37] For Hoffmann in 1810 the Fifth Symphony "unfolds Beethoven's romanticism more than any of his other works and tears the listener irresistibly away into the wonderful spiritual realm of the infinite."

By recognizing connections between movements Hoffmann identified one of the most telling features of the Fifth Symphony. The connections occur in two ways: first, through the rhythmic recurrence of the opening motif in every movement, and second, through the partial amalgamation of the Scherzo and the Finale. The three-part Scherzo, instead of ending autonomously, leads into the Finale through a colossal dominant preparation that grows from *pianississimo,* the softest of Beethovenian dynamics, to *pianissimo* and then, through a powerful crescendo, to the blazing C-major *fortissimo* opening of the Finale, with its full orchestral triadic theme.[38] But the transition directly from the Scherzo to the Finale is only half the story. At the end of the development section of the finale, the scene shifts back from the triumphal finale material to a return of the Scherzo version of the opening four-note motif, performed *misterioso,* that then gradually returns to the Finale and ushers in its recapitulation.

This attempt at integrating Scherzo and Finale by having one movement pass without a break into the next was one of Haydn's innovations in handling cyclic form.[39] It is possible that Beethoven knew Haydn's Symphonies No. 45 (the "Farewell") and No. 46, which has an explicit recall of the Minuet in the Finale. But whether or not he was making formal reference to Haydn, Beethoven appears to be invoking, to powerful effect, another tradition that had not previously appeared in the symphonic literature—the tradition of the fantasia.

Beethoven had written piano fantasias in his youth, emulating the masters and showing his improvisatory gifts in sample compositions.[40] In 1801, in the flush of experimenting with new expressive works for keyboard, he had blended sonata and fantasia in Piano Sonatas Opus 27 Nos. 1 and 2, both called "sonata quasi una fantasia."[41] Both have run-on movements, and No. 1 features the return of earlier material. The Fifth Symphony shows the same combination of principles in the Scherzo and Finale; in the explicit motivic connection of all four movements, it reveals another way of integrating a symphony.[42] It would not be wrong to call the Fifth a "sinfonia quasi una fantasia." In fact, in an early sketched movement plan for the work, Beethoven considered making it a three-movement symphony (a movement plan he only used in keyboard chamber music), with slow movement and "Menuetto" combined in a single middle movement and with a C-minor finale. That his interest in the Fantasia was strong at this time is evident in the Choral Fantasy that he premiered in 1808 alongside the Fifth, and it continued in a few later works: his curious Fantasia for Piano, Opus 77, of 1809; the first of the two Cello Sonatas of Opus 102, written in 1815; and the Piano Sonata in A Major, Opus 101, of 1816. In the latter pair of works the return of opening material late in the piece recalls his Sonata Opus 27 No. 1, and in that sense they are also "quasi una fantasia."

In even this brief appraisal, a few further points demand attention. One is the dramatic consistency of the first movement, arising not only from its incessant rhythmic motif but at least as much from its extremely limited harmonic range. The exposition leads in normal ways from the key of C minor to its relative major, E-flat, for the lyrical second theme (below which the opening motif continues). But in the development the basic harmonic range of the whole section is astonishingly restricted, and major-mode harmonies, even as chords, scarcely appear. The tension of the first movement emerges in part from the contrasting roles of two harmonic poles: C minor, the key of the movement, and F minor, its close neighbor. The first movement limits its harmonic content primarily to elements of these chords, making only the most sparing use of G major, the dominant of C minor. The primary harmonic scheme of the entire first movement can be summarized as follows:

1. Exposition	2. Development		3. Recapitulation and Coda
C minor	F minor	F minor	C minor
↓	↓	↓	↓
E♭ major	C minor	(unstable)	C major
	↓	↓	↓
	G minor	G major (brief)	C minor
	↓	↓	
	C minor	F minor	

That the harmonic plan of the development remains so rigorously in minor keys, and within a narrow band of these (witness the symmetry of the motion from F minor to C minor back to F minor) is new in Beethoven. G minor is reached as a midpoint in the cycle of minor keys moving by fifths, then returns to the more important F minor. The stress on F minor emerges in its use as the main tonality for the development and as part of the harmony from which the development springs back to C minor for the recapitulation and the return of the opening.

The Andante, consolation after tragedy, explores another range of feelings, just as it explores another range of tonal relationships. Choosing the key of A-flat major to follow a movement in C minor is a favorite scheme of Beethoven's, one he had used in such earlier C-minor works as the "Pathétique" Sonata and the Violin Sonata Opus 30 No. 2. The movement begins by recalling a slow-movement model that Haydn had perfected: variations on two alternating subjects, as in his Symphony No. 103, the "Drumroll." Beethoven starts as if he were going to proceed in the same way, and the dialectic of two basic themes soon emerges. The first is an intricate *piano dolce* in A-flat major that conceals a rising C-major triad within its coils and ends with extended cadential figures in strings and winds. This section is followed by a vigorous contrasting theme that rises from A-flat major to explode *fortissimo* in C major, setting the stage for a massive statement of the theme in C major and forcing us to realize that the basic rhythm of this theme, apart from its upbeats, is the 3 + 1 rhythm of the first movement.

From here on matters unfold in two ways: (1) through alternating variations of the first and second themes and then strangely altered extensions of both themes; and (2) through comparable extension of the second theme, leading to still another development of the first theme. A lengthy coda rounds out the whole and brings the traveler, the first theme, home to in A-flat major. The implicit conflict between the two themes has finally been resolved. As a whole, the slow movement picks up from the finale of the *Eroica* the idea of a variations movement that transforms its more rigid classical model (theme and chain of variations, each variation a closed total unit) into a more plastic form. Beethoven's freedom of formal disposition would prove as significant for the history of the symphonic slow movement as the *Eroica* fourth movement had been for the history of the symphonic finale.

The Scherzo offers contrasts that are somewhat similar to those of the slow movement in that they derive from extreme differences in character between Scherzo and Trio, even more marked than in most of Beethoven's earlier third movements.[43] The *pianissimo* Scherzo theme, marked *misterioso*, explores the C-minor chord rising through an octave and a half, a shape we can trace as far back as the E-flat minor first movement of his youthful Piano Quartet of 1785. The Scherzo then contrasts this figure with the famous "motto" (3 + 1) from the first movement, which gradually takes command of the whole movement. The Trio brings a boisterous C-major fugato in the strings, develops it in its second section, then finds new means to articulate it in the reprise. The return of the Scherzo is no mere repetition: it is a mysterious echo of the Scherzo, another "strange voice" in a Scherzo movement, with the opening theme now in pizzicato. It sets the stage for the famous Coda that will lead through a crescendo to the powerful arrival at the Finale.

The Finale, solidly in C major, crowns the work. It epitomizes all that is exultant, powerful, and wide ranging, capturing a spirit that Beethoven might have heard in some French postrevolutionary works but surpassing them in every respect. The opening theme, with its square rhythms and its basic rising triad and descending scale shape, displays the purest middle-period Beethoven thematic design. The C major of the whole movement picks up the many references to this tonality that had been heard earlier—in the first movement at the recapitulation of the second theme; in the slow movement, at the big second theme; in the third movement, in the Trio—and gathers them all in with a feeling of ultimate resolution. The triumphant tone of this movement spoke to generations of composers after Beethoven as the essence of an optimism that they could associate with Enlightenment ideals, and its way of ending offered a metaphor for the whole work as "a passage from darkness to light," as many have described it. What needs to be seen is that the "light," C major, has been gleaming distantly in the work since the recapitulation of the first movement, and that the finale, flooding the whole work with its C-major emphasis, is the summation of a process that has been unfolding since the first movement. Beethoven's decision here to end a minor-mode of work with a major-mode finale is in fact unusual, even for his C-minor works.[44] His earlier four-movement cyclic works in minor mode had minor-mode finales, even if they ended with major harmonies (as in the third piano trio of Opus 1 and the String Quartet Opus 18 No. 4). After the Fifth Symphony the only works that have full major-mode finales after a minor-mode first movement are the two-movement Piano Sonatas Opus 90 and Opus 111, and the Ninth Symphony. Indeed, this key relationship is one of the ways in which the Fifth effectively foreshadows the Ninth and provides a first symphonic presentation of a darkened world that is at last relieved by triumph. A connection to *Leonore* also suggests itself, the more so because the dark F-minor tonality of Florestan in his dungeon is eventually illuminated by the broad daylight of C major, the key of his freeing by Leonore.

The Sixth Symphony ("Sinfonia Pastorale")

After the psychological intensity of the Fifth comes a release into the tranquil world of nature. The daylight of the *Pastoral* Symphony is of quite another order than that of the finale of the Fifth, in that the work dwells on the softer experience of the countryside. As Beethoven put it in the subtitle that he finally chose for its published title page, the work is "more an expression of feelings than tone painting." The symphony evokes the quiet exaltation we feel amid the fields, streams, trees and birds; it is impregnated with a sense of communion with all that is natural and God-given in the outdoors. There is a strong religious element in Beethoven's feeling for nature. One of Beethoven's favorite books—he annotated his own copy—bore the title *Reflections on the Works of God in the Realm of Nature and Providence.*[45] That he loved the countryside and relished taking excursions into the woods and fields is clear from biographical evidence of all kinds. That he now seized on the great tradition of the musical "pastoral," with its complex connections to the pastoral tradition in literature, implies a conjoining of his personal experience with familiar and traditional modes of representing the pastoral in music.

The idea of a "pastoral" symphony in the context of Beethoven's pioneering work as a symphonic composer betokens his engagement with the popular genre of illustrative music, which was coming to be called "program music." He was, of course, aware that the prestige of "absolute" music was rising as the Romantic writers pressed its advantages home. It looks, then, as if Beethoven wanted to have it both ways. He clearly intended the work to be a "programmatic" symphony that would explore the current taste for illustrative compositions, but at the same time he meant to elevate the literature of current program music, which did little more than mimic the sound effects of battles, landscapes, storms, sea voyages, and a host of similar subjects. Although he was certainly aware of "characteristic" symphonies and even pastoral symphonies by eighteenth-century composers such as Carl Ditters von Dittersdorf and Justus Heinrich Knecht (who had written a symphony called *Portrait musical de la nature* around 1784), none of these could stand up as authentic models at Beethoven's level of musical thought and integration.[46] He despised literal program music that lacked intrinsic qualities as pure music—that is clear from the various sketch entries he made for this work as he tried to find the right way to formulate and justify his use of specific titles for each of the movements. Thus his jottings include these remarks: "One leaves it to the listener to discover the situations"; "Each act of tone-painting, as soon as it is pushed too far in instrumental music, loses its force"; and "The whole will be understood even without a description, as it is more feeling than tone-painting."[47]

The last words of this entry became the basis for the title of the work as found in an early violin part: "Sinfonia Pastorella/ Pastoral-Sinfonie/ oder/ Erinnerung an das Landleben/ Mehr Ausdruck der Empfindung als Mahlerei"; that is, "Pastoral Symphony or Memories of Country Life/ More the Expression of Feeling than Tone-Painting."[48]

Yet all his seeming embarrassment about the use of titles and the risks of tone painting did not deter Beethoven from giving a specific title to each movement, from organizing the whole work into a loosely hung narrative of pastoral experience, or from including in it copious references to the sounds of natural and human elements in nature: birds (specifically named in the score in the slow movement); the storm that interrupts a peasant dance; and country musicians, whose presence is evoked in the first movement, the Scherzo, and the finale.

The larger organization of the work and the movement titles are as follows:

1. Allegro ma non troppo, 2/4, F major, "Erwachen heiterer Empfindungen bei der Ankunft auf dem Lande" ("The awakening of joyous feelings on getting out into the countryside");
2. Andante molto moto, 12/8, B-flat major, "Scene am Bach" (Scene by the brook");
3. Allegro, 3/4 with Trio in 2/4, F major, "Lustiges Zusammensein der Landleute" ("Merry gathering of country people");
4. Allegro, 4/4, F minor, "Gewitter. Sturm" ("Thunderstorm");
5. Allegretto, 6/8, F major, "Hirtengesang. Frohe und dankbare Gefühle nach dem Sturm" ("Shepherd's song. Happy and thankful feelings after the storm").

The implicit narrative suggests the experience of an abstract protagonist or observer in nature. In the first movement, having been city bound, he gets out into the countryside and rejoices in its plenitude and wonder. As in the Fifth Symphony the first movement is the crucial basis for all that follows, and curiously it has almost the same length and formal proportional symmetry as the first movement of the Fifth: the exposition, development, and recapitulation are nearly identical in length, and they are followed by a substantial coda. More striking still is the harmonic plan. The principal contrast to the tonic key of F major is not its dominant, C major, but rather its subdominant, B-flat major, to which significant moves are made at several crucial points in the movement: in the development section (at both the beginning and end) and at the start of the recapitulation, a place for which Beethoven always reserves special treatment. Here the quiet approach to the return of the tonic is prepared by a powerful arrival on B-flat major, after which the first theme, in the tonic, slips in quietly in the second violins and violas while the first violins improvise a trill and arpeggio passage above.

Through the whole movement runs a curiously placid harmonic feeling, marked by very slow rates of harmonic change, prolonged harmonic "plateaus" on single chords, much use of repeated figures (especially in the development), and the prevalence of major-mode harmonies from start to finish. The first movement of the Fifth Symphony had been confined primarily to minor keys, above all in the development; here in the Sixth the restriction is just the opposite: there are hardly any minor harmonies in the whole movement, as Arnold Schoenberg discovered one day while listening to the symphony on the radio. The quality of the whole is carried not only by this seeming harmonic stasis, however, but by the wealth and quality of the thematic material and the motivic elements to which it gives rise. And in the coda one of the best of all Beethoven surprises turns up: after several interrupted cadences suggesting a closure that is still to come, the clarinet takes on a solo with a new thematic idea, bringing to mind a country wind player—a kind of pied piper, who is leading the orchestra to the end of the movement (*W 22). It is a touch of gentle humor, one of the varieties of the comic that abound in Beethoven and that appear at significant moments from now to the end of his life.

In the slow movement the stage shifts to a "scene by the brook." The movement is famous for the imitations of birds that appear in the coda—the nightingale (flute), the quail (oboe), and the cuckoo (two clarinets)—all of which are named in the score, a point on which Beethoven wrote an emphatic note to his copyist in the autograph manuscript.[49] These bird calls, equivalents in nature to little cadenzas by solo singers, are actually individualized representations of birds that have been evident in

the movement from the very beginning. To listen to the entire slow movement and hear the trills in high register in the violin parts as the sound of
birds is to gain a mental image of a pastoral scene by a brook. In doing so
we realize that the triplet rocking motion of the lower strings at the beginning represents the motion of the brook; that the bird sounds appear just
moments into the movement in the first violins as high trilled B♭'s; and that
the combination implies a musical distance between the brook at ground
level and the birds above, singing and trilling, flying in and out of the trees
that stand along the sides of the brook. This spatial relationship between
the ground-level brook and the birds above is not just a fanciful picture, it
represents in nature the registral span that separates the low-register
instruments (cellos and basses) from the high ones (violins).[50] The elements chosen for depiction in this seemingly placid brookside scene form
the same components for the dramatization of musical register and, more
generally, musical space, that Beethoven regularly employs in many of his
purely abstract, entirely nonprogrammatic works of this period. These procedures help to integrate the programmatic with the structural, just as we
intuitively sense to be the case in this movement.[51]

All of this representation also correlates with the larger shape of the
movement and the eventual achievement of a movement-length climax
near the end. In his initial sketch of 1804 Beethoven may have anticipated
the idea of correlating the growth of the brook with the registral growth of
the whole movement. There he had written a 12/8 theme representing the
motion of the brook, with the annotation "je grösser der Bach je tiefer der
Ton—" ("the wider the brook, the deeper the tone").[52] This entry illustrates the connection between visual image and musical register: here
"grösser" meaning "wider" must also mean "greater" and in a sense
"deeper"—as the brook, gaining force and breadth as it runs its course and
verges on becoming a river, also becomes deeper. Its greater depth is corre-
lated with the achievement of a musical climax that is registrally wider,
from bottom to top; is greater in volume; uses the full orchestra in all its
panoply; and gives the movement climactic force near the end. The grand
climax in this elaborated, quasi-sonata-form movement comes at the start
of the recapitulation, where the tonic B-flat major returns after the modulatory excursions of the development section. Now the stream has become

a river, and the birds cluster more thickly and trill more animatedly than before; the whole landscape has opened up to a four-octave span and will eventually open still further as the flutes join in.

The scene now shifts to a gathering of country people worthy of Breughel. The tone for the third movement is set by Beethoven's use of the term *lustig*—this is a "merry" and lively crowd whose collective moods emerge in the metrical animation of the Scherzo.[53] The opening F-major descending theme is immediately balanced by its countertheme in D major. The odd juxtaposition of the two major keys, F and D, continues the insistent focus on the major mode that has been running through the symphony from the start. In the middle section the oboe plays a new theme with strikingly different rhythmic features, an off-the-beat beginning and syncopation, while the bassoonist, as Tovey put it, never seems to know just how many notes to put in. To all this activity the Trio adds a violent foot-stamping dance, with powerful emphasis on the F major and B-flat major harmonies. By treating B-flat major, the subdominant, as an alternate tonic and shifting the sense of tonal balance away from the F-major–D-major harmonies of the Scherzo, Beethoven returns to the tonic-subdominant contrasts that had been postulated by the first movement, all in a powerful peasant-dance context that is *fortissimo* from start to finish.

Suddenly a storm approaches, *piano* in the cellos and basses, and quickly breaks out in a *fortissimo* fury that dominates the landscape. The storm brings the first extended use of the minor mode in the whole work, and we realize that Beethoven has been reserving the minor for the storm, along with a modulatory pattern that makes use of diminished-seventh harmonies as pivots in the chain of harmonic steps. At long last we arrive at a point of stability on C major, where we hear nothing less than a chorale phrase, suggesting a religious element both directly and intentionally—in a sketch Beethoven wrote, "Herr, wir danken Dir" ("Lord, we thank thee").

And now emerges the most beautiful and peaceful of symphonic finales, the "Shepherd's Song," labeled "Joyous and grateful feelings after the storm." "Grateful" describes the feeling of the supposed country folk but also of the ideal listener, who receives confirmation of what was implied in the first movement and thus witnesses a circular return to the tranquil conditions that initiated the entire excursion into nature. The enlarged sonata form of the Finale maintains the prominence of the tonic F major, its dominant C major, and once again the subdominant region B-flat major, thus forming a closing symmetry with the first movement. The world is set right.

The Seventh and Eighth Symphonies

With the Seventh and Eighth Symphonies Beethoven's symphonic project of the middle years comes to an end. Not that he knew it at the time—he mentioned the idea of another symphony, one that might be in D minor, but did not bring such a work even to the sketch stage then. By 1812 the Fifth and Sixth had been followed not only by new chamber music and piano sonatas but also by new orchestral theater music, above all the incidental music to *Egmont* that he wrote in 1809–10 at the request of the Court Theater director. He also composed incidental music for two patriotic plays by the Viennese playwright August von Kotzebue, written for the opening of a new theater in Pest. One was *The Ruins of Athens,* for which Beethoven wrote an overture and eight dramatic numbers as his Opus 113; the other was *King Stephen,* Opus 117, an overture plus nine numbers. He managed to finish both during the summer of 1811 while staying in Teplitz for his health. Despite some exotic ideas and striking sonority effects in these works, neither is up to his higher standards. Still, theater music brought him again to the borders of opera, and since he continued to hunt for operatic subjects that might fire his imagination, he asked Kotzebue for one in January 1812 that could be

> *romantic, serious, heroic-comic, or sentimental, as you please; in short anything to your liking. . . . True, I should prefer a big subject from history and particularly one from the Dark Ages—Attila, for example— but I should accept with thanks anything and any subject from you, from your poetical spirit, that I could translate into my musical spirit.*[54]

In 1809–12 Beethoven continued to turn out songs, long a sidelight but one that drew him in again and again as the growth of Romantic poetry challenged him and younger contemporaries to develop more imaginative ways of setting German lyric verse. In 1809 he chose poems by Friedrich von Matthison, whose "Adelaide" he had set to music years earlier, and Christian Ludwig Reissig, from whom he took as many as seven texts, most effectively Reissig's "Sehnsucht," in 1815.[55] He also set six songs by Goethe and other poets that he published in 1810 as Opus 75. More Goethe songs followed as Opus 83.

In this period Beethoven also initiated an agreement with the ambitious Scottish publisher George Thomson to compose settings of folk songs—Scottish, Irish, English, and, later, Continental songs on texts in many languages, including German, Danish, Tyrolean, Polish, Spanish, Russian, Hungarian, and Italian. These compositions add up to a very large body of works, and Beethoven took them much more seriously than later audiences have realized. Most are for solo voice, either soprano or tenor, with full-scale accompaniments for piano trio. Apart from their value in showing Beethoven's interest in folk song, many are of real musical interest. Thomson, who had earlier received some similar arrangements from Haydn, first commissioned Beethoven for forty-three settings in 1809, sending Beethoven the melodies he needed. Their contacts resumed in February 1812, then again in 1813 and 1815, and, with some lapses, Beethoven continued to supply arrangements as late as 1820. That he exceeded Thomson's expectations in the difficulty of the accompaniments is clear from their correspondence, but typically Beethoven refused to simplify his settings, except in nine cases.[56] Filled with striking moments, these little pieces show Beethoven working with the special modal and regional inflections of folk song; conceivably, these inflections and odd tonal twists formed part of their attraction for him. One of them, the Irish song "Save me from the grave and wise," to the tune of "Nora Creina" (WoO 154 No. 8) has a turn of phrase that strikingly resembles the main theme of the Seventh Symphony finale (*W 23).

The Seventh Symphony

Beethoven mentioned the Seventh Symphony in a letter of 1815 to Johann Peter Salomon in London, in which he asked for help in finding a British publisher. He told Salomon that he was ready to offer, among other works, "a grand symphony in A major (one of my most excellent works)." In contrast, he called the Eighth "a smaller symphony in F."[57] Needing no title such as "Eroica" or "Pastoral" to indicate its aesthetic category, the Seventh stands up to the Fifth in its strength and decisiveness. Unlike the Fifth it does not traverse a quasi-narrative journey from minor to major, nor does it have a cyclic return of material from one movement to another. It resembles the Fifth in that rhythmic action is of the essence in both. However, the unity of the Seventh stems not from the reappearance of a single essential rhythmic figure in all movements, but rather from the rhythmic consistency that governs each movement and the vitality, the élan, that drives the whole work.

Each movement is based on a small set of memorable rhythmic figures, with one of them singled out as the leading element. The persistence of each rhythmic set throughout each movement substantially shapes the aesthetic profile of the whole. Of course, the use of a small number of definite rhythmic cells, even of a single figure to dominate a first movement, had been a specialty of Beethoven's from early in his career. Piano Sonata Opus 2 No. 3 and the first movement of the String Quartet Opus 18 No. 1 come to mind, not to mention the first movement of the Fifth, but there are many more examples. The same had been true of many of his slow movements and finales, while in the Scherzos of his quartets and symphonies the dynamic propulsive qualities of the movements often derive from the insistent repetitions of a basic figure in compound or simple triple-meter that is designed to carry the bulk of the musical material.

But in the Seventh Symphony the projection of rhythmic action into the foreground is even more fundamental. This is why Berlioz compared the first movement to a "peasant dance" ("ronde des paysans") and why Wagner called the whole work the "apotheosis of the dance." Duple meter, in various simple and compound forms that include triplet subdivisions of two main beats per measure, dominates the whole work. The first movement features a three-note dotted figure in almost every measure. In the second, a compound figure of a quarter plus two eighth notes fills the movement from beginning to end, interwoven with other material in a rich tapestry of counterstatements. The Scherzo is driven forward incessantly by its own initial figure and by the basic Scherzo rhythm of three even quarter notes that follows. And the finale is a manic expansion of the possibilities latent in the hammering four-note figure with which it opens. In each movement ostinato passages repeat a single figure over and over again, especially in the coda of the first movement, where the bass repetitions suggested to Carl Maria von Weber that Beethoven was now "ready for the madhouse." The wide range of dynamics includes more instances of *fortississimo* and *pianississimo* than any other of his symphonic works.

As we know from the "Kreutzer" Sonata and the much later Quartet Opus 132, Beethoven liked to intermingle minor and major when his tonic was A, and he also liked to have one movement in F major. Since the first movement is in A major and the second is in A minor, the Scherzo offers contrast by shifting to F major; then its D-major Trio (with its own special rhythmic figures and character) stands in apposition to F major, somewhat in the same way that F and D major worked with one another at the opening of the Scherzo of the Sixth. Beethoven's use of F major for the Scherzo also relates well to the harmonic layout of the grand "Poco sostenuto" that introduces the first movement, one of the longest and most elaborate introductions Beethoven ever wrote.[58]

The slow movement, which ranks with the most beautiful in formal and thematic conception of any middle-period work, is primarily a set of variations superimposed on a typical slow movement form. The formal layout is A^1, B^1, A^2, B^2, Coda, with strictly alternating keys of A minor and A major. The basic rhythmic figure of the introduction haunts the entire movement, an incessant presence against which the A-minor theme emerges as a countermelody. To the bleakness of the A sections, the B sections bring repose and consolation with even-flowing quarter-note motion in the winds and lower strings, while triplets brush against them. Meanwhile, far below in the bass register, the first unit of the basic rhythmic figure of A^1 repeats throughout. Beyond all this, the entire A^1 section works out a vast scheme of incrementation, from low to high registers and from two to four octaves.

The whole plan anticipates the incrementation from low to high registers, from *piano* to *fortissimo*, that Beethoven later uses in the introduction to the first movement of the Ninth Symphony. In the Seventh the slow and deliberate style feeling of the first part of this movement begins in a quiet lower terrain, then gradually rises and gains in strength until it fills the musical space. The clear dramatization of spatial form is essential to the psychological effect of the movement, as listeners have intuitively understood from its first performances, and it partly accounts for the fame of this movement beyond any other in the symphony.

The Scherzo uses the five-part form we encountered in the Fourth Symphony and in some other middle-period works. The Scherzo is fully presented three times and the Trio twice, with room for slight modifications of the Scherzo in its second appearance; then a coda grounds the form. And the Finale, the most propulsive 2/4 Allegro con brio Beethoven had written up to that time, is in a sprawling sonata form, this time with the exposition repeated (a feature not associated with all finales) and an enormous coda that is the longest section of the movement. With its unrestrained rhythmic energy and power of sonority, rising to *fortissisimo*, the coda brings this colossal symphony to an end.

The Eighth Symphony

The Eighth Symphony surprises us with its diminutive proportions, its humor and playfulness, and its ostensible return to the world of late Haydn. The Eighth is actually the shortest of all Beethoven's symphonies, and its instrumentation is on the same reduced scale as that of the First, Second, and Fourth, with no trumpets or drums in its second movement. When the public registered puzzlement about the Eighth after the spectacular energy of the Seventh, Beethoven said, according to Czerny, "That's because it's so much better." Authentic or not, this remark catches the sense that the symphony's delicate shadings and subtle balances may have been harder for him to achieve than the direct outpouring of action in the Seventh. Furthermore, precisely because it emulates the smaller symphonic scale of Beethoven's predecessors, but from a modern perspective, this work stands in a stylistically distanced relationship to tradition and becomes an artful commentary on the historical development of the genre.[59]

As in the Seventh, the jewel in the setting is the slow movement, for

Beethoven's autograph manuscript of the Eighth Symphony, showing the last page of the slow movement. The word siml, *which appears in the next-to-last measure in many of the instrumental parts, instructs the copyist to repeat the first figure in the measure. (Staatsbibliothek, Berlin)*

many years thought to be based on a humorous canon by Beethoven, WoO 162, that refers to Johann Nepomuk Mälzel, inventor of the metronome—until the canon was shown to be a falsification of Schindler's. The movement combines two means of rhythmic motion: the steady, pulsating groups of sixteenth notes in groups of eight that establish the meter, and the anapest figure in the first violins that forms the basic theme, to which the cellos and basses provide an immediate answer that moves the harmony to the relative minor and gently propels the movement forward (*W 24).

Not to be overlooked in this delicately wrought fabric are the pizzicato figures in the second violins and violas. As in a comparable string-quartet texture, they lightly and percussively reinforce the rhythm of the first violin theme. This movement, in its tracery, anticipates later movements in which Beethoven cultivates the lightest touch: its great successor is the Andante scherzoso of the String Quartet Opus 130. In both he finds ways of working out echoes of short two-note figures between voices and registers.[60]

The other *pièce de résistance* is the Finale. Here we find a return to the rapid rhythmic action of the Seventh, but with generous hints from the finale of the "Ghost" Trio, Opus 70 No. 1. The opening theme of this Allegro vivace is in *pianissimo*. Its rapid pairs of triplets lead immediately to a three-note dactylic figure on the downbeat that is a rephrased variant of the main figure of the slow movement (where it was always on the upbeat) (*W 25). The reinforcement of this theme by violas and winds on its first appearance signals that the figure is to have a life of its own. We then witness a series of surprising events, in which the three-note dactyl figure, always in the same melodic form, seems to settle down on the dominant, C major, but then after three tries, suddenly erupts onto a *fortissimo* C♯ that is left unresolved until much later in the movement.

Paradox heaps on paradox. The form is more or less that of a sonata form but with two codas.[61] The first acts like a second development section, transforming the harmonic framework of the first theme and modulating through various keys. The second coda confirms the tonic, F major, but also supplies the longed-for resolution of that intrusive C♯ heard way back near the beginning of the movement. Now the C♯ becomes the basis for a stormy interlude in F-sharp minor, then slips back with ease into its home channel of F major and vigorously runs its course.

Touches of subtlety abound right to the end. In one passage, the winds in successive measures bring the interval of a third down through successive registers via pairs of flutes, oboes, clarinets, horns, and bassoons—and then right back up again through the same instruments. In fact Beethoven thought of this touch of comedy only at the final autograph stage of the symphony—we find him originally writing repeated chords for all the winds right through these measures; then, struck by a new idea, crossing out all the extra wind chords to leave just the falling and rising motions as they stand in the final version.[62] An element at the very end of the movement, hardly noticed, if at all, is typical of the little ways in which this symphony, in its artlessness that conceals art, predicts a detail of the late style.

The final measures hammer home the tonic harmony in the full orchestra, one chord to a measure, but the bass, *not yet finished with its cadencing functions*, at first alternates tonic and dominant under the tonic harmony above, until it too reiterates the tonic, but only in the very last two measures.

CHAPTER 11

THE MATURE CONCERTOS

❦

Beethoven wrote his first concertos, all for piano, essentially for his own use in performance. With the third, which he premiered as soloist on April 5, 1803, together with his first two symphonies and his oratorio *Christus am Ölberge*, the vocabulary and syntax of his Mozartian inheritance as a concerto composer was yielding to a more independent conception, to more varied and dramatic ways of setting up the solo-orchestra relationship. The position of the Third Piano Concerto after the first two is roughly analogous to that of the Second Symphony after the First, but in the concerto genre the spirit of Mozart was inevitably stronger and more vivid than in the symphony. Certainly the Third, as Brahms observed, is haunted by the image of Mozart's C minor concerto. Through his brother Carl, Beethoven offered the Third to the publisher André in November 1803.[1] By the time it actually appeared in print, with a dedication to Prince Louis Ferdinand of Prussia (himself an excellent pianist and sometime composer), it was the summer of the following year. By now Beethoven was occupied with the *Eroica* and with initial work on *Leonore*, as well as preliminary sketches for the "Waldstein" Sonata.

The New Symphonie concertante: *The Triple Concerto*

Beethoven returned to the concerto later in 1804 and in 1805, while he was in the midst of *Leonore* and the "Appassionata."[2] The result was a curiously passive work, the Triple Concerto for Piano, Violin, and Cello in C major, Opus 56. Dubbed by Plantinga "an interlude in the

French manner," it is a comfortable, rambling composition that aims to please but not stir its audiences, a work of easy surface qualities but no depth. We can readily connect the Triple Concerto with the *symphonie concertante* that had prospered in France and in French-influenced centers such as Bonn and Mannheim in the later eighteenth century, and which stayed alive until about 1810.[3] Beethoven had left unfinished the Romance in E minor for flute, bassoon, piano, and orchestra that he had sketched in 1786–87, and in 1802 he had tried to work out a "Concertante" in D major for piano trio soloists, the same combination as the Triple Concerto, in anticipation of a projected concert in the spring of that year. But the concert never came off and the "Concertante" remained a fragmentary torso, though it more than casually prefigures aspects of the Triple Concerto, including an "alla polacca" finale.[4]

It is surely right to associate these works with Beethoven's interest in current French traditions. He saw in postrevolutionary France that music could contribute to national pride so much more meaningfully than it could in Germany, where national feelings were rising but the sense of common identity was muted because the country was still a loose patchwork of smaller states. He admired what he knew of works by Cherubini and Méhul, and his strong turn toward French opera was reflected in his choice of *Leonore* as a subject. His encounters with French performers, especially string players, had also borne results. His dream of a potential career in France lingered on long after his angry reaction in 1804 to Napoleon's coronation. Ries predicted to Simrock in August and again in October of 1803 that within a year and a half Beethoven "will go to Paris, which makes me extremely sorry."[5] Some years later he nearly accepted the invitation from Jerome Bonaparte, and he toyed further with thoughts of a move to Paris that never came off.

The Triple Concerto may have been written for the violinist Georg August Seidler and the cellist Anton Kraft, that is "old Kraft," the father of the cellist Nikolaus Kraft. According to Schindler the original pianist was the Archduke Rudolph, but this hardly seems probable, even though Beethoven may have met the talented sixteen-year-old archduke at Lobkowitz's at about this time.[6] The intended pianist was, more likely, Beethoven himself.

Even in a symphonie concertante, the use of the piano trio as collective soloist was new. Having written three excellent piano trios and a more routine clarinet trio, Beethoven was able to transfer the total ensemble to the concerto with considerable ease, even if the musical material he settled on ranged from pleasant to banal. In sheer quality the Triple Concerto has always been regarded as marginal. Its key scheme mirrors that of the First Piano Concerto, but it is nowhere near as original. The Triple, in C major, has a long and discursive first movement, a singing Largo in A-flat major, and a rousing but ponderous Rondo alla Polacca finale. The work has a "certain indistinctness of expression and a kind of sponginess of construction"[7] to a degree not found even in the Second Piano Concerto, which Beethoven himself admitted was not one of his best. Here he was probably seeking popular appeal by keeping the thematic material simple and sequential and by limiting any form of elaboration. The work represents the easier, discursive side of Beethoven about 1804–5, with none of the intensity of the "Waldstein" and "Appassionata" Sonatas. In its Biedermeier mood and character, the Triple resembles the easy-going Andante favori that Beethoven cut away from the "Waldstein" precisely in order to sustain its taut consistency all the way through.

Nevertheless some original elements do crop up. Far from letting the piano dominate, as in a trio, Beethoven opts for the cello as the main solo instrument. It is the cello that starts off the first solo exposition in the work, presents the first new theme exploited by the solo complex, and, in its treble singing register, is the first solo voice to be heard in both the second and third movements.

After Haydn's early cello concertos and some virtuosic vehicles by Luigi Boccherini, Joseph Reicha, Anton Kraft, and others, the field lay fallow. Mozart wrote no cello concertos, nor did the later Haydn.[8] Since Beethoven himself was not moved to write one, despite his having virtually created the true cello sonata, the Triple is as close as we can come to a Beethoven cello concerto. The expanded range accorded the cello, its prominence against and with the violin, and its strong and active independence in all registers—all these foreshadow the new freedom in handling the instrument that Beethoven achieved three to four years later in his Opus 70 trios, the Cello Sonata Opus 69, and the "Archduke" Trio. The violin part in the concerto is somewhat underwritten when compared with the cello part, which successfully fulfills its leading roles both as a lyrical bass and an upper-range melodic voice.

Yet despite a few good passages, such as the A-flat-major segment in the first movement—for Tovey a "purple patch," for Leon Plantinga a "beautiful and memorable" phrase—the concerto lacks strength. Such moments are too rare to give the whole work a place in the higher scheme of things, and though it is far from being as blatant a concession to popularity as Beethoven was to commit in later years, it lags behind his other concertos in quality of thought.

The Fourth Piano Concerto

Nothing like this can be said of the Fourth Piano Concerto, in every respect a masterpiece of 1805–6. The earliest concept sketch for the opening theme of the first movement appears in the *Eroica* sketchbook, which includes notations from 1804. The main work on the concerto was put off until after *Leonore,* in late 1805 and 1806. By July 1806 Beethoven told Breitkopf & Härtel that his brother Carl would come to Leipzig with the scores in hand of the piano reduction of *Leonore,* the oratorio *Christus,* "and a new piano concerto." Beethoven played the solo part at his famous *Akademie* of December 22, 1808, along with the Fifth and Sixth symphonies, parts of the C major Mass, and the *Choral Fantasy.*[9] By that time the concerto had been in print for about four months, and its success with the public was immediate and lasting.

With this work the history of the piano concerto entered a new phase. At long last Beethoven had brought all his artistic powers to bear on the concerto, now exhibiting the fullest consistency of thought, feeling, beauty, and sensitivity. G major is a key he often associated with lightness and grace, as in the Piano Sonatas Opus 14 No. 2 and Opus 79, the Quartet Opus 18 No. 2, and the Violin Sonata Opus 31 No. 3. He never used it as primary key for a symphony, a later quartet, or a later piano sonata, and the only important middle-to-late work in this key is the idyllic Violin Sonata Opus 96 of 1812.

Although the Third Concerto has its moments of abruptness and surprise, the Fourth sustains a plateau of quiet beauty from beginning to end. If Mozart can be said to stand even distantly behind it, it is the Mozart of *The Magic Flute,* whose two vocal quintets sustain similar feelings of joy and wonder, and whose triumphal and utopian Allegro ending seems to be echoed in the ending of this concerto. Here, in its last, soft phrase, the solo piano soars into its highest octave over quiet pizzicato chords in the strings, then the horns join *pianissimo,* then flute and oboe, as a crescendo prepares for the *forte* resumption of the main motif (*W 26).

The opening is notable for beginning with the piano alone. Mozart's Piano Concerto, K. 271, had done almost the same, but Beethoven's first phrase, besides establishing the central role of the soloist from the beginning, is of a higher expressive order.[10] With this pensive, quiet phrase, which leads from its opening chord through pulsating repetitions to a pause on the dominant, the piano solo casts an unforgettable spell over the whole movement and, in a way, over the entire work. If we look back, we can see that Beethoven had begun many earlier works with quiet gestures. Indeed, opening a cyclic work with a theme or motif in *piano* was quite common with him—witness the First Piano Concerto and Piano Sonatas Opp. 27 Nos. 1 and 2, 31 No. 2, 53, and 57). But the *piano dolce* determines the quality of this opening gesture and in combination with the quasi-improvisatory feeling of the phrase produces its atmospheric effect.

From the opening gambit the rest of the movement follows. The orchestra replies to the soloist's gesture with a new version of the opening figure in the surprising key of B major, thus deviating from G major and giving the prominent upper-line B of the first theme its first harmonization as a tonic. After this striking opening, the first orchestral exposition flows forward, the remainder growing with controlled energy from the tonal contrast of G major and B major, a contrast that makes itself felt throughout the work. Beethoven's high art of transformation is especially evident in the gradual process by which a descending-fourth figure that ends the opening solo finds its way to new rhythmic forms. In the first instance, the orchestral strings regain G major in the opening passage; the figure appears later as a *forte* figure in the orchestra, the *fortissimo* theme further on, and elsewhere to the end of the movement, crowning the whole at the return in the solo piano as the movement gathers energy in readiness to end (*W 27).[11]

The slow movement has been associated with the legend of Orpheus, originally, by the nineteenth-century theorist Adolf Bernhard Marx, as Orpheus confronting the shades of Hell and later as Orpheus taming the wild beasts with his lyre, a portrayal wrongly attributed to Liszt by Tovey. There is no evidence whatsoever that this programmatic interpretation, which has been taken to extreme lengths by some writers, stems from Beethoven.[12] What is important, however, is Beethoven's way of setting up the movement as a literal dialogue between piano and strings. Each phase of the movement consists of a statement by the strings that is answered by the piano solo, with the strings at first gruff and resolute, the piano soft and yielding, using the softening *una corda* pedal throughout the movement, as directed in the score. The solo piano, figuratively turning the other cheek, reduces by stages the strings' aggressive statements, and gradually overcomes the opposing forces by a succession of dreamlike phrases, so that later in the movement the piano completely dominates, the strings are reduced to single pizzicato strokes, and the soloist can embark on an elaborate written-out cadenza that eventually prepares the final structural cadence on the tonic, E minor. There remains only a memory of the original orchestral statement, now in *pianissimo*, to close the movement, once more with the piano having the last poignant word.

The quasi-improvisatory quality of the piano part associates it with the tradition of the operatic arioso and with the eighteenth-century accompanied recitative—that is, operatic recitative accompanied not merely by a harpsichord but by the orchestra, most often strings. This device had been reserved in opera seria for moments of high dramatic importance—as when the Countess in *Figaro* comes to the bitter realization that she has lost her husband's love to her servant and prepares to sing "Dove sono i bei momenti, di dolcezza e di piacer?" ("Where are the beautiful moments of sweetness and pleasure?"); or in *Don Giovanni*, when Donna Anna compels Don Ottavio to swear to restore her honor. On the other hand this movement is not, strictly speaking, an operatic recitative transposed to an instrumental work. When he wanted to, Beethoven wrote recitatives, as he did in his Piano Sonata Opus 31 No. 2, and in later works. What we have here, rather, is more like a dramatic *scena* for solo piano and orchestra transplanted into the concerto genre and presented in a single pithy movement, with the orchestra reduced to strings alone. In this *scena,* entreaty is met at first by obdurate refusal.

Each of Mozart's earlier Italian operas always included at least one aria that was set for strings alone. *Idomeneo* had two: Electra's aria "Idol mio" and Arbace's "Se cola ne' fati." In his fully mature operas—the ones Beethoven would have known—he reduced the number to one. *Figaro* has Barbarina's mock-pathetic Cavatina as she laments over her lost pin; and in *Don Giovanni* we find "Ah fuggi il traditor," in which the half-mad Donna Elvira intercepts the innocent Zerlina and urges her in no uncertain terms to flee from Don Giovanni before it is too late. Donna Elvira's quasi-Handelian aria, often called "archaic" by commentators, has a succession of concentrated dotted rhythmic figures to which the figures in Beethoven's string parts in this concerto movement are distantly related.[13] The rhetorical character of the movement, like no other in Beethoven, invites association with traditions, and one of these may well have been that of the expressive aria with strings from Mozart's late Italian works. This is not to suggest still another "hidden program" for the movement or for the concerto as a whole, but it is, rather, to hint at the associations that such a movement evokes.

That Beethoven was interested in blending the operatic into the instrumental sphere is manifest in many of his works, not only those, mainly in his late period, that use instrumental recitatives but also those in which aria types and aria forms emerge. But he also blended the concerto principle overtly with other genres, as in the "Kreutzer" Sonata. We should remember that the gentle opening of the Fourth Piano Concerto brings the first phrase by the piano solo, then the answering phrase, with a harmonic contradiction, *by the strings alone.* Thus the beginning of the whole concerto foreshadows the opposition of forces that is worked out so dramatically and rhetorically in the slow movement—as if the piano were, in its way, an operatic soloist, and the work were a special kind of music drama.

The finale reconciles all earlier oppositions. This G-major rondo, Vivace, offers still another striking beginning—this one in C major, from which it makes its way back quickly to the tonic, G major, but not without having thus set up its own quiet tonal opposition, between C and G, that can generate later action. This lightly touched "off-tonic" opening creates a structural ambiguity that demands eventual resolution—will C or G predominate?—but the movement runs its course quite far before the inevitable answer is discovered: G, the true tonic, will triumph.

The Violin Concerto

At a crucial moment in the second act of *Leonore/Fidelio*, deep in Florestan's dungeon, the jailer Rocco and the disguised heroine Leonore dig the grave in which the starving prisoner is to be buried, when Florestan suddenly awakens. Leonore, almost speechless with hope, recognizes her husband. Florestan pleads for water. Rocco, moved by his plight, offers to give him a little wine, whereupon the great A-major trio begins, with a three-note unison figure in the strings (E–D–B) that comes down to the tonic, A, where Florestan, weakened as he is, opens the ensemble with a beautiful melodic phrase set to his words of thanks: "Euch werde Lohn in bessern Welten" ("You will be rewarded in better worlds"). This melody, saved for the first moment of emotional and physical tenderness between the reunited husband and wife, is an unforgettable expression of quiet serenity and love. And it is exactly this quality that Beethoven brings to his Violin Concerto, often noted for the ideal tranquility of its first two movements, the vivid spirit of its finale, and the sense of emotional cogency and connectedness that binds the work together. Although the *Leonore* trio is not a direct thematic source for the concerto, its striking opening figure, which recurs in various places throughout the opera—often in connection with Florestan's dream of survival—also recurs as a thematic fingerprint in this concerto as well as certain other works (*W 28).[14]

Although the concerto arose from Beethoven's contact with Franz Clement, an Austrian violinist who had come to prominence in the 1790s, Beethoven had been preparing to write a big violin concerto for some time. His first effort was an unfinished C Major Violin Concerto, WoO 5, dating probably from the early Vienna years. Then came the two Romances for Violin and Orchestra, Opp. 40 and 50, written around 1800 or a little later.

What the Germans called "Romanze" was a type of slow movement in *alla breve* (the second movement of Mozart's *Eine Kleine Nachtmusik* is the most notable), while its counterpart, the "Romance" for violin and orchestra, was a French subgenre used for slow movements by Viotti and his followers. Beethoven's two Romances have all the smoothness and polish of their French models.

Further evidence for the genesis of the D Major Violin Concerto is hard to come by: most likely the work was sketched extensively in a now-lost sketchbook of 1806–7 that probably also contained material for the Fourth Piano Concerto, the Fourth Symphony, and *Coriolanus*. Beethoven must have worked on it in the later months of 1806, since Clement was able to play its first performance at a benefit concert on December 23 of that year, but Czerny reports that Beethoven, despite frantic efforts, had barely finished the piece two days before the performance. Beethoven might have done most of his basic compositional work on it in five or six weeks during November and December 1806.[15] The autograph, which bears the date 1806, contains several layers of writing for the solo part, though whether its readings were fixed up for the December 1806 premiere or, possibly, its publication in August 1808, is impossible to say. Because of these complications the text of the work has undergone extensive scrutiny and correction in modern times, largely because of problems that arose from haste and misunderstandings on the part of early copyists, along with Beethoven's habitually rushed proofreading.

Then there is the well-known transcription of the work with a solo piano substituting for the violin. The keyboard version was contracted for by Clementi in April 1807, intended for publication in London, but it came out in Vienna in 1808 at the same time as the violin version and did not appear in London until 1810. The important question is whether Beethoven himself made the arrangement, as he was supposed to have done according to his contract with Clementi. The keyboard version has been judged to range in quality "from satisfactory to incompetent" and "more heavily weighted toward the latter."[16] The exception is the first-movement cadenza—a brilliant showpiece for solo piano with tympani that finds space for a stirring march in A major. That this march vividly recalls the march from *Leonore/Fidelio* reinforces the notion that the opera, in both its lyricism and its flashes of military music, heavily influenced this concerto. So strong is the cadenza that its retranscription for the violin version of the concerto—the only version known to concert audiences—is a potential eye-opener for listeners accustomed to the cadenzas by Joachim, Kreisler, and other virtuoso violinists, or by twentieth-century composers such as Alfred Schnittke.[17]

It is striking that Beethoven undertook a violin concerto of this character directly after the Fourth Piano Concerto. Both works create a feeling of spaciousness in their musical unfolding, in which ideas take time to develop and to fulfill their potential. This results in part from the considerable length of Beethoven's concerto first movements, in which room is needed for separate orchestral and solo expositions, for the intertwining of the two protagonists in the development, and for further interactions in the recapitulation and coda. But this spaciousness is also a consequence of the thematic ideas themselves. The five tympani strokes that open the first movement and the symmetrical first theme that follows in the winds set up a question: Do the tympani beats constitute a part of the main theme, a prologue figure, a motif that will reappear, or all of these? This question becomes increasingly urgent as the movement develops: witness the D$\sharp$ repetition of the tympani beats, now in the orchestral violins, rasping against the smooth linear flow of the D-major theme and only much later recalled and confirmed in ways that give it meaning.[18]

Listeners have never failed to feel the serenity of the slow movement, above all at that moment when its chain of variations is altered and reframed by what sounds to some like a new theme after the third variation and to others like a beautifully elaborated variant of the first theme.[19] The last movement stands as perhaps the best of Beethoven's rondo finales in 6/8 meter, a time-honored form and meter for concerto finales of which he would have known dozens of examples. These would have included Mozart's 6/8 rondo finales in every branch of his concerto writing, among them all the horn concertos and many of his piano concertos. We saw that Mozart's rondo theme from his B-flat Major Concerto, K. 595, was in Beethoven's mind when he copied it—transposed to E-flat major and written in 3/4 instead of 6/8—in the *Eroica* sketchbook. Mozart took the tradition of 6/8 rondos all the way to the rousing third movement of the Clarinet Concerto, K. 622, written in 1791. Beethoven had written a handful of 6/8 rondo finales in early works, always marking them "Rondo," as well as a few pathbreaking duple-meter examples, as in the "Pathétique" and "Waldstein" Sonatas. In later works he still wrote such finales, often blending rondo with sonata form in various and complex ways and thus inheriting and advancing the "sonata-rondo" tradition—but he never marked them "Rondo" again. This omission suggests that he passed beyond the traditional patterns of thinking that made such a form designation possible.

In the Violin Concerto rondo, the energy of the opening D-major theme is nicely contrasted with the quiet placidity of the G-minor episode, midway through the movement, that harks back distantly to Osmin's plaintive G-minor 6/8 lament in Mozart's *Entführung aus dem Serail*. Many touches of the purest middle-period Beethoven emerge as the movement proceeds, and, after a cadenza, the coda finds room for a striking harmonic move to A-flat major, from which it swings back to D major with the greatest of ease.

As late as the finale of the enigmatic F Minor Quartet Opus 95 Beethoven was still writing a 6/8 sonata-rondo finale of this type and of comparable richness. The 6/8 meter and poignant character of the Opus 95 finale, along with its thematic material, help explain why the movement has been linked to Mozart's G minor Quintet, where the 6/8 finale in G major brings serenity after turbulence. But in Beethoven's finale the 6/8 main body of the movement prolongs the darkness of F minor until the bright F-major coda in 2/2 sweeps it away.

The "Emperor" Concerto

The title of the "Emperor" Concerto, first of all, is spurious in that Beethoven had nothing to do with it.[20] And yet it carries weight: its evocation of grandeur, of the heroic, perhaps of the image of Napoleon through its connections with the *Eroica* (in the same key and with more than a few resemblances) fits well with important features of this work, especially compared with the restrained emotional worlds of the Fourth

Concerto and the Violin Concerto. Whatever else went into the making of this new E-flat Piano Concerto in 1809, it looks as if Beethoven determined to fill out his larger body of concertos with a work on the grand scale that shared elements of the heroic model. Continuing to use the three-movement plan that is normal for the concerto, he conceives for it a long and highly developed first movement, a profound and searching slow movement, and a powerful 6/8 finale that resolves all aesthetic and structural questions raised by the intensely contrasting earlier movements. A recent parallel in three movements had been the "Ghost" Trio, Opus 70 No. 1, written a year earlier, in which the slow movement, as here, had been the profound heart of the work.

In Beethoven's "Emperor," concerto and symphony virtually merge. Whereas in the Fourth Concerto trumpets and tympani enter the scene only in the finale, here the full orchestral tutti with brass and drums fills the sound space at the very beginning and remains prominent to the end. The winds and brass, especially paired horns, play a central role in defining the orchestral fabric and in supplying contrasts for the solo piano. In the slow movement, a subtle hymnlike Adagio, soft and dark colors pervade. The strings are muted throughout, brass and tympani are silent, and the interplay of strings and winds with one another and with the complex figuration patterns of the solo piano recall the slow movement of the Violin Concerto. Then the finale, emerging at the end of the Adagio through premonitions of its basic rondo theme, bursts out *fortissimo* to open the 6/8 Allegro as the finale uncoils a rising arpeggiated theme firmly in E-flat major, reminiscent in its character, syncopations, and offbeat rhythms of the Scherzo of the Fourth Symphony.

The heroic aspects of this work inevitably evoke images of the military traditions that had been associated with concertos well before Beethoven and certainly continued into his time. Particularly because this concerto was written in 1809, when the French were bombarding and invading the city, the work has seemed to some a reflection of the intensified military crises of that year—and in a broader sense, of the heightened consciousness of war that had been afflicting Europe for many years, indeed throughout Beethoven's mature lifetime. The association is plausible, since, as

Plantinga points out, the Fifth Concerto "bristles with musical topoi of a military cast and with modes of expression we easily identify as 'heroic.' "[21]

The same is true of those other occasions on which Beethoven seems to enlarge the meanings of his musical forms and genres by finding ways to let them address specific issues that are of deep human importance as the world knows them: tragic heroism and death, as in the funeral march in the *Eroica* and in *Coriolanus*; love and the contemplation of the beautiful, as in some of his major-mode slow movements, including the Adagio of the "Archduke Trio"; and fear and the otherworldly, as in the minor-mode slow movement of the quartet Opus 59 No. 1 and the "Ghost" Trio. That he can mingle softer feelings of intimacy with the strong and the powerful had always been clear even within movements of the "heroic" works, as in the second group themes in the first movements of the Third and Fifth symphonies and the melting second theme in *Coriolanus*. He certainly does so in this concerto, above all in the first movement. The first great paragraphs give us a group of powerful orchestral chords, respectively on the tonic, subdominant, and dominant seventh (thus forming a classic progression that requires resolution to the tonic), each interrupted by a vast, written-out cadenza for the solo piano, and all forming a prologue to the first theme of the exposition. This first idea opens a procession of themes, including one of haunting expressivity but brief duration, characterized by a gradually descending melodic line, diminuendo, well into the movement (*W 29).[22]

This descending theme enters above the dotted rhythms associated with the first theme and continues in the first violins while the cellos and basses propound the first theme's characteristic head motif—exactly parallel to the entrance of the lyrical second theme in the first movement of the Fifth Symphony. From here on the movement negotiates a vast trajectory in which the solo piano grapples with immensities, matching the strength of the orchestra with virtuosic figuration patterns of its own, above all a series of flying octaves in both hands in the development section.

In works such as the *Eroica* and the "Emperor" Concerto Theodor Adorno felt "exaltation"—"an expression of pride that one is allowed to be present at such an event, to be its witness." But he also saw the problem presented by works of such character in the modern world of the divided consciousness, which cannot fully sustain such unmitigated idealism. As he puts the quandary, "How far this is the *effect* of the composition—a joy which rivets the listener's attention to the dialectical logic—and how far the *expression* creates an illusion of such joy, rests on a knife's edge."[24] The separation of effect from expression, where the latter entails a genuine belief in the capacity of music to carry philosophical freight, is of the essence in the divided, self-conscious, modernist outlook that Adorno brought to bear on Beethoven, on music, and on art as a whole. To his pessimism there is no final response except that provided by listeners and musicians who seem to arise in every new generation and regard works such as the *Eroica* and the "Emperor" Concerto as among their most significant personal experiences. Listeners accept them not as antiquated expressions of a political idealism that has been cruelly banished by history, but as evocations of the human possibilities that might be realized in a better world. And by attending to the inner as well as the outer aspects of such works, such listeners still believe in the courage and beauty that they convey.

CHAPTER 12

MUSIC FOR THE STAGE

>❖❖❖⫷⫷⦗🝔⦘⫸⫸❖❖❖

Beethoven, who dreamed of mastering everything, dreamed of opera. To live up to the prediction that he would become a second Mozart, he knew that composing outstanding instrumental music would not be enough and that at some point he would have to engage with opera, the form in which Mozart had set the bar of competition unimaginably high. To Beethoven opera came hard. He had not grown up as an opera practitioner, as Mozart had since the age of twelve. Even though Bonn and Vienna provided a full menu of contemporary opera, Beethoven never had the natural feel for the theater that we find in born or experienced opera composers—many of them incapable of anything like his command of form, ideas, and proportions, but having this one gift in abundance. Furthermore, by the time Beethoven began to think about stage projects, around 1803 in Vienna, his deafness was a settled and worsening condition that made it difficult to deal with operatic people —singers, impresarios, stage directors, theater audiences, the box office—in short, the busy world of operatic production.

In his first years in Vienna he aimed to succeed first and foremost as a pianist and composer of instrumental music, not opera, and his principal patrons, even if they were opera devotees, saw him primarily as a musician of the salon and concert hall, not the stage. But as Beethoven became more and more established there was a general hope in Viennese musical circles that he would indeed turn to opera. He studied Italian text setting with Salieri, no doubt with opera in mind, and persisted in his efforts for many years, but he never managed to complete another opera besides *Leonore/Fidelio* despite many abortive ideas over many years.

When it came to subjects, Beethoven's attachment to the heroic and the ideal made him reject most contemporary opera as light and frivolous. Ignaz Seyfried reports his admiration for Cherubini ("of all living opera composers the one most worth attending to") but he thought that Weber (before *Freischütz*) "began studying too late [so that] his art could never develop in a natural way."[1] Seyfried further claimed that Beethoven regarded *The Magic Flute* as Mozart's finest work and wondered how he could have set a "scandalous" libretto like that of *Don Giovanni*. Yet Beethoven's characteristic ambivalence plays over this remark, for he did not hesitate to copy extracts from *Don Giovanni* in order to pick up secrets.[2] Further, the demonic aspects of Mozart's D-minor world, as in *Don Giovanni* and other late instrumental works, found their way into the Piano Sonata Opus 31 No. 2, the "Tempest," and the slow movement of the "Ghost" Trio, Opus 70 No. 1. When Beethoven thought about an opera based on *Macbeth* his first ideas fell easily into D minor.[3] His reluctance to tackle any but idealized subjects was not just a matter of moralistic disdain but was of a piece with his desire to integrate into opera something of the serious dramatic urgency that he had mastered in instrumental music, while at the same time he understood the need to adjust the form-building procedures of instrumental music to the formal necessities of opera.

Despite his aloofness Beethoven kept track of current developments in opera. Italian opera was the craze in Vienna, the ruling passion of the time, but German opera was gaining ground in the wake of universal admiration for *The Magic Flute*, which was so revered that Goethe actually wrote a sequel to it.[4] Beethoven had been writing concert arias from early on, had done yeoman work by contriving two arias for Umlauf's *Die Schöne Schusterin* in 1796, and had kept up with opera from a safe distance by choosing current operatic hit tunes as subjects for piano variations.

A major turn took place in 1802 when Emanuel Schikaneder presented Cherubini's *Lodoïska* at the newly founded Theater an der Wien. With this rescue opera by a serious professional composer, the new French operatic school arrived on the scene. *Lodoïska*'s success inspired other Cherubini operas that year, including *Faniska* and *Les deux journées*, also impressive and serious melodramas. *Lodoïska*, reversing *Leonore*, centers on the imprisoned heroine, who is rescued by her lover (Floreski) when the castle

The Theater an der Wien, site of the first performances of Fidelio *and other works by Beethoven, including the* Eroica *Symphony. (Historisches Museum, Vienna)*

in which she is incarcerated is attacked by the Tartars. Rescue operas had been the rage for more than twenty years, certainly since Mozart's *Entführung* in 1782, and now served as adventure stories of heroes in exotic realms and as fictional evocations of the prisons and guillotines of the French Revolution and the Terror. As in other cases, the evocation of harsh political realities in operas invited the illusion of truth while their happy endings assuaged the fears of contemporary audiences. Political imprisonment, heroism, and the restoration of freedom by the forces of liberal enlightenment is the central theme of *Leonore*.

The libretto of Beethoven's first attempt at opera, *Vestas Feuer* ("Vesta's Fire"), came from the ambitious Schikaneder early in 1803. As if to persuade himself of his real interest in operatic projects, Beethoven in the late spring of that year actually moved into a free apartment in the Theater an der Wien that was secured for him by Schikaneder as part of the commission to write an opera. He remained in it, except for the summer, through the winter of 1803–4, though, significantly, his real preoccupation at the time was not with opera but with the *Eroica*.[5] As for *Vestas Feuer*, a mediocre piece of hackwork set in ancient Rome, Beethoven got no further than the first scene and then dropped the project, although later he was able to mine it for Leonore and Florestan's duet of jubilation, "O namenlose Freude" ("O nameless joy").[6]

The Opera Leonore *and Its Overtures*

T he libretto of *Leonore, ou L'Amour Conjugale* ("Leonore; or, Conjugal Love") had originally been written in the late 1790s by Jean Nicolas Bouilly, a literary man who had been administrator of a French department near Tours during the Reign of Terror. It was widely accepted that during Bouilly's governance an episode resembling that of the opera plot had actually taken place.[7] According to the story, a woman disguised as a young man had worked her way into her husband's prison and freed him from his unjust captivity. Thus, if the tale were true, Bouilly himself would have been the minister who liberated the prisoner, and so the libretto seemed to commemorate not only actual heroism but the author's own benevolence amid the frightening atmosphere of France in those years.

The first setting of Bouilly's libretto, by the French composer Pierre Gaveaux, premiered in Paris in 1798. In an Italian translation it was then picked up by Ferdinando Paer, a capable opera composer from northern Italy. Paer had worked in Italy and in Vienna, where he had been musical director of the Kärntnertortheater in 1797 before he moved to Dresden and then finally to Paris, where he lived from 1806 until his death in 1839. Paer's *Leonore*, composed and produced in Dresden in 1804, prodded Beethoven's interest and rivalry, and when Beethoven's opera was finally ready for its premiere on November 20, 1805, it was called *Fidelio oder die eheliche Liebe* ("Fidelio, or Conjugal Love") and in the first libretto simply *Fidelio*, because Paer had used the title *Leonore* for his version thirteen months earlier. Beethoven owned a copy of Paer's score, and in several places he picked up some brief thematic ideas from Paer, then trumped him at every turn in compositional skill and dramatic intensity.[8] Paer's *Leonore* is a good jour neyman work, as we know from a modern recording; but it is essentially a patchwork of Italian operatic conventions typical of this period of transition between the light charm of Paisiello and the new brilliance of Rossini. Paer's version of Florestan's monologue and aria in the dungeon scene that opens the second act shows how a professional but unoriginal musical mind dealt with a dramatically crucial scene. Paer delivers a typical "mad scene," unusual only in being written for a male protagonist. He provides impassioned declamatory phrases for Florestan's suffering, along with handsome touches of orchestral writing throughout, including a probably half-conscious quotation from Tamino's "picture" aria in *The Magic Flute* when Florestan looks at the picture of Leonore—but nothing more, certainly nothing that matches Beethoven's gripping conception of the scene. Beethoven establishes an F-minor tonal center through alternations of *piano* and *forte* winds and works his way through diminished-seventh harmonies to remote harmonic goals as Florestan, in darkness and starvation, struggles to stay alive by conjuring up visions of former times with Leonore. The tympani, tuned at a diminished fifth (E♭, A), depicts the prisoner's beating heart as vividly as in a tale by Poe.

The 1805 libretto of *Leonore* was translated for Beethoven by Joseph Sonnleithner, secretary of the Court Theater and a prominent Viennese lawyer and musician, whom Beethoven had known through Sonnleithner's ventures in music publishing a few years earlier.[9] His libretto is well made, as we see by comparing his version with the French and Italian versions.[10] It met the demands of melodrama by intermingling minor domestic intrigue among the secondary characters (the jailer Rocco, his daughter Marzelline, and her suitor Jacquino) with scenes of power and pathos for the principals (the disguised heroine, Leonore, the suffering prisoner, Florestan, and the blackhearted prison governor, Pizarro). For the domestic scenes Beethoven provided effective set numbers that were occasionally sprinkled with Mozartian touches (sometimes even virtual quotations from Mozart, no doubt unconscious yet unmistakable)—but the scenes of serious dramatic intensity are entirely his own.[11]

Beethoven's *Leonore* failed on its first performances in November 1805, supposedly because Vienna was just then being invaded and occupied by

Joseph Sonnleithner, secretary of the Court Theater, whose translation of Leonore *from its original French source into German was used by Beethoven as the libretto for his only opera. (Historisches Museum, Vienna)*

Napoleon's armies. In fact, the audience at the first performance was well stocked with French army officers, but it may be that the opera was over the heads of many listeners accustomed to lighter stage works. Although it has long been accepted that Beethoven's alterations resulted from a committee meeting with his friends, it is more likely that such a meeting would have taken place, if at all, in 1807, after plans for a Prague performance fell through.[12] At all events, the revised version produced in March and April of 1806, with the newly rewritten *Leonore* Overture No. 3 in place of the one known as No. 2, was much more successful. The subsequent history of *Leonore* in Beethoven's lifetime was marked by abortive attempts to produce the work in Berlin and Prague, though it was eventually mounted in 1815 in Leipzig and Dresden. By far the most important step was Beethoven's agreement to revise it for a new production in Vienna early in 1814.

This final version came to be *Fidelio* as we know it. The libretto was reworked by G. F. Treitschke, an experienced hand in the theater—and Beethoven rewrote many portions of the score, a labor that occupied him from March to May of 1814. It cost him, as he said, more hard labor than if he were composing a new work, but he took pride in matching Treitschke's alterations with his own subtle splicings, in reducing redundancies, and in tightening the musical content. He also had to write several new portions, notably the final segment of Florestan's dungeon scene. All this makes the conversion of the 1805–6 *Leonore* into *Fidelio* the only time Beethoven revised a vast middle-period work during the transition to his late style.[13]

The essence of *Fidelio*, implicit in its very title, is Leonore's unwavering love for Florestan and her courage in risking her life to try to save him. The work has resonated through almost two centuries as a celebration of female heroism. Feminist criticism, while protesting the frequent suffering and death of female heroines in opera at the hands of men or from machinations hatched by men, finds in *Fidelio* a powerful exception, in that the suffering victim is the man, the agent of salvation the woman. The subtitle of the work is "Die eheliche Liebe," or "Conjugal Love," which directly translates Bouilly's "L'Amour Conjugale."

The division of the opera into two acts reflects the separate planes on which the action takes place. The dominating feature of the mise-en-scène is the prison. Thus the opera reflected heightened awareness of prisons and the miseries of incarceration that were intensified by the French Revolution and the Terror. Prison reform had been a European social concern from the mid-eighteenth century on, in works by writers such as Cesare Beccaria, who championed better conditions for prisoners. In *Leonore/Fidelio* the prison governor, Pizarro, is evil personified; his cruelty to Florestan seems to have arisen from personal and political lust for revenge and no other cause. As Florestan says in his monologue, "I told the truth, and chains are my reward."

The action is set on three floors of the prison building: (1) ground level, the world of ordinary daylight within the prison walls, where the prisoners, who emerge from below near the end of act one for a walk, grope and stagger in the unaccustomed sunlight and air; (2) a lower level, where the ordinary prisoners are kept in dark cells; and (3) the lowest level, housing the dungeon, which is reserved for prisoners of state, as Rocco tells Leonore. It is where Florestan has been kept for two years, chained to the wall, freezing and starving. "He must have done a great wrong," says Leonore to Rocco, to which Rocco replies, "Or else he has powerful enemies; it comes to the same thing."[14]

The first act takes place entirely on the ground level, and the dramatic tension arises from the presence of Leonore, disguised as Fidelio, who is unsure if Florestan can hold out much longer or is even still alive. A further twist arises from a domestic subplot in which Marzelline is pursued by Jacquino but is enamoured of Fidelio. The main plot gains additional tension from the announcement that Don Fernando, Pizarro's superior, will arrive shortly to investigate reports that prisoners are being maltreated. Meanwhile the domestic subplot carries just enough weight to generate some lesser operatic numbers, such as No. 2, in which Marzelline declares her love for Fidelio in an aria almost too big for her character; or Rocco's "gold" aria, an obligatory solo that sets up Rocco as a bluff, good-hearted peasant who does his job and has the worries of an ordinary man. But we also find numbers that lift the first act far beyond the ordinary. One is the canonic quartet "Mir ist so wunderbar" ("I feel such strange delight") which freezes the action and captures Leonore and the three minor characters in a moment of expressive contemplation. Another is the Prisoners' Chorus, one of the most moving choral utterances in opera. Theirs is the collective misery of suffering prisoners, abandoned and mistreated, reduced to the semihuman, fearful of informers, longing for light. Their raggedness compels us to imagine the lower prison level to which they must return as the chorus quietly ends. Through the heart-breaking effect of the chorus, the whole opera takes a deeper turn, from which it does not deviate.

In Act 2 Florestan becomes the central figure as the action opens with his great monologue and aria. Lying in the cold and dark of solitary confinement, he sings "Gott, welch Dunkel hier!" ("God, what darkness here!"). Beethoven establishes the atmosphere in the F-minor introduction, with horn blasts, descending chromatic bass line, and elaborate modulatory schemes that use as pivots the diminished seventh harmonies that became the stock-in-trade of Romantic operas by Weber, Marschner, and many another. After the powerful bleakness of his recitative, Florestan settles into the warmth of A-flat major for his aria, "In des Lebens Frühlingstagen" ("In the springtime of my life"), in which he remembers the happiness of earlier days (not unlike Beethoven writing from his sickbed to Wegeler in 1825). He asserts his innocence of any crime except telling the truth about Pizarro, and, at last, he looks at Leonore's image before him. We are not sure how this scene was set in 1805, though a convincing case has been made for a partial reconstruction.[15] But in the 1806 version the final section, in F minor, essentially continues and strengthens but does not change the earlier tone of reflected pain.

In 1814, however, Treitschke and Beethoven came up with another plan. Now Florestan was to end this scene with an Allegro coda in F major in which Florestan has a manic vision of Leonore actually coming to save him. "Manic" is no exaggeration: the score directs that this section is to be sung "in a quiet ecstasy bordering on madness." And Florestan now bursts loose in a passionate rising series of phrases in which he "sees" Leonore and embraces her. Here the effect of his rise to a high B♭ (his highest pitch in the opera) again demonstrates Beethoven's use of a registral extreme in a climax, as we have seen in more than one of his sonata-form recapitulations. This new coda is enormously difficult to sing and has seemed overwrought to some critics; it is certainly a sample of Beethoven taxing a voice to extremes, as he does later in some passages in the Ninth Symphony.

Leonore is ambitious and progressive for 1805–6 because the project compelled Beethoven to adapt to the necessities of operatic discourse, such as the distribution of varied set numbers between arias and ensembles, the role of the chorus, and the formation of large finales near the end of each act to sum up the action in a continuous musical setting. Text-derived sectional forms and large-scale statements and counterstatements here replace the formal traditions of sonata form, rondo, and variations that he had long been accustomed to deal with in instrumental works. Achieving large-scale growth and musical connection without the concept of a "movement"—now always an operatic "number"—was for him a new challenge. That the spirit of Mozart hovers in the background of the work should not surprise us. Most striking is Beethoven's ability to deepen expression in the serious and ethical side of the plot to such a point that the work became, as indeed it has become, one of the exceptional classics of the operatic literature, unsurpassed in its conveyance of dramatic and emotional truth. Its stature is intrinsically unrelated to Beethoven's belief that the plot conveyed a true story, not operatic claptrap. It has to do with his ability to frame the formal dynamics of the work so as to give maximum weight to the moral issues underlying the action: the physical suffering of the wretched prisoners and the system that promotes such suffering; Florestan's heroic stoicism in the face of injustice; and Leonore's love and courage, the willing risk-taking by a loving wife.

The four overtures were written in this order: *Leonore* No. 2 (1805); *Leonore* No. 3 (1806), a brilliant rewriting of No. 2; *Leonore* No. 1 (1808, for an abortive production in Prague); *Fidelio* Overture (1814).[16] The three *Leonore* overtures, all in C major, foreshadow the rescue plot. The crucial issue in all of them is how Florestan's A-flat aria should be introduced. In Nos. 2 and 3 the work opens with a slow scalewise descent, beginning on G, which defines the key of C major and then slips past it to a strange resting point on the dominant of B major before sliding smoothly into A-flat for Florestan's aria theme in the clarinets. In both overtures the aria theme dominates the slow introduction. Then the Allegro whips up new momentum with a low-register first theme in the strings, to which is contrasted the great E-major presentation of the "Florestan theme" as the secondary theme. Two trumpet calls later in both overtures signal the arrival of the minister who will save the situation, and a hymn of salvation closes the main material, followed in both cases by a tremendous coda. Wagner said of *Leonore* No. 3, "it is not the overture to the drama; it is the drama itself."

No. 1 is a weaker, smaller rewriting of the same C-major overture idea, less powerful than either No. 2 or No. 3. But the *Fidelio* overture of 1814 is a completely new work, suitable to the new concept of the work. In E major, it has no thematic foreshadowing of Florestan, but its main key is associated with Leonore's rugged solo scene of hatred for Pizarro and determination to free her husband. These feelings emerge in the great scene, "Abscheulicher, wo eilst du hin?" ("Detestable creature, where are you hastening?"), near the end of Act I, in which Leonore sets forth her love for Florestan, loathing for his captor, and vigorous resolution in her E-major aria "O Hoffnung" ("O, Hope").

The Coriolanus *Overture*

T he year of *Leonore* No. 3, 1806, also saw six other important works, none of which can be construed as "heroic" except perhaps the Quartet Opus 59 No. 1. They are: the Fourth Symphony; the three "Razumovsky" Quartets Opus 59; the Thirty-Two Variations in C Minor for Piano, WoO 80; and the Violin Concerto. We can speak in different ways of the "dramatic" in all of these works (a word without which much traditional Beethoven criticism would not exist), but in its true meaning, limited to describing music written for stage drama, the next step after *Leonore* is the *Coriolanus* Overture.

Composed early in 1807 for *Coriolanus,* a play by Heinrich Joseph von Collin, the overture was first performed at a subscription concert in March, an event that may have spurred a revival of the play itself on April 24. The play, which dates from 1802, had been given in Vienna frequently in the years up to 1805, with Joseph Lange, Mozart's brother-in-law, in the title role. Beethoven knew Collin and hoped to have him collaborate in a new opera; they talked of *Bradamante* or *Macbeth*, but nothing came of either. In any case, the overture overwhelmed the play; as Ries said of the *Eroica,* it shook heaven and earth. It evoked a thoughtful review in 1812 from E. T. A. Hoffmann, whose account of the Fifth Symphony had appeared two years earlier and for whom this second C-minor essay in Beethovenian tragedy brought recollections of Cherubini but also recognition as a "masterwork."[17]

Coriolanus, a work of gigantic strength, is a prime example of the dramatic overture as concert piece in one movement—that is, an Allegro movement with no slow introduction—a "tone poem" before the term came into existence. The rise of public symphonic concerts opened up opportunities to Beethoven to compose shorter works that could contrast with multimovement symphonies. Though opera overtures could serve this need, the genre was expanding. Thus the "concert overture" was coming into being. It is not too much to say that *Coriolanus* begins the tradition of such works, a tradition that would be taken up in the next generation by Mendelssohn and others, then developed into the programmatic symphonies of Berlioz, and, much later, the tone poems of Liszt and Strauss.

Controversy has raged for years over the true literary background of the overture. Its terse narrative structure presents the essential conditions of Coriolanus's personal tragedy. Yet although the work fits the outline of Collin's play, some have argued that it is far too big for that vehicle and that Beethoven must have had Shakespeare's *Coriolanus* in mind—a view premised on the hero-worshipping grounds that a musical star of this magnitude must have a literary analogue worthy of its composer. Its association with Shakespeare sprang up with E. T. A. Hoffmann and was later espoused by Wagner. Admittedly, it is hard to shake this view off completely, in the light of Beethoven's avowed admiration for Shakespeare, his thoughts of a possible *Macbeth,* and the clear evidence that, like any literate German artist or intellectual of the time, he knew the plays. But as for the literary analogues for the overture, an essay written in 1938 by Paul Mies went far to redeem the connection between the overture and the basic material of Collin's play.[18] In the basic story, Caius Marcius, a Roman patrician of legendary physical strength and courage, has received the laudatory name "Coriolanus" after defeating the Volscians, enemies of Rome, at Corioli. He then seeks the consulship but is repelled by the idea of currying favor with the Roman masses. The people turn against him, he denounces them, is exiled, and in his rage joins forces with the Volscian forces of Aufidius, who is planning an attack on Rome. As the Volscian armies threaten Rome, Coriolanus refuses to spare the city from devastation until his mother, Volumnia, and his wife, Virgilia, come to find him in his tent. In hopeless crisis he agrees to lift the siege, then tries to reconcile himself with the angry Volscians, but dies (either by murder or suicide, depending on the version).

As Mies shows, Collin leaves the political aspects of the plot in the background, focusing less on the outer conditions for Coriolanus's downfall than on his response to each succeeding turn of events. Collin's version includes Coriolanus's tragic meeting with his mother and his wife, who plead with him to spare Rome, its people, and themselves. This meeting determines his fate: the appeal from the woman who bore him and whose voice is somehow within him, despite himself, tears him apart as he is caught between irreconcilable necessities. In Shakespeare's play, following Plutarch, Coriolanus is murdered by the Volscians; in Collin, Coriolanus, having lost his honor and his moral courage, kills himself.

Besides the two plays another source suggests itself, namely Plutarch. We know that Beethoven read Plutarch—witness his letter to Wegeler and the Heiligenstadt Testament, in both of which he says, "Plutarch has taught me resignation." Moreover, other references to Plutarch in Beethoven's letters, Conversation Books, and account by contemporaries, have recently been unearthed.[19] Plutarch's famous *Parallel Lives*, the great biographical classic written about A.D. 100, with its pairing of the lives of Greeks and Romans, was widely read in the eighteenth and early nineteenth centuries by people at every social and educational level, and its influence on literature and moral philosophy was substantial. Editions, translations, and commentaries abounded in eighteenth-century Europe, in Germany as in Britain, in France, and as far afield as Russia.[20] The list of critics who admired and cited Plutarch is a pantheon that includes Gotthold Lessing, Johann Gottfried von Herder, and August Wilhelm Schlegel, and the parallel list of novelists and dramatists includes Friedrich Schiller and Goethe, to mention only the major German authors and those with whom Beethoven felt intellectual kinship.

Among the twenty-two pairs of lives recounted by Plutarch in his quest for understanding the tragedy of Greece and the rise of Rome are Alcibiades and Coriolanus, both celebrated military leaders of the fifth century B.C. There are some parallels between the two tragic figures. Alcibiades had been a famous Athenian general who fell into a mortal dispute with the Athenians. He escaped to Sparta but eventually lost the Spartans' confidence as well, and later met his death in Persia on orders from Sparta. Plutarch portrays Coriolanus as a military hero whose pride, rage, and arrogance presage his downfall, first through his exile, then as a result of the crucial encounter with his mother, Volumnia.

The crux of the story is the impossibility of reconciliation between the outsize strength and courage of Coriolanus as a man and general, and his vulnerability, as his mother's son, to Volumnia's eloquent declaration that if he persists in destroying Rome to satisfy his revenge, she will be among the dead. As Plutarch portrays the scene, after a further impassioned speech, she throws herself at his feet; Coriolanus raises her up, and says, "Mother, what have you done? . . . You have won your victory, you have saved Rome, but you have destroyed your son . . . no one but you could have defeated me."

This inner contradiction is writ large in Beethoven's overture. The musical image in the first theme, in C minor, depicts (no other word will do) Coriolanus as the tragic warrior, with its fortissimo unison C stated three times, each time cut off abruptly (*W 30). The theme is then contrasted with its perfect foil, the second theme, in E-flat major, the antithesis of the first in its beauty and tenderness. The second theme is perfectly balanced between its first two measures and its second pair. It hovers on the dominant of E-flat, never decisively landing but moving on into new thematic ideas. This thematic dualism—this dialectic of a son's rage and a mother's entreaty—of Coriolanus and Volumnia, remains unresolved to the end, as the failure of any resolution results in Coriolanus's fate. The whole feeling of the two principal themes is akin to that of the forthcoming Fifth Symphony's first movement, with which the whole work has much in common. Yet the two elements reflect more than the dramatic figures of Coriolanus on the one side and Volumnia on the other; both elements are within Coriolanus himself. Thus the overture ends with the two themes but in reversed order: the coda begins first with Volumnia's theme, again in C major although it has been heard in this key in the recapitulation; then to end it all, the Coriolanus theme, in C minor, as it had first been heard at the opening, as if Coriolanus is now giving his tragic answer. He is first shown in his strength, then in his disintegration as the second part of his theme slows down, repeats its first measure in ever slower forms, and finally dies away, followed by three quiet pizzicato tonic touches in the unaccompanied strings, *pianissimo.*

A look at the autograph score in the Beethoven-Archiv in Bonn discloses that, at a late stage in composing the work, Beethoven considered another way of ending, namely to have cadential dominant-tonic strokes in the first violins as the Coriolanus theme was being slowly uttered for the last time. But he took these out of the autograph and opted for the fully quiet, almost unarticulated last measures with which Coriolanus dies. Incidentally, the parallel case of thematic liquidation had taken place at the end of the *Eroica* slow movement, which as a C minor funeral march for an unnamed hero is the closest antecedent to *Coriolanus* in Beethoven's entire output. And his using the collapse of the theme to show the demise of a tragic, classical hero relates to the meaning of the Marcia funebre in the *Eroica*.

Incidental Music for Goethe's Egmont

The final dramatic work of Beethoven's middle years is the incidental music for Goethe's *Egmont*, composed in late 1809 and early 1810 on commission from the Vienna Court Theater. Goethe's play, originally written in 1786, was by now a classic drama of political liberation. In sixteenth-century Flanders, the hero, Count Egmont, is caught up in the web of political resistance to the Spanish tyranny over the Low Countries. After Egmont's capture and imprisonment, his lover, Clärchen, attempts to rescue him; failing, she poisons herself. Egmont in his cell has a transcendental vision of the image of freedom as a woman who looks like his beloved Clärchen. She puts a laurel wreath on his head while military music is heard—then Egmont is summoned to his execution and goes out to sacrifice himself for his country, knowing that freedom will prevail.

The parallels to *Leonore* are obvious: the imprisoned hero, the attempted rescue by his female beloved, and the theme of political liberation, which audiences could readily associate with Austria under Napoleonic occupation. For the drama as a whole Beethoven wrote nine numbers as well as the overture: four entr'actes to connect the five acts, two contrasting songs for Clärchen; a Larghetto in D minor for Clärchen's death; a melodrama for Egmont's vision in his cell; and an ebullient closing "victory symphony" that also ends the overture. In the first of Clärchen's two songs, "Die Trommel gerühret" ("The drum is resounding"), she declares her longing to be a soldier (like Leonore, she would then be dressed as a man); in the other, "Freudvoll und leidvoll" ("Blissful and tearful"), she sings of love and pain in a limpid aria that evokes Leonore's "Komm Hoffnung," but without a sweeping Allegro final section. In this work the female protagonist shows courage and devotion, but her lover dies a martyr. Instead, eventual triumph is predicted for the broader cause for which he fights—the freedom of the people, which must be left to the future. As Beethoven wrote on the first page of a bundle of sketches, "The main point is that the Netherlanders will eventually triumph over the Spaniards."[21]

That Beethoven originally considered writing the overture in C minor rather than F minor, its eventual key, suggests a direct derivation from *Coriolanus*, the Fifth Symphony, and his life-long C-minor mood. The final choice of F minor, with the optimistic F major "victory" music at the close, places the work in the key most commonly associated with the tragic in the vocabulary of contemporary key associations. Here, as in *Coriolanus*, it seems likely that the thematic dialectic of the overture reflects specific dramatic images: in the slow introduction, the heavy Spanish oppression and the keening pain of the people; in the Allegro, the rising tumult and revolt; in the coda, Egmont's capture and death (the *fortissimo* return of the opening oppressive figure followed by an abrupt cut-off with a hold), and then the "victory" music, which begins, significantly, *pianissimo* and then rises in eight measures to a climactic *fortissimo* tutti.[22]

Although Beethoven liked to play down the programmatic in his instrumental works, the associations are inescapable in his theater music—and even in the *Pastoral* Symphony his disclaimers about "tone painting" do not convince us that he had no pictorial images in mind for the "scenes" of the material. In *Egmont,* as there, his larger aim is to persuade audiences to attend to the structural and expressive content of the music on its own terms, but in music intended for the stage he could hardly fail to link his music directly to the dramatic action, characters, and atmosphere. In any music, the two dimensions, the programmatic and the structural, perpetually coexist, however precariously; and Beethoven's reluctance to admit his strong interest in the programmatic because he might be wrongly judged by history partly conceals his true beliefs. Though he was well aware that the age had moved decisively toward the primacy of instrumental music, toward "absolute" music and away from the "merely" pictorial, not even Beethoven's well-justified confidence in his command of musical form and content could completely repress his ambivalence.[23] As a tone poet he accepted and exploited music's power to evoke nameable, identifiable externalities; as a pure musician, he rejoiced in composing music whose structural and expressive power reinforced its claim to autonomy.

CHAPTER 13

VOCAL MUSIC

⟫⊶⊶⟪⟪⟐⟐⟐⟫⟫⊶⊶⟪

Oratorio and Mass

Beethoven's middle-period religious music for solo voices, chorus, and orchestra is limited to two works—the oratorio *Christus am Ölberge* ("Christ on the Mount of Olives"), written in 1803 and revised in 1811, and the Mass in C, written in 1807 on commission from Prince Nikolaus Esterházy and published in 1812. Different as they are, both exemplify Beethoven's respectful, thoughtful approach to sectors of religious expression to which he turned only on special occasions and for special reasons.

Beethoven later claimed that he had composed the oratorio in two weeks, working in close collaboration with Franz Xaver Huber, editor of the *Wiener Zeitung* and sometime librettist.[1] That Beethoven was able to cover seventy-five pages of the Wielhorsky sketchbook with sketches for *Christus* in a couple of weeks may seem too rapid a pace, but it is entirely imaginable for periods of intense concentration when he was working at top speed.[2] At all events the work was ready for its first performance on April 5, 1803, even though Beethoven was still working on trombone parts on the morning of the performance.[3] Haste is evident in the inconsistent quality of the work, which ranges from routine recitatives and reasonably effective arias for Jesus and the Seraph, to bombastic choral writing for the warriors and youths. Revising it for publication at long last eight years later, he described it defensively and apologetically to Breitkopf & Härtel as "my first work of that kind [a sacred oratorio] and, moreover, an early work . . . written in a fortnight during all kinds of disturbances and other unpleasant and distressing events in my life (my brother happened to be suffering from a mortal disease)."[4] Significantly, Beethoven adds that "what is quite certain is that now I should compose an absolutely different oratorio from what I composed then."

Prior to *Christus* Beethoven's only attempts at large-scale vocal works with soloists and chorus had been the two cantatas of 1790—for the death of Joseph II and the shorter one for the elevation of Leopold II. He could have looked back to the Joseph cantata as an impressive achievement for its time, and certainly he did look back to it when he took from one of its arias the great streaming melody in F major that crowns the ending of *Leonore/Fidelio*. But when we compare the arias and choruses of *Christus,* even in its improved version of 1811, with any portions of *Leonore,* the difference is clear. For the oratorio Beethoven drew on his professional competence to fashion an essentially prosaic work, while the opera caught his imagination and drove him to give it the full measure of his talents. The first aria in *Christus,* "Meine Seele ist erschüttert" ("My soul is shaken"), for the tenor role of Jesus, has rapid passage work in the strings reflecting Jesus's agitation but has little of the tautness of Pizarro's "Ha! Welch'ein Augenblick" ("Ha! What a moment"). The closing vocal trio of the oratorio, for Jesus, the Seraph, and Petrus, seems stilted and conventional when compared with either of the two trios in the opera. *Fidelio,* in its range of situations, characters, and above all its overriding moral purpose as a drama about imprisonment and freedom, is a work about which Beethoven could have said, as he did much later about the *Missa solemnis,* "from the heart—may it go to the heart." Posterity has not been able to say anything comparable about *Christus,* despite the aura of seriousness that attaches to a work in which the suffering of Jesus is the central theme. It is true that there are parallels of dramatic content between *Christus* and *Leonore* because both place at the center a suffering male figure and "in each case a long and somber prelude in the minor depicts the lone figure's plight."[5] It is also true that in the oratorio the female Seraph tries to offer Christ an alternative to the cup of sorrow, but to no avail; in the opera, as it stood in 1805–6, Leonore, after defending the weakened Florestan from Pizarro, has her pistol stripped from her by Rocco, leaving the couple defenseless. The duet that follows "is therefore sung by two people who are reconciled to death if they can die in each other's arms."[6] Yet despite these surface similarities, there are solid musical reasons why *Leonore/Fidelio* is an enduring masterpiece but *Christus* remains a hastily crafted effort to compete with Haydn as an oratorio composer. If the Joseph cantata was a major step forward for the young Beethoven in 1790, *Christus* was musically routine for him in 1803. In its revision of 1811, it remains a barely improved reconnoitering of ground from which he had long since departed. It is instructive as an example of Beethoven's response when he was working with texted music at less than his top level of concentration: a heavy reliance on tested formulas of oratorio writing, recitatives, and arias of fairly stock character, and choral numbers that rely on plain contrapuntal techniques (as in the finale chorus) or simple repetitions of obsessive rhythmic formulas.

A very different profile emerges in the Mass in C major. The artistic legacy of Haydn, now in his old age, and the long traditions of Austrian Mass composition left their imprints on it in several ways. The work was written to fulfill a request from Prince Nikolaus Esterházy, the namesake and grandson of Haydn's former patron, for performance at Eisenstadt on the name day of his wife, Princess Esterházy, née Marie von Liechtenstein. Beethoven took on the commission in the summer of 1807, promising the Mass by the needed date in September. He met the deadline despite his concern over entering into competition with Haydn in a genre that the old master had ruled to perfection but that was new to Beethoven.[7]

The gulf between Beethoven's fierce pride and the patronage ideals of tradition-minded Austro-Hungarian nobles is amply illustrated by an anecdote reported by Schindler and Thayer.[8] According to the story, the prince, after hearing the work—and probably noticing its stark differences from the styles of Mass composition he revered in Haydn—said to Beethoven, "But, my dear Beethoven, what is this that you have done again?" Whereupon, continues the story, the court chapel master was heard to laugh—this being none other than Johann Nepomuk Hummel, the composer and pianist who had himself written masses for the Esterházy court, including one in the same key, C major, just the previous year. Reacting angrily to the prince's question and furious over Hummel's pompous laughter as well as the inferior guest quarters he had been given in Eisenstadt, Beethoven left in a huff.[9]

On accepting the prince's commission Beethoven had praised Haydn's masses, calling them "inimitable masterpieces."[10] Beethoven meant it. He clearly studied Haydn's masses while composing his own, no doubt for reasons far beyond the fact that the Esterházys had commissioned it, as we see from his sketches for the Gloria. These sketches include two passages copied from the Gloria of Haydn's *Schöpfungsmesse* ("Creation Mass"), one of four late Haydn masses easily available to Beethoven in published editions.[11] Also, some thematic similarities have been noted between the Mass in C and Haydn's *Missa in tempore belli* ("Mass in Time of War"), also a C-major work. The singular gentleness of style in parts of the Mass in C, on which Beethoven himself remarked, evokes a sense of piety that he had never attempted before.[12]

To achieve the desired quality he set the text of the Mass Ordinary with remarkable restraint. He completely avoided the quasi-operatic formulas employed in *Christus* in favor of a highly diatonic, even-flowing style in the Kyrie and more powerful and varied forms of expression in the Gloria and Credo, but always remaining within what is for him a narrow range of contrasts. The last movement of the Mass, the lengthy Agnus dei, is set in three sections: a pulsating Poco andante in C minor; an energetic Allegro ma non troppo in C major for the text "dona nobis pacem" that reaches a massive height of expressivity; and a C-major Andante con moto, tempo del Kyrie, in which not only the tempo and character but the opening thematic material of the first Kyrie returns to round out the whole. Since the Kyrie itself is in a three-part ABA form, with the harmonic scheme C major (Kyrie I), E major (Christe), C major (Kyrie II), the return at the close of the Agnus dei confirms that the quiet tone of this initial C-major statement remains the dominating aesthetic quality of the work to which all else is contrasted.

In an 1813 review of the Mass, E. T. A. Hoffmann found in its C-minor Agnus dei section "a feeling of inner melancholy, which, however, does not tear the heart to pieces but rather soothes it, and, like the pain that comes to us from another world, dissolves it in unearthly joy."[13] Hoffmann, steeped in the mystical feeling characteristic of the early Romantics, was hoping to see German sacred music restored to an expressive, observant mode, as opposed to the operatic expansion of styles he found in the works of the preceding generation. Hoffmann writes that knowing Beethoven's music by now, he had expected the mass to reflect the feelings of awe and terror that he had found so clearly trumpeted forth in such works as the Fifth Symphony. And now he found, to his surprise, that the entire Mass in C breathed an atmosphere of "childlike cheerful feelings, which, building upon its purity, entrusts its faith to the goodness of God and prays to him, as to a father who wishes the best for his children and hears their supplications."[14]

The expression of personal religiosity—of an individual quest for "inner peace," to borrow the words that Beethoven inscribed on the score of the Dona nobis pacem of the much grander *Missa solemnis*—is of the essence in the Mass in C.[15] Even the choral sections, and certainly the sections in which chorus and vocal soloists combine forces, have an intimacy in the text setting for the most heartfelt passages that unmistakably foreshadows the *Missa solemnis* and that removes the work from the more traditional settings that Beethoven must have known. The Mass furnishes another example of Beethoven's experimenting in these middle years with a range of expression wholly apart from the powerful and dynamic works of the "heroic" type—now probing the world of *stille Andacht* (quiet devotion). Such qualities emerge in certain middle-period works and movements, for example, in the slow movements of the Violin Concerto and the quartets Opus 59 Nos. 1 and 2, but here the reflective, pensive lyricism of such conceptions gives way to the specific qualities associated with religious fervor and with the channeling of the subject's feeling not simply toward an aesthetic state but toward God. It is a quality that Wordsworth captured in one of his most serious sonnets, by pure chance published in 1807, the same year as the Mass in C major:

> It is a beauteous evening, calm and free;
> The holy time is quiet as a Nun
> Breathless with adoration; the broad sun
> Is sinking down in its tranquillity;
> The gentleness of heaven is on the Sea.

The Songs

Beethoven has been credited with creating the Romantic lied,[16] but except for his 1815 cycle *An die ferne Geliebte* ("To the Distant Beloved"), his songs for solo voice and piano are not much appreciated by most musicians and listeners. This neglect does not signify lack of musical substance; rather, the great outpouring of the Romantic lied repertoire in the hands of Schubert, Schumann, and later Brahms and Wolf, tended to overshadow Beethoven's vocal chamber music, as did also the massive body of his own instrumental works. This unfortunate lack of attention reinforces a historical tendency to undervalue Beethoven as a composer for whom vocality and melodic quality were of steady and vital importance, however much his developmental, processive procedures dominate our perception of his talent. Second, insufficient knowledge of his songs blurs our awareness of his important engagement with contemporary poetry. The range of texts he chose to set included older poems by Christian Fürchtegott Gellert; transforming lyric poetry of the later eighteenth century, above all that of Goethe; and new Romantic poetry of his own time, such as the work of Alois Jeitteles, the hand-picked poet of *An die ferne Geliebte*. Beethoven identified his favorite poets as Homer, Ossian, Klopstock, Schiller, and Goethe.[17] There is a discrepancy, though, between his poetic preferences and his sense of what was likely material for music, for he never set anything by Klopstock or by the supposed ancient Irish bard Ossian (actually the work of the Scottish poet James Macpherson, written about 1760).

But Beethoven, aware of his place in history, aspired to join forces with the greater poets of the age. His lifelong admiration for the "immortal Schiller," as he called him in a sketch for the Ninth Symphony finale, began in his early years. The influence of Schiller as playwright and aesthetician, above all through his 1795 *Letters on the Aesthetic Education of Man*, was profound and lasting. It was from an essay by Schiller on "The Mission of Moses" (*Die Sendung Moses*) that Beethoven copied the runic inscription "I am all that is, that was, that will be; no mortal man has lifted my veil," which he placed under glass and kept on his writing desk. Much as Beethoven admired him, however, Schiller as lyric poet seems not to have been

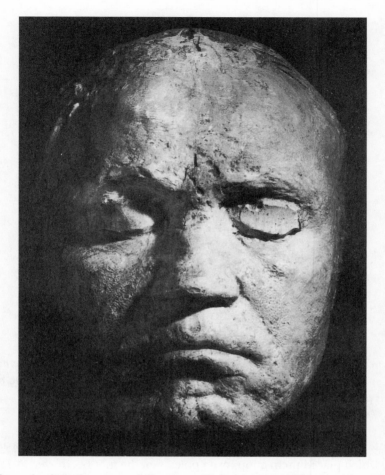

A life mask of Beethoven, made by Franz Klein in 1812, which provides valuable evidence for Beethoven's actual appearance. (Beethoven-Haus, Bonn, Collection H. C. Bodmer)

one of Beethoven's preferred moderns—among whom Goethe was foremost—but Schiller's tribute to human brotherhood in the *Ode to Joy* preoccupied Beethoven for years. Beethoven actually intended to set the *Ode* to music as early as 1793. He returned to it in sketches time after time during later years and finally found the right framework for it in the Ninth Symphony.

As for Goethe, Beethoven stood in awe of him as poet, playwright, and lawgiver of the new German artistic world. Beethoven remained loyal

Goethe

in seinem sieben und zwanzigsten Jahr.

Johann Wolfgang von Goethe in an engraving made in his earlier years. Beethoven, who met Goethe at Teplitz in 1812, admired Goethe's poetry and set some of his poems to music. (Oesterreichische Nationalbibliothek, Vienna)

despite Goethe's instinctive acceptance of the social codes of the aristocracy, which placed them at opposite poles. Goethe met Beethoven at Teplitz in 1812 and described him with an aristocrat's touch of admiration for Beethoven's stubborn resistance to polite society: "A more self-contained, energetic, sincere artist I never saw. I can understand very well how singular must be his attitude towards the world."[18] Beethoven had conveyed something of that attitude in his letter to "Emilie M." written just two days earlier.

Beethoven's reverence for Goethe as an artist, which he expressed in a later letter to the poet, was sincere and deeply rooted. Beethoven reminded Goethe that he had dedicated to him his setting of Goethe's *Calm Sea and Prosperous Voyage* for mixed choir with orchestra. He also pleaded financial need, asking Goethe to call the newly composed *Missa solemnis* to the attention of his patron, the grand duke of Weimar, in the hope that the grand duke would become a subscriber. Opening the letter with the words, "Still ever living, as I have lived since my youth, in your immortal and ever youthful works," he wrote,

> The admiration, the love and the esteem which already in my youth I cherished for the one and only immortal Goethe have persisted. Feelings like these are not easily expressed in words, particularly by such an uncouth fellow as myself, for my one aim has been to master the art of music. But a strange feeling is prompting me to say all this to you, seeing that I live in your writings.[19]

He read Goethe's novels, and late in life he planned a setting of *Faust* that, characteristically, never materialized.

Beethoven's Goethe songs are among the most eloquent of the fifty or so lieder he wrote in the early and middle years. Having composed a few songs in the earliest years under Neefe, whose meager compositional gifts were at their best in German songs, Beethoven branched out in the 1790s and early 1800s into more extended and ambitious settings in German as well as some in Italian, profiting from his lessons with Salieri in 1799–1801. In folk-song settings he went much further linguistically, finding his way into many Continental languages, but the primary language of his secular vocal music was always German, just as all his operatic projects, abortive though they were except for *Leonore/Fidelio*, were equally intended to be in German.

The principal song of the 1790s was "Adelaide," set to a text by Friedrich Matthison, to whom Beethoven sent a copy with a dedicatory letter.[20] The piece is steeped in sentimentality to fit the poem; its rolling, easy style, combined with a wider harmonic range than most contemporary lieder, made it a favorite in salon circles and a staple for tenors then and now. Much more important, though, were the songs and song groups of the years that followed: Six Gellert Songs of 1803, published as Opus 48; eight early songs published in 1805 as Opus 52, which included the first of his

Goethe settings; six new songs published in 1810 as Opus 75, which included three Goethe settings; and three more Goethe songs, Opus 83, composed in 1810, the year Beethoven completed *Egmont*.

A good way to measure Beethoven's development as a song composer in the middle years is to look at his two settings of "An die Hoffnung," a poem from Christoph August Tiedge's collection *Urania*. The first, published in 1805 as Opus 32, was composed as a gift for Josephine Brunsvik-Deym in March 1805, about the time Beethoven was working on Act 2 of *Leonore*. The second setting, which dates from 1815 (thus after the revision of *Leonore* as *Fidelio*), is a more ambitious version of the poem that was apparently intended for the opera singer Franz Wild, who sang it with Beethoven at the piano sometime after it was published as Opus 94 in April 1816.

The poem is an apostrophe to Hope (*Hoffnung*), which is first felt by the poet as a presence in the night that can softly dispel his grief; the suffering poet then calls on Hope to sustain him as he mourns his fate on earth. Beethoven's first setting of "An die Hoffnung" contains music for only the second, third, and fourth strophes of the poem; in the later setting he adds the first strophe.[21] In the first setting the whole approach is strophic; the piano accompaniment not only adjusts sensitively to the three primary melodic phrases of the song but inserts quiet arpeggiated interludes before each vocal phrase as well as at the end. The effect is one of simplicity, directness, and honesty of expression, with no vocal embellishment for any word of the text.

The 1815 setting is far more dramatic. It opens in the unusual key of B-flat minor, wanders chromatically to a new fixed point in D major, tries to settle down in G major, but then finds room to expand harmonically to E-flat major and D minor before reaching G major, which anchors the remainder. The entire spirit is that of an operatic scena, as the opening quasi-accompanied recitative makes clear (*W 31). The second is through-composed, with new music for every line of text, so each element of the poem can receive its own more sensitive musical sculpting. The keyboard writing is vastly more imaginative than that of 1805, and the whole conveys the sense of being as carefully thought through as any instrumental work of the time. It displays the delicate traceries, harmonic surprises, and romantic style feeling that is characteristic of the two Cello Sonatas Opus 102 and the oncoming Opus 101, the A Major Piano Sonata. Of course, the other, even more relevant context for the second setting is the song cycle *An die ferne Geliebte,* written in 1815–16. Every advanced element of the cycle is matched in quality in Opus 94, from its fine declamatory qualities to its use of rounded repetition at the end (in the cycle the opening of the first song returns.[22] The key phrase "O Hoffnung" comes back at the very end of the song, a single utterance by the voice over the final chord in the piano, leaving the composer's call to hope indelibly marked. Hope meant one thing to Beethoven in 1805 and something very different in 1815, in the light of his emotional crisis of 1812 and as he stood on the threshold of a new phase of artistic development.

CHAPTER 14

BEETHOVEN AT THE KEYBOARD

Improvising and Composing at the Piano

I
f Beethoven had been a pianist but not a composer he would still have been one of the preeminent musicians of his time. From childhood to old age he used the piano as his basic vehicle for improvising, composing, and performing. Inventing music at the keyboard was a prime daily activity, even more important to him than his incessant sketchbook writing. When he worked indoors he often composed at the keyboard, moving from keyboard to sketchbook and back again. In principle this procedure was not innovative in itself, as it followed, though perhaps idiosyncratically, the time-honored practices of earlier composers. Haydn, as he told Griesinger, regularly worked at the keyboard:

> *I sat down, began to improvise [phantasiren], sad or happy according to my mood, serious or trifling. Once I had seized upon an idea, my whole endeavor was to develop and sustain it in keeping with the rules of art. Thus I sought to keep going, and this is where so many of our new composers fall down. They string out one little piece after another, they break off when they have hardly begun, and nothing remains in the heart when one has listened to it.[1]*

Certainly Beethoven was not one of these hapless "new composers." The highly imaginative qualities ascribed to his improvising by contemporaries went hand in hand with his ability to sustain ideas—in Haydn's sense, to

Top: A musical sketch by Beethoven from c. 1809 containing the remark, "Real improvisation comes only when we are unconcerned [with] what we play, so—if we want to improvise in the best, truest manner in public—we should give ourselves over freely to what comes to mind." Above: Some thoughts on writing variations on a farewell song ("Lebewohl") and on a possible commission. (Beethoven-Haus, Bonn, Bodmer Collection) "keep going" within a composition, and, as Beethoven put it in a different context, "to keep the whole in view" while composing instrumental works.

Mozart, whose legendary feats of rapid composition were famous by the time Beethoven was ten years old, was accustomed to having a piano available to him at all times, whether for improvisation or composition—or for him especially, a blend of the two. He wrote to his father from Vienna in 1781 that "the room I'm supposed to be moving into is ready for me: I'm now going out to rent a piano because unless I get a piano in that room I can't live there, especially now when I have a lot to write and not a minute to waste. . . ."[2] But Mozart's wife, Constanze, later averred that "he seldom went to the pianoforte when he composed," and Niemetschek, an early biographer, wrote in 1798 that "Mozart . . . never touched the piano while writing. . . . [In approaching a vocal composition] he went about for some time, concentrating on it until his imagination was fired. Then he proceeded to work out his ideas at the piano; and only then did he sit down and write. That is why he found the writing itself so easy."[3]

While composing the overture to King Stephen in 1811, Beethoven wrote a note on a sketch leaf to remind himself to get a "small piano for composing."[4] And in 1823 he wrote a set of instructions to his longtime composition pupil, Archduke Rudolph:

> [Your Imperial Highness] must now continue, in particular, your exercises in composition, and when sitting at the pianoforte you should jot down your ideas in the form of sketches. For this purpose you should have a small table beside the pianoforte. In this way not only is one's imagination stimulated but one also learns to pin down immediately the most remote ideas. You should also compose without a pianoforte.[5]

Beethoven himself certainly worked in both ways. His extensive use of pocket sketchbooks outdoors in later years shows that composing without a piano became more habitual, perhaps as his hearing grew worse. But even so, many of the pocket sketchbooks contain preliminary ideas written in pencil that he then worked out more elaborately in ink in desk sketchbooks at home. Probably the suggestions to the archduke reflect more or less faithfully his own compositional practice at home over the years. We can easily picture Beethoven in regular, lengthy sessions at the keyboard engaged in the tactile discovery of ideas, exploring musical thoughts while his waking mind lapsed into the kind of reverie—what he would have called a *raptus*—that we associate with fantasy and daydreaming, in order to let his hands release and spread his musical imagination. In Haydn's terminology, this process was *phantasiren* ("improvising"), while the act of writing down was called *componiren* ("composing") when it referred to writing sketches and drafts, and *setzen* ("setting") when it referred to writing a full score.[6] Beethoven could easily interrupt such reveries in the service of the creative imagination to jot ideas into his current sketchbook, either short "concept sketches" often put down at the top of a blank page, or somewhat more elaborate mid-length ideas. Then if any concept sketches seized his imagination at the moment, he could readily shift to the writing table to work out longer continuity drafts and elaborate thematic and motivic ideas.

We can only imagine—and we would do well to imagine—what Beethoven's improvisations were like, extrapolating from a host of descriptions, from sketches, and from at least some improvisational patterns embedded like nuggets in a number of finished keyboard works. As early as 1791 his keyboard facility was the talk of Bonn, the Rhineland, and wider German musical circles, as described by Carl Ludwig Junker:[7]

> *Then I heard also one of the greatest keyboard players—the dear, good Bethofen [sic]. . . . It's true that he did not make a public appearance, perhaps because the instrument here [in Mergentheim] was not to his liking. It was a Spath instrument, and at Bonn he is accustomed to play only on a Steiner. However, as I greatly preferred, I heard him extemporize; indeed, I was even invited to propose a theme on which he would create variations. One can reckon the high virtuosity of this amiable, light-hearted man from his nearly inexhaustible wealth of ideas, from the quite individual style of expression in his playing, and from the great facility with which he plays. I could think of nothing that he lacks in artistic greatness. I have often heard Vogler on the fortepiano . . . heard him play by the hour altogether, and always marvelled at his astonishing facility; but Bethofen, besides his powers of execution, has*

greater eloquence, weightier ideas, and is more expressive—in short, he is more for the heart—and is equally great, as an adagio or allegro player. All the members of this remarkable orchestra are his admirers, and are all ears when he plays. Yet he is modest and without pretenses. He told me that, on the journeys that the Elector had permitted him to make, he had seldom found among the best-known keyboard virtuosi the excellence he thought he had a right to expect. His playing is so different from the usual styles of performance that it looks as if he has attained the height of perfection on which he now stands by a path of his own.[8]

By 1799, when he dueled at the piano against Joseph Wölffl, Beethoven was at the height of his first maturity as composer and had gained still more pianistic command. Johann Wenzel Tomaschek, an excellent Bohemian composer-pianist, heard him improvise and later wrote, "I did not touch my piano for several days."[9] And Johann Baptist Cramer, a pianist Beethoven admired (there were not many), said, "no one has heard improvised playing unless he has heard Beethoven."[10] Among later reports is one by Carl Czerny, the famous pianist and pedagogue, who was Beethoven's pupil and Liszt's teacher:

No one equaled him in the rapidity of his scales, double trills, skips, etc., not even Hummel. His bearing while playing was perfectly quiet, noble and beautiful, without the slightest grimace—but bent forward low, as his deafness increased; his fingers were very powerful, not long, and broadened at the tips from much playing, for he told me that in his youth he generally had to practice until after midnight. In teaching he laid great stress on a correct position of the fingers, following the principles of C. P. E. Bach, which he used in teaching me; he could scarcely span a tenth. He made frequent use of the pedals, much more than is indicated in his works. His playing of the scores of Handel and Gluck and the fugues of J. S. Bach was unique, in that in the former he introduced a full-voicedness and a spirit which gave these works a new shape. He was also the greatest sight reader of his time, even in score reading; he rapidly scanned every new and unfamiliar work like a divination and his judgment was always correct, but, especially in his younger years, very sharp, biting, and unsparing. Much that the world admired then and still admires he saw from the lofty point of view of his genius in an entirely different light.[11]

Czerny also reports an episode "in 1808 or 1810" when the pianist and composer Ignace Joseph Pleyel came from Paris to Vienna and brought with him his latest string quartets for performance at a Lobkowitz musicale.

Finally Beethoven was prevailed on to play something. As usual, he let himself be persuaded for a long time and then finally, at the entreaties of the ladies, sat down at the piano. Reluctantly he grabbed the open second violin part of the Pleyel quartets from a nearby music stand, threw it on to the piano, and began to improvise. Never had anyone heard more wonderful, more original, or greater improvising than on that evening. But through the whole improvisation there ran in the middle voice, like a thread or cantus firmus, the succession of trivial notes that he found on the accidentally open page of that quartet, while he built upon it the finest melodies and harmonies in the most brilliant concert style. Old Pleyel was so astounded that he kissed his hands.[12]

Finally we have an account by Friedrich Starke, a performer on many instruments, whose own piano method of 1821 included several Beethoven Bagatelles. Starke first heard Beethoven play in 1812 and left a description, later published by Nohl, in which he reported Beethoven's improvising in three styles: "first in a restrained manner; then fugal, where a heavenly theme in sixteenth notes was developed in the most wonderful way; and, third, in chamber style, in which Beethoven knew how to combine the greatest intricacies in projecting his special mood."[13]

All these descriptions, combined with still more anecdotal evidence of Beethoven's pianistic ability, including sight reading new works, transposing his own works at sight, and largely improvising the solo parts of his earlier piano concertos, tell us that keyboard improvisation was for him a central imaginative process. Even in March 1824, when he was too deaf to know that the audience at the Ninth Symphony premiere was loudly applauding for him, we read in the Conversation Books an entry by his nephew to the effect that "when it is known that you will improvise at the second concert, I believe, as does Schuppanzigh, Piringer, and everyone who has talked about it lately, that the hall will be much too small."[14] Beethoven once claimed to Amenda that he could recall each improvisation well enough to repeat it, and actually played one for him.[15] Even in later years Beethoven began improvisations with simple broken chords and simple figures (thus reported by Sir John Russell, who visited in 1821) and gradually warmed up to larger passages, a more fully developed flow of ideas, and, no doubt, full-length improvised compositions.[16]

How much of this music can we possibly know? The answer lies partly in his sketches and partly in his finished keyboard works, especially the different kinds of highly elaborated figuration patterns he used lifelong. In the 1780s and 90s he filled many sketch pages with sample figuration patterns, essentially on two staves for keyboard playing, that he could put to use in various compositional situations. He wrote out highly revealing cadenzas for the first four piano concertos, for the piano version of the Violin Concerto, and two for Mozart's D Minor Piano Concerto. He also alternated composing in the more strictly organized forms of multimovement sonatas with variations or, occasionally, free-form pieces that more directly reflected his improvisational skills. These were often called "Fantasia," a genre much used in the later eighteenth century by composers who followed the precepts of C. P. E. Bach; it was a genre employed sparingly but tellingly by Mozart and Haydn.[17]

The early sketch papers contain a long and sprawling D Major Fantasia for piano that Beethoven never published but that shows him trying to capture the sorts of ideas that came to him at the keyboard in a loose and extended work.[18] Around 1800 and soon thereafter his bent toward novelty resulted in the two sonatas "quasi una fantasia" and, later, in his formal public use of the term "Fantasia," as in the *Choral Fantasy,* written for a concert in December 1808, at which he also improvised a solo "Fantasia." Perhaps the solo piano "Fantasy" in G minor/B major Opus 77 of 1809 is the work he flung at the audience at that concert, or, at least, strongly resembles it.

Opus 77, the only mature solo piano piece by Beethoven called "Fantasy," is the product of the impulse to put on paper an expanded free-form example and to work free of the formal patterns he had mastered in the sonata.[19] This Fantasia is the only instrumental work by Beethoven that is unstable both in key and in thematic continuity. It begins in G minor and ends in B major. The work, easily as long as the first movement of any of his mature sonatas, opens with an abrupt pair of descending scale figures, then changes material phrase by phrase, shifting key and thematic content with dazzling quickness, each short section ending on a note or chord that is usually held and that prepares a new segment. From the abrupt descending scales of the opening we can well conjecture that Bach's *Chromatic Fantasy and Fugue* might lurk in the background. In fact we find that Beethoven knew this work, since he copied portions of it into a sketchbook that he used from the winter of 1809–10 to the fall of 1810, and his own Fantasia Opus 77 did not come out in print until November 1810.[20]

After Beethoven's Fantasy settles down in B major in a 2/4 Allegretto, it takes on somewhat more normal form as it presents an eight-measure theme plus seven variations. It cuts loose again near the end with an astonishing C-major variant of the theme, then swiftly works its way back to its B-major anchoring tonality and holds it firm to the end, though not without touches of chromatic harmonies near the conclusion that hint at some of the keys through which it has traveled.[21] The work is the father of a series of nineteenth-century piano fantasies: four by Schubert, including his grand *Wanderer* Fantasy, Schumann's great Fantasy Opus 17, and even Liszt's Fantasias.

Two other piano solo works from the middle years, neither of them a sonata, are closely related to improvising: the Thirty-Two Variations in C minor, WoO 80, of 1807, and the little-known Six Variations on a Turkish March, in D major, Opus 76, of 1809. Why Beethoven considered the little variation set worthy of publication with opus number but not the bigger one is not known. The D-major set is fairly simple for 1809, containing no special features of note other than an F-minor/major twist in the long Presto concluding variation, a trick Beethoven used to enliven earlier variations sets at similar moments.[22] The Thirty-Two Variations count for more. The first remarkable thing about the set is the theme, a mere eight measures long, which uses the traditional descending chromatic bass line C–G—a standard Baroque passacaglia theme—as its basic material, with a melody above it rising from the first to the sixth scale step. Then every variation except the last is equally brief, making the work a parade of short, brilliant pianistic transformations in the same rigorously maintained length and form. Czerny was greatly impressed by this work, and recommended to pianists that "since the theme is short, this work is best performed in public for a thinking public."[23] In the total number of units, thirty-two, it brings more variations than Beethoven or any composer of the time crowded into a single piece—which might perhaps have been the reason for his decision to surpass it by just one more in his last set, the *Diabelli Variations,* with thirty-three.

Pianos

Beethoven's early years coincided with rapid changes in the size, character, and sound of the fortepiano, which had been coming into favor since the 1760s by virtue of its dynamic flexibility, the one feature in which it inherently surpassed the otherwise excellent contemporary harpsichord.[24] Like all other keyboard instruments of the time, fortepianos were made of wood, were comparatively delicate in structure, and produced a much smaller, more refined tone than the later, metal-frame pianos of the nineteenth century. The typical range spanned sixty-three notes (five octaves plus a whole step) from the F two octaves and a fifth below middle C to the G two octaves and a fifth above. But the range soon expanded, and during Beethoven's lifetime it extended down to the lower C three octaves below middle C and to the F four octaves and a fourth above.[25] This increase coincides with Beethoven's compositional use of range as a dramatic factor in many of his works, especially from the middle period, and not only piano solo works. The dynamics that could be achieved on these instruments were finely graded, especially on the softer side, and there were degrees of difference between *forte* and *pianissimo* that are lost on modern instruments.

Beethoven's favorite instrument in the early years was a fortepiano made by Johann Andreas Streicher in Vienna, but his sense of touch and demand for tactile response was such that he could write to the maker in

1796 and say, ironically, that although his new instrument was very good, it was "too good for me . . . because it robs me of the freedom to produce my own tone."[26] But in the same year he was praising Streicher as one of the few makers "who realize and understand that, provided one can feel the music, one can also make the pianoforte sing." This stress on legato is characteristic of his approach. Beethoven commented that Mozart's playing (which he could only have heard in 1787) was "choppy," and Czerny took the same view of older keyboard playing.[27]

That Beethoven took a strong interest in the development of the instrument may be seen from his evaluations of a succession of pianos that he owned, about which he was nothing if not critical. In 1803 he received the gift of a new piano from the Parisian maker Sebastian Erard, but by 1810 he was writing to Streicher to demand fulfillment of a promise to have a new instrument from him, since "my motto is either to play on a good piano or not at all," and of his "French piano" he said that it was "certainly quite useless now." Between 1814 and 1817 he came into possession of at least three more instruments by various makers. The major advances in piano manufacturing in the late eighteenth century were centered in London, where John Broadwood produced his first instrument around 1781, boasting new and improved features. These included an equalization of string tension to stabilize the piano case and achieve a more uniform tone quality. Broadwood also extended the range to five and one-half octaves, apparently at the suggestion of Dussek, and then to six octaves. Beethoven might have seen a Broadwood in the 1790s, and actually received one in 1818 as a gift from the maker with his name inscribed on it along with that of Broadwood and other London musicians, including Frederick Kalkbrenner, Ferdinand Ries, and J. B. Cramer,[28] all active at the time in London. Beethoven's last piano was the Graf he acquired in 1825 as either a gift or a loan, made to his specifications and with a compass of six and a half octaves.[29] He seems to have been somewhat dissatisfied with his Broadwood, which Moscheles described in 1823 as having a "broad, full, though somewhat muffled tone,"[30] a view perhaps colored by feelings of national pride that were afoot at the time regarding the merits of Viennese and English pianos. Still, the Broadwood was prominently placed in his last apartment, in the Schwarzspanierhaus in Vienna, where it was depicted in a

The piano received by Beethoven in 1803 from the Parisian maker Sebastian Erard. (Kunsthistorisches Museum, Vienna)

drawing of his principal living room made just three days after his death.[31] But the chances are good that, as William Newman put it, "Beethoven seems never to have been quite satisfied with the characteristics of any piano."[32]

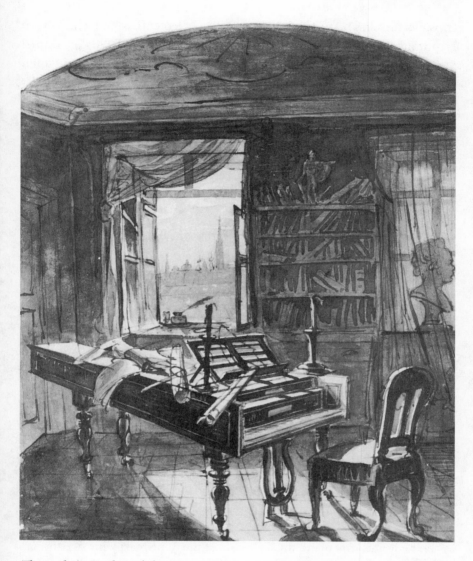

The study in Beethoven's last apartment, in which he kept his piano and some of his music, in a lithograph copy of a wash drawing made just after Beethoven's death in 1827. (Historisches Museum, Vienna)

Beethoven explored the potential of the newly developing pianoforte beyond any other composer in his time, though he was hardly the only keyboard-music innovator. Haydn, a very good pianist but not a master, much less a virtuoso, made major artistic advances in his late sonatas and piano trios. Beethoven's pianistic rivals were Muzio Clementi, John Field, Johann Nepomuk Hummel, Jan Ladislav Dussek, Georg Joseph Vogler, Daniel Steibelt, Johann Baptist Cramer, and Joseph Wölffl. Some of them could match him in technique but as composers—and probably as improvisers—none reached his level.[33] Beethoven swept the field in Vienna in the 1790s as he played the role of the conquering musical hero from the Rhineland. In 1793 he beat Josef Gelinek in a piano competition and six years later dispatched the brilliant virtuoso Wölffl in a keyboard duel that aroused an eloquent description by Seyfried.[34]

The "Waldstein" and "Appassionata" Sonatas

The major keyboard works of Beethoven's middle years are the "Waldstein" Sonata, Opus 53 and the "Appassionata" Sonata, Opus 57. Often overlooked is the minuscule Sonata Opus 54 in F major, a little masterpiece that belongs in the quiet category of Beethoven's more subtle works. But all three show Beethoven reshaping the keyboard sonata in these years. That he was self-conscious about his piano music is clear from a sketch entry of 1805, when he was working on the Finale of *Leonore* in the same sketchbook in which he had worked on Opus 54 and the "Appassionata."

> On June 2—finale always simpler—the same goes for all [my] piano music. God knows why my piano music still always makes the poorest impression on me, especially when it is badly played.[35]

When he writes "my piano music" he must mean primarily his twenty earlier piano sonatas, by now all in print. Perhaps he was also thinking about his many sets of piano variations, but these he had already transformed in 1802 in his Six Variations Opus 34 and the *Prometheus* Variations. It is curious that he writes this entry as if he were a listener to his piano music rather than its composer, and he seems not to have written so disparagingly about any other medium in which he worked. Probably through piano teaching and visits from pupils such as Ries and Czerny, as well as other pianists, he heard his piano music more often than most of his other music and he may have thought more persistently about how to improve it. The loss of confidence he expresses here about his piano compositions may also bear on their status in the light of the stylistic crisis he had passed through in 1803–4, its largest outcome being the *Eroica* Symphony. In fact, by the time of this entry he had already begun to find another new path for keyboard music, as we see in his three sonatas of 1804–5.

Beethoven began work on the "Waldstein" in December 1803–January 1804, shortly after his main sketch work on the *Eroica*; the sonata came out in Vienna a year later. It thus falls essentially between the *Eroica* and the first sketches for *Leonore*, and represents a first return to the piano sonata after his full breakthrough to the "heroic" style in orchestral music. At first the "new path" in this work stayed on familiar terrain: Beethoven originally conceived the "Waldstein" as a three-movement work in C major with a smooth and ingratiating 3/8 F-major Andante in rondo form as slow movement.

Later Beethoven cut the Andante out of the sonata, published it separately in September 1805 and republished it in 1807 under the title "Andante favori." Czerny and Ries both claimed that he removed it "because the sonata was then too long"—and certainly the newly substituted "Introduzione" is drastically shorter.[36] But even though the scale of big works was a major issue for Beethoven at the time, there were other and better reasons. One was that keeping this big Andante along with the finale would have resulted in two long rondos in succession. Another was that although this ornate and conventional Andante would have furnished a quiet contrast to the dynamic first and third movements, it fell below their level of interest. As he sketched the Andante, Beethoven considered enlivening its tonal contrast by putting it into E major, thus picking up the C major/E major tonal contrast of the first movement and extending it to the larger architecture of the work.[37] But he soon shifted it to F major, which made possible the Andante's only dramatic moment, a venture into G-flat major (a key built on the flatted second of the scale) in the coda. Then at a later stage, of which we have no record in surviving sketches, he rethought the character of the whole work and cut out the Andante altogether, replacing it with an entirely different bridge between the two big

C-major movements. His decision to insert a short mysterious Adagio molto in 6/8 meter brought about a momentous change in the character of the sonata. This substitution marks a decisive turn in Beethoven's conception of the entire genre; as Tovey put it, in this sonata Beethoven crossed the Rubicon.

The first movement begins like no other by Beethoven or anyone else. Its opening seemingly stabilizes C major as its tonic, by means of the pulsating *pianissimo* chords in low register—but almost immediately hints at a possible turn toward E minor (or major) that will bear fruit later. The array of wider harmonic implications in this opening includes not only the strange coloring of the tonic but also a strong articulation of B♭, which quickly becomes a local tonic for the pulsating chords. The B♭ destabilizes the main tonic very early in the movement but allows Beethoven to reaffirm the C-major center in a second, intensified statement of the first theme. But the main axis underlying that opening passage is a bass line moving chromatically down from C to G, with each note generating a separate harmony. Beethoven could again be distantly remembering the opening of Mozart's "Dissonant" Quartet but now in a quite different aesthetic environment.

After the first paragraph of the first movement the path opens into an exposition displaying richly developed pianistic figurations—running sixteenth-note figures, tremolos, "walking" octave figures, full chords in both hands for the second theme in E major, and brilliant changes of register.[38] The virtuoso keyboard writing and new range of pianistic colors mark the first movement as a big step beyond any earlier sonatas, even the most expressive of the Opus 20s group or those of Opus 31.

Though very brief, the dark Adagio "Introduzione" touches psychic depths. Beginning *pianissimo,* in low register, thus paralleling the dynamic and register of the first movement's beginning, it reelaborates in its first measures the descending bass line from the opening of the first movement. We also hear shades of the first movement's harmonies, as the tonic key, here F major, immediately gives way to another key, E major. From there all flows forward in a compact three-part reprise form (A, B, A') that is, however, cut off when a coda-like expansion of the first-measure figure leads to a pause on G major, the dominant that anticipates the beginning of the

Rondo. We are left not knowing if the Adagio is truly an "Introduction" to the Rondo or a truncated slow movement. Beethoven pursued this kind of ambiguity as well in the Cello Sonata Opus 69, but also, much later, in the Adagio that prepares the finale of the Quartet Opus 131. Yet both of these are firmly in the dominant, while the "Waldstein" movement is governed by a series of chromatic modulations from its tonic to various mysterious destinations. Its downward groping in the darkness, in *pianissimo,* resembles those of the introduction to the *Leonore* Overture No. 3 and the Quartet Opus 59 No. 3.

The C-major "Waldstein" cosmos is set right again as the finale opens, with smooth arpeggios and a long-phrased singing first theme (in left hand, crossing registers). The alternation of C major and C minor in the thematic expositions of the first part of the movement is picked up by the later C-minor contrasting section. All this culminates in long passages of accelerated rhythmic action in both hands, projecting the impression that the piano has expanded into a complex of instruments. We find trills combine with running sixteenths and the main theme, fantastic triplet arpeggios erupting in both hands, and a *prestissimo* coda, which combines all the previous virtuosic effects with new ones and whirls forward to five powerful C-major final chords.

This sonata could never have been played by merely competent amateurs in Beethoven's time. With its arrival the technical level of the piano sonata was elevated to that of the concerto. Accordingly, as a work for a trained solo pianist, it implies a blending of the genres of sonata and concerto—just what Beethoven had already accomplished explicitly for the violin in the "Kreutzer" Sonata. Both works give us a sense that the three-movement cycle has expanded to new technical heights.

Following the "Waldstein" is its diminutive sibling, the "little" Sonata in F Major Opus 54, about which Beethoven might perhaps have said—as he is reported to have remarked about the Eighth Symphony—"that's because it's so much better." As in other middle-period pairings, a long, powerful and brilliant work is succeeded by a short and quiet one, with Beethoven creating a double image and a deliberate contrast, a reminder of the balance between great and small, between seemingly opposed and adjacent modes of being that can complement one another, as a rare flower grows by a large tree. His contributions to the Romantic literature of aesthetic doubles are most easily seen in his piano sonatas, but he explored them as well in the symphony and in other chamber music.

This little sonata has only two movements, both in F major. The first is In tempo d'un menuetto, the second an Allegretto in 2/4. When Beethoven names a movement "Tempo di Menuetto" he means that it is not in minuet form but that it adapts the character and manner of the minuet to a larger form that resembles a rondo. To such movements he brings a sense of restrained urgency, however much the drama is set forth in period costume. Thus the opening phrase has a three-note upbeat-downbeat motif that, if it landed on a firm half-note F-major tonic, would be solid but conventional. What sets the whole phrase apart is that the first two times the harmony moves further, to the subdominant, B-flat major, thus throwing the weight of the gestural motion not onto its tonic downbeat but to the B-flat harmony just beyond it. And this shift has consequences later, as we might expect in any mature Beethoven movement.[39]

The second movement has been labeled a "perpetuum mobile," which it surely is, but it is also a path-breaking experiment in making the most of a single thematic phrase and in using it to explore the harmonic universe in a remarkable passage of harmonic expansion.[40] After this the way is clear to stay within narrower boundaries, but even at the very end the insistence of the right hand on the notes G♯-B♮, two notes entirely foreign to the key of F major, puts a special touch of color on the final tonic that was utterly modern and certainly unknown to the eighteenth century. The humor and subtlety of this gesture presage the Eighth Symphony, another exercise in modern pseudoclassicism.

The final stage of this revolution in piano sonata writing is the "Appassionata," begun in the fall of 1805 after the massive labor on *Leonore* had subsided.[41] The title, which has stuck, first appeared posthumously in 1838 in a four-hand arrangement,[42] and might have been suggested by Beethoven's later use of the term "Appassionato" for the Adagio of the *Hammerklavier* Sonata and the first movement of Opus 111. To balance the C major of the "Waldstein" and the F major of Opus 54 with a minor-mode work, he sought material of a scope that would allow the same enlargement of emotional range that he had found in the major-mode movements of the "Waldstein." The first-movement sketches show that he found the answers only after a complex search. The quest was especially arduous for the second-group theme of the exposition, which rises in an A-flat major arpeggio like consolation for the emotional darkness (akin to Florestan's F minor) implied so strongly by the first theme. This theme was not part of the early conception of the movement, a discovery that emerges from study of the sketches.[43] In fact, in its final form the second group theme is closely related rhythmically to the first theme, intensifying their differences in affect.

Dramatic tension in the first movement arises as early as the end of the first phrase. Like the Quartet Opus 18 No. 1, it opens with a quiet theme in octaves, but *pianissimo,* dark, and atmospheric. Theme 1 arpeggiates an F-minor chord, then moves to the dominant harmony and then—and this is vitally important—leaves the dominant harmony hanging and unre-solved. The next step is to repeat the first theme but now, unexpectedly, one half step higher, in G-flat major, leading to a parallel questioning half cadence before falling back to the original, unresolved cadence on the dom-inant of F minor (*W 32). There have now been three unanswered ques-tions, with more to come. In fact, this way of proceeding—to arrive at a questioning half cadence, then repeat it many times, always without reso-lution, is by now a familiar variant of one of Beethoven's most basic formal techniques: a firm entry into the musical space, arousing the need for har-monic resolution, the postponement of resolution, and then at the end of the movement, emphatic fulfillment of the necessary resolution by means of decisive full cadences on the tonic.

One metaphor is that of a great journey in which the traveler knows what the ultimate goal must be but is soon derailed, then recovers and eventually proceeds to the final destination, but does so by means that do not allow the deviation to be forgotten, since resolving it has become the point of the journey. Another parallel exists with sexual arousal, postpone-ment of fulfillment, and eventual fulfillment. Analogies with psychological models of childhood events lost to memory then later remembered through analysis in adulthood also come to mind. In the musical situation, of course, the significant element placed early in the work is not "forgotten" and later revived. But because it is planted early, it may seem unimportant or at best inexplicable. The rest of the complex process of the composition "explain" or "unravels" the feature by showing that in fact it leads to huge formal and expressive consequences that are revealed only late in the movement or later in the work.

We may seek descriptive metaphors for basic human experiences that are akin to what we hear in such a movement, but it does not follow that the music literally "means" or directly "refers" to these imagined parallels. Yet equally, there is no doubt that part of what gives a movement like this one its undeniable psychic power is the capacity to evoke metaphorical association with deep human experiences. Music of this type exposes the dynamics of emotion without our being able to name the emotions other than in the ways the music makes them emerge.

Since neither the first theme nor the lyrical second theme has a cadence that closes its local harmonic progression, the task of resolution is all the greater for the coda, and in fact it does the job by hammering home the last nail in the closing F-minor cadences.

The chorale-like slow movement, Andante con moto, is a set of variations very different from the wide-leaping arpeggios of the first movement's main themes—here the upper line barely moves, and only an active bass line keeps the rhythmic motion from being static. The key of the movement, D-flat major, is the same Beethoven had used for the major-mode final appearance in the first movement's second theme. This movement then, is an emotional oasis between storms. The last movement, in turn, begins with a lengthy insistence on an unstable chord—a diminished seventh, whose ambiguity makes it a potential pivot for modulation—which is also the basis for a descending sixteenth-note figure that sets up the eventual arrival in F minor and the first theme (*W 33).

The tremendous nervous energy of the finale links it directly to the first movement, but now the perpetual hurtling through minor-mode areas is unrelieved by any theme as consoling and stabilizing as the second theme of the first movement.[44] The finale retains its tragic power to the end.

Piano Sonatas Opp. 78–81a

The closing years of the middle period, 1809–10, brought another group of three piano sonatas. They follow works marked by full openness of expression—the Fifth and Sixth symphonies, the Fourth Piano Concerto, the Violin Concerto, *Coriolanus*, the Opus 70 trios, and the Cello Sonata Opus 69, but move in a new direction, as Beethoven entered another experimental phase that resulted in the "Harp" Quartet, Opus 74, the Piano Fantasy Opus 77, and a new series of songs. The heroic stamp is still at his disposal, as we see in the "Emperor" Concerto and in *Egmont*, but we now detect a new angle of vision that in curious ways presages the third style. This outlook is evident in the F Minor Quartet, Opus 95, but it is also evident in several other works of this time, among them the E-flat Piano Sonata Opus 81a.

The three piano sonatas are, in apparent order of composition, the "little" G major Sonata, Opus 79, and the F-sharp Sonata, Opus 78, written in the fall of 1809; then the *Lebewohl* Sonata in E-flat, written near the end of 1809 to commemorate the departure of Archduke Rudolph from Vienna the previous May. Opus 78 and Opus 79 form a pair, though not a dualism of the tragic and pastoral, like the Fifth and Sixth Symphonies. Opus 78, in two movements and on a comparatively small scale, is a rippling, black-key excursion into the realm of F-sharp major—Beethoven's only work in this obscure key. The first movement is a perfectly proportioned sonata form, the second a quirky and playful sonata form without development. Its little companion, Opus 79, is in all three of its diminutive movements the essence of ease and simplicity, an "easy sonata" that any child or amateur can play. It is a consolation prize for all the notes missed by amateurs who attempt Opus 78.

The *Lebewohl* (Farewell) Sonata is of greater magnitude, musically and biographically. In the spring of 1809 Vienna was not only under Napoleonic attack but also under siege. The Austrian regime, smarting from its previous losses of gold, men, and territories to the French in the Treaty of Pressburg in 1805, had roused itself to launch a new major campaign against the invaders. The royal commander in chief, Archduke Karl (Archduke Rudolph's brother) told the army, "Soldiers, your victories will break her [Austria's] chains."[45] But in mid-April Napoleon's forces forged new chains for the Austrians by defeating them in battles along the Danube in Bavaria and then advancing on Vienna. They reached the city by May 10 and demanded its surrender. When the new commander, Archduke Maximilian, refused, Napoleon ordered a crushing artillery barrage that lasted a full twenty-four hours. The Viennese, shocked and terrified, took whatever shelter they could find. Beethoven sought refuge from the merciless and seemingly endless bombardment by retreating to the cellar of his brother Caspar Carl's house and covering his afflicted ears with pillows.[46] The rest of the royal family, including Archduke Rudolph, had left the city on May 4, along with most of the nobility and anyone else who could escape from the battered capital as it prepared to deal with an invading French army many thousand strong. As Beethoven wrote to Breitkopf in July, "What a destructive, disorderly life I see and hear around me, nothing but drums, cannons, and human misery in every form."[47] And when the French occupation finally ended in November after a negotiated peace that left Vienna battered and depleted, he wrote again to say,

> We are enjoying a little peace after violent destruction, after suffering every hardship that one could conceivably endure—I worked for a few weeks in succession, but it seemed to me more for death than for immortality.[48]

Archduke Rudolph, born in 1788, was the youngest of the twelve sons of Grand Duke Leopold, who had succeeded Joseph II in 1790. But both Leopold and his wife died in 1792 after Leopold had been on the throne for only two years.[49] His death saw the scepter passed to his eldest son, Franz I, then twenty-four. Young Rudolph, only four years old when Franz ascended the imperial throne, was given a thorough liberal education of the kind that prepared children of the royal family for their future responsibilities. In the royal household music was more than an ornament; it was a serious interest on the part of both Franz I and his wife, Maria Therese.[50] At fifteen or sixteen (1803–4) Rudolph was an excellent pianist. He probably met Beethoven at musical soirées hosted by the Lobkowitzes and others in their circles. In 1804 he seems to have become Beethoven's pupil, beginning a long and close relationship that lasted all through the composer's life.

Although Beethoven sometimes expressed impatience with Rudolph in letters, his dealings with the archduke generally avoided the irascibility that he openly displayed to other patrons and just about everyone else. As Beethoven's only serious composition pupil, Rudolph completed more than twenty-five works under Beethoven's tutelage and continued to compose long after 1814, when epilepsy, gout, and rheumatism curtailed his piano playing. Beethoven by now had given up teaching piano to young ladies of the nobility, but he kept Ferdinand Ries as a pupil for some years, and the archduke kept up his composition lessons with him for a long time. That Beethoven took his pedagogical responsibilities seriously is evident from a notebook of "Materials on Thoroughbass" that he put together in 1809 and for which he drew on theoretical treatises by Johann Joseph Fux, C. P. E. Bach, Daniel Gottlob Türk, Johann Philipp Kirnberger, and Johann Albrechtsberger.[51]

Archduke Rudolph amassed a valuable music library, attended theater and opera, and was more serious in his piety, cultural interests, and humaneness in personal matters than many less gifted aristocratic snobs of the time and milieu.[52] He was especially helpful to Beethoven in 1809, when in March (before the French siege) he joined with princes Kinsky and Joseph Lobkowitz to pay Beethoven a yearly annuity of 4,000 florins, to keep him in Vienna and prevent his accepting Jerome Bonaparte's offer of the post of Kapellmeister in Westphalia.

Accordingly, Beethoven's dedication to Rudolph of important works—more than to any other individual—was not mere flattery. Aside from the *Lebewohl* Sonata and the *Missa solemnis,* which were expressly written for Rudolph, he was the named recipient of the Fourth Piano Concerto, the "Emperor" Concerto, the Violin Sonata Opus 96, the Trio Opus 97, the *Hammerklavier* Sonata, the Piano Sonata Opus 111, and the *Grand Fugue.* Curiously, three of these works—the *Hammerklavier,* the *Grand Fugue,* and the Credo of the *Missa solemnis*—have closing fugues in B-flat major, and all except the two concertos have overtly contrapuntal or even fully fugal passages in at least one movement. It is conceivable that these engagements with counterpoint might symbolically link to Rudolph's interests as a musician.[53] The *Missa solemnis*, perhaps the biggest single project of Beethoven's later life, was planned for Rudolph's installation as archbishop of Ölmutz in Moravia in March 1820, but Beethoven did not actually complete the Mass until 1822 and he presented it to the new archbishop the following spring.

Beethoven was proud to have a pupil who was both a serious musician and a member of the royal family. The social aspect peeps out in a letter to Gleichenstein in 1810, after Gleichenstein had missed an appointment to attend a rehearsal at which he would have met the archduke: "You have missed a great deal, not because you have not heard my music but because you would have met an amiable and talented prince and because you, as the friend of his friend, would not have been made to feel his high rank."[54]

The sketches show an entry, "The departure [that is, "Der Abschied"; crossed out is "Das Lebewohl"]—on May 4—dedicated and written from the heart to Your Imperial Highness." The work is also called *Les Adieux* because Breitkopf published it in 1810 in separate German and French editions, although Beethoven wanted a single edition with titles in both languages.[55] In German, the movements are titled "Das Lebewohl," "Abwesenheit," and "Das Wiedersehen," that is, "The Farewell," "Absence," and "The Reunion."

The sonata's overtly programmatic nature caused embarrassment to some twentieth-century analysts who wished not to believe that Beethoven could succumb to the temptations of descriptive music. Thus we are told that "the titles . . . today sound faintly comic, and Beethoven himself can hardly have meant them to be taken too seriously."[56] The facts tell a different story, for in letters to Breitkopf, Beethoven repeatedly refers to the sonata as having three movements with these precise titles and calls it a "characteristic" sonata, meaning programmatic. Later he even took the publisher to task for having published the work with French titles, since, as he told them, "'Lebewohl' means something quite different from 'Les Adieux,'" that "the first is said in a warm-hearted manner to one person, the other to a whole assembly, to entire towns."[57] That he wrote the word "Le-be-wohl" into the score, with syllables thus separated, is the surest possible sign that Beethoven wanted at least the beginning of the work to be a direct expression of a friendly gesture of parting. (There is a parallel in his writing in the names of three birds in the coda of the *Pastoral* Symphony slow movement.) The "Le-be-wohl" figure forms an unprecedented fusion of opening sonata head motif and the word it represents; it is written into the score as if it were a veiled song, of course with no further text.

Piano Sonata in E-flat major, Opus 81a (Das Lebewohl [Les Adieux]), *beginning, right hand only:*

Still, that Beethoven wanted the piece to carry the feelings he attached to his association with the young archduke does not limit its potential aesthetic meaning to the immediate biographical situation. Dahlhaus suggests a separation between the "biographical subject" and the "aesthetic subject," the latter emerging from the work itself and not from the specific factual circumstances that prompted it.[58] Indeed, it is evident that the beginning "stands for" the idea of "farewell" in a strongly Romantic sense from its use of horn fifths, the sounds associated with hunting horns echoing in the woods that signaled nostalgia to Romantic sensibilities. Charles Rosen points this out in connection with Schubert's use of horn fifths in "Der Lindenbaum," the fifth song of his cycle *Winterreise*, in which "absence and regret" are central themes.[59] The intertwining of soft horns in the distance is exactly the effect Beethoven creates in the coda of the first movement as two pairs of horns, pitched high and low, answer one another in quickening echoes (*W 34).

Lyrical and Monumental Chamber Music

The year 1808, a productive period, saw the first of three other classics of keyboard chamber music: the Cello Sonata Opus 69 (published in April 1809) and the two Piano Trios Opus 70 published in summer 1809, dedicated to Countess Erdödy. Without diminishing their individuality, we can say that the trios are clearly related as correlative opposites and that all three works can be read as a trilogy. They develop new ways of blending and opposing string and keyboard roles that radically revise earlier patterns. All three open the way to the expanded and comfortable virtuosity of Beethoven's last keyboard chamber works, the "Archduke" Trio and the Violin Sonata Opus 96.

Cello Sonata Opus 69

When Beethoven began the Opus 69 Cello Sonata in A major he had behind him the Opus 5 Cello Sonatas and nine of his ten violin sonatas. He draws on these works in shaping the levels of subtlety that appear throughout the Opus 69 Sonata, one of his most intricate and beautiful chamber music compositions. The opening theme of the first movement, in low register for cello alone, contains the motivic seeds that grow and flourish in the remainder of the movement (*W 35). It projects an anchoring tonic-fifth interval, A–E, which then shifts toward F-sharp minor (F♯–C♯). This interval succession bears fruit in the development section, whose main subordinate key areas are C-sharp minor and F-sharp minor. Whether the work has three or four movements is not a settled matter. The position of the big A-minor Scherzo as the second movement resembles the order of Quartet Opus 59 No. 1 (though without its vastness of scale), but the E-major slow movement, beginning as a full-fledged lyrical Adagio with promise of a bright future, stops short after only two melodic strains and gives way to the Finale. The plan resembles that of the "Waldstein" except that instead of a mysterious introduction to the finale we get a luxuriantly melodic opportunity to exploit the dominant, a key that is relatively neglected in the first two movements. Most important are the many forms of interaction between cello and piano in the thematic expansion and motivic development that run throughout the sonata.

The surviving autograph of the first movement—a true Beethovenian composing score—contains a wholesale revision of the relationship between the cello part and the right hand of the piano part throughout the development section. We see that at this comparatively late stage Beethoven had decided on the basic thematic content of the movement but not on its final distribution between the instruments. Along with its many other alterations on a smaller scale, the autograph portrays Beethoven wrestling with the problem of how to make these two instruments reciprocal in function, in view of their differences in range and register. Far more than in the Opus 5 Sonatas, this work brings the two instruments into equilibrium and balance of function in a large-scale cello sonata for the first time. That characteristic, along with its thematic and motivic cogency, is why the Opus 69 Sonata formed the foundation for the nineteenth-century cello sonata repertoire as it emerged in works by Mendelssohn, Brahms, and others.[60]

Piano Trios Opus 70

About the piano trios of Opus 70 much the same can be said: they raise the genre to a level from which the later piano trio literature could move forward—witness above all the trios of Schumann and Brahms. Looking back at his earlier trios as he worked on these in 1808, Beethoven could have taken some pride in his three trios of Opus 1, with their energetic and expressive challenges to Mozart and Haydn, but even their most progressive thrusts are tame in comparison with Opus 70 No. 1. This D-major trio, later called the "Ghost," is a massive three-movement work, with two very rapid movements enclosing a Largo assai ed espressivo.

The first movement hammers out its opening theme in full unison, with the piano in octaves above and below the inner octave filled by violin and cello. The vigorous pattern of descending fourths, each group coming down from successively higher starting points, contains a typical middle-period rhythmic motive (long-short-short-long) that he was to use in duple meter in the finale of the Seventh Symphony. Here it contrasts with a lyrical alternative theme in the cello, and then the dialectic of the two thematic ideas runs through the movement with rigor and passion. The finale, somewhat more relaxed than the first movement even though it is labeled Presto, is swift and smooth in its material from start to finish. Its steady marching half-note passages foretell its family resemblance to the finale of the Eighth Symphony but with a few quasi-improvisatory moments that Beethoven used only in his piano music.

The second movement, Largo, outdoes all other second-period slow movements in dramatic suspense and atmospheric effects. From the outset, with cello and violin alone followed by pulsating chords in the piano, the movement grips the listener's imagination as it slowly streams forward. Its anomalies include a strange motion from its tonic D minor to C major, extremes of register and dynamics, long cascading scalar figurations in the piano part that run through two and more octaves, tremolos in both piano and strings, sudden and abrupt stops, and silences near the close.[61] Czerny wrote in 1842 that this movement reminded him of the first appearance of the Ghost in *Hamlet*, thus coining the colloquial title "Ghost" for the whole work. Unknown to Czerny at the time, sketches for the slow movement crop up very near some ideas in D minor for an opening Witches' Chorus that Beethoven wrote down while considering a plan for an opera on *Macbeth* on a libretto by Collin.[62]

After the "Ghost," the E-flat Trio, Opus 70 No. 2, turns from the demonic to the human. It is a curious and idiosyncratic four-movement work, the only full Beethoven cycle in which two Allegretto movements stand side by side as second and third movements. The key scheme is also surprising: (1) an E-flat-major Allegro ma non troppo, with interesting slow introduction, Poco sostenuto (the same marking as the Seventh Symphony introduction); (2) a C-major Allegretto, full of humor and kindness; (3) an A-flat-major Allegretto ma non troppo, in a waltzlike pre-Romantic flowing 3/4, with Trio (not thus marked) in four-measure units alternating between strings and piano, and with superb modulatory moments that seem to spin away from the tonic and then return by legerdemain; and (4) an E-flat-major Allegro finale filled with unexpected shifts and touches of humor on every hand.

E. T. A. Hoffmann, writing in 1813, could not contain himself over the Trios' originality and brilliance.[63] Following up his review of the Fifth Symphony (which he praises for its capacity to transport the listener into the "realm of the infinite") and finding his reverence for Beethoven's gifts "confirmed by each new work of the master," Hoffmann declares that these "wonderful Trios" show how "Beethoven carries the romantic spirit of music deep into his soul and with what high geniality, with what deep sense of self-possession ["Besonnenheit"] he enlivens each work." It is no surprise that the D-major Trio evokes Hoffmann's highest praise. Most interesting, though, is his reaction to the E-flat Trio. Its first movement Allegro theme, he says, reminds him involuntarily of Mozart's Symphony No. 39 in the same key—though he quickly adds that he means only the theme, not its development, which is purely Beethovenian in its fragmentation of motives. The playful second movement reminds him of Haydn, especially the Andantes of certain Haydn symphonies. The pianistic difficulties in both trios are undeniable, but Hoffmann claims that seasoned performers steeped in Beethoven will find them entirely idiomatic. Most telling is his insistence that this is music of a higher order, music from a spirit beyond the reach of most musicians of the day:

> Since it became fashionable to employ music only as a secondary
> amusement, to drive out boredom, everything now has to be light,
> pleasing, enjoyable—that means, without any significance and depth.
> Unfortunately there are enough composers walking the earth who go
> along with the spirit of the times, and so there are plenty of easy treats
> to be had. Also, many fairly decent musicians complain about the diffi-
> culty of understanding Beethoven's works, and even Mozart's; this how-
> ever is due to a subjective imbecility which does not permit them to
> perceive and grasp the whole in its parts. Instead they praise the clarity
> of weak compositions.[64]

Hoffmann could also have remarked on Beethoven's creation of new opportunities for the trio instruments. The string parts are more difficult than those of his earlier trios; the cello parts especially are far more prominent and wide-ranging. Here, as in the quartets, Beethoven's emancipation of the cello is one of the most salient achievements of his middle-period chamber music. The greater agility and sonority this music requires from both violin and cello allows the piano part to become more expansive as well; thick chordal clusters in both hands, much use of pedal, new and complex keyboard figurations, the violin and cello playing in octaves against the piano, a heavier sound in the total ensemble—all these mark these trios as products of new ways of thinking about ensemble sonorities altogether.

The "Archduke" Trio

With the two trios of Opus 70 we enter the last phase of Beethoven's second period. His final trio, the only one to carry the archduke's name informally to posterity, was conceived on a symphonic scale and is even larger than either of the Opus 70 pair. An attempt in 1816 to write an F-minor trio failed after a few sketches. By that time Beethoven's interest in blending strings and piano had faded in the light of a broad change in his aesthetic premises that was leading him to other tasks. Similarly, the G Major Violin Sonata, Opus 96, is the last of his accompanied sonatas for any instrument.

The "Archduke" Trio was written in the earlier part of 1811, followed by his work on *The Ruins of Athens*, *King Stephen*, and, in the fall, his first work on the Seventh Symphony. The trio was not published until 1816, along with a number of earlier works. All of these compositions were sold in 1815 to the publisher Sigmund Anton Steiner, although Beethoven retained publication rights for England. Steiner apparently lent Beethoven money in 1813 and was repaid two years later with the publishing rights for this cluster of works in the Opus 90s, including the Seventh and Eighth symphonies, the Quartet Opus 95, the Violin Sonata Opus 96, and this trio. The surviving autograph manuscript, which dates from 1815, probably includes some minor revisions that Beethoven made as the work was nearing publication, but in the main the trio is the product of 1811.[65]

The "Archduke" is another monumental work, comparable in scope to the Opus 59 No. 1 quartet. Both the second-movement Scherzo and the slow movement are on a very large scale like those of Opus 59 No. 1, not condensed like the Adagio of Opus 69. The solo piano opening of the first movement, with its massive legato theme supported by full chords, sets a tone of nobility for the entire work, just as it also establishes that the basic contrast to the B-flat-major tonality in the first movement will not be its dominant, F major, but first G then E-flat major.[66] Nothing is more quietly mysterious than the *pianissimo* approach to the recapitulation, not by way of its dominant but by quiet chromatic trills on the high B♭ itself (B♭–C♭), with D–E♭ and F–G♭ in rapid alternation below it, then adding the cello with low B♭–A. From this harmonic cloud the true return to the tonic and the main theme steps forward clearly and quietly with a tiny but meaningful variant on the fourth beat of the theme that is then followed up as the theme returns.

Some adventures along the way in this complex first movement include Beethoven's longest pizzicato section (in the development section), expanding his earlier experiments with long pizzicato passages in his Quartets Opus 74 and Opus 59 No. 1. The capstone of the movement is the coda, in which the long-postponed dominant makes one insistent cadential appearance after another in a technique reminiscent of the first movement of the "Appassionata" (*W 36).

The Scherzo is on the largest scale, with the fivefold Scherzo-Trio alternation familiar from the Fourth Symphony and other middle-period works. Here three styles contrast: the brilliant sonorities of the Scherzo proper, built on its opening theme; the chromatic slithering theme of the Trio, which is a B-flat-minor fugato; and the Viennese waltz style of the Trio's second theme, attacked *fortissimo* in the piano then alternated with the head motif of the chromatic fugato theme. After all of this the D-major slow movement emerges as if from another world. Its long, chorale-like theme, Andante cantabile, is followed by four large variations and a coda. The finale, a relaxed Allegro moderato, recalls the opening of the first movement with its immediate turn from tonic to subdominant; it extends its material through a large-scale sonata-rondo form, closing at last into an astonishing Presto coda that opens in A major then shifts back through E-flat major to the home tonic, B-flat major. The coda grounds the whole work with vigorous cadences similar to those that end the first movement.

Violinists have long noticed that the violin throughout the "Archduke" Trio plays a somewhat less prominent role than the cello, which takes on major melody-bearing responsibilities far beyond the passages in which it matches the violin phrase for phrase. And because the keyboard is even more richly and heavily laden with chordal writing and figurational variety than in the Opus 70 trios, the total sonority of this work is almost that of a small orchestral ensemble in the guise of a trio. Everyone senses the nobility of conception that underlies this work; not everyone realizes how far it stands beyond the sound world of earlier keyboard chamber music, even the Opus 70 trios.

Violin Sonata Opus 96

By contrast, the G Major Violin Sonata, Opus 96, is reflective, lyrical, and subtle. Written in 1812, again for the archduke, it is Beethoven's first four-movement violin sonata since the C Minor Sonata, Opus 30 No. 2. The final version may also have been revised in 1815 before publication.[67] Just as the "Kreutzer" had been written for Bridgetower, then Kreutzer, and the concerto had been written for Clement, this sonata was written for Pierre Rode, another brilliant French violinist, who had just arrived in Vienna in 1812 and premiered it with the archduke at a Lobkowitz soirée in December of that year. Beethoven thought as carefully about fitting the work to the player as Mozart had once tailored arias to his opera singers, but in this case he seemed somewhat impatient with Rode's playing when he wrote to the archduke in December 1812:

> *I have not hurried unduly to compose the last movement merely for the sake of being punctual, the more so as in view of Rode's playing I have had to give more thought to the composition of this movement. In our finales we like to have fairly noisy passages but Rode does not care for them—and so I have been rather hampered—However, everything ought to go off well on Tuesday.*[68]

The spirit of a new romanticism hovers over the beginning of this sonata, with its quiet exchanges of a short motif between violin and piano that builds up into a more extended period (*W 37). That Schubert heard this work with admiration is clear as crystal. Anticipations of Schubert emerge in the voicing of the violin and keyboard and in the delicate tracery of their interaction. Certain musical ideas in the first movement even seem to foreshadow Schubert's E-flat-major Trio.

There is charm and beauty in every movement of this work, as Carl Flesch understood when he called it "the most perfect work in the whole series" of Beethoven violin sonatas for its deeper qualities below the lyrical surface, its avoidance of virtuoso passages for their own sake, its fineness of texture and delicacy of sonority.[69] The middle movements are mature examples of Beethoven's scherzo and slow-movement methods. The finale is a variation set on a "Gassenhauer" theme (a rollicking thematic type in 2/4 found in German light operas) generically similar to that of the "Kakadu" Variations but with a nice harmonic twist as it modulates, surprisingly, to B major for its third strain, then returns to G major to close. The variations harbor cunningly made elaborations of the theme and its motivic content as well as a highly decorated Adagio passage. They also include, as a sign of these later times, a fugato variation that quietly emerges, radically shifts the movement's perspective, then sets up the return to the main theme. An extended Poco adagio then liquidates the B-major implication within the original theme and sets up a brilliant close. In its style feeling, the humor of this 2/4 movement borrows from many an early Beethoven finale, such as the charming last movement of the Quartet Opus 18 No. 2, in the same key. It also conveys those more complex, ironic forms of humor that Beethoven later cultivates in finales, in piano movements, and in certain scherzi right into his last period. Its nearest relatives include the finale of the C Major Cello Sonata Opus 102 No. 1, a few of the rapid-tempo Bagatelles, such as Opus 119 No. 10 and Opus 126 No. 2, and the diminutive Scherzo of Opus 130.

CHAPTER 15

STRING QUARTETS

❦❦❦◈❦❦❦

The "Razumovsky" Quartets

Around 1810, an Italian couple, the violinist Felix Radicati and the soprano Teresa Bertinotti, were touring in England. In Manchester they visited the English musician Thomas Appleby, and on his piano they found the newly published parts of Beethoven's Quartets Opus 59. Said Radicati, according to an anecdote: "Have you got these here! Ha! Beethoven, as the world says, and as I believe, is music-mad—for these [pieces] are not music. He submitted them to me in manuscript and, at his request, I fingered them for him. I said to him that he surely did not consider these works to be music? To which he replied, "Oh, they are not for you, but for a later age!"[1]

The later age came quickly. Only twenty years afterward, musicians and listeners were beginning to understand that these three quartets formed a continental divide in the history of the quartet comparable to the *Eroica* and the "Waldstein." Each quartet in its own way embodies a transformation of the genre, an expansion of the realm of the possible in what contemporaries saw as the most demanding branch of chamber music. As early as 1831 Ignaz von Seyfried could write that in the period around 1806 "Beethoven sought to bring about profound achievements in quartet style, that noble genre, which had been reformed by Haydn, or, better said, conjured up by him out of nothing; which Mozart's universal genius had given much greater and deeper content and had filled with luxuriant imagination; and in which finally our Beethoven took those culminating steps that could only be attempted by one who was predestined to do so, and in which he could hardly be followed by anyone else."[2]

Seyfried's thumbnail sketch was biased by hero worship but it holds a kernel of truth. If there was a revolutionary step in Beethoven's middle-period chamber music it was in Opus 59. Although the Opus 18 Quartets had been ripe products of his first maturity, they stood in the shadow of Mozart's later quartets, especially the six of 1785 dedicated to Haydn. And if Beethoven in Opus 18 had also been directly competing with Haydn's last quartets (all but one of which had also been written in the 1790s), even the progressive features of Opus 18 predicted future greatness more than they could fully embody it. Certainly the strongest features of Opus 18 moved beyond previously established aesthetic norms: witness the motivic elaborations of the first movement and the rhetoric of the Adagio in No. 1; the smooth professionalism of No. 3; the C-minor outbursts of No. 4; or the compositional economy of No. 6, not to mention the manic rhythmic life of its Scherzo or the harmonic labyrinths of *La Malinconia*. Nevertheless, the gulf between Opus 18 and Opus 59 is as great as that separating the First Symphony from the Fifth and Sixth, or the "Pathétique" Sonata from the "Appassionata." In each category Beethoven now entered another world.

The commission for the new quartets came to Beethoven not from one of his earlier patrons such as Lobkowitz or Lichnowsky, but from the Russian ambassador to the court of Vienna, Count Andreas Kyrillovitch Razumovsky. Even among wealthy chamber-music fanatics Razumovsky stood out. A Haydn enthusiast, he played second violin in quartet ensembles, sponsored quartet concerts, and in 1808 took over from Lichnowsky the patronage of the Schuppanzigh Quartet, then the best in Vienna. According to a later biographer, Razumovsky "lived in Vienna like a prince, encouraging art and science, surrounded by a luxurious library and other collections, and envied by all; what advantages accrued from all this to Russian affairs is another question."[3] By marrying a daughter of Countess Thun in 1788 Razumovsky had moved into the top echelon of Viennese patronage, and he probably knew Beethoven more than casually before 1805. It was as well that he offered Beethoven this commission when he

Count Andreas Kyrillovitch Razumovsky, the Russian ambassador to the Austrian court, who commissioned Beethoven's three Quartets Opus 59. (Historisches Museum, Vienna)

did, because his Viennese palace burned down in 1814 and its contents were destroyed. Not much is known about his later years, but it appears that in the 1820s he traveled to Italy, France, and England, and in 1826, Beethoven's last year, he turned up again in Vienna—now "without money," as Beethoven's nephew Karl drily remarked in a Conversation Book.[4]

As the leading local violinist, Ignaz Schuppanzigh figured in Beethoven's career for many years, from the 1790s to 1816 and then again in the 1820s. A jocular fat man whom Beethoven nicknamed "Mylord Falstaff," Schuppanzigh founded his quartet and held it together, with some changing players, until 1816, when the new diplomatic openings created by the Congress of Vienna led him away to Russia to pursue his career. When he returned to Vienna in 1823 Beethoven saluted him with a Presto five-voice

Ignaz Schuppanzigh, the principal violinist in several string quartets that bore his name, who was a long-time associate of Beethoven's and performed many of his chamber works. (Österreichische Galerie, Vienna)

canon on the name "Falstafferel, lass dich sehen" ("Falstaffo, come to see me").[5] Schuppanzigh remained a prominent and influential fixture in the city, not only as quartet leader but as a regular concertmaster in orchestral and other ensemble performances, until his death in 1830. He played in premieres of new Beethoven works ranging from the Septet of 1800 to the Ninth Symphony in 1824, and he premiered several of the late quartets until the complexities of Beethoven's late style proved too much for him.

Beethoven's work on Opus 59 was held up by the complications surrounding *Leonore*, so that he could really concentrate on the new commission only from the late spring through the fall of 1806. The autograph manuscript of the first quartet, in F major, bears an inscription, "begun on May 26, 1806," a very unusual thing for Beethoven to write on an autograph. If we can believe his letters to Breitkopf & Härtel he had finished

No. 1 by July and all three by November. The period 1806 through early 1807 was a time of tremendous productivity along various lines of concentration: besides these quartets and the revision of *Leonore* he completed the Fourth Piano Concerto, the Fourth Symphony, the Violin Concerto, and *Coriolanus*, probably in that order.[6] For Opus 59 the surviving body of sketches is slim, much thinner than for any other Beethoven quartets, but we do have the three complete final autograph manuscripts. They show that the three were almost certainly composed in the consecutive order in which they were first published in 1808, when they came out adorned with a handsome title page that listed Razumovsky's titles and honors as boldly as if it were bedecked with the ribbons and medals that he wore on his ambassadorial dress uniform.

The choices of key, aesthetic character, length, and movement plans of the quartets suggest that they form a trilogy comparable in some degree to Mozart's three last symphonies, which were written in six weeks. The analogy may be more than speculative. Both sets present three innovative works—one in major, one in minor, the last a brilliant work in C major ending with a contrapuntal finale. As Mozart's symphonic testament, Nos. 39 in E-flat, 40 in G minor, and 41 (the "Jupiter") in C major follow divergent pathways. No. 39 is a profound realization of that part of Mozart's artistry that is closest to Haydn, especially in its vigorous finale. No. 40 is the classic expression of the poignancy that Mozart could summon for his most heart-breaking moments, along with the G Minor String Quintet and Pamina's aria of suffering, "Ach, ich fühl's" ("Oh, I feel it"), in *The Magic Flute*. And the "Jupiter" Symphony sums up the ideal of the sublime in the late-eighteenth-century symphonic world in combining formal clarity and the highest craftsmanship in the first movement, profound expressivity in the slow movement, and, to end the work, a matchless synthesis of sonata form and fugue, based on Mozart's elaboration of a classic contrapuntal subject that goes back to Fux.[7]

The same fraternal binding is felt in the Opus 59 Quartets. The first, in F major, is the longest and most massive, set up on the scale of the *Eroica* with four very long movements, all in sonata form. No. 2, in E minor, is highly compressed, angular, intrinsically difficult for listeners to grasp at first hearing, as Beethoven's audiences found out. No. 3 is the C major crown of the opus, the one that contemporaries found the easiest to grasp. That Beethoven saw ways of suggesting connections from work to work is apparent in his overt use of Russian themes in the first two quartets and possibly in the third, but even more in his use of key associations. Thus the finale of the E Minor Quartet, No. 2, prepares the C major of the work that follows by opening not in its own tonic, E minor, but in C major and not really providing an emphatic arrival on E minor for a long time to come.

All three works established a new and much broader range of expression for the genre. Their technical difficulties and bizarre moments alarmed and astounded performers, not only Radicati but Beethoven's old acquaintance from Bonn, Bernhard Romberg—by now a famous cellist—who trampled on the cello part of No. 1 after finding nothing to play in the solo opening phrase of the Scherzo but the single note B♭. The critics were impressed but somewhat awed. One wrote of these works as being "deeply thought through and of excellent workmanship but not comprehensible to the public, with the possible exception of the third in C major." And as late as 1821 the E Minor Quartet was being described as "important but . . . unpopular . . . bizarre."[8]

The Russian melodies were further signs of the quartets' special character, for Beethoven had not used recognizable folk tunes or national tunes in earlier instrumental works except as themes for variations, and even there they are rare. He had been aware of folk music all his life, as any serious musician would be, and his correspondence with the sometime publisher of folk and national songs, George Thomson of Edinburgh, had already begun some time before his work on these quartets. Still it was to be ten years later, in 1816, that he came back to folk music, fulfilling Thomson's requests for settings of Scottish and Irish tunes along with Polish, Portuguese, Russian, Swedish, Swiss-dialect, Spanish, and Italian melodies.[9]

For the "Razumovsky" Quartets he turned to a collection of Russian folk melodies edited by Ivan Prach and published in St. Petersburg in 1790.[10] Beethoven owned a copy of this collection, and it was evidently the source for two melodies that he employed in these works. The first is the main theme of the finale of the F Major Quartet, Opus 59 No. 1, which in its Russian version, in a minor key and marked Molto andante, was a soldier's lament on his return from the wars (we do not know if Beethoven knew any Russian or knew what the text meant) (*W 38). The second is the famous national melody "Glory be to God in Heaven," later used by Musorgsky for the chorus in the coronation scene of *Boris Godunov*, that appears in the Trio of the Scherzo of No. 2. It is possible that the slow movement of the third quartet has a Russian origin; it has, at least, a Russian flavor, and Musorgsky thought it worthwhile to make a piano transcription of this movement.[11]

The folk tunes are given real prominence. By reserving the D-minor/ F-major theme for the last movement of No. 1 Beethoven gives the "Thème russe" (so marked in the score) a place of clear significance, and his decision to use it as the finale could have been the compositional starting point for the entire quartet. In that case his broad compositional procedure would have been analogous to that of the *Eroica*, in which the final movement on a borrowed theme (his own, in that case) was the conceptual point of departure for the work as a whole. Indeed, the Thème russe has strong intervallic relationships to the first themes of movements 1 and 3 and it seems unlikely that Beethoven should first have invented these themes and then been fortunate enough to pick up the Prach collection and find a theme that was motivically related to them. As for the E Minor Quartet, on the other hand, if he was going to use the patriotic Russian coronation hymn, it had to be in a triple-meter context, and so the layout of the work left him no option other than the Scherzo movement.

Quartet Opus 59 No. 1

Like the *Eroica*, Opus 59 No. 1 explores large dimensions of musical space on an unprecedented scale, combining this expansion with innovations in form that need this greater time-space in which to unfold. The opening theme is cast in the cello, in low register, with pulsating harmonic support in the second violin and viola above it. This way of beginning is more than an innovative reversal of registral expectations:[12] it signals that in the whole movement Beethoven will explore and dramatize the use of register, which he proceeds to do in both the opening theme and throughout the movement. The whole opening paragraph thus builds gradually from its octave-wide opening melody on a harmonically unstable form of

The first page of the autograph manuscript of Beethoven's Quartet in F Major, Opus 59 No. 1, showing some annotations and corrections. (Staatsbibliothek, Berlin)

the tonic, to its first four-octave climax, anticipating the far-flung organization of the whole movement around the preparation of registral climaxes, their postponement, and their eventual arrival. By omitting the usual repeat of the exposition, Beethoven sets up the first movement to prepare for the eventual main climax, that is, when the main theme will appear in the highest register for the first time—which does not happen until the coda (*W 39).

This registral strategy resembles that of the *Eroica* first movement, except that there the long-range connections draw on the arrival of a downward descending scalar figure that refuses to descend to a dominant seventh until the coda. Here, much more overtly and audibly, it is not a transition theme but the main theme itself whose harmonically stable presentation is delayed until the coda. Although Beethoven planned the quartet movement carefully to omit the expected repeat of the exposition, he considered at a late stage enlarging the movement still further by inserting a repeat of the whole development and recapitulation. He even marked this repeat in the autograph manuscript and inserted a short transition to smooth the return to the development—but then canceled the entire repeat before releasing the work for publication. The repeat would have intensified the coda passage that forms the dynamic "resolution" of the movement by having the main theme appear in low register five times before the climactic high-register version, instead of three times. But this plan would also have rendered the movement much too long and unwieldy—the whole development repeat would have included two presentations of its fugato section. Restoring the proportions of the movement by removing the repeat still left the first movement as the longest quartet first movement written up to then.[13]

As it stands, this first movement is a monument of spaciousness and imaginative thematic design, in which every motif of the first theme generates elements suitable for elaboration over a vast and interesting harmonic layout. Thematic patterns easily emerge to create a web of interrelated elements in the exposition, marked not only by growing rhythmic intensity in moving from quarter notes to eighths to triplet figures but also by the arrival of an exotic phrase featuring antiphonal high against low unresolved dominant chords that break the flow and suggest a strange perspective, demanding confirmation at a later time.[14] This they receive in the development, where they reappear in intensified form, preparing a long excursion into a foreign harmonic territory, and they appear again in the recapitulation.[15] These antiphonal chords encapsulate in a short phrase the stark registral contrasts that in much larger terms govern the structure of the whole movement.[16]

Much the same integration of extremes is found in the Scherzo (not labeled "Scherzo" but it certainly is one), the most original in form that Beethoven ever wrote. This is not a conventional Scherzo-Trio-Scherzo or even a fivefold amplification of that scheme but a dramatic sonata-form scherzo of great length and dynamism, all in one movement.[17] Like the first movement it begins with a four-measure phrase in the cello—Romberg's *bête noire*—comprising repetitions of a motivic cell whose rhythmic profile is strong enough to generate material for the movement. From it and the contrasting Violin 2 phrase that follows it come the basic elements of the Scherzo, which develops a complex harmonic scheme with further contrasting themes. Long as the movement is, Beethoven also considered including a large repeat of what would be its development and recapitulation, but again, the plan is suppressed in the autograph at a late stage.[18] What he left in final form stands as the most elaborated Scherzo he had written up to this time, combining astonishing energy and cunning intricacy of workmanship.

The slow movement brings tragedy: the word *mesto* ("mournful") in its label Adagio molto e mesto tells us as much, and the movement eloquently fleshes out the implication of this rare term. Long and expressive, the movement plays on the two forms of the seventh note of the F-minor scale, E and E-flat. Set in sonata form, it is the longest and most complex slow movement Beethoven had written since the funeral march in the *Eroica*. In its feeling of tragedy, the strongly expressive thematic material, heard primarily in the first violin and the cello, is unmatched outside the world of Florestan's dungeon, from which it may have borrowed its F-minor tonality and its implications of death. All the more important then is the sense of salvation offered by the coda, which brings the first theme in amplified form, worked out first in close imitation in the two violin parts, then in octaves, with arpeggiated rhythmic support from the lower strings. The coda takes the first theme to its full climax in high register, somewhat paralleling the climax of the first movement. When this drama is over, the first violin embarks on a soaring cadenza of seven measures, emotionally transporting the Adagio into a new phase of preparation for the drastic change brought on by the finale.

Under a persistent trill in Violin 1, the "Thème russe" in the cello launches the finale, still another movement of grand scope and energy, a finale with a sizable development section and a long coda that exploit ensemble textures. The movement, which easily matches the breadth of the other movements, closes with vigorous gestures that ground the vast bulk of the whole. No wonder that this composition formed the primary model for quartet composers for the rest of the nineteenth century; Schumann, Mendelssohn, and Brahms understood that it opened a new world of quartet writing, and Cosima Wagner's Bayreuth diaries report Wagner in his last years listening to it with close attention.

Quartet Opus 59 No. 2

After the spacious clarity of Opus 59 No. 1, No. 2 in E minor is elusive and mysterious. Its tonal plan is almost the obverse of No. 1 in that the slow movement is in the tonic major, all other movements in the tonic minor. E minor is a bleak and distant key in the tonal system of the period. It had gained some ground in the "Sturm und Drang" 1770s when Haydn used it for his Symphony No. 44, or "Mourning" Symphony. In Mozart it is equally rare as a primary key, appearing in the strangely beautiful Violin Sonata K. 304 written for Paris in 1778. And Beethoven also keeps it at a distance, using it as a main tonic only in this quartet and the Piano Sonata Opus 90 of 1814. Middle movements in E minor are the plaintive Allegretto of the E Major Piano Sonata Opus 14 No. 1 and the dramatic Andante of the Fourth Piano Concerto.

Opus 59 No. 2 opens with a *forte* two-chord gesture, followed by a silence. Then the first "theme" breaks out of the silence in a short phrase, which again stops for another silence. The opening phrase in E minor is then repeated, a half step higher, in F major (recalling the "Appassionata" opening), then another silence! A stream of new ideas follows, now elaborating earlier figures and bringing new ones in rapid flowing sixteenth notes, leading finally to a repetition of the basic two-note chordal gesture, but on unstable harmonies—and then another silence! This discontinuous, abrupt succession of motives and figurational developments—punctuated by eloquent silences—stands in contrast to the opening of the F Major Quartet with its smooth and well-shaped melodic linearity, and it is one of the ways in which Opus 59 No. 2 presages the late quartets. Like his last quartet, Opus 135, it begins at a high level of motivic intensity and then carries the intensity to still higher levels, with resolutions kept at bay for long stretches.

The E-major Adagio takes a balanced melody of the slow-paced, small-interval, symmetrical type that has prompted the term "hymnlike" from many a commentator, and expands it into a sonata-form movement (*W 40a). Subtleties play over the surface from early on, as when the contrasting second phrase of the melody closes into what is expected to be a return to the first phrase but instead dissolves into a new dotted scalar figure that sets up the arrival of a contrasting new theme.[19] In other words, the seeming symmetry of the first large melodic paragraph breaks up, extends the form, and reaches forward into new material. The same thing happens in the recapitulation. The eventual resolution comes, as we might expect, in the lovely coda, where quiet triplet figures over a long-held E in the cello restore a sense of cadential close. Finally, the turning figure in the cello at the very end echoes the opening of the "hymn" melody (*W 40b).

The Scherzo renews the intervallic and rhythmic jaggedness of some parts of the first movement, also exploiting in a new way the severe E-minor/F-major contrast that opens the first movement. To the syncopated intensity of the Scherzo, the Russian theme of the Trio comes as a welcome return to a firm E major. Beethoven then demonstrates the capacity of the theme for contrapuntal treatment, as if he were improvising on it at the keyboard in his best fugato manner. (This contrapuntal invention on a simple theme foreshadows his way of handling the C-major Trio of the Scherzo of the Fifth Symphony, where the fugato animates a robust outbreak that contrasts with a ghost-ridden and deeply mysterious Scherzo in the tonic minor.)

The finale unleashes its Presto in C major, overtly denying the expected tonic, shifting between this C-major harmony and the dominant of E minor but not firmly landing on E minor as the central key of the movement for more than fifty measures! This opening was for Schoenberg a classic example of "fluctuating tonality."[20] That so powerful an ambiguity can begin a finale, which traditionally is the place for the reaffirmation of the home tonic, is just one more sign of the experimental vision embodied in this work. The C-major/E-minor contrast persists right to the last page of the finale, where it gives way to the final peroration, the even faster closing portion of the coda (marked "Più presto"). Here E minor finally expels its tonal rival and drives forward energetically at a steady *fortissimo* to the final chords.[21]

Quartet Opus 59 No. 3

The Opus 59 cycle closes with the C Major Quartet, evidently designed as a partial easing of the strain created by Quartets 1 and 2. The layout of the whole, which at first seemed "disjointed" to some commentators, suggests that after the innovations of the first two works Beethoven was seeking a more reduced framework, partly reminiscent of Mozart.[22] If he had specific models in mind, two are likely: Mozart's C Major Quartet, K. 465 (the "Dissonant"), which, as we saw earlier, he had been thinking about for years; and the "Jupiter" Symphony, especially its contrapuntal finale. Signs of a relationship to K. 465 appear in Beethoven's mysterious and harmonically ambiguous introduction followed by the decisive and clear-cut C-major Allegro first movement, as well as in some of the figuration patterns of the Allegro, which resemble figures in K. 465.[23] Further indications of a "classicizing" aspect to this work are found in the third movement, a C-major "Menuetto" marked "Grazioso," which Beethoven had actually sketched some years earlier. The Andante, on the other hand, sings exotically in A minor and hardly supports retrospective interpretation. Nor would the last movement, his most energetic fugato-cum-sonata-form finale, a virtual perpetuum mobile, a technical tour de force that could not fail—and never has failed—to arouse excitement.

Beethoven's plans for the work underwent some striking compositional changes. At one point the A-minor slow movement was intended to have a 2/4 theme—which, after being discarded from the quartet, resurfaced five years later as the slow-movement theme of the Seventh Symphony.[24] The Minuet was first sketched not in C major but in F major, with a projected D-flat-major Trio.[25] Beethoven also considered the possibility of a C-minor last movement for the quartet until he decided to unleash the manic energy embodied in the C-major finale.[26] And at least one of his early ideas for the first movement included a theme that traces back directly to Mozart's Clarinet Quintet (*W 41).[27]

But no matter how tradition-minded Beethoven was in fashioning the C Major Quartet, no matter how much any of its details resemble Mozart or Haydn, there are clear signs that it belongs to the same modern artistic sphere as its companions. One such indication appears in the slow introduction itself. Despite its general resemblance to the broad, intense chromatic lines of Mozart's introduction to K. 465, it actually draws even more closely on some of the same harmonic resources we find in the F-minor introduction to Florestan's dungeon scene, written in 1805–6 just before his main work on these quartets. The dynamics, mood, and of course orchestration and dramatic purpose differ, but Beethoven's strategic use in the quartet introduction of the three different diminished-seventh chords in order[28] organizes the framework of the quartet's opening section in much the same way that the identical harmonies organize the long Florestan introduction. At the same time the "wandering" lines of the quartet introduction are also reminiscent of the slow descending motions to mysterious goals that begin the second and third *Leonore* overtures. Most telling of all for the modernity of the first movement is the highly original way that Beethoven composed out the harmonic implications of the three adjacent diminished-seventh harmonies, first in the development section of the Allegro and then in the crucial transition measures that lead to the recapitulation.[29]

The "Harp" Quartet and the "Quartetto Serioso"

Between the monumental Opus 59 and the much later quartets of the last years stand two single quartets: Opus 74 in E-flat major, later called the "Harp" Quartet, and Opus 95 in F minor, which Beethoven himself labeled "Quartetto serioso." The E-flat Quartet dates from the summer of 1809, along with the "Emperor" Concerto and the *Lebewohl* Piano Sonata, both of which, it may be noted, are also in E-flat. By 1810 Beethoven had completed Opus 95, which did not appear in print until 1816 as part of the group published by Steiner, with a dedication to Nikolaus Zmeskall von Domanovecz "from his friend Ludwig van Beethoven."[30] The private character of the dedication accords well with the character of the work—deeply expressive, tightly condensed, a probing experiment—which at one time Beethoven believed "is written for a small circle of connoisseurs and is never to be performed in public."[31] Beethoven spent some time in private chamber music sessions in 1809 and 1810, often held at Zmeskall's house with Schuppanzigh and Anton Kraft performing. A sketchbook from 1809 contains the annotation "quartets every week"; it also contains at least one idea for a C-major quartet that never materialized.

The idea that Opus 74 is a light and genial diversion from the more serious Beethoven is a cliché that could not be more mistaken. This impression arises from the smooth and seemingly placid character of the first movement, along with the extended plucked-string passages that inspired its nickname and the quiet Allegretto variations finale. But it can hardly be sustained in the face of the passionate Adagio or the rough and dynamic Scherzo. These inner movements stand at extreme poles of Beethoven's middle-period universe, while the first and last surround them with high imagination and subtlety. The work prompts memories of two earlier quartets in the same key: Mozart's path-finding K. 428 of 1785 and Haydn's Opus 76 No. 6 of 1797. Haydn's E-flat masterpiece opens with a variation first movement that Beethoven could well have had in mind when he wrote the finale of Opus 74 (just as Haydn's B-major Fantasia, as a slow movement, could have influenced Beethoven's Fantasy Opus 77 a year earlier). In this quartet Beethoven's contrapuntal treatment of the Trio of the Scherzo—again, as in Opus 59 No. 2—may also reflect his interest in theoretical studies at this time, as the 1809 sketchbook indeed suggests.

The tonal plan of Opus 74 is unusual in that the two middle movements are both in keys other than the tonic, E-flat major. The slow movement is a moving and expressive Adagio in A-flat major, and the Scherzo is in C minor, with a C-major Trio. Beethoven used this kind of tonal plan for a four-movement work in only one other piece from this time, the Piano Trio Opus 70 No. 2, in which the E-flat-major first and last movements frame a second movement in C major and an Allegretto in A-flat. In Opus 74, key relationships by thirds abound at the broadest structural levels, and we are not surprised to find that in the first movement there is much exploration of C major in the development section.

The first movement, in which the introduction prepares the Allegro in a richly imaginative way, is notable for its "harp" passages, strategically placed within the movement. Here Beethoven exploits the potential of pizzicato as a special string sonority. He had begun to use it extensively and in far-flung registers in the Opus 59 Quartets—above all in the cello in the slow movements of No. 1 and No. 3—and would later do so again in the "Archduke" Trio, but in Opus 74 it gains unprecedented importance. In Haydn, Mozart, and early Beethoven quartets, plucked strings were saved for incidental contrasts, either in final cadences of slow movements or in special movements in which plucked accompaniment figures were wanted; here it becomes an essential tone color. Appearing directly after the first thematic paragraph has run its course in the exposition, the pizzicato forms a special pocket of sonority with alternating plucked quarter notes against running bowed eighth notes. In the development the passage reappears to form the transition back to the recapitulation, now with alternating plucked quarters against sustained chords. In the recapitulation the original version returns in a slightly new guise.

The coda caps the climax when the alternating pizzicato quarter notes now fill four beats at a time while the first violin suddenly tears loose with the longest and most elaborate cadenza anywhere in Beethoven's quartets. At first the lower strings, as if struggling to bring the first violinist back into the ensemble, turn to the first phrase of the first theme in Violin 2 and Viola while the cello continues to pluck away; then the cello joins in the insistent appeal, which grows in volume to a *fortissimo* cadence that finally closes the segment in the tonic and shows the way to the final tonic chords, by now all *arco* (bowed).

Of all Beethoven's quartets up to then, Opus 95 is the most fiercely concentrated and closely argued. F minor, a key of tragic feeling, always evokes a strong emotional response, not only in Beethoven but in his two great predecessors and also his followers. Witness Schubert's deeply moving Fantasy for piano four hands, D. 940, which shows some signs of potential influence from Opus 95 in its odd juxtaposition of keys. (Schubert has interior movements in F-sharp minor and D major within an F-minor context, which could well derive from Beethoven's slow movement choice of D major in this quartet.) Later examples stream down through the nineteenth century. For Beethoven himself we trace significant uses of F minor as a main key only in his piano sonatas, first in No. 1, and again, much more developed, in the "Appassionata." Otherwise Beethoven chooses it as tonic only for Florestan's dungeon scene, for the slow movement of Opus 59 No. 1, for the "Storm" in the *Pastoral* Symphony, and for the *Egmont* Overture. It is somewhat surprising that after this quartet, he never completed another full work in this key and that the only F-minor inner movement of a later cyclic work is the Scherzo of the A-flat-major Piano Sonata No. 31. The tonal and expressive range of the late works—especially the late quartets—moves beyond the classical key associations that still hovered lightly over his middle-period works.

The brief opening subject is outlined by the same scale steps, 1–3–1–5–1, as the *Eroica* opening subject but with the intervals filled in, using two forms of the minor scale in immediate succession (*W 42). Thus the melody moves down from 1 to 5 through lowered 7 and lowered 6, then moves back up from 5 to 1 through raised 6 and raised 7. This initial ambiguity sets up tonal suggestions that are immediately taken up in connection with scale step 2, that is, G; the opening subject reappears on G♭, or lowered 2, thus treating this pitch as if it were a new local tonic, and then suddenly returns to its F-minor tonic by way of a G♮ in the cello.

From here on the well-defined opening rhythmic cell of four sixteenth notes plus downbeat—with the pitches 1–2–3–2–1—takes hold as a basic figure for the movement, in which the tension once established never lets up. The phrases are frequently asymmetric and abrupt, and there is an absence of simple periodicity in the phrase relationships along with a focus on the close, insistent development of a small group of motives. This high degree of concentration allows little or no room for transition passages that could relax the discourse and define spaces between principal thematic units. The exposition is not repeated.[32] Rather, Beethoven goes on at once to the short development section, which leads to a drastically shortened recapitulation. Everywhere compression rules: the whole development section occupies only 14 percent of the whole movement, and the fiercely emphatic recapitulation and coda hold the intensity to the end (*W 43).

In contrast the Allegretto slow movement, in D major, patiently explores its thematic material, which turns out to be based on the same descending interval of a fourth that is prominent in the first movement, but now with a completely different character: it opens "mezza voce" ("with half voice") and slowly develops a web of quiet themes, gaining complexity as it accumulates more complex harmonies and relationships, including a fugal passage. The slow movement closes into a Scherzo that resumes the power and tension of the first movement, relieved only by a lyrical Trio in the odd keys of G-flat major (again the half step above the original F-minor tonic of the first movement) and D major (the key of the slow movement). All this is then capped by the Finale. A short introduction, Larghetto espressivo, prepares the 6/8 main body of the last movement, Allegretto agitato, whose basic sense is of deep gestural yearning and imploring, moving along pathways of feeling that no words can fully describe.

The coda of the Finale has baffled many a dedicated Beethovenian, as it ends the whole work with a light-fingered, nimble Allegro. Its special character is enhanced by what immediately precedes it, namely, a *pianississimo* close in F major that seemingly promises to conclude the movement on a quiet note of affirmation. But then the coda breaks out with its running figures in 2/2 meter, *sempre piano*, building gradually to two climactic arrivals on the tonic. The composer Vincent d'Indy criticized the coda harshly; others see it as perhaps a joke, even an "opera buffa finale," or as a sample of paradox and Romantic irony.[33] But behind the facade lurk elements of art, as the half-step figure F♯–G–G♯–A that starts off the coda emerges as a basic idea that is repeated three times emphatically near the end. Here it suddenly reminds us of the opening chromatic figures that had started off the first movement, now on different scale steps but with the same emphasis on two forms of the same scale step, G, which is now G and G♯ in immediate succession. Further, the F-sharp implies two forms of the tonic pitch, F; thus the implied sequence is an upward chromatic span of five notes: F–F♯–G–G♯–A. The chromatic figure forces our attention to the pitch content of the coda rather than simply letting us be carried away by its speed and finality. It ends this darkest of Beethoven quartets in a light still shadowed by the tragic features of the earlier movements. Such qualities, depths below depths, have given this work the valid reputation of being a visionary anticipation of Beethoven's late style, certainly of the late quartets. Yet if we look at the work more for what it fulfills than what it anticipates, we see that in the foliage of its interrelated clusters of ideas, it represents a deepening and thickening of Beethoven's second-period quartet style, moving from broad and open ways of expression, as in Opus 59 No. 1, into a world of pain and oppression.

PART FOUR

✦━━━━❈━━━━✦

THE FINAL MATURITY

1813–1827

CHAPTER 16

THE "FALLOW" YEARS

E xcept for the deafness crisis, no period in Beethoven's life has aroused more speculation than the years from 1813 to 1817, the lengthy twilight zone between his second and third maturities. The basic facts compel us to see this period as a major break in the larger continuity of his career, a time of psychological distress and of diminished creative energy after the extraordinary ten years that had culminated in 1812 with the Seventh and Eighth Symphonies. But it is far more fruitful to focus less on what was ending, and more on what was beginning; less on his loss of productivity and more on the progressive features of the few significant works that he completed. Once again we face the underlying question of how we can relate Beethoven's personal life to his artistic evolution and how we should construe this phase of his development—whether primarily as a lapse or as a period of quiet gestation in which the late style slowly emerges. Without denying that much depends on one's angle of vision, I will argue for the positive side of the question.

First, a few words on the main biographical developments. Beethoven's chronic physical ailments became aggravated in 1812, and his physician ordered him to seek cures at Teplitz, Karlsbad, and Franzensbrunn.[1] His deafness was growing progressively worse, intensifying his isolation and hardening the barriers that hindered social communication. July 1812 at Teplitz was the time of his passionate letter to his "Immortal Beloved," with all its implications for his acceptance of loneliness, abandonment of any lasting relationship with a woman, and withdrawal further into the self. His family obsessions broke out again, now in the form of a quixotic journey to Linz in October 1812 for the express purpose of interfering with his brother Johann's current affair with his housekeeper, Therese Obermayer. Beethoven's zealous involvement with family members was soon to take on an even more extreme form over the guardianship of his nephew, which began in a legal sense in November 1815 when his brother Carl, one day before his death, made his will appointing Beethoven and Carl's wife Johanna as coguardians of their son Karl.

Then there is Beethoven's private *Tagebuch* (diary) covering 1812–18, the most vivid testimony of his deepening isolation in these years. As Maynard Solomon wisely observed, Beethoven began keeping the *Tagebuch* just at the time when he was becoming estranged from many of his former close friends, such as Gleichenstein, Breuning, Erdödy, and others, and was now confiding his innermost feelings to the pages of his diary.[2] Finally, there was the crushing truth that his personal financial situation had taken a serious blow from the Austrian *Finanz-patent*, that is, the national currency devaluation of March 1811, which drastically reduced the value of his annuity. Compounding the bad economic news were the sudden death of his patron Prince Kinsky in November 1812 and the bankruptcy of Prince Lobkowitz, causing drastic losses in support that were only partly remedied by Archduke Rudolph's generosity.[3] It seems very clear that Beethoven was moved by genuine financial concerns as well as career ambitions in his quest for popular success in these years.[4]

The Congress of Vienna

In the outer world dramatic changes were unfolding. Napoleon's invasion of Russia in June of 1812, with "the largest army ever assembled by any one force in European history,"[5] ended in disaster three months later at Borodino. The miserable retreat of the beaten French armies from Moscow over the four months from October 1812 to January 1813, followed by Napoleon's desperate campaign in Saxony that spring and his defeat by Wellington in Spain at Vittoria in June, ended his dreams of sustaining his empire and aroused the hopes of his ill-assorted enemies that they might finish him off at last. In April 1814 he was forced to abdicate and was exiled to Elba, off the Tuscan coast, precipitating the first massive turn of the great diplomatic wheel by which the Great Powers—England, Russia, Austria, and Prussia—now readied themselves to reconstruct the old European system and set up a new balance of power that could prevent any threats to the restored or strengthened monarchies.

The result was the Congress of Vienna. Planned to begin in August 1814, it actually opened in September and met until June 1815, its last phase coinciding with Napoleon's electrifying escape from Elba, the "Hundred Days," and his final defeat at Waterloo, June 16–18, 1815. The Congress brought a swarm of high diplomats and royalty to Vienna, including Czar Alexander I, King Friedrich Wilhelm III of Prussia, and an array of titled aristocrats and their entourages. Amid glittering receptions, balls, and entertainments, Beethoven, as the most famous of Viennese composers, could draw on the backing of some of his aristocratic patrons, particularly the archduke, and play a visible role. In effect the Viennese cultural managers could show him off to visiting ambassadors and aristocrats as one of the brightest stars of Austrian artistic life, perhaps its brightest one. In 1814 Count Razumovsky and the archduke presented him to visiting royalty and others, and although Beethoven showed his customary intolerance for the pompous social life of the nobility, he let himself be persuaded to play at a concert in January 1815 in the Rittersaal. There he accompanied Franz Wild in one of his songs and presented the spellbinding first-act quartet from *Fidelio*.[6] Even though most of the gathered nobility preferred ballroom music to Beethoven, his reputation was by now so great that he could easily become the musical hero of the Congress. Despite his habitual protests, he shamelessly cultivated this role by hurriedly composing the bombastic cantata *Der Glorreiche Augenblick* ("The Glorious Moment") for the assembled heads of state, along with a flashy polonaise for piano for the czarina Elisabetha Alexievna, "Empress of all the Russias," as the title page proclaimed when it came out very soon thereafter as his Opus 89.

Taking a longer view of these years, we have to reckon with a loss of his earlier productive momentum beginning in the winter of 1812–13. Although his decline in productivity had strong inner motivations, it is curious that it coincided with the collapse of Napoleon's dreams of empire, almost as if Beethoven's conquering and heroic works of the second period might in some way have been unconsciously and symbiotically linked to the military conquests that marked Napoleon's career during these same years. We remember that Beethoven, in 1806, had remarked after Napoleon's victory at Jena that if only he understood war as well as he understood music, he could conquer the great general.

After all, in nine years he had written, along with other major works, eight symphonies that had completely revolutionized the genre, and he had enlarged the expressive capacities of instrumental music in ways that even his most admiring contemporaries had not predicted. It has been argued that Beethoven was suffering from creative exhaustion and stasis during this period, 1813–17, as if the energy of the previous years had badly faded and was not yet ready to be refired. If we measure by sheer productivity this is a reasonable hypothesis, but if we look more sharply at the works of the later second period, between 1809 and 1812, we find unmistakable features that foreshadow some aspects of the late style. Among them are the harmonic anomalies of the *Lebewohl* Sonata, Opus 81a; the motivic concentration, compression, and angularity of the first movement of Opus 95; and even the surface lyricism hiding complexity that we find in Opus 96.

Lighter Works

When we think of the popular and trivial compositions that Beethoven wrote in this fallow period we should recall that even in earlier years he had always saved some energy for accessible works that he could publish for profit, enabling him not only to dominate the musical scene with higher achievements but also to woo the public with compositions that would sell and keep him popular—simpler works that were ingratiating and easy to perform. Sometimes, paradoxically, these were modest essays in the same genres in which he was working out compositions on the grand scale. An example is the set of three Marches for Piano Four Hands, Opus 45, which Beethoven completed sketching in the *Eroica* Sketchbook, actually taking time off to compose them while he was in the thick of work on the Funeral March in the *Eroica*. For years he kept up the habit of spinning off minor works while in the heat of producing major ones. Thus in 1805 he published the two "easy" Piano Sonatinas Opus 49, works he had sketched ten years earlier; in 1806, the trio for two oboes and English horn, Opus 87, of the same vintage as the sonatinas; in 1810 the wind sextets Opus 71 and Opus 81b, dating from the mid-1790s. Apologizing to Breitkopf for offering him the sextet to publish, he had written that it was "one of my earlier works, written in one night, and one can only say that it is written by an author who has brought out at least some better works."[7] Even in the last years he would rummage among his papers for salable earlier works, as we see from his refurbishing the "Kakadu" Variations in 1824 and his exhumation of the song "Der Kuss," of 1798, which he published as Opus 128 in 1825.[8]

If we look more closely at Beethoven's actual productivity in the "fallow" period, we can distinguish several types of projects. First we find artistically insignificant works written to make money or to restore and build his broad public reputation; the two most prominent are *Wellingtons Sieg* and the cantata *Der Glorreiche Augenblick*. Then there were stylistically retrospective works that look back at second-period achievements. The biggest such project was the difficult job of reconstructing *Leonore* as *Fidelio*, but there were unfinished works that show the same style features, including the torso of what would have been a sixth piano concerto and his futile attempt at an F-minor piano trio, both in 1815. Waiting for publication in these years were a series of important compositions that had been written by 1812 but were not to be published until 1816, among them the second setting of "An die Hoffnung," the Quartet Opus 95, the "Archduke" Trio, the Violin Sonata Opus 96, and the Seventh Symphony. Finally, and most important, were the few prophetic, fully realized, and highly expressive compositions, all written between 1814 and 1816, that embodied his full creative powers: the Piano Sonata Opus 90 in E minor, the two Cello Sonatas of Opus 102, the song cycle *An die ferne Geliebte,* and the Piano Sonata Opus 101 in A major.

Celebrating Wellington's Victory

We need hardly be reminded that the battle piece *Wellingtons Sieg,* ("Wellington's Victory") is far below Beethoven's normal standards, a shameless concession to the political wave of the moment, written to win him acclaim as a patriotic Austrian artist. He wrote it at the request of Johann Nepomuk Mälzel, "Court Mechanician" for the Austrian royalty, an ingenious inventor of mechanical devices of all sorts, including the metronome, with which his name became permanently associated. Besides devising a mechanical trumpeter that played a French cavalry march with a piano accompaniment, Mälzel rigged up a new device, called the Panharmonicon, that combined military band instruments and a bellows in a case, with keys linked to pins on a revolving cylinder, as in a barrel organ or music box. Mälzel started out by producing cylinders for Cherubini's *Lodoïska* Overture, Haydn's "Military" Symphony, and a Handel chorus, but he thought he would really make a hit with the public if he persuaded Beethoven to write a patriotic battle piece for his new machine. There were already battle pieces galore in the orchestral, military band, and piano repertoires of the time, such as Georg-Friedrich Fuchs's band piece *Bataille de Gemappes* or Louis Emmanuel Jadin's piano piece *La grande bataille d'Austerlitz* of 1806, composed to celebrate Napoleon's victory. Daniel Steibelt, a composer of some reputation and sometime rival of Beethoven's as pianist, had composed a piano fantasy called *The Burning of Moscow* for Napoleon's entry into Moscow in 1812, and many more such works were being produced for an avid public.[9]

Beethoven gave in to Mälzel's blandishments and concocted his piece in two parts. Part 1 depicts the battle itself, beginning with "Rule Britannia" to represent the British forces and continuing with "Malbrouck," or "Marlborough," as the French army's march, both preceded by trumpets and drums. The battle itself is a colossal noisemaker with cannon shots for both sides marked in the score and a weakened "Marlborough" signaling the French in defeat. Part 2 consists of a "Victory Symphony" in several parts, including a new march and the melody of "God Save the King" as theme with two variations, one a tempo di menuetto, the other a fugato that leads to a smashing final coda. Ignaz Moscheles, an eyewitness, later reported apologetically that Beethoven had taken this whole plan from Mälzel, and "even the unhappy idea of converting the melody of 'God save the King' into a subject of a fugue in quick movement, emanates from Mälzel."[10]

The piece never materialized on the Panharmonicon, however, since Beethoven decided to orchestrate the work and agreed to produce it at a public concert in 1813, at which he and Mälzel would share the limelight. The program turned out to comprise the premiere of Beethoven's Seventh Symphony, two marches (by Dussek and Pleyel) played by Mälzel's mechanical trumpeter, and *Wellingtons Sieg* as the final number. The orchestra members included the best performers in Vienna, including Schuppanzigh as concertmaster, Salieri conducting the drummers and can-noneers, Ludwig Spohr, Johann Nepomuk Hummel, Joseph Mayseder, the famous double-bass virtuoso Domenico Dragonetti, and even the young Giacomo Meyerbeer. Everyone understood that the piece was nothing more than a patriotic extravaganza, not a serious composition, but Beethoven's involvement clearly embarrassed his more sophisticated admirers. For example, Wenzel Tomaschek declared that, as he understood it, Beethoven himself "declared the work to be folly and that he liked it only because with it he had thoroughly thrashed the Viennese." Thayer evaded any real eval-uation of the work by calling it "a gigantic professional frolic."[11]

Although it is possible to see *Wellingtons Sieg* as a "monument of triv-ialities" or as representing Beethoven as a "pioneer of kitsch," that is only part of the story.[12] By agreeing to devise the piece and then perform it at a major concert, Beethoven was obviously riding the euphoric wave that swept over Vienna after Napoleon's recent defeats and that seemed to promise a new era of political recovery after years of oppression and defeat. To write and produce the work at one or two major public concerts was to indulge in sincere patriotic celebration. But to then go further and publish the work, moreover to give it an opus number and place it in the series of his important compositions, showed that his deep yearning for public recognition and financial security had gone beyond any earlier limits and that his need for public acclaim, not just in the world at large or in the future but then and there, in Vienna and in his lifetime, for once overrode his normal standards of self-criticism. About *Wellingtons Sieg* he could have said the opposite of what he had told Radicati about the Opus 59 Quartets, namely that they were not for a later age but only to be patriotic, to capi-talize on current national feeling, and to make money.

The cantata for the Congress, *Der Glorreiche Augenblick* ("The Glorious Moment"), published posthumously in 1836 as Opus 136, is, like *Wellingtons Sieg,* a grotesque parody of his serious style, a plodding fabrication that falls far short of what he had achieved long ago with his youthful cantatas for Joseph II and Leopold II. The text was written by Alois Weissenbach, a Tyrolean physician and poet who came to Vienna in September 1814, met Beethoven, and persuaded him to collaborate on what has been accurately described as this "rather bombastic" piece.[13] Beethoven may have felt a special sympathy for this project since Weissenbach was also deaf and, if we can believe the poet's memoirs, spent considerable stretches of time with Beethoven discussing their mutual affliction.[14] The cantata, for four solo voices, chorus, and orchestra, shows a few faint sparks in its solo numbers that are immediately extinguished by its utterly banal choruses.[15] A couple of passages for solo violin and solo cello were no doubt written to arouse the interest of the first-desk players (probably Schuppanzigh and Joseph Linke), but they fail to sustain the work. To compare this patriotic sycophantry with the true beauty of another cantata Beethoven was writing in 1814–15—his setting of Goethe's *Calm Sea and Prosperous Voyage* for four voices and orchestra—is to see the difference between his tossing off a casual simulation and his thinking through and carefully shaping a setting of poetry that meant something to him.

The current view in modern criticism is that the success of *Fidelio* in 1814 prompted Beethoven's acceptance of a sudden new role as a famous composer in the heightened political atmosphere that was rising out of Napoleon's downfall. But there was more to it. Well aware that he was producing works such as the cantata and *Battle Symphony* that were designed for nothing but public success, Beethoven took considerable trouble to assuage his conscience and obliquely explain to his admirers what he was up to, even to do so publicly. He defended his writing such works by inserting a public statement about *Fidelio* in the *Friedensblätter* in July 1814. He may, of course, have done so to drum up business for the revival of the opera during the summer lull, but the defensive tone of the message, and its other implications, above all of his self-conscious public status, are clear enough:

A Word to His Admirers

How often, in your anger that his depth was not sufficiently appreci-
ated, have you said that van Beethoven composes only for posterity! You
have, no doubt, now retracted your error, even if only since the general
enthusiasm aroused by his immortal opera Fidelio, *in the conviction*
that what is truly great and beautiful finds kindred souls and sympa-
thetic hearts in the present without withholding in the slightest the just
privileges of posterity.[16]

That he bothered to publish such a statement at all tells the story.

Fidelio

To find a better way of understanding how Beethoven came through
this period, we can focus on his more important projects, beginning
with the *Fidelio* revision in the early months of 1814, then the line of works
that run from Opus 90 to Opus 101. Recent discussions of the 1814 *Fidelio*
have stressed its glorification of Don Fernando as a benevolent ruler whose
noble and enlightened gestures at the end reflect the supposedly benign
qualities of the European heads of state who were triumphing at last
over Napoleon.[17] In more strictly musical terms the alterations reveal
Beethoven thinking very differently about operatic material than he had
eight years earlier. This new version shows a tightening of the discourse,
much removal of repetitions, splicing of adjacent phrase units to move the
action forward, and sharpening of contrasts. Quite apart from the new
dramatic focus, the compositional changes point in the direction of his
later style. Thus the new overture in E major solves the earlier problem
he had faced in the three C-major overtures of how to anticipate Florestan's aria of hope for salvation. Here the answer is drastic: he leaves it
out, writing an overture in which the spirit but not the material of the
opera comes through in a vigorous and strongly dramatic piece of orchestral writing.

The result is that the 1814 *Fidelio* is a hybrid that combines musical material of two distinct periods, which is why he said that revising this work was so much more difficult than composing a new one.[18] While the later version strengthens the role of Leonore, it also strengthens the figure of Florestan in his representation of heroism as endurance. As we saw earlier, the great scene in the dungeon, instead of ending with Florestan's sinking back in exhaustion after dreaming of release, has a new coda in which he sees a vision of his "angel Leonore" as agent of salvation. The revision thus provides a link to Beethoven's physical and psychic struggles at the time, during which he repeatedly exhorted himself to stoic acceptance of his own limitations and the hard fate that his artistic commitment was forcing on him.[19] As he wrote in his *Tagebuch* in 1813, copying from Herder: "Lerne schweigen, O Freund" ("Learn to keep silent, O friend").[20]

The 1814 *Fidelio* constitutes a laboratory for transforming his style at the level of phrase organization and operatic formal structure. At the same time its emphasis on the lyrical—in solo and ensemble numbers above all—furnishes another basis on which Beethoven could work toward reformulating his instrumental style. To do so he turned as soon as possible to the piano sonata.

New Sonatas

The first result is the E-minor/major Sonata Opus 90, whose autograph is dated August 16, 1814. This is the first instrumental work that Beethoven wrote after the *Fidelio* revision—as if he gave himself a welcome gift, after his operatic labors, of returning to the most familiar and comfortable of his musical domains. The movement headings, which for the first time are in German, do not use the traditional tempo designations, even in translation, but instead convey character.[21] Thus the first movement, in E minor, is headed, "Mit Lebhaftigkeit und durchaus mit Empfindung und Ausdruck" ("With liveliness and throughout with feeling and expression"); the second is headed, "Nicht zu geschwind und sehr singbar vorgetragen" ("Not too quickly and to be performed in a very singing manner"). The pianist and scholar Charles Rosen describes the first movement as "despairing and impassioned, laconic almost to the point of reticence."[22] A special feature is its weak initial tonic, E minor, moving at once to its relative major, G major, and on through a lyrical counterstatement to its first cadence. We then encounter a sudden, striking use of high and low registers *within a single phrase*, a definite sign of Beethoven's late style, which is marked by discontinuities of register in unexpected ways that do not correspond with phrase endings or beginnings. Remarkably, this figure maintains its extremely strong registral contrasts not only at the recapitulation but also at the very end of the movement (*W 44).[23]

The second movement, perhaps Beethoven's longest singing rondo, reveals his renewed capacity for sustained emotional intimacy; as Tovey said, it is "devoted to the utmost luxuriance of lyric melodies."[24] Among other movements in Beethoven's middle- and later-period works committed to "absolute melody," this is the one most fully given over to a long-phrased, symmetrically structured line that is seductively "cantabile" (*singbar*) from beginning to end, in which the contrasting episodes match the spirit of the main melody and in no way ruffle the surface or mar the effect of its many repetitions. This movement might reflect a carryover into the keyboard sonata of the major-mode lyric intensity of some parts of *Fidelio*—above all Leonore's aria "Komm, Hoffnung," which is also in E major. In the same vein we might hear the opening of the C Major Cello Sonata, Opus 102 No. 1, with its cello solo marked by the terms "teneramente" (sensitively) and "cantabile," as a reflection of the voice quality, as well as the range and style of Florestan's "In des Lebens Frühlingstagen" ("In the spring days of life").[25] The same terms are used here in the second movement of this piano sonata, "teneramente" being the marking for each return of the main theme after the contrasting episodes. Another sign of Beethoven's intense exploration of melody in these years, the song cycle *An die ferne Geliebte*, was written in very close proximity to Opus 102.[26]

The two cello sonatas of Opus 102 reflect other dimensions of the emerging late style, set up as they are as correlative opposites. In No. 2 we find the concise, abrupt, brilliant discontinuities of its first movement balanced by the dark hymnlike slow movement and the bristling fugato finale. In the C-major Sonata, No. 1, Beethoven returns to his familiar formal plan of a sonata "quasi una fantasia" that brings a modified restatement of the opening Andante just before the finale, as in Piano Sonata

Opus 27 No. 1. Everywhere in the C Major Cello Sonata he focuses on the linear flow and contrapuntal integrity of the material, whether the character is romantic (as in the slower movements), vigorous and boisterous (as in the A-minor Allegro), or humorous and ironic (as in the Finale). Contemporaries were baffled; the Mannheim Hofkapellmeister Michael Frey, who heard Czerny and Linke play the premiere of one of these sonatas, wrote in his diary, "It is so original that no one can understand it on first hearing."[27]

An die ferne Geliebte

*A*n *die ferne Geliebte* ("To the Distant Beloved"), which stands alone as Beethoven's only song cycle and his only song composition on the scale of his instrumental works, is a basic step in the direction of his oncoming new style. The text is by a Viennese Jewish medical student named Alois Jeitteles. It was probably written for Beethoven and does not seem to have an existence apart from this setting.

The full text consists of six poems of differing meters in which the poet, far from his beloved, sings of desolation and loneliness. In the first song he sits on a hill "in the blue land of clouds" and mourns that his beloved cannot hear his sighs and yearnings, while the later stanzas offer images of nature that surround the poet in his misery—"the blue mountain," sun and clouds, the valley below, the wind softly blowing, the running brooks. And in the final poem, which seized the imagination of the Romantics, above all Schumann, comes the climactic strophe:

Nimm sie hin denn diese Lieder,	Take, then, these songs
Die ich dir, Geliebte, sang.	that I, beloved, sang to you.
Singe sie dann Abends wieder	Sing them of evenings
Zu der Laute stiller Klang.	to the quiet sound of the lute.

This verse is followed by three more strophes of the same type. The joining of these songs in a single narrative inaugurates the song cycle, which Schubert was within a few years of perfecting in *Die schöne Müllerin* and *Win-*

The first page of Beethoven's autograph of his only song cycle, An die ferne Geliebte *("To the Distant Beloved"). (Beethoven-Haus, Bonn)*

terreise. Beethoven's careful modeling of phrase and word to music and his concern to give the whole a sense of unity as a complex sequence of feelings in a progressive emotional and structural totality makes this work a turning point in the development of the German art song. That it coincides with a new phase in Beethoven's life situation—one of personal crisis that was giving way to resignation and to a new productive stage—is suggested more by its expressive directness than by any highly elaborated musical complexity, for which there would not have been room in the genre of the German lied.

At one point Jeitteles's poem sounds a strange note:

Denn vor Liebesklang entweichet   For at the sound of love's singing
Jeder Raum und jede Zeit.   all space and time vanishes.

The new sense of space and time that will be embodied in the late style is distantly announced in these verses, as if the poet had somehow provided Beethoven with a poetic image of the timeless forms of expression, the otherworldliness, for which his new music had already begun to strive. It is notable as well that in his *Tagebuch* of these years Beethoven occasionally copied passages from Eastern religious tracts that referred to the timelessness of mystical experience.[28]

Emergence of the Late Style

The late style in all its fullness comes forth in the Piano Sonata Opus 101, one of Beethoven's greatest compositions in any genre. Using the cyclic return form of Opus 102 No. 1, written a year earlier, Beethoven crosses the border into a new aesthetic territory, entering a sound world whose philosophical depth is new in his work and rare in music of any age. Here the contrasts between movements are substantial but less jagged than in the cello sonatas, and the whole work belongs to a sphere of intimacy beyond even his most expressive earlier piano sonatas. This sonata strikes us as being far bigger than its medium and encompassing a world in itself, thus conveying a quality that pervades the late works.

The form of the first movement, in A major, is enigmatic. It falls into a large-scale two-part framework in which the first part contains the equivalent of the exposition and development, and the second part presents the recapitulation and a short coda. But many of the traditional form-building features associated with sonata form in more traditional terms are left deliberately indistinct. These features, such as the traditionally clear division between first and second theme in an exposition, or between exposition and development—even between development and recapitulation—are disguised and elided, and are given no special emphasis. Instead they glide by without being noticed by the casual listener. A pensive, Romantic, quasi-improvisatory feeling pervades the whole of the first movement, which flows from beginning to end and, as Beethoven wrote in his tempo heading, is to be played with "the innermost expressiveness." The beginning of the movement, with its first phrase on the dominant chord, poses a question, and it implies an eventual answer. That answer might be a firm arrival on the tonic chord, but no such arrival with tonic A in the bass takes place until three-quarters of the movement has been traversed.

The remaining movements offer transcendent representations of familiar movement types. Thus the Scherzo is a fantastic march in F major with persistent imitative dialogue between high and low voices. The Trio intensifies this dialogue, the voices following each other in close canonic imitation. Then the pensive slow movement, followed by the recall of the opening of the first movement, gives way to a vigorous and energetic finale that displays further imitative dialogue and a fugal middle section. A particularly sensitive appraisal of this remarkable sonata points out that "the sheer joy of exercising a faculty that is art and craft, an intellectual activity, an emotional release, and a unique means of communicating . . . is all to be found in this sonata . . . the most physically euphoric of the last five."[29]

To judge Beethoven's productivity in this period simply by counting works and comparing totals with those achieved in the great years of his second maturity is to miss the point. It is perfectly true that between 1813 and late 1817, when he began work on the *Hammerklavier* Sonata, he had no symphonic project in hand and was far less prolific than he had been in the middle and late-middle years up to 1812. But along with the personal factors, what accounts for this change is his evolution toward the transcendental that is revealed by these works—the Piano Sonata Opus 90; the cello sonatas of Opus 102, *An die ferne Geliebte*; and the Piano Sonata Opus 101. Accordingly, what has been seen as a "fallow" period might be reconceived as a period of self-reconstruction, a necessary questioning of previous approaches and the gestation of new ones, in which a new composing personality within him was in process of emerging.

Meanwhile, the weaker works of this time—*Wellingtons Sieg* and the Congress cantata—were products of Beethoven's own ambivalence, born out of financial necessity, desire for fame, and a debilitated defense of conscience. They should be set aside as negligible byproducts, not as works in the main line.

The higher artist in Beethoven in these supposedly arid years was not dormant but, as he aged and gained deeper experience, was quietly reshaping his ways. As part of this process he reduced his reliance on the powerful, the dynamic, the developmental, and the rhetorical. Listening to the voices within himself, he yielded primarily to what was deeply personal and inward. At the same time, he began to move toward combining the melodic and contrapuntal dimensions of his thinking in a new synthesis that would enable him to come to terms with Bach. He was working toward a higher level of musical integration that would nevertheless remain organically connected to his earlier methods of composition.

CHAPTER 17

BEETHOVEN'S INNER AND OUTER WORLDS

>∘⇥∘⇥⟨⟨⟨⟩⟩⟩⇤∘⇤∘⇤

Isolation and Deafness

T wo elements of Beethoven's domestic life run through his last ten years like persistent motives from one of his major works: isolation and obsessiveness. As his hearing deteriorated he could no longer understand what people were saying without an ear trumpet, and even then sometimes badly. The need arose for others to write down their end of conversations with him. So, beginning in 1818, Beethoven kept tablets of paper and pencils ready at hand for visitors and friends to write down statements, messages, and questions instead of shouting them out. Beethoven would read what they wrote and would usually reply verbally, not in writing, unless he wanted a remark to be confidential, as once in a while he did. But by and large the Conversation Books, as they came to be called, consisted of one-way communications. Beethoven or those around him managed to collect many of these Conversation Books over the years from 1818 to 1827, and even in their one-sided form they provide a vivid reflection of his private life and of the topics of interest to him and his circle. They deal with matters personal and general, from music to politics, from wine prices to publishers' plans, from gossip to serious opinions voiced by the composer and those around him. As an example, in February 1820 Carl Bernard, a journalist who frequented Beethoven's circle, wrote that "The opera by Meyerbeer [*Emma von Leicester*] failed badly—it is a pure imitation of Rossini." A few months later the same Bernard gave Beethoven his opinion that Lord Byron "certainly has the greatest imagination and the deepest feeling of any living poet. *The*

Corsair above all would make a good opera."[1] In 1826 a remarkable exchange—that is, one side of it—is recorded between Beethoven and Karl Holz on "character" in instrumental music:

> That is what I always miss in Mozart's instrumental music.
>
> [———]
>
> Especially the instrumental music.
>
> [———]
>
> A specific character in an instrumental work, that is, one does not find in his works a representation analogous to a state of mind, as one does in yours.
>
> [———]
>
> I always ask myself, when I listen to something, what does it mean?
>
> [———]
>
> Your works have, throughout, a really exclusive character.
>
> [———]
>
> I would explain the difference between Mozart's and your instrumental works in this way: for one of your works a poet could only write one poem; while to a Mozart work he could write three or four analogous ones.[2]

Sometimes Beethoven used the sheets as memoranda or to enter items he found in current newspapers. At other times he jotted down lists of articles he needed to purchase or wrote short memos to himself of things to remember. For example, in 1820, "ask Schlemmer [his long-time music copyist] where he gets his knives sharpened," followed by "inquire what the monthly cost of a room is at Oliva's" and even "what they wear nowadays instead of an undershirt."[3]

The fate of the Conversation Books has become entangled with the posthumous reputation of Beethoven's self-promoting secretary and early biographer, Anton Schindler, who came to possess them after Beethoven's death in March 1827 and then kept them for many years before selling them to the Berlin Royal Library in 1846. In the 1970s the British music critic and scholar Peter Stadlen established that a fair number of entries in the Conversation Books had been forged by Schindler after Beethoven's

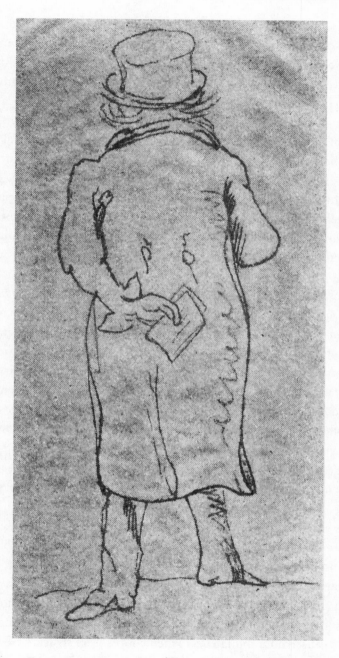

Beethoven walking, seen from the back, in a drawing by Joseph Daniel Böhm.
(Beethoven-Haus, Bonn)

death. The full extent of the Schindler forgeries was later documented by the team of scholars working on a complete edition of the German texts of the Conversation Books. The forged items were then identified and listed retroactively beginning with volume 7 of the ten-volume standard edition of the texts in German.[4]

Though Beethoven's deafness for conversation was becoming worse, he could still improvise, he could try to conduct when an orchestral work of his was being mounted, and he could even follow, in some attenuated sense, the sound of a string quartet—perhaps only when they played a work of his own, though we cannot be sure of this. A remarkable anecdote is reported about his Quartet Opus 127, when, after an unsuccessful first performance led by Schuppanzigh in March 1825 it was tried out again in Beethoven's presence. The new first violinist, Joseph Böhm, later wrote:

> [T]he unhappy man was so deaf that he could no longer hear the heavenly sound of his compositions. And yet rehearsing in his presence was not easy. With close attention his eyes followed the bows and therefore he was able to judge the smallest fluctuations in tempo or rhythm and correct them at once. At the close of the last movement of this quartet there was a meno vivace, which seemed to me to weaken the general effect. At the rehearsal, therefore, I advised that the original tempo be maintained, which was done, to the betterment of the effect. Beethoven, crouched in a corner, heard nothing, but watched with strained attention. After the last bow-stroke he said, laconically, "Let it remain so," went to the desks and crossed out the meno vivace in the four parts.[5]

A recent medical scholar has found evidence that Beethoven's deafness even in the last years was not absolute but fluctuated considerably.[6] Beethoven's use of a resonance plate on the piano along with his ear trumpet when playing and improvising is attested to by Friedrich Wieck, who visited him in 1826. The "resonance plate" was a sound-conduction device that amplified individual sounds when placed on the piano, though it may well have caused a jumbling effect when chords were struck.[7]

A famous public revelation of Beethoven's deafness took place at the first performance of the Ninth Symphony on May 7, 1824, in the Kärntnerthortheater. In the presence of a large audience that included the royal family, Beethoven tried to conduct the symphony, while the musicians quietly agreed not to follow his beat but to follow Ignaz Umlauf, who was standing by where the performers could see him. Either at the end of the Scherzo or at the end of the symphony (we are not sure which), amid tumultuous applause, Beethoven stood poring over his score while the contralto singer Caroline Unger plucked at his sleeve and pointed to the cheering audience—whereupon he turned and bowed to them all.[8]

The further decline in Beethoven's health moved in tandem with his increasing psychological withdrawal and deepening anxiety. His retreat into himself and into the inner world of his music arose partly from the intellectual and emotional demands that he continued to make on himself in order to compose the last piano sonatas, the Ninth Symphony, the *Missa solemnis*, and the last quartets. But it was also an act of self-defense against the outer world, which now pursued him more eagerly than ever as his fame continued to spread and his reclusiveness became a part of the growing Beethoven legend. Visitors sought him out in Vienna or at the spas where he went for refuge, anxious to be among those who saw and talked with the great master while he was still alive. The "pilgrimage to Beethoven," as the young Wagner later called it, became a sought-after experience in Vienna, a highly prized adventure for musicians, for cultivated and knowledgeable people, and for limelight seekers who saw the potential of writing up their visit to Beethoven for one or another cultural journal. Wagner denounced this practice in his 1840 pamphlet, "A Pilgrimage to Beethoven," in which he vilified an imaginary Englishman who wanted the glory of visiting Beethoven although he understood nothing of what was important about Beethoven as an artist.[9] The regular members of Beethoven's circle from 1820 on included at various times Beethoven's brother Johann, his nephew Karl, the ubiquitous Schindler, the violinist Karl Holz (who managed to dislodge Schindler as close confidante), and various writers, musicians, and editors whose names appear in the Conversation Books. Visitors, to mention only those recorded in memoirs, included the composers Ludwig Spohr, Carl Maria von Weber, and Gioacchino Rossini; among those who were not so recorded, perhaps the young Schubert, who had lived and worked in awe of Beethoven for years while living nearby in

Vienna.[10] Visitors from England included Sir George Smart, Sir John Russell, Cipriani Potter, and Richard Ford, and from the literary ranks Ludwig Rellstab and Franz Grillparzer, whose funeral oration for Beethoven defended the composer from the charge of misanthropy that must have been familiar gossip in Vienna.

In 1817 Beethoven wrote to Wilhelm Girard, an amateur poet, that his chronic ailments had been getting worse for the past four years.[11] He fell prey to various illnesses for periods of time: for four months in late 1816–early 1817, again in 1819, and for many weeks in 1821 and 1822.[12] Beginning in 1823 his eyes began to give him trouble, he suffered from colds and rheumatic symptoms, and signs of jaundice, most prominently a yellowing of his skin, began to appear. His letters speak more and more of physical distress and convey an atmosphere of growing infirmity during the time, in 1825 and 1826, when he was working with intense concentration on the last quartets, the summa of his artistic life.

In the three years prior to his death in March 1827 the intervals between illnesses became shorter. As Edward Larkin put it in his balanced account of Beethoven's medical history, "during 1825 he suddenly looked much older and his complexion became permanently sallow."[13] In December 1826 he began to suffer from severe symptoms of liver disease and intestinal bleeding. The physicians could find no remedies, and he died on March 26, 1827, after a final illness of four months.

Beethoven's increasing waywardness became grotesque in these years. Sometime in the early 1820s, out for a long walk, he followed a canal towpath and eventually, without knowing where he was going and with nothing to eat, made his way to a canal basin at Ungerthor. Confused and tired, he began to look in through the windows of some of the houses, and as he was dressed so shabbily some alarmed residents called in the local police. The more he complained that he was Beethoven the less they believed him: "You're a tramp; Beethoven doesn't look like this," said a policeman, and locked him up. Finally they called in the music director of the nearby town of Wiener Neustadt, a certain Herzog, who identified him, whereupon in pity and chagrin they gave him some decent clothes and sent him home.[14] Similarly, when Beethoven went to visit his nephew Karl in the hospital in

1826, he was mistaken for an "old peasant" in his seedy clothing and decrepit appearance.[15]

The Guardianship Struggle

His obsessiveness also rose to higher levels. By far the most painful and tormenting was his long-range campaign to take on the legal guardianship of his nephew Karl, the only child of his brother Caspar Carl, who died of tuberculosis in November 1815. Carl's will first appointed Ludwig van Beethoven as sole guardian of Karl, then nine years old, but a codicil written on the same day as the will canceled the exclusivity of this provision and made the boy's mother, Johanna Reiss van Beethoven, co-guardian. The codicil bluntly states that "the best of harmony does not exist between my brother and my wife."[16] That was putting it mildly, for now began a tortured emotional and legal struggle between Beethoven and his sister-in-law for the custody of the boy that lasted for more than four years and entailed perpetual rancor, court appearances, seeming successes, reversals, and appeals. He had taken on the role of family head and virtual father to his two brothers when his mother died in 1787, and he continued to play it through the years, sometimes in fantasy, sometimes in reality, often in overbearing and presumptuous terms. The family role now emerged again in his fierce determination to become a quasi-father to his nephew, if necessary demolishing the rights and reputation of the boy's mother as being unfit to be his guardian. As it happened, Johanna Reiss, whom Beethoven liked to call the "Queen of the Night," lived a life that made character assassination fairly easy, as she had been accused of theft from her parents in 1804 and had been convicted of embezzlement of jewelry in 1811.[17] Moreover, after Caspar Carl's death she took a lover and gave birth to an illegitimate daughter in 1820.

After finally gaining full guardianship of Karl in 1820, Beethoven continued to struggle for the remaining six years of his life to oversee and manage the boy's education and development. At the same time, since he was deeply immersed in his work and had to cope with publishers, his physical

generativity

Beethoven's nephew Karl, shown as a cadet in a military regiment. (Historisches Museum, Vienna)

and emotional debilitation, and his deafness, he could hardly provide an atmosphere in which the boy could thrive. As the day-to-day difficulties increased over these years, Karl's life with his uncle became increasingly intolerable. His education continued in private schools until 1823, when, aged seventeen, he went on to the university to attend lectures in philology, having apparently found ways to adjust somehow to the domestic upheavals of the previous eight years. Witnessing and taking part in the scene around Beethoven, often acting as messenger, lad-of-all-work, or music copyist, Karl, whom Beethoven called his "adopted son,"[18] still had to deal with Beethoven's unbearable demands and recriminations. Beethoven blamed Karl if he failed to provide his "adopted father" with sufficient love and attention or if Karl pursued women, gambled, or saw certain male friends whom Beethoven regarded as bad company—not to mention Karl's "disloyalty" when he paid clandestine visits to his mother.

what stage stuck?

By the summer of 1826 these conflicts reached a climax. Karl showed clear preliminary signs of potential suicide—such as leaving home with hints that he intended to take his life, and keeping a loaded pistol among his personal belongings—signs that Beethoven and those around him apparently saw but could not or did not take steps to prevent.[19] Karl then pawned his watch, bought two pistols, and in frantic desperation went to the Helenenthal, one of Beethoven's favorite places for walking in the country, to try to kill himself. The attempt failed: the bullets grazed his skull but did not deeply wound him, and he recovered in a Vienna hospital. But the psychic wounds went deep. Nothing is more telling than that the first passersby to find him took him, at his request, not to Beethoven's house but to his mother's.[20] Now Beethoven let himself be persuaded to give up the guardianship. Karl sought a way out by enlisting in the army, and, although Beethoven insisted that the youth would do better to first enroll in a military academy, he finally consented to let Karl become a cadet in a well-regarded regiment under the leadership of Lieutenant Field Marshal Baron von Stutterheim, a lifelong military officer.[21] The enlistment led to the dedication to von Stutterheim of Beethoven's C-sharp Minor Quartet, Opus 131.[22] We gain a very partial glimpse of what Karl's suicide attempt meant to Beethoven from a letter to his close associate, Karl Holz, written a month later.

> I am exhausted, and joy will be over for me for a long time to come. My terrible current and future expenses are bound to worry me and all my hopes have vanished, my hopes of having near me someone who would resemble me, at least in my better qualities![23]

"Someone who would resemble me, at least in my better qualities"—the phrase unwittingly sums up Beethoven's anguished loss of judgment and perspective in dealing with his nephew, whom he could never imagine as an independent boy trying to grope his way toward manhood in the wake of severe deprivations. Karl, after all, had lost his father, was then immediately cut off from his mother's nurturing through the willful actions of his uncle; and was further deprived of a warm environment and the personal freedom in which to find his way to maturity—all of this through the manipulative, overpowering, and suffocating embrace of that same uncle who longed to shape Karl in the image of an ideal male family member that neither Ludwig nor either of his brothers had ever been able to realize. Old Johann van Beethoven had been an absent father to his three sons; Ludwig, adopting his nephew as his son, could do no better. That this erratic uncle Ludwig also happened to be one of the greatest and most famous of living artists and thus a perpetual but unreachable model for an insecure young man only made matters worse. As it turned out later, Karl managed to become reconciled with his uncle during the latter's last illness, and when Beethoven wrote a will in early January 1827, Karl became the sole beneficiary of his estate.[24] Karl remained in military service until 1832, then obtained a job in an Austrian government office and lived quietly until his death in 1858.[25]

"The human brain . . . is not a salable commodity"

If we move from Beethoven's deeply troubled personal life to the circumstances of his career during these years, the picture is not less complicated but is certainly less depressing. In these last ten years his dealings with publishers became ever more arcane and complex. In the early years he had been making his way as virtuoso pianist and path-breaking composer, writing for the immediate public and publishing many of his works with local publishers in Vienna—Artaria, Hoffmeister, Mollo, Cappi, Traeg, and the so-called Bureau des Arts et d'Industrie. During his middle years the net widened to include publishers outside Vienna, above all Breitkopf & Härtel in Leipzig.

In the last period, his works were becoming much more difficult of immediate acceptance by even the knowledgeable public. But it was also the time in which Beethoven had become a celebrity whose fame reached abroad not only to all of Europe but also to America. Now a new group of publishers appeared, anxious to be the first to print his latest works and hoping to capitalize on his name. An early representative of the new breed was Clementi, the famous pianist and composer who was also active as a music publisher in England; he not only agreed to take on some finished works but commissioned some new ones—the Piano Sonatas Opp. 78 and

79. Less successful but interested British publishers were Birchall, which published the "Kreutzer" and Opus 96 Sonatas and the "Archduke" Trio; (Opp. 47, 96, 97), Chappell (the "Kakadu" Variations), and the curiously named "Regent's Harmonic Institution," whose address in London was "Lower Saloon, Argyll Rooms." This last publisher, at the prodding of Ferdinand Ries, brought out the British first edition of the *Hammerklavier* Sonata, Opus 106, in a curious two-part format. Part 1 comprises the first three movements, but with the second and third reversed; Part 2 consists of the finale, labeled "Introduction and Fugue," as if it were a separate composition. Beethoven's acquiescence in this strange edition gives us a partial glimpse of his legitimate uncertainty as to how the public might react to this long and unfathomably difficult sonata.

Other new firms that took hold in these later years included, most prominently, the local Viennese shop of Sigmund Anton Steiner, who came on the scene in 1813 and improved his chances by lending Beethoven money to support his sick brother, then in 1815–16 published a raft of important works. Still later Beethoven opened up connections with Adolph Martin Schlesinger, who had founded an important publishing house in Berlin in 1810 and was the major publisher of Berlin composers including Weber. Beethoven also had extensive dealings with Adolph's son, Maurice Schlesinger, who set up shop in Paris in 1821. The two Schlesingers, whom Beethoven occasionally castigated to others, in letters containing anti-Semitic remarks all too typical of the German and Austrian mentality of his time, brought out the last three piano sonatas and two of the late quartets, Opp. 132 and 135.[26] Opus 131 was published by B. Schott's Söhne at Mainz, who had also brought out the *Missa solemnis* (the publication history of which could fill a separate chapter), the Ninth Symphony, and other late works. Nearby in Vienna, Matthias Artaria, a son of Domenico Artaria, published the Quartets Opus 130 and the Grand Fugue, Opus 133, as well as the four-hand arrangement of the Fugue issued as Opus 134.

The facts and issues regarding the maze of Beethoven's later dealings with publishers can be summarized in a few words.[27] So much of Beethoven's correspondence is with publishers and about publications of his music because his career ambitions, financial worries, and obsessive mentality gave him no alternative. Rejecting or failing to obtain any permanent court position, and having as his only source of steady income the annuity bestowed on him by Kinsky, Lobkowitz, and Archduke Rudolph, Beethoven really needed to sell his works for his livelihood. Supporting himself was not easy, even if he was not badly off, but when he took on the guardianship of nephew Karl in 1816 his costs rose accordingly.

Beethoven had been very successful with publishers in his most productive early years, when he claimed that "six or seven publishers or even more" were clamoring for his works. He tried incessantly to negotiate a high fee for each work, often announcing that works were ready before they really were, in order to promote a publication contract and collect his money in hard cash. To keep up the flow of publications he wrote a fair number of accessible minor works even in his later years, or fixed up some unpublished minor early works and brought them out—all of which made it easier for publishers to do business with him and accept the increasingly difficult, at times incomprehensible major works of the last years. Plenty of later editions of his early works also remained on the market for years along with his new ones, not to mention endless arrangements for piano solo, for piano, four hands, and for small chamber ensembles, designed for the music rooms and salons of the bourgeoisie in the oncoming Biedermeier age.[28]

Since at least some chance existed of controlling the rights to a composition in other countries, Beethoven realized that he would increase his profits if he could somehow sell the rights to a given work to several publishers, each in a different country, supposedly with the understanding that they would all issue the work on the same date. On a sketch leaf in 1816 he wrote himself a memo to this effect:

> For all works, as now with the cello sonata, you must reserve for yourself the right to fix for the publisher the day of publication, without the publishers in London and Germany knowing about each other, so to speak, because otherwise they will give less, and in any case it is unnecessary that they should know. You can give the excuse that someone else has ordered this composition from you.[29]

Needless to say, this scheme could not be brought about in many cases, but it did more or less work out that way for several compositions that came out at about the same time in Vienna or Leipzig and in London. The

Napoleonic blockade of Continental commerce severely hindered such a plan for many years, but after 1815 it seemed more nearly possible than before. Thus the *Hammerklavier* Sonata, Opus 106, was issued by Artaria in September 1819 with a title page in French that also listed twelve other publishers in cities across the Continent, including Leipzig, Berlin, Bonn, Offenbach, Augsburg, Mainz (two different publishers), Zurich, Munich, Hamburg, Milan, "and the other art and book dealers of Germany, France, England, Switzerland, Russia, and Poland." At the same time Artaria issued the same work with a German title page that mentioned no other publisher, obviously intending to maintain the Austrian market for themselves.

Throughout these tortuous dealings, Beethoven and some of the more ambitious publishers thought about the idea of an authorized collected edition of his works, especially those for keyboard. The idea first surfaced as early as 1803 in correspondence with Breitkopf & Härtel (publishers of attempted "complete works" editions of Mozart and Haydn). The idea was indeed appealing to both composer and publisher, for many good reasons, but it inevitably ran aground because so many different publishers had the original publishing rights to so many of his works. One company, Zulehner in Mainz, even put out a pirated "collected edition" of his works for piano and strings, and all Beethoven could do was to register a public objection in a Vienna newspaper; he could neither prevent the edition nor stop it after it appeared.[30]

As for Beethoven's feelings about the world of music publishing, his dependence on it, and his maddening lack of control over the versions of his works that were flooding the music shops and bookstores, he put it all in a nutshell in an unpublished "Draft Statement about a Complete Edition of His Works" that he wrote in 1822 and left among his private papers. Though his actual dealings with publishers show him as a canny and wary practitioner, skilled in the unsavory practices that burnished his career but that trouble his biographers, this private document reveals the anger that he had to hide when doing actual business:

> *The law-books begin without much ado with a discussion of human rights, which nevertheless the executors trample underfoot; thus the author begins his statement: An author has the right to arrange for a*

revised edition of his works. But since there are so many greedy
brain-pickers and lovers of that noble dish, since all kinds of preserves,
ragouts, and fricassees are made from it which go to fill the pockets of
the pastry-cooks, and since the author would be glad to have as many
groschen as are sometimes paid out for his work, the author is deter-
mined to show that the human brain [Beethoven's underlining] cannot
be sold either like coffee beans or like any form of cheese, which, as
everyone knows, must first be produced from milk, urine, and so
forth—
  The human brain in itself is not a salable commodity—.[31]

The last ten words could have changed the world if only the conditions of
life had been ideal. They still could in our time, if the commercialization of
art were not a thousand times greater than in Beethoven's era. But since, for
him and for other artists through the ages, conditions have never been
ideal, this noble statement remains a utopian article of faith. In his dealings
with publishers, as in so many other aspects of his practical life, Beethoven
felt himself completely unable to reach the higher plateau of ideal behavior, the "virtue" to which he aspired. In the same vein is another draft statement, written as early as 1807, to the directors of the Imperial Theater in
Vienna, when he toyed with the idea of contracting to write an opera and
an operetta "every year"—which, of course, did not happen. He writes:

[The undersigned] has not been fortunate enough to establish himself
here in a position compatible with his desire to live entirely for art, to
develop his talents to an even higher degree of perfection, which must
be the aim of every true artist. . . . [T]he aim that he has ever pursued
in his career has been much less to earn his daily bread than to raise the
taste of the public and to let his genius soar to greater heights. . . .
[T]he inevitable result has been that the undersigned has sacrificed to
the Muse both material profit and his own advantage.[32]

The Final Projects

T he personal complications of these years, from 1818 to 1827, contributed to slowing Beethoven's creative work, but his drastically changing artistic outlook contributed even more. In the so-called fallow period, from about 1812 to 1817, he was working alternately on truly important and path-breaking works and on potboilers. The handful of major works from this time were sketched in phases between the spring of 1814, when the new version of *Fidelio* was staged, and the spring of 1816, when he completed the song cycle *An die ferne Geliebte.*

Throughout 1817 Beethoven produced only a fugue for string quintet and a few songs, besides continuing his work on arrangements of Scottish songs for Thomson. But in the fall of 1817 a new grand project began to take hold. This was to be a new piano sonata in B-flat major, on the largest scale, apparently begun with the archduke in mind as recipient. Since the first two movements were ready in fair copy by April 1818 and presented to the royal pupil, who also received the eventual dedication, the work could just as easily have come to be known as the "Archduke" Sonata, like the "Archduke" Trio Opus 97, rather than as the *Hammerklavier.* The whole work was finally completed in the fall of 1818, and now began another phase of Beethoven's career, in which he labored primarily on single works, one at a time with some overlapping, sometimes having to shift course but fundamentally aiming to create individual compositions of transcendental character, working with undiminished concentration all the way to the end of his composing career.

The late works of gigantic scope and great technical difficulty begin with the *Hammerklavier* Sonata. They continue with the "Diabelli" Variations, which were begun in 1819, put aside for work on the *Missa solemnis,* then finished in 1821–23. The *Missa solemnis* was also started in 1819 for intended completion in March of 1820, when the archduke was to be installed as bishop of Olmütz in Moravia, but Beethoven could not finish it until 1823. In 1822 he began work on the Ninth Symphony, his central preoccupation until its first performance in May 1824. Sandwiched in and around these works of enormous size were the last three piano sonatas, Opp. 109, 110, and 111—which had been commissioned by Adolph Martin Schlesinger in Berlin. Along with the overture *The Consecration of the House,* they occupied Beethoven between 1820 and late in 1822, when he returned to work on the Mass.

Beethoven's last phase was marked by his return to the string quartet, a genre about which he had said many years earlier that he wished to devote himself "exclusively" to it. Of course, he had never been able to concentrate on one genre, but now he did so. As early as May 1822 the Leipzig publisher Carl Friedrich Peters asked Beethoven for, among other things, "piano quartets and piano trios," to which Beethoven promptly replied, offering Peters some older compositions, along with a price for each, that were "all ready."[33] Some of these were old Bonn works he had never published, a few others he may have thought he could supply with a little work. Ten days later he informed Peters that "the quartet is not fully finished, because I have had other things to do." In reality the quartet, which was to be Opus 127, was only in the earliest planning stage. Peters lost headway with Beethoven when, in July 1822, he refused to meet Beethoven's price for a new quartet and tactlessly added that at present he didn't need new quartets since he had in production new ones by Spohr, Romberg, and Rode, "all of which are excellent, beautiful works." That ended the negotiation with Peters.

But on November 9, 1822, Prince Nicolas Galitzin, an amateur cellist and chamber music lover, wrote from St. Petersburg to ask Beethoven for "one, two, or three new quartets," offering to pay "what you judge appropriate" and asking for the dedication.[34] Even amidst his current grand projects, Beethoven accepted the commission. The first new quartet, in E-flat major, later Opus 127, was another momentous turning point: it is the portal to his late quartet style. After various false starts and consideration of possibilities for its material, the heavy work of composing the quartet began in earnest in 1823, but the sketches lay in gestation while he finished the Ninth and saw it performed in May 1824. It was February 1825 before the quartet was ready for a tryout. By this time Beethoven was also planning the two later quartets that would complete the Galitzin commission—namely an A-minor quartet (later Opus 132) that he promised the cellist Linke would be a "concertante for the cello," and a quartet in B-flat major, with "heavy-going introduction" and with "a fugue at the end," as he noted in a sketch.[35] It is the first hint of what would become Opus 130 in its original form. As it turned out, Opus 132 needed a full six months for its completion, from February to July 1825, and the whole of the second half of 1825 was given over to work on Opus 130 with its gigantic fugal finale. From this point on, the pattern of 1825 became the norm for each massive new quartet: Opus 131 followed as the basic focus of the six months from January to June 1826, followed by four months of concentration on completing Opus 135.

All this musical activity was taking place amid the growing crisis with nephew Karl, whose suicide attempt in early August 1826 occurred while Beethoven was immersed in Opus 135. Although we cannot date his sketches with absolute precision, Beethoven apparently found ways to protect his inner working life from even the most catastrophic problems and crises, except perhaps for short periods when he had no choice. During the fall of 1826, while staying in Gneixendorf, he put the finishing touches on Opus 131 and sent it to Schott for publication, then worked on Opus 135 and on an improved four-hand version of the final movement of Opus 130, the *Grand Fugue*, which would be published separately as Opus 133. Even then, suffering more than ever from his physical and psychological infirmities and thinking nostalgically of his youth (as he acknowledges in his December 7 letter to Wegeler), he spent the autumn months writing the last complete movement that he was to compose—namely the genial "little" or "second" finale for Opus 130, to replace the *Grand Fugue*. He began a string quintet in C major but it failed to get beyond an opening of the first movement and a few jottings for the other movements. Diabelli seized the first movement and published it in 1838 as "Beethoven's Last Musical Thought," a misstep that unfortunately precipitated a long series of attempts to finish works that Beethoven left incomplete and offer them to an eager musical world.

CHAPTER 18

BRINGING THE PAST INTO THE PRESENT

❧❧❧❦❄❦❧❧❧

The Third Maturity

In the years 1818–27 Beethoven was seeking ways of shaping larger works that would supplant the dynamic, goal-directed, wide-ranging principles of his middle-period sonata-form structures and create a new balance between the structural dimensions of harmony and counterpoint. He was looking for models that would enable him to get beyond what he had already built during his years of allegiance to Haydn and, above all, to Mozart. Even at this late stage he continued to think of his predecessors with reverence, as when he copied excerpts from the Mozart Requiem while working on the *Missa solemnis*, showing a capacity to seek appropriate compositional models that goes hand in hand with his self-critical instincts.[1] Whatever connections we may find between his early, middle, and late works in their purely musical features, we see that in broadening his reach to draw in those older predecessors who became the primary style models in his last period, he opened up new perspectives on his own development. In finding his way to Handel and especially to Bach, he was reaching back to the more distant past that lay beyond the late-eighteenth-century classicism in which he had been nurtured, but he was also returning to the contrapuntal art forms that he first knew when, at age eleven, he played and studied *The Well-Tempered Clavier*.

In these years, searching for new stimuli, he became curious about older music. His interests included music of the late Renaissance and early Baroque, which offered possibilities of experimentation with modal harmony that could augment and extend the range of his harmonic practice.[2]

Thus among the early thoughts for what became the Ninth Symphony we find the idea of a "pious song in a symphony in the old modes," and in the slow movement of the Quartet Opus 132 he realized the idea of a "Holy Song of Thanksgiving by a Convalescent, in the Lydian Mode."[3] The Conversation Books show his interest in delving into sixteenth-century treatises on the modes. Thus in December 1819 Joseph Czerny told Beethoven that "we have some old Italians," referring him to Gioseffo Zarlino, the greatest theorist of the sixteenth century. A month later another confidante, Carl Peters, told Beethoven that Heinrich Glarean's *Dodekachordon* of 1547—the treatise that officially sanctioned a twelve-mode system in place of the traditional medieval eight-mode system—could be found in the Imperial Library.[4] Beethoven found a number of works by Renaissance composers in contemporary anthologies of music of the past, and at various times he copied out pieces by Palestrina and Byrd as well as contrapuntal works by such Baroque composers as Georg Muffat and Antonio Caldara, plus instrumental works by his heroes of the past, Bach and Handel.[5]

In his first maturity he had vigorously progressed from youthful imitations of Mozart to a command of contemporary tonal language and to the realization of his own unmistakable voice within that language—all this between about 1785 and 1800. In his second maturity he had built great structures on these earlier foundations and, going beyond his post-Mozartian and post-Haydnian works of the 1790s, had moved on to broader terrain in which he put the forms of instrumental music on a new footing. Now, from 1814 on, with the *Fidelio* revision behind him and the first instrumental works of this new phase germinating, he was working to conceal or minimize the straightforward dynamic and processive features that had dominated his second period and was replacing them with musical strategies built on different ways of balancing form and content.

One of these strategies was anchored in his recourse to the lyrical. Because of the stress on motivic development in so many of his works, history has never given Beethoven his due as a purely melodic composer, but this view needs drastic revision. Melodic invention and melodic integrity, which run through his work like a spinal column, remain essential right to the end and, if anything, grow in significance. Not only do we see this happening in later years in the Ninth Symphony, the *Missa solemnis,* the late piano sonatas, and the late quartets, but he himself made the point explicit in a revealing letter to Prince Galitzin of July 1825. In answer to a question that a performer had raised about a particular viola note in the slow movement of Opus 127, Beethoven offered a lesson in his harmonic and contrapuntal methods and even a short aesthetic primer. He explained why the note had to be D♭ not C, basing his explanation on harmonic principles but insisting that the right answer to such a question could be found only in the primacy of melody: "but far beyond these [reasons for preferring D♭ to C], because of the melody, which must always be given priority above all else."[6] Elsewhere in the letter, and in a draft of it that he wrote in a sketchbook, we find the same insistence on the linear dimension. He even subscribes to the dismissive Romantic view of the "rules" when he writes, in the draft, "when the feelings open up a path to us, then away with all rules!"[7]

Alongside the dominating role of melody run other essential conditions that form the basis for the late style, as we experience it in the late piano sonatas and quartets. These include a heightened sense of musical space and time; innovative movement plans for entire works and for individual movements; radical experimentation with form and proportions, ranging to extremes of length (as in the *Hammerklavier,* the Ninth Symphony, and the *Grand Fugue*) and of brevity (as in the Bagatelles and some of the shorter movements in the last quartets); the concealment or transformation of traditional formal schemes; compression aimed at reducing repetition, redundancy, and simple parallelisms; motivic saturation, by which thematic significance is allocated to all voices in the complex (witness the cavatina of Opus 130); the use of titles and mottos to indicate the poetic and transcendental qualities for which he is striving in instrumental music; and finally, a "new kind of voice-leading," as he described it to Holz in reference to the final quartets. This last, most readily visible in the contrapuntal textures of the last works, refers on the one hand to the linearization of all voices, as in the late quartets, on the other to his expanded use of fugue and fugato beyond all previous limits. This orientation explains why in these years he turns so strongly toward Bach as a model. He judged that rigorous tonal counterpoint offered the best means of integrating all these factors in a new way, and it also strengthened his direct relationship to Bach as the greatest of contrapuntal masters. After Opus 90 a new emphasis on the contrapuntal comes sharply to the fore, embodied most clearly in Beethoven's intensive use of fugue and fugato not only for important episodes in sonata-form movements but as the dominating principle of entire movements.

In many later movements fugue and variation supplant sonata form as the primary formal means of organization. Even within sonata-form movements, mostly first movements, transformations abound, in some cases altering the defining features of traditional sonata-form procedures almost beyond recognition. The shift from late-eighteenth-century models is immediately clear in his virtual abandonment of the rondo and even the sonata-rondo for finales and occasional slow movements. After the cantabile sonata-rondo finale of Opus 90, the only other late finale that even approaches this form is the finale of the A Minor Quartet, Opus 132. But how utterly distant in character this finale is from the few earlier minor-mode sonata rondos in Beethoven, such as the finale of the E-Minor Quartet, Opus 59 No. 2, or the finale of the F Minor Quartet, Opus 95![8] And many other transformations emerge within the formal schemes of his first movements, slow movements, scherzi, and finales, not simply because of a search for innovations in formal thinking but because of the pressures on the form created by Beethoven's newly complex ways of framing and developing thematic material.

From 1815 on we find prominent use of fugue and fugato in many instrumental works, in more than a few cases as the basis for entire movements, especially finales (included here are only large-scale, finished works):

1815. Cello Sonata in D major, Opus 102 No. 2: Finale: Allegro fugato

1816. Piano Sonata in A major, Opus 101: Finale (development section)

1817. Fugue in D major for String Quintet, Opus 137

1818–19. Piano Sonata in B-flat, Opus 106, *Hammerklavier:* First movement (development section); Finale: "Fuga a tre voci, con alcune licenze"

1819–23. "Diabelli" Variations: Variations 4 (canonic), 24, and 32

1819–23. *Missa solemnis:* Gloria and Credo

1821. Piano Sonata in A-Flat, Opus 110: Finale: "Fuga. Allegro ma non troppo"

1821. Piano Sonata in C minor, Opus 111: First movement (development section)

1822. *The Consecration of the House* Overture

1821–24. Symphony No. 9: First movement (development section); Scherzo (beginning); Finale (B-flat-major section; culminating double fugue)

1825. Quartet in A minor, Opus 132: Slow movement (third primary section)

1825. *Grosse Fuge,* "tantôt libre, tantôt recherchée," in B-flat major, Opus 133 (originally the finale to Opus 130)

1826. Quartet in C-sharp Minor, Opus 131: first movement

This list omits a number of fugato episodes that appear in such lesser works as the Variations for Flute and Piano, Opus 107. It also omits a quintet fugue fragment of 1817; an idea for an "Overture on 'BACH' [that is, the notes B♭–A–C–B♮] very fugal" that Beethoven projected in 1821–25 but never finished; and Bach fugues, especially from The *Well-Tempered Clavier,* that he copied out.

Beethoven's Knowledge of Bach and Handel

The *Well-Tempered Clavier* had been a musical Bible for Beethoven since the Bonn years. He already possessed either one or both books in the 1780s, gaining access to the collection first from a manuscript copy. (The forty-eight preludes and fugues were not published until 1801, when they were issued by three different publishers—in his home town of Bonn as well as Leipzig and Zurich).[9]

His reverence for Bach was deep from early on. In 1800 he inquired about plans that were brewing for an edition of Bach's complete works—such as could then be known—and in later years, as the scope of Bach's output became gradually more visible, Beethoven tried to obtain what he could. In letters of 1810 and 1824 he asked publishers to send him

An engraved portrait of Johann Sebastian Bach, published in 1798 as the frontispiece for the first issue of the Allgemeine Musikalische Zeitung *("General Musical Journal") as a mark of its allegiance to Bach and the German tradition he was believed to represent.*

copies of the B-minor Mass.[10] Whether or not he received any of it, he could have seen quite a few Bach instrumental and vocal works, to judge from the many that were becoming available through prints and copies during Beethoven's lifetime. He owned a volume of Bach's inventions and preludes that eventually went to Count Moritz Lichnowsky along with six volumes of works by Handel that he apparently received shortly before his death.[11] Manuscripts in his possession in 1827 included, besides a pile of his own works and sketchbooks, Bach's *Art of Fugue* in both manuscript and in a printed edition, printed copies of Handel's keyboard suites, a set of selected works by Handel, and copies of Handel's *Julius Caesar* and *Alexander's Feast*.[12] He also had access to other works by Bach that were in the archduke's music library, which we know Beethoven used, and he could easily have found music by Bach and Handel in other Viennese private col-

George Frideric Handel, in an oil painting of about 1748 by Philippe Mercier. (Archiv für Kunst und Geschichte, Berlin)

lections, including those of van Swieten and Kiesewetter, with both of whom Beethoven had contact in his earlier Viennese years.[13]

Although the myth persists that Mendelssohn "rediscovered" Bach when he performed the *St. Matthew Passion* in 1829, in fact Bach's instrumental music and some of his vocal music had gradually become more and more available in prints and copies from the 1790s on. Influential as well in bringing the legend of Bach into the current marketplace of ideas were the music periodicals. Indeed, the first issue of the Leipzig *Allgemeine Musikalische Zeitung*, in 1798, bore a portrait of Bach facing its title page. Forkel's Bach biography, a very authoritative work, appeared in 1802. Between 1800 and 1809 many Bach works were issued by publishers in Leipzig, Berlin, and Zurich, including at least three competing editions of *The Well-Tempered Clavier*, several volumes of Bach's motets, and other instrumental works including *The Art of Fugue* and the "Goldberg" Variations. From 1811, publications included Bach's *Chromatic Fantasy and Fugue;* and in 1818 the B-minor Mass became available.

Beethoven was well aware that by 1800 Bach had become the musical deity of a well-informed, elite sect of worshipers. These included van Swieten (who headed a Viennese society for the promotion of ancient music) and teachers such as Albrechtsberger and others, in Vienna, Berlin, and elsewhere, who disdained most current trends toward lighter forms and styles in favor of more serious attempts to restore contrapuntal thinking into compositional styles.

Beethoven's interest in Bach, which increased greatly around 1814, coincided with a growing contemporary awareness of Bach as more than a legendary organist, master of tonal counterpoint and harmony, and composer of difficult keyboard works. More musicians were coming to understand that Bach's greatness lay not only in the formal and contrapuntal logic of his writing but in its blending of logic and expressivity. When Beethoven in 1801 referred to Bach as "the immortal god of harmony," he could base his reverence on knowledge mainly of keyboard works.[14] By the time he came to know the B-minor Mass and other works in later years he was ready to challenge Bach on Bach's own compositional ground, that of linear counterpoint. He felt impelled to master fugal writing in a way that respected and tried to match Bach's mastery but also entailed the effort to give his own fugal movements what he called a "poetic" dimension, making them part and parcel of his new sense of himself not merely as composer but as "tone poet" (*Tondichter*).[15] He conceived his later fugal movements and works not primarily as demonstrations of technique (though they succeeded in that as well) but as part of his attempt in these years to use time-honored contrapuntal fugal forms and textures to write "progressive" works and serve the cause of artistic freedom—little as the general public around 1820, lost in a craze for Rossini, could understand this.

There is a parallel in attitudes between Beethoven's late turn toward older, time-honored contrapuntal techniques and Verdi's famous dictum, uttered in his old age, "Let us go back to old times, and that will be progress."[16] A partial parallel also exists between Beethoven's assimilation of Bach in his later years and Mozart's. Like Mozart, Beethoven had been exposed to Bach in his youth; accordingly, his move toward Bach in the last decade was like a homecoming, a return rather than a discovery.[17] He also profited from having first come to grips with the Mozart-Haydn inheritance and progressed through two major phases of his own development before making his pilgrimage to Bach. Beethoven was thereby able to take part in the tendency around 1820 to couple the recovery of Bach with the glorification of Mozart, which was now also reaching its height. This viewpoint is made clear by various observers, including the Abbé Stadler, whose *Materials for a History of Music*, compiled between 1815 and 1829, treats Bach as a central figure.[18] Stadler praises Bach as a major influence, and connects his position with, surprisingly, that of late Mozart:

> *Particularly through his works written in his last ten years in Vienna, Mozart rose to such heights that not only in Vienna but in all Germany, in all of Europe, he was recognized as the greatest of masters, who united in his style the artistry of Sebastian Bach, the strength of Handel, the charming clarity and humor of Haydn.[19]*

The idea of Mozart as the mediator of the great figures of earlier times, including Bach, fits well with Beethoven's tendency to see himself as seeking "freedom and progress" in his own late work by deepening the channels that connected him to Bach and Handel yet without losing sight of his debt to Haydn and Mozart and his own impulse toward innovation. In a letter of 1819 Beethoven tells Archduke Rudolph, in his didactic manner, that he had made use of the archduke's library to look at music by older masters, "among whom only Bach and Handel had real genius," and then goes on at once to say:

> *But in the world of art, as in the whole of creation, freedom and progress are the main objectives. And although we moderns are not quite as far advanced in solidity as our ancestors, yet the refinement of our customs has enlarged many of our conceptions as well. My eminent music pupil, who himself is now competing for the laurels of fame, must not bear the reproach of being one-sided—et iterum venturus [est] judicare vivos—et mortuos ["And He shall come again to judge the living—and the dead"].[20]*

Beethoven had come to know some of Handel's choral works at van Swieten's musicales in the 1790s, where, as Mozart had put it a decade earlier, "nothing is played but Handel and Bach," especially choruses from some of the famous oratorios.[21] It was for van Swieten that Mozart had furnished new orchestrations of Handel's *Messiah* and *Alexander's Feast*, and it was van Swieten who provided Haydn with the original text for *The Creation* and inspired *The Seasons*. Van Swieten may even have persuaded Haydn to include certain "realistic" details in *The Seasons*, among them the croaking of frogs.[22] Nor could Beethoven in the 1790s, seeing Haydn's vast success in London and Vienna as symphonic and oratorio composer, have failed to realize that Handel in his oratorios had provided for Haydn's generation and now for his own the model of a powerful and original mind reaching out through religious music to audiences at large without simplifying his style, thus elevating and dignifying public musical discourse in ways that must have deeply appealed to Beethoven. He also knew that Haydn, in both *The Creation* and *The Seasons*, had matched the strength of the Handelian oratorio tradition. Beethoven copied excerpts from *Messiah* in 1808 while working on the Fifth Symphony and again around 1819 or 1820, when he was beginning work on the *Missa solemnis*.[23] At other times he copied the fugal overture to *Solomon* and contemplated a set of variations on the Dead March from Handel's *Saul*, "perhaps with voices joining in later." This notion was probably stimulated by a newspaper announcement in March 1820 that reported the performance of the Dead March and a Handel cantata at the funeral of King George III of England, duly noted at the time in Beethoven's Conversation Books.[24]

Beethoven liked to tell British visitors how much better their parliamentary system was than the stultifying monarchy that had remained in power in Austria after the fall of Napoleon, and he even dreamed of going to Britain and visiting the House of Commons. In 1817 he told Cipriani Potter, a capable English musician, that among living composers he respected Cherubini (thus pointedly omitting Weber, Rossini, and Spontini, among others), and, among dead composers, "Mozart and Handel."[25] Schindler reports a walk with Beethoven and nephew Karl in 1822 in the "lovely" Helenenthal near Baden: "Beethoven told us to go on in advance and meet him at an appointed place. Not long afterward he overtook us, saying that he had written down two motives for an overture. . . . [H]e also talked about the way in which he proposed treating them—one in the free style, one in the strict, indeed, in Handel's. . . . [H]e had long wanted to write an overture in the Handelian style."[26] And to the Englishman Edward Schulz in 1823 he commented that "Handel is the greatest composer that ever lived." Schulz continues, "I cannot describe to you with what pathos, and I am inclined to say, with what sublimity of language, he spoke of the *Messiah* of this immortal genius. . . . [Beethoven said] 'I would uncover myself and kneel down at his tomb.'"[27] Without doubting Beethoven's sincerity, we cannot help noticing that he particularly tended to praise Handel to the skies to British visitors, while expressing a desire to visit Britain. No doubt he harbored the idea in the back of his mind of a magnificent public reception by the British public and aristocracy, such as Haydn had received, and possibly a permanent position with ample salary. Among the late works, apart from passages in the *Missa solemnis* and the Ninth Symphony, the closest approach to the "Handelian manner" is the overture *The Consecration of the House* of 1822, marked by a strongly sequential double fugue in C major on subjects that unmistakably echo Handel in their directness and energy.

CHAPTER 19
LATE PIANO MUSIC

❧⟨⟨✦⟩⟩❧

The Hammerklavier *Sonata, Opus 106*

Nicknames stick. By now it is too late to call this work anything but *the* "Hammerklavier Sonata" although the term could just as well have been attached to its immediate predecessor, Opus 101, which had the same words on its autograph and on the title page of its first edition. Beethoven also used the word *Hammerklavier*—the German term for the Italian pianoforte—on the autograph of the next sonata, Opus 109. And all this arose from Beethoven's decision in 1817, in a burst of patriotic enthusiasm, to insist that "henceforth all our works on which the title is in German shall, instead of 'pianoforte,' carry the name 'Hammerklavier.'"[1]

Perversely it is right that this sonata should have its own special name. In its technical demands, its scale, and its breadth of expressive content, it is a turning point in Beethoven's third maturity and in the history of the piano sonata. It was indicative of Beethoven's change of direction after 1812 that he did not have a new symphonic project in hand after finishing the Eighth Symphony in 1812 and would not begin full-time work on what became the Ninth before 1821. Accordingly, composing the *Hammerklavier* in 1817–18 became the virtual equivalent of working on a symphony.

A notice in the *Wiener Zeitung* in 1819, surely written with Beethoven's knowledge, claims that "the work is distinguished among all other creations of the master, not only by virtue of its richness and greatness of imagination [*phantasie*] but because, in its artistic completeness and use of

Sketches for Beethoven's Piano Sonata Opus 106 (Hammerklavier), *from a pocket sketchbook of 1818. (Bibliothek der Gesellschaft der Musikfreunde, Vienna)*

strict style, it signals a new period in Beethoven's keyboard works."[2] For once journalism was justified.[3]

Its most obvious features are its length and complexity. It is immense in the way that the *Eroica* is among the symphonies or Opus 59 No. 1 is among the quartets. These are not just sizable and big-boned works; they are incomparably the longest that anyone had written in their genres. They are monuments to the part of Beethoven's vision that needed expanded scope for the expression of powerful ideas—intellectual as well as emotional—and long time-spans to provide room for a wealth of thematic ideas and harmonic procedures within a fully organized formal framework. Not that he could not achieve comparable results in shorter spans, as he often did. Rather, in these big four-movement cycles he takes pains to spread his ideas and their consequences across huge canvases. Something similar was surely in Michelangelo's mind when he decided on the great physical size of his seated Moses for the tomb of Julius II.

We remember that the sheer length of the *Eroica* had been publicly noted on the first violin part of the first edition—"this symphony having been written at greater length than is usual." Also, at the last stages of composing Opus 59 No. 1, Beethoven had reined himself in and decided not to make each of the first two movements half again as long as they already were, and not to add a long repeat that he had penciled in for the end of the last movement. Attending to proportion and balance among the segments of large-scale formal structures, whether sonata-form movements or others, was a lifetime preoccupation, and the study of Beethoven's proportions within movements is one of the many tasks for which his sketchbooks, still only partially transcribed and available, may yield valuable new knowledge.[4]

When we consider that Beethoven had produced twenty-eight highly varied piano sonatas beginning in the 1790s, the grand aesthetic model that he chooses for the *Hammerklavier* is a breakthrough. In his early published piano sonatas he had increased the genre's aesthetic weight by writing full four-movement cycles; soon thereafter, in 1800–1802, he had begun to alternate this template with three-movement sonatas or still other models, as in Opus 27 Nos. 1 and 2, or in Opus 31, where two sonatas have three movements. It is true that the "Waldstein" had greatly increased the gravity of the piano sonata, but it did so by having two quite long movements separated by a short Adagio introduction to the finale. By 1819, in fact, he had not written a four-movement piano sonata since Opus 31 No. 3, composed in 1802. Similar alternatives govern his middle period violin and cello sonatas, as we see from the three-movement "Kreutzer" Sonata and the pseudo-four-movement Cello Sonata Opus 69, in which the decision to abbreviate the beautiful slow movement seems to take place as the sonata unfolds. Thereafter he produced two large, four-movement cycles in his keyboard chamber music, the "Archduke" Trio in 1811 and the G Major Violin Sonata in 1812, each of them his last word in its genre.

Of the two, the "Archduke" Trio, in the same key of B-flat and dedicated to the same patron, comes closest to being a model for the *Hammerklavier*, the largest of all Beethoven piano sonatas.[5] The analogy in length is clear.

Less clear is that in their first movements the two works share important features of their harmonic plans, in both cases using chains of descending thirds from the tonic, B-flat major, across the scope of the exposition and development sections. In this sonata, as Charles Rosen has vividly shown, descending thirds play an important role in integrating the whole work; their employment here is a later realization of Beethoven's earlier uses of descending-third chains, a process he had derived from Mozart and Haydn, and which he may also have found in Bach as well, especially at this Bachian stage of his development, when he would have been looking for it.[6] In the "Archduke," the subdominant is the first harmonic contrast to the tonic, and a descending-third chain governs the big second theme in the cello, thus anticipating the thirds of the *Hammerklavier*. Further in the "Archduke," as we saw, the tonal plan of the exposition moves not from the B-flat tonic to its dominant, F, as we would normally expect, but rather to G major.[7] From there an abrupt shift is needed at the end of the exposition either to restore the tonic for the repeat of the whole section or to go on into the development. In the development the next goal is indeed E-flat major, in which the cello arrives with an expressive variant of the first theme to seal the moment. The final steps bring a rare touch of the minor mode—C minor—then finally settle back into the orbit of the tonic B-flat major well before the *dolce* recapitulation.[8] This comparative absence of harmonic tensions before the recapitulation differs altogether from the situation in the *Hammerklavier*, signaling the more relaxed and leisurely character of the "Archduke" 's first movement. But the harmonic planning is essentially the same in the exposition and early parts of the development.

Certainly the two works differ sharply in other ways. The piano trio impresses for its nobility and optimism—like the *Pastoral* Symphony before the storm, it makes hardly any use of minor mode. As we saw earlier, the first movement of the trio is followed by an enormous Scherzo with fugato Trio, the slow movement is a well-crafted set of variations, and the finale is in a relaxed 2/4 meter animated by rhythmic shifts that come in fits and starts between the stringed instruments and the piano. The *Hammerklavier*, on the other hand, builds through three enormous movements to its fugal finale, giving the work an end-orientation quite different from that of the "Archduke" Trio.

The *Hammerklavier* starts with a classic Beethovenian physical opening gesture, an eight-note *marcato* figure, memorable for its rhythm alone, that rises in thirds as it is repeated and comes to a stop; then the legato main theme emerges and comes to another stop. A sketch for this opening idea has the words "Vivat Rudolphus," showing that the eventual dedication was anything but perfunctory. The two elements—opening motif and main theme, both demanding continuation—establish a high state of tension, somewhat like the opening of the Fifth Symphony, with its two pauses, or the *Fidelio* Overture, with its incisive rhythm and repetitions rising through the tonic triad. In the *Hammerklavier* opening this tension increases as the movement progresses, partly owing to the large number of rhythmically profiled thematic ideas and to the long fugal episode that marks the development section. It also arises from the movement's further harmonic advances into distant regions (G-flat major, B minor) as well as to its stark contrasts of dynamics. *Forte* accents on weak beats appear like explosions at the end of the first movement, and nothing could be more characteristic of this sonata than the dynamics in the last seven measures, in which a diminuendo moves down from an already established *piano* to *piano sempre* and then to the very rare *pianissimo*; then the registrally extreme *fortissimo* tonic chord breaks out suddenly, just preceding the final unison B♭.

This sonata was written just after Beethoven had received Broadwood's handsome gift of a six-octave grand piano from London, in 1817. If the Broadwood tone was perhaps less brilliant than that of Viennese pianos, its capacities for a wide range of dynamics and tonal shading compensated well. And modern performances of Beethoven's later sonatas on a restored Broadwood should convince anyone that tonal shading, subtlety of dynamics, and beauty of sonority, were now more vital than ever in Beethoven's conception of keyboard writing.[9]

The spaciousness of the *Hammerklavier* is further apparent in its Scherzo and Trio, and even more in the heavily freighted F-sharp-minor *Adagio sostenuto*, one of Beethoven's longest brooding slow movements, of which Adorno curiously remarked that its opening melody "lacks plasticity," shows "the disappearance of surface articulations," and is "stretched over long arches."[10] Had this been a second-period work, even a late one like the "Archduke" Trio, its finale might have been light, to balance the whole work, rather than even more monumental. But Beethoven made the latter choice and added greater weight at the end. After an improvisational Largo and Allegro introduction in the manner of a fantasia, itself a succession of strange and seemingly unrelated figures that mysteriously point the way to a new aesthetic state, that new state indeed emerges as a vast fugue for three voices, "con alcune licenze" ("with some deviations from strict writing"). It is the biggest and most complicated fugue that Beethoven had yet written.

This fugue was conceived on a grand scale, compared with the fugal finale of the D Major Cello Sonata Opus 102 No. 2 written a couple of years earlier, which is an amply dissonant fugato movement, not a strict fugue, with three large segments welded together into a whole. The *Hammerklavier* fugue subject is unusually long. After some intervallic anticipations it begins with a great leap of a tenth, which clearly recalls the emphatic leap that opened the first movement, while a trill intensifies the leading-tone-to-tonic motion in a startling way (*W 45). (Beethoven would later use a similar figure in his other late B-flat-major fugue, the *Grand Fugue*, Opus 133—in many ways the great descendant of this one—where insistent trills on isolated note pairs play a powerful role.) In the fugue of Opus 106, after the opening upward gesture, the descending-third chain of the ensuing figures closes into a series of running sixteenth patterns that form a larger melodic shape through which the descending thirds in fact continue to be heard.

The fugue unfolds in two ways. One is in its contrapuntal transformations of its subject in a time-honored manner. We find passages devoted to the subject in augmentation, the subject in retrograde with a new countersubject, and the subject in inversion.[11] Far from supposing that Beethoven is "merely displaying erudition" or "submitting" to so-called constructivist principles of fugue writing in using augmentation, retrograde, and inversion to manipulate thematic material, we see that their characteristic functions as developmental features of fugue are essential to the aesthetic he is embracing in this finale. His aim in this movement is to rival Bach's capacity to expand and rejoice in displays of rigorous formal logic and contrapuntal skill while infusing them with that "poetic" element (as Beethoven himself called it) that is fully his own.

After the first section, we encounter a new and contrasting second subject, made of steadily flowing quarter notes in 3/4 meter, as even and regular as the first subject had been abrupt and barely predictable. The new subject receives a full exposition,[12] and once this thematic antithesis is established, even the least sophisticated Hegelian can predict the outcome: the two themes will eventually be combined and then give rise to new and more intensified contrapuntal combinations that will form the peroration of the movement. It is exactly the principle that Beethoven later used in the finale of the Ninth Symphony, where the "Ode to Joy," the theme of brotherhood, and the great second theme, speaking to the millions under God, combine in a climactic double fugue. In the *Hammerklavier*, the combinational features include not only the two themes in a consonant contrapuntal relationship to one another, but the renewed appearance of Theme 1 in both its original form and its inversion. All this, and the sonata as a whole, is then crowned by a lengthy coda that caps all previous climaxes: low roaring trills in the bass register, a short Poco adagio to set up the dynamic finish, rushing unison scales on the original Theme 1, and trilled *fortissimo* octave pairs, all of this working out to the last possible degree the implications of the upward leap that started the fugue off in the first place—and had also started off the whole sonata. As in many a mature work, Beethoven seeks to draw the last ounce of meaning from even the simplest figures and develops the material of a vast movement through to an ending that feels and sounds as absolute as it is inevitable.

As indicated earlier, a remarkable feature of this sonata is that Beethoven, in sending it to Ries in 1819 for publication in London, authorized him to publish it in one of three ways: (1) "you could . . . omit the Largo and begin straight away with the Fugue"; (2) "you could use the first movement and then the Adagio, and then for the third movement the Scherzo"; or (3) "you could take just the first movement and the Scherzo and let them form the whole sonata."[13] What are we to make of this? Has Beethoven "momentarily lost confidence in the value of his effort[?]"[14] Perhaps, though it seems unlikely. We are aware of the perpetual economic factor in

Beethoven's shrewd and calculating ways with publishers. To gain a quick British edition of so difficult a work was so important that he would accept virtually any partial or variant published version. Not only did he urgently need money to finance Karl's education, but his principal supporter, the archduke, was in some financial straits at this time. As Beethoven tells Ries in this same letter, "my income has vanished." He also makes clear that he wants the fee for any British version as soon as possible so that he can release the work to the Viennese publisher, "who has really been kept waiting too long." As usual he could expect only a one-time payment, and he urgently wanted to get one from each publisher before piracy set in.

In any event, the sonata came out in Britain in a two-part version: the first part contained the first three movements (with the second and third in reversed order!) and the second part consisted of the Introduction and Fugue. This concession for an unusually long and difficult work could have been in his mind seven years later, when he was urged to detach the even longer, even more arcane, fugal finale from his B Flat Quartet, Opus 130, and he agreed, creating the *Grand Fugue*, Opus 133, as a separate work.

Piano Sonatas Opp. 109–111

With the publication of Opus 106, seemingly unfathomable and to most musicians unplayable, the piano sonata could never be the same again. It is against the background of this monumental achievement that we must see the last three piano sonatas. Resolutely original, independent, fully realized masterpieces that they are, we can nevertheless dimly perceive that they form a trilogy, the more so as they originated as a group from a commission by Adolph Martin Schlesinger in Berlin in a letter to Beethoven of April 11, 1820. Although Schlesinger's letter is lost we know what it must have said, since Beethoven told him on April 30 that, in addition to their discussions about other, lesser works, for forty ducats each he could supply "an opus of three sonatas."[15] As usual he was rushing ahead of himself, for he had only just begun to jot down some ideas for what turned out to be the first movement of Opus 109 while the others were at best dimly imagined visions waiting to be fleshed out. Beethoven was then in the midst of work on the *Missa solemnis*, and when the deadline for its presentation passed on March 9, 1820, with Archduke Rudolph's inauguration as archbishop of Olmütz, it was clear that he would need much more time for the completion of the Mass but also that he could turn his attention to some smaller-scale projects—like the three piano sonatas. The first to be finished was the E Major Sonata, Opus 109, which became his main project during the summer of 1820 and was ready by the fall. He then began the next sonata, Opus 110, in the spring of 1821, finishing it by December. Then came his first work on the C Minor Sonata, Opus 111, which he finished much more quickly than the previous two, and he was able to send both Opus 110 and Opus 111 to Schlesinger around February 1822. Still, there was work to do, as Beethoven then revised the second movement of Opus 111 and dispatched the revision in early April 1822. Besides his continuing preoccupation with the Mass, the magnum opus of these years, he managed to finish a set of Eleven Bagatelles for Piano, Opus 119, early in 1821 and also, in the fall of 1822, his overture for the reopening of the Josephstadt Theater, *The Consecration of the House*.

Beethoven's pianistic imagination is stamped on every page of these three sonatas. Deaf as he was, his sustained ability to compose at the keyboard—to use his fingers to unleash his imagination—must have released a wealth of new ideas. Undreamed-of sonorities and multivariate figuration patterns appear in each of these works, exploiting both keyboard and pedals in ways that went beyond even his most innovative earlier keyboard works. We find arpeggiated cadenzalike passages through several octaves; rapid parallel thirds and sixths; delicate figurations; use of *una corda* pedal effects; and sustained trills in extreme registers against continuing melodic and contrapuntal lines in other parts. In each case these pianistic effects were grounded in the structural marrow of the individual movement and of the work as a whole. Moreover, each sonata has an idiosyncratic design in which the form arises even more dramatically from the material than it had in even the most original middle-period works. Here the macroscopic formal shaping is even more fully detached from the expected norms because Beethoven had moved away from the processive developmental methods that tended to govern his major works before 1815 (except those experimental, fantasialike works such as the "Moonlight" and "Tempest"

Sonatas). In the late sonatas we feel that the form is in process of emerging as the material of a given movement realizes its potential from beginning to end. Though such a feeling can always be inferred from true master-works, here it is more palpable than almost anywhere else in Beethoven. The psychological aspect of what I call the "process of emergence" is given primacy, and the traditional means by which formal expectations were cre-ated and satisfied in classical sonatas, even in his most path-breaking ear-lier ones, are often suspended, elided, or concealed. This concealment of formal junctures is a basic aspect of the late style, and it is in its glory in these three works.

Sonata Opus 109

If we consider the three sonatas as totalities we see that Opus 109 is somewhat ambiguous in the weight and balance of its movements. It has a curious three-movement plan: Vivace, a short and intense rapid-tempo first movement in the tonic, E major; Prestissimo, a still more rapid Scherzo in the tonic minor; and Andante molto cantabile ed espressivo in E major (theme and six variations plus coda), a calm, deeply expressive movement, the longest of the three, to conclude. The sequence of tempos is unprecedented: Beethoven had previously used a first-movement Vivace only in the Seventh Symphony, reserving it mainly for finales, as in the Fourth Piano Concerto and the *Lebewohl* Sonata. Even for this purpose he had only begun to use Vivace to replace Allegro or Presto as a finale tempo in a few middle-period works; it was becoming more frequent in his last works, above all in the Scherzos of the last quartets. As for Prestissimo as a faster variant for Presto, he had used it as a main tempo in three early piano works but not since.[16] And as for ending with a variation set, this in itself is not a radical step, but the intensity of this movement and its many tempo changes breaks with its precedents (such as the finale of the "Harp" Quar-tet, Opus 74). The theme itself, which Beethoven labeled in German "Gesangvoll, mit innigster Empfindung" ("Songlike, with the greatest inwardness of feeling"), is a magnificent specimen of "hymnlike" melodies in Beethoven slow movements. Each variation then carries its own tempo or character designation and in some cases a new meter: (1) Molto espressivo; (2) Leggiermente; (3) Allegro vivace, 2/4; (4) "Etwas langsamer als das Thema" ("A little slower than the theme"), 6/8; (5) Allegro, ma non troppo, 4/4; and (6) "Tempo I del thema" ("Original tempo of the theme") for the final peroration. There is evidence in Beethoven's autograph that the first movement goes right on to the second without pause, despite his having written "attacca" and then canceled it. And Nicholas Marston has shown that the same immediacy of connection is wanted between the Prestissimo and the variations finale.[17]

Even more surprising is Marston's discovery that the order of composition of the movements, as disclosed in the sketches, is quite unusual. To begin with, the first movement was apparently planned as a separate composition, intended for a piano method by Friedrich Starke, and Beethoven's friend Franz Oliva spurred him to use the "little new piece" as the first movement of the new sonata he needed for Schlesinger.[18] It seems clear that, once he decided on the change, Beethoven went ahead and composed, first, the third-movement theme; then the second movement; then the third-movement variations. Afterward he undoubtedly revised the whole to bring it all into its fully mastered coherence, in which, as Marston remarks, the third-movement theme "effectively recomposes the first movement and concludes its [structural] 'unfinished business' while also foreshadowing the structure of the third movement."[19]

Sonata Opus 110

The compactness and brevity of the first movement of Opus 109 is mirrored in that of Opus 110 (a fairly short Moderato cantabile movement), but the continuation of this second sonata brings an entirely different pattern. The F-minor Scherzo is a fierce counterpart to the Prestissimo of Opus 109, but then the sonata turns in a wholly new direction. A short Adagio introductory phrase gives way to a dramatic and atmospheric Recitativo that closes into a "Klagender Gesang" ("Song of Lament") in A♭ minor. This "arioso," of transcendent beauty and depth, turns out to be a lyrical preparation for the main body of the finale, which emerges as a fully developed fugue in the home tonic of A-flat major on a subject that clearly derives from the opening theme of the first movement.

This poetic fugue is another example of Beethoven's late-period blending of cunning contrapuntal artifice with his most expressive modes of utterance. It finds room halfway through for a return of the "Klagender Gesang" in G minor, a key remote from the home tonic, even in Beethoven's uses of extended tonality. The fugue subject then returns in inverted form in G major. After further modulatory and contrapuntal adventures, including augmentation and diminution, the subject finds its way back to A-flat major and launches into a coda that synthesizes all earlier complexities, while it also confirms the sense of homecoming by bringing the subject triumphantly in high register and in full chordal style while the left hand rolls sixteenth-patterns below. Finally the whole suggests a circular time-space by its closing reference back to the cascading tonic arpeggios of the first movement.

Sonata Opus 111

The last sonata gives every sign of being a self-consciously final statement. There is no evidence that after Opus 111, Beethoven ever thought of writing another piano sonata, as he moved on to complete his other grand projects. Nothing in the general literature is more familiar than speculation as to why this C-minor sonata has "only" two movements, and no controversy is more useless. In July 1822 Maurice Schlesinger, by now established in Paris, wrote to Beethoven to thank him for entrusting "your masterworks" to him and his father for publication, but also asked "most submissively, if you wrote for the work only one Maestoso and one Andante; or if perhaps the [final] Allegro was accidentally forgotten by the copyist."[20] Ten days later his father wrote from Berlin with the same question.[21] If Beethoven bothered to reply we don't know; the chances are that he simply passed it over in grim silence. Schindler also claimed to have been worried about the absence of a third movement, and writes that he asked Beethoven for an explanation. This time Beethoven replied that he hadn't had time to write one, an answer whose irony was probably lost on Schindler.[22] The lack of any sketches or even jottings for a potential third movement makes it apparent that Beethoven never intended the Arietta to be anything other than the final movement.[23] Even so, the question continued to be asked, as when Wendell Kretzschmar, Thomas Mann's Pennsylvania-born music teacher in *Doctor Faustus*, found himself lecturing to a bored general audience on just this issue, stuttering violently as he tried to convey to his lay audience what premonitions of greatness and death lay in this movement, which could not possibly be followed by anything else.[24]

The opening of the Maestoso, with its *forte* jagged downward leap of a diminished seventh followed by a full diminished seventh chord on F♯, creates an immediate instability, a harmonic crisis that defines no tonic, until it finds its way in a softer dynamic to an apparent clarifying cadence in C minor (*W 46). But then in succession we encounter the other two diminished sevenths of the tonal system, those on B♮ and on E♮, expanding the last of these through winding ways until, finally, the dominant of C minor breaks the suspense, preparing the way to the Allegro first movement. The diminished-seventh leaps of this extraordinary opening have a strong impact on the later course of the first movement.[25] So striking and pre-Romantic, this opening has a precedent in another genre: it is, again, the introduction to Florestan's dungeon scene that opens Act 2 of *Fidelio*, which uses all three diminished-seventh chords of the tonal system and a two-note, heartbeat figure in the tympani tuned to a diminished fifth.[26] The larger shape of the sonata grows organically from this opening Maestoso. The C-minor Allegro movement not only has strong affinities with other representatives of Beethoven's "C-minor mood" but its opening theme was consciously associated by Beethoven with two great precedents—one is the fugue subject of the Kyrie in the Mozart Requiem, the other is the subject of the fugal finale of Haydn's F Minor String Quartet, Opus 20 No. 5; Beethoven wrote both of these out on a sketch leaf that contains a draft of the beginning of the Maestoso.[27] There are indications that at a preliminary stage of composition Beethoven considered writing the first movement of the sonata as a fugue, based on a subject he had originally sketched as early as 1801 while working on the Opus 30 violin sonatas.[28] He even wrote out a full fugal exposition, which was suppressed in favor of the sonata-form movement as we have it. What these drafts show is the decisive importance of contrapuntal thinking in his last piano sonatas and in his last maturity altogether.[29] It also appears that the Maestoso introduction only emerged in the plan of the work when Beethoven had given up the idea of a fugal first movement and reshaped it into sonata form, thus providing an introduction that would be integral to the whole work. "[H]e considered using it at the end of the development section, to prepare the recapitulation of the main theme, [and] he contemplated bringing it back towards the end of the second movement."[30] We see here the malleability of Beethoven's formal thinking in mapping out the larger plans of his late works, something we also find in the late quartets, in which at least two movements were transferred from one work to another.

The Arietta with its variations is in every sense a slow finale, not a slow movement that lacks a further movement as confirmation. Labeled "Adagio molto semplice e cantabile" ("Adagio, to be played very simply and in a singing manner"), it presents a theme of absolute directness and clarity. It is followed by four intricate variations that, as always, closely follow the contour and harmonic pattern of the theme, then a modulatory episode that breaks out of the C-major framework for an excursion to E-flat major and C minor, then a vast reprise of the theme with new figuration patterns streaming forth in the lower voices, and at the end a soaring conclusion with high trills in the upper register over a final statement of the first part of the theme, plus a poignant chromatic inflection (*W 47).[31] Mann's fictional music teacher, Wendell Kretzschmar, is speaking of this moment when he says that it represents

> something entirely unexpected and touching in its mildness and good-
> ness . . . [T]his added C♯ is the most moving, consolatory, pathetically
> reconciling thing in the world. It is like having one's hair or cheek
> stroked, lovingly, understandingly, like a deep and silent farewell look.
> It blesses the object, the frightfully harried formulation, with overpow-
> ering humanity, lies in parting so gently on the hearer's heart in eternal
> farewell that the eyes run over.[32]

The Arietta's ending, in which the basic melody, now wreathed in accompanying figures, soars to higher regions, raises the conclusion of this work to the level reached at the end of Opus 109 by the quiet return of its Andante theme, and to the end of Opus 110 by its arpeggiated harmonies flying downward and then upward in a vast registral arch. In each instance we have the feeling that an incomparable musical experience has come to its end, has reached a wisdom that is granted only to the greatest artists. In early February 1820, Beethoven wrote the Conversation Book entry quoting Kant: "The moral law within us, and the starry heavens above us. Kant!!!"[33] It is just this spirit, of the mortal, vulnerable human being striving against the odds to hold his moral being steady in order to gather strength as an artist to strive toward the heavens—it is this conjoining that we feel at the end of Opus 111 and in a few other moments in Beethoven's last works. They are moments that few composers before or after him ever quite achieved.

The "Diabelli" Variations

The strength of purpose behind Beethoven's large-scale late works makes it biographically useful to know that some of them came about through special circumstances, such as the archduke's elevation to a high church position and the reopening of the Josephstadt theater; or through commissions from patrons such as the Philharmonic Society of London and Prince Galitzin. Some came from publishers, including Schlesinger, Schott, and Diabelli. Of these only Diabelli stumbled into immortality by having his name affixed to Beethoven's last, and by far greatest, set of variations for piano, to which Beethoven once referred as "grand variations on a German waltz," begun in 1819 and not completed until 1823. In 1817 Anton Diabelli, a journeyman composer and sometime proofreader for Steiner's publishing house, set up shop, with Pietro Cappi as his partner, in a new music-publishing venture located in the Kohlmarkt, a square in Vienna. By early 1819 he was doing a brisk business in arrangements of operatic and dance tunes for piano and for guitar. A little later he established a connection with a promising younger Viennese composer, Franz Schubert, and in 1821 published his lieder "Erlkönig" as Schubert's Opus 1 and "Gretchen am Spinnrade" as Opus 2. Early in 1819 Diabelli conceived the sure-fire idea of combining popular appeal with patriotism, though less flamboyantly than Mälzel had done with his Panharmonicon and *Wellington's Sieg*. Diabelli, who had a background as a piano teacher

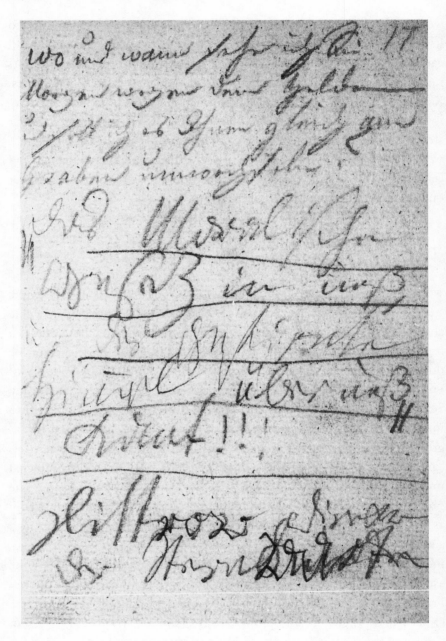

A page from a Conversation Book of 1820 showing Beethoven's inscription, "The moral law within us and the starry heavens above us. Kant!!!" (Staatsbibliothek, Berlin)

and composer, wrote a thirty-two-bar waltz tune in C major and sent it off to every important or would-be important composer in Austria, asking each of them to contribute a variation on the tune for a collection to be entitled "Vaterländischer Künstlerverein" ("Patriotic Association of Artists"). Not all replied, and Beethoven went his separate way, but by 1824 fifty composers had sent in one variation each, and Diabelli proudly published them in 1824 with a handsome title page. The roster, ranging alphabetically from Assmayer to Worzischek, included Czerny, Gelinek, Hummel, Friedrich August Kanne, Conradin Kreutzer, Ignaz Moscheles, W. A. Mozart the younger, Schubert, Tomaschek, and the child prodigy Franz Liszt. One variation is ascribed to "S.R.D." ("Serenissimus Rudolphus Dux") on the title page; in fact the archduke contributed a very professional fugal variation.[34] Czerny was not only the first to come on board (his variation is dated May 7, 1819, on the autograph), he also rounded out the collection with a coda.[35]

Obviously struck by Diabelli's waltz, a simple springboard for his imagination, Beethoven decided in the spring of 1819 to work up a full-scale set of variations, and we now know that he sketched as many as nineteen of the eventual thirty-three variations before he put the project aside. He had to in order to continue his work on the *Missa solemnis* and then the last three piano sonatas, and he did not return to the variation cycle until 1823.[36] In other words, when Beethoven began the "Diabelli" Variations he had just finished the *Hammerklavier* Sonata and had begun work on the Mass; by the time he finished it the Mass was complete, as were the last piano sonatas, and he was moving into work on the Ninth Symphony and contemplating a quartet in E-flat major that would become Opus 127.

Why thirty-three? Many reasons have been advanced, mainly drawn from analytical studies of the growing complexity of structure and expression in the course of the work, but it should also be noted that in the year before the "Diabelli" Variations Archduke Rudolph, as part of his training, had composed a set of forty variations on a theme by Beethoven. It is possible that Beethoven's own plan for a large variation set could be related to a letter of 1819, in which Beethoven tells Rudolph that he is at work on the great Mass for the archduke's installation, but also that "in my writing-desk there are several compositions that bear witness to my remembering Your Imperial Highness and I hope to work on them under more favorable conditions."[37] This suggests that in writing his longest variation set, one variation longer than Bach's "Goldberg" Variations (counting Bach's two presentations of the theme plus thirty variations) and his own Thirty-two Variations of 1806, Beethoven could also have had it in mind to create a panoramic set of elaborations upon a simple tune, demonstrating a wide range of approaches to variation in his ripest manner and showing his contemporaries and future audiences what immense possibilities lay within Diabelli's sequential "cobbler's patch." The whole would show how a monumental musical experience could be carved out from this seemingly trivial little dance number. It is highly probable that Beethoven knew the "Goldberg" Variations, as they had been published in 1817 in Zurich, and a manuscript copy could have reached him even before that.[38]

Diabelli's waltz is actually a well-crafted, symmetrical little piece, not just a simple tune (*W 48). From this slender stalk Beethoven builds a variation set that grows aesthetically in stature from beginning to end, putting the most traditional of genres on a completely new footing. As much as he had made innovations in some of his earlier independent sets of piano variations—the Six Variations of Opus 34 and the Fifteen Variations and Fugue of Opus 35—here he goes beyond precedents, his own or anyone else's. There are changes of tempo and character not just for some variations but for almost every one. The range extends across the Alla Marcia of No. 1, the swirling, pre-Romantic waltz of No. 8, the Grave e maestoso of No. 14, and the Presto scherzando of No. 15. Number 20 brings a strange and dissonant chorale, to which No. 22 opposes a naked parody of Leporello's "Notte e giorno faticar" from the opening of *Don Giovanni*, chosen for its obvious affinity to the opening intervals of Diabelli's tune. The final three variations expand in feeling and depth, reaching out in new directions. No. 31 is a Bachian arioso that is followed by a rigorous fugue (thus paralleling the Arioso and fugue of the Opus 110 finale). The whole is crowned by simplicity: the final word in No. 33 is reserved for a freely developed "Tempo di Menuetto," a graceful and gentle conclusion that steps back historically from the waltz era to that of the minuet, then builds up at the end to a sublime ending in C major with familiar late-Beethoven keyboard figurations interwoven with fragments from Diabelli's tune. The path to the transcendental has once again been traversed, now all the way from the Viennese ballroom through human tragedy and comedy, finally arriving once more, and by a different route, at the starry heavens.

The Late Bagatelles

Opus 33

The term "bagatelle" from the French means "trifle" but also refers to a game something like billiards, played with four to nine balls on a flat table with cups at the corners. The word was rare in music before Beethoven. It first appeared in a few French titles in the eighteenth century, for example, a 1717 rondeau by Couperin and a set of dances issued by the publisher Boivin around 1753. Later, and more relevantly for Beethoven, a certain Carl Wilhelm Maizier issued a set of *Musikalische Bagatellen* in 1797 that combine dance pieces with songs. But Beethoven was the first to use the term for detached, short piano pieces, at first for his collection of seven *Bagatelles pour le Pianoforte* (using the French form of the term), Opus 33, published in 1803 by the Viennese Bureau d'Arts et d'Industrie. In it he brings together a selection of the many short piano pieces he had been writing since the Bonn years, and one of the seven (No. 1, a simple rondo in E-flat major) actually bears the date 1782 (originally written 1788). Beethoven put these dates on his autograph manuscript in 1802 when he was assembling this set, no doubt trying to remember just when he had originally written the piece. The main point about Opus 33 is that it was an assemblage of disparate little pieces that Beethoven brought together, not a set that he planned as a collection having any special unity. He always had a raft of little piano pieces somewhere at hand, some of them rejects from piano sonatas, some just advanced exercises. The "Kafka" miscellany contains many of them.

Opus 33 displays a small wealth of pianistic figurations used as bases for little pieces, but only two numbers have real expressive merit: No. 6, a D-major Allegretto quasi Andante, which Beethoven marks "Con una certa espressione parlante" ("With a certain speaking quality of expression"), is the only one of the set that has a pensive, touching quality; the other is No. 7, a Presto quasi-scherzo piece in A-flat major in Beethoven's most brilliant and rhythmically exciting manner, some of it a counterpart to the angular Scherzo of the "Pastorale" Piano Sonata, Opus 28, and in its quiet, arpeggiated octaves a parallel to the Scherzo of Opus 10 No. 2 and the first Allegro of the Sonata Opus 27 No. 1.

Opus 119

Beethoven came back to the idea of the bagatelle in 1820 to 1822, the period of his main work on Opp. 110 and 111, just after the *Missa solemnis* and probably just before his return to the "Diabelli" Variations in 1823. The result was the collection of eleven Bagatelles, Opus 119, issued in 1823 by Maurice Schlesinger in Paris, curiously bearing the Opus number 112 (it took until the middle of the nineteenth century before the final opus number 119 was established).[39] Beethoven had actually published five of the pieces, Nos. 7–11, in 1821 in a piano pedagogy book by Friedrich Starke, with a note using the German word *Kleinigkeiten* ("trifles") rather than the French *bagatelles,* no doubt in keeping with his patriotic preference for German terms and titles in these years (e.g., *Hammerklavier*). The note in Starke's publication told the performer to see in these pieces that "the unique genius of the famous master shines through in every piece, and that these pieces, modestly labeled 'Trifles' by Beethoven, will be as instructive for the player as they will provide the most perfect insight into the spirit of composition."[40] Actually Beethoven culled the first five from a portfolio of such pieces he had been keeping over the years, marked "Bagatellen," of which the cover still survives in Bonn.[41] He looked at pieces he had first sketched as long before as 1791–1802, then selected what he wanted for his new collection as Nos. 1–6, adding Nos. 7–11 from the Starke collection already published.

Some aspects of the Opus 119 Bagatelles show Beethoven thinking about how to order them effectively and establish a modest degree of unity in the set, but what appeals most about the collection is found not in the set as a whole but in the single pieces. Like decorative ornaments to the great jewels of Opp. 110 and 111, these bagatelles show Beethoven's ability to convey a sense of completeness within the smallest boundaries. The longest piece in the set totals seventy-four measures (No. 1 in G minor), the shortest, No. 10 (marked "Allegramente") in D major, is a mere thirteen, and six more pieces are less than thirty measures long. That he would take pains with them when he was working out the *Missa solemnis*, the "Diabelli" Variations, and the Ninth Symphony shows that these are serious little compositions, representing his miniaturist side as explorer of aesthetic extremes. The same tendency crops up here and there in the late quartets: witness the tightly compressed Scherzo of Opus 130.

Opus 126

When we come to Opus 126 we see Beethoven deepening the expressive qualities of his short piano pieces once more, and now thinking of them as a cycle, not merely an assemblage. These six Bagatelles were not dredged up from earlier times but were written in February and March of 1824, directly after his completion of the Ninth Symphony. Once again composing elegantly for the piano was a welcome break from his fierce concentration on the Ninth, just as in 1814 he had turned to the songlike Opus 90 directly after the revision of *Fidelio*. These pieces were planned as a unit; they appear in a group on successive leaves of a sketchbook and are labeled "Ciclus von Kleinigkeiten" ("cycle of trifles"). The term "cycle" indicates that they are intended to be movements of a single work, but it may also refer to the major-third cycle that connects their keys.[42] Performing them as an integral whole has become an appropriate modern practice, and thus their convincing sequence of expressive and psychological moods comes forth with something of the same artistic conviction we find in a larger complex work—the closest we come to this set is, indeed, the short middle movements of the quartet Opus 130, not only with its diminutive

Scherzo but its other little movements that culminate in the aria-like cavatina, just prior to the finale.

In Opus 126 we find the following key scheme:

No.	1	2	3	4	5	6
Key	G major	G minor	E-flat major	B minor	G minor	E-flat major

The descending cycle of major thirds is obvious. What seems not to have been noticed is that this type of falling-third sequence, with major thirds descending in order, also governs the main key scheme of the development section of the *Eroica* first movement, whose key-scheme is C major–A-flat major–E minor–C major. That this same sequence remained in memory is shown by its use in another E-flat-major work, the Quartet Opus 127, which Beethoven was planning just at the time he was writing the Bagatelles of Opus 126. In the coda of the finale, a surprising "Allegro con moto,"[43] he turns from the tonic E-flat major that had already been established, to the following scheme: E-flat major–C major–A-flat major–E major–E♭ major. This sequence convincingly unfolds in modulatory moves that occupy just a few measures each—another mark of the compactness that is part of Beethoven's late style.[44]

Such weighty predecessors help justify placing Opus 126 in the main line of Beethoven's late achievements. These bagatelles are individually longer than most of those in Opus 119, and they are stronger espressively as well: thus No. 3, an Andante cantabile in E-flat major, ranks with the Adagio of Opus 127 and the Lento of Opus 135 in its slowly flowing thematic quality.

Of the late bagatelles it has become a commonplace to say that they anticipate the later Romantic interest in the single song or piano piece, as in Schumann and Chopin, the "fragment," about which Charles Rosen has written with great insight. Rosen notes, however, that Opus 126 is a genuine cycle, and that when compared with Beethoven's earlier bagatelles, its pieces have such weight that they "are no longer miniatures.[45] What the bagatelles offered Beethoven was a museum of small forms. Also, writing them offered him a chance to look back imaginatively at his compositional methods from much earlier periods of his life, to put himself back even into his earlier child's world of playing and writing easy piano pieces in his apprentice years. Having long since left that world behind, he could now heighten the features of these playthings that would ensure their place in his later world.

CHAPTER 20

THE CELESTIAL AND THE HUMAN

❧◦❀◦❈❀❈◦❀◦❧

The Missa solemnis

The impetus to writing a great Mass in D major was the news in early March 1819 that Archduke Rudolph had been elected archbishop by the cathedral chapter of Olmütz in Moravia and would be officially installed in a great ceremony a year later.[1] At once Beethoven wrote to congratulate him, characteristically combining, in a single letter, expressions of homage, some avuncular advice, stoic wisdom, firm reminders of Beethoven's artistic superiority, and resistance to any hint of subordinate status.

Congratulations:

> *When I consider . . . what an enlarged sphere of activity is going to be thereby opened to you and to your fine and noble qualities, I too cannot but add my congratulations to the many others which Your Imperial Highness must have received.[2]*

Stoicism:

> *There is hardly any good thing that can be achieved . . . without a sacrifice; and it is precisely the nobler and better man who seems to be destined for this more than other human beings, no doubt that his virtue may be put to the test.*

Archduke Rudolph, for whose 1820 installation as Archbishop of Olmütz Beethoven set out to write the Missa solemnis; *the work was not finished until two years later. (Historisches Museum, Vienna)*

Teacher to student:

Beethoven thanks the archduke for the forty variations he had written on a theme Beethoven had given him, then reminds him who his teacher is by mentioning "several slips" in the work, adding bluntly in Italian, "La Musica merita d'esser studiata" ("music deserves to be studied"). That he had also used this expression in a letter to nephew Karl's boarding school teacher, Cajetan Gianattasio del Rio, in 1817, suggests a parallel between his deeply paternal view of his young nephew and his more complex feelings about his royal pupil, at least in the necessities of their musical education.[3]

Advice on how to be both an artist and a public benefactor:

> *Your Imperial Highness can . . . create in two ways, both for the happiness and welfare of so many people and also for yourself. For creators of*

music and benefactors of humanity have not hitherto been found in the world of monarchs.

Reminder of Beethoven's stubborn individuality:

The meaning of Your Royal Highness's command that I should come, and again your indication that Your Imperial Highness would let me <u>know when</u> I should do so [Beethoven's underlining] I was quite unable to fathom, for I never was, still am not, and never will be, a courtier.

Pleasure and admiration:

The day on which a High Mass composed by me will be performed during the ceremonies solemnized for Your Imperial Highness will be the most glorious day of my life.[4]

This letter conveys part of the spirit in which this immense Mass was then composed. In an immediate sense it was a tribute to his royal pupil's new stature, the crowning work among those he had already dedicated to him. In a larger sense it offered Beethoven an opportunity to reenter the sphere of liturgical music in the wake of his artistic progress since the Mass in C of 1807. It was also an invitation to make a new contribution to the Mass tradition that he had formerly conceived in relation to the Masses of Haydn and Mozart, especially Haydn, but which he could now reframe against a broader background that included Bach's B Minor Mass, Handel's *Messiah*, and Mozart's Requiem. Further, the Mass project enabled Beethoven to forge an affirmation of his personal religiosity and his broad belief in humanity's relationship to God. Though born a Catholic, Beethoven was not a regular churchgoer, but he had a lifelong leaning to religious experience that took many forms. In the later years his introspective temperament and the many crises of his life had intensified his spiritual awareness and tendency to belief, and if he thought of the Hamlet he had once quoted in a letter about false friends, he could summon faith in a divinity that shapes our ends, rough-hew them as we may. "Oh God, you look down into my innermost soul" he had written in the Heiligenstadt Testament, and similar bursts of religious fervor arise in his letters, in the *Tagebuch*, and in his music, as in the "Holy Song of Thanksgiving" in the Quartet Opus 132 as well as in song texts. Along the way his devotion to Nature and to a pantheistic belief in the presence of God in natural things, shown in his annotations to the writings of Christoph Christian Sturm, betoken a wider horizon, as do his readings in Eastern religious writings, some of which he copied into the *Tagebuch*.[5] We see something of his otherworldly, abstracted demeanor in the Waldmüller portrait made in 1823.

During the same year in which he began work on the *Missa solemnis* he was in touch with the orator and theologian Johann Michael Sailer, a prominent figure in the anti-establishment wing of German Catholicism. Sailer, an ex-Jesuit, spent the years from 1799 to 1821 as teacher in the university at Landshut in Bavaria, going on from there to the important German Catholic post at Regensburg in 1821 where he became bishop in 1829. Rejecting the more orthodox official frameworks of Catholicism, Sailer insisted on the primacy of the individual believer's interior experience of faith and spirituality. He distinguished three forms of religiosity: first, mechanical, literal observance, which he thought was no better than heresy; second, a scholastic mode, that was almost entirely conceptual in nature; and third, a highly personal spirituality, through which alone an individual could approach the inner world of religious feeling and meaning.[6]

As a nineteenth-century commentator on Sailer expressed it,

The basic experience of modern man, since he began to stretch his awareness, beginning in the middle of the century of the Enlightenment and even in Catholic southern Germany, was the conviction that human dignity was incompatible with the [individual's] remaining a passive and mechanical element in the larger traditional scheme of relationships. . . . [W]hat counted was to realize the inalienable right and reasonable duty of personal freedom. A man who is conscious of his own personal worth can only accept as true and as real that part of the traditional body of belief that he has made his own, either through the workings of his own mind or by the most inward feeling [durch innerste Empfindung]. Everything else is dangerous heresy, empty literal orthodoxy.[7]

Beethoven in an 1823 portrait by Ferdinand Georg Waldmüller, who made at least two versions of this portrait. One was destroyed during World War II; the other is evidently in a private collection. (Archiv für Kunst und Geschichte, Berlin)

Such views formed the backbone of the movement that was coming to be known as "Fideism," a trend that stressed the personal and subjective character of religious practice and that, predictably, sustained heavy attacks from the official Austrian Catholic hierarchy. There were other competing post-Enlightenment strains in Austrian religious thought at this time, and other anti-establishment figures. One was Clemens Maria Hofbauer, the head of the so-called Liguorians, a clerical Redemptorist party founded in 1816, and his disciple, the playwright and poet Zacharias Werner, whose extravagant sermons mingled references to sex, religion, and art and attracted wide audiences in Vienna in these years.[8]

But it was Sailer who commanded the respect and admiration of German intellectuals such as the Brentanos, and of Beethoven as well. Sailer admired Beethoven, and Beethoven at one point took preliminary steps to send his nephew Karl to be Sailer's pupil. Though nothing came of that plan, Beethoven's awareness of this new stress on individual experience in German Catholic worship may have helped to motivate the strong expressions of personal devotion that he employed in this abundantly varied mass setting, such as his insertion of the personal exclamations "O" and "Ah" before certain clauses in the Gloria and the lyrical feeling with which he imbues the more personal and less massive portions of the text.

Writing a solemn mass offered Beethoven a way of achieving a summa of his faith, a personal interpretation of the mass Ordinary text that by this time had five centuries of polyphonic music in its traditions, reaching back as far as Beethoven could know to Palestrina and Lassus in the sixteenth century and, in reality, more than a hundred years earlier. Yet his vision is not that of a composer writing an obligatory setting of a traditional text. The Mass in C had been marked by deep repose and avoidance of the operatic. It had turned a page in Beethoven's sacred music toward the newly pious and archaizing sacred styles being espoused by the Romantics.[9] But in grandeur of scale and conception, the Missa solemnis moves far beyond the Mass in C. It is a wide-ranging, intricate composition by a master at the height of his powers, drawing on all the complexities of his late style to construct a monumental work that could be heard in the concert hall as well as in the church. It offered him a chance finally to acknowledge his need "to come to terms with God."[10] It also shows him coming to terms with the visionary spirituality that lay behind the larger choral works of Bach and Handel, an approach that was intertwined with a long-standing interest in studying older music, from which he believed he could increase his ability to represent holiness in music.[11]

Beethoven studied Handel's Messiah and Mozart's Requiem, as we know from copies he made of portions of both works.[12] For his knowledge of the B Minor Mass the evidence is less secure but there are circumstantial reasons to believe that it was available to him.[13] In 1810 he wrote to Breitkopf asking for all the works of Carl Philipp Emanuel Bach that they could supply, and requesting in particular "a Mass by J. S. Bach that has the following Crucifixus with a basso ostinato as obstinate as you are" (here Beethoven quotes the four-measure ostinato from the Crucifixus of Bach's B Minor Mass, which very likely he had seen in a theory treatise).[14] An edition of the B Minor Mass was announced by Nägeli in 1818, and Beethoven asked Nägeli for a copy of it in 1824—but the promised edition failed because there were not enough subscribers and the work was finally published only in 1833.[15] Still, the great work was becoming known. Between 1811 and 1815 Zelter attempted performances of the whole Mass at the Berlin Singakademie, and though these were not public events they must have helped spread the word among musicians of the work's magnitude. Between 1810 and 1819 Beethoven could have had access to copies of the B Minor Mass, as Nägeli had actually owned the autograph since 1805 and a copy could have come from him. There was a copy in Haydn's library in Vienna at his death in 1809, and another was owned by Johann Traeg, one of Beethoven's publishers, from whom we know that Beethoven borrowed a *Messiah* score in 1809.[16] At this time, as Beethoven told Breitkopf, he was holding "a little singing party in my rooms every week."

In 1819, when Beethoven had his portrait painted by Josef Karl Stieler, he was shown in the act of working on the score of the *Missa solemnis*, a clear indication of the importance he attached to the project and the prestige of showing his relation to the archduke and thus also the royal family.[17] In a letter of 1824, when the work was finished, he said of it that "my chief aim when I was composing this grand Mass was to awaken and instil enduring religious feelings not only into the singers but also into the listeners."[18]

In his autograph manuscript, above the opening Kyrie of the Mass, Beethoven placed an inscription—a very unusual thing for him to do—which reads, "From the heart—may it again—go to the heart" (*"Von Herzen—möge es wieder—zu Herzen gehen!"*). It has long been assumed that this inscription is addressed to mankind, that it fits with Beethoven's wish to make the Mass a universal art work. But a close look at the source situation regarding this inscription casts doubt on its universality and suggests another view.[19] The inscription appears on Beethoven's autograph manuscript but not on any of the other early manuscript sources of the work, including the numerous copies made for him as he began to circulate the work to publishers. Above all, the inscription does not appear in the main copy that Beethoven corrected and that also contains some compositional changes in addition to those he made in the autograph. Nor did Beethoven include it in the copy sent to Schott for the engraver. From all this it appears that the inscription carried a more limited, private meaning, and was not explicitly intended for the publicly available text of the Mass.[20] It also turns out that Beethoven tried out the inscription on a sketch leaf while sketching the Gloria. So it seems likely that the intended recipient of the inscription was not the public at large but rather the archduke himself—that Beethoven meant once more to express his personal affection for his royal patron, as he had done in 1811 in the *Lebewohl* Piano Sonata, Opus 81a.[21] Accordingly, it has been plausibly suggested that both the sketches for the Gloria and the inscription over the Kyrie could have been entered while Beethoven was still hoping to finish the work for the archduke's installation in March 1820, but that once that deadline had passed he no longer had it included in later manuscript copies.[22]

In choosing the wording of the inscription, Beethoven may also have consciously or unconsciously remembered a sentence in E. T. A. Hoffmann's review of the Fifth Symphony: "A more profound relationship, however, which cannot be described in such terms [that is, in terms of the formal or thematic unity of a larger work] is often communicated *from the heart to the heart* [italics mine]."[23] Even if the inscription was not intended to appear on the Mass as published, this was clearly a work of special personal importance and its dedication to Rudolph was a sincere gesture to the patron and nobleman Beethoven most admired. He had reasons for calling it "my greatest work," above all for its capacity to engender a spirit of exaltation in ever-widening circles, including worshipers in church congregations, lay audiences in concert halls, and the world of listeners in his own time—all of which has in fact happened since then.

The work exemplifies Beethoven's attempt to unify a mass setting, inevitably less organically than he could unify a large instrumental composition, owing to the disparity in length and type of its movements. He approached the task with great awareness of the special requirements demanded by the declamation of the text and its religious meanings. The musical discourse grows in complexity from beginning to end. The Kyrie, an appeal for God's mercy, is by far the simplest and most direct movement, and it may be that the opening static chords symbolize the unalterable presence of God the Creator.[24] Beginning with the Gloria the material becomes more arcane and ramified, suiting the greater length and complexity of the words. Beethoven sets each clause of text in a way that reflects its rhetorical shape and also represents its symbolic and liturgical meaning, at times making use of traditional musical figures, familiar over the centuries.[25] The vast space established by the Kyrie continues to be exploited in the Gloria, which erupts in its first part in an Allegro vivace choral explosion, then moves through strongly contrasting passages and at last gives way to the slower tempo and delicate brushwork of the Qui tollis, leading eventually to the majestic D-major closing fugue on "in gloria Dei patris, Amen." As if this fugue were not overwhelming in itself, the final measures return to the opening choral statements of "Gloria in excelsis Deo," now marked Presto, ending with the word "Gloria" heroically ringing out from the chorus after the last emphatic orchestral chord.

The Credo, with a text even longer and more complex than the Gloria, receives a comparably massive treatment, with numerous turnings and windings as the words are treated in various ways as doctrinal and suggestive of time-honored musical-rhetorical associations. Beethoven opens the Credo with a great leaping motif reminiscent of the opening of the *Hammerklavier* sonata (we may recall that behind the *Hammerklavier* opening lay the sketched idea "Vivat Rudolphus"!)(*W 49). Then he uses a short motif of four notes, first sounded by the choral basses with the word "Credo, Credo" to connect the disparate and far-flung parts of the Credo. Indicative of Beethoven's ways of binding large-scale structures together is his way of bringing back this motif at two of the crucial important statements of the Creed, at the words "Credo in unum Dominum" and "Credo in spiritum sanctum." Thus this figure serves as a kind of choral motto that unifies the vast movement and also attaches it distantly to predecessors that used similar repetitions in the Credo, such as Haydn's "Saint Cecilia"

Mass.[26] Such insights into the complex unity of the work argue against the view of Theodor Adorno, for whom the *Missa solemnis* is an "alienated masterpiece" whose surface fragmentation is symptomatic of inner conflicts in the work that point to Beethoven's increasing disillusionment with the ideals of the Enlightenment. Adorno's view is a radical reversal of Richard Wagner's. Wagner who saw the Mass as a "strictly symphonic work of the truest Beethovenian spirit," in which "the vocal parts are handled quite in that sense of human instruments that Schopenhauer very rightly wished to see alone assigned to them."[27] In other words, and with modifications of Wagner's view, it is possible to see in the dramatic complexities of this work and its many and varied uses of the orchestra some indications of its status as a symphonic choral work, though one in which all elements of instrumental material and tone color are influenced by its text interpretation. With that difference it is a companion to the Ninth Symphony despite its being, at the same time, a true mass in a tradition going back to Bach and through him to the earlier polyphonic mass tradition.

The Sanctus and Agnus dei hold further treasures. In the Sanctus the traditional question of form turns on the divisions of the text: Sanctus, Pleni, Osanna I, Benedictus, Osanna II. Of the many ways of formally dividing this sequence, which coincides with the most solemn passages of the liturgy—the consecration of the bread and wine as the body and blood of Christ—Beethoven chooses one that yields him maximum space for contrast and elaboration.

Part I: Sanctus (Adagio) + Pleni (Allegro pesante) + Osanna I (Presto); B minor–D major

Part II: Praeludium (Sostenuto ma non troppo); reduced orchestra alone, G major

Part III: Benedictus (Andante molto cantabile); full orchestra with solo violin + Osanna II grafted on; G major

The Praeludium has been aptly associated with a long-established tradition in which the silence during the elevation of the host was filled by an organ in a quiet improvisation.[28] The unusual scoring of this short section, in which we might hear Beethoven imagining his own improvisational practice at this point, is organlike. It has no violins, the flutes and violas double one another in their low registers, and the slowly drifting harmonies create the sense of the unearthly while no singing takes place. Then this "prelude" is retrospectively heard as preparation for the arrival of the solo violin, which occupies the unfilled orchestral high register.

Nothing in Beethoven's orchestral work, not the slow movements of any of his mature quartets or of the violin concerto, surpasses the intimate expressivity of the solo violin passages in the Benedictus, a pure expression of "blessedness."

The final movement is the Agnus dei, set in two large sections:

Agnus dei, qui tollis peccata mundi, miserere nobis; 4/4, B minor
Dona nobis pacem; 6/8 and changing meters and tempos, D major

Since the Benedictus, like a symphonic slow movement, had ended the Sanctus in G major, the Agnus section must reestablish the home tonic, D major. It does that and much more. Its large-scale three-part design is fixed to end each part with the words, "miserere nobis." The Dona nobis section also has an inscription (this one fully intended in all copies): "Prayer for inner and outer peace" (*Bitte um innern und äussern Frieden*). The autograph score contains the words "Dona nobis pacem darstellend den innern und äussern Frieden" ("Dona nobis pacem *presenting* inner and outer peace [my italics]"). Beethoven clearly thought of this movement as a frankly programmatic depiction, a full expression of the yearning for personal tranquility and for peace on earth. These ideas are symbolized by two sets of orchestral forces: one in D major, the other (the "military" component) in B-flat major (foreshadowing his contrast of just these keys for antagonistic and reconciling forces in the Ninth Symphony). Inserted into a large-scale variant of sonata form is the first "war" interlude, whose obsessive tympani on F presages a development of the opening theme, which then, after a second warlike passage, leads on to a massive recapitulation and to a lengthy coda that restores the tonic D and rounds out the movement and the whole vast structure in peace. Beethoven's depiction of "outer" war and peace reflects the capacity of the work to refer to the collective battles and struggles through which his generation had labored; it can also refer to the collective struggles that threaten and destroy peace in every age. (The *Lebewohl* Sonata had been written for the same archduke in the wake of the fearful bombardment of Vienna in 1809.) Peace here would be the *pax humana*, the condition of life unblemished by war.

But "inner" in the heading signifies a deeper, personal plea for peace; it refers to the peace of the soul, his own and that of every human being. It reflects his awareness of psychic turmoil in his own life, of the individual's struggle for equilibrium and tranquility; and it reflects the individual who lives in search of respite from the harsh contingencies of existence and the fear of death. For Beethoven, this therapeutic goal seemed to be unattainable in the circumstances of life outside of art, but he could represent it in an artwork of the spiritual magnitude of this one, itself a surrogate for the "one day of pure joy" he had yearned for in the Heiligenstadt Testament. The Mass is thus not only his largest contribution to the expression of the spiritual, in the various senses of the term, it is also a symbolic representation of humanity's search for peace that can only be discovered through religious feeling, collectively and personally. From here it is only one more step to his next great work, the Ninth Symphony. In setting selected stanzas of Schiller's "Ode to Joy," the composer chose texts that would stress, first, the human brotherhood entering into the realm of holiness in search of joy, then the voice of the composer (as before him the poet) who passionately throws his arms around the multitudes and urges them to look upward: "Brothers, above the starry tent of heaven, a beloved Father must dwell."

The Ninth Symphony

In 1998 at the Winter Olympics in Nagano, Japan, Seiji Ozawa appeared in what may have been the largest electronic simulation of a concert hall ever imagined. He conducted six choirs that were located in New York, Berlin, Cape Town, Sydney, Beijing, and Nagano (six cities on five continents) in a televised simulcast in which all of them sang the "Ode to Joy," the principal theme of the finale of the Ninth Symphony, electronically synchronized to overcome time differences. Remarkable as this achievement was, it had a background.

The "Ode" has been sung at every Olympic Games since 1956. By the 1990s it had become a common practice in Japan for massed choral groups and orchestras to come together in December of each year to give performances of *Daiku*—"The Big Nine."[29]

The newly achieved world status of the "Ode to Joy" melody is only one of the most visible ways in which the Beethoven legend that was created in the nineteenth century has been reshaped and enlarged many times over in the twentieth. The very name Beethoven has attained cult status beyond that of almost any other classical composer; the cult has spread through many levels of high, middle, and popular culture in music, art, television, and film. The Beethoven image, now all too commercially viable, is itself the subject of a sizable literature. And no work has been more fertile in creating and maintaining this image than the Ninth Symphony.

In the mind of the general public there are actually two "Ninth Symphonies." One is the "Ode to Joy" itself, as choral anthem; that is, just the melody, not the elaborate and complex movement from which it comes. The other is the symphony as a complete work, a large-scale four-movement cycle in which the enormous finale brings solo and choral voices into the symphonic genre for the first time. Seen as a whole, the movement plan of the work forms a progressive sequence in which the three earlier movements balance each other but also prepare the finale and give it much of its structural and aesthetic meaning. Beethoven's setting of the first strophe of Schiller's poem, beginning "Freude, schöner Götterfunken" ("Joy, beautiful spark of divinity"), is the admitted centerpiece of its finale, but it is matched in significance by a second, contrasting section in a radically different style that sets the first chorus of the "Ode," "Seid umschlungen, Millionen" ("Be embraced, you millions"). The theme and text of "Freude, schöner Götterfunken" is eventually combined contrapuntally with that of "Seid umschlungen, Millionen" to form the great climax of the movement. The "Seid umschlungen" theme has no chance whatever of being selected as a singable anthem by amateur choral groups because it is melodically difficult and harmonically obscure, and is of a totally different type and character. In other words, it is an important feature of the modern history of the Ninth Symphony that at popular levels it is barely known as a symphony at all but is represented only by its most famous melody.[30]

The Political Background of the Ninth

With the collapse of the Napoleonic empire and the return of the monarchies to power, retrenchment and repression closed in on Europe.[31] The Congress of Vienna in 1814–15 was attended by the political movers and shakers from all the major powers, including France. From England came Castlereagh and Wellington; from Prussia, Hardenberg and Humboldt; from France, Talleyrand; from Russia, Czar Alexander I. Their Austrian host was the brilliant manipulator Prince Clemens von Metternich, chancellor of Austria and effective ruler of the country and its empire. The delegates carved out a European settlement that imposed a new conservative order on Continental politics, earnestly and quixotically doing all they could to return Europe not only to its pre-Napoleonic status but to the way it had been before 1789, setting up a system that lasted for most of the nineteenth century. Austria and Prussia, the two major German powers, were unable to form a nation that would embody *Grossdeutschland* (that would have to await Bismarck and eventually Hitler), but Prussia gained new territories in the Rhineland and Westphalia as well as in the east, while Austria regained control of Lombardy and the Veneto in northern Italy. The smaller German territories remained a patchwork of some thirty-nine states that were loosely bound together in the so-called German Confederation but were dominated by Vienna and Berlin; actually there were now far fewer minor German states than there had been before 1806, when Napoleon had consolidated most of the German territories, except Austria and Prussia, into his Confederation of the Rhine. Beginning in 1815 and lasting down to the revolutions of 1848, stretched out what later came to be called the "Vormärz" period (literally the period "before March" 1848), essentially an era of political stagnation.

In France the Bourbons got back the government but found that the country's social and political mentality had been totally transformed several times over since the Revolution and that they could not turn back the clock. The victorious powers saw to it that France, as the earlier cockpit of revolution and Continental invasion, would now be surrounded by a newly enlarged Holland, by the newly Prussian-dominated Rhineland, by other German states, and by Austrian-ruled northern Italy. Poland, which Napoleon had rescued temporarily as the grand duchy of Warsaw, was once more swept under Russian control. Spain and Portugal, which were losing their Latin American colonies to revolution, were restored to their royal families.

The leaders of the aristocratic restoration did all they could to repress the patriotic nationalist movements that were burgeoning in every country, especially movements led by students and workers that were sowing the seeds for the uprisings of 1848. In Germany student groups led the fight, inspired by the teachings of the chauvinist Ludwig ("Father") Jahn and by the preaching and writing of Johann Gottlob Fichte and Ernst Moritz Arndt. These spokesmen called upon Germans to convert their sense of cultural identity into political unity, not without mystical overtones of the glorification of the German *Volk*.[32] Some major German artists and thinkers, including Goethe and Hegel, had been sympathetic to Napoleon and thought that he had represented a force for unity and progress, but the fervor of the nationalist movements, beginning in 1806 with the formal end of the Holy Roman empire, soon swept such moderate views aside.[33] All this was also taking place against the background of the oncoming Industrial Revolution, which was irreversibly changing the economic conditions of life, transforming the means of production from agrarian to industrial, moving workers from farms and little workshops to factories and production lines, reshaping the traditional social order and its established values, and intensifying social inequalities, as Karl Marx later explained to the world. European culture was moving into a new phase dominated by the entrenched bourgeoisie, typified in Germany and Austria by the epithet "Biedermeier," applied retroactively when the period was named for a fictional character named Gottlob Biedermeier, who was invented at mid-century by the satirist Ludwig Eichrodt. "Biedermeier" culture, effectively emerging around 1815, reflected the middle-class world of

German society: economically comfortable, politically conservative, and interested in art primarily as cultivated entertainment. In music this meant having a piano at home in the parlor, and playing and singing familiar works of the past—both easy works written for amateur enjoyment and performable arrangements of more difficult music. Though many of Beethoven's works were beyond the reach of such amateurs, his easier sonatas and trifles could be included alongside readily playable and singable compositions by his younger contemporaries, whether operatic numbers, works by Schubert, Mendelssohn, or lesser fabricators of this type of music. The great changes that were taking place in society, increasingly stratified into highbrow and lowbrow in the age of rising industrial capitalism, were manifestly reflected in contemporary literature, above all in writings that directly centered on social concerns, but also in painting and music.

Across Europe liberals bitterly opposed the resurgence of harshly conservative governments and gave allegiance to national movements fighting for liberation. Byron's passionate attachment to the nationalist movements in Greece and Italy, from 1816 to his death in 1824, epitomized the hopes of many sympathizers.[34] In Britain economic misery brought on mass demonstrations in the years after Napoleon's downfall, and in 1819 a crisis erupted with the Peterloo massacre of working-class demonstrators. Enraged by the violence of Peterloo, Shelley wrote "The Mask of Anarchy," a long poem of protest. Politics and the fate of individuals dealing with the inequities of life in newly modernizing societies were coming to form the central themes of playwrights and novelists, from Victor Hugo to Honoré de Balzac, Charles Dickens, and Nikolai Gogol.[35] As early as 1820 there were uprisings in Naples against the Bourbons and in Piedmont against Austria. The year 1830 saw the division of the Netherlands into a newly formed Holland, to which its former Austrian lands had been restored, along with a newly created Belgium, half French, half Flemish. And in the July revolution of that year, Parisian radicals went to the barricades in an attempt to bring down the regime of Charles X. Though the revolution failed, it set the pattern for 1848.

Austria under Metternich, who endured as chief minister from 1809 to 1848, became the leading model of repression. To him as Austrian chancellor all nationalist movements were anathema. In 1819 he called a meeting of the principal states of the German Confederation and passed the reactionary "Karlsbad Decrees," which set up regulatory commissions at all universities to try to hold the radical students in check, to spy on faculty members considered subversive, and to suppress political societies. The decrees even set up a system of censorship, by which any published material longer than twenty pages had to be submitted to the censors for approval. Many German liberals fled into exile.

In 1815, during the Congress of Vienna, perpetual spying was the order of the day, and police informers were everywhere. Artists such as Beethoven who were known for their republican views were suspect, and the Conversation Books reflect the atmosphere of suspicion that ruled the city. An 1820 entry that was probably made in a cafe says, "another time—just now the spy Haensl is here."[36] This situation, combined with Austria's difficult economic recovery, Beethoven's personal financial reverses, and the disappearance or death of many of his traditional aristocratic supporters, fueled his habitual anxiety. When Dr. Karl von Bursy, recommended by his old friend Amenda, visited him in June 1816, Beethoven ranted loudly about the state of things in Vienna:

> [V]enom and rancor raged in him. He defies everything and is dissatisfied with everything, blaspheming against Austria and especially Vienna. . . . Everyone is a scoundrel. There is nobody one can trust. What is not down in black and white is not observed by anyone, not even by the man with whom you have made an agreement.[37]

In a Conversation Book of 1820, Schindler wrote (in a passage not regarded as a later addition):[38]

> Before the French Revolution there was great freedom of thought and politics. The revolution made the government and the nobility distrust the common people, which has led to the current repression. . . . The regimes, as they are now constituted, are not in tune with the needs of the time; eventually they will have to change or become more easy-going, that is, become a little different.[39]

It is against such a background that we can take the measure of Beethoven's decision in 1821–24 to return to his old idea of setting Schiller's "Ode to Joy" and to present it, not as a solo song to be heard in the private salons of music lovers but as an anthem that could be performed on the grandest possible scale in the concert hall, the most public of settings. His further plan, to make that melody the climax of a great symphony, distantly recalls Haydn's use of his famous patriotic hymn, "Gott erhalte Franz den Kaiser," as a slow movement with variations in his C Major Quartet Opus 76 No. 3, composed in 1797 just a few months after he had written the anthem itself. Beethoven, in this new symphony that would have Schiller's "Ode" as centerpiece, meant to leave to posterity a public monument of his liberal beliefs. His decision to fashion a great work that would convey the poet's utopian vision of human brotherhood is a statement of support for the principles of democracy at a time when direct political action on behalf of such principles was difficult and dangerous. It enabled him to realize in his way what Shelley meant when he called poets the "unacknowledged legislators of the world."[40]

Changing Views of the Ninth

The Ninth Symphony, of all Beethoven's works, has had the broadest impact and the widest range of interpretations. From Beethoven's time to ours, generations of commentators, musicians, artists, and critics have stepped forward to give voice to their interpretations, many of them focusing only on the "Ode" rather than on the symphony as a whole. Very few have explored what may seem to some critics in our time the historicizing and anachronistic question of what it was, or could have been, that Beethoven himself intended this work to mean and to express.

The interpretive trend began effectively with Wagner, whose entire career was conditioned by his fascination with the Ninth: in his early years he copied the entire score, arranged it for piano, performed it many times, rescored some passages, and claimed it as the starting point of his lifetime aesthetic mission to equal and surpass Beethoven by reshaping opera along symphonic lines into music-drama. As Beethoven transformed the symphony and spoke to the world by combining instrumental music with words, Wagner would reshape culture, especially German culture, by means of music-drama based on national myths.

In *My Life*, Wagner writes that he was impelled by the "mystical influence of Beethoven's Ninth Symphony to plumb the deepest recesses of music."[41] On another front, every German composer of symphonies after Beethoven, from Mendelssohn and Schumann to Brahms, Bruckner, and Mahler, understood that the Ninth had come to be a central bulwark of musical experience that each would have to confront in carving out a personal path as a symphonist. In fact each composer also confronted the Ninth in individual works, whether by the choice of key or scale, by the use of solo and choral voices, or by thematic content. Schumann, for example, who worshipped Beethoven like a god, quotes Karl Voigt, the husband of Schumann's friend Henriette Voigt and portrayed by Schumann as an enthusiastic common listener, as saying about the Ninth as a monumental experience, "I am the blind man who is standing before the Strasbourg Cathedral, who hears its bells but cannot see the entrance."[42]

Worship of Beethoven, above all the symphonies, was rampant in the more conservative nineteenth-century centers of American musical culture. The Ninth, which had received its first London performance in 1825, was given its American premiere in New York in 1846 by the recently founded New York Philharmonic Society. In Boston, Brahmins and transcendentalists alike acclaimed Beethoven as a godlike figure (said Margaret Fuller, "the mind is large that can contain a Beethoven"). A major purpose in founding the Boston Symphony Orchestra in the 1880s, in addition to rivaling New York, was to make possible the performance of Beethoven's symphonies, with the Ninth as the capstone of the great tradition.[43] Though other Western musical traditions, especially in the earlier twentieth century, were less enthralled with the Beethoven symphonies, especially the Ninth, as these works receded further into the past, still the power of mass media and the message of brotherhood in the finale continued to make the Ninth a natural symbol at great political events celebrating freedom, as at the concert led by Leonard Bernstein on December 25, 1989, celebrating the tearing down of the infamous Berlin Wall. At this concert Bernstein substituted the word "Freiheit" ("freedom") for Schiller's "Freude" ("joy").

As an example of the way in which the Ninth has been used by political regimes of every stripe, including the most loathsome, consider the Nazis between 1933 and 1945. After making certain that Beethoven himself had no suspicious racial or national tinge of the non-Germanic in his background (the clear evidence of his Flemish ancestry was denied in a series of articles), the masters of the Nazi propaganda and cultural machinery promoted his works, especially his more powerful and public ones, as the essence of Germanic and Aryan strength. To quote a passage from an article by a Nazi "race expert":

> Nordic are, above all, the heroic aspects of his works, which often rise to titanic greatness. It is significant that today, in a time of national renovation, Beethoven's works are played more often than any others, that one hears his works at almost all events of heroic tenor.[44]

Among others in Germany who knew better but shamelessly sold out to the Nazi regime was the musicologist Arnold Schering, who in 1934 associated Beethoven with Hitler as a "Führer-type."[45] It was easy enough for musical propagandists to harness the Third and Fifth Symphonies as emblems of the Third Reich, but the Ninth at first gave them some trouble, since its message of human brotherhood could hardly be squared with the doctrine of Aryan racial superiority. The Nazi-tainted musicologist Hans Joachim Moser figured out that Schiller's and Beethoven's "kiss to the whole world" could not really mean "every Tom, Dick, and Harry, as it was too often misunderstood back in Germany's red years," but must refer to "the simple idea of a humanity conceived in as German a way as possible."[46] With foresight that now seems ironic, the "Ode to Joy" was performed in 1936 at the Olympics in Berlin and was announced not as a symbol of international brotherhood but as a "proclamation of the Nazi *Volksgemeinschaft* ["people's culture"]."[47] With equal prudence, the Ninth was performed frequently at concerts in Germany but was kept out of concerts for those living in occupied territories, especially in Eastern Europe, obviously to prevent their getting its message.[48] In April 1942 Wilhelm Furtwängler conducted the Ninth at a celebration for Hitler's birthday.[49]

More recently, as other intellectual and social ideologies have competed for domination, the Ninth has been reinterpreted in other ways. Adorno regarded its optimism as awkward and old-fashioned, out of phase with the inwardness of Beethoven's other late works, above all the last quartets, owing to the naked directness of its finale and its obvious bid for popular acceptance. Since the late quartets, more than any other Beethoven works, stood as essential objects of artistic value for Adorno—above all the late quartets as mediated through their importance to the music of Arnold Schoenberg—it is not surprising that the Ninth Symphony disappointed him. Although in certain of his writings Adorno had sensitive things to say about the first movement and slow movement, he was blind to the ways in which the Ninth brought aspects of Beethoven's earlier symphonic style forward into his late period, and so for him the Ninth (by which he really means the finale above all) "falls outside the late style altogether."[50]

On another front, and with great éclat, a feminist critic has denounced the first movement as an example of "horrifyingly violent" masculine rage, and a feminist poet reviled the entire work as a "sexual message" written by a man "in terror of impotence or infertility, not knowing the difference."[51] The list of political interpretations is long and will inevitably lengthen in time. One critic, running a substantial risk in using encomia, wrote that a "great work such as the Ninth Symphony cannot be protected from those who would abuse its immense power."[52] In fact, against the strong, totally committed forms of ideological interpretation in the current phase of ascendant "cultural studies," in which modern political and social content is read into every work of art or literature, there is no recourse or final court of appeal; to a convinced ideologue, objections are simply the product of an opposed ideology and cannot possess any special claim to "truth," a word that can now be used in some critical circles only with quotation marks.

Accordingly, those looking for ground to stand on outside ideology may be able to do so only by recommitting themselves to analysis, which concerns itself exclusively with the structural, or recommitting to history, that is, to understanding the Ninth not as a disembodied art product out of time and space, but as the work of an artist living in a particular period and context, who carried out a project that had personal meanings that we can reconstruct from the accumulated debris that has covered his tracks since then. Our job would then be not only to try to understand the work in the context of its origins but to make that understanding, as nearly as possible and with minimal distortion and loss of content, meaningful in the present. This is the essential direction of this discussion, offered with the hope that by perceiving what Beethoven wanted us to understand, as an engaged artist caught up in the conflicts of his own time, we can gain a little respite from the regressive cycles of strong ideological claims and counterclaims, covering our ears as best we can to the howls from outside telling us that we are simply different kinds of ideologues. It is not that the potential meanings of such a work are remotely exhausted by those we can uncover in its origins; it is, rather, that some knowledge of its origins can help inform and solidify a broad range of other hypotheses and viewpoints that can otherwise lapse into postmodern solipsism.

Among recent interpretations that do exhibit interest in the historical context of the work is one that sees the Ninth in the context of "political Romanticism," a term that refers to a putative synthesis of Schillerian optimism about humanity's aspirations to freedom and joy, and to the post-Enlightenment Romantic aesthetics of writers such as E. T. A. Hoffmann.[53] This view perceives a steady progression through several of Beethoven's major works, which are seen first and foremost as vehicles of political philosophical thought, emerging in the *Eroica* as a musical translation of the "*universal history*," that is, the idea of the "education . . . of humanity from an instinctual harmony with nature to a state of rational, civilized, freedom."[54] Since *Prometheus* was manifestly devoted to showing the triumph of education and civilization over the state of nature, the parallel fits to some degree. Certainly it is plausible that in the *Eroica* "we behold the fiercest rays of the French Revolution refracted through the cooling ether of German idealism."[55] The progression is not presented as a steady one, in which the Ninth was simply the end product of a consecutive series of enlightened statements about human progress and brotherhood. Quite the contrary: by the time of the Ninth, the manifest abandonment of Enlightenment ideals by all post-1789 regimes from the 1790s to the 1820s—first the Terror and its adversaries, then Napoleon and his adversaries, then the newly victorious autocratic governments—led to political stasis and retrenchment. The light had failed.

But the situation was more drastic than this viewpoint proposes. The Ninth, in my view, was written to revive a lost idealism. It was a strong political statement made at a time when the practical possibilities of realizing Schiller's ideals of universal brotherhood had been virtually extinguished by the post-Napoleonic regimes. Beethoven's decision to complete the work was thus intended to right the balance, to send a message of hope to the future, and to proclaim that message to the world.

Another aspect of the Ninth in its creative context has nearly been lost sight of in most modern discussions—its religious dimension. Schiller's poem emulates one type of classical ode form in its alternation of stanza and chorus (strophe and refrain), the two dividing between them the two forms of imagery that dominate the poem: one portraying a circle of friends praising Joy as a spiritual and moral condition, a kind of Bacchic celebration; the other widening the poet's outreach in the choruses to embrace all humanity, which aspires through human Joy to reach God, who dwells above the stars. Thus, as we saw earlier, the first stanza is uttered by a communal group (it speaks of "we"), while the first chorus implies a personal "I" who reaches out at once to embrace the millions, and urges on his "brothers" the unseen presence of God "above the starry tent." This theme is even stronger in chorus 3, in which the poet-composer's individual voice asks, "Do you prostrate yourselves, you millions? Do you sense the Creator, World?" The stanzas and choruses of the "Ode" work out aspects of these images along somewhat separate lines (though not with an absolutely clear division) and gradually intertwine and strive to unite them. As Schiller said in a commentary about the poem, "Let us be conscious of a higher ideal unity and by means of brotherhood we will attain to this state. . . . Joy is beautiful because it provides harmony; it is 'god-descended' because all harmony is derived from the Master of Worlds and flows back to him."

From the "Ode" Beethoven selects primarily stanzas 1–3 and choruses 1 and 3, with chorus 4 used also in the tenor solo in B-flat that furnishes contrast in the extensive first part of the finale. Thus the stanzas emphasize the first image, that of the communal circle singing in praise of Joy, while the second image, with its references to God the Creator, who dwells above the stars, belongs to the choruses. Accordingly there are two basic topics in the text—secular and religious—and Beethoven's choice of poetic material shows him laying stress on the balance between the two. The secular image is the subject of Part 1 of the finale; the religious one is the subject of Part 2. The point of Part 3 is to unite the two worlds of feeling, the communal and the religious, by combining the two disparate themes in a double fugue that brings together both their melodies and their texts, progressing from this climactic point to the end of the work in a powerful synthesis.

One of the few to understand this basic progression of ideas was Tovey, who saw "the central thought of the Ninth Symphony, . . . [which] also underlies his treatment of the Gloria, Credo, and Sanctus of the *Missa solemnis* 1) the divine glory; 2) always in direct contrast, the awe-struck prostration of mankind; 3) the human divinity of Christ."[56] In the *Missa solemnis*, with its fixed liturgical text, Beethoven had gone far in giving personal feeling and perception to his interpretation of the text; in the symphony, which stems from a secular poem celebrating joy, communality, and political freedom, Beethoven goes to some lengths to bring the religious message of the poem into view, first as contrast, then as part of the great synthesis in which humanity's ideal state can be found only by reaching toward the heavens to find God. Similarly, Solomon captures the essence of this perception when he writes, "Together they [the *Missa solemnis* and the Ninth Symphony] exemplify Beethoven's desire to hold both religious and secular-humanist ideas in one hand."[57] At this point we should remember that the Mass reflected much of the personal feeling for sacred experience that Beethoven could find in current reformist religious doctrines, notably those of Sailer, while secular experience has primacy in the Ninth Symphony. Here the religious dimension is drawn from Schiller's secular "Ode" and given prominence. Thus the two works gain virtually parallel status.

We must remember that the Ninth Symphony was not an occasional work like the *Missa solemnis*. If Archduke Rudolph had not been made archbishop of Olmütz, the Mass might never have been written. But as for a symphony, Beethoven had been looking for a reason and opportunity to compose a ninth as early as 1813. As a musical venture, the work looks like a confluence of two ambitions: one was to write a new symphony in D minor, in his late style, worthy of standing up to his earlier ones; the other was to create a cantatalike setting of Schiller's "Ode." The two goals finally coalesced in 1823, when Beethoven set to work intensively on the project.[58]

Composing the Ninth

Although Beethoven's compositional work on the Ninth took place in stages between 1818 and 1824, becoming his main preoccupation in 1823 once the *Missa solemnis* was finished, in some ways it has a much longer prehistory—indeed, the longest of any of his works. Beethoven's idea of setting Schiller's poem to music is mentioned by a Bonn acquaintance as early as 1793; five years later, Beethoven jotted down a sketch for the words "Muss ein lieber Vater wohnen" ("A dear Father must reside") from the first chorus of the "Ode." His *Choral Fantasy* of 1808 anticipates the Ninth finale in combining chorus and orchestra in a set of variations that culminate in a plain melody on an uplifting and benign text on "Fried und Freude" ("peace and joy"). In 1824 Beethoven himself said that the Ninth's finale was "in the style of my fantasia for piano with chorus but on a far grander scale, with vocal solos and choruses based on the words of Schiller's immortal and famous song *An die Freude*."[59] At the time of the Eighth Symphony, in 1812, we find a brief setting of the opening words of the poem as Beethoven began to think about the possibility of a D-minor symphony to follow the Seventh and Eighth; had he carried out this idea, the three symphonies would have formed a trilogy with one work in minor, like the quartets of Opus 59 (and at long range, like Mozart's last three symphonies).[60] Three years later he jotted down a verbal description for a symphony that would open "with only four voices at the beginning . . . [and] if possible bring in all the instruments gradually one by one," anticipating the gradual entrance of instruments at the beginning of the Ninth, probably before he had fixed on its pitch content.[61] In the same sketchbook we find the idea in D minor that eventually became the main theme of the Scherzo.

In 1818, after completing the *Hammerklavier* Sonata, Beethoven began to sketch a D-minor symphony, getting some material down for the first movement and adding some speculative jottings for the other three.[62] Some of these ideas lasted through to the final version, though at this time the finale was to be purely instrumental. He also considered the idea of a symphony "in the old modes," with voices entering in one or more movements. The vision of a second symphony in 1818 is prophetic:

> *Adagio Cantique—A Pious Song in a symphony in the old modes—Lord God we praise thee—Hallelujah—either by itself alone or as an introduction to a fugue. Perhaps the whole second symphony could be characterized in this way, where the voices enter either in the last movement or already in the Adagio. The orchestral violins will be increased tenfold in the Finale. Or the Adagio will in some way be repeated in the last movement and then the singing voices will enter one after the other . . . in the Adagio the text of a Greek myth, a Cantique ecclesiastique—in the Allegro, a celebration of Bacchus.*[63]

This description is rich in implications, among them the stress on the religious dimension, the inclusion of voices in one or more movements, the increased sonority of the last movement, and the repetition of the slow movement in the finale, inevitably suggesting the Fifth Symphony—and, above all, the fleeting notion of invoking a Greek myth by means of a religious song and a Bacchic celebration.

No second symphony ever got off the ground, but in 1821–23 he went back to work on the D-minor project while still putting the finishing touches on the Mass and the "Diabelli" Variations. The first movement came first; then the others grew slowly, in order, between the spring of 1823 and the end of the year, some of the work being done during Beethoven's summer retreats in Hetzendorf and Baden and the rest after his return to Vienna in October. The shaping of the finale in definitive form took extensive labor before the melody was achieved, and the different versions that Beethoven tried out in his sketch pages show the many stages of work he needed to arrive at the principal melody, which seems in its final form to be such a paragon of melodic simplicity.[64]

The great work was ready for its premiere performance—a much-anticipated event in Vienna—on May 9, 1824, along with the overture *The Consecration of the House* and three movements of the *Missa solemnis*. This was the famous concert at which, with the audience cheering, the deaf Beethoven had to be turned around to see them.

Other events spurred him to complete the symphony. In the summer of 1817 the Royal Philharmonic Society, then only a few years old, asked Ferdinand Ries to negotiate with Beethoven for two "new symphonies to remain the property of the Society," for a fee of three hundred guineas. They invited Beethoven to come to London in the winter of 1818 for the expected premieres of these works during the society's season, which ran from February to June.[65] In a warm-hearted letter, Ries proposed the commission with an advance of a hundred guineas, trying to attract Beethoven with the prospect of other engagements in England. To all this Beethoven replied in his most enthusiastic bargaining mode, accepting in principle but asking for a higher fee and a larger advance; but his request failed to move the society, and the plan collapsed. Beethoven came back to it in a letter to Ries in July 1822, and in November 1822 the society renewed its proposal, now offering him fifty pounds for a "manuscript symphony" which they would keep as their property for eighteen months, after which he would be free to have it performed by other orchestras and published.

On December 20 Beethoven accepted the commission, "even though the fee . . . cannot be compared with the fees paid by other countries . . . yet I would compose even without a fee for the leading European artists, if I were not that poor Beethoven. For, thank God, Beethoven can compose—even if he can't do anything else in this world."[66] And he spoke of other commissions from European countries and from North America, which, if only his health would enable him to fulfill them, "might yet make a success of my life."[67] In July 1823 he wrote to the archduke that he hoped to finish the symphony in "less than a fortnight;" in fact it was not ready before February 1824, and Beethoven delivered a copy to the Philharmonic Society through an emissary with a note saying that he had composed it for them. It took months to actually reach the Society, and in December 1824 Charles Neate, an English musician who had come to know Beethoven in Vienna in 1815, wrote to acknowledge its arrival and renew the idea of a visit to England. By that time, of course, the Ninth had been premiered in Vienna. When it was published by Schott in August 1826 it bore a dedication to King Friedrich Wilhelm of Prussia, a choice that emerged after consideration of other royal dedicatees, including those of France and Russia.[68] Beethoven sent the king a handsome copy with an elaborate dedication. In recognition he received what looked like a diamond ring. Unfortunately a court jeweler reported that the diamond was false, and Beethoven's friends had a hard time persuading him not to send it back.[69] His lifelong dependency on aristocratic patrons had taken another bad turn.

The Character of the Ninth

T he choice of key for the Ninth Symphony is telling. D minor had been the key of the slow movements of two early piano sonatas, of an early quartet, and of the Largo of the "Ghost" Trio Opus 70 No. 1. But the only other full-scale Beethoven work in D minor, surprisingly, is Sonata Opus 31 No. 2, the "Tempest." Associated with despair and especially with turbulence, D minor had been a powerful key for Mozart (which might have had something to do with Beethoven's hesitation in using it). Witness its role in late Mozart alone as the key of Electra's aria in *Idomeneo*, as the primary key of *Don Giovanni*, of the String Quartet K. 421, the Piano Concerto K. 466, and the Requiem, which, as we saw, Beethoven had been studying while working on the Credo of the *Missa solemnis*.[70] Years earlier he had copied out lengthy excerpts from *Don Giovanni*, of all Mozart's D-minor works the one whose demonic power most nearly anticipates the first movement of the Ninth. The portentous opening of the *Don Giovanni* overture, with its restless syncopated opening chords over steady half notes, with its falling fourth from D to A, with its opening focus on the tonic D minor and on the dominant A minor with a C♯ in the bass, all leading to chromaticism and to E-flat minor—all these factors distantly foreshadow the expressive world brought forth by the first movement of the Ninth.

First Movement

Mozart's way of connecting the opening of the overture with the eventual climax of the opera—when the commendatore's statue arrives as the agent of retribution for Don Giovanni's crimes—lies somewhere behind the first movement of the Ninth, with its mysterious opening in open fifths (we hear only A and E, raising the question of whether the key will be major or minor), its gradual creation of a powerful theme from motivic hints, the domination of the movement by the fully created theme and its fragments, the tremendous unfolding of tragic events, and above all the colossal return of the introduction in altered form at the recapitulation. That the movement ends with a short powerful single statement of its opening D-minor theme could also connect with Mozart's ending of the tragic portion of his finale, when Don Giovanni goes down to hell, with the descending D-A interval that has permeated the work from the very beginning.

The only earlier Beethoven symphonic first movement that even partly adumbrates the dramatization of musical space and time that Beethoven achieves here is that of the Fifth Symphony, which is also his only earlier minor-mode symphonic first movement. But in the Ninth, instead of a shattering opening gesture with a single short motif, Beethoven gradually creates the opening theme, with its clear-cut rhythmic elements, before the listener's very ears. He brings the material gradually into being by passing from silence to the vast filling of the sonorous space and with the time spans of the entrances of the instruments calibrated in such a way as to arouse what has been called "an awareness of the eternal."[71]

After the opening sixteen measures—we hardly know if the opening is an "introduction" or an integral part of the movement—the first theme erupts with chthonic force, the most powerful of all descending triadic themes in Beethoven's music (*W 50). Not only the accelerating descent through the D-minor triad (D–A–F–D) but the great leap up a tenth for its last motivic unit marks this as a true late-Beethoven theme, from which all hints of simple periodicity have disappeared. He had written many primarily triadic opening themes but none like this one, which would have been inconceivable in early works or even in the most forceful thematic statements of his second maturity, such as the opening of the F Minor Quartet, Opus 95. The shape of the tail-end motif of the theme emphasizes the scale steps 5–4–2—the same downward turn, outlining a dominant seventh harmony, that we hear in the Cello Sonata Opus 102 No. 1 as the phrase ending of the first theme and in the first phrase of the A Major Piano Sonata Opus 101. But here the downward turn is the main stem of the culminating figure that will bring about the close of this theme and ultimately the close of the movement.

The basic forms of discourse in the music are extremely complex as the movement develops from its otherworldly opening through the narrative of its exposition, presenting twisting labyrinths of thematic ideas. The main subject is stated twice, first in the tonic D minor, then in its primary contrasting key, B-flat major—and the key remains B-flat to the end of the exposition, where for the first time in a Beethoven symphonic first movement exposition, there is no repeat sign. Instead the movement proceeds into a large development section that, typically for Beethoven's heroic symphonies, has room for a fugato, this time on several subjects, one of them a variant form of the opening theme's motivic ending. And all this eventually leads to the recapitulation by way of still another return of the "introduction" but now fortissimo for full orchestra, tympani rolling, in D major but with an F sharp in the cellos and basses, a moment that has occasioned amazed and sometimes amazing reactions from its time to ours. For Tovey, writing in 1935, this

> catastrophic return reveals fresh evidence of the gigantic size of the opening. Now we are brought into the midst of it and instead of a distant nebula we see the heavens on fire. There is something very terrible about this triumphant major tonic.[72]

For Leo Treitler, writing in 1989,

> [the] moment of reprise constitutes a correction of the development, but an escalation, not merely a restoration, of the tone of the exposition. . . . [I]t is the antithesis of what that moment had been in the convention of the genre—a moment of arrival and resolution.[73]

And after working carefully through the "rapidity of tonal action" in this extraordinary passage, Treitler sees the "moment of recapitulation as the high point of dramatic conflict and tension."

Tovey's metaphor of stars and nebulas is reminiscent of Beethoven's Kantian "starry heaven above us." Though Tovey disdained the biographical and liked to use celestial metaphors of planets and stars to convey the vast spatial aspects of great tonal music, he would probably have accepted that there could be a connection. As to Treitler's portrayal, it effectively characterizes Beethoven's ways of dramatizing formal, emotional, and structural elements in the work, in this case the reversal of expectations in the formal and emotional character of the recapitulation compared with the memory of the movement's opening. Treitler also allows that the opening of the movement, which is neither clearly an "introduction" nor clearly a "theme," receives in this gigantic climax a transformation that serves to "make the moment of recapitulation the high point of dramatic conflict and tension, rather than the moment of release."[74] The recapitulation, if anything, intensifies the ambiguities that had been raised earlier at the opening of the movement and in its later reassertions.

Second Movement

Looking at the larger shape of the whole work as it unfolds in relation to the first movement, we find that Beethoven has placed the Scherzo second, not third, as he did in a few other larger works in which he wanted an unusually expansive slow movement. He used this order in big works such as the Quartet Opus 59 No. 1; the "Archduke" Trio, Opus 97; and the *Hammerklavier* Sonata (we may remember Beethoven's seeming ambivalence about the order of the movements for his English edition). He also used this order in works where the four-movement cycle is ambiguous because the slow movement serves as an introduction to the finale and is itself incomplete—examples are the A Major Cello Sonata, Opus 69, and the A-flat Major Piano Sonata, Opus 110. The Ninth Symphony layout belongs to the first category, but this scherzo dwarfs all of them in length.

Actually the movement is not labeled "Scherzo" in the autograph manuscript, but "Molto vivace." Beethoven stopped using the term *scherzo* in symphonies as early as the Fourth, and he also dropped it in a number of other later works. Even when he was still writing movements that are clearly scherzos in every respect, he apparently disliked the term, perhaps because of a literal-minded distrust of its meaning of "joke" or lighter movement, even though that meaning was by then outmoded. The character of this huge movement in its first part is one of enormous speed and headlong forward motion, with fugal textures, great use of symmetries in phrase structure, emphatic repetitions of its main rhythmic cells, use of hypermeters of three-measure or four-measure units (all so labeled, "rhythm of three bars" or "four bars") in the middle part of the Scherzo itself. The Trio, on the other hand, is short, quiet, and bucolic—a D-major section in 2/2 time that brings an interlude of pastoral grace between the stormy outbursts of the Scherzo. In its full form, with all internal repeats, this movement spans more than fifteen hundred measures, longer than even the longest Scherzos in the earlier symphonies (the Seventh, third movement, has a total of 653 measures in its five-part form of Scherzo-Trio-Scherzo-Trio-Scherzo-Coda).

Third Movement

The slow movement, in B-flat major (exploiting the relationship of D minor and B-flat major that had occupied much of the first movement) is a lyrical outpouring on a comparably large scale, exploring at least two types of melodies. The first is the beautiful main theme that opens the movement, a fully mature example of Beethovenian "absolute melody" and also a fully integrated musical entity with beginning, middle, and end. With its phrases amply spaced and with woodwind echoes after each such phrase, its opening member pauses on the dominant with what we have come to recognize as one of Beethoven's favorite downward melodic turns (5–4–2) (*W 51). The other kind of lyricism appears when the B-flat major first section gives way to D major and presents a passionate new melodic phrase that sweeps upward sequentially to a climax, then returns to its starting point to make the same ascent again and closes on the tonic. The alternation of these two themes generates the basic form of the piece, parallel in some respects to the form of the slow movement of the Fifth Symphony in offering the appearance of a set of variations on a principal theme plus an alternating theme that plays a crucial contrasting role. The basic formal structure here is as follows (measure numbers are provided to show the relative lengths of the sections):

Section	Measure	Key	Meter	Tempo
Introduction	1–2			
Theme 1	3–24	B-flat major	4/4	Adagio molto e cantabile
Theme 2	25–42	D major	3/4	Andante moderato
Variation 1 (Theme 1)	43–64	B-flat major	4/4	Tempo I
Theme 2	65–82	G major	3/4	Andante moderato
Transition to Variation 2	83–98	E-flat major C-flat major		Adagio
Variation 2 (Theme 1)	99–120	B-flat major		[Adagio]
Coda	121–157	B-flat major		[Adagio]

After the great storms of the first and second movements this Adagio and its lyrical extensions bring an oasis of peace and contemplation. It has a kinship with the slow movements of the Quartet Opus 59 No. 2, the Fifth Symphony, and the "Archduke" Trio, Opus 97. It also connects with the Trio's Andante in both key and long-breathed melodic structure, but there is nothing in the Trio or the earlier slow movements quite like the upward rushing vocality of the D-major theme of this movement. Its wonders include a fourth-horn solo that dominates the great "transition" section in E-flat and C-flat major—Beethoven's longest horn solo, perhaps written for the newly invented valve horn. In the hushed close of the movement, the final completion of the melodic aspect gives way to simultaneous upward and downward scales and the tympani brings its tonic and dominant notes simultaneously as a "double stop," probably for the first time in the history of the symphony (*W 52).

Fourth Movement

The finale erupts. Its scale is enormous not merely because it must match the size of the preceding three movements but because Beethoven needs room in which to justify the use of solo voices and chorus singing Schiller's "Ode," and then to lay out an immense choral-orchestral finale that affords space for the equivalent of a cantata that is also a symphonic finale. He solves the problem by presenting these sections, indicated in the following overview.[75]

Introduction (measures 1–91). After two cacophonous outbreaks from the orchestra, each followed by instrumental recitatives, this section recapitu-

A sketch for the finale of Beethoven's Ninth Symphony. At the top left are the words, "Presto bleibt meilleur" ("Presto remains [the] better [tempo]"). (Gesellschaft der Musikfreunde, Vienna)

lates thematic ideas from within the first three movements, rejecting each one with instrumental recitatives. Then the winds foreshadow the finale main theme. Nothing is more indicative of Beethoven's aim of harnessing operatic expression in the service of instrumental music than these recitatives by the cellos and basses, which strain to arrive at the border of human speech and use the expressive gestures and rhythms of speech sounds but remain "inarticulate" in the sense—though it is a crucial sense—that they cannot speak with words.

Orchestral Exposition (mm. 91–207). The "main theme" (to become the theme of the "Ode to Joy") is presented in full in the cellos and basses, those same lower orchestral voices whose recitatives had answered each of the preceding musical ideas, rejecting them all until the main theme had been foreshadowed. Now they are the first voices to present it. The full theme, in D major, is followed by a series of three variations (measures 116–187), rising in successive presentations through the orchestra and adding more instruments with each presentation. We soon realize that this is the same method of "creating the theme" that took place at the very beginning of the symphony, when the crushing first theme of the first movement was created out of silence—thus the idea of thematic creation is built into both first and last movements. The presentation of the theme also entails the idea of rising gradually through an enormous musical space, which Beethoven had made a hallmark of his second-period style.

The orchestral exposition, as presentation of the main theme in successively higher and fuller registers, could form the basis for a full instrumental finale. But when the third variation is completed the whole apparatus breaks down. The coda (mm. 188—207) leads to the dominant, A major, and gives way to the chaos that had opened the movement, now intensified.

Vocal Exposition with Solo Voices and Choir (mm. 208–594). This breakdown brings on the human voice—first the baritone solo, with the words, written by Beethoven, "O Freunde, nicht diese Töne! Sondern lasst uns angenehmere anstimmen, und freudenvollere" ("Oh, Friends, not these tones! Let us instead tune our voices more pleasantly and joyfully"). This is the crux of the finale, on which everything now depends. The baritone, as if stepping outside the picture frame, in effect addresses the other singers, soloists and chorus, and beckons them to join in what now must be not just a symphonic finale but a specifically vocal celebration of joy and brotherhood.[76] He rejects not just the cacophony of the last phrase but the whole idea of the orchestral exposition of the main theme, and, asking them to "tune" their voices, proceeds himself to apply the main theme to the first stanza of Schiller's poem, which reads:

Freude, schöner Götterfunken,	Joy, beautiful spark of divinity,
Tochter aus Elysium,	daughter of Elysium,
Wir betreten, feuertrunken,	We enter thy sanctuary,
Himmlische, dein Heiligtum;	Heavenly one, drunk with fire;
Deine Zauber binden wieder,	Your magic binds again
was die Mode streng geteilt;	what custom rudely divided;
alle Menschen werden Brüder,	all mankind become brothers,
wo dein sanfter Flügel weilt.	where your gentle wing abides.

The further structure of the finale continues the variation process. Because the orchestral exposition presented the main theme (that of the first stanza) as theme and three variations, the vocal exposition that now follows can be construed as continuing the variation set.

Vocal Exposition with Solo Voices and Choir (mm. 208–594)

Introduction	*mm. 208–240*	*Free*	*Baritone recitative and transition*
Stanza 1	*mm. 241–268*	*Variation 4*	*Baritone answered by lower voices of choir*
Stanza 2	*mm. 269–296*	*Variation 5*	*Solo quartet; second part repeated by full choir*
Stanza 3	*mm. 297–324*	*Variation 6*	*Solo quartet in ornamentation of theme; second part answered by full choir*

Transition	*mm. 325–330*		*Short transition to B-flat major with unexpected harmonic motion to F major*
Chorus 4	*mm. 331–430*	*Variation 7*	*Alla marcia, 6/8, B-flat major; tenor solo with male voices of choir*
Interlude	*mm. 431–542*		*Orchestral expansion of main theme material in 6/8, forming transition from B-flat major to D major to prepare return of Stanza 1*
Stanza 1	*mm. 543–594*	*Variation 8*	*Full choir, full orchestral accompaniment* fortissimo, *D major*

Andante maestoso, choir only, no soloists (mm. 595–694)

To Stanza 1 Beethoven juxtaposes Chorus 1 of the Ode:

Seid umschlungen, Millionen!	You millions, I embrace you
Diesen Kuss der ganzen Welt!	This kiss goes to the whole world;
Brüder—überm Sternenzelt	Brothers—above the starry canopy
Muss ein lieber Vater wohnen.	A beloved father must surely dwell.

With this stanza and the text of chorus 1 of the "Ode" ("Seid umschlungen, Millionen"), Beethoven builds the gigantic finale, first by making the most of the contrasts in setting and tone between the two texts—the secular and the sacred—and then eventually combining them to show their symbolic interdependence.

Chorus 1	*mm. 595–626*	*New theme, full choir; Andante maestoso, 3/2; G major, then B-flat major*
Chorus 3	*mm. 627–654*	*Adagio ma non troppo, ma divoto (closes with orchestral representation of the heavenly father*

who "dwells above the stars," pianissimo, all
voices and instruments in high register

Recapitulation and Coda, D major (mm. 655–940)

Stanza 1 and chorus 1 texts combined	mm. 655–729	Climactic double fugue on the two main themes, the "Ode to Joy" and the theme of "Seid umschlungen" (second section)
Interlude	mm. 730–762	Sudden interruption of text of Chorus 3 (as at end of second section), leading again to the portrayal of the heavenly father above the stars and closing quietly in G major
Stanza 1, lines 1–2, incomplete	mm. 763–782	Soloists, D major
Stanza 1, lines 5–8	mm. 783–813	Soloists and choir
Stanza 1, lines 5–8	mm. 814–842	Soloists and choir (with expanded coloratura passages for the four soloists at the end of this segment)
Transition	mm. 843–850	Orchestral transition to coda
Chorus 1 with Stanza 1, lines 1–2 at end	mm. 851–940	Prestissimo coda, full orchestra

---

The form of the finale, beyond the shape that emerges from its successive settings of the stanzas and choruses selected from the poem, can be only distantly or analogously connected to any of the paradigmatic formal schemes that governed classical instrumental music—principally variants of sonata form or rondo. Its overt use of variation procedure helps to clarify Beethoven's formal intentions. Thus the entire first part can be construed as consisting of an introduction (in which the main theme is gradually discovered), followed by the main theme and a set of eight variations; then a strongly contrasting second section ("Seid umschlungen, Millionen," etc.), then the final section, beginning with the double fugue combining them. In this view the finale would relate closely to the most innovative of Beethoven's earlier symphonic finales, that of the *Eroica*, in which the main theme is also "discovered" in the introduction and is followed by a freely developing set of variations.

In another way the Ninth finale also harks back to the *Eroica* finale's progenitor, the Piano Variations Opus 35, which had been structured as a massive set of fifteen variations with a culminating fugue. Some have seen the Ninth finale as, in effect, itself a large-scale cyclic four-movement form, others as a variant of sonata form; but the sectional contrasts of the finale should not admit the dominance of any single formal interpretation that blurs the basic dialectic of its two main themes and their eventual reconciliation in the great double fugue.[77]

Looked at in another way, however, and with the whole of the symphony in view rather than the finale alone, the form, except for the cyclic return of the Scherzo, reflects the same broad aesthetic model that Beethoven used in the Fifth Symphony. Here in the Ninth, as in the Fifth, we have a tragic first movement in minor, a songlike slow movement that freely employs the variation principle using two contrasting themes; and a triumphant finale—here, of course, on a much larger scale and with its protagonist enlarged from an imagined hero to the whole "brotherhood of humanity" striving for union under God.

The Ninth Symphony came down on later nineteenth-century symphonic composers like an avalanche. As we saw earlier, no symphonist after Beethoven could avoid its impact, and many who were not symphonic composers were spellbound by it. Consider, for example, Berlioz's program symphonies, such as *Harold in Italy*, with its thematic reminiscences of earlier movements and its climactic combining of principal themes, a true Berliozian feature. In a more literal vein, Mendelssohn wrote an overt imitation of the Ninth in his *Lobgesang*, while Wagner's obsession with the work ran through his entire career. Later D-minor orchestral works of size, whether Schumann's Fourth Symphony, Wagner's *Faust Overture*, Liszt's *Faust Symphony*, Bruckner's Third Symphony, or Franck's Symphony are inconceivable without it. The Ninth set a precedent that enabled Mahler to build his immense symphonic structures, with their wide-ranging rhetoric and their exemplification of his concept of the symphony as an art form that "must have something cosmic in itself, must be inexhaustible, like the world and life."[78] It is not surprising that no major composer of symphonies after Beethoven down to the early twentieth century wrote more than nine, as if this work had set up a virtually permanent standard. It was not for nothing that Brahms' First Symphony was called "Beethoven's Tenth" or that when someone pointed out a resemblance between the middle strain of the main theme of his finale and the middle strain of the "Ode to Joy," Brahms said, "any jackass can see that."[79] By building his finale as the farthest-reaching, most massive movement of the work, containing a slow introduction, an anthemlike Allegro main theme, and a great brass chorale near the end, Brahms in effect restored faith that the symphonic tradition laid down by Beethoven could indeed be continued.[80]

Yet there were dissenting voices, even in the nineteenth century. Spohr, a conservative who had known Beethoven, could barely abide the first three movements and found the finale "monstrous . . . tasteless, and in its handling of Schiller's Ode so trivial, that I cannot, even now, comprehend how such a genius as Beethoven could have written it."[81] It took until mid-century for the work to gain public approval, mainly because the finale to many seemed incongruous and the whole work contradicted narrow concepts of symphonic tradition. Since even the most ambitious local orchestras across Europe could not readily get to know it, as they did the earlier eight, and since every performance of it became a kind of civic event (as performances still are), harnessing singers and players on a grand scale—the Ninth took on a near-mythic status from which it has not been displaced even in the twenty-first century. To cite one acerbic commentator, it has survived despite the fact that "the canon has become the ossified object of a wholly distracted, automatic genuflection, and . . . Beethoven's technical and stylistic advances have long since been absorbed into the language and [been] vastly exceeded."[82] To which one can reply that the "canon" may be ossified in the minds of critics through overexposure but its bones have a strange ability to regain flesh and blood when new generations are given access to its best works and are moved by the intelligence and humane values they embody.

The Ninth continues to attract both formal analyses and critical interpretations on every side, some of which accept, some reject, its forthright, naive, powerful assertions of ethical and political ideals. Some rejections stem from current disillusionment in the face of modern history and a twentieth century in which monumental crimes against humanity were committed, above all the Holocaust, carried out by the Nazi leaders of the supposedly civilized nation that professed to believe that Beethoven and Goethe were the bearers of its national cultural identity. Others in our secular age are no longer able to give credence to the idealistic verities that Schiller so boldly proclaimed in his poem celebrating joy and freedom, above all under a God who dwells "above the stars." But if we look at the Ninth as the product of an attempted revival of these ideals, written at a time when political tyranny had returned to the European world after 1815, a symphony that originated as an effort to reinstill some hope into a world even then desperate for assurances of the survival of such ideals—then we can see that modern skepticism unwittingly tends to replicate the political despondency of the time in which it came into being. Of course the symphony is open to many interpretations, and it seems to have the strength to withstand admiration and blame about equally well. A telling view of its many meanings is voiced by Solomon, for whom "it encompasses larger relevancies and manifold meanings that have given it unassailable status as a model of human transformation."[83] Among these is the sense that its sublime, uplifting symbolism embraces not only the millions but a belief in a world in which their fate matters, just as does that of every individual. It can well be seen as the largest musical expression Beethoven ever made of what he told the unknown "Emilie M." in that letter of 1812—that "art has no limits," that the artist strives endlessly because "he has not yet reached the point to which his better genius only lights the way for him like a distant sun." By using Schiller's "Ode" to directly address humanity at large, Beethoven conveys the struggle of both the individual and of the millions to work their way through experience from tragedy to idealism and to preserve the image of human brotherhood as a defense against the darkness.

CHAPTER 21

TIMELESS MUSIC:
THE LAST QUARTETS

≻○≺⫷⫸≻○≺

Introduction

In 1857, thirty years after Beethoven's death, the violinist Karl Holz gave Wilhelm von Lenz some written reminiscences about the last quartets, which Lenz published three years later.[1] Holz had credentials. He had joined the Schuppanzigh Quartet as its second violinist in 1824, just when Beethoven was working on Opus 127. In 1825 he became a trusted member of the inner circle, replacing the officious Schindler as personal assistant, factotum, and unpaid manager of Beethoven's business affairs.[2] Holz was a musician of independent judgment who did not hesitate to tell Beethoven what he thought on any subject.[3] His testimony to Lenz on the quartets is as follows:

> *During the time when he was composing the three quartets commissioned by Prince Galitzin, Opus 127, Opus 130, Opus 132, such a wealth of new quartet ideas streamed forth from Beethoven's inexhaustible imagination that he felt almost involuntarily compelled to write the C♯-minor and F-major quartets [Opus 131 and 135]. "My dear friend, I have just had another new idea," he used to say, in a joking manner and with shining eyes, when we would go out for a walk; and he wrote down some notes in a little pocket sketchbook. "But that belongs to the quartet after the next one [i.e., the C♯ minor quartet], since the next one [Opus 130, with six movements] already has too many movements." . . . When he had finished the B♭ major quartet [Opus 130] I said that I thought it the best of the three. To which he*

replied, "Each in its own way! Art demands of us that we don't stand
still" (he used to speak this way, in an imperial style). "You will find
here a new kind of voice-leading, and, as to imagination [Phantasie], it
will, God willing, be less lacking than ever before!" Later he said that he
thought the C♯ minor Quartet his greatest. On the score he sent to
Schott he wrote, ironically, "Pilfered together from various odds and
ends" ["Zusammengestohlen aus Verschiedenem, diesem und Jenem"].[4]

The passage is rich in implications behind the humorous veil. Whether
Beethoven actually said that he had "another new idea . . . in a joking manner and with shining eyes" might be an invention or a wishful memory, but
it gives a feeling of what his immersion in his composing life meant for him
as an aging, misanthropic artist for whom joy in any other aspect of life was
a fleeting dream at best. Beethoven's hope that in these quartets "imagination [will be] less lacking than ever before," has been called an "understate-
ment to leave us all speechless."[5] Striking too is that Holz approaches the
three Galitzin quartets and even the next two (Opus 131 and Opus 135) not
only as individual works but as an aggregate. His vignette of Beethoven jotting down an idea for one of them, well in advance of settling down to work
on it in earnest, fits well with what we find in the sketchbooks. Of course
he had had such habits all his life, but the last quartets impress us more
than any other closely related group of Beethoven compositions as being
mature individual artworks that nevertheless are bound to each other like
family members who look somewhat alike and have some common features, traits, and gestures. Some of these are shared thematic and motivic
ideas, some are contrapuntal, some are rhythmic; the sum of their presence
is that these works belong to a special and rarefied plane of musical
thought. Beethoven's further comment, that these quartets present a "new
kind of voice-leading," is at the heart of what is rich and strange in their
textures. Holz's memoir reinforces the feeling, felt by listeners from Beethoven's time to ours, that the last quartets form a *summa* of his creativity,
that they give access to higher regions of thought and feeling that lie
beyond even his farthest-reaching earlier achievements. The response of
twenty-first-century lay listeners and of musicians, writers, visual artists,

and filmmakers, speaks volumes about the qualities of experience that the last quartets reveal to the perceiving world.[6]

Years earlier, while preparing the Opus 59 Quartets for publication, Beethoven had claimed that he was thinking about "devoting myself almost entirely to this type of composition."[7] Yet after Opus 95, composed in 1810, his only token before the last quartets was a little B-minor quartet movement that he wrote for an English visitor in 1817.[8] After accepting Galitzin's commission for three quartets in November 1822, he started drafting a quartet in E-flat, then turned back to the completion of the *Missa solemnis,* the "Diabelli" Variations, and the Ninth Symphony. Only after the premiere of the Ninth in May 1824 was he ready to bury himself in work on the quartet that became Opus 127, completing it in time for its first performance in March 1825.

From then on, and especially beginning in 1825, the story of Beethoven's compositional life centers on these quartets, each of which became a full-time creative project, not really interrupted by a few little works written or jotted down along the way, such as joking canons, two little piano pieces (WoO 85 and 86), some random ideas for unfinished works that barely got beyond the planning stage, alternative movements, and plans for movements. No other major projects, and few external distractions (not even his nephew's attempted suicide!) interfered with his riveted concentration on these quartets. Never had there been a period in his life during which he chained himself so exclusively to work on a single genre as he now did for two and a half years.

In order of composition, the first three quartets, as promised to Galitzin, were Opus 127 in E-flat major, Opus 132 in A minor, and Opus 130 in B-flat major, with its long fugal finale that he later removed and published separately as the *Grand Fugue,* Opus 133. Composing the A-minor quartet took him from February to July of 1825 but was interrupted when he fell prey in April to a serious abdominal illness that lasted a month. The illness, evidently more threatening than most of his chronic debilitating ailments, is reflected in the celebrated "Holy Song of Thanksgiving by a Convalescent, in the Lydian Mode," the slow movement of Opus 132. He was now in the hands of a stern and demanding physician, Dr. Anton Braunhofer, who bullied Beethoven into submission to the regime he prescribed for recovery, apparently with good results. In May Beethoven sent Braunhofer a letter of "respect and gratitude" in the form of a comic dialogue between doctor and patient, along with a canon on the text "Doctor, close the door against Death, notes [*Noten*] will help him who is in need [*Not*].⁹ In this case the connection between life situation and compositional idea is unusually direct. The canon text, which Beethoven wrote himself, gives every hint that during this illness, his sense of mission, his urgent desire to complete these quartets, and—not stated but implied—his obsessive love for his nephew Karl and yearning for Karl's reciprocation of that love, were now (with much difficulty and with Braunhofer's help) holding the door closed against death.

With the A-minor Quartet finished by July 1825 he turned directly to Opus 130 and its fugue, planning it at a very early stage as the "Last quartet [that is, last of the three for Galitzin] with a serious and heavy-going introduction," a jotting that he then followed with a sketch for a "Finale" in B-flat major that forms the kernel for the beginning of the *Grand Fugue* (*W 53).¹⁰ This shows that Beethoven was building the frame of the structure by first envisaging its beginning and its ending, along with the character of its "introduction" (which indeed turned out to be "serious and heavy-going") and that of the finale, which he then conceived as a fugue but with a subject that had a close intervallic kinship to that of the introduction's opening.¹¹

Again the project lasted half a year, not the few weeks that Beethoven imagined in the late summer of 1825, and it was first performed with the fugue as the finale in March of 1826. We can see that if Beethoven had written the three "Galitzin" quartets and stopped there, leaving Opus 130 with its enormous fugal finale, the resultant trilogy would have distantly resembled his Opus 59 trilogy in its larger pattern: the first is a sturdy and lengthy work in a major key (Opus 127); the second (Opus 132) is in a little-used minor key and has an idiosyncratic layout and diversity of movement types; and the third is in major and culminates in a fugal finale (though one that differs vastly from that of Opus 59 No. 3). Despite their radical differences, there is some affinity of aesthetic balance in these trilogies, and we should remember that in Beethoven's later lifetime the Opus 59 quartets were still regarded as difficult to understand, above all No. 2. As with Opus 18, if the three members of Opus 59 had been published separately, we would see them quite differently and more independently. And the opposite would hold if the three "Galitzin" Quartets had been, imaginably, grouped under one opus number.[12]

In the early months of 1826, Beethoven's last full year of life, he embarked on the C-sharp Minor Quartet, Opus 131, again completing it in six months or so. It turned out to be so difficult to play that a performance planned for September of that year was abandoned. We can gauge the circumstances when we realize that early in 1826, while he was working on Opus 131, Beethoven had to cope with the difficult decision to uncouple the *Grand Fugue* and publish it separately; and in July and August he had to deal with Karl's attempted suicide. The crisis occurred just as Beethoven was reaching an artistic summit, the completion of the C-sharp Minor Quartet. It sharpens our awareness of Beethoven's ability to deflect psychological pain from his artistic life, to cover the pain through creative work and to "close the door against Death," that in these same months, midsummer of 1826, he started on Opus 135, the epitome of subtlety, brevity, and humor. Opus 135 took less time than the others, only the four months from July to October, the last part of which he spent in refuge, along with Karl, at his brother Johann's estate in the country village of Gneixendorf near the Danube.[13] After this there remained the composition of the substitute finale for Opus 130 to replace the *Grand Fugue*—a labor of love that was finished by November. He tried to launch a string quintet in C major but made little progress. In December his health failed again, and though he rallied for a while it became progressively worse in the early winter of 1827. Seeing a few visitors, writing a few letters, complaining about current trends in music and politics, bravely offering the Philharmonic Society a "new symphony, a new overture, or some other work," none of which existed, he tried to keep the flame alive. But it was all too late, and he died on March 26, 1827. Of the last quartets there had been performances of the first three (127, 132, 130) while he was still alive but not of Opus 131 or 135.

Opus 127

The traditional four-movement layout of Opus 127 is the only feature of the work that might be construed (that is, misconstrued) as conservative. In the long course of planning and writing the quartet Beethoven thought at one time that it might have as many as six movements, including a slow introduction to the finale and a middle movement to be called "La Gaieté." Strangely enough this heading was applied to a sketch for a jocular movement in 2/4 whose theme he transformed into the profoundly moving 12/8 main theme of the Adagio movement of the quartet.[14] The final movement plan of the work, with its tightly condensed slow introduction to the first movement, has a fair number of antecedents. Perhaps most relevant are two important chamber works in the same key: the Trio Opus 70 No. 2 and the "Harp" Quartet, Opus 74. The first movement Allegro, with its smooth, flowing melodic motion in 3/4, recalls the first movement of the Violin Sonata Opus 96 and the Piano Sonata Opus 90, but in his earlier works, triple-meter Allegro first movements had been a minority compared to those in duple.[15]

The very brief opening Maestoso sets up the first movement with a clenched-fist opening gesture in which the basic tonic chord of E-flat major appears three times with the upper line rising through each statement on the scale steps 1, 3, and 5, spaced out between restless syncopated figures in the intervening measures and leading to a firm subdominant (A-flat major) chord. There may have been Masonic overtones in this elaborated use of the rising tonic triad to open the work; similar conspicuous uses of the rising triad, all progeny of the symbolic rising triadic chords that open the overture to *The Magic Flute*, had appeared in earlier Beethoven works in this key.[16] Slow introductions in middle and later Beethoven works are often extended sections with well-developed frameworks of their own, but here, as in at least one earlier example—the Piano Sonata in F-sharp Major, Opus 78—the introduction is short and firm but subtle in content and consequence. The Allegro rises smoothly out of the subdominant harmony that ends the introduction and feels more like a continuation than a wholly new theme. In fact, somewhat as in the *Eroica*, this exposition has no single, fully shaped main theme; rather, a succession of well-crafted thematic ideas lead from the tonic area to a transition that moves out, not to the traditional dominant (B-flat major), but to G minor and then to G major.

There is little or no use of the dominant as a key area in the entire work, a mark of late Beethoven harmonic planning in which the time-honored use of the dominant as basic opposition to the tonic is supplanted by other contrasting tonal centers. Sometimes the main contrasting harmony is the subdominant, as in the *Missa solemnis;* sometimes the flat sixth degree, as in the first movement of the Ninth Symphony and that of the Sonata Opus 111. Here the central contrast is formed on the third degree, G, as root of both major and minor harmonies. The formal dynamics of the movement take advantage of the opening contrast of Maestoso and Allegro. The Maestoso returns in G major to signal the beginning of the development section; it returns another time, now in C major and in truncated form, near the end of the development section, thus dramatizing the harmonic move to C major that Beethoven will use to set up the eventual return to the tonic E-flat major.

A typical paradox of the late style, met with here for the first time, is that the three statements of the Maestoso appear in three different keys and serve three entirely different structural functions: to open the piece; to open the development, and to mark a turning point as the development moves to C major. Most important is that the Maestoso never returns in the tonic. Thus it does not round off the form, as it so readily would have in earlier works using this strategy—and it does not appear in the recapitulation. Whereas the opening of the recapitulation in many an earlier and middle-period work had always been a moment of vital articulation, whether attacked forcefully or smoothly, here it is virtually concealed within the ongoing discourse at the end of the development; the listener has to know it is there in order to hear it.[17] In other words, traditional formal junctures and dividing points are now either signaled by an introductory passage that is never exactly the same twice or are concealed in the name of continuity. That is why there is no repeat of the exposition and no use of the Maestoso at the recapitulation or the coda. Another element of long-range structural planning does emerge, however, and this one harks back in various ways to earlier works, especially Opus 59 No. 1. It is the gradual enlargement of registral space as the movement progresses, from the opening two-octave span of its beginning, to the three octaves of the G-major Maestoso, to the four octaves of the C-major Maestoso, and finally, to the maximum span, four octaves and a sixth—from low C of the cello to the high A♭ of the first violin—at the apex of the coda. From this moment of maximum spatial expansion, the final beautiful and intimate phrases take their point of departure and finish the movement with grace and sensibility on a tonic chord that spans four octaves.

From the very opening of the Allegro we see what Beethoven meant when he spoke to Holz about "a new kind of voice-leading." It is true that the upper line, Violin 1, is the leading voice in the sense of carrying the most distinctive melodic content. But the lower voices are no mere accompaniment. Each is a smoothly written, stable melodic or quasi-melodic voice. No matter to what degree they are simpler than the top voice and seemingly subordinated to it, they are individualized and linearized to a degree surpassing what we find characteristically in the earlier quartets, except in earlier fugal and fugato writing. The texture is saturated with motivic content, overt or latent, and is inherently linear in all voices, while at the same time it makes perfect harmonic sense. Not only this counterpoint of voices but also another factor strikes the ear and helps account for the density of the content. Although there are four instruments in the quartet there are often many more than four voices. Sudden leaps in register within individual string parts, abrupt shifts that can occur in the current leading voice or in any other voice, above all the viola and cello, give rise to the realization that a single part can often imply more than one contrapuntal line. For example, in one cadence on the tonic E-flat major, both Violin 1 and cello suddenly leap down from a high B♭ to an E♭ an octave and half lower, instead of resolving conventionally to the E♭ a fifth below. Moreover, to reach this higher B♭ the cello has to leap up an octave to reach it, when it could perfectly well have remained on the lower B♭ (*W 54). Why? Because in both string parts Beethoven wants to prepare the middle register in which the next thematic material will occur; the cello picks up the middle-range B♭ for the next phrase, and Violin 1 answers it two bars later in the same range. Meanwhile the high B♭ in Violin 1 is being "saved" or held in reserve until it reemerges a bit later.[18] The texture is filled with mysterious suggestions, hints, and allusions to voices that come and go in the four-instrument texture, which is perpetually resonant with content, infused with even more motivic and thematic material than it overtly presents.

The slow movement, transformed from "La Gaieté" to a profoundly beautiful variation movement, exemplifies the *cantabile* aspect of quartet writing but shares the development of thought that marks all of Beethoven's mature variations. As it fills out its ample space it has room for striking shifts of affect, from the jocular to the tragic. The opening "curtain" in *pianissimo*, which slowly steals into the mind of the listener by building a dominant seventh chord from the bottom up, is acutely calculated to prepare the arrival of the main theme, a long and winding melody whose first and second strains are each presented first in Violin 1, then in the cello, with a short codetta to softly round off the whole.[19] Now begins a set of variations, five in all plus a surprising interlude between Nos. 4 and 5, and with a breathtaking coda to finish the movement.

It is no accident that the variations are not numbered in the score. By omitting the numbering, as he had already done in other variation movements, such as the finale of Opus 74, Beethoven signals his departure from the traditional formal codes that belonged to the variation as a classical genre, with its familiar succession of tonally closed sections.[20] The same is true in late independent sets of variations, above all the "Diabelli" Variations, but there he has no choice but to number each variation since they make up the whole work. The same avoidance of labels for each variation is found in the slow movement of Opus 132 (the "Heiliger Dankgesang"), the Andante of Opus 131, and the Lento assai of Opus 135.[21]

Gone too in this mature phase is Beethoven's earlier adherence to the older method of variation writing in which the first few variations of a set in turn created new versions of the theme by having each variation proceed in shorter note values than the one before, then altering the material in new ways such as a change to minor (for a major-mode theme) and a change of tempo. Now in the first variation, while retaining the 12/8 meter of the theme, Beethoven plunges directly into elaborate figurations in all four instruments, weaving fantastic patterns from the simpler melodic lines of the theme. In the second variation he shifts the tempo from Adagio to Andante con moto and brings a new meter, 4/4, for a marchlike section with even more complex writing in the two violin parts, which form an animated dialogue. The third variation restores the Adagio tempo, maintains the duple meter, but moves the entire harmonic content into the key of E major—extremely distant from the basic tonic of A-flat major. In this new environment he develops a rich body of melody from the earlier material, with Violin 1 soaring into new expressive regions and with a harmonic climax on a C-natural harmony in Beethoven's ripest style. The fourth variation slips back easily into the home tonic, A-flat major, and unfolds a dialogue between cello and first violin in the original meter, followed by a strange interlude, perhaps an extended coda, at the end of this section that leads once more from A-flat major to E major. This move in turn leads back to the final variation, in which first Violin 1 and then the three other instruments sing in arabesques of sixteenth-note diminutions of the phrases of the original theme. The coda revives echoes of the rising arpeggios of variation 4, then works its way gently through reminiscences of earlier sixteenth-note patterns to the final measure, where the last cadence closes the vast circle of the movement with a reference back to the opening phrase of the theme. And fully indicative of Beethoven's departure from convention is that the last cadence, rather than having the traditional dominant to tonic (5–1) motion in the bass, moves from scale degree 2 to 1, keeping its melodic role alive to the very end, as do all the voices.

In its third and fourth movements Opus 127 sails into uncharted waters, making full use of the Scherzo-Trio and sonata-form templates but with a new relation between content and form. The opening measures announce a new paradigm in Scherzo writing, as Beethoven finds ways of supplying inner contrasts to this movement type that is seemingly limited by its adherence to a single basic metrical format throughout its length.

The opening phrases give us a clear sample of how he achieves such variety (*W 55). First comes a short "curtain" made up of four plucked chords in a regular 3/4 rhythm, simple tonic and dominant in a two-octave span. A paradox follows: neither the opening harmonic sequence, nor the short chords on the beat, nor the pizzicato sonority provides the main stuff of the movement: in fact they are never heard again within it. The cello theme that follows, with its sequential rising repetitions of a rhythmically jagged, four-note upbeat-downbeat figure (3 + 1) moving on to a smooth legato phrase with conspicuous trills on the third beat of each measure, is answered by the viola with an inverted form of the figure that also descends in its main melodic line, replying to the cello's ascent. They join as a contrapuntal pair. In complementary style, the tossing back and forth of short phrases (always with trill) spreads to the upper voices and higher registers; just as the first big cadence is to be reached, the cello makes a rhythmic shift and brings the jagged rhythm on the first instead of the third beat. This introduces a new form of the rhythm that then has a life of its own, and we realize with astonishment how freely new rhythmic cells and placements of already known rhythmic cells can be worked into the texture. This scherzo in fact resembles some other late Beethoven scherzos (certainly that of the Ninth Symphony) in having enough differentiated material to form an approximation of a sonata form. Not that this formal shape is new here, but a sonata-form scherzo with such ample material and density of textures had not been seen since the large, one-movement Scherzo of Opus 59 No. 1. In Opp. 74 and 95, and in the Seventh Symphony, Beethoven worked out the scherzi along different lines.

The larger pattern of the whole third movement is:

Scherzo	Trio (Presto)	Scherzo repeated	Coda
E-flat major (sonata form)	E-flat minor	E-flat major	E-flat minor–major
143 measures	125 mm.	146 mm.	21 mm.

This makes up a large, three-part Scherzo-Trio-Scherzo form with coda, but the coda alludes to both Trio and Scherzo at the end, somewhat as in the Seventh Symphony, and thus hints at Beethoven's middle-period five-part Scherzo form. No change of scene in any Beethoven movement is more vivid than that between this intricate, active, contrapuntal Scherzo and the mysterious Trio that flies in like a distant storm, passing from its opening *pianissimo* to its *fortissimo* climax and then receding; it breaks off abruptly to give way to the return of the Scherzo, briefly reappears, and then breaks off again in the coda.

The finale, massive like its fellow movements, is in a highly elaborated sonata form with remarkable features, most of all a pseudo-recapitulation in the subdominant immediately followed by the real recapitulation. The opening gesture, an octave leap from G to G, is a hallmark of the late quartet style, in its anticipation of the leap that opens the Grand Fugue (on the same pitch, G), and even that of the D-major second movement of Opus 131) (*W 56). But even more striking is Beethoven's way of opening this E-flat major finale with an off-tonic phrase that then wends its way down to E-flat through sinuous motions that suggest a related key area, C minor; in fact C minor is a goal of the development section. The opening gesture also anticipates the movement of the first theme to its dominant note, B♭, by way of its own leading tone, the raised fourth A♮.

The coda is a telling example of Beethoven's sensitivity to the effects of harmonic shift and tone color. Anticipating Impressionism by three generations, it blends the strings in a gossamer web of new sonorities, some of which were heard by Schubert and used to wonderful effect in his last piano trio, in the same key, and in his own late quartets, written in the next few years. The coda is no mere completion of the final tonic harmony: it has its own tempo and meter, starts in C major with a new version of the first theme, and explores, in order, a series of keys descending by major thirds before moving chromatically into the home tonic. It is exactly the scheme that Beethoven used for the Bagatelles Opus 126, as we saw earlier. It was this coda that the deaf Beethoven, "crouched in a corner," heard being rehearsed by Joseph Böhm and the other members of the Schuppanzigh Quartet, and, by following their bowings, attended so carefully to the tempo that he changed it then and there from "Meno Vivace" to "Allegro con moto."[22]

Opus 132

As noted earlier, A minor as a principal key is surprisingly rare in Beethoven's works and in those of his predecessors. Despite its ready playability on stringed and wind instruments, neither Haydn nor Mozart wrote more than a very few works in this key, a pattern that seems to fit in with a general inhibition in the later eighteenth century against minor keys containing sharps as principal keys. Preferred instead are the flat-side minor keys: D minor, G minor, and C minor (with F minor as an extreme possibility).[23] Although Beethoven wrote interior movements in A minor, he avoided it as a primary key except in two cases, one of which is slightly ambiguous. Altogether in A minor is the quirky and peculiar Violin Sonata Opus 23 of 1800; largely in A minor but interestingly mixed with major is the "Kreutzer" Sonata of 1801–3.[24] The movement plan of Opus 132 has some surprising parallels with the "Kreutzer":

Opus 132, Movement Plan
1. Assai sostenuto [Introduction], 2/2, and Allegro, 4/4, in A minor
2. Allegro ma non tanto [Scherzo], 3/4, in A major
3. Molto adagio: "Holy Song of Thanksgiving to the Deity by a Convalescent, in the Lydian Mode,"[25] 4/4, in Lydian F major
4. Alla marcia, assai vivace, 4/4, A major, plus Più allegro and Presto [recitative]
5. Allegro appassionato, 3/4, in A minor (with A major close)

This cycle of five movements yields a simple tonal arch-form: A minor–A major–F major–A major–A minor. In the proportions of the quartet's movements, however, we can construe the scheme as having four principal elements:

1.   a slow introduction and Allegro first movement
2.   a substantial Scherzo (three-part form)
3.   a slow movement, as double variation movement
4a. A short Alla marcia plus recitative, all of which can be heard as an introduction to the finale
4b. the 3/4 finale itself

The tonal layout, with its long slow movement in the Lydian mode (for Beethoven a special archaizing form of F major using a B-natural instead of a B-flat) extends the tonal plan of the "Kreutzer" (first movement in A major/minor; slow movement in F major; finale in A major). It shows a kinship with the Piano Sonata Opus 101, in A major, which also has an

F-major middle movement; there the sequence is A major–F major–A minor–A major. For inner tonal contrast Beethoven often used the major key on the flat sixth degree in minor-mode works; thus a number of C-minor works have A-flat-major slow movements, (e.g. Opus 10 No. 1, Opus 13 ("Pathétique"), Violin Sonata Opus 30 No. 2, and the Fifth Symphony, among others). Equally, D-minor works can have B-flat-major slow movements (Opus 31 No. 2 and the Ninth Symphony). This choice allowed Beethoven to reinterpret the tonic pitch of the home key as the major third of the slow-movement key, with expressive consequences, often consolatory, as the slow movements begin. In major-mode works he also used the major key on the flat sixth as a tonal foil in, for example, the Violin Sonata in G major, Opus 30 No. 3 (slow movement in E-flat major); the Triple Concerto in C major (slow movement in A-flat major) and, far closer to the late quartets, the *Hammerklavier* Sonata in B-flat major, with its slow movement in F-sharp *minor*—the only example in Beethoven in which a major-mode work uses its flat sixth in minor rather than major. In late quartets other than Opus 132, the wider harmonic range prompts other uses of this relationship. In Opus 131, the most experimental of his works in tonal plan, the C-sharp-minor home tonic has as its primary slow movement an Andante in A major (the flat sixth); and in Opus 135 in F major the slow movement is in D-flat major.

Some precedents for this tonal layout in minor-mode works came down from Mozart (though not for A minor). For example, his great D-minor Piano Concerto, K. 466 has its pensive slow movement in B-flat major; and in several of Mozart's late works in G minor (above all the String Quintet and the Symphony No. 40), a slow movement in E-flat major is an anchoring major-mode element of stability. But in the major mode Mozart does not normally choose an internal contrast so dramatic as that of a slow movement in the flat-sixth key, preferring one in the subdominant or the dominant.[26] Haydn is characteristically more adventurous in choosing keys that for Mozart (and even for Beethoven) would be extreme.[27]

The opening measures of Opus 132 project us into a dark terrain in which multiple pathways open up the musical space, all using the same initial four-note figure but in several different forms and scalar positions, both successively and in combination with each other. The slow introduction begins with a four-note figure (call it "x") that will permeate the first movement and in various ways become its fundamental idea (*W 57). For this view of the first movement no complex analysis is needed, since the statements and elaborations of the opening figure are manifest throughout the slow introduction and the Allegro. Less obvious, though listeners have always felt it and can hardly fail to sense it, is that it also exerts a profound influence on the later movements. We should also stop for a moment to consider that this four-note figure—a latent shape more than a motif—appears in various forms, all of them closely related, in all the late quartets after Opus 127, stated and elaborated in different ways in each of them but always playing a substantial role.

In the slow introduction that begins Opus 132 the figure "x" is on the tonic in the cello; it is answered by an immediate restatement of "x" on the dominant in Violin 1 (thus at once implying a potential fugal exposition, which, however, does not materialize) while simultaneously the viola brings the inversion of "x" on the dominant. This same inversion is then repeated by the cello, but in the tonic. Above, two-note cells, as halves of the original four-note unit, are divided between Violins 1 and 2. To close this densely packed opening phrase, the registrally extreme Violin 1 and cello present the two halves ("x1" and "x2") in E minor simultaneously twice, while the inner voices remember different earlier versions. All this plays out in the space of some twenty seconds, within a harmonic context that oscillates between the tonic A minor and its dominant, E minor.

The Allegro grows out of this mystery by posing a new one that combines two basic ideas: one is the arabesque of descending and then rising sixteenth-note figures in Violin 1, the other is a distinctive figure in the cello, a short quasi-theme that will be elaborated throughout the movement. Everything is fluid and elusive, shapes and quasi-motives appear only to melt back into the texture, and no clear-cut tonic arrival is offered for a long time to come—in fact not until the very end of the movement, where at last a series of cadential figures resolve forcefully to the tonic. Creating expectation of the tonic and then postponing its arrival is a plan we have encountered in Beethoven's earlier works, certainly in the second period; but here it is magnified as the tonal scheme interacts with the other asymmetries that suspend expectations and give the work its complex larger shape. The formal plan of the first movement itself poses a problem as it appears to have two recapitulations: the first in E minor, the second, or "real" one marked by the return to A minor, which runs its course and is then followed by the emphatic Coda that finally gives firm shape to the whole.[28]

At one point in the composition process Beethoven wrote out in nearly full form a draft of a 3/8 movement in A major, "Alla allemande," which he later deleted from Opus 132 and which then found a home in Opus 130 in G major, as the "Alla danza tedesca."[29] The Scherzo of Opus 132 shows us why. Here he created one of his most convincing new scherzo types, a quasi-waltz that elaborates its opening figure, combines it with a second figure, and expands both in complementary ways to form the sections of an expanded compound binary form in A major. The full-bodied Scherzo is followed by a dreamlike musette, with a long drone on A and easy melodic motions in tenths in the high violin registers. It hints at similar quasi-pastoral evocations from the late Baroque, above all the musettes in Bach's suites, which normally function as counterparts to gavottes that imitate their own French models in Bach's masterly way. Examples include the "Gavotte ou la musette" in Bach's English Suite No. 3, and that in the Sixth Violoncello Suite in D major. So Beethoven's "pastoral" sections in late works not only point to a quiet utopian aesthetic state (as in the comparable Trio of the Ninth Symphony Scherzo) but also to historically memorable antecedents of an earlier period, namely that of Bach, the "immortal God of harmony," as Beethoven called him.

From here the quartet moves into a different world—that of the poetics of prayer and thanksgiving for recovery "by a convalescent." That he chooses the Lydian mode betokens not only a desire to frame this poignant movement with a modal cantus firmus that has an archaic character, but to use the time-honored Lydian mode in one of its historical associations, as the mode associated with healing and recovery.[30] To portray this experience, like no other in his works or those of any predecessor, Beethoven finds new means. One is the creation of a chorale melody in five phrases that can serve as the basic prayer and can later be elaborated in variations. Although some surmised that the melody must have come from his studies of early music, possibly Palestrina, the sketches show that Beethoven invented it. It is his own, fully realized chorale, "archaic" in sound because it is built, like the whole movement, on an F major foundation that has no B♭. In short, it uses the Lydian mode in the strict form that was, ironically, almost unknown in the sixteenth century except as a theoretical construct but that Beethoven chose because he wanted the movement to oscillate between a feeling of F as tonic and a feeling of C not as dominant but as an alternate tonic. The result is a new kind of harmonic polarity quite different from his various ways of making tonal contrasts in late works, such as substituting a contrasting key built on the third, sixth, flat sixth, or even the fourth scale step for the traditional role of the dominant. The stages of prayer are intensified by two means: one is the increasing animation and tension as the chorale elaborations are successively presented, the other emerges through the contrasting passages in D major, marked "Feeling new strength," in 3/8, that he alternates with the chorale segments.

After this great stillness the work resumes its motion, as the Alla marcia restores the tonic, now as A major, and the little march, with its off-beat accents (which we have learned to expect in this quartet from the very beginning) restores the atmosphere to vivid life. But after two brief, repeated sections it is quickly supplanted by a wholly new genre piece, a quasi-operatic recitative in which the first violin is clearly the solo voice. Its purpose, like that of all recitatives, is to prepare an aria, or in this case a finale. Sure enough the final cadence of the recitative, amazingly reminiscent of the opening of the first movement, brings in the final movement.

The rondo form of the finale disguises its own subtleties, but one of great importance is the harmonic oscillation that governs the main theme itself. We can get outside the work to remember that the theme had surfaced years earlier as a possible main theme for an instrumental finale to the Ninth Symphony, where its ending worked differently from the way it does here. Now the ending of the theme opens out from its A-minor to a C-major harmony, then slides back to A minor with ease. This harmonic motion also has a quasi-modal feel to it, though less an archaism than in the "Heiliger Dankgesang," but the basic sense of the movement is an exploration of the tonal space of a special version of A minor. At first this version of A minor engages in destabilizing relationships to C major but at last gives way to a firm and clear A major for the extremely long coda, which settles the harmonic questions of the finale and of the whole quartet. To strengthen the coda Beethoven made a basic compositional change in his autograph manuscript, extending it from its original close (at measure 351) for an additional fifty-four measures. In this late phase of his thinking, sectional proportions were more important than ever in compositional planning, and the need for a full thematic completion of the movement grew on him at a late stage of composition, as it often had before.

Opus 130 and the Grand Fugue

Two ideas that Beethoven jotted on sketch leaves as he began to plan this quartet were an entry for a possible finale, written in 6/8 meter, marked "Fugha"; and as we saw earlier, an entry in words for the slow introduction to the first movement: "Last quartet, with a serious and heavy-going Introduction."[31] Along with other preliminary sketches these ideas show that from the beginning Beethoven was trying to reach a synoptic idea of how the quartet should begin and end. He wanted a weighty and portentous introduction to his first movement; although he also tried out a number of short ideas for possible finale themes, he foresaw that the work should end with a fugal finale.[32]

The shape of the quartet in its original complete form is new. It is a cyclic work in B-flat major that has no extended transitions like those in Opus 132 and 131 but instead presents a deliberately unbalanced succession of six movements. The first and last, sonata form and fugue, are equally weighty though entirely different in form and length. Between them are four brief or moderate-length movements of different "characteristic" types. The whole is thus much more nearly a string of pearls of different colors and facets of light than any of the other late quartets; although comparisons with the eighteenth-century divertimento seem far fetched, we can understand why this superficial association springs to mind. The first movement, defined by its opening slow introduction contrasted with its Allegro main section, is tightly developed within its moderate framework; in performance time it comes to little more than half the length of the fugal finale.[33] It is followed by the shortest and tightest of all Beethoven's quartet scherzi, a mere two-minute Presto of streaking light. Then comes an equally compact D-flat major movement of grace and subtlety, as gentle as the little Presto is gruff. The fourth movement is a waltz, the 3/8 Alla danza tedesca lifted from an early plan for Opus 132. The sequence of middle movements then closes with a slow movement "Cavatina" in E-flat major. Capping the whole and integrating the cycle is the role of the multisectional fugue in B-flat major, a leviathan of 741 measures that dwarfs the preceding movements in weight, duration, level of difficulty, and scope. It comprises a whole series of contrasting sections that differ in tempo and key; it is a "fugue" in the larger sense but like no other, since it is, as Beethoven's subtitle later put it, "tantôt libre, tantôt recherchée"—"partly free, partly in strict counterpoint." This is the finale that Beethoven later removed from the quartet and published separately as the *Grosse Fuge*, Opus 133. He thus gave it a life of its own and sparked a controversy that has lasted ever since as to which finale is "correct," that is, the replacement finale that he wrote for the quartet—a genial deft, and humorous 2/4 Allegro—or the *Grand Fugue*.

Grasping the reasons behind the replacement may help resolve the question, though in a sense it can never be resolved in a simple either/or. The ambiguity of a work with two viable finales, each a plausible ending, is the central issue that needs to be understood by performers and listeners alike. A brief chronology will clarify the basic facts:

May–September 1825: Beethoven works on composing Opus 130, with the fugue as his only intended finale.

July 6, 1825 (approximately): Beethoven informs Prince Galitzin that the A Minor Quartet (Opus 132) is ready and that "the third quartet is nearly finished."

August 24: Beethoven writes to both Karl and Holz to say that the third quartet will have six movements and tells Karl that it will be "quite finished in ten or at most twelve days."[34]

January 1826: Schuppanzigh and the other members of his quartet rehearse the B-flat Quartet in Beethoven's apartment and find it very difficult to play, above all the fugue.[35] The work, originally offered to

Schlesinger in Berlin, is now accepted for publication in Vienna by Matthias Artaria, who pays Beethoven eighty ducats for it. The actual publication of the first edition, both in parts and in score, with the fugue as finale, takes six more months to appear.

March 21, 1826: The first performance of Opus 130 takes place in Vienna, played by the Schuppanzigh Quartet, with the fugue as finale.[36] The Presto and Alla danza tedesca are repeated; the audience is totally bewildered by the fugue. A reviewer in the *Allgemeine Musikalische Zeitung* writes that for him the fugue was "incomprehensible, like Chinese." He sympathizes with what seemed to be the performers' struggle to master its dissonances and registral extremes, and hints darkly that Beethoven's deafness must have led him astray.[37] Sometime in March Beethoven sends the completed quartet to Prince Galitzin.

April 24: A piano four-hand arrangement of the fugue is completed by Anton Halm, who is paid for it by Matthias Artaria on May 12 (Artaria no doubt intended to publish it). But Beethoven is dissatisfied with Halm's work and makes his own four-hand arrangement, giving it to Artaria for separate publication in August.

August: An engraving of Opus 130 with the fugue as finale is prepared for Matthias Artaria.[38] Word begins to circulate in Beethoven's circle, led by Holz and Johann van Beethoven, that the other quartet movements but not the finale are being well received, and that the fugue is extremely difficult for players and incomprehensible to the public. Holz later tells Lenz that, at the publisher's explicit request, he approached Beethoven with the idea of writing a new and more accessible finale, separating the fugue and publishing it separately with its own opus number, for which Artaria would pay a separate fee. Beethoven, according to Holz, "wanted time to think it over, but the next day he sent me a note in which he said that he was willing to comply . . . and that for the new finale I should negotiate a fee of fifteen ducats."[39] Although Holz makes it seem as if Beethoven came to this decision in something of a hurry, the whole question of separating the fugue, if it came up first in August, was posed about five months after the first performance in March. In all probability Beethoven thought about it carefully during these five months and the project likely gained credibility for him once the notion of a separate four-hand version was agreed on. In addition, an entry in the Conversation Books in August 1826 indicates that Artaria actually had a plan in mind to bring out each single movement of the quartet in a separate edition.[40]

September: Holz continues to encourage Beethoven to separate the fugue and write the new finale: "It would be more money for you and the publisher would have to pay the costs."[41] In late September, just as Beethoven is preparing to leave for Gneixendorf, Holz tells him, "You should work further on the finale. . . . [Y]ou'll have it done in an hour."[42]

Late September–November: At Gneixendorf Beethoven writes the new finale. He delivers it to Matthias Artaria on November 22, 1826.

March 26, 1827: Beethoven dies.

May 10: Artaria publishes first editions of Opus 130 (with the substitute finale, in score and parts) and of the *Grosse Fuge* as Opus 133, plus a four-hand arrangement of the fugue as Opus 134.

The two sides of the "finale" controversy regarding Opus 130/133 have hardened over the years. Some argue that since Beethoven authorized the separation of the fugue from the rest of the work, published it separately, and wrote the "little" finale in its place, this final decision to separate it should prevail. Another view, championed by Arnold Schoenberg and his associates in the Kolisch Quartet, is that Beethoven's conception of the work entailed the great fugue as its finale from the outset, that his agreement to separate it was not an artistic one but was more or less forced on him by his publisher and close associates—in short, that he let himself be persuaded to publish it with its own opus number and write the new finale, but not as a matter of deep artistic conviction. On this view the "right" version of the quartet has the *Grand Fugue* as finale.

There is justice on both sides, but except in performance we do not have to make an absolute choice. This is not the only case in which Beethoven changed movements after he thought a work was finished and used the excluded movement in another work or as a separate composition. An early example is the finale of the "Kreutzer" Sonata, originally planned as the finale for the A Major Violin Sonata, Opus 30 No. 1 and replaced there by the variations movement. Another is his excision of the *Andante favori* from the "Waldstein" Sonata in favor of the "Introduzione" to the finale. Anecdotal evidence suggests that at one time after the completion of the Ninth, Beethoven even considered substituting a purely instrumental finale for the vocal finale.[43]

The two finales are so different that what results from performing one or the other is an entirely different proportional and aesthetic structure for the whole work. The *Grand Fugue* originated as the largest and most radical of Beethoven's fugal finales. It is driven by the same impulse to use fugal textures to finish large cyclic works that brought about the finales of the Cello Sonata Opus 102 No. 2, the *Hammerklavier* Sonata Opus 106, and the A-flat Major Piano Sonata Opus 110. Its compositional scale is so large that we can compare it without exaggeration to the finale of the Ninth Symphony, with which it also has some direct affinities—one of them, and not the only one, is the B-flat-major "March" in 6/8 that inhabits a middle position in both.

That the work is dedicated to the archduke, coming in the wake of the great mass for his investiture, arouses further reflections, among them a link to other lengthy works in B-flat major that Beethoven dedicated to him, especially "his" Piano Trio and the *Hammerklavier* Sonata with its closing fugue. Like the finale of the Ninth, but without its humanitarian texts and political program, this work exemplifies Beethoven's commitment to writing great polyphonic works that transcend their traditions.

In the case of the *Grand Fugue,* the tradition includes Bach, and it has been argued that this fugue, with its exhaustive use of arcane fugal devices poured out in a movement of passionate energy and enormous expressive contrasts, is Beethoven's "Art of Fugue."[44] Without assurance that Bach's *Art of Fugue* could literally have been a model, or even that the features of the fugue must have resulted directly from Beethoven's close study of fugal procedures in the work of Albrechtsberger—though the evidence that he knew his old teacher's work is persuasive—nevertheless the figure of Bach looms over this movement, as it does over the other fugues and fugal finales of the late works. Beethoven's spiritual kinship to Bach in these years, his reverence for Bach's musical wisdom coupled with his own sense of purpose as both inheritor and innovator, is summed up perfectly in his urge to come to grips with what has been called the "nemesis" of fugue.[45] It has already been speculated that Beethoven's use of the Italian term "Overtura" for the introduction to the Grand Fugue, a term he used nowhere else, links to the tradition of the French "Ouverture," that long-familiar Baroque genre in which a slow section, often in "dotted" rhythm, passes into a swiftly moving contrapuntal Allegro.[46] Examples in Handel and Bach are legion, as they are in the works of many other Baroque composers, but Beethoven might well have known the examples in Bach's *Clavierübung*, the D-Major Suite, and the sixteenth variation in the "Goldberg" Variations.[47]

Whatever the terminology, the "Overtura" sets the stage for the entire vast structure that follows it, presenting its primary thematic material with the biggest of all his "off-tonic" openings, in four rhythmic versions that move harmonically down the circle of fifths, from G to C to F to the tonic destination, B-flat major (*W 58). Each of these versions is an instance of the basic intervallic material that will emerge in the two fugue subjects that constitute the main body of the first fugue. They provide preliminary visions of the later large sections of the work—almost as if, in opposition to the Ninth Symphony finale, they are "prefaces" to its sectional design, showing at once its vast diversity of material and its unity.

Decoding the larger form of the *Grand Fugue* presents as many problems as does studying the finale of the Ninth Symphony, and for many similar reasons. It is not a fugue in Bach's sense—the relentless working out of the combinatorial possibilities inherent in a single subject, or even at times two subjects. It is, rather, a poetic discourse of enormous size, a behemoth in which the fugal principle plays a leading role but is complemented by other textures. Also, a dialectic is worked out from start to finish that can be read into many formal templates without quite satisfying the basic requirements of any one of them. It is pretty well agreed that the work encompasses ten sections, as follows:

Section	Measures	Key	Tempo
1. "Overtura"	1–30	G–B-flat major	Allegro; Meno mosso; Allegro
2. Double fugue	31–158	B-flat major	Allegro 4/4
3. Double fugato	159–232	G-flat major	Meno mosso 2/4
4. Episode ("March")	233–272	B-flat major	Allegro molto e con brio 6/8
5. Double fugue	273–414	A-flat major	Allegro molto e con brio 6/8
6. "Fantasy"	415–492	E-flat major	Allegro molto e con brio 6/8
7. Double fugato + Transition	493–510 511–532	A-flat major Preparing B-flat	Reprise of Section 3 (Meno mosso 2/4)
8. "March"	533–564	B-flat major	Reprise of Section 4 (Allegro molto e con brio, 6/8)
9. Coda I	565–662	B-flat major	(Allegro molto e con brio, 6/8; brief contrasting tempos at 657–662)
10. Coda 2	663–741	B-flat major	Allegro molto e con brio, 6/8

The enormous reprises of Sections 7 and 8 suggest that a version of sonata form underlies the work. Thus the work has also been construed in the following way:

Overtura = introduction
Sections 2 and 3 = exposition of theme groups A and B
Section 4 as a coda to the exposition
Sections 5 and 6 = development
Sections 7 and 8 = recapitulation
Sections 9 and 10 = coda

The *Grand Fugue* has also been described as being the equivalent of a multi-movement work:

Overtura + Allegro (Sections 1 and 2) = the first movement
Section 3 = a slow movement
Section 4 = an interlude
Sections 5 and 6 = the equivalent of a Scherzo
Sections 7–10 = more or less a composite finale

Vincent D'Indy construed the work along Hegelian lines as revealing a mighty dialectic in which there is an opposition of two antagonistic views of Nature, represented by the primary themes that form the opening double fugue: "one gently melancholy" (the "A" theme), the other "exuberant in its gaiety" (the "B" theme). As D'Indy sees it, "after the presentation of the two subjects, open war begins between careless merriment and serious thought," the latter gradually winning over its thoughtless and frivolous opponent.[48]

As superficial as this viewpoint may be, it has the advantage over formal taxonomies of stressing the dynamic, outsized, Armageddon-like character of much of the work, in which powerful forces contend in a struggle for supremacy. This struggle reaches a first peak in the later portions of the first double fugue and rises to still higher tensions at later points, such as a passage where lengthy trills on extreme high and low pitches pile heavily on one another, playing out in enormous gestures the little trill that had appeared at the end of the opening theme of the entire piece.[49] The immense dialectic seems to strive for completion when the Meno mosso theme (originally Section 3) is given a full reprise at Section 7, now not in the smooth flowing *pianissimo* dynamic of Section 3 but rather in *forte* with heavy accents on every quarter note and with new fragments of the opposing theme, Theme "B," with its vast leaps in the cello, then the viola. At long last the whole settles down to a succession of closing phases, first exploring distant spiritual regions and then returning to a forceful, emphatic statements of the thematic material[50] before the last page rises to a final crescendo and brings the whole gigantic structure to rest.

How utterly different is the "second" finale, the "little" movement that Beethoven wrote as a substitute, ostensibly to satisfy his publishers, the performers, and the listening public, and perhaps to make a little extra money. Received opinion about this finale is that it is a light-hearted, easily digested, charming sonata-rondo movement in 2/4 with memorable tunes and an air of the Viennese tavern about it. Proponents of the *Grand Fugue*, above all from the Schoenbergian side, denounce it as an easygoing concession to necessity and see the publication and performance of the quartet with the fugue as an act of restoration. Thus a very serious and experienced Beethovenian writes,

> *Beethoven's agreement to write a new finale was an act of resignation.*
> *. . . [D]espite all its geniality, which cannot be denied to the new finale,*
> *we must absolutely declare that this movement has no inner relation-*
> *ship to the rest of the work. To any sensitive musician, the beginning of*
> *the light rondo finale after the dying away of the unearthly Cavatina*
> *must always come as a dreadful shock.*[51]

Schindler notoriously hated the *Grand Fugue* and joined the throng of admirers who breathed relief on hearing this new finale, persuading himself that its accessibility arose from its "similarity in style and clarity to many of the quartet movements of an earlier period."[52]

He could not have been more wrong. The undeniable air of charm and insouciance in the "little finale" is deceptive. It conceals a subtlety and intricacy of thematic interplay and sectional contrast that fits well with the earlier movements of the quartet, not as a big finale but as a clever, dancelike, beautifully proportioned closing movement that distributes the weight of the whole work back generously toward its predecessors. Beethoven not only devoted scrupulous care to its planning and execution, he saw to it that its material stands up to the previous movements and also reflects in subtle ways the basic thematic interval sequence that inhabits not only several of the last quartets but even the *Grand Fugue* itself.

The opening figure, a playful, two-note octave leap in the viola, has several functions (*W 59). It emphasizes the pitch G, thus stressing the same opening pitch that starts the *Grand Fugue*, but in a totally different way. The figure is a persistent accompaniment for the theme that enters in Violin 1 (though later the two-note octave leap turns out to have motivic functions as well). And the various returns of the two-note figure in the course of the movement enable Beethoven to fashion some Haydn-like jokes, as he uses it in different ways each time.[53] The main theme is intricate enough in its interior motives (no two of the first four measures have the same rhythm), and the speed and verve of the whole movement take their departure from the *pianissimo* character of the opening ten measures.

The exposition of the movement brings not two contrasting sections but three: the first in the tonic; the second in the dominant (so far all is normal), but the third in A-flat major, the flat seventh degree of the tonic, B-flat major.[54] This third segment of the exposition is the capstone of the movement, for not only does it bring new streaming legato thematic material into play, but it also makes room for groups of alternating four-note figures that have a familiar ring (*W 60).[55]

The four-note figure, with its characteristic shape (two notes in stepwise relationship, then a large upward leap, then downward by step) is nothing less than a nonchromatic version of the same shape that underlies the opening of the Quartet Opus 132, the principal subject of the *Grand Fugue*—and (before this finale was written) in the great fugato first movement of Opus 131! With all this, the movement rolls smoothly to its appointed ending without any of the emotional stress that is rampant in the *Grand Fugue*.

The little finale once more evokes the issue of dualism in Beethoven's art. Already in his second maturity we saw pairings of works in the same genre—often back to back and at times published consecutively—that exemplify aesthetic dualism: weight versus lightness; density versus lucidity; complexity versus simplicity. Examples include the "Waldstein" Sonata, Opus 53, and its companion, the F Major Sonata, Opus 54; the Fifth and Sixth Symphonies, which are correlative antipodes in so many ways; the Seventh and Eighth Symphonies; and the Trios Opus 70 No. 1 (the "Ghost" Trio) and its curiously romantic mate, Opus 70 No. 2. In many other cases, contrasts we can call dualistic appear in the relations of movements to one another within a cyclic work—here the most palpable examples are the abbreviated two-movement piano sonatas, such as Opus 54 itself, Opus 78, and the almost late Opus 90, with its enigmatic E-minor first movement and its full-throated lyrical second movement. With the finale of Opus 130 and the Grand Fugue, Opus 133, the dualism is one of alternatives, since in performance we must have one not the other, and this concept is new in Beethoven's output. But if we consider that the second finale brings a lightness of touch and intricacy of connections against the monumental weight, relentless intellectual earnestness, and heavy dissonance of the *Grand Fugue,* we can imagine that Beethoven was in effect giving the world two choices, not absolutely displacing one with another. And that legacy has not been lost on performers, many of whom now, in Beethoven quartet cycles, play the whole work twice, once with each finale. In effect, they are being true to the spirit with which Beethoven, in his last months, came to a complex vision of this great work.

Opus 131

Directly following his completion of Opus 130 Beethoven embarked on the C-sharp Minor Quartet, Opus 131. This means, and the sketches show, that he moved directly from work on the *Grand Fugue* to his first sketches for this new quartet, "as if," as one writer puts it, "the profound catharsis of the former had released the serene lyricism of the latter."[56] To which we can add that the immediate move from the expansive variety of the *Grand Fugue* to the single-minded concentration of the first movement of Opus 131 shows Beethoven adapting fugal principles to two entirely different aesthetic situations that he created in immediate succession. Since he had now fulfilled Galitzin's commission for three quartets—and done it with a trilogy of depth and scope such as the world had not seen before—this new quartet was an independent venture, for which he was offered a fee of eighty ducats by Schott in Mainz, thirty more than he had been promised by Galitzin (if he could collect it from Galitzin) for each of the three previous quartets.[57] Schott had stepped forward as Beethoven's major publisher in the preceding few years.[58] That he needed the money, as he always did, is a basic biographical truth, but it does not remotely suffice to "explain" his purposes in writing Opus 131.[59] Beethoven told Schott in May that the new quartet was finished, but he delayed sending it to them for several months, finally dispatching it in August. Despite the shock brought on by Karl's attempted suicide on July 30, he was able to regain his footing by turning back to his work, not only in composing but in seeing to the usual round of publication arrangements. He never saw the quartet in print, since the first edition did not come out until June 1827, almost three months after his death. Nor did he hear it in a public setting, as it was never played in concert during the short remainder of his lifetime. It was, however, rehearsed privately by the quartet now being led by Joseph Böhm, and in November 1828 Holz apparently led a quartet that played it for Franz Schubert, whose last musical request is said to have been to hear Opus 131.[60]

That he now chose the odd key of C-sharp minor was a vital condition for the new quartet, a mark of its special sound image. He had not used this key for any work other than the "Moonlight" Sonata, Opus 27 No. 2; nor had Haydn used it more than once (in the Piano Sonata Hob. XVI/36, apparently written in the mid-1770s), while Mozart avoided it entirely.[61] Choosing C-sharp minor for a quartet meant that the semitone motion B♯–C♯ would entail B♯ (= C♮) as the open string in viola and cello, especially in the cello at the bottom of the quartet's registral span. And Beethoven makes good use of this effect in the cello at the end of the first movement (with cello B♯ against a high D♮ in Violin 1) as well as in the basic theme of the finale. Accordingly this extreme use of the open string as leading tone is reserved for the two C-sharp-minor movements that anchor the work.

As with Opus 132 and 130, another radically new formal plan dominates the work. Because Beethoven was persuaded to add numbers to the movements (just as he was to put rehearsal letters in the first great double fugue of the *Grand Fugue*), the number of separate movements in the work was fixed at seven. Ever since, seven has been graven in stone in the critical literature despite the fact that it hardly accounts for the true organization of the work. The movement plan of the finished work (published, as always, using Beethoven's numbers) is this:

1. Adagio ma non troppo e molto espressivo; C-sharp minor; 2/2; closes into
2. Allegro molto vivace; D major; 6/8; closes into
3. Allegro moderato; B minor–A major; 4/4; actually a short transition to
4. Andante ma non troppo e molto cantabile; A major; 2/4
5. Presto; E major; 2/2; marked "attacca" at end, to move without pause to
6. Adagio quasi un poco andante; G-sharp minor; 3/4; moves directly to
7. Allegro; C-sharp minor; 2/2.

If we recognize that movement 3 is simply an eleven-measure transition between D major and A major—a formal and psychological bridge but not really an independent movement—and also that movement No. 6 is a short, slow introduction to the finale (although it is in the dominant minor), then the quartet becomes a peculiar type of five-movement work, somewhat akin to Opus 132.[62]

But another view can be advanced, construing the work in four large units:

Unit 1. Movements 1 and 2, where the first, fugal Adagio is construed as an immense slow introduction to an Allegro (although it is an introduction that outweighs the Allegro). The tonal sequence C-sharp–D for a pair of adjacent movements is unheard of in Beethoven and almost unique in the literature; only the adventurous Haydn had done it in his last piano sonata, where an E-major slow movement is flanked by E-flat-major movements. But in Opus 131 the C-sharp–D sequence is just the beginning of a tonal motion to far-flung regions. The short transition ("No. 3") leads from Unit 1 to Unit 2.

Unit 2. The Andante, a variations movement in 2/4; A major (one step up in the circle of fifths from movement 2).

Unit 3. The Scherzo; E major (another step upward in the circle of fifths).

Unit 4. The Adagio and Allegro form a second paired slow introduction and Allegro, entirely different from the pairing of movements 1 and 2; the keys are now G-sharp minor (relative minor of the E-major Scherzo) and the home tonic of C-sharp minor.

And there are grounds for hearing the whole as an enormously expanded four-movement structure, leaving out No. 3 as an independent entity and construing the slow sections as introductions. In that sense it seems like a distant parallel to Opus 127 or Opus 132 rather than to the authentic six-movement plan of Opus 130.

That all these ideas and more were in Beethoven's mind as he worked is clear from the five different movement plans that have been unearthed from the sketches.[63] In the first one Beethoven considered making the work a true four-movement composition consisting of the C-sharp-minor fugue; a recitative leading to the Andante in A major; a scherzo in D major; and a tonic finale in duple meter. Other sketched plans included reducing the work to a three-movement cycle, with an opening fugue in C-sharp minor, then an Allegro in C-sharp major, and a last movement in C-sharp minor, a sequence that recalls the "Moonlight" Sonata of twenty-five years earlier.[64] But all the remaining plans bring back the 2/4 Andante, showing that he clearly wanted to keep the variations middle movement as a foil to the fugal first movement. Movement plan no. 3 sways the harmonic path toward F-sharp minor after the opening C-sharp minor fugue; this was to be followed by an F-sharp minor 6/8 Allegro; then the A-major slow movement; then a scherzo in F-sharp minor; and finally a fifth movement in C-sharp minor. At the end of this third sketched movement plan is the notation "end of the last movement," showing a close in D-flat major! And this plan connects to a surprising finale score sketch in which it is clear that Beethoven was thinking of ending the work with a D-flat-major postlude whose theme is identical to the theme of the slow movement of Opus 135![65] This transfer is even more remarkable than his shifting the Alla danza tedesca from Opus 132 to Opus 130 (changed from A major to G major). Of course the idea of ending the gigantic work as a whole in the major mode (final paragraph and final chords in C-sharp major) does survive in the final version. The remaining movement plans (fourth and fifth) include other elaborate fantasies about the middle movements, but all the plans keep the opening fugue intact.

The opening of the first movement is unearthly (*W 61). The slow unfolding of the four statements of the main subject, in strict fugal order and from top to bottom, gradually fills the registral space; we suddenly realize that the composer of this deeply expressive exposition had, three years earlier, written the opening measures of the Ninth Symphony in which a filling out of a large registral space also takes place gradually and systematically, though of course using entirely different means.

A central feature of the subject is its division into two parts: the four-note head motive "a," with its motion 5–7–1–6 (bringing a focus on the semitones 5–6 and 7–1); and its tail, the "b" motive, a gradual turning motive around scale step 5 (G♯). The special expressive quality of the initial crescendo leading to an accent on the A in measure 2, followed by a steady *piano* on the tail of the theme, dramatizes the division between the two parts and prepares the way for the contrasting use of these two types of gestures—the dynamic crescendo-to-accent gesture and the placid, flowing gesture—throughout the entire movement.

Once the exposition is accomplished the movement proceeds by a series of closely packed segments, some of them strettos (close imitations) on the head motive, some using the tail motive, and finally an augmentation in the cello to end the movement. All of these are woven into a continuous fugal fabric while at the same time the larger harmonic and thematic plan ranges much more widely than most traditional fugues—and it presages the wider harmonic trajectory of the quartet's movements. In the first movement the modulatory scheme leads from the initial C-sharp minor to B major and D-sharp minor, to E major and A major, to D major, and then returns to its home tonic, C-sharp minor, fixing firmly on the tonic key all the way to the end despite a few inflections.[66] This return somewhat resembles that of a sonata-form recapitulation, a feeling that is reinforced when the viola then brings back the first subject in complete form in the home tonic, C-sharp minor, *for the first time since the beginning*, and is answered by Violin 2 in close imitation in the subdominant (F-sharp minor) with the head motive, with exactly the same pitches we heard right near the beginning of the movement. Through the movement the main subject, especially the tail motive, has appeared in various forms, including diminution, stretto, and close imitation. One passage

in particular has always struck deep into the minds of listeners for its sensuous beauty: the two violins alone answer one another with an altered
vision of the tail motive (*W 62).[67]

The larger pattern of dynamics in the movement at first oscillates
between periods of crescendo-to-accent patterns and periods of placid
flow. But in the last large segment, the harmony having settled down in the
tonic, the crescendo phrases become more and more frequent, more and
more insistent. As the movement reaches its climax, the rising and falling
waves of intensity coincide with the extremes of dissonance created by the
high D♮ in Violin 1 against the low B♯ in the cello (*W 63). No moment of
harmonic resolution anywhere in music is stronger than the arrival of the
C-sharp-major chord in these closing measures, for this chord has not been
heard before in the movement, and will not be heard again until the very
end of the last movement.

It is by now a commonplace of the literature that the intervallic substance of the main fugue subject (two semitones a major third apart, with
the four notes variously interchangeable in order) is nearly identical to a
traditional fugue subject that stems from antecedents that go back to Bach.
Other composers, including Haydn and Mozart, also used it. In all of these
examples, as in Opus 131, the two semitones occur in the pitch relationships 7–1 and 6–5 in minor, which Kirkendale called a "pathotype."[68] What
has not been adequately considered, however, is the likelihood that Bach
alone is the true background figure for this movement, in particular his
Well-Tempered Clavier with its array of fugal masterpieces. We remember,
of course, that Beethoven had known the collection (at least Book I and
perhaps both books) since childhood.[69] The theme of Bach's own
C-sharp-minor Fugue, No. 4, in Book I, has an obvious affinity to Beethoven's subject.

(a) Bach, The Well-Tempered Clavier, *Book I, Fugue No. 4 in* C♯ *Minor, beginning:*

[etc.]

(b) Beethoven, String Quartet in C# minor, Opus 131, first movement, beginning:

But there is more. Another fugue of exceptional importance is the last in Book I, No. 24, in B minor. Bach organized the collection not only to show the viability of all major and minor keys (thus showing that the keyboard is "well-tempered" and fully usable) but also to demonstrate a wide range of subjects and what he could do with them in a correspondingly rich and varied set of fugues. The first fugue in the book opens with a rising figure in C major that recalls the "natural" hexachord of medieval and Renaissance music, in its normal position on C, rising from C to A, then moving onward. For the last fugue in the book Bach uses a "modern" subject that includes all twelve tones of the chromatic scale and is also shaped in such a way that, after its initial use of chord tones on the B-minor tonic triad, it forms four-note groups with increasingly chromatic content and widening interval spans. If we mark off the components as units "a," "b," and "c," some affinities to Beethoven's subject become clear.

Bach, The Well-Tempered Clavier, *Book I, Fugue No. 24 in B minor, beginning, with initial motives labeled "a," "b," "c":*

After the initial triad motion of "a," figure "b" has the exact pitch content of Beethoven's subject; and the figure "c" presents the related figure that he uses for the opening of Opus 132; from here it is only a step to the form he uses for the subject of the *Grand Fugue*. And a passage mentioned earlier from Beethoven's first movement is also prefigured in an episode within Bach's B-minor fugue:[70]

Bach, The Well-Tempered Clavier, *Book I, Fugue No. 24 in B minor, excerpt, with motif labeled "m":*

Ex. 7

It is certainly striking to discover that Beethoven copied this B-minor fugue from *The Well-Tempered Clavier, on four staves,* for string quartet. The copy may date from about 1817, a time when Bach fugues were very much on his mind, as we see from the fact that at about the same time, while composing the *Hammerklavier* Sonata, he copied the B-flat Minor Fugue from Book I of the same collection.[71]

In one way or another each of the remaining movements reflects the influence of the main subject of the fugue, in that the intervallic content of the main theme of each successive movement contains unmistakable elements of the semitones-and-leap configuration of the head motive of the fugue subject. The D-major Allegro movement, No. 2, contrasts sharply with the deep windings of the preceding fugue. Its opening moves in smoothly shaped symmetrical phrases in a clear-cut D major with sustained chords in the lower strings. Though the theme gains in urgency and complexity as it goes, its broad outlines are as clear as its melodic substance.

From the Allegro's quiet ending emerges the curious short transition

Fugue No. 24 from J. S. Bach's Well-Tempered Clavier, Book I, *copied around 1817 by Beethoven, who used its primary subject as a source of ideas for his last string quartets. (Bibliothek der Gesellschaft der Musikfreunde, Vienna)*

("No. 3") that first establishes B minor and then shifts course toward E major and then E as the dominant of A major. The little piece starts out in Allegro as if it were quoting the opening of Opus 59 No.2, then through short figures (as at the opening of the first movement, moving down in imitation from Violin 1 to cello) it cadences firmly on B minor. From here the tempo changes to Adagio, in which Violin 1 takes off on a long roulade (we have seen such cadenzas before in Beethoven's quartet writing, as in Opus 59 No. 1 to prepare the finale)—the whole little passage paves the way for the lyricism to come.

What follows is the centerpiece of the whole work—the A-major Andante variations movement. Its larger shape is that of a theme and six variations plus coda, but that is merely the skeleton. Its theme is a lyric tune in A major, divided between the two violin parts so as to give prominence to the pitches 1–7–4–3 (A–G♯–D–C♯), thus reflecting the semitones-plus-leap figure. The variations shed every kind of new light on the theme's inherent possibilities, carrying out the process of variation as a kind of formal counterpart to what the fugal first movement does combinatorially for its first theme, of which this A-major tune is a relative. And the coda of the movement breaks free from the variation process and moves into a succession of short phrases built on the opening of the theme, first in C major then again in A major. It then moves suddenly into F major then accelerates into an outburst in Violin 1 that leads by a fantastic swooping cadenza to the emotional high point of the entire movement, an A-major chord in extreme registers with its high-placed 7–1 in Violin 1. It recalls the 7–1 that had been prominent in the fugue subject, then lapses downward to its quiet and serene close in high range for all four strings.[72]

The Scherzo erupts as a low, barking triadic figure in the cello, then a silence; then the main theme picks up this figure and sweeps it forward. Duple-meter scherzi are more common in late Beethoven than earlier, where a rare specimen had been the 2/4 Scherzo of the clever Piano Sonata Opus 31 No. 3. Others are found in Opus 110, the Opus 130 Quartet, and the Trios of the Scherzi of the Ninth and of the *Pastoral* Symphony (the *Pastoral* occurred to Wagner when he wrote a program note for this quartet). The range of experiment with sonorities in this movement goes beyond even Beethoven's most expansive previous quartet scherzi— witness the various uses of pizzicato and the final statement of the main theme *sul ponticello*, a first use of this rubric in quartet writing that tells the players to play close to the bridge, producing a strange nasal effect and a parody of the theme. But the movement recovers its gravity and normal bowing shortly before the end, and in a smashing crescendo the final cadence ends it all *fortissimo*. Then come three portentous G♯ strokes to prepare another new key and movement.

The new movement is the 3/4 Adagio in G-sharp minor. The Adagio provides the statement and three repetitions of a clear-cut thematic phrase. It is a dirge that ends on the tonic, the second time with a pungent flatted second degree (A♮) that intensifies the semitone inflection at the cadence each time it appears. The brief movement also includes a short figure, derived from the main theme and used in imitation.[73] Before it can all expand further, the work plunges into the finale.

The finale has to ground the work as a tonal, cyclical, formal, and psychological whole. It does all of that. First it restores C-sharp minor absolutely; second, its main theme has clear intervallic affinities with the opening of the fugue subject (*W 64). It has a compact head motive (this time twofold, statement and answer) and a scalar tail motive in a dotted rhythm that has no precedent in the work. After this a third important theme springs up, also clearly derived in intervals *and rhythm* from the head motive of the fugue subject (now the four-note sequence begins 1–7–6–5), and a full-scale eight-measure phrase emerges (*W 65).

The larger form of the finale oscillates between rondolike returns of the opening theme (though not in the home tonic until halfway through) and sonata-form features. This rondo- and sonata-form ambiguity is not new in Beethoven's finales, as the last movements of the Second and Eighth Symphonies bear witness. But here it appears in a context in which only the most abstract formal outlines govern the action. I opt for the sonata-form interpretation, which makes better sense of the situation. It is, after all, no accident that the biggest and strongest return of the main theme is reserved for its reappearance in the tonic, C-sharp minor,[74] where it returns *fortissimo* in the cello under powerful contrasting figures in the higher strings, as if there were too much material to be accounted for to have a simple and direct repetition of the opening unison statement of the theme.

The fury of the final Allegro acts to release the pent-up energy that is so lyrically controlled in three earlier movements: the fugue, the D-major Allegro, and the Andante. In the Scherzo, hell breaks loose but in a subsidiary key, and with wit and humor. The G-sharp-minor introduction returns the work to the contemplative seriousness of the first movement, so it remains for the finale to find new reserves of energy with which to resume the note of courage with which the work ends. The turn to C-sharp major at the end, with its threefold chords with the tonic in the bass, takes possession of the whole work and brings it to its homecoming on a note of grandeur, no longer (and not possibly) the ending in triumph of earlier heroic works but with a deeper quality of affirmation that emerges from tragedy in its highest form.

Opus 135

In sketches, in Beethoven's autograph fair copies of both the score and all four parts, and in the first edition of his last quartet—Opus 135, in F major—stands an enigmatic heading followed by a musical staff containing two musical phrases, both with text.

The opening of the autograph violin 1 part of Beethoven's Quartet, Opus 135, Finale. The heading, inserted by the composer in all four string parts, reads (in translation), "The resolution reached with difficulty." The words below the music read, "Must it be?" and "It must be!" (Beethoven-Haus, Bonn, Bodmer Collection)

Transcription of the autograph heading for the finale of Opus 135:

Der schwer gefaßte Entschluß.

This heading translates as "The resolution reached with difficulty"; "Must it be?" "It must be!" It relates directly to a canon (WoO 196) that Beethoven is supposed to have written several months before starting work on the quartet. The joking four-voice canon, on the text "Es muss sein! Ja, heraus mit dem Beutel!" ("It must be! Yes, take out your wallet!") uses the same basic theme as the finale. According to Holz the story concerns an amateur named Ignaz Dembscher, who held chamber-music sessions at his house in Vienna. It seems that Dembscher had failed to attend the premiere of Opus 130 in March 1826 but wanted to have the work performed at his home, since, as Thayer reports, "it was easy for him to get manuscripts from Beethoven."[75] But Beethoven refused to let him have it because he had not come to Schuppanzigh's concert, so Holz told Dembscher to send Schuppanzigh fifty florins, the subscription price of the concert. Dembscher is supposed to have asked in joking fashion, "Muss es sein?" Whereupon, when Holz told all this to Beethoven, he supposedly sat down at once and wrote out the four-voice canon.[76]

But sketch evidence suggests another dating. Received opinion is that Beethoven wrote the canon in April but did not embark on Opus 135 before the late summer and fall of 1826. During the spring of 1826 he was heavily engaged in writing Opus 131, which he finished (he said in a letter) on July 12. Sketches show that drafts for the canon (including fragments of its text, such as "heraus mit dem Beutel") occur on leaves containing sketches for the conclusion of the Opus 131 finale, and the physical and handwriting evidence point to their being written in close proximity.[77] If this is true, then the canon might have been worked out later than April, for it also appears from the sketch material that the canon and the finale were both written near the end of Beethoven's labors on the C-sharp Minor Quartet.[78] This general dating is confirmed by the Conversation Books, which contain an entry in July in which Beethoven mentions to Holz plans for a new quartet in F, to which Holz notes that "it will be the third in F major ... there is still none [i.e., a quartet] in D minor."[79] At times sketches for the canon and for the finale are so tightly intermingled that they cannot be, or at least have not yet been, fully separated from one another.

All this is by way of explanation for the startling inscription that Beethoven placed at the head of the music, "Der schwer gefasste Entschluss." These words have been variously interpreted by scholars as a joke, as a terse German phrase out of daily life, or, in a serious vein, as a reference to Beethoven's alleged difficulty in deciding to finish the work in the light of Karl's suicide attempt and his own despair and debilitation.[80] The expression "Der schwer gefasste Entschluss" has a formal and legalistic ring to it, and therefore it recalls Beethoven's gruff and aggressive use of legal-sounding language when he wanted to be bitter and ironic, as in the draft of the attack on publishers regarding a complete edition of his works that he left among his posthumous papers. As a formal expression, the phrase "Unterzeichnete den Entschluss gefasst" ("the undersigned have reached the decision") had been used by the archduke and the princes Lobkowitz and Kinsky in 1809 in the legal agreement by which they agreed to pay Beethoven his annuity of four thousand florins.[81] Since Beethoven's sketches for the finale include a pair of alternative phrases—"der gezwungene Entschluss" ("the forced decision") and "der harte Entschluss" ("the hard-won decision")—we can see him trying out other possibilities in his usual vein, much as he did when trying to find the right way of introducing the baritone soloist in the finale of the Ninth Symphony with his sententious "O Freunde."[82] At all events, the final version of the heading refers directly to the two texted musical phrases that follow, which are in bass clef, in Grave tempo and 3/2 meter. They consist of the three-note figure on the question "Muss es sein?" and its answer, in treble clef, Allegro, 2/2, "Es muss sein!" which is given twice. The two phrases directly anticipate the openings of the main sections of the finale.

Although Beethoven's legendary humor is plentifully represented in his works, and although the whole inscription could be seen as a joke, there is more here than meets the eye. Other late quartet movements with special titles include the "Heiliger Dankgesang" ("Holy Song of Thanksgiving") of Opus 132 and the "Cavatina" of Opus 130; but they differ in that they signify these movements as special instances of generally known song types, prayer and aria. Closer to the Opus 135 heading as personal statement is the inscription over the Dona nobis pacem of the *Missa solemnis*, namely "Prayer for inner and outer peace." This is also deeply personal, and we know that here too Beethoven labored long over its wording before he found the right solution.[83] An earlier instance—notably, for a quartet finale—is *La Malinconia* as a title for the last movement of Opus 18 No. 6.

Accordingly, we should take the inscription seriously as a personal statement about the content of the movement and its meanings. One of these emerges from its "prefatory" function; the phrases show that the movement will be based dialectically on two musical elements—or two forms of the same element—that go with this question and answer. The question falls and rises. The answer, its near inversion both musically and verbally, rises and falls. The answer comes twice, to make the reply more emphatic but also because the second phrase brings the motif down a full step. The question (as the opening shows in its signature) is in F minor; the answer is in F major. So the polarity is one of minor followed by major; of doubt followed by assertion; of uncertainty followed by an emphatic twofold gesture of determination. There is no personified speaker; it is, as Kerman put it, the quartet that speaks.[84]

What is the meaning of the inscription? We do not know, and are not meant to know in any specific sense, what is being asked and answered. We cannot miss the feeling that something basic is afoot, but we cannot define it in words or concepts. That may be the point. As in the Ninth Symphony cello-bass recitatives and at various points in other late works, Beethoven is driving instrumental music to the limits of speech, making instruments "almost speak"—as he had done in recitatives and other quasi-sung instrumental movements and works from early on—but with this runic inscription he raises the semantic potential of two vital musical figures to an even higher peak by using prefatory versions of these figures as settings of bits of text.

A number of decodings have been suggested. One is that this inscription refers to Beethoven's own sense of the struggle for meaning in life, which for Beethoven is found in art. He had written the following to Prince Galitzin in his letter about the correction in Opus 127:

Believe me when I say that my supreme aim is that my art should be welcomed by the noblest and most cultured people. Unfortunately we are dragged down from the supernatural element in art only too rudely

*into the earthly and human sides of life. Yet is it not precisely they who
are related to us?*[85]

The inscription may connect as well to those runic sayings in the *Tagebuch*
of 1811–18, in which Beethoven had sought refuge from his isolation and
psychic anguish in mottos and statements of stoic resignation. Thus:
"Learn to keep silent, oh friend," or "Live only in your art, for you are so
limited in your senses; this is nevertheless the only existence for you." And
elsewhere, "Endurance—Resignation—Resignation. Thus we profit by the
deepest misery and make ourselves worthy, so that God [can forgive us]
our mistakes."[86] The question and answer, "Must it be?" "It must be!" is like
a *Tagebuch* entry in a finished work. We should also remember Holz's comment to von Lenz that when he told Beethoven that his favorite among the
three Galitzin quartets was Opus 130, Beethoven replied "Each in its own
way! Art demands of us that we don't stand still"; as Holz added, "he used
to speak this way, in an Imperial style." It is not far-fetched to imagine Beethoven asking and answering the question "Must it be?" to himself and perhaps to others, expecting no explanation and giving none.

The formal layout of the whole work has occasioned comment, much
of it wedded to the view that Opus 135 is a throwback, a retreat to classical
models and compositional techniques. The basis for this judgment lies
essentially in externals, in Beethoven's return in this work to a smaller compositional scale, his reestablishment of the traditional four-movement
model, the apparent renewal of sonata-form procedures in the first and last
movements. Kerman places it among works he calls "nostalgic—elusive
spiritual 'parodies' of an earlier style, evocations of the artistic world of
Haydn and Mozart," and Ratner hears "much in this work that reminds the
listener of an earlier style, the eighteenth-century *galant*."[87] But these comments fail to look behind the mask of affability that the quartet wears on
its surface, disclosing unmistakable features of his late quartet style and
much that moves in new directions within that style.[88] We might also consider that, earlier, when Beethoven wanted to balance a big heroic or tragic
work with a more modest and intimate one, he often turned comfortably
to F major—consider Opus 54 after the "Waldstein," the Sixth Symphony
after the Fifth, the Eighth after the Seventh.

The opening phrase of the first movement discloses subtleties that could not possibly come from earlier times (*W 66). If we look at the curiously laconic opening figure in the viola, several features emerge. The most obvious is the off-tonic opening in F major, with two main subfigures. One is a little three-note figure that flips upward from G to B♭ (at once echoed in Violin 1); the other is the dotted figure F–G–E that immediately follows.

Furthermore, the first notes of the viola phrase, moving upward from G to B♭ and down to F, outline the "Es muss sein" figure from the canon and finale—literally identical to its second statement beginning on G. The perfect-fourth intervals are ubiquitous in the movement, as well as being prominent in the "Es muss sein" figure. The second figure, heard in both viola and cello, which mixes F major and minor, is a compressed form of the same basic theme type that dominates the late quartets—two semitones with inner leap—that we know from the openings of Opus 132, Opus 131, and the *Grand Fugue.*

The further development of the first movement is filled with quirks and odd moments that have stimulated questions about its use of discontinuous, short, pithy phrases whose order and positions are susceptible of curious interchanges, as if phrases heard earlier could in imagination be placed later, scrambling the sense of time. The view has been proposed that this movement makes use of several orders of time and does so "polyphonically" by embedding "nonlinear" as well as "linear" events within the work by separating its clock time from its "gestural time." As an example, the strong cadence shortly after the movement opens has been cited, a moment that has the impact but not the function of a final cadence, a cadence that is found again right after the beginning of the recapitulation and at the end of the movement.[89] It is not merely that these cadences are identical but that in effect the movement "ends three times" and that "these moments do not so much seem to refer to or repeat one another as they seem to be exactly the same moment in gestural-time, experienced time."[90] The first movement's ability to sustain such interpretations while maintaining the logic and continuity of its phrase elements and themes only begins to suggest the range of its subtleties. That the movement shares procedures familiar in other late quartets appears from its use of contrapuntal artifice. Thus the development begins with a fugato built on the opening figure and a curious leap-and-step theme (which first appears right after the first of the three cadences), which now combine in fugue-like fashion before giving way to other contrasting processes that move the section through its harmonic paths.

The Scherzo is another sample of Beethoven's mordant humor, now unleashed on a colossal scale through rhythmic displacement in the first phrase (*W 67). The syncopation and displacement distantly recall an early F-major Scherzo, that of the Violin Sonata Opus 24. There the violin is persistently off beat with the piano in a similar way in the Scherzo; also as here, the Trio relieves the rhythmic strain by bringing all parts together in regularity before the reprise of the Scherzo again tears them apart. The harmonic expansion of the Scherzo marks it as true late Beethoven: the larger harmonic layout of the movement, with its big sections in F major, G major, and A major, mirrors in the larger span the rising melodic motion from F to G to A that is prominent in the first phrase in Violin 1. And, beyond the irresistible momentum of the whole movement, its obsessive attention to certain odd elements (for example, the E♭ repeated on off beats that starts the second part of the Scherzo and the incessant repetition of the same figure for more than fifty measures at the end of the Trio!) rests a feeling that, even more than some of the other late scherzos, this one is laden with inner complexities that only now and then flash out as moments of surprise. The greatest such surprise is surely the ending. Repeating the tonic chord three time on off beats (in the rhythm of enigmatic E-flats that appear earlier), the ending simmers down through successive levels of dynamics from *forte* through a diminuendo to *piano* to *più piano* to *pianissimo* and then to a sudden *forte* downbeat that takes our breath away (*W 68). Thinking back, we recall that this way of ending a movement, with "terraced" dynamics becoming progressively softer, was his way of ending several late-quartet slow movements—the "Heiliger Dankgesang" of Opus 132, the Cavatina of Opus 130, and the Adagio first movement of Opus 131.[91]

To leaven the wit and brilliance with depth of feeling, Beethoven brings on the slow movement, Lento assai, cantante e tranquillo ("Quite slow, singing and tranquil"). This D-flat-major movement matches the other movements in packing density of thought into a short time span, now in the form of a beautiful melody plus variations that range over Beethoven's time-honored variation procedures, each one adding a new layer of emotional meaning to the movement as it proceeds. The opening "curtain," building a D-flat-major tonic chord by adding an instrument on each beat, reminds us of the opening of the Opus 127 variation slow movement, and we can also recall that this entire D-flat-major Lento, which is as centered and "settled" as any Beethovenian slow movement, was once under consideration as a tranquil ending for Opus 131. Further evocations of other late quartets are found in its "Più lento" variation, No. 2, which is notated in C-sharp minor and reminds us of the "oppressed" (*beklemmt*) section in the Cavatina of Opus 130. The canonic imitation between cello and Violin 1 in the third variation binds the movement by association to some of the deepest moments of the Opus 131 first movement, a connection that will return in the finale.

And at last "The resolution reached with difficulty" brings us to the finale (*W 69). The contrast of the question and answer, with their two versions of the same basic motive, form the essence of the movement, Beethoven's last adventure in dialectic. The Grave insists on the question, always presenting it in bass register and repeating it four times insistently on rising scale steps of F minor; at first the upper strings reply softly with scalar figures in F minor and then B-flat minor, but soon reduce their material to a three-note *forte* figure that they repeat to the end. This figure seems to soften the dialogue of lower and upper strings in the last three measures of the Grave when the "question" disappears and only the figure remains; significantly this happens as the upper strings reach the note D♭, for the figure D♭–C will be among the important elements of the whole finale. And now the "answer" erupts in the F major of the Allegro main section of the finale, over a rising bass that manages to insert an E♭ into its F-major scale content.

The continuation of the "Es muss sein" phrase is one of those passages in Beethovenian discourse that turn out to have much greater importance then they seem to at first. This second figure of the Allegro has been noted as having the form of the descending fourth and rising third that relates it to both the slow movement main theme and to the contour of the "Es muss sein" itself; but what has not been noticed is that it also harks back to the tail of the main theme of the first movement of Opus 131, which is used throughout that movement. We see this figure in Opus 131 both in diminution and where it emerges in canon between the two violins, singing in upper register. How closely the Opus 135 finale follows this structural model, however different the emotional and aesthetic context. The figure, at various places in the movement, combines with itself as a canon, but with the canonic answers at a different pitch level; the culminating such moment is in the D major section in the recapitulation, which replicates the A major section but with the cello now as leading voice. As to the import of this figure, it reflects back to Opus 131—but we have seen that in turn it also has a long-range connection to the B-minor fugue of *The Well-Tempered Clavier,* Book I. I do not propose a "Bach quotation" in either work, although the spirit of Bachian polyphony, in Beethoven's hands, is certainly palpable in the fugato movement of Opus 131. But when it appears here, it is as if the same Bachian antecedent can be reincarnated within a composition whose style and spirit seems utterly removed from Bach. That the same figure can live in both styles may be the point.

A further mark of the dramatic character and structure of this finale is this: the Grave returns in an intensified form of its earlier state, not a simple repeat (just as the recapitulation in the first movement intensifies and magnifies the opening). In the return of the Grave the upper strings roar repeated-note harmonies that are partly dissonant with the "question" below. A further mark of the growth we feel now is that the "answer" ("Es muss sein") does not wait for the Allegro but now appears *in* the Grave for the first time, so that question and answer are in close juxtaposition, seemingly vying for supremacy. And from here the Allegro recapitulation takes off once more, but reharmonized by the lower strings over a dominant pedal that breathes a spirit telling us that all's right with the world. The same confirmation comes at the end, where "Es muss sein" is the last word, first twice in *pianissimo,* then in a *fortissimo* gesture that triumphs over all earlier questions.

Final Thoughts

In the brief time that remained to him after finishing Opus 135 at Gneixendorf in October 1826, Beethoven took a month to compose the "little" finale for Opus 130 and then ceased writing quartets. His efforts in the last months focused on a C-major string quintet, for which he had accepted a commission from Diabelli a few years earlier, and some sketches toward a tenth symphony that never got off the ground.[92] Schindler claimed that Beethoven worked on the quintet until twelve days before his death, but we have no basis for believing him. At all events, the surviving quintet fragments show several efforts at a slow introduction to the first movement, but nothing sufficiently articulated to warrant considering it a developed conception. What is important, though, is that by turning to other genres, Beethoven left Opus 135 as his final quartet. Conceivably he regarded it as such, and even if we can never be sure that he would not have returned to quartet writing had he lived some years longer, it remains that at the time of completing it (and then writing the Opus 130 finale) he was in effect designating Opus 135 as the last work in this cycle, that is, the Galitzin trilogy plus Opus 131 and 135.

If we regard the last two—the C-sharp minor and this F major—as a complementary pair, they embody the highest tragedy and subtlest comedy that he ever achieved. They stand as the last word in Beethovenian dualism. That Opus 131 is a tragic work hardly needs further explication; the critical literature from Wagner's time to our own shows that it has long been understood as the most inward and searching of his late works while it is also, in content and form, the most innovative and most integrated of the late quartets. The whole work, but certainly its first and last movements, stand with Beethoven's explorations of dark emotions—the *Eroica* Funeral March; the "Appassionata;" the Fifth Symphony; the F Minor Quartet, Opus 95; Florestan's "Dungeon" scene; and the first movement of the Ninth Symphony—as his final word on the ways in which the human soul, confronted by an implacable world, comes to terms with fate and mortality through struggle but at last through endurance and resignation.

By common consent Opus 135 is its polar opposite—a work that steps forward into the light of day, raising serious questions but framing them in wholly different ways: by directness, humaneness, and what Kundera calls the "unbearable lightness of being." With its enigmatic question and answer as to whether or not "it must be," the work stands between joke and parable, between quotidian humor and allegory of necessity. In its four movements four categories of feeling prevail: in the first, wit, dislocations, and incongruities that surprise and please; in the Scherzo, manic comic energy bordering on the burlesque; in the slow movement, lyrical reflection; in the finale, the dialectic of darkness and light, of deep questioning followed by its transformation into joyous, brilliant resolution. For Beethoven, as for the greatest literary artists, above all his beloved Shakespeare, comedy is not a lesser form than tragedy but is its true counterpart, the celebration of the human in all things.

NOTES

><del><><><><>|<><>|<><><><</del>

For bibliographic abbreviations, see pages 559–60.

Prologue

1. *Briefwechsel*, No. 3. The translation is modified from those in TF, 89, and Anderson No. 1.
2. Maynard Solomon has shown that the Beethoven family's financial situation in the Bonn years was not so difficult as had previously been believed. See M. Solomon, "Economic Circumstances of the Beethoven Household in Bonn," *JAMS* 50 (1997): 331–51. At the same time, it is clear that from at least 1784 on, acquaintances in Bonn realized that Johann was increasingly unable to care for and support his family. It is possible that in September 1787 the young Beethoven did not really know if the family had any resources to speak of, and he may well have been telling von Schaden the literal truth when he said that his journey had cost him a great deal of money and that he presently had little or none. But as Solomon points out, he fails to tell von Schaden that his Vienna trip had been subsidized by the Elector.
3. *Briefwechsel*, No. 585; Anderson No. 376 (translation slightly modified). First published by Thayer (TDR 3:318f., TF, 535), who had Beethoven's letter from a certain Matthias Sirk of Graz along with the information Thayer transmits about her age and her letter and gift to Beethoven. Emilie's letter is not preserved; according to Thayer she wrote it "with the help of her governess." As Sieghard Brandenburg notes in *Briefwechsel*, No. 585, n. 1 and 586, n. 14, following Anderson, 1:381, n. 2, this letter may very well be the one that Beethoven enclosed the next day (July 18) in a letter to Breitkopf & Härtel (*Briefwechsel*, No. 586) asking them to "forward the enclosed letter to Hamburg . . ." [and adding], "I have been owing this reply for at least five months." Although one Beethoven scholar in private conversation has questioned whether the letter might or might not be genuine, owing to the absence of an autograph and in view of its style, Beethoven's reference the next day to a letter intended for delivery in Hamburg argues in its favor. So does its congruence with his earlier letter to Christine Gerhardi (see note 4).
4. For the Gerhardi letter see Anderson, No. 23; *Briefwechsel*, No. 33. For the passage in the "Immortal Beloved" letter see Solomon, *Beethoven*, 210, in the part written in the "Evening, Monday, July 6." The relevant passage reads, "What a life!!!! thus!!!! without you—pursued by the goodness of man hither and thither—which I as little want to deserve as I deserve it—Humility of man towards man—it pains me—and when I consider myself in relation to the universe, what am I and what is He—whom we call the greatest—and yet—herein lies the divine in man. . . ."

5. Karol Berger, "Beethoven and the Aesthetic State," *BF* 7 (1999): 17–44.

6. Berger, "Beethoven and the Aesthetic State," 39.

7. On the alleged incident see A. Comini, *The Changing Image of Beethoven: A Study in Mythmaking* (New York, 1987), 16–18. The shaky basis for the incident, a letter supposedly written by Beethoven to Bettina Brentano but probably fabricated by her, became a staple of the legend of Beethoven as the ruggedly independent artist, in comparison to Goethe, who still savored the appreciation of the aristocracy and maintained the role of an artist who could defer to them without loss of honor. But as Comini notes, p. 17, whether or not the incident took place, the divergence in attitudes it presents is fortified by Goethe's description of Beethoven, written from Teplitz on September 2, 1812, as "an utterly untamed personality."

8. See J. May, "Beethoven and Prince Karl Lichnowsky," *BF* 3 (1994): 36. Though May doubts its authenticity, I share Frimmel's view that it fits with what we know of Beethoven's pride and audacity in dealing with his patrons. Evidence for the incident and remark originated with Lichnowsky's physician, Anton Weiser. Weiser was present at a banquet given by Lichnowsky at his castle in Gräz, near Troppau in Silesia, for some French officers at which Beethoven refused to improvise after feeling insulted by one of them. According to Weiser's testimony he had to leave Gräz for Troppau before the incident; Beethoven, feeling insulted by Lichnowsky, packed up and went on foot and in the rain to Troppau, where he asked Weiser to put him up for the night. The next day another annoying problem arose, in that Beethoven could not return to Vienna without a permit from Lichnowsky. Before leaving Troppau, Beethoven allegedly wrote a note to Lichnowsky containing these words. Weiser's account was first published by his grandson in 1873 and was apparently written by his son; see Theodor von Frimmel, *Beethoven*, 4th ed. (Berlin, 1912), 44; and Frimmel, *Beethoven-Handbuch* (Leipzig, 1926), 1:347.

9. *Briefwechsel*, No. 2236. Solomon notes that by chance the letter may not actually have been sent, as we see from *Briefwechsel*, No. 2257 (February 17, 1827), another letter to Wegeler, in which Beethoven replies to Wegeler's apparent reference to "not having received anything." However, this may primarily refer to music and a portrait that Beethoven wished to send to his old friend but which had not yet been sent by Schott in Mainz.

10. Presumably a room in the von Breuning house in which the young Beethoven frequently stayed.

11. *Briefwechsel*, No. 11, dated November 2, 1793, exactly a year after his arrival in Vienna, as he himself notes in the letter.

12. For a searching account of Beethoven's troubled relationship with Karl see Solomon, *Beethoven*, especially 297–330; also the well-documented narrative by S. Wolf, *Beethovens Neffenkonflikt* (Munich, 1995).

13. For the full text see O. G. Sonneck, *Beethoven: Impressions of Contemporaries*, 229–31; also Comini, *The Changing Image of Beethoven*, 75ff., with interesting commentary.

14. The "three-period" concept goes back as early as 1818 (an anonymous essay in *Janus*, 1 (1818): 10; and to the first Beethoven biographer, Johann Aloys Schlosser (1828); see M. Solomon, "The Creative Periods of Beethoven," in his *Beethoven Essays*, 116 and n. 1. It

was then picked up by Schindler and popularized by Lenz in his *Beethoven et ses trois styles* (St. Petersburg, 1852). For a critical appraisal of this periodization see J. Webster, "The Concept of Beethoven's 'Early' Period in the Context of Periodizations in General," *BF* 3 (1994): 1–28.

15. P. Rosenfeld, "Beethoven," *The New Republic*, May 12, 1917, later reprinted in his *Discoveries of a Music Critic* (New York, 1936), 67–72.

16. A. Schopenhauer, *The World as Will and Representation*, trans. E. F. J. Payne (New York, 1966), 1:256–57.

17. Quoted by Schopenhauer, *The World as Will and Representation*, 1:256.

18. Schopenhauer, 1:260.

19. Schopenhauer, 1:450.

20. D. F. Tovey, *Beethoven*, 1; see my review of Solomon's *Beethoven*, 1st ed., in *19th-Century Music* 3 (July 1979): 80; and L. Lockwood, "Beethoven's Emergence from Crisis: the Cello Sonatas Opus 102 (1815)," *Journal of Musicology* 16 (1998): 301.

21. C. Dahlhaus, *Beethoven: Approaches to His Music*, trans. Mary Whitall (Oxford, 1991), 1.

22. M. Piercy in *The New York Times*, December 20, 1999: sec. B, 1–2.

23. A telling example is his letter of October 9, 1813, to Zmeskall, in which he asks Zmeskall to please write the "attached address" on an enclosed letter, because the addressee is "always complaining about not getting a letter from me, and yesterday I went to the post office where they asked me where this letter should be sent. Thus my request to you." As he says despondently in this note to Zmeskall, "You see that my handwriting is misunderstood as often as I am myself." *Briefwechsel*, No. 675; cited by Max Unger in his *Beethovens Handschrift* (Bonn, 1926), 5.

24. W. Leppmann, *Rilke: A Life* (New York, 1984), 170.

25. E. Young-Bruehl, *Creative Characters* (New York, 1991).

26. G. Flaubert, *Correspondance* (1852), 2:155. Compare Virginia Woolf in *Orlando* (London, 1928), 189f: "Every secret of a writer's soul, every experience of his life, every quality of his mind, is written large in his works, yet we require critics to explain the one and biographers to expound the other." For both quotations I am indebted to C. Spurgeon, *Shakespeare's Imagery and What It Tells Us* (New York, 1935), xviii.

27. I. Ritter von Seyfried, *Ludwig van Beethovens Studien*, 19.

28. See L. Lockwood, "On Beethoven's Sketches and Autographs: Some Problems of Definition and Interpretation," originally published in 1970 and included in Lockwood, *Studies*, 4–16.

29. Lockwood, *Studies*, 12.

30. D. Johnson, Introduction to JTW, 4.

31. O. Sonneck, *Beethoven: Impressions of Contemporaries* (New York, 1926), 70 (translation slightly modified).

32. Letter of July 1825; *Briefwechsel*, No. 2003.

Chapter 1

1. For detailed portraits of Bonn in Beethoven's time see TF, chapters 1–6; L. Schiedermair, *Der Junge Beethoven* (Leipzig, 1925), 3–90; and Solomon, *Beethoven*, chapters 1–4.

Further work is needed on the careers and music of Beethoven's fellow musicians at Bonn.

2. TF, 14, 16, quoting Henry Swinburne, whose letters to his brother were published in 1841 as *The Courts of Europe at the Close of the Last Century* (London, 1841), 371–72. The reference in Swinburne's 1780 description to the "archduke" is to Max Franz, who was then Max Friedrich's new coadjutor and established successor.

3. TF, 17.

4. TF, 48. This much-reproduced portrait of grandfather Ludwig by Radoux was kept by Beethoven all his life; see Solomon, *Beethoven,* 21.

5. Solomon persuasively ascribes to the young Beethoven the concept of the "family romance," in that the fantasy of replacement of his forlorn father by an "elevated substitute" seems to have been expressed in his admiration for his grandfather at the expense of his father. See Solomon, *Beethoven,* Part I, Chapters 1–2.

6. See Solomon, "Economic Circumstances of the Beethoven Household in Bonn," 341.

7. On Andrea Lucchesi see *NG2,* 15:269–76. On Cajetan Mattioli, whom Neefe praised for his excellence as an orchestral conductor, even preferring him to Cannabich at Mannheim, see TF, 33ff. Neefe's admiration for Mattioli's stress on accentuation, orchestral dynamics and "all the degrees of light and shade" is conceivably reflected in Beethoven's strong feeling for the importance of these factors in even his earlier music, certainly including the First Symphony.

8. On the operas rehearsed at Bonn in 1781–83 and performed there in 1789–91 see TF, 31, 32, 97ff.; Schiedermair, *Der Junge Beethoven,* 50ff., 65.

9. On the orchestra personnel in 1783 see Schiedermair, 47.

10. Schiedermair, 58, 86 (Junker report of 1791).

11. On Andreas Romberg see *NG2,* 21:603.

12. On Joseph Reicha see *NG2,* 21:136.

13. On Bernhard Romberg, who continued to have some contact with Beethoven in later years see *NG2,* 21:603–5, and H. Schäfer, *Bernhard Romberg, sein Leben und Wirken* (Lübben, 1931).

14. Simrock remained on good terms with Beethoven for many years, as we know from letters. On him and the history of the firm see *NG2,* article "Simrock."

15. On Neefe as musician the best study is still that of I. Leux, *Christian Gottlob Neefe* (Leipzig, 1925); on his role at Bonn, see Schiedermair, 140–62; Solomon, *Beethoven,* 33–35; and A. Becker, *Christian Gottlob Neefe und die Bonner Illuminati* (Bonn, 1969). It is interesting to note Wegeler's remark that Beethoven "frequently complained about the too severe criticisms [by Neefe] of his first efforts in composition;" TF, 65 and Solomon, *Beethoven,* 437, n. 9.

16. *NG2,* 15:270.

17. *Briefwechsel,* No. 6.

18. See Solomon, *Beethoven,* 50; also his "Beethoven, Freemasonry, and the *Tagebuch,*" BF 8 (2001): 101–46.

19. Solomon, *Beethoven,* 34, translated from Cramer's *Magazin der Musik;* for the original German see *TDR,* 1:150 and Schiedermair, 161f.

20. For an overview of Bach editions in the eighteenth century see M. Zenck, *Die Bach-Rezeption des späten Beethoven* (Stuttgart, 1986), 6.

21. *Briefwechsel,* No. 408 (November 2, 1809) to Breitkopf & Härtel.

22. Schiedermair, 196.

23. *Briefwechsel,* No. 84.

24. Review of the first performance of *The Robbers* (*Die Räuber*), quoted and translated by Leslie Sharpe, *Friedrich Schiller: Drama, Thought and Politics* (Cambridge, 1991), 29.

25. See E. Bücken, *Anton Reicha* (Munich, 1912), 21; Schiedermair, 195ff.

26. On Eulogius Schneider see Frimmel, *Beethoven-Handbuch,* 2:136; Schiedermair, 29, 196, 219ff., 319, 326. Also E. Nacken, *Studien über Eulogius Schneider in Deutschland* (Bonn, 1933).

27. See M. Braubach, *Maria Theresias jüngster Sohn, Max Franz* (Vienna, 1961), 179.

28. Quoted from *Quellen zur Geschichte des Rheinlandes im Zeitalter der französischen Revolution,* ed. J. Hansen (Bonn, 1931–38), 1:348; cited in R. Aris, *A History of Political Thought in Germany from 1789 to 1815* (London, 1936), 41.

29. *Konversationshefte,* 1:326. This may be a quotation but its source is not known.

30. Solomon, *Beethoven,* 57, where the contradictions are noted.

31. Schiedermair, 84.

32. R. L. Marshall, *Mozart Speaks* (New York, 1991), 44.

33. A. Reicha, "Notes sur Antoine-Joseph Reicha," 16.

34. On the Bonn court library see S. Brandenburg, "Die kurfürstliche Musikbibliothek in Bonn und ihre Bestände im 18. Jahrhundert," *BJ* 8 (1971/72): 7–48. Brandenburg corrects some dates given earlier by Sandberger, *Ausgewählte Aufsätze,* vol. 2. Some portions of the Bonn music library were dispersed when the Elector died in 1801; in 1836, through his nephew Maximilian Joseph, they made their way to Modena. As Brandenburg notes (p. 46) the task of determining which portions of the Bonn music library still survive in the Biblioteca Estense in Modena remains to be carried out.

35. TF, 37. See also H. C. Robbins Landon, *Haydn: Chronicle and Works* (Bloomington, Ind., 1976–80), 5:64n., in which Landon offers the view that the influence of Haydn's music on the young Beethoven was "practically negligible" in the Bonn years, and asks: "Can a Beethoven have ignored deliberately all this amount of Haydn's music [in the Mastiaux collection]? Knowing his later character, it is entirely possible." I disagree emphatically, though neither Landon nor I can document the point. It seems to me totally unlikely that Beethoven ignored Haydn's music, either in Bonn or at any time, but, to the contrary, that his absorption in attaining knowledge of the best possible models in the language of his time would have led him inevitably to Haydn, as it did to Mozart. However, in the 1780s he was not yet ready to move beyond keyboard-dominated chamber music into the string quartet, nor ready yet to write symphonies. In the 1790s we find concrete evidence of his knowledge of Haydn (e.g., a passage from a Haydn symphony in the "Kafka" sketch papers, identified by Alan Tyson in his review of Kerman's edition of the "Kafka" Miscellany in *The Musical Times* 111 [1970]: 1194–98); his copy of Haydn's Quartet Opus 20 No. 2 and, later, his copy of Haydn's *Schöpfungsmesse* at the time of composing the Mass in C (I am indebted for this last point to Jeremiah McGrann).

36. G. von Breuning, *Memories of Beethoven,* ed. M. Solomon (Cambridge, 1992), 29.

37. For the petition of 1789 see TF, 95 and Solomon, *Beethoven,* 42; for the 1793 letter see *Briefwechsel,* No. 7.
38. See D. Busch-Weise, "Beethovens Jugendtagebuch," *Studien zur Musikwissenschaft* 25 (1962): 68–88.
39. See the translations of the later *Tagebuch* by M. Solomon, in *BS* 3:193–288; and in Solomon's *Beethoven Essays* (Cambridge, Mass., 1988), 233–95.
40. TF, 135–37.
41. Wegeler later reports (Wegeler-Ries, 10) that "Beethoven was treated as a child of the house, spending not only the greater number of his days there but also many nights."
42. G. von Breuning, *Memoirs of Beethoven,* 33–35.
43. On editions of Wegeler-Ries see Solomon, *Beethoven,* 497.
44. The abbreviation "WoO" stands for "Werke ohne Opuszahl," i.e., "Work with no opus number."
45. TF, 92, contributed by E. Forbes.
46. TF, 747, inserted by Forbes following Joseph Heer. On Waldstein at the time of the album, and for all its material and its authors, see M. Braubach, *Die Stammbücher Beethovens und der Babette Koch* (Bonn, 1970). See also TF, 114–17.
47. G. von Breuning, *Memories of Beethoven,* 33.
48. See, most recently, M. Solomon, *Mozart* (New York, 1995), 395.
49. TF, 88.
50. See E. Hertzmann et al., eds., *Thomas Attwoods Theorie- und Kompositionsstudien bei Mozart,* in W. A. Mozart, *Neue Ausgabe sämtliche Werke,* X/30/1 (Kassel, 1965). For an overview, see D. Heartz, "Thomas Attwood's Lessons in Composition with Mozart," *PRMA* 100 (1973–74): 175–84.
51. See Thayer in TF, 112, who sustains this view.
52. TF, 97ff.
53. TF, 101.
54. Wegeler-Ries, 15.
55. TF, 106.
56. TF, 104ff.
57. TF, 105.
58. Forbes in TF, 114ff.
59. TF, 167 (Forbes commentary).
60. The entire album, or *Stammbuch,* was published in facsimile by Max Braubach, *Die Stammbücher Beethovens und der Babette Koch.* For Waldstein's entry see 18–19, including a silhouette of the count. The italicized words follow Waldstein's text exactly.
61. Solomon, *Mozart,* 499; G. Gruber, *Mozart and Posterity,* trans. R. S. Furness (Boston, 1994), chapter 1 (to 1800).
62. Gruber, 13ff.
63. A. Berger in the *Boston Globe,* December 4, 1990 (one day after Copland's death), 65.
64. On Beethoven's relations with the Elector following his journey to Vienna see F. von Reinöhl, "Neues zu Beethovens Lehrjahr bei Haydn," *NBJ* 6 (1935): 36–47; also TF, 144ff.

Chapter 2

1. See H. Boettcher, *Beethoven als Liederkomponist* (Augsburg, 1928), especially 147ff. on Neefe as lieder composer and as Beethoven's early guide.

2. Kinsky-Halm, 570 notes that the poet of *Schilderung eines Mädchens* is not G. A. Bürger, as claimed by Boettcher, Table 1.

3. See Kinsky-Halm, 509f. (WoO 63). The two versions are published in *Beethoven Werke*, Abt. VII, Bd. 5 (Munich, G. Henle Verlag, 1961), 1–8 and 239–46.

4. Kinsky-Halm, 491–94.

5. Wegeler-Ries, 125.

6. The original order is not as published in the 1828 first edition and in the older complete-works edition, but rather as in the modern *Werke*, namely No. 1 in C, No. 2 in E-flat, and No. 3 in D.

7. On the "signs of a man's power" in these works see D. F. Tovey, "Beethoven," *Encyclopaedia Britannica*, 11th ed. (Cambridge, 1910), 3:647.

8. This discussion is partly drawn from my "Beethoven before 1800: The Mozart Legacy," *BF* 3 (1994): 39–53.

9. "Diese ganze Stelle ist gestohlen aus der Mozartschen Sinfonie in c wo das Andante in 6 8tel aus den . . ."; "Beethowen ipse." This appears in J. Kerman, ed., *Ludwig van Beethoven: Autograph Miscellany from circa 1786 to 1799: British Museum Additional Manuscript 29801, ff. 39–162 (The "Kafka" Sketchbook)* (London, 1970), 1: fol. 88v; 2:228; and comment, 293. See also 2:246 for "some alterations of some passages in [a] Mozart concerto" (the concerto is as yet unidentified).

10. Reicha, "Notes sur Antoine Reicha," 44.

11. For these examples and commentary see L. Lockwood, "Beethoven before 1800," *BF* 3 (1994): 39–41.

12. See J. Kerman, *The Beethoven Quartets* (New York, 1967), 57–59; the example has been known since T. Helm, *Beethovens Streichquartette* (Leipzig, 1885), 26; Czerny remarked on Beethoven's admiration for K. 464. More recently see J. Yudkin, "Beethoven's 'Mozart' Quartet," *JAMS* 45 (1992): 30–74.

13. J. Webster, "Traditional Elements in Beethoven's Middle-Period String Quartets," in R. Winter and B. Carr, eds., *Beethoven: Performers and Critics . . . Detroit, 1977* (Detroit, 1980), 94–133.

14. The passage, from the E-flat-minor exposition of the first movement of the quartet, mm. 76–84, appears in C minor in the exposition of the first movement of the piano trio, mm. 110–18.

15. See D. Johnson, *Beethoven's Early Sketches in the "Fischof Miscellany," Berlin Autograph 28* (Ann Arbor, 1980), 1:315ff. (published version); 527f. (original version of dissertation).

16. It is at least possible that the young Beethoven connected the viability of E-flat minor with its use in *The Well-Tempered Clavier;* I am indebted for this idea to Robert Marshall. We also see Beethoven using it conspicuously in the first number of the oratorio *Christus am Ölberge*. But it is rare in later works.

17. See M. Tusa, "Beethoven's 'C-Minor Mood': Some Thoughts on the Structural Implications of Key Choice," *BF* 2 (1993): 1–28.

18. Wegeler-Ries, 17.

19. See J. Kerman, *Beethoven: Autograph Miscellany from c. 1786 to 1799,* 2 (transcription): 137–45.

20. On all three early concerto attempts, see L. Plantinga, *Beethoven's Concertos* (New York, 1999), 31–38.

21. For details see J. Kerman, *Beethoven: Autograph Miscellany from c. 1786 to 1799.*

22. See Kerman, *Beethoven: Autograph Miscellany,* 2, part 2: "Shorter Sketches, Exercises, and Miscellaneous Notations," 185–274.

23. Quoted by Solomon, *Beethoven,* 68f.; the first to cite the letter was Elliot Forbes in TF, 120.

Chapter 3

1. For entries from his travel diary see TF, 116ff.; for the full text and commentary, D. Busch-Weise, "Beethovens Jugendtagebuch," *Studien zur Musikwissenschaft* 25 (1962): 68–88.

2. See G. Lefebvre, *The French Revolution,* trans. E. M. Evanson (New York, 1962), vol. 1, especially chapters 13 (August-September 1792) and 14 (September 1792–January 1793).

3. Older titles from the massive body of writings on the effects of the French Revolution are G. P. Gooch, *Germany and the French Revolution* (London, 1920), and *Quellen zur Geschichte des Rheinlandes im Zeitalter der französische Revolution, 1780–1801,* ed. J. Hansen (Bonn, 1931–38). More recent discussions include T. Saine, *Black Bread, White Bread: German Intellectuals and the French Revolution* (Columbia, S.C., 1988); G.-L. Fink, "The French Revolution as Reflected in German Literature and Political Journals from 1789 to 1800," *The Internalized Revolution: German Reactions to the French Revolution, 1789–1989,* ed. E. Bahr and T. P. Saine (New York, 1992), 11–32. On German political thought in relation to the revolution see R. Aris, *History of Political Thought in Germany from 1789 to 1815,* 21–205.

4. E. Wangermann, *From Joseph II to the Jacobin Trials* (Oxford, 1969), 37, from Austrian secret instructions of 1786.

5. See Wangermann, *From Joseph II,* 94ff., on Sonnenfels and his attempted defense of enlightened ideas against the entrenched bureaucrats of the regime.

6. Wangermann, *From Joseph II,* 149–71.

7. For the original German and commentary see J. Schmidt-Görg, "Ein Schiller-Zitat Beethovens in Neuer Sicht," in *Musik, Edition, Interpretation: Gedenkschrift Günter Henle* (Munich, 1980), 423–26, where the recipient, identified by Max Unger, is shown to be Theodora Johanna Vocke rather than "A. Vocke" as given in Anderson, No. 4. See also M. Solomon, *Beethoven Essays,* 344, n. 45.

8. Letter to Simrock of August 2, 1794; *Briefwechsel,* No. 17; Anderson, No. 12.

9. See B. Witte, "The Beautiful Society and the Symbolic Work of Art: The Anti-

Revolutionary Origin of the Bildungsroman," in Bahr and Saine, eds., *The Internalized Revolution*, 80.

10. Schiller's *Letters on the Aesthetic Education of Man* were first published in his periodical *Die Horen* in 1795; modern edition New York, 1954. See Kinderman, *Beethoven*, 5–9.

11. See M. S. Morrow, *Concert Life in Haydn's Vienna* (New York, 1987), xiv. The Gesellschaft der Musikfreunde was founded only in 1812, and its concert hall opened as late as 1831; see Otto Biba, "Concert Life in Beethoven's Vienna," in R. Winter and B. Carr, *Beethoven, Performers and Critics* (International Beethoven Congress, Detroit, 1977), (Detroit, 1980), 77–93.

12. Biba, "Concert Life," 78–84.

13. See Morrow, *Concert Life*, 54ff.

14. Morrow, *Concert Life*, 2.

15. See T. DeNora, *Beethoven and the Construction of Genius* (Berkeley, 1995), 21–23, Table 2: "Key Viennese Music Patrons in the 1790s and 1800s"; the list is incomplete but serves as a useful starting point.

16. That Josephine Deym can be identified as the "Immortal Beloved" is a thesis long propounded by various scholars, especially M.-E. Tellenbach, *Beethoven und seine "unsterbliche Geliebte"* (Zurich, 1983). I favor the hypothesis advanced by Maynard Solomon that the probable recipient of the "Immortal Beloved" letter was Antonie Brentano. In light of the currently known evidence Solomon's view is by far the most convincing.

17. See J. May, "Beethoven and Prince Karl Lichnowsky," *BF* 3 (1994), 29–38.

18. Solomon, *Beethoven*, 86. Reported by Lulu Thürheim, *Mein Leben*, vol. 2 (1788–1819) Munich, 1913), 19.

19. Solomon, *Beethoven*, 86, and TF, 212.

20. Solomon, *Beethoven*, 86.

21. Madame de Staël, *De l'Allemagne* (London, 1813), 1:78.

22. Beaumarchais, *Les Noces de Figaro*, Act I. Mozart's "replacement" for this famous monologue is Figaro's first-act cavatina, "Se vuol ballare, signor Contino," ("If you want to dance, dear Count") in which the servant Figaro expresses resentment of his master's pretensions and determination to beat him at his own game. That Beethoven composed a set of variations on "Se vuol ballare" for violin and piano (WoO 40) in 1791–93 can be seen as merely an example of his choosing a well-known tune but can also be read as a reflection of his sympathy with its well-known antiaristocratic message. As late as the 1890s, Sigmund Freud reports associating this tune with the same meaning, in his *Interpretation of Dreams;* S. Freud, Standard Edition (1900), (London, 1953), 4:208f.

23. On Beethoven's "nobility pretense" see Solomon, *Beethoven*, 117–20.

24. Kerst, *Die Erinnerungen an Beethoven* (Stuttgart, 1913), 1:24.

25. G. A. Griesinger, *Joseph Haydn, Eighteenth-Century Gentleman and Genius*, trans. by V. Gotwals of *Biographische Notizen über Joseph Haydn (1810)* (Madison, 1963), 17.

26. Griesinger, *Joseph Haydn*, 22.

27. Dies in Griesinger, *Joseph Haydn*, 114f.

28. On Mozart's economic status in his free-lance years in Vienna, see M. Solomon, *Mozart* (New York, 1995), 427–32, and Appendix, "Mozart's Vienna Earnings," 521–28. For Haydn's letter, undated but evidently from December 1787, see Haydn, *Gesammelte Briefe und Aufzeichnungen* (Kassel and New York, 1965), 185f.

29. Wegeler-Ries, 33, as translated by C. S. Jolly in Schindler, *Beethoven as I Knew Him: A Biography,* ed. D. W. MacArdle (Chapel Hill, N.C., 1966), 61; see also Solomon, *Beethoven,* 84.

30. A. Tyson, "Beethoven to the Countess Susanna Guicciardi: A New Letter," in *BS* 1: (1973), 9.

31. The exact membership of the Schuppanzigh quartet in the 1790s is open to some question. Schindler reports that Lichnowsky's musicians included Schuppanzigh, the violist Franz Weiss and the two cellists Anton and Nikolaus Kraft, father and son. Schindler says that the first three of these especially influenced Beethoven's early understanding of string writing. In a footnote to Schindler's account, MacArdle notes that in 1793 Schuppanzigh was only sixteen, Weiss and Nikolaus Kraft were both fifteen, and that Louis Sina, later second violinist in the Razumovsky quartet with these three, would have been only nine years old at this time. See Schindler, ed. MacArdle, 59 and n. 35.

32. Wegeler-Ries, quoted in Schindler, ed. MacArdle, 45.

33. From the autobiography of Johann Schenk, quoted by TF, 140. It seems likely that Schenk's reference to Beethoven's having studied with Haydn for "six months" is an error, and should have read more like "six weeks." For a thorough review of the evidence for the personal side of Beethoven's relationship to Haydn see James Webster, "The Falling-Out between Haydn and Beethoven: The Evidence of the Sources," in L. Lockwood and P. Benjamin, eds., *Beethoven Essays: Studies in Honor of Elliot Forbes* (Cambridge, Mass., 1984), 3–45. Webster offers a close reading of all the verbal testimony about their relationship, concluding that it may not have been as bad as traditionally portrayed during the 1790s, and perhaps deteriorated only between 1800 and 1804, when Haydn's failing health and productivity coincided with Beethoven's full rise to artistic independence. On the other hand, the general tenor and weight of the evidence support the traditional view that the personal feeling between the young Beethoven and the mature Haydn was never comfortable and was at times a bit antagonistic. One senses that Haydn expected Beethoven to develop a career that would advertise him as having been Haydn's pupil, but that the older man reckoned without Beethoven's egotism, his resistance to the aristocratic tradition of patronage, and his demand that he be seen as a natural talent. At the same time, it is more important for Beethoven as a composer that he never ceased to admire Haydn, learned immensely from his works, and assimilated aspects of Haydn's style into his work through the 1790s and down into the first part of his second maturity (c. 1802–6).

34. Nottebohm, *Beethovens Studien* (Leipzig, 1873), 196.

35. Nottebohm, *Beethovens Studien,* 201 (my translation).

36. J. Kerman, ed., "Autograph Miscellany . . . ," 2:130. On other early fugal efforts see R. Kramer, "'Das Organische der Fuge': On the Autograph of Beethoven's String Quartet in F Major, Opus 59 No. 1," in *The String Quartets of Haydn, Mozart and Beethoven: Studies of the Autograph Manuscripts,* ed. C. Wolff (Cambridge, Mass., 1980), 233–65, esp. 225–27.

37. I. von Seyfried, *Beethovens Studien,* Anhang, 23: Seyfried reports a moment in Haydn's later life when, in ill health, he knew that Beethoven was moving in a compositional

direction of which Haydn "did not entirely approve." "Nevertheless the kindly old man often inquired about his 'Telemachus' and often asked, "what is our Grand Mogul up to?" Translation from Webster, "The Falling-Out," 44.

38. Wegeler-Ries, 85; quoted in TF, 164.

39. See Solomon, *Beethoven*, 101.

40. For an account of this duel, using contemporary material by Seyfried and the *AMZ*, see DeNora, *Beethoven and the Construction of Genius*, 147–69.

41. DeNora, 156.

42. The original text is in Kerst, *Die Erinnerungen an Beethoven*, 1:30. A full reprint of the *Jahrbuch* was published in 1976, edited by Otto Biba, and a complete translation by Katherine Talbot is included in *Haydn and His World*, ed. E. Sisman (Princeton, 1997), 289–320.

43. For details of this journey see H. Loos, "Beethoven in Prag 1796 und 1798," in *Beethoven und Böhmen*, ed. S. Brandenburg and M. Gutierrez-Denhoff (Bonn, 1998), 63–90. Loos thinks it possible that the original idea was to go only to Prague, but that after Lichnowsky's departure in February Beethoven himself may have decided to go on to the other cities, following in Mozart's footsteps. Loos (71f.) thinks it possible that he may have been looking for a permanent position in one of these places, not yet having found one in Vienna.

44. *Briefwechsel*, No. 20; Anderson, No. 16 (February 19, 1796).

45. See D. Johnson, *Beethoven's Early Sketches in the "Fischhof Miscellany"* (Ann Arbor, Mich., 1978), 1:674.

46. On his stay in Dresden see H. Volkmann, *Beethoven in seinen Beziehungen zu Dresden* (Dresden, 1942); on his visit to Leipzig we have almost no information.

47. See Volkmann, *Beethoven in seinen Beziehungen zu Dresden*, 21ff. for letters from Dresden confirming his performance for the Elector.

48. For a brief survey of the cellists connected with Friedrich Wilhelm II, see V. Walden, *One Hundred Years of Violoncello* (Cambridge, 1998), 10–15.

49. See A. Weissmann, *Berlin als Musikstadt* (Berlin, 1911), 89ff.

50. See the documents in Weissman, 92.

51. I am indebted for this information to Christoph Wolff.

52. For an excellent overview of his dealings with publishers see A. Tyson, "Steps to Publication—and Beyond" in *The Beethoven Reader*, ed. D. Arnold and N. Fortune (New York, 1971), 459–89.

53. *Briefwechsel*, No. 11.

54. *Briefwechsel*, No. 65 (June 29, 1801).

55. The basic modern catalogue of Beethoven's works is that of Georg Kinsky and Hans Halm, *Das Werk Beethovens* (Munich, 1955), which replaced catalogues compiled in the nineteenth century by Nottebohm and by Thayer.

56. See A. Tyson, "The Authors of the Op. 104 String Quintet," in *BS* 1:158–73.

57. Albrecht, No. 47 (November 3, 1802).

58. See Tyson, "Steps to Publication," 474ff.

59. See this letter and commentary in Lockwood, *Studies*, 32.

60. *Briefwechsel*, No. 496.

Chapter 4

1. For an excellent overview of Beethoven's early exposure to late-eighteenth-century theorists, see R. Kramer, "Notes to Beethoven's Education," *JAMS*, 28 (1975): 71–101; on Beethoven's early experiments with fugal writing, see Kramer, "'Das Organische der Fuge,'" in C. Wolff, ed., *The String Quartets of Haydn, Mozart, and Beethoven*, 223–65.

2. D. Johnson, "Beethoven's Early Sketches in the 'Fischhof' Miscellany," vol. 1, pt. 1, 506–9. Johnson persuasively argues against earlier claims by Ries, followed by Thayer, that the trios of Opus 1 had all been composed and even performed in private for Haydn before his departure for England in January 1794. Johnson's view is that No. 1 might have been ready that early but that Nos. 2 and 3 were not composed before 1794–95, in the months prior to their publication in July-August 1795.

3. D. F. Tovey, "Beethoven," in *Encyclopaedia Brittanica*, 11th ed., 3:648.

4. For a thorough discussion of this revision see D. Johnson, "1794–1795: Decisive Years in Beethoven's Early Development," *BS* 3:1–14.

5. Gardiner, *Music and Friends* (London, 1853), 3:142ff.

6. On Beethoven and contemporary piano literature see A. Ringer, "Beethoven and the London Pianoforte School," *The Musical Quarterly* 56 (1970): 742–58, reprinted in Lang, ed., *The Creative World of Beethoven*, 240–56.

7. I am indebted here to Robert Marshall.

8. See D. Johnson, *Beethoven's Early Sketches in the 'Fischof' Miscellany*, 1:527–29.

9. See M. Tusa, "Beethoven's 'C-Minor Mood,'" *BF* 2:1–28.

10. For the phrase "absolute melody" see H. Gál, "Die Stileigentümlichkeiten des jungen Beethoven," *Studien zur Musikwissenschaft* 5 (1916): 61ff.

11. See L. Lockwood, "Beethoven's Early Works for Violoncello and Contemporary Violoncello Technique," in *Beethoven-Kolloquium 1977*, ed. R. Klein (Kassel, 1978), 174–82; and L. Lockwood, "Beethoven's Early Works for Violoncello and Pianoforte: Innovation in Context," *Beethoven Newsletter* 1, no. 2 (1986): 17–21.

12. *Essai sur le doigté du violoncelle* (Paris, c. 1813).

13. For a précis of this lost letter of September 16, 1798, from Jean Louis Duport to Beethoven, thanking him for these two cello sonatas, see Albrecht, 1, No. 28, 52ff. The sonatas were formally dedicated to King Friedrich Wilhelm II, no doubt for good diplomatic reasons but also as a reflection of the king's cellistic ambitions.

14. Wegeler-Ries, 86.

15. *AMZ* (1799), cols. 570–71, quoted by S. Kunze, *Ludwig van Beethoven: Die Werke im Spiegel seiner Zeit* (Laaber, 1987), 18.

16. *Zeitung für die elegante Welt*; see Kunze, *Beethoven: Die Werke*, 15ff.

17. Mm. 64–65.

18. "Largo" is found as tempo for the slow movements of the Trio Opus 1 No. 2; the piano sonatas Opus 2 No. 2 and Opus 7; the First Piano Concerto; and then later works such as Opus 31 No. 2, Introduction; the Third Piano Concerto; the Triple Concerto; and the famous slow movement of the "Ghost" Trio, Opus 70 No. 1; finally, for the introduction to the finale of the *Hammerklavier* Sonata, Opus 106.

19. See L. Finscher, "Zur Interpretation des langsamen Satzes aus Beethovens Klaviersonate Opus 10 Nr. 3," in *International Musicological Society, Report of the Eleventh Congress. Copenhagen 1972* (Copenhagen, 1974), 1:84.

20. Schindler, *Beethoven*, 2nd ed. (Münster, 1845), 80; see Schindler, *Beethoven as I Knew Him*, 406.

21. There were at the time three countesses Thun: the elder was a patron of Haydn's; the two younger ones were, respectively, the wife of Count Razumovsky and the wife of Prince Karl Lichnowsky. See B. Cooper, *The Beethoven Compendium* (London, 1991), 223. For a portrait of all three made by Heinrich C. Füger c. 1788 see *Ludwig van Beethoven*, edited by Joseph Schmidt-Görg and Hans Schmidt (Bonn, 1974), 131.

22. Mozart to his father, letter of April 10, 1784, after the first performance at a concert at which he produced a new piano concerto and three symphonies; see R. Spaethling, *Mozart's Letters, Mozart's Life*, 366f.

23. Letter of Constanze Mozart to Johann André of May 30, 1800, quoted by Alfred Einstein, *Chronologisch-thematisches Verzeichnis sämtlicher Tonwerke Wolfgang Amadé Mozarts . . . von Dr. Ludwig Ritter von Köchel*, 3rd ed., edited by A. Einstein (Leipzig, 1980), 572.

24. On Zmeskall's ownership of the autograph around 1800 see the Köchel Catalogue as edited by A. Einstein, *Chronologisch-thematisches Verzeichnis sämtlicher Tonwerke Wolfgang Amadeus Mozarts* (Leipzig, reprint 1980), 572. For a comparison of the two see D. F. Tovey's program note on Mozart's Quintet in his *Essays in Musical Analysis: Chamber Music* (Oxford, 1944), 106–20.

25. See Michael Tusa, note 9 above.

Chapter 5

1. On Goya's illnesses and artistic reactions, see M. Gedo, "The Healing Power of Art: Goya as His Own Physician," in M. Gedo, ed., *Psychoanalytic Perspectives on Art* (Hillsdale, New Jersey, 1985), 1:75–106. Gedo's description of Goya at one point reminds us of Beethoven: "a man with a powerful but compact physique . . . [with] stamina and force . . . [capable of] prodigious productivity . . . [who made] a rapid rise to a position of eminence and power in the artistic world of his era" (77). For a critical overview of Goya as artist see Fred Licht, *Goya: The Origins of the Modern Temper in Art* (New York, 1979).

2. For a recent medical review of his illnesses and deafness throughout his life, year by year, see H. Bankl and H. Jesserer, *Die Krankheiten Ludwig van Beethovens* (Vienna, 1987). The source of the early illness theory is the "Fischof-Manuscript," which describes him as suffering a "dangerous illness in the summer of 1796 and that during his convalescence his hearing began to deteriorate"; quoted by Bankl and Jesserer, 11.

3. *Briefwechsel*, 65; Anderson 51. In the Heiligenstadt Testament, dated October 1802, Beethoven writes that he has been "hopelessly afflicted" by deafness "for six years now," which might place his earliest awareness of the problem as far back as the latter part of 1796. We cannot be sure that this reference to a date of onset is exact, however, and at present can say only that "between 1796 and 1798" he became aware of the problem.

4. For a broad sampling of comparable responses to deafness by writers see the anthology compiled by B. Grant, *The Quiet Ear: Deafness in Literature* (London, 1987). In her

introduction to this volume, Margaret Drabble observes that "it is not just the deaf person that suffers, but family, friends, teachers, and all who come into contact." Grant's anthology includes the Heiligenstadt Testament, 71–73.

5. *Briefwechsel*, 67; Anderson, No. 53. Anderson seems to be the only editor of the Beethoven letters who identified this reference to *Hamlet*, III, ii, 388–96, in which Hamlet ironically accuses Guildenstern of treachery, saying "You would play upon me; you would seem to know my stops; you would pluck out the heart of my mystery; you would sound me from my lowest note to the top of my compass," etc. Beethoven knew Shakespeare in the Schlegel translation, of which eight volumes had appeared by 1801. In 1810 he has these volumes in hand, and offers to send some of them and Goethe's *Wilhelm Meister* to Therese Malfatti; see *Briefwechsel*, No. 442; Anderson, No. 258.

6. Anderson, No. 53, translation slightly changed here.

7. The letter is *Briefwechsel*, No. 70; Anderson, No. 54. For the Heiligenstadt Testament, much discussed, a full facsimile edition has been published more than once, as by H. Müller von Asow, *Beethoven, Heiligenstadter Testament: Faksimile* (Vienna, 1969); translations are found in Anderson, *Letters*, 3: 1351–54; TF, 304; and Solomon, *Beethoven*, 151–54. Solomon offers a penetrating interpretation of the "curiously uneven" tone of the document, "alternating between touching expressions of Beethoven's feelings of despair . . . and stilted, even literary formulations emphasizing his adherence to virtue." He notes that the document is a "carefully revised 'fair copy' which has been scrubbed clean of much of its original emotion."

8. On Giulietta Guicciardi see TF, 288–92; Solomon, *Beethoven*, 196ff., and A. Tyson, "Beethoven to the Countess Susanna Guicciardi," *BS* 1:1–17.

9. The significance of the Heiligenstadt Testament lies not only in its importance for Beethoven's life and character but as an account of the experience of oncoming deafness and its consequences.

10. *AMZ* 29 (October 17, 1827): 705. See Schindler, *Beethoven as I Knew Him*, 188, n. 62.

11. *Briefwechsel*, No. 106 (Heiligenstadt Testament), 124, n. 2. The editor of the *Briefwechsel*, Sieghard Brandenburg, attributes this point to Hedwig Müller von Asow.

12. Solomon, *Beethoven*, 155–57.

13. Ries, in Wegeler-Ries, *Notizen*, 78–79 confirms such an incident while on a walk with Beethoven. A shepherd was piping and "for half an hour Beethoven could hear nothing."

14. The reference to his age as twenty-eight stems from Beethoven's belief, until about 1810, that he had been born in 1772.

15. The rhetorical aspect is stressed by Claus Canisius, *Beethoven* (Munich, 1992), 155–64. But Canisius goes too far in interpreting the Testament as primarily "an example of Beethoven's close relationship to literature," not as a primarily personal statement.

16. See M. Solomon, ed., "Beethoven's Tagebuch of 1812–1818," *BS*, 3:193–288, especially 212.

17. On the possibility of Beethoven's having joined the Masonic Order, see Frimmel, *Beethoven-Handbuch*, 1: 151ff. For a searching account of Beethoven and the Masonic movement see M. Solomon, "Beethoven, Freemasonry, and the *Tagebuch of 1812–1818*," *BF* 8 (2001): 101–46. On the temple scene in *The Magic Flute* see the remarks by N. Till, *Mozart and the Enlightenment* (New York, 1993), 282ff. It is possible, as I indicated above

in discussion of the Trio Opus 1 No. 1, that a number of Beethoven's works in E-flat major (and to a lesser extent in C and B-flat major) contain references to the rising triadic chords familiar from *The Magic Flute* as symbols of Masonic ritual.

18. For an overview of the letters as evidence of his ill health see Bankl and Jesserer, *Die Krankheiten Ludwig van Beethovens*, 8–66.

Chapter 6

1. Czerny, *Erinnerungen aus meinem Leben,* as excerpted in Carl Czerny, *Über den richtigen Vortrag der sämtlichen Beethoven'schen Klavierwerke,* ed. P. Badura-Skoda (Vienna, 1963), 19. The remark dates from 1852, very late in Czerny's life, as one of the anecdotes he added to his memoirs ten years after first compiling them.

2. Czerny, *Über den richtigen Vortrag,* 10: "I was ten years old when I was brought to Beethoven by Krumpholz," i.e., sometime in 1800. That Beethoven liked Krumpholz is evident from other hearsay evidence but is also attested by the "Gesang der Mönche," WoO 104, which Beethoven wrote down in the notebook of Franz Kandler "in memory of the abrupt and unexpected death of our Krumpholz." Krumpholz died around May 1, 1817; see Kinsky-Halm, 566ff.

3. For an overview see JTW, 511–23.

4. *Briefwechsel,* No. 870; Anderson, No. 553.

5. In addition to the sketches for Opus 18 but in the absence of autographs, we can learn about their origins from a preliminary version of Opus 18 No. 1 that was preserved by Amenda, and from some manuscript copies of the parts preserved in the Lobkowitz archive in the Czech Republic that contain earlier readings of certain passages. The Grasnick 1 sketchbook is to be published in a transcription by Clemens Brenneis that will be issued by the Beethoven-Archiv in Bonn. I am grateful to the members of my Spring 2001 Beethoven seminar at Harvard for their assiduous work on this sketchbook, and to Sieghard Brandenburg of the Beethoven-Archiv and Dr. Brenneis for providing the seminar with a prepublication copy of the new transcription.

6. See JTW, 48ff.

7. Credit for this method of restoring leaves to sketchbooks goes to Alan Tyson, Douglas Johnson, and Robert Winter, whose results are embodied in the catalogue of the reconstructed sketchbooks published as *The Beethoven Sketchbooks* (Berkeley, 1985), with Johnson as principal editor. On the reconstruction of the first gathering of Grasnick 1 I am indebted to JTW, 78–83; to Clemens Brenneis for his transcription and proposed order; and to Aaron Allen, a member of the seminar mentioned in note 5.

8. JTW, 77–83, gives a reconstruction of the sketchbook, including its scattered first gathering; and 82 gives an overview of its contents.

9. The history of scholarship on the Beethoven sketches is itself a long and complex story, with many turnings. To put it briefly, it begins with the first descriptions of the sketchbooks, between 1865 and 1880, by Gustav Nottebohm. In the century and a quarter since then, reliable publication of their contents has been sporadic, and most of the material still awaits publication. For a brief history of the field and survey of the main collections see *JTW,* Introduction and chapter 1, 3–65.

10. *Briefwechsel,* No. 1021 (letter to Steiner of, apparently, December 30, 1816). In May 1817 Steiner published three quintets by Onslow as that composer's Opus 1.

11. *Briefwechsel,* No. 1782 (February 25, 1824, to Maurice Schlesinger).

12. See O. Biba, "Schubert's Position in Viennese Musical Life," *19th Century Music* 3 (1979): 106–13.

13. For a recent summary of the Schubert-Beethoven relationship in 1827 see B. Newbould, *Schubert: the Music and the Man* (Berkeley, 1997), 258.

14. Mm. 167–71 and 175–79.

15. E. Sisman, "Pathos and the Pathétique: Rhetorical Stance in Beethoven's C-Minor Sonata, Op. 13," *BF* 3 (1993), 81–105.

16. *Briefwechsel,* No. 97, a fragmentary letter known through Thayer. It is not known what arrangements by Haydn or Mozart Beethoven could have been referring to, or if he was simply speaking in general.

17. See L. Lockwood, "Reshaping the Genre: Beethoven's Piano Sonatas from Op. 22 to Op. 28," *Israel Studies in Musicology* 6 (1996): 1–16.

18. See R. Kramer, ed., *A Beethoven Sketchbook from the Summer of 1800* (Bonn, 1999).

19. Kunze, *Beethoven, Die Werke,* 25.

20. W. Gardiner, *The Music of Nature* (London, 1832), 235–40.

21. For this movement plan, from the sketchbook Landsberg 7 of 1800, see Lockwood, *Studies,* 148.

22. For a piano score of Paer's march, in its entirety though with some minor errors, see G. Biamonti, *Catalogo cronologico e tematico delle opere di Beethoven* (Turin, 1968), 312ff. I have compared Biamonti's version with the original piano score of Paer's opera housed in the Eda Kuhn Loeb Music Library of Harvard University.

23. Beethoven uses D-flat major to avoid placing the middle movement in the wholly unconventional key of C-sharp major, with its signature of seven sharps.

24. The famous title "Moonlight" seems to come from the poet Rellstab, who compared the quality of the first movement to the experience of a boat trip on the Vierwaldstättersee in the moonlight; see TDR, 2: 257 and J. Uhde, *Beethovens Klaviermusik* (Stuttgart, 1980), 2: 361. Its early fame was such that there were transcriptions of all kinds, including one for chorus and orchestra with the text "Kyrie eleison," and a later arrangement by Liszt in 1835 with a Paris orchestra playing the first movement and Liszt alone the second and third.

25. See the review of 1802 in Kunze, *Beethoven, Die Werke,* 2, and L. Lockwood, "Reshaping the Genre."

26. See D. Coren, "Structural Relations between Op. 28 and Op. 36," *BS* 2:66–83.

27. See J. Schmalfeldt, "Form as the Process of Becoming: The Beethoven-Hegelian Tradition and the 'Tempest' Sonata," *BF* 4 (1995): 37–72.

28. On the compositional background of Opus 47 see Suhnne Ahn, "Genre, Style, and Compositional Procedure in Beethoven's "Kreutzer" Sonata, Op. 47" (Ph.D. diss., Harvard University, 1997).

29. In turn Tolstoy's story inspired Janáček's String Quartet No. 1 (1923), called the "Kreutzer Sonata."

30. The dating of the Third Piano Concerto is uncertain, owing to the discovery of the jottings for a first-movement cadenza and a 2/4 rondo finale in the "Kafka" papers, probably made between 1796 and early 1798. It is perfectly conceivable that Beethoven thought of a C-minor concerto as a companion to his C-major concerto but then let the project lapse for four or five more years, since the writing out of concertos was closely tied to opportunities for public performance. In addition, speculation about the date on the autograph of the C Minor Concerto—i.e., whether it reads "1800" or "1803"—has been resolved by Leon Plantinga in favor of 1803, thus strengthening the view that its real period of gestation was 1802–3, in the context of the Second Symphony, the Opus 31 Piano Sonatas, the Variations Opus 34 and Opus 35, and other works representative of the major style changes centered around 1802. See Plantinga, *Beethoven's Concertos*, 113–35. Although William Kinderman (*Beethoven* [Berkeley, Calif., 1995], 64ff.) has sustained the older view that the Third Concerto could have been composed as early as 1796–1800, I find Plantinga's arguments convincing.
31. On Beethoven's copying the finale theme of K. 595 while working on the *Eroica*, see chapter 2.

Chapter 7

1. The opening progression, beginning with the tonic C^7 as the dominant seventh of its subdominant, F, condenses a familiar move in which an opening tonic chord adds its flat seventh, becomes V of IV, moves to IV then to V and back to I. Examples abound, from the first prelude of the *Well-Tempered Clavier* to the first measures of Mozart's E-flat Major Piano Quartet and Haydn's big E-flat Major Piano Sonata. Beethoven had already used the traditional form in the first measures of his own E-flat Major Piano Trio, Opus 1 No. 1, and he used it in a more dramatic way, as in the First Symphony, in the opening measures of his *Prometheus* Overture, there with the even more unstable chord of V^2 of IV as initial sonority.
2. See L. Lockwood, "Beethoven's First Symphony: A Farewell to the Eighteenth Century" in *Essays in Musicology: A Tribute to Alvin Johnson*, ed. L. Lockwood and E. Roesner (Philadelphia, 1990), 235–46.
3. See H. Berlioz, *A Critical Study of Beethoven's Nine Symphonies* (Urbana, Ill., 2000), 30f. Translation modified.
4. C. Ritorni, *Commentari della vita e delle opere coredrammatiche di Salvatore di Viganò e della chirografia e de' coropei scritti da Carlo Ritorni* (Milan, 1838), 47. For a translation see T. Sipe, *Beethoven: Eroica Symphony* (Cambridge, 1998), 117ff.
5. Ritorni, *Commentari*, 49.
6. On the connection between Viganò's ballet and Napoleon see C. Floros, *Beethovens Eroica und Prometheus-Musik* (Wilhelmshaven, 1978), 73–81; also P. Schleuning, "Beethoven in alter Deutung: Der 'neue Weg' mit der Sinfonia Eroica," *Archiv für Musikwissenschaft* 44 (1987): 165–94.
7. *Briefwechsel*, No. 176 (January 4, 1804).
8. See M. S. Morrow, *Concert Life in Haydn's Vienna*, 391.

9. J. Mongredien, *French Music from the Enlightenment to Romanticism: 1789–1830,* trans. S. Fremaux (Portland, 1986), 278, from an article on Baillot in Vienna published in *Le Menestrel,* 1864.

10. See David Charlton's excellent article in *NG2,* "Revolutionary Hymn."

11. S. Schama, *Citizens: A Chronicle of the French Revolution* (New York, 1989), 598. See also Laura Mason, *Singing The French Revolution* (Ithaca, N.Y., 1996).

12. R. Rolland, *Goethe and Beethoven* (New York, 1931), 192. Rolland reports that Klopstock said almost the same thing to Rouget de Lisle when he met him in Hamburg in 1797.

13. In the score Beethoven labels the music for the French side as simply "Marcia: Marlborough."

14. See "March," *NG2.*

15. See Plantinga, *Beethoven's Concertos,* 7ff.

16. "National Anthems," under "Germany," *NG2.*

17. "The Star-Spangled Banner" was not adopted as the national anthem of the United States until 1931.

18. R. Locke, "Paris: Centre of Intellectual Ferment," in A. Ringer, ed., *The Early Romantic Era* (Englewood Cliffs, N.J., 1990), 37.

19. Beethoven used the designation "Allegro con brio" for a number of first movements of orchestral works, among them the First Piano Concerto; the Symphonies Nos. 3 and 5; and the *Coriolanus* and *Egmont* overtures.

20. Berlioz, *A Critical Study,* 36. Translation modified.

21. Wegeler-Ries, 77.

22. Kunze, *Beethoven, Die Werke,* 35–38, presenting reviews ranging from 1804 to 1812.

23. I. Ritter von Seyfried, *Ludwig van Beethovens Studien . . . ,* 2nd ed. (Leipzig, 1853), 6. Despite the questions justifiably raised by Nottebohm about Seyfried's presentation of Beethoven's study material in counterpoint and composition, his "Biographical Sketch" attached to this volume is valuable testimony by a contemporary.

24. On Haydn's Opus 20 Quartets see W. Drabkin, *A Reader's Guide to Haydn's Early String Quartets* (Westport, Conn., 2000).

25. The view goes back to Riemann and abounds in the later literature, including Kerman, *The Beethoven Quartets,* 68.

26. See R. Kramer, "Counterpoint and Syntax: On a Difficult Passage in the First Movement of Beethoven's String Quartet in C Minor, Op. 18 No. 4," in S. Brandenburg and H. Loos, eds., *Beiträge zu Beethovens Kammermusik* (Munich, 1987), 111–24.

27. On a proposed lost sketchbook of this year see S. Brandenburg, "Beethovens Streichquartette Op. 18," in *Beethoven und Böhmen* ed. S. Brandenburg and M. Gutierrez-Denhoff (Bonn, 1998), 282.

28. On the earlier version, first movement, see Janet Levy, *Beethoven's Compositional Choices;* and my liner notes for the Laurel Recording of the early version made by the Pro Arte Quartet.

29. *Briefwechsel,* No. 67 (July 1, 1801).

30. This observation—that fugue and fugato are more common in the quartet than the piano sonata—holds true despite occasional fugato passages in Beethoven's earlier sonatas. The two cases in point are the Scherzo of the C Major Sonata, Opus 2 No. 3, and

the finale opening of Opus 10 No. 2. The central point is that at this stage Beethoven does not find room in the elaborative processes of his piano sonatas for fugue or fugato, as he will in late sonatas; but he does in Opus 18 No. 1, both first movement and finale.

31. Owen Jander surmised that Beethoven could have had in mind in 1793 a French opera on Romeo and Juliet by his rival Daniel Steibelt (paper delivered at a chapter meeting of the American Musicological Society in September 1988).

32. TDR 2, 186; TF, 261. See also Bernd Edelmann, "Die poetische Idee des Adagio von Beethovens Quartett Op. 18, Nr. 1," in *Rudolph Bockholdt Festschrift*, ed. N. Dubowy and S. Meyer-Eller (Pfaffenhofen, Germany, 1992), 247–67.

33. See S. Brandenburg, "The First Version of Beethoven's G Major String Quartet, Op. 18 No. 2," *Music and Letters* 58 (1977): 127–52. See also D. Greenfield, "Sketch Studies for Three Movements of Opus 18, Nos. 1 and 2" (Ph.D. diss., Princeton University, 1982).

34. Sketchbook Grasnick 1, fol. 27v. The note indicates that Beethoven was thinking not only about the individual work but about the order he might decide to use for the set of six quartets.

35. In favor of the connection is J. Yudkin, "Beethoven's 'Mozart' Quartet," *JAMS* 45 (1992): 30–74.

36. Kerman, *The Beethoven Quartets*, 76, connects the movement with Beethoven's heartfelt letter to Amenda of July 1, 1801, in which Beethoven speaks of the "sad resignation" with which he is preparing to meet his oncoming deafness. From another viewpoint, C. Dahlhaus, "La Malinconia," in *Ludwig van Beethoven*, ed. L. Finscher (Darmstadt, 1983), 200–211, proposes that biographical factors must be minimized and that the idea of the movement is to present a "philosophical melancholy." A. Forchert, "Die Darstellung de Melancholie in Beethovens Opus 18 No. 6," in *ibid.*, 212–39, argued, I believe correctly, that the movement presents "melancholy" in two guises—of sadness and happiness, in its contrast of Adagio and Allegro. This view has recently been followed up by Elaine Sisman in her paper "C. P. E. Bach, Beethoven, and the Labyrinth of Melancholy" (unpublished paper, 2000), which shows that Beethoven's sources for this twofold view of the topos could well have included C. P. E. Bach's Trio Sonata in C Minor, H. 579, of which the first movement is a dialogue between a "Sanguineus" and a "Melancholicus."

37. I owe this observation to Professor Richard Kurth, who discussed it in an unpublished paper that originated in a seminar at Harvard.

Chapter 8

1. C. Burney, *A General History of Music* (London, 1776), 1:xvii.

2. Burney (London, 1789), 3:v.

3. For relevant excerpts from Burke's *Philosophical Enquiry into the Origin of Our Ideas of the Sublime and the Beautiful* (London, 1757) and Christian Friedrich Michaelis's articles in the *Leipziger allgemeine musikalische Zeitung* (1806–7) and the *Berlinische musikalische Zeitung* (1805), see P. le Huray and J. Day, *Music and Aesthetics in the Eighteenth and Early Nineteenth Centuries* (Cambridge, 1981), 69–74 and 286–92, especially 289.

4. See V. Gotwals, ed., *Joseph Haydn*, 60–61. Gotwals translates Griesinger's *Biographische*

Notizen über Joseph Haydn, originally published in the *AMZ,* Nos. 41–49 (July–September 1809), then as a separate volume (Leipzig, 1810). See also J. Webster, *Haydn's "Farewell" Symphony and the Idea of Classical Style* (Cambridge, 1991), 227–32, on extramusical aspects of Haydn's aesthetics.

5. A parallel may be seen in the other important Haydn biography by a contemporary, Albert Christoph Dies, in which Dies places Haydn's keyboard music directly after his symphonies and quartets in importance, then says that "many new clavier composers (besides Mozart) might contest the place with him, especially Muzio Clementi with his fire and spirit (even perhaps in the future, *if his wild rioting subsides* [my italics], Beethoven)." See Griesinger, 200.

6. *The Letters of Mozart and his Family,* 2nd ed., ed. and trans. Emily Anderson (New York, 1985), II, 769.

7. *Letters,* ed. Anderson, 833.

8. That art is essentially an imitation of nature is the centerpiece of the Aristotelian view, echoed and elaborated for centuries in literary and then aesthetic writings of the sixteenth to eighteenth centuries; for a pithy summary see N. Marston, "Intellectual Currents: Philosophy and Aesthetics," in *The Beethoven Compendium,* ed. B. Cooper, 62–65.

9. See the section on "Aesthetic Premises" in Robert Marshall's annotated compilation *Mozart Speaks,* 181ff. See also Till, *Mozart and the Enlightenment,* 172–88.

10. See A. Tyson, *Mozart: Studies of the Autograph Scores* (Cambridge, Mass., 1987), especially 23–35.

11. That Beethoven knew and read Sulzer's encyclopedic treatise is apparent from his use of the article on "Recitative" for his own studies of dramatic vocal music c. 1800–1802; see R. Kramer, "Beethoven and Carl Heinrich Graun," *BS* 1:18–44.

12. J. G. von Herder, *Reflections on the Philosophy and History of Mankind* (1784–91), abridged English trans. by T. Churchill, ed. F. Manuel (Chicago, 1968), 40.

13. J. G. Herder, *Sämtliche Werke,* ed. by B. Suphan, IV (Berlin, 1877–1913), 161f., quoted by F. Blume, *Classic and Romantic Music* (New York, 1970), 13.

14. From *The Remarkable Musical Life of the Tone-Poet Joseph Berglinger,* included in Wackenroder and Tieck's *Outpourings of an Art-Loving Friar,* trans. E. Mornin (New York, 1975), 105ff., 107ff. That musicians and literary people around Beethoven, and Beethoven himself, knew Wackenroder's writings is clearly evident from a letter sent to Beethoven in 1819 by the Bremen literary man Carl Iken, who quotes a passage by "Joseph Berglinger" to Beethoven without having to explain to him who Berglinger is; see *Briefwechsel,* 1359.

15. See Prologue for the letter to "Emilie M." of July 17, 1812.

16. Richard Heuberger, *Erinnerungen an Johannes Brahms,* 2nd ed., ed. K. Hofmann (Tutzing, 1971), 93.

17. According to Heuberger, Brahms went on to compare Beethoven's treatment of dissonance in his earlier works unfavorably with that of Mozart and Bach.

18. Review of Opus 1 in *Wiener Jahrbuch* 1 (1806), Heft 2, 53–54; quoted in Kunze, *Beethoven, Die Werke,* 13.

19. From *AMZ* review of 1805, quoted in Kunze, *Beethoven, Die Werke,* 36.

20. Review in the *AMZ* (1799), cols. 541ff., quoted in Kunze, *Beethoven, Die Werke*, 18.
21. *Briefwechsel*, No. 59; Anderson No. 48 (April 22, 1801.)

Chapter 9

1. Of the vast number of books on Napoleon I mention only two. One is the classic account by G. Lefebvre, *Napoleon*, trans. H. F. Stockold (New York, 1969); the other is the overview by A. Schom, *Napoleon Bonaparte* (New York, 1997), with an ample bibliography.
2. E. Hobsbawm, *The Age of Revolution, 1799–1848* (New York, 1962), 99.
3. TF, 403; Solomon, *Beethoven*, 181.
4. *Briefwechsel*, No. 84; Anderson, No. 57. Napoleon's concordat with the pope reconciled the French regime's policies with those of the church. The concordat declared, among other things, that Roman Catholicism was to be regarded as the religion of the majority of the French people as well as of the consuls who were then seen as its rulers in the future. The accord spelled the end of the separation of church and state, a concept in the secular tradition of the Revolution. See Lefebvre, *Napoleon* 1:133ff.
5. For the original text see F. Ries, *Briefe und Dokumente*, 61–63; for a translation, see Albrecht, No. 71.
6. On the relationship between Austria's war-making capacities and its financial situation see Josef Karl Mayr, *Wien im Zeitalter Napoleons* (Vienna, 1940), 16; also Lefebvre, *Napoleon* 1: 206. On the cautious and wavering attitude of the Austrian regime toward Napoleon in the years 1802–5 see Sipe, *Beethoven: Eroica Symphony*, 44f.
7. For a personal portrait, especially on his education, see W. Langsam, *Francis the Good* (New York, 1949). Beethoven had dedicated his Septet Opus 20 to the Empress Maria Theresa, Francis's second wife; and of course he intended his cantata *Der Glorreiche Augenblick*, Opus 136 as a tribute to the reigning heads of state at the Congress of Vienna, which included Emperor Francis. In 1815 he did decide to use his C-major Overture as a belated "Name-day" work for the emperor, but the work (later Opus 115) had been begun in 1814 as an overture "for any purpose, or for use in concerts." But he did not explicitly dedicate any major work to the emperor, even after Francis's dissolution of the faded Holy Roman empire in 1806 and his assumption of the rank of hereditary emperor of Austria. By this means, incidentally, "Francis II" as Holy Roman emperor became "Francis I" as emperor of Austria.
8. On Francis's ineffectual management and further on the financial problems that beset his regime, see Lefebvre, 1:206–8.
9. See Ries's letter, note 5 above.
10. There were numerous pieces written in this period that celebrated battles and victories, by a host of composers; see B. Arnold, *Music and War: A Research and Information Guide* (New York, 1993), 52–87.
11. On the possible connections of these French works to the *Eroica*, see C. Palisca, "French Revolutionary Models for Beethoven's *Eroica* Funeral March," in *Music and Context: Essays for John Ward*, ed. A. D. McLucas (Cambridge, Mass., 1985), 198–209.

12. Sonneck, 74ff.; Solomon, 181.

13. TF, 920.

14. See TF, 339. We have to remember as well that the idea of a "complete edition" also implied an edition that might counteract the rampant piracy of his music by unauthorized publishers, and thus was an attempt to protect his income.

15. See TF, 328ff.

16. TF, 330.

17. On Klinger's marble monument, with the naked Beethoven enthroned, see Comini, *The Changing Image of Beethoven,* especially 403–15.

18. See Comini, *The Changing Image of Beethoven,* 34–36.

19. See R. Bory, *Beethoven: His Life and His Work in Pictures,* trans. W. Glass and H. Rosenwald (Zurich, 1960), 97 and 163.

20. See Comini, 35. I am not persuaded by the argument of Owen Jander that the faded leaves at the lower left-hand corner of the picture symbolize Beethoven's deafness. See his " 'Let Your Deafness No Longer Be a Secret—Even in Art:' Self-Portraiture and the Third Movement of the C-Minor Symphony," *BF* 8:60–68 (on the Mähler portrait).

21. *Briefwechsel,* No. 206. See TF, 337, where Thayer records his own conversation with Mähler sometime before 1860. Mähler was a sometime musician, a singer, and a man of varied talents in addition to his painting. He told Thayer that his first meeting with Beethoven in the fall of 1803 coincided with Beethoven's immersion in the composition of the *Eroica* and that Beethoven played the finale of the new symphony and then improvised for two hours. Thayer owned a copy of the earlier Mähler portrait that is now in the New York Public Library.

22. Sonneck, *Beethoven,* 8–9. Fischer (1780–1864), a baker, was a decade younger than Beethoven and outlived him by many years. His handwritten memoirs, begun in 1838 with the help of his sister, are an important biographical source for Beethoven's youth. His reference to Beethoven's "dark complexion" was used to argue that Beethoven was of African ancestry, a belief promulgated in the twentieth century that lacks any foundation in all we know of Beethoven's forebears. For further commentary on this question see Dominique-René de Lerma, "Beethoven as a Black Composer," *Black Music Research Newsletter,* 8/1 (1985): 3–5.

23. See Edward Larkin, "Beethoven's Medical History," in M. Cooper, *Beethoven: The Last Decade* (London, 1970), 449, n. 1. Larkin writes of "lesions and indurations of the skin at the root of the nose, on the cheeks and around the mouth and chin . . . as well as 'disfigurement' about the mouth and chin." This passage is quoted and discussed by Comini, 33ff. As she notes, a diagnosis of Beethoven's "pustular facial eruptions" is "admittedly difficult," but, as she also shrewdly observes, the "formidable impression conveyed by [Klein's] austere life-mask of seriousness and intense concentration . . . would be seized upon by all later image makers as appropriate to the Beethoven aura."

24. The only other truly well-known composer who suffered deafness was Bedřich Smetana, who, however, became deaf at fifty, near the end of his productive career.

25. D. Wright, *Deafness: A Personal Account,* in Grant, ed., *The Quiet Ear,* 44. See chapter 5, note 4. I omit from Wright's account of sounds he could hear that did not exist in Bee-

thoven's time, such as "low-flying aeroplanes, cars backfiring, motor-bicycles, heavy lorries." We have to remember that Beethoven lived in a world much quieter than ours, in which softer and more delicate gradations of sound were part of the experience of daily life to a far higher degree than they have become since.

26. N II, 89. Although Jander (see note 20) claims that the expression "even in art" (*auch bey der Kunst*) means that Beethoven was now willing to "reveal" his deafness symptoms through dissonant and muffled passages in some of his works, I believe that this view overinterprets the meaning of the expression. Beethoven might simply have meant that from this point on he was resolved not to hide his deafness from musicians and others with whom he would have to be in contact—especially if he was to write operas—but that he would face the consequences of letting others know that he was deaf. I read *bey der Kunst* as meaning "in relation to art" rather than "*in* art." The fact that he makes this point in connection with his intention to write operas is telling.

27. Beethoven-Archiv, Bonn, MS Mh 83, fol. 1r, with sketches for the overture to *König Stephan*, Op. 117.

28. *Briefwechsel*, No. 65 (June 29, 1801).

29. Larkin, "Beethoven's Medical History," 448. See also Bankl and Jesserer, *Die Krankheiten Ludwig van Beethovens*. These authors agree with Larkin that a long-held belief that Beethoven had syphilis lacks any clear foundation. Contrary to Larkin, however, they believe in a probable diagnosis of cirrhosis of the liver and in the likelihood of chronic colon inflammation. That Beethoven drank alcohol in quantities is not to be doubted, but whether he had cirrhosis of the liver remains speculative. For a recent review of the literature on Beethoven's deafness and other disorders see M. Saffle and J. R. Saffle, "Medical Histories of Prominent Composers: Recent Research and Discoveries," *Acta Musicologica* 65 (1993): 82–86.

30. The most recent effort to determine the causes of his ill health have centered on the analysis of strands of hair that were apparently removed from Beethoven's lifeless body by Ferdinand Hiller; see Russell Martin, *Beethoven's Hair* (New York, 2000). Preliminary tests of these strands seem to have indicated unusually high levels of lead, suggesting the possibility of lead poisoning. As Martin observes, it remains to be seen whether the laboratory tests that produced these results may be corroborated by DNA comparison with bone remains, and for now the entire question of lead poisoning must be left open. I am grateful to Dr. Raymond Firestone for sharing with me his views on the lead-poisoning hypothesis based on the analysis described in Martin's book. Many further questions would have to be resolved in order to determine the validity of the entire lead-poisoning hypothesis. A similar lead-poisoning hypothesis was offered as an explanation for Goya's major illness of 1792, but that case is seemingly fortified by Goya's use of lead-based pigments; see Gedo, "The Healing Power of Art: Goya as His Own Physician," 81, and further references given there.

31. TF, 248.

32. *Briefwechsel*, No. 303.

33. This dedication is confirmed by the rediscovery of the long-missing corrected copy of Opus 69, found by Dr. Albert Dunning in a Dutch library and described by him at the

International Conference on Beethoven's Music for Violoncello, held at Bonn in July 1989 (proceedings forthcoming). The copy explicitly bears a dedication to Gleichenstein in Beethoven's hand.

34. See Kinsky-Halm, 269, and *Briefwechsel*, No. 1014. Zmeskall's sixteen unpublished string quartets remain in manuscript at the Gesellschaft der Musikfreunde, Vienna.

35. *Briefwechsel*, Nos. 414 (dated by Brandenburg to 1809) and 35 (c. 1798). In the latter, as in other notes of the same year (Nos. 37 and 39), Beethoven plays with the word *baron*, reversing letters to make combinations such as "nor," "orn," "rno", "onr"—and sometimes, as in *Briefwechsel* No. 39, setting "Ba-ron" to short musical phrases.

36. See A. Tyson, "The 'Razumovsky' Quartets: Some Aspects of the Sources," *BS* 3 (Cambridge, 1982), 134ff. and plates 3 and 4. Tyson shows a draft dating from the summer of 1807 in which Beethoven considered revising the titles and dedications of seven major works from Opus 58 to Opus 62.

37. See TF, 432–5.

38. *Briefwechsel*, No. 523 (October 9, 1811, to Breitkopf).

39. Wegeler-Ries, 42, 43.

40. TF, 232, based on a conversation between Thayer and Willmann's niece. See also Solomon, *Beethoven*, 111 and his letter to the *Beethoven Journal* 12/1 (Spring, 1997), 48.

41. Letter apparently dating from 1805, translated in Albrecht, No. 99. See also Solomon, 198 and TF, 379.

42. Albrecht, No. 100.

43. Solomon, *Beethoven*, 198f. As noted in chapter 3, note 16, Josephine Deym (later Deym-Stackelberg) has been advanced as the likely recipient of the "Immortal Beloved" letter, most vigorously by Elisabeth Tellenbach and Harry Goldschmidt. But this proposal remains improbable, given the lack of any persuasive evidence that their relationship continued after 1804–7 or that they even had any contact after that year. See Solomon's "Recherche de Josephine Deym," in his *Beethoven Essays* (Cambridge, Mass., 1988), 157–65.

44. Anderson, No. 254, translation modified by Solomon, *Beethoven*, 202; see *Briefwechsel*, No. 445, attributed to June 1810, though a somewhat earlier date is not excluded by the editors.

45. Solomon, *Beethoven*, Chapter 15, 207–46. The list of candidates was subsequently widened by Gail Altman to include Countess Marie Erdödy, but the case is altogether unconvincing; see Barry Cooper's review in *Beethoven Journal* 11/2 (Fall 1996): 18–24. The whole subject reached a new low in Bernard Rose's 1994 film *Immortal Beloved*, in which the supposed recipient is presented as Johanna van Beethoven, the widow of the composer's brother Carl and the mother of his beloved nephew Karl. In actuality, Johanna was the object of Beethoven's deep animosity in his later years as he battled her for custody of Karl.

46. Solomon, *Beethoven Essays*, 179; letter of Antonie Brentano to Bishop Johann Michael Sailer, February 22, 1819.

47. Sonneck, *Beethoven: Impressions of Contemporaries*, 230.

48. Solomon, *Beethoven Essays*, and his communication to the *Beethoven Journal* 12/1 (Spring 1997): 48. Most recently another new candidate has been proposed, namely, the

Countess Almerie Esterházy (1789–1848), the daughter of Count Valentin Esterházy, a member of a branch of the large Esterházy family that had settled in France in the early eighteenth century. In 1815 she married Count Albert Joseph Murray von Melgum, a military man of Scottish descent who was born in Vienna and was a decorated officer in the Austrian army. See O. Pulkert, "Beethoven's 'Immortal Beloved,'" *Beethoven Journal* 15/1 (2000): 2–18, rev. H.-W. Küthen and trans. W. Meredith. A lengthier account is that of J. Čeleda and O. Pulkert, "Beethovens 'Unsterbliche Geliebte,'" in *Ludwig van Beethoven im Herzen Europas,* ed. O. Pulkert and H.-W. Küthen (Prague, 2000), 383–408. Although the evidence presented in this article is more generally promising than that in many previous essays on the subject—for example, it shows that in July 1812 the twenty-two-year-old Almerie Esterházy was listed as arriving in Karlsbad as one of the two daughters of Count Valentin Esterházy—the arguments in her favor are entirely circumstantial. Nor is any other evidence known that would connect Almerie Esterházy with Beethoven. For Antonie Brentano, on the other hand, there is substantial evidence of her emotional allegiance to Beethoven.

49. For the original German text see, most conveniently, *Briefwechsel,* No. 582. These words in German, "was für unss seyn muss und seyn soll," are like a distant premonition of the runic phrases that Beethoven placed over the finale to his Quartet in F major, Opus 135: "Muss es sein? Es muss sein!"

Chapter 10

1. Tovey, "Beethoven," *Enclylopedia Britannica,* 11th ed., 1911. That the "heroic" works of this period continue to be defining parts of musical experience is the thesis of S. Burnham's *Beethoven Hero* (Princeton, 1995).

2. See "The Earliest Sketches for the *Eroica* Symphony," in Lockwood, *Studies,* 134–50.

3. See H. Schenker's vast analysis of the symphony in his *Das Meisterwerk in der Musik* (Munich, 1930), 3:25–99 and especially 74ff. on the finale. Also K. von Fischer, "Eroica-Variationen Op. 35 und Eroica-Finale," *Schweizerische Musikzeitung* 89 (1949): 282–6.

4. On the origins of the finale see "The Compositional Genesis of the *Eroica* Finale," in Lockwood, *Studies,* 151–66.

5. See Kinsky-Halm, 130.

6. This important segment, at mm. 57–64, has been overlooked by many commentators; the transition figure that introduces it ends on a diminished-seventh chord with F-sharp in the bass.

7. See my "*Eroica* Perspectives: Strategy and Design in the First Movement," in Lockwood, *Studies,* 118–34.

8. These events occur at mm. 655–673.

9. Wegeler-Ries, 79. On the whole passage and its sketches and significance, see my "Planning the Unexpected: Beethoven's Sketches for the Horn Entrance in the *Eroica* Symphony, First Movement," in Lockwood, *Studies,* 167–80.

10. See Paul Bekker, *Beethoven,* 2nd ed. (Berlin, 1912), 220ff.; English translation by M. M. Bozman (London, 1925), 163; and Lockwood, *Studies,* 119.

11. Berlioz, *A Critical Study,* 41.
12. Biamonti, *Catalogo cronologico,* 312ff., reproduces the Paer march in piano score. As Biamonti explains, in the opera the funeral march is undertaken by a cortege of Greek warriors who bear the body of the fallen hero Patroclus before the tent of Achilles. Thomas Sipe suggests that, following this precedent, we can understand the *Eroica* second movement to reflect the image of Achilles lamenting the death of Patroclus, thus it would represent a "hero lamenting the death of his comrade" (Sipe, *Beethoven: Eroica Symphony,* 105). But that theory is purely speculative, like all specific programmatic interpretations of the movement.
13. A number of general books on Beethoven thus label the second period "heroic," including the major books by Solomon (chapters 12 and 14, "The Heroic Decade" I and II) and Kinderman (chapters 4 and 5, "The Heroic Style I and II"), though in the latter the terminal boundary is given as 1809, and the years from 1809 to 1812 are captured under the term "Consolidation." A book devoted to exploring the emergence of the "heroic style" is M. Broyles, *Beethoven: The Emergence and Evolution of Beethoven's Heroic Style* (New York, 1987). Though Broyles's book contains many valuable observations on style and compositional technique, its title forces the concept on some works that do not belong to this category.
14. See L. Lockwood, "Beethoven, Florestan, and the Varieties of Heroism," in *Beethoven and His World,* ed. S. Burnham and M. P. Steinberg (Princeton, 2000), 27–47. I try to correct what I regard as an inevitable imbalance in the title and import of so intelligent and interesting a book as Scott Burnham's *Beethoven Hero,* which is primarily an analytical study of the *Eroica* and the Fifth Symphonies, with occasional references to a few other works. It is not that these two works are not "heroic"—they certainly are. But the basic premise of the book is that Beethoven's "heroic style has come to dominate our discourse about Western art music" (158) and the book explores the ramifications of this viewpoint. Yet the heroic view has not dominated all of our discourse by any means, and certainly not that of many commentators on major composers and styles from the late nineteenth century through the twentieth. All of which is not to denigrate Burnham's insight into the specific works he discusses, but rather to insist on releasing into the light the other major works of this time that are inevitably omitted since they do not fit—for example, the Violin Concerto, the Fourth Piano Concerto, the Quartets Opus 59 Nos. 2 and 3; the Piano Sonatas Opp. 54, 78, and 81a; and the Piano Trio Opus 70 No. 2. A broader view of Beethoven's approach to genre, style, and aesthetic models, on a much wider scale, seems to me more revealing.
15. This point is noted by Solomon, *Beethoven,* 174.
16. *Briefwechsel,* No. 165; Ferdinand Ries, *Briefwechsel und Dokumente* (Bonn, 1982), No. 14, 61f. As Solomon notes, 175, this letter hints that Beethoven's enthusiasm for dedicating the work to Bonaparte had already cooled somewhat by this time, and, in order to insure his fee, he was now willing to let Lobkowitz have it for six months with the understanding that it would be *titled* "Bonaparte." It is impossible to avoid the impression that Beethoven was cautiously attempting to have it both ways, protecting his fee yet leaving open the possibility of gaining favor with Napoleon.
17. Lefebvre, *Napoleon,* 1: 183.

18. *Briefwechsel,* No. 188. Beethoven spells it "Ponaparte."

19. Lefebvre, 186. The quotation is from the Napoleonic administrator Jean-Antoine de Chaptal.

20. The words in German are "Geschrieben auf Bonaparte."

21. This view is well stated in the excellent and still highly readable book by A. Schmitz, *Das Romantische Beethovenbild* (Berlin, 1927), 153–76. Schmitz puts the case as clearly as I believe it can be put: "For his symphony he now chooses, instead of the name of a specific person, by whom he has been deceived, the indication of the idea [of the heroic], by which he cannot be deceived: Eroica" (p. 162). Schmitz is also one of the first major commentators to link the idea of the "heroic" in music to Sulzer's *Allgemeine Theorie der Schönen Künste* (1792) and to show that the category of the "heroic," with varying shades of meaning but always stressing "uncommon" and "exceptional" qualities of mind and heart, is found in literature and opera of the period, as well as in the music of the French Revolution.

22. See Lefebvre, *Napoleon* 1: 208.

23. On David and Napoleon see P. Johnson, *The Birth of the Modern* (New York, 1991), 145; W. Roberts, *Jacques-Louis David: Revolutionary Artist* (Chapel Hill, 1989); and S. Lee, *David* (London, 1999).

24. See Fred Licht, *Canova* (1983), 104.

25. The reference to a "strange voice" is from Beethoven's sketches for the scherzo in the sketchbook Landsberg 6, fol. 10. The word "voice" (*Stimme*) is admittedly conjectural but makes sense; see Nottebohm, *Ein Skizzenbuch von Beethoven aus dem Jahre 1803* (Leipzig, 1880), 44.

26. Wegeler-Ries, 78.

27. *Briefwechsel,* No. 395, letter of August 8, 1809, to Breitkopf & Härtel, requesting that the publisher send him the complete works of Goethe and Schiller, says they are his "favorite poets" along with Ossian and Homer, "whom unfortunately I can only read in translation."

28. J. R. Schultz, *The Harmonicon,* January 1824; see Sonneck, *Beethoven: Impressions of Contemporaries,* 153 (Sonneck misattributes the essay to "Edward Schulz"; see B. Cooper, *The Beethoven Compendium,* 53.

29. On the introduction see Hillary Tann Presslaff, "The Investigation," *Perspectives of New Music,* 20 (1981–82): 526–59.

30. R. Schumann, *On Music and Musicians* (New York, 1946), 99.

31. T. Adorno, *Beethoven, The Philosophy of Music* (Stanford, 1998), 99 (No. 228).

32. See A. Tyson, "Das Leonoreskizzenbuch (Mendelssohn 15): Problems der Rekonstruktion und Chronologie," *BJ* 9 (1977): 490ff. See also the excellent critical score of the work edited by Bathia Churgin (London, 1998).

33. Especially striking in their use of rhythmic and metrical shifts is the comparison between the Allegro movements of the symphony and the march in *Leonore,* also in B-flat major, by far the most rhythmically interesting march Beethoven wrote before his last period.

34. Kinderman, *Beethoven,* 123.

35. Nottebohm, *Ein Skizzenbuch . . . 1803,* 70–71, where at the end of the *Eroica* sketchbook

we find, along with first ideas for the Fourth Piano Concerto and amid first thoughts for *Leonore,* early sketches for what became the Scherzo of the Fifth and for the first movement, here marked "Sinfonia." The first-movement idea encompasses the motto-like opening on tonic and dominant, then a bare outline of part of an exposition down as far as the legato second theme, which is already complete. Much earlier in the same sketchbook of 1803–4 (p. 93, N II 375), we find the first sketch that we can associate with the *Pastoral* Symphony slow movement: a gentle C-major Andante molto labeled *Murmeln der Bäche* (Murmurs of the brooks) with repeated triplets on C as the basic idea. This is the sketch that contains the significant marginal note, "je grösser der Bach, je tiefer der Ton" ("the wider the brook, the deeper the tone").

36. The review appeared in the *Allgemeine Musikalische Zeitung* 12 (July 4 and 11, 1810), 30 and 41, and is reprinted in S. Kunze, *Beethoven, Die Werke,* 100–112. For an English translation see *Beethoven, Symphony No. 5 in C Minor,* ed. E. Forbes (New York, 1971), 150–63. For a modern commentary on the review see P. Schnaus, *E. T. A. Hoffmann als Beethoven-Rezensent der Allgemeinen Musikalischen Zeitung* (Munich, 1977), 89–101.

37. As expressed here and elsewhere in his voluminous writings on music, Hoffmann's idea of "romanticism" in music entails the view that instrumental music, by virtue of its independence from text or specified programmatic purposes, is innately "romantic," that is, it evokes nameless but powerful emotions in the listener, who can thereby be transported to a sense of the infinite, beyond the expressive boundaries of texted or particularized programmatic music.

38. The immediate predecessor of this vast growing crescendo preparation is the retransition in the first movement of the *Eroica* (mm. 338–397). The difference here is that although the motivic content of the Fifth is simpler, the harmonic content is more complex, in that the tympani sound an incessant tonic C against the growing mass of the dominant harmony in the other instruments (mm. 324–373). When the Scherzo returns, the tympani C again reenters four bars before the end (Finale, m. 203) to build the final crescendo preparing the climactic return of the triumphant finale theme.

39. See Webster, *Haydn's "Farewell" Symphony,* especially 6, "Integration of the Cycle," and 366–73, comparing Haydn's and Beethoven's uses of cyclic form.

40. See the very long work in D major for piano solo in the "Kafka" sketch collection, the largest surviving group of Beethoven's early sketches and studies, published by Joseph Kerman as *Ludwig van Beethoven, Autograph Miscellany from circa 1786 to 1799 . . . the "Kafka" Sketchbook* (London, 1970), 2:110–25, including variant passages. Kerman observes that the piece could bear the title "fantasia" and its three sections suggest a three-movement Allego—Andante—Allegro piano sonata, but with transitions (II, 285). The work is both ambitious and unfinished, and may, as Kerman notes, "record a successful improvisation" that also anticipates the idea of a "sonata quasi una fantasia."

41. See Paul Mies, "Quasi una fantasia," in *Colloquium Amicorum: Joseph Schmidt-Görg zum 70. Geburtstag,* ed. S. Kross and H. Schmidt (Bonn, 1967), 239–49.

42. For references to late-eighteenth- and earlier nineteenth-century commentators on cyclic integration in the symphony with particular reference to Beethoven's Fifth, see Webster, *Haydn's "Farewell" Symphony,* 179–81.

43. Beethoven considered using a five-part form in this scherzo, resembling that of the

Fourth Symphony, and this form for the movement is actually indicated in some of the early sources; but he changed his mind for the first performance in 1808. See S. Brandenburg, "Once Again: On the Question of the Repeat of the Scherzo and Trio in Beethoven's Fifth Symphony," in *Beethoven Essays: Studies in Honor of Elliot Forbes,* ed. L. Lockwood and P. Benjamin (Cambridge, Mass., 1984), 146–98.

44. See J. Kerman, "Beethoven's Minority," in *Haydn, Mozart and Beethoven: Essays in Honor of Alan Tyson,* ed. S. Brandenburg (Oxford, 1998), 151–74.

45. *Betrachtungen über die Werke Gottes im Reiche der Natur* by Christoph Christian Sturm, originally published in 1785, Beethoven's copy published 1811; the information is from Schindler. See Solomon, "The Quest for Faith" in his *Beethoven Essays* (Cambridge, 1988), 216–32, especially 220ff.; and C. C. Witcombe, "Beethoven's Private God: An Analysis of the Composer's Markings in Sturm's 'Betrachtungen'" (M. A. thesis, San Jose State University, 1998).

46. On antecedents of the *Pastoral* Symphony see Richard Will, *The Characteristic Symphony in the Age of Haydn and Beethoven* (Cambridge, 2002).

47. For these and other entries see the *Pastoral* Symphony Sketchbook, as partially published by D. Weise, *Ein Skizzenbuch zur Pastoralsymphonie Op. 68 und zu den Trios Op. 70, 1 und 2* (Bonn, 1961), vols. 2 and 5, and N II, 375 and 504.

48. N II, 378, reports the survival of a violin part made from Beethoven's autograph, in which he had instructed the copyist to enter the movement headings into the first violin part.

49. See *Ludwig van Beethoven: Sechste Symphonie F-Dur Opus 68 . . . Faksimile nach dem Autograph BH 64 im Beethoven-Haus Bonn,* ed. S. Brandenburg (Bonn, 2000), 45.

50. As the autograph shows, Beethoven's way of setting up an orchestral score in 1808 still followed the eighteenth-century convention of having the violin and viola parts at the top of the score, then the winds and brass below, and the low-register strings (cellos and basses) at the bottom. Thus the score layout graphically shows the spatial distance between low strings and high strings, i.e., between the brook (cellos) and birds trilling (Violin I and, in the course of the movement, Violin II).

51. Similar observations are found in O. Jander, "The Prophetic Conversation in Beethoven's 'Scene by the Brook,'" *The Musical Quarterly* 77 (1993): 508–59. However in my view Jander's interpretation suffers from several shortcomings: (1) his belief that the "resumption" theme in the movement, returning after every major incise, is to be associated with Beethoven personifying himself; (2) his literal programmatic account of every segment of the movement; and (3) the absence of any reference to the spatial and registral aspects of the movement. Regarding (1), there is no evidence that the "resumption" theme characterizes Beethoven or anyone else; (2), a detailed programmatic narrative is just what Beethoven regarded as "going too far," by the evidence of his own entries in the Pastoral Symphony Sketchbook (see above). As for (3), this combination of the evocative with the structural is to me the essence of any analytically sound interpretation.

52. See note 35.

53. As in the Fifth, this third movement is not marked "Scherzo."

54. TF, 524, letter of January 28, 1812, translation modified; *Briefwechsel,* No. 546.

55. See "Beethoven's Sketches for *Sehnsucht* (WoO 146)," in Lockwood, *Studies*, 95–117.
56. For a brief overview see B. Cooper, "Folksong arrangements" in *The Beethoven Compendium*, ed. B. Cooper (London, 1991), 267–72.
57. *Briefwechsel*, No. 809 (June 1, 1815).
58. There the opening theme in the oboe brings the pitch sequence 1–5–3–6–5, a rearrangement of the pitch collection Beethoven had used to open the A Major cello sonata, Opus 69 (1–5–6–3–5); for this introduction a basic unifying feature is the bass-line, which descends from the tonic to the dominant via chromatic steps: 1–7–♭7–6–♭6–5 (mm. 1–8) and then makes extensive use of each member of this descending series in what follows. Thus, the note G-natural (♭7) when taken up again at m. 24, becomes the dominant of C major, to which the motion turns for a long and important portion of the Introduction. And in the vast Allegro that follows, the harmonic goals are closely related to those of the Introduction.
59. See C. Dahlhaus, "Bemerkungen zu Beethovens 8. Symphonie," *Schweizerische Musikzeitung* 110 (1970): 205–9.
60. At mm. 26–29 in the symphony slow movement.
61. Mm. 267–354 and 355–502.
62. See Lockwood, *Studies*, 220–25.

Chapter 11

1. On the dating and other aspects of the Third Concerto, see Plantinga, *Beethoven's Concertos*, 133–35.
2. On the dating of the sketches see JTW, 140, 143, and 148.
3. Plantinga, 159–84; B. Brook, "The Symphonie Concertante: Its Musical and Sociological Bases," *International Review of the Aesthetics and Sociology of Music* 6 (1975): 9–28.
4. See R. Kramer, "An Unfinished Concertante by Beethoven," *BS*, 2: 33–36.
5. Plantinga, 183ff.; Ries, No. 11, letter of August 6, 1803; No. 14, of October 22, 1803.
6. S. Kagan, *Archduke Rudolph, Beethoven's Patron, Pupil and Friend* (Stuyvesant, N.Y., 1988), 3. For the view that Beethoven did not know the archduke before about 1808 see Sieghard Brandenburg, "Die Beethoven-Handschriften in der Musikaliensammlung des Erzherzogs Rudolph," *Zu Beethoven* 3 (Berlin, 1988): 141–66.
7. Plantinga, 161.
8. On cello concertos of this period see the summary in R. Stowell, ed., *The Cambridge Companion to the Cello* (Cambridge, 1999), 92–95. Anton Kraft's importance as a cellist is suggested not only by his role for eleven years as leading cellist at Esterházy with Haydn but also by his having participated in the first performance of Mozart's great E-flat Flat Major Divertimento for String Trio, K. 563, at Dresden in 1789. Kraft's later career included concert tours to major capitals and performances in Vienna as a soloist and orchestral section leader, as in the premieres of Beethoven's Seventh Symphony and *Wellingtons Sieg*. He was the regular cellist in the Schuppanzigh Quartet until 1808. His son Nikolaus Kraft (1778–1853) was also a successful cellist, a member of Lobkowitz's Kapelle and, for a time, of the Schuppanzigh Quartet. He may have given the first per-

formances of Beethoven's Opus 69 in 1809. On the two Krafts see, most recently, Walden, 43–45.

9. Kinsky-Halm, 136 refers to the premiere as having taken place in March 1807 at a subscription concert at Lobkowitz's, but the evidence is weak, and Plantinga, 211, finds it unconvincing. The only surviving evidence reports that "a piano concerto" was played at one of these concerts, but not which one, nor who was the soloist. Furthermore, as Plantinga points out, Reichardt calls the Fourth concerto "new" after hearing it at Beethoven's concert in 1808 while sitting in Lobkowitz's box.

10. See J. Kerman, *Concerto Conversations* (Cambridge, Mass., 1999), 62.

11. See mm. 4–5 (the original figure), 11–12, 51–52, and 348–349.

12. For a summary of views associating the slow movement with the Orpheus legend see Plantinga, 185–94. Plantinga's list includes A. B. Marx, *Ludwig van Beethoven: Leben und Schaffen* (Leipzig, 1902, originally published 1859), 2:78f.; D. F. Tovey, *Essays in Musical Analysis* (London, 1944), 3:80f.; and two essays by O. Jander: "Beethoven's 'Orpheus in Hades': the Andante con moto of the Fourth Piano Concerto," *19th Century Music*, 8 (1985): 195–212, and "Orpheus Revisited: A Ten-Year Retrospect on the Andante con moto of Beethoven's Fourth Piano Concerto," *19th Century Music* (1995): 31–49. An important critical view of Jander's programmatic interpretation is E. T. Cone, "Beethoven's Orpheus—or Jander's," *19th Century Music* 8 (1985): 283–86. Summarizing, Plantinga wisely observes that despite the obvious dramatic quality of the movement, with its "pleading" soloist and its "stern, rejecting" orchestra (these terms are my own), there is no basis in Beethoven writings or known conversations for associating the movement specifically with the Orpheus legend.

13. In *Così fan tutte* there are two short arias with strings alone, both for Don Alfonso: the first is "Vorrei dir," in which Don Alfonso feigns anguish as he tells the two women that their lovers have met a "great disaster," i.e., have supposedly been called to the army; the other is Don Alfonso's ottava, "Tutte accusan le donne," in which he explains to everyone the ways of the world, namely, "all women do it" ("così fan tutte").

14. E.g., in the consoling D-flat-major passage in the slow movement of Opus 59 No. 1, and repeatedly in the Cello Sonata in C Major, Opus 102 No. 1; further on this figure see Lockwood, "Beethoven's Emergence from Crisis," especially 317–19.

15. Plantinga, 235.

16. Plantinga, 246.

17. For a brief survey of the known cadenzas see R. Stowell, *Beethoven: Violin Concerto* (Cambridge, 1998), 90–97. Stowell lists retranscriptions or adaptations of the piano concerto cadenza by Nováček, Rostal, M. Abbado, Schneiderhan, Swensen, and, in part, Hellmesberger.

18. See mm. 65–68ff. and later reappearances of the figure including its diminution as four sixteenths leading to a sharply accented eighth, or its mysterious appearances at dramatic moments, such as mm. 480–485.

19. Mm. 45–55. Tovey, *Essays in Musical Analysis*, 3: 94; Stowell, *Beethoven: Violin Concerto*, 77.

20. Plantinga, 255.

21. Plantinga, 256.
22. Mm. 94ff.
23. T. W. Adorno, *Beethoven,* 76f.

Chapter 12

1. Seyfried, *Ludwig van Beethovens Studien* (Leipzig, 1853), 20.
2. See JTW, 419, 598.
3. N II, 225f.
4. This unfinished effort was fixed up by Emanuel Schikaneder, the librettist and Papageno of *The Magic Flute,* and was given a mediocre setting by Peter Winter, an older contemporary of Beethoven's. On Goethe's libretto and Winter's setting see Gruber, 74ff.
5. See K. Smolle, *Wohnstätten Ludwig van Beethovens von 1792 bis zu seinem Tod* (Bonn, 1970), 23–27.
6. See Nottebohm, *Ein Skizzenbuch . . . 1803,* 56.
7. Bouilly later claimed this was not the case, but in the period 1798–1806, when the Gaveaux, Paer, and Beethoven settings were written, it could readily be assumed that the plot was based on a real event. Indeed, the libretto of Paer's setting carries the subtitle "fatto storico in due atti" ("historically factual drama in two acts"). For a careful assessment of the credibility of Bouilly's claims see D. Galliver, "Jean-Nicolas Bouilly (1763–1842), Successor of Sedaine," *Studies in Music* (Nedlands, Australia) 13 (1973): 16–33; and Galliver's "Leonore, ou L'amour conjugale: a celebrated offspring of the French Revolution," in *Music and the French Revolution,* ed. Malcolm Boyd (Cambridge, 1992), 157–68.
8. See R. Engländer, "Paer's 'Leonora' und Beethoven's 'Fidelio,'" *Neues Beethoven Jahrbuch* 4 (1930): 118–32.
9. In 1801 Sonnleithner had helped found the Bureau d'Arts et d'Industrie, a Viennese publishing firm that brought out a number of Beethoven's works, including several important early piano sonatas. His enterprises also included a tour of Europe to collect material for a historical anthology of music of older periods, an idea he had picked up from Forkel, the first biographer of Bach.
10. W. Hess, *Beethovens Oper Fidelio und ihre drei Fassungen* (Zurich, 1953), 22–33. This is only one of many studies of the *Leonore-Fidelio* material by Hess, who also published an extensive amount of music that he believed to stem from the 1805 and 1806 versions. More recent scholarship by Helga Lühning and Michael Tusa has tended to cast some doubt on the versions of Beethoven's opera that Hess ascribed to 1805 and on the traditional view that the 1805 version is the "original" *Leonore* that modern performers should strive to recreate. Dr. Lühning's work discloses a rather different picture in that the primary early version that we possess is essentially that of 1806, while exactly what was performed in 1805 remains, in her view, a "torso, which one can only perform in a filled-out, corrected version that is in need of revisions." See H. Lühning, "Vom Mythos der Ur-Leonore," in *Von der Leonore zum Fidelio,* ed. H. Lühning and W. Steinbeck (Frankfurt, 2000), 41–64; this quotation is from p. 64.
11. For a sample of a Mozart quotation in the opera see M. Brunswick, "Beethoven's Trib-

ute to Mozart in *Fidelio*," *The Musical Quarterly* 36 (1945): 29–32; Brunswick's quotation, which is found in the terzett in Act I, echoes a passage in the duet between Papageno and Papagena in the second-act finale of *The Magic Flute*. Other similar quotations or near quotations occur in *Leonore/Fidelio* in the domestic passages, often recalling Mozartian characters in comic or everyday scenes.

12. See Lühning, "Vom Mythos der Ur-Leonore," 52ff., and her "'Fidelio' in Prag," in *Beethoven und Böhmen*, ed. S. Brandenburg and M. Gutierrez-Denhoff (Bonn, 1988), 349–91.

13. Letter to Treitschke, apparently from early March 1814 (*Briefwechsel*, No. 707; Anderson, No. 479): "I shall now continue to work until it is completely finished, and . . . exactly in the way you have altered and improved everything . . . but it does not go as easily as if I were writing something new."

14. I am indebted here to Daniel Beller-McKenna.

15. See M. Tusa, "The Unknown Florestan: The 1805 Version of 'In des Lebens Frühlingstagen,'" *JAMS* 46 (1993): 175–220.

16. See Alan Tyson, "The Problem of Beethoven's 'First' *Leonore* Overture," *JAMS* 28 (1975): 292–334.

17. See review by Hoffmann in Kunze, *Beethoven, Die Werke*, 83–90.

18. Paul Mies, "Beethoven—Collin—Shakespeare: Zur Coriolan-Ouverture," *BJ* 6 (1965), 260–68; reprinted from *Zeitschrift für Musik* (February 1938): 156–61.

19. See the excellent article by E. Kerr Borthwick, "Beethoven and Plutarch," *Music and Letters* 79 (1998): 268–72.

20. See M. W. Howard, *The Influence of Plutarch in the Major European Literatures of the Eighteenth Century* (Chapel Hill, N.C., 1970).

21. Entry on folio 1r of a sketch leaf in the Hannover Kestner-Museum, quoted by A. Fecker, *Die Entstehung von Beethovens Musik zu Goethes Trauerspiel Egmont* (Hamburg, 1978), 17.

22. See mm. 261–264 and 281.

23. On the early-nineteenth-century trend away from mimesis and toward the autonomous view of music, see J. Neubauer, *The Emancipation of Music from Language* (New Haven, 1986).

Chapter 13

1. See T. Albrecht, "The Fortnight Fallacy: A Revised Chronology for Beethoven's *Christ on the Mount of Olives*, Op. 85, and Wielhorsky Sketchbook," *Journal of Musicological Research*, 11 (1991): 263–84. Albrecht's proposed chronology for the sketchbook suggests that work on the oratorio began in the fall of 1802.

2. Albrecht, 266, speculates that when Beethoven was "physically and mentally healthy" he was able to produce about eighty sketch pages a month, whereas at less productive times about half this number might have been the norm. At times when other major tasks (copying, orchestrating, etc.) claimed his attention, the number could have dropped to about fifteen pages a month or even to none. Albrecht suggests the latter situation for January to June 1805, when he was scoring the first two acts of *Leonore*.

3. Wegeler-Ries, 76.

4. *Briefwechsel,* No. 523 (October 9, 1811). According to Tyson, Beethoven was probably referring to his brother Carl, who in March 1803 had contracted rheumatic fever.

5. Alan Tyson, "Beethoven's Heroic Phase," *The Musical Times* 110 (1969): 139.

6. Tyson, "Beethoven's Heroic Phase," 140.

7. As observed by Tyson in JTW, 159.

8. See TF, 423.

9. Solomon, *Beethoven,* 456, n. 15, doubts the story because of evidence that Beethoven stayed on at Eisenstadt for three days after the premiere of the Mass, on September 13, 1807. But apart from this fact it has a reasonable ring of credibility as a reflection of the differing tastes and characters of Beethoven and the prince, not to mention other conservative patrons of the time. Elliot Forbes points out (TF, 424) that the story takes on more credibility when we find that the dedication of the mass went not to Esterházy but to Prince Kinsky.

10. *Briefwechsel,* No. 291 (July 26, 1807).

11. The Haydn passage was discovered by J. McGrann, "Beethoven's Mass in C, Opus 86: Genesis and Compositional Background" (Ph.D. diss., Harvard University, 1991), and independently found by A. Tyson, in JTW, 157, n. 1. There is, however, good reason to agree with E. T. A. Hoffmann, who regarded Beethoven's Mass as quite distant from those of Haydn; see J. McGrann, "An Exegesis of the Kyrie from Beethoven's Mass in C, Opus 86," in *Religion and the Arts* 2 (1998): 185ff.

12. *Briefwechsel,* No. 484 (letter to Breitkopf of January 16, 1811).

13. For Hoffmann's complete review see Kunze, *Beethoven, Die Werke,* 252–65.

14. Kunze, *Beethoven, Die Werke,* 254; see also Schnaus, 111–17.

15. On this aspect see M. Fillion, "Beethoven's Mass in C and the Search for Inner Peace," *BF* 7 (1999): 1–16.

16. E. Sams and G. Johnson, "The Romantic Lied," *NG2.*

17. Letter to Breitkopf of August 8, 1809 (*Briefwechsel,* No. 395), asking for volumes of their poetry; again in 1824 he tells Kiesewetter that he "prefers to set to music the works of poets like Homer, Klopstock, and Schiller" (*Briefwechsel,* No. 1773).

18. TF, 536.

19. *Briefwechsel,* No. 1562; Anderson, No. 1136.

20. Anderson, No. 40; *Briefwechsel,* No. 47.

21. For a discussion of the two settings see H. Lühning, "Gattungen des Liedes," in *Beiträge zu Beethovens Kammermusik: Symposion Bonn 1984,* ed. S. Brandenburg and H. Loos (Munich, 1987), 197–202.

22. See Joseph Kerman, "An die ferne Geliebte," in BS 1 (1973), 123–57.

Chapter 14

1. Griesinger, 61; see also H. A. Schafer, "'A Wisely Ordered Phantasie': Joseph Haydn's Creative Process from the Sketches and Drafts for Instrumental Music" (Ph.D. diss., Brandeis University, 1987).

2. W. A. Mozart, *Mozart's Letters, Mozart's Life: Selected Letters,* ed. and trans. R. Spaethling (New York, 2000), 277.
3. The quotations from Constanze Mozart and Niemetschek are from R. Marshall, ed., *Mozart Speaks,* 24.
4. H. Schmidt, *Verzeichnis der Skizzen Beethovens, BJ* 6: 60, MS Bonn Mh 83, fol. 1r: "kleines klawier zum componieren." This leaf contains sketches for the *King Stephen* Overture.
5. Kagan, 32; *Briefwechsel,* No. 1686.
6. On this important distinction between "componiren" and "setzen" see Schafer, *passim.*
7. See chapter 1 for a brief excerpt from this passage.
8. For the original text see Schiedermair, 88ff.; my translation. Junker was then the chaplain at Kirchberg, the residence of Prince Hohenlohe, and an accomplished musician.
9. TF, 207.
10. TF, 209.
11. C. Czerny, *Über den richtigen Vortrag der sämtlichen Beethoven'schen Klavierwerke,* ed. Paul Badura-Skoda (Vienna, 1963), 22. My translation.
12. Czerny, 21. My translation.
13. L. Nohl, *Beethoven nach den Schilderungen seiner Zeitgenossen* (Stuttgart, 1877), 114–15; also TF, 525–26.
14. S. Kross, "Improvisation und Konzertform bei Beethoven," *Beethoven-Kolloquium 1977* (Kassel: Barenreiter, 1978), 133; *Konversationshefte,* 5: 192. Compare 5: 185, where Karl writes, "Linke said today, that if it says on the placard for the second concert that you will improvise, they [the public] will storm the house."
15. Kross, 134.
16. For Russell's account of his visit in 1821, published in 1828, see Sonneck, 114–16.
17. Mozart left three Fantasies for piano, one of which, K. 394, is followed by a fugue, while another Fantasy remained unfinished. He also wrote a C minor Fantasie, K. 475, that stands as prologue to the Sonata K. 457. Haydn used the term *capriccio* interchangeably with *Fantasie* for certain works, and his later compositions include the F-Minor Fantasia Hob. XVII:4 as well as the astonishing B major Fantasie that serves as slow movement of the E-flat Major Quarter, Opus 76 No. 6. It is possible that Beethoven's Opus 77, with its eventual settling down to B major, reflects this Haydn quartet's slow movement, though its tonal plan otherwise differs. On Haydn's keyboard fantasies, see A. P. Brown, *Haydn's Keyboard Music* (Bloomington, 1986), 220–28.
18. For this work see above, chapter 10, note 40.
19. According to a catalogue entry by Archduke Rudolph, the Fantasie was written in close proximity to the F-sharp Major Piano Sonata No. 24, Opus 78, a work that is also unconventional in choice of key and subtly integrates two highly contrasting movements. See Kagan, 13, fn. 47.
20. On Beethoven's copying of portions of Bach's *Chromatic Fantasy and Fugue* see N II, 286; on the potential importance of this work for Beethoven's late sonatas see M. Zenck, *Die Bach-Rezeption des späten Beethoven* (Stuttgart, 1986), 216ff.
21. On the anomalies of the work see H. MacDonald, "Fantasy and Order in Beethoven's Phantasie Op. 77," in *Modern Musical Scholarship,* ed. E. Olleson (Stocksfield, 1980), 141–50.

22. See the F major Cello Variations on a Theme from *The Magic Flute,* Opus 66. (The opus number is problematic since the work was issued without a number in 1798.)

23. Czerny, 64.

24. For a recent brief survey of the early history of the fortepiano see Laurence Libin, "The Instruments," in *Eighteenth-Century Keyboard Music,* ed. R. L. Marshall (New York, 1994), 1–32.

25. On the ranges of Beethoven's pianos see D. Melville, "Beethoven's Pianos," in *The Beethoven Reader,* ed. D. Arnold and N. Fortune (New York, 1971), 42. T. Skowroneck points out that in early sketches Beethoven at times exceeded the range of five octaves plus a whole step common at the time; see his "The Keyboard Instruments of the Young Beethoven," in *Beethoven and His World,* ed. S. Burnham and M. P. Steinberg (Princeton, N. J., 2000), 177.

26. Letter of November 10, 1796; *Briefwechsel,* No. 22.

27. See G. Barth, *The Pianist as Orator* (Ithaca, N.Y.), 5.

28. See W. S. Newman, *Beethoven on Beethoven* (New York, 1988), 52.

29. Newman, 53.

30. Newman, 56.

31. See Comini, Fig. 23, for Gustav Leybold's lithograph of the original wash drawing by J.N. Höchle; see also Comini's discussion, 44f.

32. Newman, 54.

33. For a convenient listing of important pianists in Vienna and London between 1790 and 1810, see DeNora, 120.

34. For Seyfried's text see TF, 206ff; on the social basis of Beethoven's reputation in Vienna see DeNora.

35. See JTW, 150. Nottebohm (N II, 446) had assigned the entry to June 1804, but Tyson opts for 1805 in the light of other evidence concerning the Opus 32 "An die Hoffnung" that Nottebohm could not have known. The reference to bad playing of his piano music can refer to any number of current pianists; but the primary point of this moment of self-criticism concerns compositional matters.

36. Wegeler-Ries, 101; Czerny's memoirs were published in *Neues Beethoven Jahrbuch* 9 (1933): 65.

37. For brief excerpts from the E-major sketches for the original slow movement see Nottebohm, *Ein Skizzenbuch . . . 1803,* 61.

38. For example, a massive shift to the treble at mm. 68–77.

39. One is found in the first long episode (mm. 25–69) in which its first large unit, in octaves and then sixths, moves from F major to D minor and then to its proper goal, V (C major) at 38, whereupon there is a sudden harmonic shift to A-flat major (moving then to F minor) for what follows. This big motion to the flat side had been presaged by that unobtrusive opening B-flat in m. 1.

40. At mm. 83–98 the theme, finding itself on the dominant of D-flat, careens down by one-measure leaps through a chain of dominant harmonies through seven steps of the circle of fifths, coming to earth on the dominant of the home tonic, F.

41. See M. Frohlich, *Beethoven's "Appassionata" Sonata* (Oxford, 1991).

42. Kinsky-Halm, 136.

43. This discovery was first noted by Nottebohm, then by Tovey, and confirmed by Frohlich, 63ff.

44. A striking feature of the finale is that it repeats its development section and recapitulation (mm. 118–303, first ending), and that the autograph manuscript is expressly marked, "la seconda parte due volte" (the second part twice). Beethoven had written the same instruction in the autograph of Opus 59 No. 1, first movement, when he was still thinking of carrying out a similar large-scale repeat.

45. On the military situation of 1809 and Napoleon's campaign against Austria see Schom, 493–504.

46. G. Marek, *Beethoven* (New York, 1969), 397, says Beethoven sought shelter in the house of Ignaz Castelli, but Wegeler-Ries, 121, reports it was Caspar Carl's house. According to Smolle, 42, Beethoven was probably then living in the Wallfischgasse but sought refuge in a cellar in Rauhensteingasse 987, now Ballgasse No. 4. Smolle accepts that Beethoven's place of refuge was with his brother, but does not explicitly say that the Rauhenstein address was Caspar Carl's house. For a vivid account of the fear and suffering of the Viennese under the bombardment see excerpts from the diaries of Joseph Rosenbaum, quoted in Marek, 396ff.

47. *Briefwechsel*, No. 392 (July 26, 1809).

48. Letter assigned by Anderson (No. 228) to November 2, 1809; *Briefwechsel*, No. 408, assigns it to November 22 instead.

49. Beethoven's two cantatas of 1790 had commemorated these events.

50. Kagan, 2ff. Emperor Franz was a good enough violinist to play Haydn quartets, and his wife sang soprano arias in performances of *The Seasons* and *The Creation* in 1801.

51. See Kagan, 54ff.

52. Kagan, 9ff., offers evidence from the Archduke's correspondence with his lifelong secretary and confidant, Rudolph Baumeister, that confirms these impressions.

53. See W. Drabkin, *Beethoven: Missa Solemnis* (Cambridge, 1991), 4.

54. Anderson No. 248; *Briefwechsel*, No. 435, dated April 1810.

55. Kinsky-Halm, 216ff.

56. W. Riezler, *Beethoven*, trans. G. D. H. Pidcock (London, 1938), 81.

57. Letters of July 2, 1810 (*Briefwechsel*, No. 451), and September 23, 1810 (*Briefwechsel*, No. 468). By "characteristic sonata" Beethoven means that it is descriptive and programmatic, with titles, just as he called the *Pastoral* Symphony a "sinfonia caracteristica" in one of his sketchbook entries. Sonatas of this type were being composed in some numbers at this time. Examples are Dussek's piano sonata of 1807, which is an elegy for Prince Louis-Ferdinand, and his sonata "Le Retour à Paris" of the same year.

58. Dahlhaus, 35.

59. C. Rosen, *The Romantic Generation* (Cambridge, Mass., 1995), 116ff.

60. On the autograph see my article "The Autograph of the First Movement of the Sonata for Violoncello and Pianoforte, Opus 69," in Lockwood, *Studies*, 17–94; also my paper, "Beethoven's Opus 69 Revisited: The Place of the Sonata in Beethoven's Chamber Music," in proceedings of the Symposium on Beethoven's Music for Violoncello, held at Bonn in 1998 (forthcoming).

61. On Beethoven's revisions of the end of the slow movement see my article "The Problem

of Closure: Some Examples from the Middle-Period Chamber Music," in Lockwood, *Studies,* 181–97.

62. N II, 225–7.

63. For the full text of Hoffmann's review, originally published in the *AMZ* (1813), cols. 141–54, see Kunze, *Beethoven, Die Werke,* 129–50.

64. Hoffmann in Kunze, *Beethoven, Die Werke,* 138ff. The italics are Hoffmann's. My translation.

65. See S.-C. P. Ong, "Source Studies for Beethoven's Piano Trio in B-flat Major, Op. 97 ('Archduke')" (Ph.D. diss., University of California, Berkeley, 1995), 297–387 (on the sources). That an autograph of 1811 was lost appears from Beethoven's letter of 1815 to the archduke requesting the loan of the parts to Opus 97 and 96 in order to have them copied; see *Briefwechsel,* No. 801; Anderson, No. 592.

66. The trajectory of the first movement in fact unfolds in a large downward arc from B-flat major to G major (second group, mm. 43–94, the bulk of the exposition), then moves down another third to E-flat major (mm. 107ff) at the beginning of the development section, and then by many steps makes its eventual return to the tonic for the recapitulation at m. 191.

67. On the probability of a revision see S. Brandenburg, "Bermerkungen zu Op. 96," *BJ* 9 (1933/77): 11–26.

68. *Briefwechsel,* No. 606; Anderson, No. 392.

69. Carl Flesch, *Kunst des Violinspiels* (Berlin 1923), 171.

Chapter 15

1. TF, 409. Thayer does not give a source but it is probably from Samuel Appleby, son of Thomas Appleby and a collector of biographical material on the violinist George Polgreen Bridgetower.

2. I. von Seyfried, *Biographische Notizen . . .* published in *Beethoven, Studien in Generalbasse . . . ,* ed. by Seyfried (Vienna: Haslinger, 1832), appendix, 6f. For a facsimile of Seyfried's *Notizen* see the sales catalogue of L. H. Niemeyer, Bonn, 1990.

3. TF, 401. The biography, which appeared in *Historisches Tagebuch,* ser. 4, no. 4 (1863), was written by "Schnitzler," according to TDR, 2:546, n. 1. Further on Razumovsky see Lulu Thürheim, *Mein Leben,* vol. 2, *passim.*

4. *Konversationshefte,* 10:70.

5. See Kinsky-Halm, 687, on WoO 184.

6. A. Tyson, "The 'Razumovsky' Quartets: Some Aspects of the Sources," *BS* 3:107–40.

7. See Peter Gülke, *"Triumph der Neuen Tonkunst": Mozarts späte Sinfonien und ihr Umfeld* (Kassel, 1998).

8. *AMZ,* reviews of 1807 and 1821; see Kunze, *Beethoven, Die Werke,* 72.

9. See WoO 157 and 158.

10. For a modern edition of the Prach collection see *A Collection of Russian Folk Songs,* complied by N. K. Lvov and I. Prach, ed. by Malcolm H. Brown (Ann Arbor, Mich., 1987).

11. See J. Leyda and S. Bertensson, eds, *The Musorgsky Reader* (New York, 1947), 41, n. 82. The transcription dates from 1859.

12. Partial antecedents in string chamber music include Haydn's Quartet Opus 20 No. 2, in which the cello begins with the main theme, but in tenor register; and Mozart's C Major Quintet, K. 515, which opens with pulsating middle voices while the cello rises in an arpeggiated theme from low C to the E above middle C, two octaves and a third. But neither Mozart nor Haydn presented a main opening theme fully in bass register in a quartet, as in Opus 59 No. 1.

13. On this whole strategy see my article, "Process vs. Limits : A View of the Quartet in F Major, Opus 59 No. 1," in Lockwood, *Studies,* 181–97.

14. See mm. 73–84 and 85–90.

15. Mm. 144–149 and 331–337.

16. These high and low chords are anticipated in *La Malinconia* (Opus 18 No. 6, finale), mm. 12–17, where contrasting dynamics reinforce the registral shifts.

17. See L. Lockwood, "A Problem of Form: The 'Scherzo' of Beethoven's String Quartet in F major, Op. 59 No. 1," *BF* 2 (1993): 85–96.

18. See Lockwood, "A Problem of Form," as well as Jonathan Del Mar's comments on this article and my reply, in *BF* 8 (2001): 165–70 and 170–72.

19. At mm. 23–24 and 27.

20. A. Schoenberg, *Theory of Harmony,* trans. R. E. Carter (New York, 1978), 383.

21. In these chords, the descending motion from the fifth degree to the tonic reminds us that the work has come full circle from the opening chords, which are I–V^6.

22. On the "retrospective" aspects of Opus 59 No. 3 see Webster, "Traditional Elements in Beethoven's Middle-Period String Quartets," 94–133. See chapter 2 above.

23. For examples see Webster, "Traditional Elements," 106ff., with examples from Mozart, K. 465, first movement, mm. 59–61 and 87–91, compared with Beethoven, Opus 59 No. 3, first movement, mm. 59–64 and 88–91.

24. See Tyson, "The 'Razumovsky' Quartets," 126ff.

25. See Mies, *Beethoven's Sketches: An Analysis of His Style Based on a Study of His Sketch-Books,* trans. D. L. Mackinnon (New York, 1974), 73, and Webster, "Traditional Elements," 127.

26. See A. Tyson, "The Problem of Beethoven's 'First' *Leonore* Overture," 326ff.

27. See N II, 86 and Tyson, "The Razumovsky Quartets," 121.

28. On F-sharp in m. 1, on F-natural in m. 10, and on E-natural in m. 15; a further diminished seventh on B in m. 22 resolves to the dominant seventh of C minor at m. 29.

29. That is, the diminished seventh on E (mm. 176–177), on F-sharp (mm. 182–183), on F-natural (m. 190).

30. For a silhouette of Zmeskall see O. Biba, "Zu Beethovens Streichquartett Opus 95, in *Münchener Beethoven-Studien,* ed. J. Fischer (Munich, 1992), 40. The first known public performance was in 1814 by the Schuppanzigh Quartet.

31. Letter to Sir George Smart, apparently October 7, 1816, written in English with the aid of Johann von Häring; *Briefwechsel,* No. 983.

32. As Robert Marshall pointed out to me, Mozart also has no formal repeat in the first movement of his "Haffner" Symphony, K. 385, the most concentrated monothematic first movement in Mozart's late symphonies. But there is no reason to suppose that Beethoven had the "Haffner" Symphony in mind as model when he wrote Opus 95.

33. Kerman, *The Beethoven Quartets,* 182; R. Longyear, "Beethoven and Romantic Irony," in *The Creative World of Beethoven,* ed. P. H. Lang (New York, 1971), 147.

Chapter 16

1. *Briefwechsel,* No. 592; Anderson, No. 381; letter to the archduke of August 12, 1812.
2. Solomon, "Beethoven's Tagebuch of 1812–1818," 206.
3. See Solomon, *Beethoven,* 194; also B. Cooper, *The Beethoven Compendium,* 121.
4. See, e.g., Alan Tyson in Kerman and Tyson, *The New Grove Beethoven* (New York, 1983), 58.
5. Schom, 595.
6. TF, 610.
7. *Briefwechsel,* No. 395 (August 8, 1809).
8. See L. Lockwood, "Beethoven's "Kakadu" Variations, Op. 121a: A Study in Paradox," in *Pianist, Scholar, Connoisseur: Essays in Honor of Jacob Lateiner,* ed. B. Brubaker and J. Gottlieb (Stuyvesant, New York, 2000), 95–108. I believe that the introduction to Opus 121a was a late addition to an earlier set of variations.
9. TF, 560f. For a substantial listing of war pieces composed during this period see Arnold, 51–87. They include Benjamin Carr's *The Siege of Tripoli: An Historical Naval Sonata,* written c. 1801 (published Philadelphia, n.d.); and Ferdinand Kauer's, *La conquete d'Oczakow: Sonata Militaire,* written in 1788 to commemorate the war between the Russians and Turks. Kauer composed many other battle pieces that depicted such events as Nelson's sea victory in 1798, the destruction of the city of Algiers, and one on *Wellington's and Blucher's Famous Battle near Waterloo* (1815). Other battle pieces include works by Mozart, Vanhal, Dussek, Koczwara, and Viguerie.
10. TF, 561, quoting Moscheles's English translation of Schindler's biography as *The Life of Beethoven* (London, 1841), 153f.
11. For this material and still more detail see TF, 561–66.
12. The expression "monument of trivialities" is from Solomon, *Beethoven,* 287; on "kitsch," see Kinderman, *Beethoven,* 195. Further on the piece see Dahlhaus, *Beethoven: Approaches to his Music,* xxiii and 17, and on its background, H.-W. Küthen, "Neue Aspekte zur Entstehung von *Wellingtons Sieg,"* BJ 8 (1971/72): 73–92.
13. Kinsky-Halm, 413.
14. See TF, 595 for an excerpt; also Nottebohm, *Beethoveniana,* 145–53.
15. See TF, 593f. for Thayer's quotations from the text, with translations and appropriate critical views.
16. TDR, III, 432ff.; TF, 586–87; Solomon, *Beethoven,* 288–89. Translation modified here.
17. See, e.g., W. Dean, "Beethoven and Opera," in *The Beethoven Reader,* ed. D. Arnold and N. Fortune (New York, 1971), especially 364–73; Solomon, *Beethoven,* 288.
18. For a recent conspectus of critical work on the various versions of the opera see H. Lühning and W. Steinbeck, *Von der Leonore zum Fidelio* (Frankfurt, 2000).
19. For a longer discussion of this point see L. Lockwood, "Beethoven, Florestan, and the Varieties of Heroism," in *Beethoven and His World,* ed. S. Burnham and M. P. Steinberg (Princeton, N.J., 2000), 27–47.

20. M. Solomon, "Beethoven's *Tagebuch* of 1812–1818," *BS*, 3:215. In 1816 Beethoven entered a canon on this text into Charles Neate's personal album.
21. See, e.g., Uhde, 300f; W. Mellers, 130–42.
22. C. Rosen, *The Classical Style: Haydn, Mozart, and Beethoven,* expanded ed. (New York, 1997), 403.
23. Another special moment occurs at mm. 131–43, with its liquidation of the three-note figure, 3–2–1, that opens the movement. Here the figure prepares the recapitulation by appearing in more than twenty consecutive rhythmic forms, in imitation between the two hands, again with sudden registral shifts, as if it were a page of sketches on which Beethoven tries out a series of versions of a simple motif. The motivic process is further dramatized by a diminuendo from *fortissimo* to *pianissimo.*
24. D. F. Tovey, *A Companion to Beethoven's Pianoforte Sonatas* (London, 1931), 198.
25. See my "Beethoven's Emergence from Crisis: the Cello Sonatas of Op. 102 (1815)," 305.
26. The autograph of the Cello Sonata Opus 102 No. 1 is dated "1815 gegen Ende Juli," ("toward the end of July 1815"), that of No. 2 is headed "anfangs August 1815" ("beginning of August 1815"), while that of *An die ferne Geliebte* is headed "1816 im Monath April" ("1816, in the month of April"). Finally, the autograph of Opus 101 has the heading "1816 im Monath November" ("1816 in the month of November"). But the sketches for *An die ferne Geliebte* in the Scheide sketchbook seem to coincide with later work on Opus 102 No. 2.
27. J. Schmidt-Görg, "Das Wiener Tagebuch des Mannheimer Hofkapellmeisters Michael Frey," *BJ* 6 (1965/68): 182.
28. See M. Solomon's edition in his "Beethoven's *Tagebuch* of 1812–1818," Nos. 61, 62, 63, 64; it was Solomon who discovered the original sources for these quotations in the *Tagebuch.*
29. M. Cooper, *Beethoven: The Last Decade,* rev. ed. (Oxford, 1985), 156.

Chapter 17

1. *Konversationshefte,* 1:262; 2:174.
2. *Konversationshefte,* 8:268 (written between January 16 and 22, 1826).
3. *Konversationshefte,* 1, Heft 8 (c. February 25 to c. March 12, 1820), 287f. (= fols. 25v–26).
4. See P. Stadlen, "Zu Schindlers Fälschungen in Beethovens Konversationshefte," *Oesterreichische Musikzeitung* 32 (1977): 246–52; also his "Schindler und die Konversationshefte," *Oesterreichische Musikzeitung* 34 (1979): 2–18; and in English, "Schindler's Beethoven Forgeries," *The Musical Times* 118 (1977): 549–52 and other writings. Stadlen's priority in this discovery, originally ignored by German scholars but later admitted, was confirmed by him in a letter to me of April 14, 1983.
5. TF, 940–1. According to TDR, 5: 180, n. 1, the anecdote comes from an article entitled "Eine Soiree bei Prof. Böhm" in the *Brünner Zeitung* of June 18 and 20, 1863. Other material from Böhm, including an account of Beethoven hurling rotten eggs through a window at a restaurant, was transmitted by members of Böhm's family to Theodor Frimmel, who acknowledges them in his *Beethoven* (Berlin, 1900), 101. Frimmel got the story from a surviving niece of Böhm's in Vienna who reported having heard her uncle

tell many anecdotes about Beethoven. The passage in question, from the finale of Opus 127, is marked "Allegro comodo" in the autograph manuscript, but "Allegro con moto" in the Breitkopf & Härtel complete edition.

6. G. T. Ealy, "Of Ear Trumpets and a Resonance Plate: Early Hearing Aids and Beethoven's Hearing Perception," *19th Century Music* 17 (1994): 262–73.

7. Thus Schindler, as quoted by Ealy, 271.

8. For this anecdote, reported to Thayer by the pianist Sigismund Thalberg in Paris in 1860 see TF, 909.

9. Richard Wagner, "Ein Pilgerfahrt zu Beethoven," in *Sämtliche Schriften und Dichtungen,* 6th ed. (Leipzig, 1911), 1: 90–114 (originally published in 1840).

10. Schubert's friend Josef von Spaun is recorded as having denied that Schubert visited Beethoven in 1827; see O. E. Deutsch, *Schubert: Memoirs by His Friends,* trans. R. Ley and J. Nowell (London, 1958), 366; also Newbould, 259.

11. *Briefwechsel,* No. 1141; Anderson, No. 788.

12. For brief accounts of the evidence for Beethoven's illnesses from 1795 to 1827 see Bankl and Jesserer, 10–66.

13. Larkin, 445.

14. TF, 777f. For variant versions of the story see T. Frimmel, "Beethoven's Spaziergang nach Wiener-Neustadt," in *Beethoven-Forschung: Lose Blätter* 9 (1923): 2–12.

15. Larkin, 456.

16. TF, 625.

17. For a full account of Johanna's crimes and punishments see S. Brandenburg, "Johanna van Beethoven's Embezzlement," in *Haydn, Mozart, Beethoven: Essays in Honor of Alan Tyson,* ed. S. Brandenburg, Oxford, 1998, 237–51.

18. *Briefwechsel,* No. 2187; Anderson, No. 1498 (August 19, 1826 to Schott).

19. TF, 995.

20. TF, 996; M. Cooper, 76.

21. See *Briefwechsel,* No. 2197; Anderson, No. 1521 (letter of September 9, 1826, to Holz).

22. Beethoven had planned to dedicate the quartet to a Viennese friend and businessman, Johann von Wolfmayer, who instead received the dedication of Opus 135.

23. *Briefwechsel,* No. 2197; Anderson, No. 1521.

24. *Briefwechsel,* No. 2246; Anderson, No. 1547 (letter of January 3, 1827 to attorney Johann Baptist Bach).

25. Karl's son, born in 1839 and named Ludwig Johann, eventually emigrated to America after various misdemeanors in Germany, began a new life in New York that included a stint in the railroad business under the name "von Hoven," then returned to Europe, where he died near Paris in the 1890s. His only surviving son, Karl Julius, lived for a time in the ancient family surroundings in Belgium, later worked as a correspondent for various French and English newspapers, and in 1916, as an Austrian citizen, was called to the Austrian army. He died in a Viennese hospital in 1917, thus ending the male succession in the family line. For this and other material, including a long letter in German written by "Louis von Hoven" from Philadelphia on September 19, 1875, to his sister Maria Anna, then living in Vienna, see the Beethoven-Haus pamphlet *Ein Brief von*

Beethovens Grossneffen Louis von Hoven an seine Schwester Marie Weidinger in Wien aus dem Jahre 1875, ed. S. Brandenburg (Bonn, 1984).

26. All of Beethoven's recorded references to "Jews" and "Jewishness" occur in relation to music publishers, a subject on which he was, for obvious reasons, hypersensitive. These remarks occur as early as December 15, 1800, when he tells Hoffmeister that, in setting prices for his works, Hoffmeister is "neither a Jew nor an Italian," and that he, Beethoven, is also neither one of these—thus "perhaps we shall come to some agreement" (*Briefwechsel*, No. 49; Anderson, No. 41). Such references become more plentiful in his later years, when he is hard at work trying to secure publishers for the *Missa solemnis,* and when he had dealings with the Schlesingers, his only publishers who were actually Jewish. As Siegmund Kaznelson points out in his *Beethovens ferne und unsterbliche Geliebte* (Zurich, 1954), 286–95 and 430–36, the word *Jew* as used colloquially at this time in Germany and Austria, before the emancipation of the Jews, could loosely refer to anyone engaged in commerce ranging from a peddler to a businessman. Sometimes, of course, it was used in direct and harsh anti-Semitic ways, as when C. F. Peters complained bitterly to Beethoven in 1822 that he should not give his Mass to the Schlesingers because such a "Christian Mass cannot come into the hands of a Jew, and especially such a Jew" (Albrecht, No. 290 [June 15, 1822]). I am inclined to agree with Albrecht that although Beethoven was perfectly capable of launching remarks such as "Schlesinger 'has played me a Jewish trick'" he was not deliberately or self-consciously anti-Semitic, certainly not in any degree approaching the paranoid, obsessive anti-Semitism of Wagner. I am also inclined to agree with Albrecht that, in these comments, "he was merely dealing in tasteless stereotypical remarks that, although mildly prejudicial, do not reflect deeper intent" (Albrecht, 214, n. 5). That Beethoven had no prejudice about collaborating with a Jewish contemporary is shown by *An die ferne Geliebte* (1816), which is set to poems by Alois Jeitteles, a Jewish poet, medical student, and friend of Grillparzer and Castelli. Jeitteles, unlike several other members of his family, did not convert and change his family name but remained faithful to his Jewish identity all his life; see Kaznelson, 390.

27. This summary is indebted to Alan Tyson, "Steps to Publication—and Beyond," in *The Beethoven Companion,* ed. D. Arnold and N. Fortune (New York, 1971), 459–89.

28. A good example is provided by the many arrangements of Beethoven symphonies for small ensembles, including more than a few by so prominent a musician as Johann Nepomuk Hummel. I am indebted to Mark Kroll for calling my attention to these arrangements.

29. Quoted by A. Tyson, *The Authentic English Editions of Beethoven,* 17.

30. *Briefwechsel,* No. 166, fn. 1; Anderson, III, Appendix H, 1435.

31. Anderson, III, Appendix I, 1450f.

32. Anderson, III, Appendix I, 1444.

33. Letter from Peters to Beethoven, May 18, 1822; known through a summary made by Thayer; in Albrecht, No. 268. For Beethoven's reply see *Briefwechsel,* No. 1468.

34. Albrecht, No. 299.

35. From De Roda Sketchbook, fol. 6. See K. Kropfinger, "Das Gespaltene Werk: Beethoven's

Streichquartett Op. 130/133," in S. Brandenburg and H. Loos, eds., *Beiträge zu Beethovens Kammermusik* (Munich, 1987), 305.

Chapter 18

1. See Churgin, 457–77.
2. See R. Kramer, "In Search of Palestrina: Beethoven in the Archives," in *Haydn, Mozart, and Beethoven: Essays in Honor of Alan Tyson*, ed. S. Brandenburg (Oxford, 1998), 283–300.
3. For the idea of the "pious song" see N II, 163.
4. *Konversationshefte*, 1:108, 196f.
5. For an overview of Beethoven's copies of older music and knowledge of it beyond what he copied, see W. Kirkendale, *Fugue and Fugato in Rococo and Classical Chamber Music*, trans. M. Bent and the author (Durham, N.C., 1979), 211–19.
6. *Briefwechsel*, No. 2003, with draft in De Roda sketchbook. The passage reads, "jedoch noch über diess des gesanges wegen, welcher allzeit verdient allem übrigen vorgezogen zu werden."
7. *Briefwechsel*, No. 2003 (from De Roda draft).
8. On minor-mode rondos in Beethoven see M. Cole, "Techniques of Surprise in the Sonata-Rondos of Beethoven," *Studia Musicologica Academiae Scientiarum Hungaricae* 12 (1970): 232–62.
9. See Zenck, 40ff.
10. *Briefwechsel*, Nos. 474, 1263 (Nägeli to Beethoven, 1818), 1873.
11. TF, 1061.
12. TF, 1069f.
13. See Zenck, 78–108, on Bach in the major Viennese collections of the time.
14. *Briefwechsel*, No. 59.
15. On the title page of his overture *Zur Namensfeier*, Opus 115, published in 1825, the work is indicated as having been "poeticized by Ludwig van Beethoven" (*gedichtet . . . von Ludwig van Beethoven*) (Kinsky-Halm, 332f.). And in a review in *Cecilia* (July 1826), the reviewer made special mention of the fact that this was "the first time that a composer, that Beethoven himself, as I think, used the word 'gedichtet' [made into poetry] instead of the word 'komponiert' [composed]." I am indebted here to Maynard Solomon. Elsewhere we find evidence of the same impulse, as when Beethoven is reported by Holz to have said that "in my youth and years of study I made dozens of fugues. But fantasy also has its rights, and today a truly poetic element must be included in traditional forms." See W. von Lenz, *Beethoven: Eine Kunststudie* (Cassel, 1855–60), 5:219.
16. On Verdi's admiration for Palestrina see L. Lockwood, ed., *Palestrina: Pope Marcellus Mass* (New York, 1975), 140.
17. On Mozart's exposure to Bach in his earlier years, before 1782 and his acquaintance with van Swieten, see R. Marshall, "Bach and Mozart's Artistic Maturity," *Bach Perspectives* 3 (1998): 47–79.
18. On this see Zenck, 82–84.

19. Zenck, 83.

20. *Briefwechsel,* No. 1318; Anderson, No. 955. Beethoven is evidently telling the archduke that there must be a balance between the modern demands for freedom and progress on the one hand, and a deep knowledge of the "older composers," chiefly Bach and Handel.

21. W. A. Mozart, *The Letters of Mozart and His Family,* 2nd ed. (New York, 1985), No. 800 (letter to Constanze Mozart of April 19, 1782).

22. TF, 157ff.

23. JTW, 525. These *Messiah* excerpts appear in Artaria 197, but on the outside leaves of gatherings, leaves that were in use sometime before the sketchbook proper, which dates from 1821.

24. See N. Marston, *Beethoven's Piano Sonata in E. Op. 109* (Oxford, 1995), 23.

25. TF, 683.

26. Schindler, 234.

27. TF, 871.

Chapter 19

1. *Briefwechsel,* No. 1071; Anderson, No. 737.

2. Kinsky-Halm, 294; Uhde, 3: 385.

3. Indicative of the status of this work as presenting unparalleled technical demands among all Beethoven's piano sonatas is Fred Hoyle's use of it in his science-fiction novel *The Black Cloud* (London, 1957), 196ff. When the Black Cloud, an extraterrestrial force of vast size, invades the solar system and makes contact with earth, it speaks to earth's scientists about many things, reporting that it understands literature but not music. When the scientists play it a recording of the *Hammerklavier* Sonata, the Cloud, in its superior intelligence, asks that the first part "be repeated at a speed increased by thirty percent." Then the scientists remember that Beethoven's metronome marking for the first movement is a nearly unplayable MM. half note = 138. Hoyle volunteers support for the view that "musical rhythms reflect the main electrical rhythms that occur in the brain" (297).

4. See D. H. Smyth, "Codas in Classical Form: Aspects of Large-Scale Rhythm and Pattern Completion" (Ph.D. diss., University of Texas at Austin, 1985). Dr. Smyth works primarily from finished compositions in this study, but the prospective value of adding information from the sketches is clear.

5. D. B. Greene compares the "Archduke" Trio with the *Hammerklavier* in his *Temporal Processes in Beethoven's Music* (New York, 1982), 99–124.

6. His earlier uses of descending-third chains include those in the Sonata Opus 22 (as Charles Rosen notes in *The Classical Style*) and in the introduction to the finale of the *Eroica*. In Mozart a prominent use of the process occurs in the A major quartet K. 464, which Beethoven admired, but there are many others. A Haydn example is the introduction to the "Drumroll" Symphony, No. 103. And Bach's Sarabande in the Fifth Suite for unaccompanied cello is a marvel of successive overlapping descending-third patterns.

7. This is already clear at m. 4 of the opening, with its powerful upper-line G over a sub-dominant chord, at first over a tonic pedal (m. 5) but later given root support by the low cello E-flat at mm. 16–17 and, in the coda, at the grand, confirming restatement of the opening theme, now with a low E-flat in the piano (mm. 270–271).

8. The C-minor passage is at mm. 144–152. The return to B-flat begins at m. 162, and the development starts at m. 191.

9. I particularly recall Kenneth Drake's performance on a restored Broadwood at Princeton University in 1976. For an overview of Beethoven's pianos see Melville, 41–67. On Beethoven's earlier instruments see Skowroneck, 151–92.

10. Adorno, 128 [No. 266].

11. In tonal fugues, "augmentation" refers to the presentation of the subject in longer note values; "retrograde" to its presentation in reverse order; and "inversion" to its presentation with its intervals reversed in direction.

12. In his *Companion to the Beethoven Pianoforte Sonatas*, Tovey, 239, calls this a "third subject," since he ascribes the role of a "second" subject to what I am calling the "countersubject" that accompanies the retrograde at mm. 153ff. Uhde, 446ff., agrees with my terminology.

13. *Briefwechsel*, No. 1295; Anderson, No. 939. The Bonn edition dates it March 19, Anderson "c. March 20." No reply from Ries appears to be preserved.

14. Solomon, *Beethoven*, 394.

15. See the reconstruction of Schlesinger's letter (now lost) as *Briefwechsel*, No. 1381; and the full text of Beethoven's letter as *Briefwechsel*, No. 1388; Anderson, No. 1021. As it turned out (*Briefwechsel*, No. 1393, Beethoven to Schlesinger, May 31, 1820) he had to accept a fee of 30 ducats each for the three sonatas. From this letter it is definitely clear, however, that Schlesinger's request had been for three piano sonatas, as Beethoven offers to send Schlesinger one "right away" and the other two in July. Neither promise was fulfilled.

16. See the Prestissimo finale tempi of Opus 1 No. 3; Opus 2 No. 1; and Opus 10 No. 1. There are no others until Opus 109.

17. See Marston, 4ff., fns. 4 and 5 (on Schenker's "explanatory" edition of 1913), and 9–12 on the closing bar lines of each movement and variation, and their implications for analysis of the larger structure of the work.

18. Marston, 30.

19. Marston, 259. This study exemplifies the ways in which the study of sources can amplify understanding of the structure of a composition.

20. Albrecht, No. 293.

21. Albrecht, No. 296.

22. Schindler, *Biographie*, 3rd ed. (Münster, 1860), II, 3ff.; *Beethoven as I Knew Him*, 232. William Drabkin, "The Sketches for Beethoven's Piano Sonata in C Minor. Opus 111" (Ph.D. diss., Princeton University, 1977), 251–58, discusses the issue thoroughly.

23. Drabkin, "Sketches," 257f.

24. T. Mann, *Doctor Faustus*, trans. H. T. Lowe-Porter (New York, 1948), 51–56.

25. Rosen, *The Classical Style*, 442ff.; Drabkin, 6ff.

26. I mentioned in chapter 15 the influence of the Florestan introduction on the slow introduction of the Quartet Opus 59 No. 3.

27. Drabkin, "Sketches" 26ff. Drabkin also suggests that in looking at Haydn's Opus 20 quartets as providing three models of cyclic works with fugal finales, Beethoven could readily have come across the opening theme of the C Major Quartet, Opus 20 No. 2, which presents the same three-note motif as the first Allegro theme of Opus 111. See also W. Drabkin, *A Reader's Guide to Haydn's Early String Quartets*, 46–47, on other aspects of Opus 111 in comparison to early Haydn quartets.

28. "Kessler" Sketchbook, f. 37v., Brandenburg edition, transcription, 88; first quoted by Nottebohm, *Ein Skizzenbuch von Beethoven, beschrieben und in Auszügen dargestellt* (Leipzig, 1865), 19. As this entry directly follows a concept sketch for the opening of Opus 30 No. 2, in A major, it is conceivable, as Nottebohm suggests, that it may have originated as a possible theme for an F-sharp-minor slow movement for that sonata.

29. For more on this matter see Drabkin, "Sketches," 69–76.

30. Drabkin, "Sketches," 89f.

31. Mm. 170–171.

32. Mann, 55.

33. *Konversationshefte*, 1:235. This conversation book has been dated to the period from c. January 22 to February 23, 1820, and consists of a total of ninety leaves; since the quotation appears on fol. 17 and is taken from a notice in the *Wiener Zeitung* dated February 1, it was most likely entered sometime during the first week of February—the more so as the next datable reference, to the Kaiserin's birthday, February 8, occurs on fol. 45. The article in the *Wiener Zeitung*, by the astronomer Joseph Littrow and titled "Cosmological Considerations," ascribes the quotation to Kant. Littrow's sentence, as quoted in *Konversationshefte*, 1:473, n. 538, epitomizes Beethoven's lifelong adherence to the Enlightenment belief that humankind must strive to rise above its frailties and reach as high as it can: "There are two things that raise men above themselves and lead to eternal, ever upward-striving wonder: the moral law within us and the starry sky above us."

34. On the archduke's variation see Kagan, 140–46.

35. Kinsky-Halm, 348.

36. See W. Kinderman, *Beethoven's Diabelli Variations* (Oxford, 1987).

37. *Briefwechsel*, No. 1291, dates it March 3, 1819, on the basis of the date that appears at the end of the letter; Anderson, No. 948, dates it in early June 1819, apparently working from a copy on which the date and signature had been cut off.

38. Zenck, 18.

39. For the complicated history of the publishers and opus number for this set of bagatelles see Kinsky-Halm, 346f.

40. Friedrich Starke, *Wiener Pianoforte Schule* (Vienna, 1821)

41. For this and other material on the assembling of Opp. 119 and 126 see B. Cooper, *Beethoven and the Creative Process* (Oxford, 1990), 263–82.

42. E. T. Cone, "Beethoven's Experiments in Composition: The Late Bagatelles," *BS*, 2: 84–105.

43. Astonishingly, the finale appears in the traditional standard editions of Opus 127 with

no tempo marking! See *Beethoven Werke*, Series 8 No. 48, finale, (71) 25, where it is simply labeled "Finale." However, the autograph shows the tempo marking "All[ergo]," which was somehow lost in the published editions.

44. Schubert was deeply influenced by this model, as is apparent in his E-flat Major Piano Trio, composed in November 1827, seven to eight months after Beethoven's death.

45. Rosen, *The Romantic Generation*, 88.

Chapter 20

1. As early as 1805 Rudolph was named coadjutor to the Archbishop of Olmütz, with the right of succession. He was elected by the chapter of Olmütz Cathedral on March 23, 1819, and confirmed by the pope on June 4. His installation took place on September 3, 1820. See *Briefwechsel*, No. 1292, fn. 1.

2. *Briefwechsel*, No. 1292.

3. *Briefwechsel*, No. 1091; Anderson, No. 767, fn. 1.

4. See note 1.

5. For an overview see M. Solomon, "The Quest for Faith," in his *Beethoven Essays*, 216–29; on Beethoven's annotations of Sturm see Witcombe. On the *Tagebuch* entries see Solomon, *Beethoven Essays*, 233–95, and especially 356–58, the index of the *Tagebuch*.

6. Schmitz, 94ff.

7. Karl Eschweiler, "Die Erlebnistheologie Johann Michael Sailers als Grundlegung des theologischen Fideismus in der vorvatikanischen Theologie," quoted by Schmitz, 85 and partly translated by M. Cooper, 113.

8. A Conversation Book of March 1819 (*Konversationshefte*, I, 352) shows disparaging commentary in Beethoven's inner circle about Hofbauer and the "so-called Ligorianer." In the same year the Conversation Books show various references to Werner's sermons, mostly unfavorable. Further on Hofbauer see Schmitz, 83; M. Cooper, 107–10. On Werner, see also Schmitz, 31–35, and Solomon, "The Quest for Faith," in his *Beethoven Essays*, 222.

9. Especially relevant here is the 1814 essay by E. T. A. Hoffmann, *Alte und neue Kirchenmusik*, which Beethoven could well have read. The relevance of Hoffmann's essay to the *Missa solemnis* was advocated especially by Dahlhaus, *Beethoven*, 194ff.

10. Drabkin, *Beethoven: Missa Solemnis*, 2.

11. A telling piece of evidence for this is the remark Beethoven entered on a sketch leaf concerned with fugal writing: "The sense of devotion [die Andacht] in the old church modes is divine; I called out, and may God permit me to produce it one day [my translation]." I owe this item to R. Kramer, "In Search of Palestrina," 294.

12. On Beethoven's copying of passages from *Messiah* see Drabkin, *Beethoven's Missa Solemnis*, 21 and 92, and JTW, 267, 270 and 525. For his copying from the Mozart Requiem see B. Churgin, 457–77. On a sketch leaf, apparently from 1819 or 1820, Beethoven made a précis and analysis of portions of the Kyrie fugue from the Requiem.

13. One prominent doubter is R. Fiske, in his *Beethoven's Missa Solemnis* (New York, 1979), 7. The positive evidence cited here is more amply summarized by Zenck, 232–63, to which I am much indebted.

14. *Briefwechsel,* No. 474; Anderson, No. 281 (October 15, 1810); Kirkendale, *Fugue and Fugato,* 215.

15. Zenck, 233. See also H.-J. Schulze and C. Wolff, eds., *Bach Compendium* (Leipzig, 1989), 4: 1151–85.

16. *Briefwechsel,* No. 392; Anderson, No. 220 (June 26, 1809); "At Traeg's office I borrowed the *Messiah,* using a privilege that you had already granted me here" (Traeg was a Vienna agent for Breitkopf & Härtel).

17. For this frequently reproduced painting see Bory, 173; or Comini, Plate 4 and, for an incisive commentary, 46–48.

18. *Briefwechsel,* No. 1876; Anderson, No. 1307 (September 16, 1824).

19. B. Lodes, *Das Gloria in Beethovens Missa Solemnis* (Tutzing, 1997), 322–34, especially 331ff.

20. See Lodes, 331ff.

21. *Briefwechsel,* No. 523; Anderson, No. 325. Beethoven wanted a title page in two languages, French and German, but Breitkopf published it with two different title pages, one in French and one in German. Brandenburg, *Briefwechsel,* No. 523, n. 9 suggests Beethoven might have been alluding to such titles as "Les Adieux de Paris" or "Les Adieux de Londres," which were appearing in the piano music of the time. Lodes, 332, also points out that from sketches for Opus 81a, we see that Beethoven had planned to dedicate the sonata to Rudolf with the words, "gewidmet und aus dem Herzen geschrieben" ("dedicated and written from the heart.").

22. Lodes, 332ff. and n. 118.

23. See Hoffmann's review, as translated by F. John Adams, Jr., in *Beethoven: Symphony No. 5 in C Minor,* ed. E. Forbes (New York, 1971), 163.

24. J. McGrann, program notes for a performance of the *Missa solemnis* at Harvard University by the Harvard-Radcliffe Chorus, conducted by Jameson Marvin, on April 22, 1990.

25. See W. Kirkendale, "New Roads to Old Ideas in Beethoven's *Missa solemnis,*" in *The Creative World of Beethoven,* ed. P. H. Lang (New York, 1971), 163–99.

26. N. Waldvogel, "'Symphonic Unity' and the Organization of Individual Movements in Beethoven's *Missa Solemnis*" (B.A. thesis, Harvard University, 1988), calls these passages "choral ritornellos."

27. R. Wagner, "Beethoven" (1870), *Prose Works,* trans. W. A. Ellis (New York, repr. 1966), 5: 104, quoted by Waldvogel, 6.

28. See Kirkendale, "New Roads" 186.

29. On the "Ode" in Japan see D. B. Levy, *The Ninth Symphony,* 6, and R. Solie, "Beethoven as Secular Humanist: Ideology and the Ninth Symphony in Nineteenth-Century Criticism," in *Explorations in Music, the Arts, and Ideas: Essays in Honor of Leonard B. Meyer,* ed. E. Narmour and R. A. Solie (Stuyvesant, N. Y., 1988), 3, n. 6. At the 1956 Olympics the East and West German teams were united, for the first time since the end of World War II in 1945, in an all-German team that marched under a single flag and sang the "Ode to Joy" in place of their respective national anthems. This practice was repeated in 1960 and 1964, but in 1968 the two Germanys split on this point; each had its own German anthem and argued over the use of the "Ode" to represent both. As David Dennis notes, this split corresponds to what were, in 1968 and afterward until 1989, more or less

established East German and West German views of Beethoven as a cultural and historical figure. I am indebted here to D. B. Dennis, *Beethoven in German Politics, 1870–1989* (New Haven, Conn., 1996), 177 and n. 5. I am also indebted to a paper on the "Ode" as Olympic anthem by Alexis Koutrovelis, a student in a course on the Ninth Symphony I gave at Harvard University in 1998.

30. It is entirely characteristic of current American usage that at the Yale University Baccalaureate Exercises, in Spring 2001, the melody, with suitable words in English, was included in the program, to be sung by the audience, and was simply identified as "Hymn of Joy," with no composer's name given.

31. For well-documented overviews of this period and its political conditions see H. Kohn, *The Mind of Germany* (New York, 1960), especially chapters 3 and 4; M. Dill, *Germany: A Modern History*, rev. ed. (Ann Arbor, 1970); and Hobsbawm, *op. cit.* Among writings on Beethoven that offer some insight into his reactions to current political developments see M. Cooper, *op. cit.*, and E. Rumph, "Beethoven after Napoleon: Political Romanticism in the Late Works" (Ph.D. diss., University of California, Berkeley, 1997).

32. See Kohn, 75–80.

33. For a summary on Goethe's and Hegel's views of Napoleon, see Kohn, 34–75.

34. References to Byron appear in Beethoven's circles in the 1820s, as we see especially in the Conversation Books of 1820 (2:89, 173f., 248f.). See above, chapter 17.

35. On Shelley and contemporary politics see P. M. S. Dawson, *The Unacknowledged Legislator: Shelley and Politics* (Oxford, 1980). For a summary on "political art" in the time of the Romantic revolutionaries see Hobsbawm, 317f. On the Romantic writer as "prisoner," see V. Brombert. The *Romantic Prison* (Princeton, N.J., 1978).

36. M. Cooper, 18; *Konversationshefte*, 1:333; Schünemann, *Ludwig van Beethovens Konversationshefte* (Berlin, 1941), 1:328. Schünemann thinks the spy might be Peter Hensler, a member of the Royal Life-Guards.

37. From the diary of Karl von Bursy, as published by M. Cooper, 20.

38. This passage is not among those listed as later additions by Schindler, published in v. 7 of the *Konversationshefte* retroactively for vols. 1, 2, 4, 5, and 6.

39. *Konversationshefte*, 2:172 (June 1820); see M. Cooper, 93. Cooper says that the entry is "probably in Bernard's hand," but in the foreword to vol. 2 of the *Konversationshefte*, 10, it is ascribed to Schindler. The context of this remark is the heightened concern in Beethoven's circle of acquaintances, earlier in 1821, over the political situation in Spain, where the harsh regime of King Ferdinand VII had been actively suppressing revolutionary activities since 1814. News of revolutionary actions in Italy and attacks on Carbonari by Austrian troops are also found in a Conversation Book for 1821. See the foreword cited above, 11.

40. P. B. Shelley, *A Defense of Poetry*, in his *Works*, 7:20. The passage is paraphrased from Shelley's mentor, William Godwin; see Dawson, 218. See above, chapter 9.

41. Quoted by K. Kropfinger, *Wagner and Beethoven*, trans. P. Palmer (Cambridge, 1991), 31.

42. Schumann, 98ff.

43. On the New York premiere of the Ninth see O. F. Saloman, *Beethoven's Symphonies and J. S. Dwight* (Boston, 1995), 162–71. On the Boston Symphony, founded in 1881, and the

construction of Symphony Hall (1900) see "Boston," *NG2,* and M. A. de Wolfe Howe, *The Boston Symphony Orchestra* (Boston, 1931).

44. From an article on Beethoven's (supposedly) Aryan racial characteristics by Walther Rauschenberger, "Rassenmerkmale Beethovens und seiner nächsten Verwandten," ("Beethoven's racial characteristics and those of his closest relatives") in *Volk und Rasse* . . . 9 (1934), reprinted in 1939. I quote it from Dennis, 149.

45. Dennis, 151.

46. Dennis, 152.

47. Dennis, 162.

48. Dennis, 168.

49. D. B. Levy, 16.

50. Adorno, 144.

51. S. McClary, *Feminine Endings: Music, Gender, and Sexuality* (Minneapolis, 1991), 127–30; A. Rich, "The Ninth Symphony of Beethoven Understood at Last as a Sexual Message," in her *Diving into the Wreck* (New York, 1962), 43. For discussion see D. B. Levy, 15–17. For a critique of McClary's interpretation see P. van den Toorn, *Music, Politics, and the Academy* (Berkeley, 1995), *passim.*

52. D. B. Levy, *Beethoven's Ninth Symphony,* 17.

53. See Rumph, *passim.*

54. Rumph, 42f.

55. Rumph, 75.

56. D. F. Tovey, *Essays in Musical Analysis* (London, 1935–39), 2:42ff.

57. Solomon, "The Quest for Faith," in his *Beethoven Essays,* 228.

58. For an overview of the genesis of the finale see R. Winter, "The Sketches for the Ode to Joy," *Beethoven, Performers, and Critics,* ed. R. Winter and B. Carr. (Detroit, 1980), 176–214. For a close study of the sketches for the first movement see J. Kallick, "A Study of the Advanced Sketches and Full Score Autograph for the First Movement of Beethoven's Ninth Symphony" (Ph.D. diss., Yale University, 1987).

59. Letter to Schott of March 10, 1824; *Briefwechsel,* No. 1787; Anderson, No. 1270.

60. My thanks to Robert Marshall for the Mozart parallel.

61. Scheide sketchbook; N II, 329.

62. N II, 157–92 is still the basic account because it is based primarily on the Boldrini sketchbook, which has been lost since the late nineteenth century.

63. N II, 163.

64. For these sketches see Winter, "The Sketches for the Ode to Joy," 182–90. Winter notes that the actual time it took to compose and revise the melody may not have been very long.

65. Albrecht, No. 239.

66. *Briefwechsel,* No 1517; Anderson, No. 1110.

67. In a Conversation Book of April 1823 there is mention of a commission from the Handel and Haydn Society of Boston for an oratorio on a biblical text; see *Konversationshefte,* 3:148 and 449ff, fn. 407.

68. TF, 1001.

69. TF, 1002. It is still not known if the fraud originated with the king or his agents, or if someone exchanged stones before the gift reached Beethoven.

70. Churgin, 457–77. Churgin's Appendix A, 475–77, lists all the known Mozart works copied by Beethoven; as she suggests, there may have been many more that are now lost.

71. L. Treitler, *Music and the Historical Imagination* (Cambridge, 1989), 23ff; the quotation is from 24. A parallel is found in the way in which the "Prometheus" Variations, Opus 35, and also the opening of the *Eroica* Symphony finale "create" the bass and then the theme by stages, also through rising registers that gradually fill the whole space.

72. Tovey, *Essays in Musical Analysis*, II, 18.

73. Treitler, 23.

74. Treitler, 24.

75. This outline is my own modification of the larger view proposed by H. Schenker in his *Beethoven: Neunte Sinfonie* (Vienna, 1912, reprinted 1969), 242–375. For other views of the form of the finale see especially and most recently J. Webster, "The Form of the Finale of Beethoven's Ninth Symphony," *BF* 1 (1992): 36–44; and M. Tusa, "*Noch einmal:* Form and Content in the Finale of Beethoven's Ninth Symphony," *BF* 7 (1999): 113–37.

76. For a sensitive discussion of the recitative see S. Hinton, "Not *Which* Tones: The Crux of Beethoven's Ninth," *19th Century Music* 22 (1998): 61–77.

77. Webster, "The Form of the Finale of Beethoven's Ninth Symphony," summarizes many of the major analyses of the work published since the early twentieth century and argues for a "multivalent" approach that seeks to account for the coherence achieved in the movement by means of its combining of various "domains." The attempt to avoid the reductionism characteristic of traditional formalistic thinking is the chief virtue of this approach, and Webster's article certainly yields a number of new insights. But even so, it remains only one of many possible attempts to construe the movement under the heading of form, an approach that Beethoven's freedom of procedure in this movement renders exceptionally difficult.

78. Cited in M. E. Bonds, *After Beethoven* (Cambridge, 1996), 16.

79. See Bonds, 1.

80. I emphatically disagree with R. Taruskin's view, in his "Resisting the Ninth," *19th Century Music* 12 (1989): 247, that Brahms's finale "as it were, corrected the wrong turn Beethoven had taken. . . ."

81. See D. B. Levy, 165. Levy's critical study provides an ample survey of early responses to the Ninth; see also Robin Wallace, *Beethoven's Critics*, 73–92.

82. Taruskin, 247.

83. Solomon, *Beethoven*, 409.

Chapter 21

1. W. von Lenz, *Beethoven: Eine Kunst-Studie* (Kassel, 1855–60), 4:216–28.

2. Schindler, who had met Beethoven in 1814, became his man of all work from 1822–23 until his dismissal by Beethoven in the spring of 1824, after a brutal dispute with the composer over the receipts from the concert of May 7. Beethoven believed that Schindler

and Umlauf had cheated him; see TF, 911. Schindler was again associated with Beethoven from December 1826 until Beethoven's death in March 1827.

3. On Holz and his character see TF, 942–44.

4. Lenz, *Beethoven: Eine Kunst-Studie*, 1:216f.

5. Kerman, *The Beethoven Quartets*, 349.

6. See C. Reynolds, "From Berlioz's Fugitives to Godard's Terrorists: Artistic Response to Beethoven's Last Quartets," *BF* 8 (2000): 147–63.

7. Letter to Breitkopf & Härtel of July 5, 1806; *Briefwechsel*, No. 254; Anderson, No. 132.

8. Discovered in 1999, written for Richard Ford, a critic and writer, later the author of a *Handbook for Travellers in Spain* (1845). The little piece was offered for sale by Sotheby's on December 8, 1999. It carried the inscription, "This quartette was composed for me in my presence by Ludwig v. Beethoven at Vienna Friday 28th November 1817[.] Richard Ford."

9. TF, 946. "Noten" in German refers, as usual with Beethoven, to musical "notes" but also to money (*Banknoten*).

10. For a recent account of the genesis of Opus 130 see K. Kropfinger, "Das gespaltene Werk—Beethovens Streichquartett Op. 130/133," in *Beiträge zu Beethovens Kammermusik*, ed. S. Brandenburg and H. Loos (Munich, 1987), 296–335; also B. Cooper, "Planning the Later Movements: String Quartet in B flat, Op. 130," in his *Beethoven and the Creative Process*, 197–214.

11. See Kropfinger, "Das gespaltene Werk," 305–7. An earlier example of his planning a movement by starting with its first idea (a "concept sketch") and then moving to its final measures, was shown by Peter Cahn in his study of the slow movement of the "Kreutzer" Sonata; see Cahn, "Aspekte der Schlussgestaltung in Beethovens Instrumentalwerken," *Archiv für Musikwissenschaft* (1982): 9–28.

12. The commissioning of both sets of three quartets by Russian aristocrats is no more than a coincidence, since there is no hint in the "Galitzin" quartets of any use of Russian melodies.

13. For a vivid account of Beethoven's stay at Gneixendorf, its natural surroundings, and his dealings with his brother and his wife (whom Beethoven had long despised) see TF, 1005–9. Among the reminiscences of this stay, reported by Thayer from his own visit to Gneixendorf, is that of a servant named Michael Krenn, who recalled that every day Beethoven would get up at 5:30 A.M., "seat himself at a table and write while he beat time with hands and feet and sang." After breakfast Beethoven "hurried out into the open air, rambled across the fields shouting and waving his arms, sometimes walking very rapidly, sometimes very slowly and stopping at times to write in a sort of pocket book" (a pocket sketchbook, such as he had used since 1815 or so). On one occasion a couple of peasants encountered Beethoven shouting in the fields, "took him for a madman and kept out of his way." On another occasion his cries and gestures frightened a pair of oxen.

14. For a transcription of "La Gaieté" see N II, 218–20; also S. Brandenburg, "Die Quellen von Beethovens Streichquartett Es-dur Op. 127," *BJ* 10 (1978/81): 238.

15. Excluding the *Eroica* first movement, which has a vast variety of types of motion, we find

other Allegro first movements in 3/4 mainly in a cluster of early works before 1802; the early sextet Opus 71, the cello sonata Opus 5 No. 2; the piano sonatas Opp. 28 and 31 No. 3) the Quintet for Piano and Winds, Opus 16, and the Violin Sonata Opus 30 No. 1.

16. For example, at or near the beginnings of the first movements of the Piano Sonata No. 4, Opus 7; the Septet Opus 20; the *Eroica;* the "Emperor" Concerto, and the Quartet Opus 74.

17. Compare the Piano Trio Opus 70 No. 2, first movement, where the opening short introduction comes back in abbreviated form to begin the coda. There are certainly other cases of first movements in which a slow introduction does not return (e.g., Opus 59 No. 3, Opus 78) but in each case the content of the introduction subtly influences the Allegro material; in Opus 59 No. 3 the harmonic ambiguity of the introduction is the source for comparable mystifying moments in the development section.

18. See mm. 27–32 and 41.

19. The expression, "steals into the mind of the listener" is from Cicero, *De inventione,* Loeb Classical Library (Cambridge, Mass., 1949), I, xv. 20, 43, cited by E. Sisman, *Haydn and the Classical Variation* (Cambridge, Mass., 1993), 256.

20. For a parallel view of Beethoven's originality in variation writing, far beyond his use or nonuse of numbers for the successive sections, see Sisman, *Haydn and the Classical Variation,* 235–62.

21. The absence of variation numbers in Beethoven's later works at times conceals their formal schemes from the view of even very seasoned performers.

22. See Böhm's anecdote on p. 352.

23. I am indebted to James Webster for pointing out to me that Haydn wrote only thirteen works in sharp-side minor keys; see his *Haydn's "Farewell" Symphony* 223. Haydn's only works in A minor are his Baryton Trio Hob. X:87 and the Baryton Octet Hob. X:3, plus the winds introduction to Part 2 of *The Seven Last Words of Christ.* As for Mozart, the A Minor Piano Sonata, K. 310, is a solitary example in its genre. The E Minor Violin Sonata, K. 304, is again unique; F-sharp minor is exotic for Mozart, as we see from his memorable use of it in the slow movement of the A Major Piano Concerto, K. 488.

24. Even among Beethoven's little individual works the only one in A minor is the piano piece known as "Für Elise" (perhaps a mistake for "Für Therese") WoO 59, written in 1810 for Therese Malfatti. On the key scheme of the "Kreutzer" Sonata see W. Drabkin, "The Introduction to Beethoven's 'Kreutzer' Sonata: A Historical Perspective," a paper delivered at the Boston Conference on the Beethoven Violin Sonatas in October 2000 (to be published).

25. Beethoven's title in German is: "Heiliger Dankgesang eines Genesenen an die Gottheit in der Lydischen Tonart."

26. On Mozart's key choices in general see A. Einstein, *Mozart: His Character, His Work,* trans. A. Mandel and N. Broder (New York, 1945), 157–63. For a more general picture see Rita Steblin, *A History of Key Characteristics in the Eighteenth and Early Nineteenth Centuries* (Ann Arbor, Mich., 1983).

27. For example, Haydn's choice of F♯ major for the Minuet of the "Farewell" Symphony, No. 45, or the flat sixth in his Piano Trios Nos. 14 and 27 (Hob. XV:14 and Hob.

XV:29). As James Webster has pointed out, remote keys also appear in Haydn's Quartets Opus 71.

28. The two recapitulations are at mm. 103–192 and 193–231; the coda at 233 to the end. Other views of the movement abound. Thus Leonard Ratner, *The Beethoven String Quartets* (Stanford, Calif., 1995), 263, posits two expositions: a tonic exposition, mm. 1–73, a "parenthesis," mm. 74–102, then a second exposition in E minor, mm. 103–192; recapitulation, mm. 193–231; and coda, mm. 232–264. He omits a development. The Procrustean bed of traditional sonata form has trouble with this shape no matter how it is cut to fit.

29. See S. Brandenburg, "The Autograph of Beethoven's Quartet in A minor, Opus 132," in *The String Quartets of Haydn, Mozart and Beethoven*, ed. C. Wolff (Cambridge, Mass. 1980), 283–84, following up on Schindler and Nottebohm.

30. For a view of the earlier history of modal affects see C. V. Palisca, *Humanism in Italian Renaissance Musical Thought* (New Haven, Conn., 1995). On the history of the "Lydian" see Harold Powers, "Lydian," *NG2*.

31. "Letztes quartett mit einer ernsthaftigen und schwergängigen Einleitung." See chapter 17, note 35, and Kropfinger, "Das gespaltene Werk," in *Beiträge zu Beethovens Kammermusik*, ed. S. Brandenburg and H. Loos (Munich, 1987), 296–335, especially 305. Kropfinger followed up this article with his contribution "Streichquartett B-Dur Op. 130" in *Beethoven: Interpretationen seiner Werke*, ed. A. Riethmüller et al. (Laaber, 1994), 2:299–316.

32. For the B-flat 6/8 entry, quite diatonic, see Kropfinger's article in Riethmüller, *Beethoven: Interpretationen seiner Werke*, 304. Although there are a number of early ideas for a possible finale, not all of them apparently fugal, I agree with Kropfinger's argument that a fugal finale was an important early idea for framing the whole work.

33. In the excellent recording by the Fine Arts Quartet (EVC 9056/58, 1969, reissued 1996), the first movement takes 9' 36", the *Grosse Fuge* 15' 23". Significantly, the substitute finale takes 7' 47", almost two minutes less than the first movement. Obviously the entire balance and proportions of the work are drastically altered by the new finale, not to mention the difference in weight that the finale brings.

34. *Briefwechsel*, No. 2042; Anderson, No. 1416 (to Karl); *Briefwechsel*, No. 2043; Anderson, No. 1415 (to Holz). It is interesting to see that Beethoven—writing to Karl and with no need to exaggerate, as he often would to a publisher—could estimate his own speed of composition.

35. The account of the rehearsal is from Holz's testimony to Lenz; see Lenz, *Beethoven: Eine Kunststudie*, 5:218. Holz says that Beethoven usually sat between the first and second violinists, "for although he could no longer hear low-pitched sounds, his ear still caught the higher notes; Beethoven specified the tempos, the ritardandos, and so forth, and also demonstrated certain passages for us at the piano. . . . [O]ften Schuppanzigh had quite a struggle with the difficult first violin part, at which Beethoven broke into peals of laughter."

36. Holz to Lenz, *op cit.*, 218ff: "Beethoven was not present. The audience was by turns delighted, astonished, or puzzled, though out of respect there were no disparaging com-

ments." The "short transition movements," i.e., the Scherzo and Alla danza tedesca, were repeated. "The fugue passed by uncomprehended. Beethoven was waiting for me after the performance in a nearby tavern. I told him that the two [inner] movements had been encored. 'What, those trifles?' he said in exasperation. 'Why not the fugue?'"

37. "Perhaps so much would not have been written into the piece if the master could hear his own works." But hedging his bets, the reviewer allowed for the possibility that "perhaps there will come a time when what at first glance seems to us so turbid and confused will be seen as clear and perfectly balanced." *AMZ* 28 (1826): 310.

38. Kinsky-Halm, 394. The evidence for this engraving comes from Artaria's expense book.

39. Lenz, *Beethoven: Eine Kunststudie,* 219.

40. *Konversationshefte,* 10:107 (first half of August 1826).

41. *Konversationshefte,* 10:185 (September 1826).

42. TDR, 5:405, n. 1.

43. See TF, 895, where this opinion is attributed to Czerny, who told it to Jahn in 1852. On the quartet finale issue see R. Kramer, "Between Cavatina and Ouverture," *BF* 1 (1992): 165–90, to which this discussion is much indebted.

44. See W. Kirkendale, "The 'Great Fugue' Op. 133: Beethoven's 'Art of Fugue,'" *Acta Musicologica* 35 (1963): 14–24; and his *Fugue and Fugato in Rococo and Classical Chamber Music,* 255–71.

45. I am indebted for this phrase to Richard Kramer.

46. Beethoven actually wrote "Ouverture" in the autograph, which was altered to the Italian "Overtura" in the early prints and remained that way.

47. I am indebted here to Richard Kramer, "Between Cavatina and Ouverture," 172. The "Goldberg" Variations had been published in Vienna c. 1803. To Kramer's conjecture, fn. 13, that Beethoven could also have known the orchestral suites, we can speculate on the further possibility of his knowledge of Bach's G Minor Sonata for solo violin and C Minor Suite for solo cello.

48. Vincent D'Indy in *Cobbett's Cyclopedia of Chamber Music,* 104.

49. The passage is mm. 368–414.

50. Mm. 661–681.

51. Erwin Ratz, *Die Originalfassung des Streichquartettes Op. 130 von Beethoven* (Vienna, 1957), 4.

52. Schindler, *Beethoven as I Knew Him,* 308.

53. Compare mm. 158ff., where the figure introduces the development section but is divided between viola and cello; mm. 223f., where it introduces a false reprise of the main theme; mm. 232f. where it presages the real recapitulation but is now combined with the main theme after one measure instead of two; and its permeation of the coda, as at mm. 402ff., 407ff., and 414ff., where it combines with fragments of the main theme as the movement picks up momentum and heads toward its close.

54. Mm. 109–160.

55. Mm. 131–140.

56. R. Winter, "Plans for the Structure of the String Quartet in C Sharp Minor," *BS,* 2: 114.

57. On the commission see *Briefwechsel,* No. 2154; Anderson, No. 1485 (Beethoven to Schott, May 20, 1826).

58. Schott published a series of late works, including all the works with opus numbers from Opus 121b to Opus 128.

59. Favoring the financial explanation is Barry Cooper in his review of R. Winter and R. Martin, eds., *The Beethoven Quartet Companion,* in *Music and Letters,* 76 (1995), 447.

60. Deutsch, *Schubert: A Documentary Biography,* 820. Deutsch records a notice reporting that on November 14, 1828, just five days before Schubert's death, Opus 131 was played for him in the presence of Johann Dolezálek, a composer and teacher, by Karl Holz, Karl Gross, Baron König, and an unnamed fourth player. Deutsch questions the story, which apparently came from Holz, but we have no other evidence for either viewpoint.

61. On Haydn's C-sharp Minor Piano Sonata see Brown, *Joseph Haydn's Keyboard Music,* 64, 320–24.

62. We saw earlier an example of a long, slow introduction to a finale that is in the dominant key—the Adagio of the Cello Sonata in A major, Opus 69.

63. R. Winter, *Compositional Origins of Beethoven's Opus 131* (Ann Arbor, 1982). Winter's study is the first to catalogue exhaustively the massive sketch material for this work. Beethoven made more than six hundred pages of score sketches, plus others yet to be sorted and integrated, plus the autographs and copies. Winter offers a detailed study of three aspects of the work: the movement plans for the whole, the finale, and the fourth movement. The remaining material awaits further study.

64. Winter, "Plans for the Structure of the String Quartet in C Sharp Minor," 120. Such a three-movement plan would also have agreed, by reversal of major and minor, with earlier three-movement works in major with the slow movement in tonic minor including the "Ghost" Trio, Opus 70 No. 1; among late works the Cello Sonata Opus 102 No. 2 (D major–D minor–D major fugato).

65. See Winter, *Compositional Origins,* 124 and Ex. 13.

66. See mm. 35–52, 55–72, 73–80, and 83.

67. Mm. 67–72.

68. Kirkendale, *Fugue and Fugato,* 91f. and *passim.*

69. See above, chapter 1.

70. I am indebted for this observation to Matthias Bieber, who pointed it out during a course I gave on the late Beethoven quartets at the University of Munich in January 1998. The relationship of the initial fugue subject to Beethoven's late quartets is my own observation.

71. Beethoven's copy of the B-minor fugue from *The Well-Tempered Clavier, Book I,* is at the Gesellschaft der Musikfreunde in Vienna, MS A 81; for a facsimile of one page see p. 476, and Bory, 63. For a list of Bach fugues copied by Beethoven, seen Kirkendale, *Fugue and Fugato in Rococo and Classical Chamber Music,* 212–15.

72. See mm. 231ff., 243–253, and 266.

73. The cadential inflection is at mm. 9, 17, and 25; the short figure is at mm. 1–14 and 20–22.

74. At mm. 160ff.

75. TF, 976. Holz reported on the whole matter in an article in a German periodical in 1844 (see Kinsky-Halm, 697f.) and included a facsimile of the autograph of the canon. For further details see TDR, 5:301–3.

76. WoO 196. For a reliable transcription see MacArdle-Misch, *New Beethoven Letters,* 512.
77. L. K. Bumpass, "Beethoven's Last Quartet" (Ph.D. diss., University of Illinois, 1982). Volume 2 contains extensive transcriptions from the sources.
78. Bumpass, 230.
79. TF, 1009; *Konversationshefte,* 10:26 (fol. 8v). Since an entry on fol. 4v can be dated July 7, this exchange is likely to have taken place a few days later, about July 10.
80. This last view was promoted by the publisher Maurice Schlesinger in a lost letter that he later claimed to have received from Beethoven. Schlesinger reproduced it from memory twice, in 1859 and 1867. In one of these texts Beethoven is reported to have said that he had great trouble in composing the finale, which is why he had written the inscription. The factual faults in the letter and its unreliability as evidence are obvious, and it has no serious basis as evidence. See Anderson, No. 1318, n. 4, and Kinsky-Halm, 409.
81. The similarity of phrasing to the inscription in Opus 135 was noted by Albrecht, 1:207, n. 4. The original German text is readily available in TDR, 3:125f.
82. For these alternatives in the sketches see Bumpass, 243ff.
83. W. Drabkin, "The Agnus Dei of Beethoven's *Missa Solemnis:* The Growth of its Form," in *Beethoven's Compositional Process,* ed. W. Kinderman (Lincoln, Nebraska, 1991), 131–59, especially 137. Table 10.2 gives a set of "programmatic" remarks from the sketches on peace and war in this section of the Mass.
84. Kerman, *The Beethoven Quartets,* 362.
85. *Briefwechsel,* No. 2003.
86. Solomon, "Beethoven's Tagebuch," 272, 274, 275.
87. Kerman, *The Beethoven Quartets,* 376; also Ratner, 291.
88. For a similar objection see Robert Winter's remarks in C. Wolff, ed., *The String Quartets of Haydn, Mozart, and Beethoven,* 324.
89. The cadences are at mm. 10, 104, 109, and 188–193. For insight into the opening content of Opus 135 I am indebted to Curt Cacioppo, "Color and Dissonance in Late Beethoven: The Quartet Op. 135," *Journal of Musicological Research* 6(1986): 207–12.
90. Jonathan Kramer, "Multiple and Non-linear Time in Beethoven's Opus 135," *Perspectives of New Music* 11/2 (1973), 122–45; also Judy Lochhead, "The Temporal in Beethoven's Opus 135: When are Ends Beginnings?" *In Theory Only,* 4/7 (1979): 3–30.
91. On these endings and their dynamics see Emil Platen, "Ein Notierungsproblem in Beethovens späten Streichquartetten," *BJ* 8 (1971/72): 147–56. The Opus 135 example is not mentioned by Platen and has not been discussed earlier, to my knowledge. Nor has another similar passage that occurs in the *Grand Fugue,* mm. 511–530, which is also "poco a poco sempre più allegro ed accelerando il tempo" ("little by little becoming faster and accelerating the tempo").
92. See M. Staehelin, "Another Approach to Beethoven's Last String Quartet Oeuvre: The Unfinished String Quintet of 1826/27," in *The String Quartets of Haydn, Mozart, and Beethoven,* ed. C. Wolff (Cambridge, Mass., 1980), 302–28. Beethoven's preliminary ideas for a Tenth Symphony, which never got beyond an incipient stage, were assembled and amplified by Barry Cooper in a speculative "realization" in 1988 as "Beethoven's Symphony No. 10" (actually an attempted reconstruction of the first movement only)

recorded by MCA Classics, MCAD-6269, with a recorded lecture by Cooper. The musically inadequate results of this quixotic project were discussed by Robert Winter in his article, "Of Realizations, Completions, Restorations, and Reconstructions: From Bach's *The Art of Fugue* to Beethoven's Tenth Symphony," *Journal of the Royal Musical Association* 116 (1991): 96–126. The article definitively demolished Cooper's claims that the surviving sketches add up to a coherent first movement worthy to be taken seriously by scholars, critics, and the musical public. Cooper replied to Winter in his "Beethoven's Tenth Symphony," *JRMA* 117 (1992), 324–29, and Winter then responded in the same issue, 329–30.

CHRONOLOGY

><><><<[ᴓᴄ]]>><><><

1770 December 17: Ludwig van Beethoven, second son of Johann van Beethoven and his wife, Maria Magdalena Keverich Leym, baptized at Bonn; he had probably been born the previous day, December 16. An older brother, Ludwig Maria, born on April 2, 1769, had died in infancy; there were two surviving younger brothers, Caspar Carl (born 1774) and Johann (born 1776).

1773 December 24: Death of Beethoven's revered grandfather, Ludwig van Beethoven, age sixty-one. From 1761 to his death the elder Ludwig had been Kapellmeister to the Elector Max Friedrich. For many years Beethoven kept a portrait of his grandfather in his rooms.

1778 Apparently the first public appearance of the child Ludwig as performer, in Cologne; he was presented as being six years old, owing to his father's claim that he was born in 1772, made in order to enhance his status as a prodigy. Beethoven himself apparently believed in this birth year for many years. In 1778 he had his first music lessons with the organist Gilles van den Eeden.

1779 Arrival in Bonn of Christian Gottlob Neefe, Beethoven's first important teacher.

1781 Mozart settles in Vienna. The young Beethoven travels to Holland with his mother; he begins lessons with Neefe at Bonn.

1782 First musical publication: the Piano Variations on a March by Dressler "par un jeune amateur Louis van Betthoven, âgè de dix ans." In 1782–83, he composes the three "Electoral" Sonatas for fortepiano.

1783 Neefe's laudatory notice on Beethoven appears in Cramer's *Magazin der Musik,* mentioning the boy's remarkable pianistic talent, that he plays Bach's *Well-Tempered Clavier* "at the instigation of Herr Neefe," that Neefe is currently training him in composition, and that "he would certainly become a second Wolfgang Amadeus Mozart if he progresses as he has begun."

1784   Death of Elector Max Friedrich, succeeded by Max Franz. Beethoven appointed court organist at 150 florins per year.

1785   Beethoven composes three Piano Quartets WoO 36. Anton Reicha arrives in Bonn.

1787   In the spring Beethoven travels to Vienna, probably meets Mozart or at least hears him play the piano; the illness of Beethoven's mother forces him to return to Bonn. On July 17 his mother dies.

1788   Count Ferdinand von Waldstein arrives in Bonn.

1789   Beethoven, now a violist in the court orchestra, petitions the Elector to pay him half of his father's wages for the necessary support of the family.

1790   Death of the Emperor Joseph II; Beethoven writes two cantatas, one for Joseph's death (WoO 87), the other for the coronation of his successor, Leopold II (WoO 88). December: Haydn stops in Bonn on his way from Vienna to London.

1791   Beethoven writes music for a "Ritterballet" (WoO 1) performed in Bonn, allowing it to appear that Waldstein was the composer. Publication of "Righini" Variations, WoO 65. December 5: death of Mozart in Vienna.

1792   July: Haydn again in Bonn, probably agrees to accept Beethoven as his student if Beethoven comes to Vienna. Early November: Beethoven departs from Bonn for Vienna; his friends inscribe an album for him, including Waldstein's remark that he is going to Vienna "to receive the spirit of Mozart from the hands of Haydn." December 18: Death of Johann van Beethoven in Bonn.

1793   Beethoven continues counterpoint studies with Haydn. Publishes "Se vuol ballare" Variations (WoO 40) and Variations on a theme by Dittersdorf (WoO 66).

1794   Haydn leaves for England. Beethoven continues his counterpoint lessons with Johann Georg Albrechtsberger; begins studies of Italian text setting with Salieri; begins composing Piano Trios, Opus 1.

1795   March 29: Beethoven's first public concert, at the Burgtheater in Vienna; he plays the B-flat Major Piano Concerto, later titled No. 2. Publication of Opus 1 Piano Trios; composes three Piano Sonatas, Opus 2.

1796   Opus 2 Piano Sonatas published. February: Beethoven travels with Prince Karl Lichnowsky to Prague, Dresden, Leipzig, and on to Berlin, where he plays for King Friedrich Wilhelm II and meets the French cellists Jean Louis and Jean Pierre Duport. For Jean Louis he writes the two Cello Sonatas Op. 5. Summer: journey to Pressburg and Pest.

1797   First performance of the Quintet for Piano and Winds, Opus 16

1798   Beethoven composes Piano Sonatas Opus 10; String Trios Opus 9; Clarinet Trio, Opus 11. He begins first systematic use of sketchbooks in connection with composition of Opus 18 Quartets, on commission from Prince Lobkowitz.

1799   Piano competition with Joseph Wölffl. Beethoven composes First Symphony, Opus 21, and Septet, Opus 20. Publication of "Pathétique" Sonata, Opus 13.

1800   April 2: Beethoven's first concert of his own music in the Hoftheater, including First Symphony and C Major Piano Concerto, later titled No. 1. His compositions include Violin Sonatas Opp. 23 and 24 and Piano Sonata Opus 22.

1801   Stephan von Breuning comes to Vienna, as does Ferdinand Ries, who is to be one of Beethoven's pupils. Beethoven sends first letters revealing his deafness to his trusted friends Franz Gerhard Wegeler (June 29) and Karl Amenda (July 1). Compositions include the Piano Sonatas Opus 26, Opus 27 Nos. 1 and 2, and Opus 28; Opus 29 Quintet. He begins work on Second Symphony and composition of ballet *Prometheus*.

1802   May 24: First performance of "Kreutzer" Sonata for Violin and Piano, with George Augustus Polgreen Bridgetower. Composes oratorio *Christus am Ölberge;* Piano Variations, Opp. 34 and 35; Piano Sonatas Opus 31. October: writes Heiligenstadt Testament.

1803   1803–4: Beethoven composes Third Symphony, later entitled *Eroica;* also Piano Sonatas Opus 53 ("Waldstein") and Opus 54. April 5: Beethoven holds a concert in the Theater an der Wien, with premieres of *Christus am*

Ölberge, Second Symphony, and Third Piano Concerto. Plans an opera with Schikaneder on *Vestas Feuer.*

1804 Beethoven begins composition of *Leonore.* May 20: Napoleon crowns himself emperor. Summer: first private performance of Third Symphony in Vienna, in palace of Prince Lobkowitz. Composes Triple Concerto.

1805 Close relationship with Josephine Deym-Brunsvik; Beethoven gives her the song "An die Hoffnung," Opus 32. Composes "Appassionata" Sonata, Opus 57. Completes *Leonore,* and its premiere takes place on November 20. Count Razumovsky commissions Opus 59 Quartets.

1806 Beethoven composes Piano Concerto No. 4; second version of *Leonore* performed in March and April. Brother Caspar Carl marries Johanna Reiss. Composes Opus 59 Quartets, Fourth Symphony, Violin Concerto.

1807 Prince Esterházy commissions Mass in C. Beethoven completes *Coriolanus* Overture. He signs contract with Clementi for rights to publish six of his works in England, and, apparently, a contract with the Bureau des Arts et d'Industrie for the Continental rights to the same works.

1808 Beethoven composes Cello Sonata Opus 69; Fifth and Sixth Symphonies; Trios Opus 70 Nos. 1 and 2; *Choral Fantasy.* Brother Johann van Beethoven moves to Linz, where he sets up an apothecary shop. Beethoven sketches some ideas for an opera on *Macbeth* with libretto by Collin. Jerome Bonaparte invites Beethoven to become his Kapellmeister at Kassel.

1809 Beethoven rejects Jerome Bonaparte's offer to move to Kassel when Archduke Rudolph, Prince Lobkowitz, and Prince Kinsky combine to give him an annuity contract of 4,000 florins to persuade him to stay in Vienna. Vienna under siege by Napoleonic armies. Beethoven composes Fifth Piano Concerto, Piano Sonata *Das Lebewohl,* Opus 81a, for Archduke Rudolph. May 31: death of Haydn. Beethoven prepares teaching materials for his instruction of Archduke Rudolph, composes Quartet Opus 74, and, for piano, Fantasia Opus 77 and Sonata Opus 78.

1810 Beethoven's hopes of marrying Therese Malfatti fail; he meets the Brentano family. Composition and performance of *Egmont* music; Beethoven sends first batch of folk-song arrangements to George Thomson. Composition of Quartet Opus 95, Goethe Songs Opus 83.

1811   Composition of "Archduke" Trio, Opus 97; music for *King Stephen* and *The Ruins of Athens,* for new theater in Pest. The Austrian government, in financial straits after years of war, issues a Finanz-Patent that depreciates the national currency; Beethoven's income suffers, but the archduke compensates for the loss by increasing his annuity. Death of Collin; Beethoven in contact with Goethe.

1812   Napoleon invades Russia. Beethoven presents autograph of song "An die Geliebte" ("To the Beloved"), WoO 140, to Antonie Brentano. Composes Seventh and Eighth Symphonies. In summer Beethoven goes to spa at Teplitz, where he writes a letter to an unnamed woman called the "Immortal Beloved" (almost certainly identified as Antonie Brentano). Beethoven meets Goethe at Teplitz, and writes in a letter of August 9, 1812, "Goethe enjoys the air at court too much, more than is proper for a poet."

1813   Beethoven persuades his brother Carl, gravely ill, to declare him guardian of his nephew Karl in the event of Carl's death. June 21: Wellington defeats French at Vittoria, and Beethoven accepts proposal by Johann Nepomuk Mälzel to write a piece for Mälzel's mechanical instrument, the Panharmonicon. *Wellingtons Sieg* ("Wellington's Victory") is performed in December at a charity concert along with the Seventh Symphony. Mälzel also invents an early form of the metronome in October 1813, which is praised by Beethoven and others.

1814   Viennese theater managers agree to revive *Leonore* and Beethoven revises it thoroughly, now calling it *Fidelio;* the first performance takes place on May 23. Beethoven quarrels with Mälzel over the performing rights to *Wellingtons Sieg.* Compositions include the Piano Sonata Opus 90, the *Elegischer Gesang* ("Elegiac Song") Opus 118, and the cantata *Der Glorreiche Augenblick* ("The Glorious Moment") for the newly assembled Congress of Vienna.

1815   Napoleon escapes from Elba, regains power during the "Hundred Days," and suffers final defeat at Waterloo. Beethoven writes a Polonaise Opus 89 for the empress of Russia, in Vienna for the Congress. Compositions include the *Namensfeier* ("Name Day") Overture, Opus 115, and the Cello Sonatas Opus 102 Nos. 1 and 2. Beethoven's brother Carl dies on November 15. His wife Johanna is named guardian and Beethoven associate guardian, whereupon Beethoven appeals to the courts to exclude her from this responsibility. Beethoven makes his first use of pocket sketch-books.

1816   Rossini, *II Barbiere di Siviglia;* in 1822 Beethoven tells a visitor that Rossini's music, though it is tuneful and attractive, "suits the frivolous and sensuous spirit of the time." Composes song cycle *An die ferne Geliebte*, Opus 98; Piano Sonata Opus 101. The court gives Beethoven sole custody of his nephew Karl; Beethoven places him in a boarding school, then plans to have the young man live with him. A series of important works composed earlier are published by Steiner in Vienna, including the Seventh Symphony.

1817   Beethoven's poor health continues, along with problems with nephew Karl. Through Ferdinand Ries the Philharmonic Society of London invites Beethoven to come to London and to write two new symphonies for them. Composes Fugue in D for string quintet, Opus 137; begins work on the *Hammerklavier* Sonata, Opus 106.

1818   Nephew Karl comes to live with Beethoven; he gives up the idea of a trip to London, citing poor health. *Hammerklavier* Sonata completed. The courts reject appeals by Johanna van Beethoven to regain guardianship of Karl, but in December the boy runs away to her and Beethoven calls out the police to get him back. Beethoven's deafness now requires the use of Conversion Books by his visitors, who write down their side of their conversations with him.

1819   The Austrian regime promulgates the Carlsbad Decrees, increasing police surveillance and restricting freedom of speech. Beethoven's guardianship case is heard in the Magistrat, the lower court of Vienna, resulting in Beethoven's temporary loss of custody of his nephew. Archduke Rudolph named archbishop of Ölmutz. Beethoven begins work on the *Missa solemnis*, intended for performance at Rudolph's installation the following year. He stops work on the "Diabelli" Variations, begun in March when the publisher Diabelli sent out an invitation to a large number of composers to write one variation each on Diabelli's waltz tune.

1820   Beethoven prepares a lengthy appeal to the courts over Karl's guardianship, and in April the court rules in his favor. He continues work on the *Missa solemnis*, but also accepts a request from the publisher Schlesinger to write three piano sonatas, which causes the Mass to be put aside until the fall.

1821   Amid recurring illnesses, Beethoven completes the Piano Sonatas Opp. 109, 110, and 111.

1822   After completing the *Missa solemnis,* Beethoven offers it to a number of publishers. He composes the overture *Consecration of the House* for the opening of the Josephstadt Theater in Vienna; he starts work on the Ninth Symphony. Prince Nicolai Galitzin commissions Beethoven to write three new string quartets, and the Philharmonic Society of London offers him 50 pounds for a new symphony. He continues work on the "Diabelli" Variations and the Bagatelles Opus 119.

1823   Beethoven plans to sell manuscript copies of the *Missa solemnis* by subscription, at 50 ducats each, to all the major courts of Europe, and receives orders from ten of them. He accepts Galitzin's commission for three quartets, completes the "Diabelli" Variations, and begins full-scale work on the Ninth Symphony. He discusses possible opera projects with Grillparzer, but nothing comes of them.

1824   A group of Viennese admirers petition Beethoven to perform his Mass and Ninth Symphony in Vienna, and plans are made for a concert in March. He finishes the symphony in February, and on May 7 the concert takes place; at the end Beethoven, unable to hear the applause, is turned around to face the audience. He begins work on the Quartet Opus 127 and, later, Opus 132.

1825   Beethoven completes Opus 127, whose first performance in March is not successful, and then composes Opus 132 (February–July). In the second half of the year he composes the Quartet Opus 130, with the long fugue as finale.

1826   Karl attempts suicide but escapes with only slight injury and is taken to his mother's house. Beethoven soon thereafter begins work on his last quartet, Opus 135. He also agrees to detach the *Grand Fugue* from the Quartet Opus 130, publish it separately as Opus 133, and write a new finale for Opus 130. He composes the second finale in the fall, at Gneixendorf, while staying there at the house of his brother Johann, accompanied by his nephew Karl. He begins work on a string quintet that remains unfinished. His health deteriorates sharply in December, and he undergoes an abdominal operation.

1827   Despite further medical efforts his health continues to decline. Karl, now a cadet in a military regiment, leaves Vienna. Beethoven dies on March

26. A massive funeral takes place three days later, on March 29, at which a funeral oration written by Grillparzer is delivered by Heinrich Anschütz, an actor. The funeral is a major event at which from ten to twenty thousand people march in procession. The pallbearers include his friends Stephan and Gerhard von Breuning with eight leading Austrian musicians (Hummel, Eybler, Kreutzer, Gyrowetz, Gänsbacher, Würfel, Seyfried, and Weigl) while the many torchbearers include Czerny, Grillparzer, Holz, Linke, Schuppanzigh, and Schubert. Beethoven was originally buried in the cemetery at Währing, near Vienna, but his remains were later transferred to the Central Cemetery of Vienna.

BIBLIOGRAPHY

Abbreviations

AMZ   *Allgemeine musikalische Zeitung.* Leipzig, 1798–1848.

Albrecht   Albrecht, Theodore, ed. *Letters to Beethoven and Other Correspondence.* 3 vols. Lincoln, Neb., 1996.

Anderson   Beethoven, Ludwig van. *The Letters of Beethoven.* Translated and edited by Emily Anderson. 3 vols. London, 1961.

BF   *Beethoven Forum.* Lincoln, Neb., 1992–.

BJ   *Beethoven Jahrbuch.* 10 vols. Bonn, 1953/54–1978/81.

Briefwechsel   Beethoven, Ludwig van. *Briefwechsel: Gesamtausgabe.* Edited by Sieghard Brandenburg. 7 vols. Munich, 1996–98.

BS   Tyson, Alan, ed. *Beethoven Studies.* New York (vol. 1), 1973; London (vol. 2), 1977; Cambridge (vol. 3), 1982.

JAMS   *Journal of the American Musicological Society.* 1948–.

JTW   Johnson, Douglas, Alan Tyson, and Robert Winter. *The Beethoven Sketchbooks: History, Reconstruction, Inventory.* Berkeley, 1985.

Kinsky-Halm   Kinsky, Georg, and Hans Halm. *Das Werk Beethovens: Thematisch-bibliographisches Verzeichnis seiner sämtlichen vollendeten Kompositionen.* Munich, 1955.

Konversationshefte   Beethoven, Ludwig van. *Konversationshefte.* Edited by Karl-Heinz Köhler, Grita Herre, Dagmar Beck, and Günter Brosche. 11 vols. Leipzig, 1968–2001.

Lockwood, *Studies*   Lockwood, Lewis. *Beethoven: Studies in the Creative Process.* Cambridge, Mass., 1992.

NG2   *The New Grove Dictionary of Music and Musicians.* 2nd ed. Edited by Stanley Sadie. 29 vols. London, 2001. Online ed. at www.grovemusic.com.

N II   Nottebohm, Gustav. *Zweite Beethoveniana: Nachgelassene Aufsätze.* Leipzig, 1887.

TDR   Thayer, Alexander Wheelock. *Ludwig van Beethovens Leben.* Edited by Hugo Riemann from the revised edition of Hermann Deiters (1901). Leipzig, 1917.

TF   Thayer, Alexander Wheelock. *Thayer's Life of Beethoven.* Revised and edited by Elliot Forbes. Princeton, N.J., 1964.

Wegeler-Ries   Wegeler, Franz, and Ferdinand Ries. *Biographische Notizen über Ludwig van Beethoven.* Coblenz, 1838.

WoO   Werk ohne Opuszahl (Work without Opus number), as listed in Kinsky-Halm (see above).

NOTE: The lists above and below include only items cited in this book. The enormous scholarly and critical literature on Beethoven is covered in the following bibliographies:

Kastner, Emerich. *Bibliotheca Beethoveniana.* 2nd ed., revised by Theodor Frimmel. Leipzig, 1925. Covers the years 1778–1924.

"Beethoven-Literatur." *Neues Beethoven-Jahrbuch* 1–9 (1924–39). Covers 1924–38.

"Beethoven-Schrifttum." *Beethoven-Jahrbuch* 1–10 (1953/54–1978/81). Covers 1939–75.

Beethoven Bibliography Database (www.sjsu.edu/depts/beethoven/database/database.html). Compiled and maintained by the Ira F. Brilliant Center for Beethoven Studies, San José State University. A computerized database containing a fully indexed bibliography of published and some unpublished materials by and about Beethoven, covering both primary and secondary literature.

Works Cited

Adorno, Theodor W. *Beethoven, The Philosophy of Music: Fragments and Texts.* Edited by Rolf Tiedemann, translated by Edmund Jephcott, Stanford, Calif., 1998.

Ahn, Suhnne. "Genre, Style, and Compositional Procedure in Beethoven's 'Kreutzer' Sonata, Opus 47." Ph.D. diss., Harvard University, 1997.

Albrecht, Theodore. "The Fortnight Fallacy: A Revised Chronology for Beethoven's *Christ on the Mount of Olives,* Op. 85, and Wielhorsky Sketchbook," *Journal of Musicological Research* 11 (1991): 263–84.

Aris, Reinhold. *A History of Political Thought in Germany from 1789 to 1815.* London, 1936; reprinted 1965.

Arnold, Ben. *Music and War: A Research and Information Guide.* New York, 1993.

Bankl, Hans, and Hans Jesserer. *Die Krankheiten Ludwig van Beethovens: Pathographie seines Lebens und Pathologie seiner Leiden.* Vienna, 1987.

Bahr, Ehrhard, and Saine, Thomas P. *The Internalized Revolution: German Reactions to the French Revolution, 1789–1989.* New York, 1992.

Barth, George. *The Pianist as Orator: Beethoven and the Transformation of Keyboard Style.* Ithaca, N.Y., 1992.

Becker, Alfred. *Christian Gottlob Neefe und die Bonner Illuminaten.* Bonn, 1969.

Beethoven, Ludwig van. *Autograph Miscellany from circa 1786 to 1799: British Museum Additional Manuscript 29801, ff. 39–162 (The Kafka Sketchbook).* Edited by Joseph Kerman. 2 vols. London, 1980.

———. *Konversationshefte.* Edited by Georg Schünemann. Vol. 1, Februar 1818–März 1820. Berlin, 1941.

———. *New Beethoven Letters.* Edited by Donald MacArdle and Ludwig Misch. Norman, Okla., 1957.

———. *Ein Notierungsbuch von Beethoven aus dem Besitze der Preussischen Staatsbibliothek zu Berlin.* Edited by Karl Lothar Mikulicz. Leipzig, 1927.

———. *A Sketchbook from the Summer of 1800.* Edited by Richard Kramer. 2 vols. Bonn, 1996.

———. *Studien im Generalbass, Contrapunct und in der Compositions-Lehre.* Edited by Ignaz Seyfried. Vienna, 1832.

———. *Symphony No. 5 in C Minor.* Edited by Elliot Forbes. New York, 1971.

———. *Werke.* Edited by the Beethoven-Archiv Bonn, under the direction of Joseph Schmidt-Görg. Munich, 1961–.

Bekker, Paul. *Beethoven.* 2nd ed. Berlin, 1912.

Berger, Arthur. Obituary of Aaron Copland, *The Boston Globe,* December 4, 1994, 65.

Berger, Karol. "Beethoven and the Aesthetic State." *BF* 7 (1999): 17–44.

Berlioz, Hector. *A Critical Study of Beethoven's Nine Symphonies.* Translated by Edwin Evans. Urbana, Ill., 2000.

Biamonti, Giovanni. *Catalogo cronologico e tematico delle opere di Beethoven, comprese quelle inedite e gli abbozzi non utilizzati.* Turin, 1968.

Biba, Otto. "Concert Life in Beethoven's Vienna, 1780–1810." In *Beethoven: Performers, and Critics: The International Beethoven Congress, Detroit, 1977,* edited by Robert Winter and Bruce Carr, 77–93. Detroit, 1980.

———. "Schubert's Position in Viennese Musical Life," *19th Century Music* 3 (1979): 106–13.

———. "Zu Beethovens Streichquartett Opus 95." In *Münchener Beethoven-Studien,* edited by Johannes Fischer, 39–45. Munich, 1992.

Blume, Friedrich. *Classic and Romantic Music.* New York, 1970.

Boettcher, Hans. *Beethoven als Liederkomponist.* Augsburg, 1928.

Bonds, Mark Evan. *After Beethoven: Imperatives of Originality in the Symphony.* Cambridge, Mass., 1996.

Borthwick, E. Kerr. "Beethoven and Plutarch." *Music and Letters* 79 (1998): 268–72.

Bory, Robert. *Ludwig van Beethoven: His Life and His Work in Pictures.* Translated by Winifred Glass and Hans Rosenwald. Zurich, 1960.

Brandenburg, Sieghard. "The Autograph of Beethoven's String Quartet in A Minor, Opus 132." In *The String Quartets of Haydn, Mozart, and Beethoven,* edited by Christoph Wolff, 278–301. Cambridge, Mass., 1980.

———. "Die Beethovenhandschriften in der Musikaliensammlung des Erzherzogs Rudolph." *Zu Beethoven* 3 (1988): 141–66.

———. "Beethovens Streichquartette Op. 18." In *Beethoven und Böhmen,* edited by Sieghard Brandenburg and Martella Gutierrez-Denhoff, 259–310. Bonn, 1998.

———. "Bemerkungen zu Beethovens Op. 96." *BJ* 9 (1973/77): 11–26.

———. "The First Version of Beethoven's G Major String Quartet, Op. 18 No. 2." *Music and Letters* 58 (1977): 127–52.

———. "Johanna van Beethoven's Embezzlement." In *Haydn, Mozart, Beethoven: Studies in Music of the Classical Period: Essays in Honor of Alan Tyson,* edited by Sieghard Brandenburg, 237–51. Oxford, 1998.

———. "Die kurfürstliche Musikbibliothek in Bonn und ihre Bestände im 18. Jahrhundert." *BJ* 8 (1971/72): 7–48.

———. "Once Again: On the Question of the Repeat of the Scherzo and Trio in Beethoven's Fifth Symphony." In *Beethoven Essays: Studies in Honor of Elliot Forbes,* edited by Lewis Lockwood and Phyllis Benjamin, 146–98. Cambridge, Mass., 1984.

———. "Die Quellen zur Entstehungsgeschichte von Beethovens Streichquartett Es-Dur Op. 127" *BJ* 10 (1978/81): 221–76.

Braubach, Max. *Maria Theresias jüngster Sohn, Max Franz, Letzter Kurfürst von*

Köln und Fürstbischof von Münster. Vienna, 1961. First published under title *Max Franz von Österreich* (Münster, 1925).

Braubach, Max, ed. *Die Stammbücher Beethovens und der Babette Koch.* Bonn, 1970.

Breuning, Gerhard von. *Memories of Beethoven: From the House of the Black-Robed Spaniards.* Edited by Maynard Solomon, translated by Henry Mins and Maynard Solomon. Cambridge, 1992. Translation of Breuning's *Aus dem Schwarzspanierhause* (Vienna, 1874).

Brook, Barry S. "The Symphonie Concertante: Its Musical and Sociological Bases." *International Review of the Aesthetics and Sociology of Music* 6 (1975): 9–28.

Brown, A. Peter. *Joseph Haydn's Keyboard Music: Sources and Style.* Bloomington, 1986.

Broyles, Michael. *Beethoven: The Emergence and Evolution of Beethoven's Heroic Style.* New York, 1987.

Brunswick, Mark. "Beethoven's Tribute to Mozart in *Fidelio.*" *The Musical Quarterly* 36 (1945): 29–32.

Bücken, Ernst. *Anton Reicha: Sein Leben und seine Kompositionen.* Munich, 1912.

Bumpass, Laura Kathryn. "Beethoven's Last Quartet." 2 vols. Ph.D. diss., University of Illinois, 1982.

Burney, Charles. *A General History of Music: From the Earliest Ages to the Present Period.* 4 vols. London, 1776–89.

Burnham, Scott. *Beethoven Hero.* Princeton, N. J., 1995.

Busch-Weise, Dagmar. "Beethovens Jugendtagebuch." *Studien zur Musikwissenschaft* 25 (1962): 68–88.

Cahn, Peter. "Aspekte der Schlussgestaltung in Beethovens Instrumentalwerken." *Archiv für Musikwissenschaft* (1982): 9–28.

Canisius, Claus. *Beethoven, "Sehnsucht und Unruhe in der Musik": Aspekte zu Leben und Werk.* Munich, 1992.

Čeleda, Jaroslav, and Oldřich Pulkert. "Beethoven's 'Unsterbliche Geliebte.'" In *Ludwig van Beethoven im Herzen Europas,* edited by Oldřich Pulkert and Hans-Werner Küthen, 383–408. Prague, 2000.

Charlton, David. "Revolutionary Hymn." *NG2* 15, 776–78.

Churgin, Bathia. "Beethoven and Mozart's Requiem: A New Connection." *Journal of Musicology* 5 (1987): 457–77.

Cole, Malcolm. "Techniques of Surprise in the Sonata-Rondos of Beethoven." *Studia Musicologica Academiae Scientiarum Hungaricae* 12 (1970): 232–62.

Comini, Alessandra. *The Changing Image of Beethoven: A Study in Mythmaking.* New York, 1987.

Cone, Edward T. "Beethoven's Experiments in Composition: The Late Bagatelles." In *BS,* 2:84–105.

———. "Beethoven's *Orpheus*—or Jander's." *19th Century Music* 8 (1985): 283–86.

Cooper, Barry. *Beethoven.* Oxford, 2000.

———. *Beethoven and the Creative Process.* Oxford, 1990.

———. *The Beethoven Compendium: A Guide to Beethoven's Life and Music.* London, 1991.

———. "Beethoven's Tenth Symphony." *Journal of the Royal Musical Association* 117 (1992): 324–29.

———. Review of G. Altman, *Beethoven: A Man of His Word. Beethoven Journal* 11/2 (1996): 18–24.

———. Review of *The Beethoven Quartet Companion. Music and Letters* 76 (1995): 445–47.

Cooper, Martin. *Beethoven: The Last Decade, 1817–1827.* Revised ed., Oxford, 1985.

Coren, Daniel. "Structural Relations between Op. 28 and Op. 36." In *BS,* 2:66–83.

Czerny, Carl. *Über den richtigen Vortrag der sämtlichen Beethoven'schen Klavierwerke.* Edited by Paul Badura-Skoda. Vienna, 1963.

Dahlhaus, Carl. *Beethoven: Approaches to His Music.* Translated by Mary Whittall. Oxford, 1991.

———. "Bemerkungen zu Beethovens 8. Symphonie." *Schweizerische Musikzeitung* 110 (1970): 205–9.

———. "La Malinconia." In *Ludwig van Beethoven,* edited by Ludwig Finscher. 200–211. Darmstadt, 1983.

Dawson, P. M. S. *The Unacknowledged Legislator: Shelley and Politics.* Oxford, 1980.

Dean, Winton. "Beethoven and Opera." In *The Beethoven Reader,* edited by Denis Arnold and Nigel Fortune, 331–86. New York, 1971.

De Lerma, Dominique René. "Beethoven as a Black Composer." *Black Music Research Newsletter* 8/1 (1985): 3–5.

Dennis, David B. *Beethoven in German Politics, 1870–1989.* New Haven, Conn., 1996.

DeNora, Tia. *Beethoven and the Construction of Genius: Musical Politics in Vienna, 1792–1803.* Berkeley, 1995.

Deutsch, Otto Erich. *Schubert: A Documentary Biography.* Translated by Eric Blom. London, 1946.

Deutsch, Otto Erich, ed. *Schubert: Memoirs by His Friends.* Translated by Rosamond Ley and John Nowell. London, 1958.

Dies, Albert Christoph. *Biographische Nachrichten von Joseph Haydn.* Vienna, 1810.

Dill, Marshall. *Germany: A Modern History.* Revised ed. Ann Arbor, Mich., 1970.

Drabkin, William. "The Agnus Dei of Beethoven's *Missa Solemnis:* The Growth of Its Form." In *Beethoven's Compositional Process,* edited by William Kinderman, 131–59. Lincoln, Neb., 1991.

———. *Beethoven: Missa Solemnis.* Cambridge, 1991.

————. "The Introduction to Beethoven's 'Kreutzer' Sonata: A Historical Perspective." In *Beethoven's Violin Sonatas*. Edited by Lewis Lockwood and Mark Kroll. Forthcoming.

————. *A Reader's Guide to Haydn's Early String Quartets*. Westport, Conn., 2000.

————. "The Sketches for Beethoven's Piano Sonata in C Minor, Opus 111." Ph.D. diss., Princeton University, 1977.

Duport, Jean Louis. *Essai sur le doigté du violoncelle*. Paris, c. 1813.

Ealy, George T. "Of Ear Trumpets and a Resonance Plate: Early Hearing Aids and Beethoven's Hearing Perception." *19th Century Music* 17 (1994): 262–73.

Edelmann, Bernd. "Die poetische Idee des Adagio von Beethovens Quartet Op. 18 Nr. 1." In *Festschrift Rudolph Bockholdt zum 60. Geburtstag*, edited by Norbert Dubowy and Sören Meyer-Eller, 247–67. Pfaffenhofen, 1992.

Einstein, Alfred. *Mozart: His Character, His Work*. Translated by Arthur Mendel and Nathan Broder. New York, 1945.

Engländer, Richard. "Paer's 'Leonora' und Beethoven's 'Fidelio.'" *Neues Beethoven-Jahrbuch* 4 (1930): 118–32.

Fecker, Adolf. *Die Entstehung von Beethovens Musik zu Goethes Trauerspiel Egmont: Eine Abhandlung über die Skizzen*. Hamburg, 1978.

Fillion, Michelle. "Beethoven's Mass in C and the Search for Inner Peace." *BF* 7 (1999): 1–16.

Fink, Gonthier-Louis. "The French Revolution as Reflected in German Literature and Political Journals from 1789 to 1800." In *The Internalized Revolution: German Reactions to the French Revolution, 1789–1989*, edited by Erhard Bahr and Thomas P. Saine, 11–32. New York, 1992.

Finscher, Ludwig. "Zur Interpretation des langsamen Satzes aus Beethovens Klaviersonate Opus 10 Nr. 3." In *International Musicological Society, Report of the Eleventh Congress, Copenhagen, 1972*, edited by Henrik Glahn, Søren Sørensen, and Peter Ryom, 1:82–85. Copenhagen, 1974.

Fischer, Kurt von. "Eroica-Variationen Op. 35 und Eroica-Finale." *Schweizerische Musikzeitung* 89 (1949): 282–86.

Fiske, Roger. *Beethoven's Missa Solemnis*. New York, 1979.

Flaubert, Gustave. *Correspondance*. Paris, 1893.

Flesch, Carl. *Kunst des Violinspiels*. Berlin, 1923.

Floros, Constantin. *Beethovens Eroica und Prometheus-Musik: Sujet-Studien*. Wilhelmshaven, 1978.

Forchert, Arno. "Die Darstellung von Melancholie in Beethovens Opus 18 Nr. 6." In *Ludwig van Beethoven*, edited by Ludwig Finscher, 212–39. Darmstadt, 1983.

Freud, Sigmund. *The Interpretation of Dreams*. Standard Edition, vol. 4. London, 1953.

Frimmel, Theodor von. *Ludwig van Beethoven*. 4th ed. Berlin, 1912.

————. *Beethoven-Handbuch*. 2 vols. Leipzig, 1926.

————. "Beethoven's Spaziergang nach Wiener-Neustadt." In *Beethoven-Forschung: Lose Blätter.* 9 (1923): 2–12.

Frohlich, Martha. *Beethoven's "Appassionata" Sonata.* Oxford, 1991.

Gál, Hans. "Die Stileigentümlichkeiten des jungen Beethoven." *Studien zur Musikwissenschaft* 5 (1916): 58–115.

Galliver, David. "Jean-Nicolas Bouilly (1763–1842), Successor of Sedaine." *Studies in Music* (Nedlands, Australia) 13 (1973): 16–33.

————. "Leonore, ou L'Amour Conjugale: A Celebrated Offspring of the French Revolution." In *Music and the French Revolution,* edited by Malcolm Boyd, 157–68. Cambridge, 1992.

Gardiner, William. *Music and Friends; or, Pleasant Recollections of a Dilettante.* 3 vols. London, 1838–53.

————. *The Music of Nature.* London, 1832.

Gedo, Mary Mathews. "The Healing Power of Art: Goya as His Own Physician." In *Psychoanalytic Perspectives on Art,* edited by Mary Mathews Gedo, 1:75–106. Hillsdale, N.J., 1985.

Gooch, G. P. *Germany and the French Revolution.* London, 1920.

Grant, Brian, ed. *The Quiet Ear: Deafness in Literature.* London, 1987.

Greene, David B. *Temporal Processes in Beethoven's Music.* New York, 1982.

Greenfield, Donald. "Sketch Studies for Three Movements of Beethoven's String Quartets Opus 18, Nos. 1 and 2." Ph. D. diss., Princeton University, 1982.

Griesinger, Georg August. *Joseph Haydn: Eighteenth-Century Gentleman and Genius.* Translated by Vernon Gotwals. Madison, Wisc., 1963. Translation of Griesinger's *Biographische Notizen über Joseph Haydn* (Leipzig, 1810).

Gruber, Gernot. *Mozart and Posterity.* Translated by R. S. Furness. London, 1991.

Gülke, Peter. *"Triumph der neuen Tonkunst": Mozarts späte Sinfonien und ihr Umfeld.* Kassel, 1998.

Hansen, Joseph, ed. *Quellen zur Geschichte des Rheinlandes im Zeitalter der französischen Revolution, 1780–1801.* 4 vols. Bonn, 1931–38.

Haydn, Joseph. *Gesammelte Briefe und Aufzeichnungen.* Edited by Denes Bartha. Kassel, 1965.

Heartz, Daniel. "Thomas Attwood's Lessons in Composition with Mozart." *Papers of the Royal Musical Association* 100 (1973–74): 175–84.

Helm, Theodor. *Beethovens Streichquartette.* Leipzig, 1885.

Herder, Johann Gottfried von. *Reflections on the Philosophy of the History of Mankind.* Abridged and edited by Frank Manuel. Chicago, 1968. Translation of Herder's *Ideen zur Philosophie der Geschichte der Menschheit* (1784–91).

Hertzmann, Erich, C. B. Oldham, Daniel Heartz, and Alfred Mann, eds. *Thomas Attwoods Theorie- und Kompositionsstudien bei Mozart.* In *Neue Ausgabe sämtlicher Werke,* by Wolfgang Amadeus Mozart, vol. X/30/I. Kassel, 1965.

Hess, Willy. *Beethovens Oper Fidelio und ihre drei Fassungen.* Zurich, 1953.

Heuberger, Richard. *Erinnerungen an Johannes Brahms: Tagebuchnotizen aus den Jahren 1875 bis 1897.* 2nd ed. Edited by Kurt Hofmann. Tutzing, 1971.

Hinton, Stephen. "Not *Which* Tones: The Crux of Beethoven's Ninth." *19th Century Music* 22 (1998): 61–77.

Hobsbawm, Eric. *The Age of Revolution. 1789–1848.* New York, 1962.

Hoffmann, Ernst Theodor Amadeus. *Schriften zur Musik.* Edited by Friedrich Schnapp. Munich, 1963.

Hoven, Louis von. *Ein Brief von Beethovens Grossneffen Louis von Hoven an seine Schwester Marie Weidinger in Wien aus dem Jahre 1875.* Edited by Sieghard Brandenburg. Bonn, 1984.

Howard, Martha Walling. *The Influence of Plutarch in the Major European Literatures of the Eighteenth Century.* Chapel Hill, N.C., 1970.

Hoyle, Fred. *The Black Cloud.* London, 1957.

Howe, Mark A. de Wolfe. *The Boston Symphony Orchestra.* Boston, 1931.

Indy, Vincent d'. "Beethoven." In *Cobbett's Cyclopaedia of Chamber Music.* Oxford, 1929.

Jander, Owen. "'Let Your Deafness No Longer be a Secret—Even in Art:' Self-Portraiture and the Third Movement of the C-Minor Symphony." *BF* 8 (2000): 25–70.

———. "Beethoven's 'Orpheus in Hades': The Andante con moto of the Fourth Piano Concerto." *19th Century Music* 8 (1985): 195–212.

———. "Orpheus Revisited: A Ten-Year Retrospect on the Andante con moto of Beethoven's Fourth Piano Concerto." *19th Century Music* 19 (1995): 31–49.

———. "The Prophetic Conversation in Beethoven's 'Scene by the Brook.'" *The Musical Quarterly* 77 (1993): 508–59.

Johnson, Douglas. *Beethoven's Early Sketches in the "Fischhof Miscellany," Berlin Autograph 28.* 2 vols. Ann Arbor, Mich., 1978. Partially published with the same title: Ann Arbor, UMI Research Press, 1980.

———. "1794–1795: Decisive Years in Beethoven's Early Development." In *BS*, 3:2–14.

Johnson, Paul. *The Birth of the Modern: World Society, 1815–1830.* New York, 1991.

Kagan, Susan. *Archduke Rudolph, Beethoven's Patron, Pupil, and Friend: His Life and Music.* Stuyvesant, N.Y., 1988.

Kallick, Jenny. "A Study of the Advanced Sketches and Full Score Autograph for the First Movement of Beethoven's Ninth Symphony." Ph.D. diss., Yale University, 1987.

Kaznelson, Siegmund. *Beethovens ferne und unsterbliche Geliebte.* Zurich, 1954.

Kerman, Joseph. "An die ferne Geliebte." In *BS*, 1:123–57.

———. "Beethoven's Minority." In *Haydn, Mozart and Beethoven: Essays in Honor of Alan Tyson,* edited by Sieghard Brandenburg, 151–74. Oxford, 1998.

———. *Concerto Conversations.* Cambridge, Mass., 1999.

————. *The Beethoven Quartets.* New York, 1967.

————. ed. *Ludwig van Beethoven: Autograph Miscellany from Circa 1786 to 1799: British Museum Additional Manuscript 29801, ff. 39–162 (The "Kafka" Sketchbook).* 2 vols. London, 1970.

Kerman, Joseph, and Alan Tyson. "Beethoven." In *NG2*, augmented by Scott Burnham.

Kerst, Friedrich, ed. *Die Erinnerungen an Beethoven.* 2 vols. Stuttgart, 1913.

Kinderman, William. *Beethoven.* Berkeley, Calif., 1995.

————. *Beethoven's Diabelli Variations.* Oxford, 1987.

Kirkendale, Warren. *Fugue and Fugato in Rococo and Classical Chamber Music.* 2nd ed. Translated by Margaret Bent and the author. Durham, N.C., 1979.

————. "The 'Great Fugue,' Op. 133: Beethoven's 'Art of Fugue.'" *Acta Musicologica* 35 (1963): 14–24.

————. "New Roads to Old Ideas in Beethoven's 'Missa Solemnis.'" In *The Creative World of Beethoven,* edited by Paul Henry Lang, 163–99. New York, 1971.

Köchel, Ludwig Ritter von. *Chronologisch-thematisches Verzeichnis sämtlicher Tonwerke Wolfgang Amadé Mozarts.* 3rd ed., edited by Alfred Einstein. Leipzig, 1937.

Kohn, Hans. *The Mind of Germany: The Education of a Nation.* New York, 1960.

Kramer, Jonathan. "Multiple and Non-linear Time in Beethoven's Opus 135." *Perspectives of New Music* 11 (1973): 122–45.

Kramer, Richard. "Beethoven and Carl-Heinrich Graun." In *BS,* 1:18–44.

————. *A Beethoven Sketchbook from the Summer of 1800.* Bonn, 1999.

————. "Between Cavatina and Ouverture." *BF* 1 (1992): 165–90.

————. "Counterpoint and Syntax: On a Difficult Passage in the First Movement of Beethoven's String Quartet in C Minor, Op. 18 No. 4." *In Beiträge zu Beethovens Kammermusik; Symposion Bonn 1984,* edited by Sieghard Brandenburg and Helmut Loos, 111–24. Munich, 1987.

————. "Notes to Beethoven's Education." *JAMS* 28 (1975): 72–101.

————. "'Das Organische der Fuge': On the Autograph of Beethoven's String Quartet in F Major, Opus 59 No. 1." In *The String Quartets of Haydn, Mozart, and Beethoven: Studies of the Autograph Manuscripts,* edited by Christoph Wolff, 223–65. Cambridge, Mass., 1980.

————. "In Search of Palestrina: Beethoven in the Archives." In *Haydn, Mozart, and Beethoven: Essays in Honor of Alan Tyson,* edited by Sieghard Brandenburg, 283–300. Oxford, 1998.

————. "An Unfinished Concertante by Beethoven." In *BS,* 2:33–36.

Kropfinger, Klaus. "Beethoven." In *MGG: Personenteil* 2, cols. 667–915.

————. "Das gespaltene Werk: Beethovens Streichquartett Op. 130/133." In *Beiträge zu Beethovens Kammermusik,* edited by Sieghard Brandenburg and Helmut Loos, 296–335. Munich, 1987.

————. *Wagner and Beethoven: Richard Wagner's Reception of Beethoven.* Translated by Peter Palmer. Cambridge, 1991.

Kross, Siegfried. "Improvisation und Konzertform bei Beethoven." In *Beethoven-Kolloquium 1977: Dokumentation und Aufführungspraxis,* edited by Rudolf Klein, 132–39. Kassel, 1978.

Kunze, Stefan, ed. *Ludwig van Beethoven, Die Werke im Spiegel seiner Zeit: Gesammelte Konzertberichte und Rezensionen bis 1830.* Laaber, 1987.

Küthen, Hans-Werner. "Neue Aspekte zur Entstehung von *Wellingtons Sieg,*" *BJ* 8 (1971/2): 73–92.

Landon, H. C. Robbins. *Haydn: Chronicle and Works.* 5 vols. Bloomington, Ind., 1976–80.

Lang, Paul Henry, ed. *The Creative World of Beethoven.* New York, 1971.

Langsam, Walter. *Francis the Good: The Education of an Emperor.* New York, 1949.

Larkin, Edward. "Beethoven's Medical History." In *Beethoven: The Last Decade, 1817–1827,* by Martin Cooper. London, 1970. Revised ed., 1985.

Lee, Simon. *David.* London, 1999.

Lefebvre, Georges. *The French Revolution.* Translated by Elizabeth Moss Evanson. 2 vols. New York, 1962–64.

————. *Napoleon, from 18 Brumaire to Tilsit, 1799–1807.* Vol. 1. Translated by Henry F. Stockhold. New York, 1969.

Le Huray, Peter, and James Day, eds. *Music and Aesthetics in the Eighteenth and Early-Nineteenth Centuries.* Cambridge, 1981.

Lenz, Wilhelm von. *Beethoven: Eine Kunststudie.* 5 vols. Cassel, 1855–60.

————. *Beethoven et ses trois styles.* 2 vols. St. Petersburg, 1852–53.

Leppmann, Wolfgang. *Rilke: A Life.* Translated with the author by Russell M. Stockman. New York, 1984.

Leux, Irmgard. *Christian Gottlob Neefe (1748–1798).* Leipzig, 1925.

Levy, David Benjamin. *Beethoven: The Ninth Symphony.* New York, 1995.

Levy, Janet M. *Beethoven's Compositional Choices: The Two Versions of Opus 18, No. 1, First Movement.* Philadelphia, 1982.

Leyda, Jay, and Sergei Bertensson, eds. *The Musorgsky Reader: A Life of Modeste Petrovich Musorgsky in Letters and Documents.* New York, 1947.

Libin, Lawrence. "The Instruments." In *Eighteenth-Century Keyboard Music,* edited by Robert L. Marshall, 1–32. New York, 1994.

Licht, Fred. *Canova.* New York, 1983.

Licht, Fred. *Goya: The Origins of the Modern Temper in Art.* New York, 1979.

Lochhead, Judy. "The Temporal in Beethoven's Opus 135: When are Ends Beginnings?" *In Theory Only* 4/7 (1979): 3–30.

Locke, Ralph. "Paris: Centre of Intellectual Ferment." In *The Early Romantic Era: Between Revolutions, 1789 and 1848,* edited by Alexander Ringer, 32–83. Englewood Cliffs, N.J., 1991.

Lockwood, Lewis. "The Autograph of the First Movement of the Sonata for Violoncello and Pianoforte, Opus 69." In Lockwood, *Studies*, 17–94.

———. "Beethoven before 1800: The Mozart Legacy." *BF* 3 (1994): 39–53.

———. "Beethoven, Florestan, and the Varieties of Heroism." In *Beethoven and His World*, edited by Scott Burnham and Michael P. Steinberg, 27–47. Princeton, N.J., 2000.

———. "Beethoven's Early Works for Violoncello and Contemporary Violoncello Technique." In *Beethoven-Kolloquium 1977: Dokumentation und Aufführungspraxis*, edited by Rudolf Klein, 174–82. Kassel, 1978.

———. "Beethoven's Emergence from Crisis: The Cello Sonatas Opus 102 (1815)." *Journal of Musicology* 16 (1998): 301–22.

———. "Beethoven's First Symphony: A Farewell to the Eighteenth Century." In *Essays in Musicology: A Tribute to Alvin Johnson*, edited by Lewis Lockwood and Edward Roesner, 235–46. Philadelphia, 1990.

———. "Beethoven's 'Kakadu' Variations, Op. 121a: A Study in Paradox." In *Pianist, Scholar, Connoisseur: Essays in Honor of Jacob Lateiner*, edited by Bruce Brubaker and Jane Gottlieb, 95–108. Stuyvesant, N.Y., 2000.

———. "Beethoven's Opus 69 Revisited." Paper given at International Conference on Beethoven's Music for Violoncello (Bonn, 1998), to be published in the conference proceedings.

———. "On Beethoven's Sketches and Autographs." In Lockwood, *Studies*, 4–16. Originally published in 1970 with subtitle: "Some Problems of Definition and Interpretation."

———. "The Problem of Closure: Some Examples from the Middle-Period Chamber Music." In Lockwood, *Studies*, 181–97.

———. "A Problem of Form: The 'Scherzo' of Beethoven's String Quartet in F Major, Opus 59 No. 1." *BF* 2 (1993): 85–96. See also Jonathan Del Mar's comments on this article and my reply, in *BF* 8 (2001): 165–72.

———. "Process vs. Limits: A View of the Quartet in F Major, Opus 59 No. 1," in Lockwood, *Studies*, 198–208.

———. "Reshaping the Genre: Beethoven's Piano Sonatas from Op. 22 to Op. 28." *Israel Studies in Musicology* 6 (1996): 1–16.

———. Review of *Beethoven*, by Maynard Solomon, *19th Century Music* 3 (1979): 76–82.

Lodes, Birgit. *Das Gloria in Beethovens Missa Solemnis*. Tutzing, 1997.

Longyear, Rey M. "Beethoven and Romantic Irony." In *The Creative World of Beethoven*, edited by Paul Henry Lang, 145–62. New York, 1971.

Loos, Helmut. "Beethoven in Prag 1796 und 1798." In *Beethoven und Böhmen*, edited by Sieghard Brandenburg and Martella Gutierrez-Denhoff, 63–90. Bonn, 1998.

Lühning, Helga. "'Fidelio' in Prag." In *Beethoven und Böhmen*, edited by Sieghard Brandenburg and Martella Gutierrez-Denhoff, 349–91. Bonn, 1998.

————. "Gattungen des Liedes," in S. Brandenburg and H. Loos, eds., *Beiträge zu Beethovens Kammermusik,* edited by Sieghard Brandenburg and Helmut Loos, 191–204. Munich, 1987.

————. "Vom Mythos der Ur-Leonore." In *Von der Leonore zum Fidelio: Vorträge und Referate des Bonner Symposions 1997,* edited by Helga Lühning and Wolfram Steinbeck, 41–64. Frankfurt, 2000.

Lühning, Helga, and Wolfram Steinbeck, eds. *Von der Leonore zum Fidelio: Vorträge und Referate des Bonner Symposions 1997.* Frankfurt 2000.

Lvov, Nikolai Aleksandrovich, and Ivan Prach, eds. *A Collection of Russian Folk Songs.* Edited by Malcolm Hamrick Brown and Margarita Mazo. Ann Arbor, Mich., 1987.

Macdonald, Hugh. "Fantasy and Order in Beethoven's Phantasie Op. 77." In *Modern Musical Scholarship,* edited by Edward Olleson, 141–50. Stocksfield, England, 1980.

Mann, Thomas. *Doctor Faustus: The Life of the German Composer Adrian Leverkühn, as Told by a Friend.* Translated by H. T. Lowe-Porter. New York, 1948.

Marek, George R. *Beethoven: Biography of a Genius.* New York, 1969.

Marshall, Robert L. "Bach and Mozart's Artistic Maturity." *Bach Perspectives* 3 (1998): 47–79.

————. *Mozart Speaks: Views on Music, Musicians, and the World, Drawn from the Letters of Wolfgang Amadeus Mozart and Other Early Accounts.* New York, 1991.

Marshall, Robert L., ed. *Eighteenth-Century Keyboard Music.* New York, 1994.

Marston, Nicholas. *Beethoven's Piano Sonata in E. Op. 109.* Oxford, 1995.

Martin, Russell. *Beethoven's Hair.* New York, 2000.

Marx, Adolph Bernhard. *Ludwig van Beethoven: Leben und Schaffen.* Leipzig, 1859.

May, Jurgen. "Beethoven and Prince Karl Lichnowsky." *BF* 3 (1994): 29–38.

Mayr, Josef Karl. *Wien im Zeitalter Napoleons: Staatsfinanzen, Lebenserhältnisse, Beamte, und Militär.* Vienna, 1940.

McClary, Susan. *Feminine Endings: Music, Gender, and Sexuality.* Minneapolis, 1991.

McGrann, Jeremiah. "Beethoven's Mass in C, Opus 86: Genesis and Compositional Background." Ph.D. diss., Harvard University, 1991.

Mellers, Wilfrid. *Beethoven and the Voice of God.* London, 1983.

Melville, Derek. "Beethoven's Pianos." In *The Beethoven Reader,* edited by Denis Arnold and Nigel Fortune, 41–67. New York, 1971.

Mies, Paul. *Beethoven's Sketches: An Analysis of His Style Based on a Study of His Sketch-Books.* Translated by Doris L. Mackinnon. New York, 1974.

————. "Beethoven—Collin—Shakespeare: Zur Coriolan-Ouverture," *BJ* 6 (1965): 260–68.

————. "Quasi una fantasia." In *Colloquium Amicorum: Joseph Schmidt-Görg zum 70. Geburtstag,* edited by Siegried Kross and Hans Schmidt, 239–49. Bonn, 1967.

Mongredien, Jean. *French Music from the Enlightenment to Romanticism: 1789–1830*. Translated by Sylvian Fremaux, Portland, 1986.

Morrow, Mary Sue. *Concert Life in Haydn's Vienna: Aspects of a Developing Musical and Social Institution*. Stuvesant, N.Y., 1989.

Mozart, Wolfgang Amadeus. *The Letters of Mozart and His Family*. Edited and translated by Emily Anderson. 2nd ed. 3 vols. London, 1985.

———. *Mozart's Letters, Mozart's Life: Selected Letters*. Edited and translated by Robert Spaethling. New York, 2000.

Müller von Asow, Hedwig. *Beethoven, Heiligenstadter Testament: Faksimile*. Vienna, 1969.

Neubauer, John. *The Emancipation of Music from Language: Departure from Mimesis in Eighteenth-Century Aesthetics*. New Haven, Conn., 1986.

Newbould, Brian. *Schubert: The Music and the Man*. Berkeley, 1997.

Newman, William S. *Beethoven on Beethoven: Playing His Piano Music His Way*. New York, 1988.

Nohl, Ludwig. *Beethoven nach den Schilderungen seiner Zeitgenossen*. Stuttgart, 1877.

Nottebohm, Gustav. *Beethoveniana: Aufsätze und Mittheilungen*. Leipzig, 1872.

———. *Beethovens Studien*. Leipzig, 1873.

———. *Ein Skizzenbuch von Beethoven aus dem Jahre 1803, in Auszügen dargestellt*. Leipzig, 1880.

———. *Ein Skizzenbuch von Beethoven, beschrieben und in Auszügen dargestellt*. Leipzig, 1865.

Ong, Seow-Chin Peter. "Source Studies for Beethoven's Piano Trio in B-flat Major, Op. 97 ('Archduke')." Ph.D. diss., University of California, Berkeley, 1995.

Palestrina, Giovanni Pierluigi da. *Pope Marcellus Mass*, edited by Lewis Lockwood. New York, 1975.

Palisca, Claude V. "French Revolutionary Models for Beethoven's *Eroica* Funeral March." In *Music and Context: Essays for John M. Ward*, edited by Anne Dhu McLucas, 198–209. Cambridge, Mass., 1985.

———. *Humanism in Italian Renaissance Musical Thought*. New Haven, Conn. 1995.

Piercy, Marge. "A Writer's Notebook." *The New York Times*, December 20, 1999, sec. B, 1–2.

Plantinga, Leon. *Beethoven's Concertos: History, Style, Performance*. New York, 1999.

Platen, Emil. "Ein Notierungsproblem in Beethovens späten Streichquartetten." *BJ* 8 (1971/72): 147–56.

Presslaff, Hilary Tann. "The Investigation." *Perspectives of New Music* 20 (1981–82): 526–59.

Pulkert, Oldřich. "Beethoven's 'Immortal Beloved,'" *The Beethoven Journal* 15/1 (2000): 2–18.

Ratner, Leonard G. *Beethoven String Quartets: Compositional Strategies and Rhetoric.* Stanford, 1995.

Ratz, Erwin. *Die Originalfassung des Streichquartettes Op. 130 von Beethoven.* Vienna, 1957.

Reicha, Antoine. "Notes sur Antoine-Joseph Reicha." Ms. in the Bibliothèque Nationale, Paris. [1824.]

Reinhöl, Fritz von. "Neues zu Beethoven's Lehrjahr bei Haydn." *Neues Beethoven-Jahrbuch* 6 (1935): 36–47.

Reynolds, Christopher. "From Berloiz's Fugitives to Godard's Terrorists: Artistic Responses to Beethoven's Last Quartets." *BF* 8 (2000): 147–63.

Rich, Adrienne. "The Ninth Symphony of Beethoven Understood at Last as a Sexual Message." In her *Diving into the Wreck,* 43. New York, 1962.

Ries, Ferdinand. *Briefe und Dokumente.* Edited by Cecil Hill. Bonn, 1982.

Riethmüller, Albrecht, Carl Dahlhaus, and Alexander L. Ringer, eds. *Beethoven: Interpretationen seiner Werke.* 2 vols. Laaber, 1994.

Riezler, Walter. *Beethoven,* Translated by G. D. H. Pidcock. London, 1938.

Ringer, Alexander L. "Beethoven and the London Pianoforte School." *The Musical Quarterly* 56 (1970): 742–58.

Roberts, Warren. *Jacques-Louis David, Revolutionary Artist: Art, Politics, and the French Revolution.* Chapel Hill, N.C., 1989.

Rolland, Romain. *Goethe and Beethoven.* Translated by G. A. Pfister and E. S. Kemp. New York, 1931.

Rosen, Charles. *The Classical Style: Haydn, Mozart, Beethoven.* Expanded ed. New York, 1997.

———. *The Romantic Generation.* Cambridge, Mass., 1995.

Rosenfeld, Paul. "Beethoven." *The New Republic,* May 12, 1917; reprinted in his *Discoveries of A Music Critic,* 67–72. New York, 1936.

Rumph, Stephen Charles. "Beethoven after Napoleon: Political Romanticism in the Late Works." Ph.D. diss., University of California, Berkeley, 1997.

Saffle, Michael, and Jeffrey R. Saffle. "Medical Histories of Prominent Composers: Recent Research and Discoveries." *Acta Musicologica* 65 (1993): 77–101.

Saine, Thomas. *Black Bread, White Bread: German Intellectuals and the French Revolution.* Columbia, S.C., 1988.

Saloman, Ora Frishberg. *Beethoven's Symphonies and J. S. Dwight: The Birth of American Music Criticism.* Boston, 1995.

Sams, Eric, and Graham Johnson. "The Romantic Lied." In *NG2.*

Sandberger, Adolf. *Ausgewählte Aufsätze zus Musikgeschichte.* 2 vols. Munich, 1924.

Schäfer, Heinrich. *Bernard Romberg, Sein Leben und Wirken: Ein Beitrag zur Geschichte des Violoncells.* Lübben, Ger., 1931.

Schafer, Hollace Ann. " 'A Wisely Ordered "Phantasie" ': Joseph Haydn's Creative

Process from the Sketches and Drafts for Instrumental Music." Ph.D. diss., Brandeis University, 1987.

Schama, Simon. *Citizens: A Chronicle of the French Revolution.* New York, 1989.

Schenker, Heinrich. "Beethovens Dritte Sinfonie zum erstenmal in ihrem wahren Inhalt dargestellt." In *Das Meisterwerk in der Musik,* 3:25–101. Munich, 1930. English translation, *The Masterwork in Music: a Yearbook,* edited by William Drabkin, translated by Ian Bent, vol. 3 (Cambridge, 1994–97).

—————. *Beethovens Neunte Sinfonie: Eine Darstellung des musikalischen Inhaltes unter fortlaufender Berücksichtigung, auch des Vortages und der Literatur.* Vienna, 1912 (reprinted 1969).

Schiedermair, Ludwig. *Der Junge Beethoven.* Leipzig, 1925.

Schiller, Friedrich. *On the Aesthetic Education of Man in a Series of Letters.* Translated by Reginald Snell. New York, 1954.

Schindler, Anton. *Beethoven as I Knew Him: A Biography.* Edited by Donald W. MacArdle, translated by Constance S. Jolly. Chapel Hill, N.C., 1966.

Schleuning, Peter. "Beethoven in alter Deutung: Der 'neue Weg' mit der Sinfonia Eroica." *Archiv für Musikwissenschaft* 44 (1987): 165–94.

Schlosser, Johann Aloys. *Ludwig van Beethoven: Eine Biographie.* Prague, 1828.

Schmalfeldt, Janet. "Form as the Process of Becoming: The Beethoven-Hegelian Tradition and the 'Tempest' Sonata." *BF* 4 (1995): 37–72.

Schmidt, Hans. "Verzeichnis der Skizzen Beethovens." *BJ* 6 (1965/68): 7–128.

Schmidt-Görg, Joseph. "Ein Schiller-Zitat Beethovens in neuer Sicht." In *Musik, Edition, Interpretation: Gedenkschrift Günter Henle,* edited by Martin Bente, 423–26. Munich, 1980.

—————. "Das Wiener Tagebuch des Mannheimer Hofkapellmeisters Michael Frey." *BJ* 6 (1965/68): 129–204.

Schmidt-Görg, Joseph, and Hans Schmidt, eds. *Ludwig van Beethoven.* Hamburg, 1974.

Schmitz, Arnold. *Das Romantische Beethovenbild.* Berlin, 1927.

Schnaus, Peter. *E. T. A. Hoffmann als Beethoven-Rezensent der Allgemeinen Musikalischen Zeitung.* Munich, 1977.

Schoenberg, Arnold. *Theory of Harmony.* Translated by R. E. Carter, New York, 1978.

Schom, Alan. *Napoleon Bonaparte.* New York, 1997.

Schopenhauer, Arthur. *The World as Will and Representation.* 2 vols. Translated by E. F. J. Payne. New York, 1966.

Schulze, Hans-Joachim, and Christoph Wolff. *Bach Compendium: Analytisch-bibliographisches Repertorium der Werke Johann Sebastian Bachs.* 7 vols. Leipzig, 1986–.

Schumann, Robert. *On Music and Musicians.* Edited by Konrad Wolff, translated by Paul Rosenfeld. New York, 1946.

Seyfried, Ignaz von. *Beethovens Studien.* 2nd ed. Leipzig, 1853.

Sharpe, Lesley. *Friedrich Schiller: Drama, Thought, and Politics.* Cambridge, 1991.

Sipe, Thomas. *Beethoven, Eroica Symphony.* Cambridge, 1998.

Sisman, Elaine R. "C. P. E. Bach, Beethoven, and the Labyrinth of Melancholy." unpublished paper.

———. *Haydn and the Classical Variation.* Cambridge, Mass., 1993.

———. "Pathos and the Pathétique: Rhetorical Stance in Beethoven's C-Minor Sonata, Op. 13." *BF* 3 (1993): 81–105.

Sisman, Elaine R., ed., *Haydn and His World.* Princeton, N.J., 1997.

Skowroneck, Tilman. "The Keyboard Instruments of the Young Beethoven." In *Beethoven and His World,* edited by Scott Burnham and Michael P. Steinberg, 151–92. Princeton, N.J., 2000.

Smolle, Kurt. *Wohnstätten Ludwig van Beethovens von 1792 bis zu seinem Tod.* Bonn, 1970.

Smyth, David H. "Codas in Classical Form: Aspects of Large-Scale Rhythm and Pattern Completion." Ph.D. diss., University of Texas at Austin, 1985.

Solie, Ruth. "Beethoven as Secular Humanist: Ideology and the Ninth Symphony in Nineteenth-Century Criticism" In *Explorations in Music, the Arts, and Ideas: Essays in Honor of Leonard B. Meyer,* edited by Eugene Narmour and Ruth A. Solie, 1–42. Stuyvesant, N.Y., 1988.

Solomon, Maynard, *Beethoven.* 2nd ed. New York, 1998.

———. "Beethoven, Freemasonry, and the *Tagebuch.*" *BF* 8 (2001): 101–46.

———. "The Creative Periods of Beethoven." In his *Beethoven Essays,* 116–25. Cambridge, Mass., 1988.

———. "Economic Circumstances of the Beethoven Household in Bonn." *JAMS* 50 (1997): 331–51.

———. *Mozart: A Life.* New York, 1995.

———. "Recherche de Josephine Deym." In his *Beethoven Essays,* 157–65. Cambridge, Mass., 1988.

———. "The Quest for Faith." In his *Beethoven Essays,* 216–32.

Solomon, Maynard, ed. "Beethoven's *Tagebuch* of 1812–1818." In *BS,* 3:193–288; also in Solomon's *Beethoven Essays.* 233–95. Cambridge, Mass., 1988.

Sonneck, Oscar G. *Beethoven: Impressions of Contemporaries.* New York, 1926.

Spurgeon, Caroline F. E. *Shakespeare's Imagery and What It Tells Us.* New York, 1935.

Stadlen, Peter. "Schindler und die Konversationshefte." *Oesterreichische Musikzeitung* 34 (1979): 2–18.

———. "Schindler's Beethoven Forgeries." *The Musical Times* 118 (1977): 549–52.

———. "Zu Schindlers Fälschungen in Beethovens Konversationshefte." *Oesterreichische Musikzeitung* 32 (1977): 246–52.

Staehelin, Martin. "Another Approach to Beethoven's Last String Quartet Oeuvre: The Unfinished String Quintet of 1826/27." In *The String Quartets of Haydn,*

Mozart, and Beethoven, edited by Christoph Wolff, 302–28. Cambridge, Mass., 1980.

Staël, Germaine de. *De l'Allemagne.* 3 vols. London, 1813.

Steblin, Rita. *A History of Key Characteristics in the Eighteenth and Early Nineteenth Centuries.* Ann Arbor, 1983.

Stowell, Robin. *Beethoven, Violin Concerto.* Cambridge, 1998.

Stowell, Robin, ed. *The Cambridge Companion to the Cello.* Cambridge, 1999.

Sulzer, Johann Georg. *Allgemeine Theorie der schönen Kunste.* Leipzig, 1792.

Swinburne, Henry. *The Courts of Europe at the Close of the Last Century.* Edited by Charles White. 2 vols. London, 1841.

Taruskin, Richard. "Resisting the Ninth." *19th Century Music* 12 (1989): 241–56.

Tellenbach, Marie-Elisabeth. *Beethoven und seine "Unsterbliche Geliebte" Josephine Brunswick: Ihr Schicksal und der Einfluss auf Beethovens Werk.* Zurich, 1983.

Thürheim, Lulu, Mein Leben : *Erinnerungen aus Osterreichs grosser welt*, German tradition, 4. Munich, 1913–14.

Till, Nicholas. *Mozart and the Enlightenment: Truth, Virtue, and Beauty in Mozart's Operas.* New York, 1993.

Tovey, Donald Francis. *Beethoven.* Oxford, 1945.

———. "Beethoven." *Encyclopaedia Britannica,* 11th ed., 647ff. Cambridge, 1910.

———. *A Companion to Beethoven's Pianoforte Sonatas: Bar to Bar Analysis.* London, 1931.

———. *Essays in Musical Analysis.* 6 vols. London, 1935–39.

———. *Essays in Musical Analysis: Chamber Music.* London, 1944.

Treitler, Leo. *Music and the Historical Imagination.* Cambridge, Mass., 1989.

Tusa, Michael. "Beethoven's 'C-Minor Mood': Some Thoughts on the Structural Implications of Key Choice." *BF* 2 (1993): 1–28.

———. "Noch einmal: Form and Content in the Finale of Beethoven's Ninth Symphony." *BF* 7 (1999): 113–37.

———. "The Unknown Florestan: The 1805 Version of 'In des Lebens Frühlingstagen.'" *JAMS* 46 (1993): 175–220.

Tyson, Alan. *The Authentic English Editions of Beethoven.* London, 1963.

———. "The Authors of the Op. 104 String Quintet." In *BS,* 1:158–73.

———. "Beethoven to the Countess Susanna Guicciardi: A New Letter." In *BS,* 1:1–17.

———. "Beethoven's Heroic Phase." *The Musical Times* 110 (1969): 139–41.

———. "Das Leonoreskizzenbuch (Mendelssohn 15): Probleme der Rekonstruktion und Chronologie." *BJ* 9 (1977): 469–500.

———. *Mozart: Studies of the Autograph Scores.* Cambridge, Mass., 1987.

———. "The Problem of Beethoven's 'First' *Leonore* Overture." *JAMS* 28 (1975): 292–334.

———. "The Razumovsky Quartets: Some Aspects of the Sources." In *BS*, 3: 107–40.

———. Review of *Autograph Miscellany from circa 1786 to 1799: British Museum Additional Manuscript 29801, ff. 39–162 (The Kafka Sketchbook)*, by Ludwig van Beethoven, edited by Joseph Kerman. *The Musical Times* 111 (1970): 1194–98.

———. "Steps to Publication—and Beyond." In *The Beethoven Reader*, edited by Denis Arnold and Nigel Fortune, 459–89. New York, 1971.

Uhde, Jürgen. *Beethovens Klaviermusik*. 2nd ed. 3 vols. Stuttgart, 1980.

Unger, Max. *Beethovens Handschrift*. Bonn, 1926.

Van den Toorn, Pieter C. *Music, Politics, and the Academy*. Berkeley, 1995.

Volkmann, Hans. *Beethoven in seinen Beziehungen zu Dresden: Unbekannte Strecken seines Lebens*. Dresden, 1942.

Wackenroder, Wilhelm Heinrich, and Ludwig Tieck. *Outpourings of an Art-Loving Friar*. Translated by Edward Mornin. New York, 1975.

Wagner, Richard, "Beethoven." In his *Gesammelte Schriften und Dichtungen*, 6th ed., 9:61–126. Leipzig, 1911. Originally published in 1840. English trans. in Wagner's *Prose Works*, translated by William Ashton Ellis, 6:57–126. London, 1893–99. Reprinted 1966.

———. "Eine Pilgerfahrt zu Beethoven." In his *Gesammelte Schriften und Dichtungen*, 6th ed., 90–113. Leipzig, 1907.

Walden, Valerie. *One Hundred Years of Violoncello: A History of Technique and Performance Practice, 1740–1840*. Cambridge, 1998.

Waldvogel, Nicolas. "'Symphonic Unity' and the Organization of Individual Movements in Beethoven's *Missa solemnis*." B.A. thesis, Harvard University, 1988.

Wallace, Robin. *Beethoven's Critics*. Cambridge, 1986.

Wangermann, Ernst. *From Joseph II to the Jacobin Trials: Government Policy and Public Opinion in the Habsburg Dominions in the Period of the French Revolution*. London, 1969.

Webster, James. "The Concept of Beethoven's 'Early' Period in the context of Periodizations in General." *BF* 3 (1994): 1–28.

———. "The Falling-Out Between Haydn and Beethoven: The Evidence of the Sources." In *Beethoven Essays: Studies in Honor of Elliot Forbes*, edited by Lewis Lockwood and Phyllis Benjamin, 3–45. Cambridge, Mass., 1984.

———. "The Form of the Finale of Beethoven's Ninth Symphony." *BF* 1 (1992): 36–44.

———. *Haydn's "Farewell" Symphony and the Idea of Classical Style: Through-Composition and Cyclic Integration in his Instrumental Music*. Cambridge, 1991.

———. "Traditional Elements in Beethoven's Middle-Period String Quartets." In *Beethoven: Performers and Critics; The International Beethoven Congress, Detroit, 1977*, edited by Robert Winter and Bruce Carr, 94–133. Detroit, 1980.

Wegeler, Franz Gerhard, and Ferdinand Ries. *Biographische Notizen über Ludwig van Beethoven.* Koblenz, 1838.

Weise, Dagmar. *Ein Skizzenbuch zur Pastoralsymphonie Op. 68 und zu den Trios Op. 70,1 und 2.* 2 vols. Bonn, 1961.

Weissmann, Adolph. *Berlin als Musikstadt.* Berlin, 1911.

Will, Richard. *The Characteristic Symphony in the Age of Haydn and Beethoven.* Oxford, 2001.

Winter, Robert. *Compositional Origins of Beethoven's Opus 131.* Ann Arbor, 1982.

———. "Plans for the Structure of the String Quartet in C Sharp Minor." In *BS* 2: 106–37.

———. "Of Realizations, Completions, Restorations, and Reconstructions: From Bach's *The Art of Fugue* to Beethoven's Tenth Symphony." *Journal of the Royal Musical Association* 116 (1991): 96–126.

———. "The Sketches for the Ode to Joy." In *Beethoven, Performers, and Critics; The International Beethoven Congress, Detroit 1977,* edited by Robert Winter and Bruce Carr, 176–214. Detroit, 1980.

Winter, Robert, and Robert Martin, eds. *The Beethoven Quartet Companion.* Berkeley, Calif., 1994.

Witcombe, Charles C. "Beethoven's Private God: An Analysis of the Composer's Markings in Sturm's 'Betrachtungen.'" M.A. thesis, San Jose State University, 1998.

Witte, Bernd. "The Beautiful Society and the Symbolic Work of Art: The Anti-Revolutionary Origins of the Bildungsroman." In *The Internalized Revolution: German Reactions to the French Revolution, 1789–1989,* edited by Erhard Bahr and Thomas P. Saine, 79–98. New York, 1992.

Wolf, Stefan. *Beethovens Neffenkonflikt: Eine psychologisch-biographische Studie.* Munich, 1995.

Wolff, Christoph, ed. *The String Quartets of Haydn, Mozart, and Beethoven. Studies of the Autograph Manuscripts.* Cambridge, Mass., 1980.

Woolf, Virginia. *Orlando.* London, 1928.

Young-Bruehl, Elisabeth. *Creative Characters.* New York, 1991.

Yudkin, Jeremy. "Beethoven's 'Mozart' Quartet." *JAMS* 45 (1992): 30–74.

Zenck, Martin. *Die Bach-Rezeption des späten Beethoven: Zum Verhältnis von Musikhistoriographie und Rezeptionsgeschichtsschreibung der "Klassik."* Stuttgart, 1986.

CLASSIFIED INDEX
OF BEETHOVEN'S WORKS

>─○─◦─◦⋘✕⋙◦─◦─○─<

Boldface page numbers indicate the principal discussion of each work; *italic* numbers indicate a musical example.

INDEX OF BEETHOVEN'S WORKS BY OPUS NUMBER

❧⟶⟶⬖⟨❦⟩⬗⟵⟵❧

Boldface page numbers indicate the principal discussion of each work; *italic* numbers indicate a musical example.

GENERAL INDEX

Page numbers in *italics* indicate an illustration or musical example.

Washington, George, 212
Weber, Carl Maria von, 233, 353
  bassoon concerto, 102
  operas of, 253
Webster, James, 500n33, 542n77, 545n27
Wegeler, Franz Gerhard, 44, 46, 48, 80, 115
  on Beethoven and women, 197
  on Beethoven as pianist, 63
  on Beethoven's grandfather, 27
  on Beethoven's obstinacy, 81–82
  Biographical Notes about Ludwig van Beethoven, 44
  letters from Beethoven, 12–13, 89–90, 260, 264, 365, 492n9, 494n15
Wegeler, Lorenz, 44
Weidinger, Maria Anna (née Beethoven), 532n25
Weigl, Joseph, 85, 108
Weimar, grand duke of, 277
Weiser, Anton, 492n8
Weiss, Franz, 81, 500n31
Weissenbach, Alois, 340
Wellington, Duke of, 155, 186, 334, 413
Werner, Zacharias, 405

Westphalia, 413
Wieck, Friedrich, 352
Wiener Zeitung, 269, 377–78
Wild, Franz, 278, 335
Willman, Magdalena, 197
Winneberger, Paul Anton, 48
Winter, Peter, 140, 522n4
Winter, Robert, 547n63
Wolf, Hugo, 274
Wölffl, Joseph, 85, 284, 292
Wolfmayer, Johann von, 532n22
Woolf, Virginia, *Orlando*, 493n26
Wordsworth, William, 70, 273
Worzischek, Jan-Hugo, 393
Wranitsky, Anton, 85
Wright, David, 192
Württemberg, duke of, 37

Zarlino, Gioseffo, 367
Zelter, Carl, 406
Zmeskall von Domanovecs, Baron Nikolaus von, 109, 114, 194, 325–26, 493n23